THE
VIETNAM WAR

AN EYEWITNESS HISTORY

THE
VIETNAM WAR

AN EYEWITNESS HISTORY

SANFORD WEXLER

Facts On File

New York • Oxford

The Vietnam War: An Eyewitness History

Copyright © 1992 by Sanford Wexler

Facts On File, Inc.   Facts On File Limited
460 Park Avenue South   Collins Street
New York NY 10016   Oxford OX4 1XJ
USA   United Kingdom

Library of Congress Cataloging-in-Publication Data
Wexler, Sanford
 The Vietnam war : an eyewitness history / Sanford Wexler.
  p. cm.—(The Eyewitness history series)
 Includes bibliographical references and index.
 ISBN 0-8160-2617-3
 1. Vietnamese Conflict, 1961–1975. I. Title. II. Series.
DS557.7.W48 1992
959.704′3—dc20   91-25996

A British CIP catalogue record for this book is available from the British Library.

Facts On File books are available at special discounts when purchased in bulk quantities
for businesses, associations, institutions or sales promotions. Please call our Special
Sales Department in New York at 212/683-2244 (dial 800/322-8755 except in
NY, AK or HI) or in Oxford at 865-728399.

Jacket design by Keith Lovell
Composition by the Maple-Vail Book Manufacturing Group
Manufactured by the Maple-Vail Book Manufacturing Group
Printed in the United States of America

10 9 8 7 6 5 4 3 2 1

This book is printed on acid-free paper.

To those who were there

Contents

Preface **xi**

Introduction **xiii**

Prologue: Setting the Stage **1**

1. The War with the French: 1945–1959 **13**
2. Days of Hope: 1960–1963 **47**
3. Year of Decision: 1964 **77**
4. America Takes Over: 1965 **95**
5. Escalation: 1966 **117**
6. An Expanding War: 1967 **141**
7. The Tet Offensive: 1968 **163**
8. Fighting for Time: 1969 **189**
9. Vietnamizing the War: 1970–1971 **213**
10. Peace Is at Hand: 1972–1973 **237**
11. The Fall of the South: 1974–1975 **261**
12. Legacies and Reflections **285**

Appendix A, Documents **301**

Appendix B, Biographies of Major Personalities **321**

Appendix C, Maps **343**

Appendix D, Statistics on the War **347**

Appendix E, Glossary **349**

Bibliography **357**

Credits **377**

Index **385**

Acknowledgments

No book like this one could have been completed alone. In addition to thanking all of the authors, journalists and veterans whose work is excerpted here, I would especially like to acknowledge the following people who provided me with invaluable assistance and advice: Don Bowden and Patricia Lantis, Wide World Photos; Dale Connelly, Sharon Culley, Fred Pernell and Gary Stern, Still Picture Branch, the National Archives; Vincent Demma, Joel Myerson and Ronald Spector, Center for Military History; Stephen Denney and Douglas Pike, the Indochina Archive, Berkeley, California; Maja Felaco and George Hobart, Prints and Photographs Division, the Library of Congress; Gayle Garmise, Marc Leepson, Mark Perry and publisher Mary R. Stout, the *Veteran*, Vietnam Veterans of America; William Conrad Gibbons, Congressional Research Service, Library of Congress; and Kim LeJuez, Philip Yockey and the many helpful staff members and librarians at the New York Public Library.

Special thanks to Bernard Edelman and Robert Santos, the New York Vietnam Veterans Memorial Commission; Katherine Graham, chairman of the board, the Washington Post Company; Michael Davies, publisher, *The Baltimore Sun*; and Mortimer B. Zuckerman, editor-in-chief, *U.S. News & World Report*.

I would also like to thank Colonel Harry G. Summers Jr., whose *Vietnam War Almanac* was an indispensable source of information.

At Facts On File, vice president and associate publisher Gerard Helferich was the inspiration for this volume; project editor Gary Krebs expertly oversaw the book's production; and copy editor Paul Scaramazza, a former U.S. Army journalist, put at my disposal his encyclopedic knowledge of military terminology.

Finally, I would like to express my appreciation to Carl and Molly Waldman, Alan, Cliff and Gloria Wexler, and my parents, Minnie and Nathan, for their insightful comments and encouragement.

The Eyewitness History Series

Historians have long recognized that to truly understand the past we must relive it. We can see past eras and events clearly only when we free our minds from the knowledge of what unfolded between then and now and permit ourselves to experience events with the fresh vision of a contemporary participant or observer.

To stimulate our powers of historical imagination we must begin by immersing ourselves in the documents of the period, so that we can view events as eyewitnesses. The Eyewitness History Series offers readers and students the opportunity to exercise their historical imaginations by providing in a single volume a large collection of excerpts from what historians call "primary sources," the memoirs, diaries, letters, journalism and official documents of the period.

To give these historical raw materials a framework, each chapter begins with a brief summary of the "Historical Context" followed by a detailed "Chronicle of Events." However, the bulk of each chapter consists of a large selection of quotations from eyewitness accounts of the events of the time. These have been selected to give the reader the widest range of views possible. Each has a specific source in the Bibliography to facilitate further study. To further stimulate the reader's historical imagination, a selection of contemporary illustrations is included in each chapter. Modern maps have been included in an appendix for the convenience of readers.

Rather than interrupt the main text with lengthy official documents, we have included them in an appendix. Another appendix includes brief biographies of the major personalities referred to in the text.

Eyewitness Histories are intended to encourage students and readers to discover the powers and the pleasures of historical imagination, while also providing them with comprehensive and self-contained works of reference to significant historical periods.

Preface

"The real war will never get in the books," said Walt Whitman about the Civil War. His observation is probably true of any war. The closest we can come to reliving the experiences of those who witnessed war is through their first-person accounts, whether they be letters, personal diaries, memoirs or oral histories. At best, this eyewitness testimony can simulate the experience of war so vividly that we can almost appreciate General William Tecumseh Sherman's comment that war "is all hell." "Almost" appreciate, for those of us who have never experienced war can never fully comprehend the true nature of war.

The eyewitness accounts assembled here trace the evolution of U.S. involvement in Vietnam, beginning with U.S. support for the French war against the Vietminh, to the landing of American combat troops in 1965, to the helicopter evacuation of Saigon 10 years later. The last chapter discusses the legacy of Vietnam and includes reflections on the war by some of those who participated in it, either directly or indirectly.

The firsthand accounts excerpted in this volume are from a diverse group of people who fought, lived and worked in Vietnam in peace and in war: French, American and Vietnamese soldiers and officers, POWs, reporters, doctors and nurses, diplomats, missionaries, relief workers and spies. The quotations from letters, journals and news dispatches describe events as they unfolded, while the excerpts from memoirs and oral histories are generally more reflective. Taken all together, these unique voices and unique experiences illuminate the strange land that was Vietnam.

To illustrate the "war" that was taking place 8,000 miles away, in the United States, firsthand accounts by those who had family members and friends in Vietnam are included, as well as excerpts from official memos and speeches by many prominent figures who either directed, supported or protested the war—for example, presidents Kennedy, Johnson and Nixon, secretaries McNamara, Rusk and Kissinger, senators Barry Goldwater and Eugene McCarthy and activist Dr. Benjamin Spock.

The Vietnam War: An Eyewitness History attempts to be objective, yet some readers may object to the space given either to antiwar protesters or North Vietnamese, or to the truly heroic exploits of some U.S. military personnel. I have endeavored to give each perspective enough coverage to ensure that no important aspect of the Vietnam experience is omitted.

There is such an abundance of firsthand material on the Vietnam War, including scores of personal accounts by veterans and news correspondents, thousands of collected letters and hundreds of thousands of pages of oral histories, that the sheer volume boggles the mind of well-intentioned chronicler and reader alike. In addition, every year at least a few dozen books are published as well as innumerable magazine and newspaper articles.

Here you will find excerpts from many of the classic accounts by Vietnam veterans and combat journalists as well as several quotations from lesser-known books, some of which were privately published by veterans themselves or are from collections of letters home compiled by parents who lost their sons in Vietnam. These vivid and spontaneous voices from the "boonies," base camps and evacuation hospitals are often raw, honest and personal. Some are sad; a few will evoke a laugh. It is hoped that these authentic voices will give a picture of the Vietnam War as it was for those who fought and died in it.

Introduction

The word "Vietnam" is likely to trigger images of American soldiers slogging through rice paddies and of helicopter gunships flying over dense Southeast Asian jungles in search of the elusive Vietcong. For many who lived through this turbulent time, whether they were for or against the war, names and places like Danang, Khe Sanh, Hue, the DMZ, Tet, Cambodia and Saigon, as well as Chicago and Kent State, are likely to stir up the same kind of passions that Bull Run, Shiloh and Gettysburg evoked for Americans after the Civil War.

While no comparison can be made between the battlefield carnage of the Civil War and that of Vietnam, the Vietnam War did eventually divide a nation against itself. It certainly was the most divisive conflict for Americans since the Civil War.

It was also America's longest war, lasting from 1965 to 1973. Although it is sometimes referred to as the first war the United States ever lost, it was South Vietnam that actually lost the war. The U.S. won almost every battle thanks to superior firepower and mobility. What the United States did lose was prestige.

It was the first television war, as scenes of Americans in combat were brought into living rooms at dinnertime via the evening news. Unlike previous American wars, there was no front line. The enemy often wore civilian clothes, and the only clear objective was "body count," rather than retaking or occupying territory.

The cold numbers speak for themselves. The Vietnam War cost the lives of 58,183 Americans and wounded 300,000 more; it also produced a million and a half Vietnamese deaths on both sides, with an estimated 4.5 million more left wounded and nine million becoming refugees. It is a human tragedy of unspeakable proportions for those who suffered and died in Indochina, and for the survivors who suffer still.

Indeed, Vietnam was a war nobody won. Although North Vietnam achieved a military victory by "liberating" South Vietnam, it has become at least as corrupt and repressive as the regime it overthrew. Mismanagement of the economy has transformed Vietnam into one of the poorest nations in the world.

For the Vietnamese, the war was yet another chapter in their long struggle for independence, from the Chinese and then from the French and Japanese. For the United States, the war was another attempt to reorganize the world order after World War II and to halt the spread of communism.

U.S. involvement began in 1945 when President Truman decided to support France's request to retain its former colony at the end of the

Second World War. Each succeeding president made a further commitment. President Eisenhower supported the installation of Ngo Dinh Diem as South Vietnam's first leader after the 1954 Geneva agreement that ended France's rule. President Kennedy increased the number of American advisers, and President Johnson made the fateful decision in 1965 to bomb North Vietnam and to dispatch U.S. combat troops to the south.

There was never any plan to win the war, only to contain it. Each administration feared being blamed for the fall of Vietnam to the communists, and at the same time feared provoking either China or the Soviet Union into the conflict. Hanoi calculated that in a war of attrition, the United States would eventually lose patience.

It is now believed that the critical turning point of the war may have been the communists' Tet Offensive in 1968. Hanoi expected it would capture Saigon, but the exact opposite actually occurred. The communists suffered over 50,000 killed, a devastating military defeat. However, the intensity of the communist attack astonished Americans, who had been led to believe that the U.S. was winning the war. As a result, Tet significantly reduced popular support for the war at home.

It is ironic that after Tet the United States finally began to make some substantial progress in the war. The local Vietcong were largely decimated while the North Vietnamese who came south to replace them were fatigued. By 1970, 90% of the countryside was officially "pacified," compared with only 33% in 1965.

By the time Richard Nixon was sworn in as president, the American public had grown tired of the war, liberals believing that the U.S. was waging a war in a country it had no business being in and conservatives feeling that the conflict was unwinnable. Increasing domestic pressure to end the war motivated President Nixon in 1973 to agree to the Paris Peace Accords, which ultimately proved only a face-saving device for American withdrawal.

American interest in Vietnam quickly evaporated after all of the U.S. combat troops and the POWs returned home. Congress drastically cut back U.S. aid to Saigon and corruption substantially increased. The fall of Saigon in 1975 surprised even the communists, who intended the attack only to be a preliminary offensive for a full-scale invasion the following year.

For the post-Vietnam generation, "the domino theory," pacification, "search-and destroy-missions," napalm, "winning hearts and minds," "seeing light at the end of the tunnel," "the best and the brightest," "Hell no, we won't go" and "Peace with honor" are all phrases from history. But the trauma of Vietnam is still with us. Two million Americans a year visit the black, monolithic Vietnam Veterans Memorial in Washington, on which the names of 58,183 Americans who died in the Vietnam War are enshrined.

Has the U.S. victory in the Persian Gulf kicked the "Vietnam syndrome" once and for all? Or, rather, was America's concern with heavy casualties in a potentially long ground war an example of the "Vietnam syndrome" in action? Did Americans express a sense of jubilation for their nation's triumph over Iraq, or were they simply relieved that the war did not turn out to be "another Vietnam?" Have subsequent events in Southeast Asia given validity to what the U.S. originally set out to do?

It seems that any attempt to answer one question about Vietnam simply leads to several more. Did the political limitations placed on the military prevent the United States from winning a decisive victory? Were the Vietcong fighting for their country's independence or were they simply terrorists, willing to use any means necessary in order to gain power? Was Vietnam a noble cause, as President Ronald Reagan once said, or was it a vast and tragic mistake?

These questions may never be completely answered. While the causes and lessons of Vietnam will continue to be debated, it is agreed by all sides that the Vietnam War remains the most misunderstood and complex conflict in American history. The broad selection of eyewitness accounts in this book, ranging from foot soldiers, officers and government officials to protesters and journalists will, we hope, enable you to shape your own interpretation of the Vietnam experience.

THE
VIETNAM WAR

AN EYEWITNESS HISTORY

Prologue: Setting the Stage

FIRST CONTACT WITH THE WEST

The first Europeans to establish a permanent settlement in Vietnam were the Portuguese. In 1535, under the command of Captain Antonio da Faria, the Portuguese entered the Bay of Tourane, now the city of Danang. Fifteen miles south of Tourane, da Faria found a suitable site for a harbor at Faifo.

In the 16th century, Portuguese explorers and conquerors, prodded by merchants and missionaries, became the pioneers of Western imperialism in the Far East. When Vasco da Gama succeeded in reaching India in 1498 after sailing around the Cape of Good Hope, he opened up a direct route to the Asian world for the West. The Portuguese immediately began to settle portions of the Indian coast and soon pushed eastward to capture Malacca, the gateway to the China Sea. From this pivotal Malayan port they fanned out to assert their presence nearly everywhere in Asia.

Although da Faria failed to make Faifo into a stronghold similar to Goa or Malacca, by 1540 it had become the main port of entry for foreign goods into "Cauchichina," the name given by the Portuguese to Vietnam. They derived "Cauchi" from "Gia Chi," the Chinese characters for Vietnam, and added "China" to distinguish it from Cochin, another of their colonies in India. To portray Vietnam as disunified, the French later referred only to the southern third of the country as Cochinchina, and called the center "Annam" and the north "Tonkin."

After a century of dramatic expansion, the Portuguese began to lose their grasp on Asia. Their position as a world power was declining. Toward the end of the 16th century the Dutch and the English began to sail in search of new trade routes and new worlds. The Dutch, wealthier than the English, and with more experienced navigators and traders, became the heirs of the Portuguese, chiefly by concentrating their efforts on Southeast Asia.

The Dutch made their appearance in Vietnam exactly 100 years after the Portuguese. In 1636, they established their first trading post in the southern half of the country. A year later, when the government in Hanoi permitted them to set up a post in Pho Hien, the Dutch immediately switched the bulk of their trading activities to the north, the wealthier region of the country.

Next to appear at the gates of Vietnam were the English, who in 1672 opened an office in Pho Hien, which they later moved to Hanoi, hoping that the trade thus gained would justify their efforts. By the time the French arrived in Pho Hien in 1680, trade with Vietnam was becoming unprofitable.

As it would be three centuries later, Vietnam was then torn by a civil war between regional factions. Europeans sold weapons to both sides—the Trinh dynasty in the north and the Nguyen in the south. But they were unable to subdue the Vietnamese as they had the Malayans and Javanese. Despite their own differences, the Vietnamese despised foreigners. Their sophisticated administrative system, modeled on China's, effectively rallied support for resistance against intruders. Besides, the Europeans were too preoccupied with fighting among themselves to wage campaigns of the sort that would have been required for conquest.

By the end of the 17th century, the Dutch and the English had closed the small offices they had opened earlier in Hanoi, and the French had disbanded their post at Pho Hien. But if the merchants had failed, Catholic missionaries considered the Vietnamese, with their melange of Confucianism, Taoism, ancestor worship and remnants of Hinduistic beliefs, ripe prospects for conversion.

MISSIONARIES IN VIETNAM

The first Italian and Portuguese Jesuit missionaries landed in Danang on January 18, 1615. Their initial successes led the Pope to send a permanent mission to Vietnam, headed by a French Jesuit, Alexandre de Rhodes. Within six months he had mastered the language and began to preach in Vietnamese. Monsignor de Rhodes remained in Vietnam for 22 years, and by the time he was banished in 1649, tens of thousands of Vietnamese had embraced Catholicism.

Rhodes soon realized that hearts and minds could be more effectively won by Vietnamese priests than by European missionaries. He submitted to the Vatican a training program for indigenous priests. However, the Vatican bureacracy, fearing a conflict with Portugal, did not act, whereupon Rhodes turned to France for support.

To succeed, Rhodes would have to persuade French religious and commercial leaders to underwrite his project. He lobbied both, describing Vietnam as ripe for Christian conversion and portraying it as an El Dorado of boundless wealth. The Vatican finally accepted his program, though Rhodes died before it was implemented. In 1664, four years after his death, French religious leaders and their commercial sponsors formed the Society of Foreign Missions to advance Christianity in

Jesuit missionary Alexandre de Rhodes, who traveled through Asia in the 17th century. Courtesy of the Boston Public Library.

Asia. In the same year, French business and religious leaders created the East India Company to increase trade.

Throughout the 18th century the French accomplished little in Vietnam, since the Vietnamese emperors continued to harass or restrict foreign missionaries and merchants. Moreover, back in France the public was not supportive of the idea of acquiring overseas territories. But the dream was kept alive by a handful of determined individuals and groups.

In 1789, French missionary Pierre Pigneua de Behaine sailed from France with a single privately bought warship and 300 French volunteers attracted by the promise of land. The week that Parisians stormed the Bastille, the colonists landed in Vietnam.

TAY SON REBELLION

In the meantime, three brothers from Tay Son village in the south had risen against the Nguyen, an imperial family, with demands for social reforms and reunification. They were supported by the landless peasants who were oppressed by their feudal lords. By 1776, the Tay Son had murdered all the Nguyen rulers save one young prince, Nguyen Anh. The Tay Son were masters of most of South Vietnam.

The tide eventually turned with the arrival of Behaine and his infusion of military know-how. After more than a dozen campaigns the Tay Son were defeated. In 1802, Nguyen Anh proclaimed himself emperor of Vietnam, taking the name of Gia Long. For the first time in almost two centuries Vietnam was a single country, from the China Gates in the north to the Ca-Mau Peninsula at its southernmost tip.

Emperor Minh Mang, who ruled Vietnam in the early 19th century. Courtesy of the New York Public Library.

Vietnam turned against the West in Gia Long's lifetime. Although he respected and honored his French benefactors, he did not trust any European power. The reign of the last Vietnamese dynasty, the Nguyen, did not end until the abdication of Emperor Bao Dai in 1955.

Influenced by their Confucian backgrounds, both Gia Long and his son Minh Mang, who ruled from 1820 to 1841, decided that Vietnam's national interest required strict isolation from the West. Soon after succeeding his father, Minh Mang outlawed the Catholic religion. He suspected collusion between missionaries and Western traders, who had begun using military means to gain economic control over Asia.

The French Conquest

From 1817 to 1831, France tried through diplomatic efforts to obtain trading privileges and to persuade Vietnam to forge closer political bonds with Paris. Both these efforts failed. After a series of setbacks the French abandoned their attempts to gain a foothold in Vietnam by diplomatic and peaceful means.

The antimissionary policy of the Nguyen ultimately provided France with its opportunity to intervene in Vietnam. In 1843, gunboats sailed into Tourane, present-day Danang, and secured the release of five jailed missionaries. Four years later, in 1847, unaware that two French missionaries who were condemned to death were pardoned and departed to Singapore, French naval forces boarded and disabled two Vietnamese warships. Fearing imminent attack, the French then bombarded three Vietnamese vessels, killing hundreds of local inhabitants.

In 1857, Napoleon III appointed a commission to recommend further action in the Far East. This panel declared that France must enter the race for Asian possessions or be reduced to a second-rank power. They argued for establishing a French port in Southeast Asia, pointing out that Vietnam was not an area of English interest.

On August 31, 1858, the French fleet in the Far East reached the Bay of Tourane, attacked the harbor's defenses and occupied Danang. The French established a beachhead but were devastated by heat and disease. In addition, the French forces were provided with misleading intelligence reports and lacked an understanding of the Vietnamese people. Missionaries had informed Admiral Rigault de Genouilly, the commander of the expedition, that the Vietnamese Christians would rise against the authorities, that the natives would labor for the French and that mandarin control over the Vietnamese had declined. None of these proved true.

Genouilly dispatched one missionary to Hong Kong to secure reinforcements and then sailed south to attack Saigon. On February 17, 1859, the citadel at Saigon fell to the French. However, the Vietnamese refused to negotiate despite the occupation of Saigon. Genouilly was replaced by Admiral Theogene-Francois Page, who recommended that a stronger effort be made for annexing Saigon and the surrounding territory.

In February 1861, 3,000 French troops arrived in Saigon to relieve Admiral Page's garrison. Six months after launching the campaign, the French claimed the city for France. Vietnamese guerrillas harassed the French, but by 1862 France was firmly in control of the three provinces surrounding Saigon: Dinh Tuong, Gia Dinh and Bien Hoa.

Faced with a civil war that had broken out in Tonkin, led by supporters of the old Le dynasty, Emperor Tu Duc agreed to sacrifice the south in order to retain his throne. He gave France the three provinces adjacent to Saigon and the island of Poulo Condore and agreed not to cede any part of Vietnamese territory to another power. France finally had its Asian port. Although France's latest conquest was not ratified by its Parliament until 1874, France's occupation of the south was complete: Cochin China became a French colony.

UNDER COLONIAL RULE

France's foreign policy took a bold turn in 1879 when popular forces finally won an election and took control of the Third Republic from the conservatives. The new republican leaders enjoyed the strongest domestic support of any French government in the 19th century, and the confidence of their foreign policy reflected this fact.

In August 1883, taking advantage of the confusion after Tu Duc's death, a French fleet entered the mouth of the Perfume River, not far from Hue. The French warships opened fire, inflicting such heavy casualties that a chief mandarin emerged personally under a flag of truce to negotiate. A treaty was signed that granted France a "protectorate" over all of Vietnam with the exception of Cochin China, already a French colony. Consequently, the French installed officials and garrisons to exercise jurisdiction over the Vietnamese authorities, including the emperor. They regulated Vietnam's commerce, collected its custom duties, assured its defenses and managed its foreign relations. Vietnam had become a virtual French possession.

THE GUERRILLA WAR BEGINS

But French control of Tonkin was not entirely secured and perhaps never would be. The young Emperor Ham Nghi, together with his Court, fled Hue in 1885 and issued an edict calling for a popular uprising against the French. For 10 more years the Vietnamese engaged French troops in guerrilla wars in the jungles, mountains and villages of Tonkin. Loyalty to the monarchy and hatred of the French resulted in a decade of resistance. It was known as the "Scholars' Revolt," because its leaders were drawn from loyal mandarins and other local scholars.

With the French in pursuit of the fleeing Court, the Vietnamese were unable to reach the mountain retreat they had selected in advance. They moved farther into the mountains, where they quickly became dependent on the support of small villages. In the early years the rebels were highly effective, and their ambushes prevented French troops from gaining a significant foothold in the mountains. The classic pattern of guerrilla warfare emerged. By day the forces kept to the security of the mountains; at night they entered villages to resupply and enlist new recruits. The French appeared to be in control of the villages, but no French soldiers were safe.

Like the Americans nearly a century later, the French exploited the guerrillas' reliance upon Vietnam's ethnic minorities in the mountains. In November 1888, the French were able to capture Ham Nghi by offering opium and a military title to a Muong chieftain in return for his betrayal of the 16-year-old emperor. Ham Nghi spent the rest of his life in exile in the French colony of Algeria.

THE END OF THE SCHOLARS' REVOLT

The capture of Ham Nghi was a turning point for the French. More and more mandarins accepted French rule and returned to their duties, this time in the service of the French. For a minority, however, the struggle against the French intensified. They developed sophisticated guerrilla tactics and began manufacturing replicas of the most advanced French weapons. But French forces overcame the guerrilla resistance by building a series of fortifications around the rebels' mountain base. French forces slowly moved in and eventually trapped the guerrillas. By 1897 the last of the rebels in the mountains of Tonkin had been subdued. Despite its failure, the Scholars' Revolt marked the beginning of the Vietnamese resistance movement.

Although peace dominated the years following the Scholars' Revolt, by 1903 a new generation of intellectuals had emerged who began plotting an independence movement. The struggle of this new generation centered around two Vietnamese with different strategies. Phan Boi Chau, a radical monarchist, believed that with Chinese and Japanese aid a powerful emperor could unite the opposition. Phan Chu Trinh rejected royalism and contended instead that cooperation with the French would lead Vietnam toward democracy.

THE POISON PLOT

In 1907, Phan Boi Chau developed a plan by which French officers at the Hanoi garrison would be poisoned by low-ranking native troops, who then would seize crucial points in the capital. The French officers were poisoned as planned, but the colonial authorities discovered the plot and executed 13 of Phan's followers, sending scores more to prison. Phan himself, already wanted by the French police, avoided arrest by remaining in Japan during the revolt.

PHAN CHU TRINH'S WESTERN ALTERNATIVE

Phan Chu Trinh sent an open letter to the French governor in 1906, warning of an eventual rebellion unless the Vietnamese could express themselves politically, economically and socially. He argued that colonial rule violated the very principles that French democracy represented. These ideas were supported by progressives in France itself, and with the permission of the French authorities, Phan Chu Trinh organized and opened the Hanoi Free School in 1907. The Free School's theory held that scholars must renounce their elitist traditions by learning from the masses and that peasants must be given a modern education.

Within a year, the French closed the school, and Trinh was arrested for inciting tax riots. He was condemned to death, but his progressive supporters in France intervened. His sentence was commuted to life imprisonment, and after three years he was released. For the next decade he lived in Paris, where he symbolized the anticolonial resistance for both Vietnamese expatriates and their French sympathizers.

THE COMMUNIST PARTY IN VIETNAM

Following the end of World War I, the initial blow for Vietnamese independence was struck in Paris. A 29-year-old Vietnamese by the name of Nguyen Ai Quoc (Nguyen the Patriot) presented a petition for Vietnamese independence to the Versailles Peace Conference. The conference quickly dismissed it, but the young petitioner, who would later change his name to Ho Chi Minh, "He Who Enlightens," was determined to dedicate his life to relentlessly pursuing the goal of Vietnamese independence.

But the 1920s was not a decade of anticolonial politics in Vietnam. Instead, the prosperity of the post-World War I period created a new Vietnamese elite—the increasingly wealthy urban middle class. Many relied on the French for their wealth, and accepted their dependent status.

The increased landlessness and indebtedness of the peasantry under French rule resulted in the growth of a resistance movement in the villages, which eventually emerged into a Vietnamese Communist Party. The French, after making a study of Vietnamese land laws, decided that private ownership of land did not exist in Vietnam, that all the land belonged to the emperor. The peasant, at least in theory, was only a tenant of the state. In practice, however, the peasant functioned as the owner of the land because the emperors had allotted land to the peasant's ancestors in the course of creating new villages.

French authorities ignored custom in favor of theory that they, as heirs of imperial power, had the right to dispose of all unoccupied lands. Peasants who were displaced due to war and civil war were the first ones to have their land taken away and given to colonists and to wealthy Vietnamese collaborators. When the peasants returned to their

Saigon, ca. 1930. Courtesy of the Library of Congress.

villages, they were appalled to find that their fields no longer belonged to them. The new owners offered to have them work the land or rent small portions of the land at excessive rates. Thus was created the new class of landless tenants, or *tadien*.

In February 1930, Ho Chi Minh attended a conference in southern China, where the Vietnamese Communist Party was formed. Six months later, under instructions from Moscow, the party changed its name to the Indochinese Communist Party (ICP). The communist flag waved for the first time in Vietnam during the revolt of the so-called Red Soviets in Nghe An and Ha Tinh provinces in 1930 and 1931.

When the worldwide Depression reached Vietnam in 1930 its effect was devastating to the economy: The market price of rice in Saigon fell 50%, tax revolts broke out in central Annam, and in the countryside peasant bands formed, waving red flags. Although the French succeeded at controlling the revolts in the cities, they were unable to subdue the rebellions that were taking place in the rural villages. Soon French rule in the countryside disappeared.

Local "soviets" replaced the French-controlled administration over a wide territory of Annam. The communist leaders developed a five-point program that called for: (1) the formation of peasant associations; (2) the organization of a village for militia; (3) the annulment of all taxes and reduction of rents; (4) the redistribution of former communal lands taken by French colonists; and (5) the distribution of excess rice to the destitute.

The French responded with the first use of air power in Vietnam. Almost 200 Vietnamese died in air attacks. On the ground, the French Foreign Legion moved in to subdue the soviets. The Vietnamese re-

Haiphong, ca. 1930. Courtesy of the Library of Congress.

sorted to guerrilla tactics. Not until the summer of 1931 did the French succeed in restoring what they called normal conditions. Although the legionnaires waged a campaign of terror, the going was slow. Finally, a famine came to the aid of the French. The soviets were unable to feed their people. The guerrillas were forced to come out of hiding or starve.

The decimation of the Communist Party in Vietnam did not mean its demise. The party was rejuvenated by Comintern officials in Moscow and by political developments in France. New recruits were sent to Moscow for training, supplying the ICP with a growing leadership cadre. Paris aided the cause by granting amnesties to those arrested for communist activities.

WORLD WAR II—OCCUPATION AND LIBERATION

When France surrendered to the Nazi armies in May 1940, the remaining leadership of the Vietnamese Communist Party, centered in Saigon, thought their moment had arrived. In November 1940 they staged an uprising in Cochin China. However, the French secret police were well aware of their plot. Within 15 days the rebellion was crushed; over 6,000 arrests followed. When word of the insurrection reached the party leadership in southern China, the actions of the Cochin China leaders were condemned. It was decided that the party would again have to be reorganized. Ho Chi Minh returned from his world travels to take over personal supervision of the reconstruction. He was joined by two young leaders: Vo Nguyen Giap, the mastermind of the communist guerrilla strategy, and Pham Van Dong, later to become premier of North Vietnam.

On September 22, 1940, France's Vichy government concluded an agreement that permitted Nazi ally Japan to station troops and use facilities in Tonkin. Although the French administrative machinery was left intact, Vietnam remained a virtual colony of Japan for the duration of World War II.

THE BIRTH OF THE VIETMINH

In late 1940 and early 1941, members of the Vietnamese Communist Party infiltrated Cao Bang Province along the Chinese border. They established ties with the mountain peoples of the area, and made the village of Pac Bo their base of activities in Vietnam. In May 1941, the eighth party conference was held in Pac Bo, where, under the leadership of Ho Chi Minh, a new organization was formed—the Vietnam Doc Lap Dong Minh (Vietnam Independence League), or Vietminh. The party's goals were to organize all Vietnamese, "whether workers, peasants, rich peasants, landlords, or native bourgeois, to work for the seizure of independence."

Communist and Vietminh activity between 1941 and 1945 had no spectacular results. Despite frequent appeals to the peasants to rebel, the Vietminh carefully avoided risking their own organization in local actions. Their primary goal was to command a politically organized following when the proper moment arrived.

THE U.S. STRIKES IN SOUTHEAST ASIA

As Asia headed into its last year of World War II, it became apparent that the Japanese empire was doomed. By late 1944 Allied victories in Malaya, Indonesia and especially the Philippines had forced the Japanese into a steady withdrawal. In November 1944, the headquarters of the Japanese Southern Army moved from Manila to Saigon. On January 12, 1945, American fighter-bombers flying from Vice Admiral William F. "Bull" Halsey's Third Fleet struck at Saigon as thousands of French and Vietnamese watched, hundreds from the city's rooftops. Five hundred American fighter-bombers sank four cargo ships and two oil tankers in Saigon harbor. In all, 14 enemy warships and 33 merchant ships were destroyed, the most sunk by the U.S. Navy in any one day in the entire war.

On March 9, 1945, Japan ended nearly 100 years of French rule in Indochina by granting independence to Vietnam under Japanese protection and reinstalling Emperor Bao Dai as head of state. With the French defeated, the Vietminh moved to consolidate their position. In April 1945, the Vietminh began to plan for national liberation, placing the Vietnam Liberation Army under the command of Vo Nguyen Giap.

THE U.S. SUPPORTS HO CHI MINH

During the latter stages of World War II, OSS (Office of Strategic Services) teams were operating in Vietnam, cooperating with the anti-Japanese efforts of the Vietminh. One of the most unusual American commando missions was the so-called Deer Mission, where a team of American OSS officers parachuted into Ho Chi Minh's jungle camp on July 16, 1945. They were met by a Vietminh official who escorted them to a nearby village, on whose bamboo gateway was posted the simple sign: "Welcome to our American Friends." The commandos were soon joined by Ho Chi Minh and treated to a banquet, including fatted calf and Hanoi beer.

INDEPENDENCE FOR VIETNAM

The final capitulation of the Japanese empire in August 1945 eliminated the last force between the Vietminh and independence. On August 18th, the Japanese transferred power in Indochina to the Vietminh. The ranks of the Vietminh National Salvation Association swelled. Hanoi, Hue and Saigon were soon governed by Vietminh committees.

The author of Vietnam's Declaration of Independence was none other than Ho Chi Minh. On September 2, 1945, he addressed a crowd assembled in Hanoi, proclaiming the Independent Democratic Republic of Vietnam (DRV). Quoting from the American Declaration of Independence and the Declaration of the French Revolution, he launched a bitter attack on French colonialism.

There would be a year of negotiations with Vietnam, an attempt to create a new relationship between that country and France. But France, now under the political leadership of Charles de Gaulle, was simply unwilling to give away the "jewel" of its empire. The revolution of August 1945 did not usher in a new era of peace for the Vietnamese but rather 30 more years of war.

1. The War with the French: 1945–1959

THE BRITISH OCCUPATION OF VIETNAM

After World War II the Vietnamese expected the Allies to support their claims for independence. The United States in principle favored the formation of a provisional international trusteeship for Vietnam. However, at the Potsdam Conference of July 1945, the question of whether France would be permitted to repossess its colonies was deliberately kept ambiguous. The Allied leaders agreed to divide the country at the 16th parallel. The British would take the south, the Chinese Nationalists the north. It was a formula for disaster.

The first British troops arrived in Saigon on September 12, 1945. With them came the first French troops, a company from Calcutta, where the French had assembled about 1,800 men. The British occupation troops were under the command of General Douglas D. Gracey, who regarded the right of the French to reoccupy Vietnam as self-evident. He had been clearly told by Lord Louis Mountbatten, the Allied commander for Southeast Asia, to avoid Vietnam's internal problems and to disarm only the Japanese, repatriate the prisoners of war and maintain order. But before leaving for Vietnam he said publicly, "The question of the government of Indochina is exclusively French." Only a week after his arrival, he took measures that enabled the French to evict the Vietnamese from the administration of Saigon.

THE FRENCH RETURN

Colonel Jean Cédile, whom De Gaulle had sent to Indochina, met repeatedly with Gracey and argued that the majority of Vietnamese supported the French regime and lived in fear of the Vietminh. The Vietminh countered this argument by staging a general strike in Saigon on September 17. In response, Gracey proclaimed martial law. He banned public meetings, imposed a curfew, closed down the Vietnamese newspapers and ordered all Vietnamese disarmed.

With only 1,800 British, Indian and Gurkha soldiers at his disposal, Gracey lacked the might to enforce his decree. Encouraged by Cédile, he released and armed 1,400 French army troops, most of them legionnaires who had been interned by the Japanese.

On September 22, a day after their release, French paratroopers and Foreign Legionnaires poured into the Saigon city hall and ousted the Vietminh's so-called Provisional Executive Committee. These French soldiers later went on a rampage. They took over police stations, broke into Vietnamese homes and shops, and brutally attacked innocent Vietnamese they found in the streets. The violence disgusted Cédile and infuriated Gracey, who ordered the French soldiers back into their barracks.

THE VIETMINH STRIKE BACK

On September 24, the Vietminh retaliated against the French by staging a general strike that effectively shut down Saigon. The city's 20,000 French civilians barricaded their houses or fled in panic to the security of the old Continental Palace Hotel. The crackle of gunfire and the thud of mortars could be heard throughout the city, as armed Vietminh squads attacked the airport, burned the central market and stormed the local prison to free hundreds of Vietnamese inmates.

The Vietminh blockaded the roads leading out of Saigon and urged the entire Vietnamese population to evacuate the city, much as their ancestors had done in 1859 when the French first claimed it. The Indian troops of the British army then began a slow, village-by-village pacification effort. They made some progress, but as the next 30 years would show, progress is elusive in guerrilla warfare. As Gracey described the problem of pacification to his troops, "There is no front in these operations. We may find it difficult to distinguish friend from foe."

By the end of 1945, when their obligations to supervise the Japanese surrender ended, the British began to withdraw their troops. By April 1946, the final British soldiers had left, replaced by French troops, supported with supplies from the British. With the British economy devastated by six years of war, they could provide the French only with lend-lease materials given them by the United States.

A CHANCE FOR PEACE

In March 1946, the French government and Ho Chi Minh signed an agreement by which the Democratic Republic of Vietnam was recognized as a "free state" within the Indochinese Federation (yet to be created) and the French Union. The new state, which was not precisely defined in the agreement, was interpreted by the Vietnamese as consisting of Tonkin, Annam and Cochin China. Vietnam was to have its own finances and maintain its own army. However, the French did not appear to imply recognition of any single government to rule the three regions, and details of the new state's relationship to France remained to be decided.

As a result of this agreement, French forces were permitted to reenter the north. Although no deadline had been set for a plebiscite, Ho Chi Minh was pleased with this arrangement, which confirmed his legitimacy and bought him time to strengthen the Vietminh. Moreover, he succeeded at expelling the Chinese, an achievement he considered most important. He told his critics in Hanoi, "The French are foreigners. They are weak. Colonialism is dying. The white man is finished in Asia. But if the Chinese stay now, they will never go. As for me, I prefer to sniff French shit for five years than eat Chinese shit for the rest of my life."

Differences between the French government and the Democratic Republic of Vietnam immediately developed over the question of defining the "free state." On June 1, 1946, a conference attended by Ho Chi Minh and a Vietnamese delegation at Fontainebleau was derailed when Vietnam High Commissioner Georges Thierry d'Aregenlieu violated the March agreement by proclaiming a separate government for Cochin China. The conference was concluded in September 1946 when Ho Chi Minh signed an agreement covering a cessation of hostilities and facilitating French resumption of economic and cultural activities in return for a more liberal regime.

This agreement did not include recognition of Vietnamese unity or independence and was opposed by many within Ho Chi Minh's regime. He predicted that unless the French proved more flexible in the future, war was inevitable. After Ho Chi Minh initialed a partial agreement, which the French entitled a modus vivendi, an interim understanding, he murmured to his bodyguard as he left, "I've just signed my death warrant."

THE FRENCH INDOCHINA WAR BEGINS

The fragile peace was shattered in mid-November 1946. French and Vietnamese customs officials clashed in Haiphong over who had the legal right to collect import duties. During the next few days isolated gunfire was exchanged between Vietminh militia and French soldiers The Vietminh were given two hours to evacuate the Chinese quarter of Haiphong. Two hours were not enough time even to forward the message to Hanoi for consideration by the government, and when the deadline expired, the French shelled the city, killing at least 6,000 Vietnamese civilians.

On November 28, 1946, the French demanded full control of the Hanoi-Haiphong road, until then shared with the Vietminh. General Vo Nguyen Giap prepared his troops for war. He removed his regular troops from Hanoi and other large cities. In Hanoi, the Vietminh began to erect barricades, dig trenches, fell trees and bore tunnels for safe passage between their various strongholds.

In early December, Ho Chi Minh radioed an appeal to the French parliament to honor the accord he had signed. He told a French correspondent that neither France nor Vietnam "can afford the luxury of a bloody war," but he warned that the Vietnamese would endure an "atrocious struggle" rather than "renounce their liberty." The French presented Ho Chi Minh with a demand to disarm the Vietminh and place security in their hands. He continued to request that the French rescind the order.

The exact unfolding of events is still unclear, but the Vietminh militia probably struck first on the evening of December 19, 1946, destroying the electric power plant in Hanoi, plunging the city into darkness. Homes of French civilians were attacked and mines exploded in Hanoi's streets. Also that night, French installations throughout Vietnam were attacked. Ho Chi Minh and his government fled to a preselected mountain retreat even before the attack was staged, much as the Emperor Ham Nghi had tried to do 62 years earlier, when the Vietnamese had fought their first war of resistance against the French.

General Giap issued a virtual declaration of war: "I order all soldiers and militia in the center, south, and north to stand together, go into battle, destroy the invaders, and save the nation . . . The resistance will be long and arduous, but our cause is just and we will surely triumph." French officials predicted the war would be over in three months. What came to be known as the First Indochina War would last for the next eight years.

The Guerrilla War

By April 1947, the French military forces had expelled the Vietminh forces from almost all the towns in Tonkin and northern Annam. The Vietminh Army prepared for a long war and moved into the Viet Bac, the mountainous region north of Hanoi. They resorted to guerrilla tactics against the French forces. The Vietminh were fighting in terrain they knew, under conditoins that were part of their daily life, and they had the advantage of being able to make allies of the population. A French soldier surveying the situation said, "We can't live in the jungles like the Annamites. We get cholera and malaria, and die. Or they sneak into our camps and cut our throats. There are ten thousand Annamites for every hundred Frenchmen. Out of every hundred soldiers only five go home alive."

In the early years of the war the French believed that the capture of Ho Chi Minh would decisively defeat the rebellion, as the capture of Emperor Ham Nghi in 1888 had ended an earlier uprising. In the fall of 1947, Operation Lea was launched. Fifteen-thousand men and reserves in three columns waged an attack on Ho Chi Minh's mountain outpost. The third column, consisting of 1,137 paratroopers, landed directly over Ho Chi Minh's headquarters at dawn on October 7. The paratroopers captured a ranking Vietminh official, but Ho Chi Minh and General Vo Nguyen Giap managed to escape.

Although the French had gained an enormous expanse of territory, they failed to secure the area from Vietminh regiments, who were able to penetrate the French lines by passing at night on secret jungle paths. The belief in a quick victory soon faded, and the French Union forces settled in for a long war of pacification. The French high command positioned troops in isolated outposts—known as hedgehogs—in hostile territory. The troops would then spread out in pursuit of the guerrilla forces. But the Vietminh army refused to engage in direct combat. Pacification proved elusive, as the Vietminh troops slipped away from French patrols only to return when the French had left. After three years of fighting, the Vietminh controlled large areas throughout the country, while the French controlled only the large cities.

By 1950, two governments had emerged, both competing for popular support. First was the Democratic Republic of Vietnam (DRV), led by Ho Chi Minh; the other was what later became the Republic of Vietnam (RVN) in 1955. Although the United States maintained a public policy of neutrality toward Indochina, it pressed the French to implement reforms in Vietnam that would result in a national movement leading to eventual independence. In January 1949, the American ambassador told the French government that the State Department "is desirous of the French coming to terms with . . . any truly nationalist group which has a reasonable chance of winning over the preponderance of the Vietnamese" from the Vietminh.

THE "BAO DAI SOLUTION"

On March 8, 1949, France finally approved limited independence for the state of Vietnam within the French Union. The Elysée Agreement, as this pact was known, was signed by Emperor Bao Dai, who assumed the role of chief of state. He received the right to raise an independent army but could enjoy full diplomatic relations only with Nationalist China, Thailand and the Vatican. The French also ensured that their economic and military interests were preserved.

On April 10, 1949, the Bao Dai solution was put to a popular vote in Cochin China to decide whether the southern colony would join Annam and Tonkin to form a unified Vietnam. The Vietminh declared the Bao Dai government a fraud and called for a boycott of the election. Of the 3 million qualified voters in Cochin China, only 1,700 voted. In the French-authorized Cochin assembly votes were obtained through pressure, including bribery and threats of death. After four days of debate before the assembly, on April 23, it was decided that Cochin China would become part of Vietnam. But the state of Vietnam was still not totally independent from France. On December 30, 1949, a Franco-Vietnamese agreement was signed that spelled out numerous restrictions and responsibilities limiting Vietnam's independence.

While Great Britain and the United States recognized the state of Vietnam headed by the former Emperor Bao Dai as the legitimate government, communist China became the first state to recognize the DRV in North Vietnam as the sole government of all Vietnam. By 1950, there were two Vietnams: Bao Dai's state of Vietnam and Ho Chi Minh's Democratic Republic of Vietnam (DRV).

AMERICA BECOMES INVOLVED

After a National Security Council meeting on February 27, 1950, the council and President Harry S Truman formulated the basis for a new American policy toward Indochina: "It is recognized that the threat of Communist aggression against Indochina is only one phase of anticipated Communist plans to seize all of Southeast Asia." On May 1, 1950, President Truman signed a bill authorizing $10 million in military assistance for the Bao Dai government, all to be controlled by the French. With the recognition of the Bao Dai regime, the United States established an embassy in Saigon.

American foreign policy makers were becoming increasingly concerned about changes in the global balance of power that might result from communist gains in Southeast Asia. It was believed that winning the Indochina War was crucial to deterring China from invading Vietnam. However, this policy did not take into account the colonial character of the Indochina War. The United States also underestimated the strength and will of the Vietminh, and American officials were certain that U.S. military assistance would bring victory to France and the free world.

THE GUERRILLA ARMY BECOMES A PEOPLE'S ARMY

Originally a guerrilla force, the Vietminh army had grown into a sizeable military unit, able to fight the French in large-scale engagements, mostly in the thick jungles of northern Vietnam. The region favored the Vietminh, whose troops could easily hide and ambush French columns. The Chinese communists began supplying the Vietminh with advisers and modern American weapons captured from Chiang Kai-shek's defeated Nationalists. Ho Chi Minh and his commander, Vo Nguyen Giap, believed the element of time was on their side. A long struggle would exhaust the French both on the battlefield and at home, where the French public would lose patience as the war dragged on.

As the Vietminh's leading military tactician, Giap modeled his strategy on Mao Zedong's theory of revolutionary warfare. The war would be waged in three stages. In the first stage, the revolutionaries would inflict hit-and-run guerrilla raids. Their only objective was to survive, avoid confrontation and frustrate the enemy. This would lead directly to the second stage, mounting larger actions. Finally, after gaining numerical and military superiority, they would move on to the third stage—the general counteroffensive (GCO)—and stage conventional battles.

One of Giap's initial aims was to open the supply roads to China, which meant driving the French from their strategic posts near the border. In September 1950, he took Dongkhe, located on Route 4 between Caobang and Langson, wiping out two French columns as they rushed to its rescue. One month later, having cut the French supply line from Langson, Giap attacked Caobang and succeeded in driving its defenders south to Langson. The French forces abandoned valuable artillery, mortars, 8,000 rifles and more than 1,000 tons of ammunition. Giap began assembling his regular troops at the perimeter of the Tonkin Delta. He was preparing to enter into the general counteroffensive (GCO), and Hanoi was his target.

THE FRENCH STRATEGY

Although suffering from its defeat, the French government refused to give in. Instead, on December 17, 1950, it reinforced its commitment to the Expeditionary Force with the appointment of General Jean de Lattre de Tassigny as both high commissioner and commander-in-chief of the French Union forces. De Lattre was a World War II hero, a French version of MacArthur.

De Lattre had little time to turn conditions around for the French. On January 13, 1951, Giap began the GCO. He attempted to take the French fortified city of Vinh Yen, the last major French stronghold west of Hanoi. If Giap were successful, Hanoi might be in Vietminh hands by the Tet festival, the lunar New Year that began in February. In the first day of fighting the Vietminh completely surrounded Vinh Yen. But the next day, de Lattre personally took charge, flying into the besieged outpost in his private two-seater plane, accompanied by reinforcements. After being bombarded for three days, Giap retreated, leaving 6,000 Vietminh dead and carrying off another 8,000 wounded. Hanoi was safe for the time being.

De Lattre, now eager to go on the offensive, flew to Washington to request more American aid. He warned that the loss of northern Vietnam would open the rest of Southeast Asia to the advance of communism, which would eventually engulf the Middle East and Africa. The United States, now committed to the Korean War, could give only partial help. Although De Lattre got more transport airplanes, trucks and other equipment, it was not enough to turn the tide for France. Five months later, he died of cancer in Paris. For the next two years the war was at a stalemate.

In 1951, France's increasing war weariness resulted in a new policy. The French did not give it a name, but 15 years later Richard Nixon would call the more extensive American version of the same policy "Vietnamization." The U.S. plan was to create an independent army for the state of Vietnam, which was to be equipped and supported with American aid. However, the French distrusted these Vietnamese soldiers, fearing they might defect to the Vietminh, and most were assigned to passive military duties.

By 1953, after seven years of war, France had lost 74,000 troops in Vietnam, and nearly 200,000 were bogged down. The public was quickly withdrawing its support for *la sale guerre*, "the dirty war." The controversy had entered France's National Assembly, where debates were conducted over new appropriations for the Indochina conflict.

THE NAVARRE PLAN

In March and April 1953, high-level French and American defense planners met in Washington and devised a scheme that would regain the initiative for the French. Known as the Navarre Plan, after General Henri Navarre, who took command of the Expeditionary Corps in May 1953, its first part consisted of the Vietnamese army assuming a larger role, with the United States assuming the financial costs. The second part included the concept of a *mole d'amarrage*, or mooring point, from which the French forces would penetrate the Vietminh's rear areas, trying to ambush and engage the guerrillas in pitched battles. Navarre decided to establish his base of operations at Dien Bien Phu, but it first had to be recaptured.

On November 20, 1953, the French began their 290-day reoccupation of Dien Bien Phu. Meanwhile, Giap had encircled the valley, moving 33 infantry battalions, six artillery regiments and a regiment of engineers toward Dien Bien Phu. It was not until the battle began some hundred days later that the French realized how completely outnumbered and outgunned they were.

THE SIEGE BEGINS

Dien Bien Phu soon proved itself useless as a land-air base. By late December, it became apparent that Giap had begun to build up a huge siege force. By March 12, the French had lost 1,037 troops, on patrols that ventured outside the safety of the garrison. Navarre had underes-

Genevieve de Garland-Terraube, a 29-year-old French Air Force nurse, tends to a wounded soldier at Dien Bien Phu. She was the only woman to stay in the valley throughout the battle. She became known as the "Angel of Dien Bien Phu." Courtesy of the National Archives.

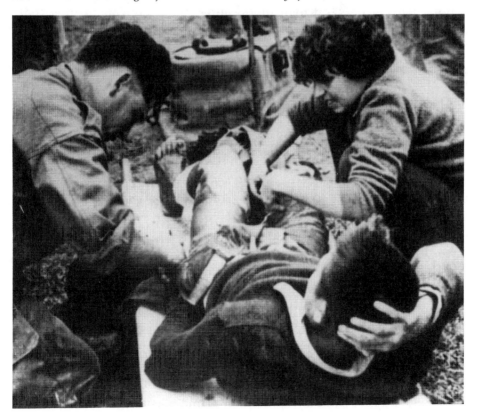

timated Giap's ability to move a huge force rapidly through the jungle. He had also failed to anticipate how Giap's howitzers, positioned within easy range of his airstrip, could cut off incoming and outgoing flights, making it difficult for his besieged troops to receive supplies, evacuate the wounded and withdraw themselves, if necessary.

Giap's army was now far different from the one that had engaged the French for over eight years. Total Vietminh forces had grown from 150,000 to almost 350,000. Moreover, Giap's troops were no longer organized into small units, but had grown to regiments and 12,000-man divisions, equipped with sophisticated Russian and Chinese arms, including antiaircraft weapons.

On the afternoon of March 13, 1954, Giap ordered his force of 40,000 troops surrounding Dien Bien Phu to begin their attack on the French garrison. His first target, stronghold Beatrice, fell immediately, and stronghold Gabrielle collapsed the next day, as Vietminh guns ravaged the airstrip. With the airstrip closed, the garrison had to depend on parachute drops for supplies and reinforcements. The monsoon clouds hindered French aircraft from bombing the Vietminh and made parachuting supplies to the besieged post difficult. The French knew that they were doomed on the battlefield unless they received more aid from the United States.

While the battle raged, on March 20 General Paul Ely, French chief of staff, flew from Paris to Washington. U.S. aid had grown to represent 80% of France's war costs, and now Ely requested that the U.S. respond with airpower if the Chinese intervened. He was assured that the U.S. would respond immediately if air power was needed.

OPERATION VULTURE

Admiral Arthur W. Radford, chairman of the Joint Chiefs of Staff, met with Ely and proposed a plan named Operation Vulture, which called for American bombers to conduct several raids around the perimeter of Dien Bien Phu. Ely returned to Paris under the impression that Radford was speaking for President Eisenhower. On March 31, Eisenhower told the American people that he could "conceive of no greater tragedy than for the United States to become involved in an all-out war in Indochina." He would authorize the strike around Dien Bien Phu, but only with congressional approval. The request was rejected by several influential senators and representatives, among them Senator Lyndon Johnson of Texas.

However, Congress indicated that it might support an air strike if it were part of a multinational effort, either through the United Nations or with the support of a group of allies. Time was too short to go to the U.N., so Eisenhower sent Secretary of State John Foster Dulles to line up allied support. Convincing Australia, New Zealand, Thailand and the Philippines was not difficult. But the British refused to endorse the strike around Dien Bien Phu, fearing that it would sabotage the upcoming Geneva talks on the future of Vietnam.

While France approved of a unilateral strike by the United States, it feared that a joint action would remove it from the basic decisions concerning the war. The French preferred to negotiate a settlement at the Geneva Conference rather than risk losing control. Meanwhile, by early April the situation at Dien Bien Phu had deteriorated.

Hell in a Very Small Place

Giap had adopted a new tactic of building a series of trenches so that his troops could choke off the outer French strongholds one by one. Every night the Vietminh would move a little closer and dig in. The French, by now short on ammunition, were also being bombarded with Vietminh loudspeakers that endlessly blared "Surrender or die" in Vietnamese, French, Arabic and German.

On April 21, the French renewed their request for American intervention to break the siege. They had agreed to withdraw their opposition to a multinational action. But the British flatly refused. Thus faded any chance for France receiving any help in saving Dien Bien Phu.

Giap launched a dual attack on May 1 against the central sector and the isolated southern stronghold. The Vietminh now outnumbered the French 10 to one. Nearly 2,100 French troops were killed in action and more than 5,000 were wounded. The Vietminh had lost an estimated 7,900 men and had 15,000 wounded. On the afternoon of May 7, 1954, the Vietminh's red flag went up over the French command bunker at Dien Bien Phu. Ten thousand French troops were taken as prisoners-of-war, but only 6,500 of them survived. The next day in Geneva, nine delegations assembled around a conference table at the old League of Nations building to begin their discussion of the Indochina problem.

Compromise in Geneva

The conference was cochaired by Great Britain and the Soviet Union, with representatives from the United States, France, China, the state of Vietnam (which was to become South Vietnam, officially the Republic of Vietnam [RVN]), the Democratic Republic of Vietnam (DRV) (which was to become North Vietnam), Cambodia and Laos.

A French Foreign Legionnaire goes to war along the dry rib of a rice paddy, during a mission through communist-held areas in the Red River Delta, between Haiphong and Hanoi, ca. 1954. Courtesy of the National Archives.

After three months of tense negotiations a cease-fire agreement was reached on July 20, 1954, between France and the Democratic Republic of Vietnam. The agreement fixed a provisional demarcation line roughly along the 17th parallel (which was to become the DMZ), pending countrywide elections in July 1956. The Geneva Accords also included a provision for the movement of civilians between the zones within a 300-day period. An International Control Commission (ICC) was formed with representatives from India, Canada and Poland to enforce these provisions, including the scheduled elections.

The cease-fire agreement turned out to be the only document signed at the Geneva Conference. The armistice agreement was reached over the objection of South Vietnam, which did not sign the Final Declaration. When the United States joined South Vietnam in refusing to sign the document, so did the communist nations refuse. The United States pledged not to upset the accords by "threat or use of force." However, it declared that it would look upon any renewed aggression in violation of the agreement "with grave concern."

TWO VIETNAMS

The only real accomplishment of the Geneva Conference was the end of hostilities between France and the Democratic Republic of Vietnam. Vietnam was neither united nor fully independent. A military truce was achieved that awaited a political settlement, which never really occurred. The conference was merely an interlude between two wars, or, rather, a pause in the same war. Within five years North and South Vietnam would be openly at war.

While the government of Ho Chi Minh, centered in Hanoi, moved to implement its program of communism north of the 17th parallel, France transferred the remnants of its administration to the state of Vietnam, with its capital in Saigon. Bao Dai, as chief of state, called on Ngo Dinh Diem, who was living in exile in Paris, to become the prime minister of the new government. Shortly after he took office on July 7, 1954, Diem was confronted with the overwhelming challenge of bringing order and stability to a country on the brink of anarchy and economic collapse.

The new regime was under attack not from communists, who Diem had always expected to face, but from the Binh Xuyen, the mob of gangsters who controlled most of Saigon. The government was also being challenged by such armed political-religious dissidents as the Cao Dai and the Hoa Hao sects. By April 28, 1955, Saigon was in an uproar. A shootout between Diem's forces and the Binh Xuyen was ravaging the streets of the city.

DIEM TAKES CHARGE

After two days of house-to-house combat, which subjected thousands of panic-stricken residents to waves of crossfire, wounding and killing some, the Diem army had broken the Binh Xuyen forces. Encouraged by his success, Diem took the offensive against the Hoa Hao and Cao Dai strongholds. Within a few months, Diem's troops had eradicated any sect resistance. Diem's astonishing victory over the Binh Xuyen and the sects made him into something of an instant hero in South Vietnam.

The American response to Diem's success in defeating the armed opposition was quick and enthusiastic. The Eisenhower administration was now convinced that Diem was the only man to build a new state. On the Senate floor, Hubert Humphrey echoed the president's admiration for the new leader: "Premier Diem is the best hope that we have in South Vietnam . . . He deserves and must have the wholehearted support of the American government and our foreign policy."

After subduing the Binh Xuyen and the sects, Diem denounced the French for their "collusion" in a conspiracy to topple his government. On January 19, 1956, he informed the French that "the presence of foreign troops, no matter how friendly . . . was incompatible with Vietnam's concept of full independence." In April 1956, the last 10,000 soldiers of the French Expeditionary Corps, which had numbered nearly 150,000 in 1954, bid their final adieu to Vietnam.

With the French gone, the United States was the only foreign military presence in the country. The Geneva Accords permitted the U.S. to have a limited number of troops, 342, stationed in Vietnam until nationwide elections were held in the summer of 1956. The United States did not sign these declarations, but it did agree that it would refrain from using force or the threat of force to disturb these provisions.

In the late spring of 1956, the Americans reorganized their military advisory program, the Military Assistance Advisory Group (MAAG). MAAG's new mission was to streamline the Vietnamese army of 250,000 troops into a smaller conventional force of 150,000 soldiers, capable of repelling an invasion from the north. The U.S. equipped and trained this army and now dispensed its funds for the armed forces directly through Diem.

THE REVOLUTION CONTINUES

When Ho Chi Minh returned to Hanoi in October 1954, after eight years in the jungle, his problems differed from those that faced Diem. The French army was leaving the north, and the massive flight of the Catholics to the south made his control easier. But he was beset by severe economic difficulties. Starting in 1955, he set up a land-reform program that touched off atrocities throughout the country. Anyone suspected of having worked for the French was executed as a "traitor," and other victims included those who had shown insufficient support for the Vietminh. The communists have never published an official count of those killed in the land reform, but thousands died, and thousands more were interned in forced labor camps.

The Hanoi government, having anticipated that the 1956 nationwide election would reunify the country, organized a group of Vietminh soldiers to remain in the south and represent their interests. The "stay behinds" conducted organizational and propaganda activities throughout the countryside, working with the peasants and explaining the clauses of the Geneva Accords. In urban areas, cadres formed political groups to criticize Diem's policies and mobilize support for the elections.

In response to the Vietminh propaganda, Diem initiated the Anti-Communist Denunciation Campaign. Diem's government no longer called the cadres Vietminh but used the derogatory term "Vietcong," or "Vietnamese Communist." Diem's own corps of cadres, members of the National Revolutionary Movement dominated by his brothers Nhu and Can, organized mass meetings in the countryside to incite the peasants to expose and condemn communists. In 1956, a presidential ordinance authorized the arrest and detention "of all pesons deemed dangerous to the state." This measure inflicted hardship and suffering on tens of thousands of people, both communists and noncommunists. It did, however, succeed in crushing the Communist Party structure in the south.

By July 20, 1956, the deadline had passed for the elections set by the Final Declaration at the Geneva Conference. With complete support from the United States, Diem announced that he would not meet with the North Vietnamese to discuss the elections and that those elections would not be held. His explanation, and that of the United States, was that his government had not been a party to the Geneva Declaration in which the election was stipulated, and that elections were not possible unless they could be genuinely free.

A NATION AT WAR

When the political struggle for elections failed, North Vietnam began to consider other means for achieving its goal of unification. Despite the cease-fire agreement, a well-organized Vietminh underground network was based in the jungle regions of the southern Mekong Delta and along the Cambodian and Laotian border regions. In May 1959, at the Fifteenth Plenum of the Central Committee of the North Vietnamese Communist Party, Hanoi's fateful decision was announced. It called for a "strong North Vietnamese base for helping the South Vietnamese overthrow Diem and expel the United States."

By the end of 1959, approximately 2,500 village officials in the south had been assassinated. Moreover, there was a growing number of armed attacks on highway traffic and government military outposts. At Bien Hoa, 20 miles north of Saigon, on July 8, 1959, Major Dale R. Buis and Master Sergeant Chester M. Ovnand became the first American advisers killed in the Vietnam War when guerrillas struck their MAAG compound. The Second Indochina War had begun.

CHRONICLE OF EVENTS

1945

September 2: After the departure of Japanese occupation forces, Ho Chi Minh and the communist-dominated Vietminh Independence League establish the Government of the Democratic Republic of Vietnam in Hanoi.

September 22: French troops return to Vietnam to assert France's sovereignty.

September 26: In Saigon, Lieutenant Colonel A. Peter Dewey, head of the OSS mission in Vietnam, is driving a jeep to the airport when he is shot by Vietminh troops (who evidently mistake him for a Frenchman). He is the first American to die in Vietnam.

November: The Indochinese Communist Party is dissolved and replaced by the Association for Marxist Studies, as Ho Chi Minh tries to broaden his base.

1946

March 6: Ho Chi Minh signs an agreement with France, which recognizes the Democratic Republic of Vietnam as a "free state" within the French Union. French troops are permitted to return to the north to replace the Nationalist Chinese.

June 1: A conference in Fontainbleau, attended by Ho Chi Minh and a delegation of Vietnamese, hoping to clarify the status of the "new state," breaks up when Vietnam High Commissioner Georges Thierry d'Argenlieu violates the March agreement by proclaiming a separate government for Cochin China.

September: Ho Chi Minh signs modus vivendi covering economic issues and agrees to cessation of hostilities. He returns to Vietnam.

November 23: Amid growing tensions, French warships bombard Haiphong.

December 19: In Hanoi the Democratic Republic of Vietnam launches its first attack against the French. What will come to be known as the Indochina War begins.

1947

April: Preparing for a long war, the Vietminh army moves into Viet Bac, the mountainous region north of Hanoi.

October: General Etienne Valluy, leading the biggest French colonial operation to date, fails to overcome the Vietminh army.

1948

June 5: High Commissioner Bollaert and General Nguyen Van Xuan sign the Baie d'Along Agreement. The agreement names Bao Dai as chief of state and France recognizes the independence of Vietnam within the French Union; however, Ho Chi Minh and Ngo Dinh Diem denounce the Xuan government as a French tool.

1949

March 8: Bao Dai and President Vincent Auriol of France sign the Elysée Agreement, making Vietnam an "associated state" within the French Union.

Vietnamese parading in 1948, following their independence from France within the French Union. Courtesy of the Library of Congress.

1950

January 14: Ho Chi Minh declares that the Democratic Republic of Vietnam is the only legal government. The Soviet Union and China extend recognition, and China starts supplying modern weapons to the Vietminh.

May 8: The U.S. announces it will provide military and economic aid to the French in Indochina, starting with a grant of $10 million.

June 27: President Truman announces the dispatch of a 35-member military mission to Vietnam.

July 26: President Truman signs legislation granting $15 million in military aid to the French for the war in Indochina.

December 23: The United States signs a Mutual Defense Assistance Agreement with France, Vietnam, Cambodia and Laos (the French Associated States).

1951

September 7: The United States signs an agreement with Saigon for direct aid to South Vietnam. American presence in Saigon is increased as civilian government employees join the military already there.

1952

July: President Truman promotes the American Legation in Saigon to an embassy—one sovereign country dealing with another.

November 4: Dwight David Eisenhower is elected president; with his administration the Indochina War is no longer regarded as a colonial war, but as a war between communism and the free world.

1953

May 20: General Henri Navarre assumes command of French Union forces. He advances a plan for a buildup of French forces preparatory to a massive attack against the Vietminh.

September 30: President Eisenhower approves a budget of $385,000,000 for military aid to the French forces in Vietnam.

November 20: General Vo Nguyen Giap is forced out of Dien Bien Phu, which he had taken from the French a year before. He sets up a supply base at Taum Gio near Dien Bien Phu.

December: Vietminh forces push into Laos.

1954

March 13: The Vietminh attack the French garrison at Dien Bien Phu. A force of 40,000 Vietminh with heavy artillery ring the 15,000 French troops stationed behind enemy lines. Vietminh shell the airstrip. French troops face defeat, for all their supplies must arrive by air.

April 29: President Eisenhower announces that the United States will not intervene in Indochina.

May 7: Dien Bien Phu falls to the Vietminh. Nearly 2,100 French troops are killed during the 55-day siege. Ten thousand French troops are taken as prisoners-of-war, but only 6,500 survive. An estimated 7,900 Vietminh are killed; 15,000 wounded.

May 8: Indochina phase of the Geneva Conference begins; attending are the Big Four—the United States, Britain, France and the Soviet Union. For six weeks negotiations are held on ending the Indochina War.

June 1: Colonel Edward G. Lansdale, USAF, arrives in Saigon as chief of the Saigon Military Mission. He is in fact a member of the CIA assigned to paramilitary operations against the communist Vietnamese.

June 18: At his chateau in Cannes, France, Bao Dai selects Ngo Dinh Diem as the new prime minister of Vietnam.

July 7: Diem returns to Saigon.

July 20: French and Vietminh representatives sign Geneva cease-fire agreement. Vietnam is divided into northern and southern zones pending reunification elections in 1956.

August: Under the terms of the Geneva Agreement, a flow of almost 1 million refugees from North to South Vietnam begins. France and the United States provide aircraft and ships for transportation. The majority of the refugees are Catholic; others include various factions opposed to the Vietminh.

September 8: The Southeast Asia Treaty Organization (SEATO) is formed by the United States, Britain, France, Australia, New Zealand, Pakistan, Thailand and the Philippines.

October 9: French forces leave Hanoi.

October 11: The Vietminh formally take over Hanoi and North Vietnam.

October 24: President Eisenhower advises Premier Ngo Dinh Diem that the U.S. will provide assistance directly to South Vietnam.

November 3: General J. Lawton Collins arrives in Saigon to coordinate the operations of all U.S. agencies in South Vietnam.

1955

May 10: South Vietnam makes a formal request for U.S. military advisers.

July 20: South Vietnam refuses to participate in Vietnam-wide elections as called for in the Geneva Agreements on the grounds that the elections would not be free in the north.

October 23: Diem defeats Bao Dai in a referendum and becomes chief of state.

October 26: Diem proclaims the Republic of South Vietnam with himself as its first president.

1956

April 28: The last French soldier leaves Vietnam and the French High Command for Indochina is officially dissolved. The U.S. Military Assistance Advisory Group (MAAG) assumes responsibility for training South Vietnamese military forces.

July 20: The deadline set at Geneva in 1954 for nationwide elections passes. Diem declares South Vietnam is in favor of elections but states that the absence of freedom in North Vietnam makes it impractical to hold elections.

1957

January 3: The International Control Commission reports that neither North Vietnam nor South Vietnam is complying with the Geneva Agreements.

May 5–19: Diem visits the United States. President Eisenhower reaffirms support for his regime.

October: Communist insurgent activity in South Vietnam begins when a decision is reached in Hanoi to organize 37 armed companies in the Mekong Delta.

October 22: U.S. military personnel suffer their first casualties in the Vietnam War when 13 Americans are wounded in three terrorist bombings of MAAG and U.S. Information Service installations in Saigon.

1958

June: The communists form a coordinated command structure in the eastern Mekong Delta.

1959

May: U.S. advisers are assigned to the regimental level of South Vietnamese armed forces.

At the 15th plenum of the Central Committee, North Vietnam's leaders formally decide to take control of the growing insurgency in the South.

July: Hanoi sets up 559 Group to organize the Ho Chi Minh Trail to supply routes to South Vietnam. The activities of the group are kept secret, as they are in clear violation of the Geneva agreements.

July 8: Major Dale R. Buis and Master Sergeant Chester M. Ovnand become the first Americans killed in the Vietnam War when guerrillas strike a MAAG compound in Bienhoa, 20 miles northeast of Saigon.

August: Diem promulgates a law authorizing severe repression of communists and other dissidents.

September 26: Vietcong ambush two companies of Saigon's 23rd Division, killing 12 soldiers and capturing most of their weapons. The attack demonstrates Hanoi's decision to switch from a "political struggle" to an "armed struggle."

December 31: Approximately 760 U.S. military personnel are now in Vietnam. South Vietnamese Armed Forces (SVNAF) now total 243,000 personnel.

Eyewitness Testimony

I still do not want to get mixed up in any Indochina decision . . . From both the military and civil point of view, action at this time is premature.

President Franklin D. Roosevelt, to Secretary of State Edward R. Stettinius, memorandum of January 1, 1945, in U.S. Department of State's Foreign Relations of the United States, 1945 *(1967–1969).*

To me, he was just another old Vietnamese. Except for one thing, that in parting he had said: "Now if you need any help, contact the following people," and he gave me a list of names which at the time meant nothing to me, in Kunming [China]. Well sure enough those people started to come into Kunming headquarters at our compound and brought us some interesting order of battle information on the Japanese in Indo-China. So we were beginning to get information which was free—no charge connected with it, which was unusual. It was reasonably accurate. At first we paid no credence to it. But it contradicted French intelligence. And we were more or less compelled after a while to really read the information that was coming from Vietnam, and it was good.

Archimedes Patti, OSS officer, on meeting Ho Chi Minh during field operations in southern China in April 1945, in Charlton and Moncrieff's Many Reasons Why *(1978).*

On August 11, 1945, the Japanese invaders completely disintegrated and asked to surrender to Allied Forces. The Soviet, British, and American conference meeting in Moscow has accepted the surrender of Japan. Thus the Pacific war is about to end.

The hour and minute of the general uprising has arrived, the general struggle has come to a decisive time; you, comrades, must calmly and determinedly carry out the orders which follow:

1. Mobilize troops to strike into the cities where there are sufficient conditions for victory.

2. Deploy to attack and cut off withdrawing troops of the enemy . . .

General Vo Nguyen Giap, commander of the Vietminh army, to the Vietminh, message of August 12, 1945, on behalf of the Provisional Executive Committee of the Liberated Zone, in Orders of the Day *(1952).*

You would understand still better if you could see what is happening here, if you could feel the will for independence which has been smoldering in the hearts of all and which no human force can hold in check any longer. Even if you were to come to reestablish French government here it would not be obeyed: each village would be a nest of resistance, each former collaborator an enemy, and your officials and your colonists themselves would ask to leave that unbreathable atmosphere.

I beg you to understand that the only means of safeguarding French interests and the spiritual influence of France in Indochina is to recognize unreservedly the independence of Viet-Nam and to renounce any idea of re-establishing French sovereignty or French administration here in any form.

Emperor Bao Dai, to General Charles de Gaulle, letter of August 18, 1945, in Devillers' Historie du Viêt-Nam de 1940 à 1952 *(1952).*

As for the United States, it is a democratic country which has no territorial ambitions but has contributed particularly to the defeat of our enemy, Japanese fascism. Therefore we regard the United States as a good friend.

General Vo Nguyen Giap, speech of September 2, 1945, in Trang Su Moi *[A New Page of History] (1945).*

The Provisional Annamese Government in Indo-China is in full control and so well organized that several attempts by French from Calcutta to parachute into the country have been frustrated. The parachutists, although not maltreated, were held as prisoners. According to the Annamese Prime Minister, should the French attempt a return, the Annamese are determined to maintain their independence even at the cost of lives. They feel they have nothing to lose and all to gain. Meanwhile, however, the Prime Minister has promised the OSS representative in Hanoi that no organized violence against Europeans will occur until the Chinese assume control in the area.

William J. Donovan, OSS director, to Secretary of State James Byrnes, memorandum of September 5, 1945, Department of State Central Files, National Archives, 851G.0019-545.

Our team left by foot, car, and boat and arrived at Hanoi about 4 PM. We obtained quarters through

Saigon street, 1952. Courtesy of the National Archives.

the Vietminh party, which was authorized by the Patti mission.

We spent the time from 9 Sept to 16 Sept seeing the city buying souvenirs, saying good-bye to our Vietminh friends, and making arrangements to return to Kunming. Hanoi was an extremely festive city for everyone except the French.

Vietminh flags were flying from almost every house. Banners were stretched across the streets with various "slogans" in Annamese, English, Chinese, Russian, Indian, etc. French was noticeably absent.

Some of the slogans seen everywhere were as follows: "Welcome Allies," "Welcome Peace Commission," "Down with French Imperialism," "Let's kick out French Imperialism," "Independence or Death," "2,000,000 people died under French domination," "Vietminh for the Vietnamese."

Our friend of the forest, Mr. C. M. Hoo, now Mr. Ho Chi Minh, was President of the Provisional Government and Minister of Foreign Affairs. Another friend of the forest, Mr. Van, now Vo Nguyen Giap became Minister of Interior.

Major Allison K. Thomas, OSS officer, to the U.S. Senate, report of September 17, 1945, in Senate Committee on Foreign Relations, Hearings on Causes, Origins and Lessons of the Vietnam War (1973).

How would the Vietnamese, already bloodied in skirmishes with the French in various parts of the country, react to the sight of a French reinvestment of their capital city? I sat in a waterfront cafe in Haiphong and watched the incoming heavy cruiser "Richelieu", then the only capital ship in the French navy, lob shells into the foothills behind the port city. These, it turned out later, constituted a show of force rather than an attack but the shelling served to heighten tensions another notch.

Frank M. White, OSS officer, in December 1945, Senate Committee on Foreign Relations, Hearings on Causes, Origins and Lessons of the Vietnam War.

. . . security and freedom can only be guaranteed by our independence from any colonial power, and our free cooperation with all other powers. It is with this firm conviction that we request of the United States as guardians and champions of World Justice to take a decisive step in support of our independence.

What we ask has been graciously granted to the Philippines. Like the Philippines our goal is full independence and *full cooperation with the United States*. We will do our best to make this independence and cooperation profitable to the whole world.

President Ho Chi Minh, Provisional Government of the Democratic Republic of Vietnam, to President Harry S Truman, letter of February 16, 1946, in Porter's Vietnam: The Definitive Documentation of Human Decisions *(1979).*

Hanoi looked like a city already at war. The Vietnamese troops under General Vo Nguyen Giap . . . had turned the capital into a maze of trenches and bunkers under the eyes of the French. What the French did not see was the network of tunnels constructed secretly under the city. These underground passages connected secret command posts in various private homes at key locations, including the house of the Vietnamese mayor.

Robert Trumbull, Southeast Asia correspondent, 1946, in The Scrutable East *(1964).*

. . . there is the occasional crack of gunfire, the thud of exploding grenades, the mad run of automatic rifle or machine gun-fire close in or toward the environs. Or the sky glows with fire where a gasoline dump goes up or a French barracks is set ablaze. For Saigon is under seige . . . Out there along the roads and waterways French and British and Indian—and Japanese—troops meet Annamite guerrilla attacks . . . There the thatch of Annamite village every day goes up in smoke and the people flushed out come into Saigon in those long straggling lines of prisoners.

Harold R. Isaacs, Far East correspondent, in Harper's, *article of March 1946.*

He spoke of his friendship and admiration for the United States and the Americans he had known and worked with in the jungle, etc., and how they had treated the Annamese as equals. He spoke of his desire to build up Vietnam in collaboration with the French so that his people might be better off, and to that end they wanted independence to seek friends

among other countries as well as France and to secure the capital needed to develop their country, which France was now too poor to give them. He said he knew that the United States did not like communism, but that that was not his aim. If he could secure their independence that was enough for his lifetime. "Perhaps fifty years from now the United States will be communist; and then the Vietnam can be also" or "then they will not object if the Vietnam is also."

Abbott Low Moffat, chief of the Division of Southeast Asian Affairs, to the U.S. State Department, letter of December 1946, on his meeting with Ho Chi Minh, in U.S. Senate's Committee on Foreign Relations, the United States and Vietnam: 1944–1947 *(1972).*

If those gooks want a fight, they'll get it.

General Etienne Valluy, commander of French Union Forces in Indochina, upon landing in Haiphong, December 17, 1946, in Karnow's Vietnam: A History *(1983).*

Every minute, hundreds of thousands of people die all over the world. The life or death of thousands of human beings, even if they are compatriots, represents very little.

General Vo Nguyen Giap, 1946, in Fall's Vietnam Witness *(1966).*

Compatriots, stand up!

Men and women, old and young, regardless of religious creed, political affiliation and nationality, all Vietnamese must stand up to fight the French colonialists and save the Fatherland. Those who have rifles will use their rifles; those who have swords will use their swords; those who have no swords will use spades, hoes or sticks . . .

The hour for national salvation has struck! We must shed even our last drop of blood to safeguard our country . . . with our determination to face all sacrifices, we are bound to win.

President Ho Chi Minh, to the people of Vietnam, appeal of December 20, 1946, in Selected Works *(1961–1962).*

Under the cover of darkness, members of the Vietminh front, many of whom were daytime peasants, had grabbed their guns and set out to assassinate designated enemies, either French or Vietnamese who were known supporters of the French, in the villages around Saigon or in the city itself. The night before I arrived, fifteen murders had taken place, and this, I discovered, was an average toll. On my first morning, I had surveyed the area in a light plane and had seen scores of burnt-out houses in the villages—this, too, was part of the campaign of terror, and of its inevitable consequence, reprisal. There were already more than fifty thousand French colonial troops in the country, including some twelve thousand members of the famous French Foreign Legion.

Robert Shaplen, journalist, 1946, in The Lost Revolution *(1965).*

. . . we declare solemnly that the Vietnamese people desire only unity and independence in the French Union, and we pledge ourselves to respect French economic and cultural interests . . . If France would but say the word to cease hostility immediately, so many lives and so much property would be saved and friendship and confidence would be regained.

President Ho Chi Minh, to the French government, message of March 1, 1947, in Selected Works.

We must protect the life and possessions of Frenchmen, of foreigners, of our Indochinese friends who have confidence in French liberty. It is necessary that we disengage our garrisons, re-establish essential communications, assure the safety of populations which have taken refuge with us. That we have done.

Premier Paul Ramadier of France, March 1947, in Gravel's The Pentagon Papers *(1971).*

You may kill ten of my men for every one I kill of yours, but even at those odds, you will lose and I will win.

President Ho Chi Minh, to the French, statement of 1948, in Wintle's The Dictionary of War Quotations *(1989).*

Determined to safeguard their national independence from the French colonialists, the Vietnamese people and army are fighting heroically and are nearing final victory. Throughout these years of resistance, Viet Nam has won the sympathy and support of the people of the world. The Government of the Democratic Republic of Viet Nam declares to the Governments of the countries of the world that it is the only lawful Government of the entire Vietnamese people. On the basis of common interests, it is ready to establish diplomatic relations with the Governments of all countries which respect the equality,

territorial sovereignty and national independence of Viet Nam in order to contribute to safeguarding peace and building world democracy.

President Ho Chi Minh, to the governments of the world, declaration of January 14, 1950, in Selected Works.

We shall attack without cease until final victory, until we have swept the enemy forces from Indochina. During the first and second stage, we have gnawed away at the enemy forces; now we must destroy them. All military activities of the third stage must tend to the same simple aim—the total destruction of French forces.

General Vo Nguyen Giap, pamphlet of February 2, 1950, in Nhiem Vu Quan Su Truoc Mat Chuyen Sang Tong Phan Cong *[Immediate Military Tasks for Switching to the General Counteroffensive] (1950).*

The Viet Minh has secret cells in Hanoi and in every city we hold. There must be at least three thousand Viets here in Hanoi. They throw grenades, set fires, and murder wherever they can. And nobody knows who is the Viet Minh chief. He may be that little clerk there, so intent on his papers, or he may be the servant at home now with my wife and children. Who knows? This rebellion is like a plant that you cut and cut, and it still comes back. You can't kill it. The only way would be to bring half a million troops and go from village to village, sweeping the whole thing clean.

Anonymous French official in Hanoi, quoted in Berrigan's Saturday Evening Post *article of March 18, 1950.*

The United States Government, convinced that neither national independence nor democratic evolution exist in any area dominated by Soviet imperialism, considers the situation to be such as to warrant its according economic aid and military equipment to the Associated States of Indochina and to France in order to assist them in restoring stability and permitting these states to pursue their peaceful and democratic development.

Secretary of State Dean Acheson, statement of May 8, 1950, in U.S. Department of State's American Foreign Policy 1950–1955: Basic Documents *(1957).*

The attack upon Korea makes it plain beyond all doubt that communism has passed beyond the use of subversion to conquer independent nations and will now use armed invasion and war. It has defied the orders of the Security Council of the United Nations issued to preserve international peace and security. . . .

I have similarly directed acceleration in the furnishing of military assistance to the forces of France and the Associated States in Indochina and the dispatch of a military mission to provide close working relations with those forces.

President Truman, statement of June 27, 1950, in U.S. Department of State's American Foreign Policy 1950–1955: Basic Documents.

To gain independence, we, the Indochinese people, must defeat the French colonialists, our enemy number one. At the same time, we will struggle against the U.S. interventionists. The deeper their interference the more powerful are our solidarity and our struggle.

We will expose their manoeuvres before all our people, especially those living in areas under their control.

We will expose all those who serve as lackeys for the U.S. imperialists to coerce, deceive and divide our people.

The close solidarity between the peoples of Viet Nam, Cambodia and Laos constitutes a force capable of defeating the French colonialists and the U.S. interventionists.

President Ho Chi Minh, July 25, 1950, in Selected Works.

All of a sudden a sound can be heard in the sky and strange birds appear, getting larger and larger. Airplanes. I order my men to take cover from the bombs and machine-gun bullets. But the planes dived upon us without firing their guns. However, all of a sudden, hell opens in front of my eyes. Hell comes in the form of large, egg-shaped containers, dropping from the first plane, followed by other eggs from the second and third plane. Immense sheets of flames, extending over hundreds of meters, it seems, strike terror in the ranks of my soldiers. This is *napalm*, the fire which falls from the skies.

Ngo Van Chieu, Vietminh officer, on the battle of Vinh-Yen, January 1951, in Journal d'un combattant Vietminh *(1954).*

Today there is in the world a city whose importance is great, it is the capital of Tonkin: Hanoi.

Ho Chi Minh, 1948. Courtesy of the National Archives.

Morally this city has become, in the eyes of all peoples of Southeast Asia, the test of the will and of the power to stop Communism. Militarily its loss would open to the Communist invasion the road to Bangkok, to Singapore, and many other roads that you can easily guess. Gentlemen, Hanoi today is for the free world of Southeast Asia both the Bastogne of December 1944 and the Berlin of June 1947.

And the loss of Southeast Asia would mean that Communism would have at its disposal essential strategic raw materials, that Japanese economy would forever be unbalanced and that the whole of Asia would be threatened.

General Jean de Lattre de Tassigny, French Army, to the National Press Club in Washington, D.C., speech of September 20, 1951, French Press and Information Service (Document #61).

Accompanied by General Jean de Lattre de Tassigny, General J. Lawton Collins, the U.S. Army chief of staff (second from left), visits French forces in Hanoi in October 1951. De Lattre wears a black arm band for his son, killed in Vietnam. Congressman John F. Kennedy (rear, second from right) is on a private tour of Indochina. Courtesy of the National Archives.

It became increasingly evident after my arrival in Indo China and seeing the terrain, visiting the troops, and knowing the type of combat, that the most important and immediate need to the successful conclusion of the war in Indo China was more troops. During the past year, the Vietnamese Army has been organized as scheduled. However, most of these units have been activated by merely transferring and renaming units in the Vietnamese Army which were already in being in the French Colonial Army. I am convinced that additional Vietnamese battalions, over and above the units approved for support by the Joint Chiefs of Staff, should be activated.

Brigadier General T.J.H. Trapnell, USA, Chief Military Assistance Advisory Group (MAAG), Indochina, to U.S. Army Chief of Staff J. Lawton Collins, letter of December 20, 1952, in U.S. Department of Defense's United States-Vietnam Relations *(1971).*

Shortly after midnight, the steady stream of small-arms fire stopped. The flashlights twinkled across the endless vista of soggy paddy fields as the Reds signaled each other from village to village. Two hours later, the Vietminh opened up again . . . the sergeant ordered out fifteen men to de-mine the muddy trails between the paddy fields and to find out what happened.

Back in the safety of the press camp in beleaguered Hanoi, the French High Command's daily communiqué boldly announced: "Situation normale sur l'ensemble du territoire." And so the war goes on, night after night, in the northern delta, a rice-rich mud bath which war maps usually claim as French territory.

Arnaud de Borchgrave, correspondent, report in April 20, 1953 issue of Newsweek.

Of course, the Communists had been informed of the operation, as they usually are, either by the cumbersomeness of our preparations or by spies infiltrating among the Vietnamese cooks and shoe-shine boys and girl friends and other paraphernalia with which the French units in Indochina are always bogged down. Like clockwork, each such mop-up operation begins by an aerial reconnaissance, which only puts the Commies on notice that something is afoot; then this is followed up by long columns of trucks carrying the troops necessary for the operation. And as if all this weren't sufficient to wake up the whole neighborhood, there generally come along a few tanks to provide for artillery support, I suppose, whose clanking can be heard five miles around.

Bernard Fall, author and journalist, diary entry of June 2, 1953, in Street Without Joy *(1961).*

Genuine independence as we understand it is lacking in Indochina . . . local government is circumscribed in its functions . . . the government of Vietnam, the state which is of the greatest importance in this area, lacks popular support, that the degree of military, civil, political, and economic control maintained by the French goes well beyond what is necessary to fight a war . . . It is because we want the war to be brought to a successful conclusion that we should insist on genuine independence . . . Regardless of our united effort, it is a truism that the war can never be successful unless large numbers of the people of Vietnam are won over from their sullen neutrality and open hostility to it and fully support its successful conclusion . . . I strongly believe that the French cannot succeed in Indochina without giving concessions necessary to make the native army a reliable and crusading force.

Senator John F. Kennedy (D–Mass.), to the U.S. Senate, speech of June 30, 1953.

. . . when the United States votes $400 million to help that war, we are not voting for a giveaway program. We are voting for the cheapest way that we can to prevent the occurrence of something that would be of the most terrible significance for the United States of America—our security, our power and ability to get certain things we need from the riches of the Indonesian territory, and from southeast Asia.

President Dwight D. Eisenhower, speech of November 4, 1953, in Public Papers of the Presidents of the United States.

. . . as far as the war in Indochina is concerned, I was there, right on the battlefield or close to it, and it's a bloody war and it's a bitter one. And may I make the position of the United States clear with regard to that war. The United States supports the Associated States of Indochina in their understandable aspirations for independence. But we know as they do that the day the French leave Indochina, the Communists will take over. We realize as they do that the only way they can assure their independence and the only way they can defend it is to continue the fight side by side with their partners in the French Union against the forces of Communist colonialism which would enslave them.

Vice President Richard M. Nixon, speech of December 23, 1953, in U.S. Department of State's Bulletin *(January 4, 1954).*

The war must stop being a French war supported by Vietnam and become a Vietnamese war supported by France.

Vice Premier Paul Reynaud of France, 1953, in Karnow's Vietnam: A History *(1983).*

A year ago none of us could see victory. There wasn't a prayer. Now we can see it clearly—like light at the end of a tunnel.

Lieutenant General Henri Navarre, upon assuming command of French Union Forces in Vietnam, speech of May 20, 1953, in Fall's Hell in a Very Small Place *(1966).*

Q. Marvin Arrowsmith, Associated Press: Mr. President, to go back for a moment to that question on Indochina, there seems to be some uneasiness in Congress, as voiced by Senator [John] Stennis [D–Miss.] for one, that sending these technicians to Indochina will lead eventually to our involvement in a hot war there. Would you comment on that?

THE PRESIDENT: I would just say this: no one could be more bitterly opposed to ever getting the United States involved in a hot war in that region than I am; consequently, every move that I authorize is calculated, so far as humans can do it, to make certain that that does not happen.

. . . . .

Q. Daniel Shorr, CBS Radio: Mr. President, should your remarks on Indochina be construed as meaning that you are determined not to become involved or, perhaps, more deeply involved in the war in Indochina, regardless of how that war may go?

THE PRESIDENT: Well, I am not going to try to predict the drift of world events now and the course of world events over the next months. I say that I cannot conceive of a greater tragedy for America than to get heavily involved now in an all-out war in any of those regions, particularly with large units.

So what we are doing is supporting the Vietnamese and the French in their conduct of that war; because, as we see it, it is a case of independent and free nations operating against the encroachment of communism.

President Eisenhower, to a news conference of February 10, 1954, in Public Papers of the Presidents of the United States.

Q. James J. Patterson, New York Daily News: Mr. President, Senator Stennis said yesterday that we were in danger of becoming involved in World War III in Indochina because of the Air Force technicians there. What will we do if one of those men is captured or killed?

THE PRESIDENT: I will say this: there is going to be no involvement of America in war unless it is a result of the constitutional process that is placed upon Congress to declare it. Now, let us have that clear; and that is the answer.

President Eisenhower, to a news conference of March 10, 1954, in Public Papers of the Presidents of the United States.

We are undertaking at Dien Bien Phu a battle in which the whole fate of the Indochina War will be decided.

Colonel Christian de La Croix, to French Union forces, order of March 16, 1954, in Fall's Hell in a Very Small Place.

There is a very gallant and brave struggle being carried on at Dien Bien Phu by the French and Associated States Forces. It is an outpost. It has already inflicted very heavy damage upon the enemy. The French and Associated States Forces at Dien Bien Phu are writing, in my opinion, a notable chapter in military history. Dien Bien Phu is, as I say, an outpost position where only a very small percentage of the French Union forces is engaged and where a very considerable percentage of the forces of the Viet Minh is engaged.

Broadly speaking, the United States has, under its previously known policy, been extending aid in the form of money and materiel to the French Union Forces in Indochina. As their requests for materiel become known and their need for that becomes evident, we respond to it as rapidly as we can.

Secretary of State John Foster Dulles, to a news conference of March 23, 1954, in U.S. Department of State's Bulletin *(April 15, 1954).*

French Colonel Christian de Castries at his bunker at Dien Bien Phu, 1954. Courtesy of the National Archives.

During the past three months, from the time the enemy forces parachuted into Diebienphu, our army has surrounded and confined their main force in there, creating conditions for continuously defeating the enemy on all battlefields in the entire country.

Today Lai-chau was liberated, the Nam-hu River defense line of the invaders was broken, and there is no shadow of an invader in Phong Saly. Dienbienphu has become a collection of important points completely isolated, standing alone in the middle of our broad rear area.

Today, the time has come for our main forces to begin the attack on Dienbienphu.

If we are victorious at Dienbienphu, we will annihilate a very important part of the invaders' manpower, liberate the entire Northwest territory, widen and consolidate the broad rear area of our resistance war, and help to insure that the land reform achieves success.

General Vo Nguyen Giap, to all cadres and fighting units, message of March 1954, in Orders of the Day.

An artillery barrage would usually begin around six in the evening, then die down to start again about eleven. From fifty to a hundred guns would hail down shells on a piece of ground only a few hundred square yards in extent. A shelter stood up to the first shell, crumbled at the second, collapsed at the third, so that towards midnight half the shelters had fallen on their occupants and their weapons, which they could no longer use. Then the storm of metal would come to an end and the Viets, who all this time had been digging under the barbed wire, would burst suddenly into the middle of the support post, which was already shattered with half its men either wounded or dead.

Major Paul Grauwin, French Union army doctor, March 1954, in Doctor at Dien Bien Phu *(1955).*

I am gravely fearful that the measures being taken by the French will prove to be inadequate and initiated too late to prevent a progressive deterioration of the situation. The consequences can well lead to the loss of all of S.E. Asia to Communist domination. If this is to be avoided, I consider that the U.S. must be prepared to act promptly and in force possibly to a frantic and belated request by the French for U.S. intervention.

Admiral Arthur Radford, chairman of the Joint Chiefs of Staff, to President Eisenhower, memorandum of March 24, 1954, in U.S. Department of Defense, United States-Vietnam Relations.

Those fighting under the banner of Ho Chi Minh have largely been trained and equipped in Communist China. They are supplied with artillery and ammunition through the Soviet-Chinese Communist bloc. Captured materiel shows that much of it was fabricated by the Skoda Munition Works in Czechoslovakia and transported across Russia and Siberia and then sent through China into Viet-Nam. Military supplies for the communist armies have been pouring into Viet-Nam at a steadily increasing rate.

Secretary of State John Foster Dulles, to the Overseas Press Club of America in New York City, speech of March 29, 1954, in Gravel's The Pentagon Papers.

I can conceive of no greater disadvantage to America than to be employing its own ground forces, and any other kind of forces, in great numbers around the world, meeting each little situation as it arises.

President Eisenhower, to a news conference of March 31, 1954, in Public Papers of the Presidents of the United States.

In the plane to Hanoi, I thought of what the doctor had told me, for in the plane were many crippled Tonkinese returning home after being patched in the South. One had seen just such faces, patient, gentle, expecting nothing, behind the water buffaloes plowing the drowned paddy fields: it seemed wrong that war should have picked on them and lopped off a leg or an arm—war should belong to the brazen battalions, the ribboned commanders, the goose step and the Guards' march.

Graham Greene, author and journalist, article of April 5, 1954, in The New Republic.

In my opinion, the Congress of the United States, Democrats and Republicans, have a responsibility to support the administration in trying to save southeast Asia. I think the administration should come to Congress with a resolution stating in no uncertain terms our wishes and aspirations for the people of Indochina and for all Asia and to outline the policy to be pursued . . . I do not believe we can wait much longer lest we lose southeast Asia to the Communist forces which are about to take over.

Senator Henry Jackson (D–Wash.), to the U.S. Senate, speech of April 6, 1954.

Q. Robert Richards, Copley Press: Mr. President, would you mind commenting on the strategic importance of Indochina to the free world? I think there has been, across the country, some lack of understanding on just what it means to us.

THE PRESIDENT: You have, of course, both the specific and the general when you talk about such things.

First of all, you have the specific value of a locality in its production of materials that the world needs.

Then you have the possibility that many human beings pass under a dictatorship that is inimical to the free world.

Finally, you have broader considerations that might follow what you would call the "falling domino" principle. You have a row of dominoes set up, you knock over the first one, and what will happen to the last one is the certainty that it will go over very quickly. So you could have a beginning of a disintegration that would have the most profound influences.

President Eisenhower, to a news conference of April 7, 1954, in Public Papers of the Presidents of the United States.

The United States is less and less disposed to risk sending her own men into the melee . . . Well satisfied that the French are carrying the weight of the battle in Indo-China, she is ready to contribute matériel and money, but wants to decide how that battle is carried on and appears to be ready to throw in contingents of yellow and white peoples supplied by her allies in Asia and Australasia and even to employ her own long range weapons. But she has no thought of contributing battalions.

President Charles De Gaulle, to a Paris news conference of April 7, 1954, in The New York Times *(April 8, 1954).*

The newcomers have ceased to be objects of curiosity. There are so many of them they have become commonplace—uniformed officers and men assigned to the U.S. military mission and aircraft crews here overnight after ferrying war equipment from U.S. bases in Japan and the Philippines.

Anonymous Saigon correspondent, in U.S. News & World Report *article of April 9, 1954.*

I am frankly of the belief that no amount of American military assistance in Indochina can conquer an enemy which is everywhere and at the same time nowhere, "an enemy of the people" which has the sympathy and covert support of the people.

Senator John F. Kennedy, to the U.S. Senate, speech of April 16, 1954, during a debate over aid to Indochina.

Dien Bien Phu is a valley, and it's completely surrounded by mountains. The cream of the French expeditionary corps are down there, and we are around the mountains. And they'll never get out.

Ho Chi Minh, to Wilfred Burchett, Australian journalist, 1954, in Maclear's The Ten Thousand Day War *(1981).*

No more reserves left. Fatigue and wear and tear on the units terrible. Supplies and ammunition insufficient. Quite difficult to resist one more such push by Communists, at least without bringing in one brand-new battalion of excellent quality.

Anonymous senior French army commanders, to General René Cogney, dispatch of May 1, 1954, from Dien Bien Phu, in Fall's Hell in a Very Small Place.

. . . at 5 p.m. our troops attacked Hill A-1. In the preparatory stage our sappers had dug an under-

ground trench leading to the centre of the hill and introduced there one ton of explosives. With the powerful co-ordination of this explosion, our troops attacked this position from various directions, put out of action the defending unit composed of paratroopers of the foreign legion, and occupied the last height.

General Vo Nguyen Giap, recalls the Vietminh victory at Dien Bien Phu on May 6, 1954, in Dien Bien Phu *(1964).*

The situation of the wounded is particularly tragic. They are piled up on top of each other in holes that are completely filled with mud and devoid of any hygiene. Their martyrdom increases day by day.

Brigadier General Christian de Castries, French commander at Dien Bien Phu, to General René Cogny, French commander in Hanoi, message of May 5, 1954, in Fall's Hell in a Very Small Place.

What is American policy in Indochina?

All of us have listened to the dismal series of reversals and confusions and alarms and excursions which have emerged from Washington over the past few weeks.

We have been caught bluffing by our enemies, our friends and Allies are frightened and wondering, as we do, where we are headed.

We stand in clear danger of being left naked and alone in a hostile world.

Senator Lyndon Johnson (D–Tex.), to a Democratic fund-raising dinner in Washington, D.C., speech of May 6, 1954, in Gibbons' The U.S. Government and the Vietnam War *(1984).*

We must make clear to France we are not going to enter into any agreement which will result in shiploads of coffins draped in American flags being shipped from Indochina to the United States in any attempt to support colonialism in Indochina.

Senator Wayne Morse (D–Ore.), to the U.S. Senate, speech of May 7, 1954.

We lack ammunition. Our resistance is going to be overwhelmed. The Vietminh are now within a few meters from the radio transmitter where I am speaking.

Brigadier General Christian de Castries, French commander at Dien Bien Phu, to General René Cogny, in Hanoi, message of May 7, 1954, in Fall's Hell in a Very Small Place.

We will destroy the cannons . . . We will fight to the end. Au revoir, mon General. Vive la France.

*Brigadier General Christian de Castries, to
General René Cogny, last message of May 7,
1954, in Fall's* Hell in a Very Small Place.

In five minutes, everything will be blowing up here. The Viets are only a few minutes away. Greetings to everybody.

*Sergeant Millien, to French army headquarters
in Hanoi, the last message from Dien Bien Phu,
May 7, 1954, in Fall's* Hell in a Very Small
Place.

The fortress of Dien Bien Phu fell today.

Human avalanches of screaming Communist swarmed over the outnumbered French Union defenders after 56 days of siege.

With the enemy at his throat, the commander, Brigadier General Christian de Castries radioed, "We will not surrender"—then the radio went dead.

*Anonymous correspondent, United Press dis-
patch of May 7, 1954, from Hanoi.*

The Government has been informed that the central position of Dien Bien Phu has fallen after twenty hours of uninterrupted violent combat.

*Prime Minister Joseph Laniel of France, to the
National Assembly, speech of May 7, 1954, in
Fall's* Hell in a Very Small Place.

Under the influence of [Communist] Chinese advisers, the Viet-Minh command had used processes quite different from the classical methods. The artillery had been dug in by single pieces. The guns had been brought forward dismantled, carried by men, to emplacements where they had direct observation of their targets. They were installed in shell-proof dugouts, and fired point blank from portholes or were pulled out by their crews and pulled back as soon as our counterbattery fire began. Each piece or group of pieces was covered by massed antiaircraft artillery put into position and camouflaged in the same manner as the guns. This way of using the artillery and AA guns was possible only with the "human ant hill" at the disposal of the Viet-Minh and was to make shambles of all the estimates of our own artillerymen. It was the major surprise of the battle.

*General Henri Navarre, commander of French
Union Forces in Indochina, recalling the French
defeat at Dien Bien Phu, in* Agonie de l'Indochine *(1956).*

President Eisenhower has repeatedly emphasized that he would not take military action in Indochina without the support of Congress. Furthermore, he has made clear that he would not seek that unless, in his opinion, there would be an adequate collective effort based on genuine mutuality of purpose in defending vital interests.

*Secretary of State John Foster Dulles, to the
nation, radio and television address of May 7,
1954, in the U.S. Department of State* Bulletin
of April 5, 1954.

Our army has liberated Dien Bien Phu. The Government and I convey our cordial greetings to you, cadres, fighters, war service workers, shock youth, and local people who have gloriously fulfilled your tasks.

This victory is big, but it is only the beginning. We must not be self-complacent and subjective and underestimate the enemy. We are determined to fight for independence, national unity, democracy, and peace. A struggle, whether military or diplomatic, must be long and hard before complete victory can be achieved.

*President Ho Chi Minh, to the Viet Minh,
proclamation of May 8, 1954, in* Selected
Works.

The Dien Bien Phu victory is the most prestigious which our Army has ever achieved . . . In liberating this strategic northwestern region of our country we have further expanded our zone of resistance and contributed to the success of land reform.

*General Vo Nguyen Giap, to the Vietnamese
people, proclamation of May 13, 1954, in* Orders of the Day.

Now that France has recognized the independence of Vietnam, no one can have any doubts as to the unselfish nobleness of her defense of the Vietnamese people and of the Free World . . . The French can be assured that Vietnam shall not forget the sacrifices of France.

*Emperor Bao Dai, from Nice, on the French
Riviera, statement of May 15, 1954, in* Vietnam *(a French-language bulletin, May 1954).*

We fought desperately against partition . . . Absolutely impossible to surmount the hostility of our enemies and the perfidy of false friends. Unusual procedures paralyzed the action of our delegation.

All arrangements were signed in privacy. We express deepest sorrow in this total failure of our mission.

Tran Van Don, senior officer in Diem regime, to President Ngo Dinh Diem, on the conclusion of the Geneva Conference, message of July 1954, in Warner's The Last Confucian *(1965).*

We felt apprehensive about the return journey to Hanoi. Countless mines buried in the roads had not yet been removed. Columns of smoke rose into the air at regular intervals every time a vehicle exploded. The stoical calm everyone had displayed until the ceasefire came into force had vanished. Now the words on everyone's lips were: "Just so long as I'm not the last man killed in this war."

Peter Scholl-Latour, French journalist, July 1954, in Death in the Rice Fields *(1985).*

I am glad, of course, that agreement has been reached at Geneva to stop the bloodshed in Indochina.

The United States has not been a belligerent in the war. The primary responsibility for the settlement in Indochina rested with those nations which participated in the fighting. Our role at Geneva has been at all times to try to be helpful where desired and to aid France and Cambodia, Laos, and Viet-Nam to obtain a just and honorable settlement which will take into account the needs of the interested people. Accordingly, the United States has not itself been party to or bound by the decisions taken by the Conference, but it is our hope that it will lead to the establishment of peace consistent with the rights and the needs of the countries concerned. The agreement contains features which we do not like, but a great deal depends on how they work in practice.

President Eisenhower, to a news conference of July 21, 1954, in U.S. Department of State's American Foreign Policy 1950–1955: Basic Documents.

Although the Geneva accord is being ostensibly observed in the entire country and the fighting has come to an end, the cease fire does not preclude a subsurface continuation of the Communist advance in south Vietnam. Vietminh sympathizers are to be found throughout that region and it is likely that their number is growing. It must also be presumed that Vietminh activists are being left behind as the Vietminh withdraw their regular forces from south

Vietnam in accordance with the terms of the cease fire. One observer described the situation to me in these terms: "Bring a brush down on the map of south Vietnam. Wherever the bristles touch you will find Vietminh."

Senator Mike Mansfield (D–Mont.), to the U.S. Senate, on his visit to Vietnam, October 15, 1954, in U.S. Senate Committee on Foreign Relations' Report on Indochina *(1954).*

We have been exploring ways and means to permit our aid to Vietnam to be more effective and to make a greater contribution to the welfare and stability of the Government of Vietnam. I am, accordingly, instructing the American Ambassador in Vietnam to examine with you in your capacity as Chief of Government, how an intelligent program of American aid given directly to your Government can serve to assist Vietnam in its present hour of trial . . .

President Eisenhower, to President Ngo Dinh Diem, letter of October 23, 1954, in U.S. Department of State's Foreign Relations of the United States *(1952–1954).*

Several days after my first meeting with Ngo dinh Diem, a group of perhaps fifty U.S. military men arrived in Saigon and reported for duty at MAAG. Their arrival was in anticipation of a more active role by Americans in the training of the Vietnamese armed forces, an expectation based upon the recent final initialing in Paris of the treaty providing independence for Vietnam. Twelve of the new arrivals had been assigned as my "team." Soldiers, sailors, and marines, they had been selected for me by personnel officers in Washington who must have had a Korean-style conflict in mind and disregarded my own written list of requirements. They were an ideal crew for guerrilla combat, for blowing up things, for jumps behind enemy lines, and for sensitive intelligence work against Communist infiltrators, saboteurs, and terrorists. But none had an inkling of psywar, the one activity in which I already was helping the Vietnamese Army . . .

Colonel Edward G. Lansdale, USAF, chief of the Saigon Mission, in In the Midst of Wars *(1972).*

Withdrawal [of] our support would hasten [a] Communist takeover [in] Vietnam and have adverse repercussions [throughout] all [of] Southeast Asia. Consequently, [our] investment in Vietnam [is] justified even if only to buy time [to] build up strength elsewhere in the area.

Secretary of State John Foster Dulles, to General Lawton J. Collins, American representative in Saigon, message of December 24, 1954, in Gravel's The Pentagon Papers.

I was deeply concerned to hear individuals of great influence, both in and out of government, raising the cry that now was the time, and here, in Indo-China, was the place to "test the New Look," for us to intervene, to come to the aid of France with arms. At the same time that same old delusive idea was advanced—that we could do things the cheap and easy way, by going into Indo-China with air and naval forces alone. To me this had an ominous ring. For I felt sure that if we committed air and naval power to that area, we would have to follow them immediately with ground forces in support.

I also knew that none of those advocating such a step had any accurate idea what such an operation would cost us in blood and money and national effort.

General Matthew B. Ridgway, chief of staff, USA, recalls his opposition to a ground war in Asia in 1954, in Soldier: The Memoirs of Matthew B. Ridgway *(1956).*

What Vietnam needs is not millions of dollars but thousands of experts. It needs technical advice and aid. It needs political support. It needs our help in freeing itself from the remnants of a decaying colonialism. We should send there an ambassador with sympathy for the people's national aspirations, and understanding of their social and political problems, and the authority and strength required for a difficult political job.

Joseph Buttinger, International Rescue Committee worker, Reporter *article of January 27, 1955.*

. . . there has never been any President of the United States who was not able, if he wanted to, to involve this United States in war . . . There is nothing that the Congress can do to diminish effectively that danger, because if the President wants to get us into a war, resolution or no resolution in my opinion he can do it.

Secretary of State John Foster Dulles, to the U.S. Senate Foreign Relations and Armed Services Committee, testimony of January 1955, in U.S. Department of State's American Foreign Policy 1950–1955: Basic Documents *(1957).*

On the shore the refugees [from Haiphong] watched the beaching with open-mouthed wonder. A new world, the world of the sea and modern ships, was about to open for them. Four hours away, lying quietly at anchor among the churchlike rocky islands of the Baie D'Along, a U.S. Navy transport waited to load these refugees, in number about two thousand, in order to take them to South Vietnam.

Howard R. Simpson, USIA press officer, Commonweal *article of January 21, 1955.*

The average person in Southeast Asia doesn't know much about Communism. He's interested in where he's going to get his next meal, whether he is going to have a decent shelter for his family. That is the reason why I think that if this agrarian-reform program of Diem's works out, gets beyond the talking stage and is really implemented, he can demonstrate to the people that his Government is looking after the welfare of the ordinary poor people, the common peasant of Vietnam, that will be one of the finest things that could be done to combat Communism.

General J. Lawton Collins, to U.S. News & World Report, *in an article of March 4, 1955.*

In the harbor nearby, almost ignored by the city, 2,000 refugees poured down gangplanks of the U.S.S. *Mountrail,* which had evacuated them from Haiphong in the north.

Wearing conical hats, dark tunics, and peasant trousers, barefooted and weary, mothers handed down

South Vietnamese Premier Ngo Dinh Diem (right) meets with U.S. General J. Lawton Collins (left), special representative to Vietnam, at the Independence Palace, on May 13, 1955. Courtesy of the National Archives.

their babies first; sympathetic young sailors helped old people at the gangplanks. The refugees swarmed on the dockside, uncertain, silent, confused. Even as they stumbled away, the bluejackets aboard were cleaning the ship, preparatory to going back for more.

Gertrude Samuels, journalist, on refugees from North Vietnam arriving in Saigon, in National Geographic *article of June 1955.*

Fellow-countrymen,

The national government has on many occasions stressed the value it attaches to the defence of the Unity of our country and of true democracy.

We did not sign the Geneva agreements.

We are in no way bound by these agreements, which were concluded against the will of the Vietnamese people.

Our policy is one of peace. No stratagems, from wherever they may come, will divert us from our goal: the Unity of our land, but Unity in freedom, not in slavery. In service to the national cause we are striving more than ever for territorial unification.

We do not reject the principle of elections as a peaceful and democratic means of realising this unity. Still, though elections may form one of the pillars of true democracy, they are senseless if they are not absolutely free.

When we see the system of oppression practised by the Viet-Minh, we cannot but be sceptical as to the possibility of obtaining conditions for a free vote in the North.

Premier Ngo Dinh Diem, to the people of Vietnam, declaration of July 16, 1955, in Gravel's The Pentagon Papers.

Oddly enough M. Diem has borrowed from his enemies what is most reprehensible in their methods: the denial of freedom of opinion, the deification of the man who incarnates the regime and also that form of hypocrisy which attributes to the "people's will" measures taken against those whom one considers as political opponents . . . The Viet Minh dictatorship is at least as odious as that of M. Diem. But it can show results in the political and economic fields. It is up to Diemism to show concrete achievements. This has not yet been done in South Vietnam.

Max Clos, French journalist, article in Le Monde, *December 1, 1955.*

Vietnam represents the cornerstone of the Free World in Southeast Asia, the keystone to the arch, the finger in the dike. Burma, Thailand, India, Japan, the Philippines and obviously Laos and Cambodia are among those whose security would be threatened if the red tide of Communism overflowed into Vietnam.

Senator John F. Kennedy, to the American Friends of Vietnam, a citizens' lobby group, speech of June 1956, in Gibbons' The U.S. Government and the Vietnam War.

. . . our *sacred* duty is resolutely to continue to struggle for the execution of the Geneva Agreements and for the reunification of the country on the basis of independence and democracy through peaceful means, and to make the glorious cause of national liberation triumph.

Our line of struggle at present is to achieve the broad and close unity of the entire people from South to North within the Viet-nam Fatherland Front, and to strive to consolidate North Viet-nam into a strong base of the struggle for the reunification of our country.

President Ho Chi Minh, to the Vietnamese people, letter of July 6, 1956, in Selected Works.

My concept is that the advisor should take the field with the Headquarters of the Unit he is advising and there advise the Vietnamese Commander and his Staff as to preparation of daily plans, monitor the day-to-day conduct of the operations and render on-the-spot advice based on the situation as it exists at the time. This to include logistical as well as tactical matters. The logistical questions that come up normally have to do with medical support, evacuation of wounded, transportation problems, road and trail construction, bridging, supply procedures, maintenance of equipment, etc.

General Samuel T. Williams, USA, chief of the Military Assistance Advisory Group (MAAG) in Vietnam, to General H.D. Riley, commander in chief, Pacific, letter of April 14, 1959, in U.S. Department of State's Foreign Relations of the United States 1958–1960, Vietnam *(1986).*

. . . held back in her development by 100 years of foreign domination, exhausted by 15 years of war and destruction, the northern half of her territory given to the Communists, Free Viet-Nam is in a more menaced and critical position than other Asian countries.

At great human sacrifice and thanks to the aid given by the generous American people, Free Viet-Nam has succeeded, in record time, to overcome the chaos brought about by war and the Geneva Accords. The national rehabilitation and stability which have been achieved have permitted the integration of over 860,000 refugees into the economy of the other 11 million people in Free Viet-Nam and have permitted the adoption of important economic and political reforms.

President Ngo Dinh Diem, to a joint session of the U.S. Congress, speech of May 9, 1957.

You are proud of having created for Viet-Nam a regime that you think is similar to that of the United States. If those regimes are similar, then they are as related as a skyscraper is to a tin-roofed shack, in that they both are houses to live in.

In the U.S.A., Congress is a true parliament and Congressmen are legislators, i.e., free and disinterested men who are not afraid of the government, and who know their duties and dare to carry them out. Here the deputies are political functionaries who make laws like an announcer in a radio station, by reading out loud texts that have been prepared [for them] beforehand . . .

Nghiem Xuan Thien, publisher of Thoi-Luan, *South Vietnam's largest daily newspaper, editorial of March 15, 1958.*

Strategically, South Viet-Nam's capture by the Communists would bring their power several hundred miles into a hitherto free region. The remaining countries in Southeast Asia would be menaced by a great flanking movement. The freedom of twelve million people would be lost immediately, and that of 150 million others in adjacent lands would be seriously endangered. The loss of South Viet-Nam would set in motion a crumbling process that could, as it progressed, have grave consequences for us and for freedom.

Viet-Nam must have a reasonable degree of safety now—both for her people and for her property. Because of these facts, military as well as economic help is currently needed in Viet-Nam.

President Eisenhower, speech of April 4, 1959, at Gettysburg College, in Public Papers of the Presidents of the United States.

Diem impressed me deeply by his grasp of the problems, not only of his own country but of Asia as a whole. He remains, of course, an unflinching foe of communism. On his record, he must be rated as one of the ablest free Asian leaders. We can take pride in our support.

Ernest K. Lindley, Newsweek correspondent, article of June 29, 1959, in Newsweek.

Following a reckless, foolish, made-in-Washington policy of noninterference, we've forked over bundles of American cash to the fledging, inexperienced Vietnam Government, and then looked piously at the ceiling while the money melted away.

Thanks to our hands-off attitude, we've done little to guide Vietnam toward the day when she can support herself. This country has a terrible financial problem. Our solution has been to put her on the dole. She may be there 10 years, 25 years—or forever.

Why has all this happen?

It has happened because the byword of most high American officials here is: "Keep your mouth shut, smile, and don't rock the boat."

Albert Colegrove, Scripps-Howard reporter, newspaper article of July 20, 1959, reprinted in U.S. Congress, House Committee on Foreign Affairs' Current Situation in the Far East *(1959).*

. . . the area around Ban Methuot, offers some of the finest hunting in the world. You have to go on foot or on elephant back, and you don't see the big herds you do in Africa, but there's plenty of game: elephant, leopard, Himalyan bear. However, the Vietnamese haven't been able to reinstate the tourist attraction of hunting—they have so much to do all at once . . . They are working hard in this new nation, and what we feel was sort of a preview peak at its advancement has convinced us that beautiful Vietnam will take its rightful place as a true traveler's goal in tomorrow's world of easy access by jet.

Richard Tregaskis, author and journalist, in Travel *article of March 1959.*

. . . six Communist terrorists (who obviously had cased the place well) crept out of the darkness and surrounded the mess hall . . . In the first murderous hail of bullets, [Sergeant] Ovnand and Major Buis fell and died within minutes. Captain Howard Boston of Blairsburg, Iowa, was seriously wounded, and two Vietnamese guards were killed . . . Within minutes Vietnamese troops arrived, but the rest of the assassins had already fled.

Stanley Karnow, journalist, on the first Americans killed in Vietnam (July 8, 1959), in Time *article of July 20, 1959.*

2. Days of Hope: 1960–1963

INSURGENCY IN THE SOUTH

Until 1959, Ho Chi Minh had discouraged insurgents living in South Vietnam from engaging in armed attacks against the Diem regime. He argued that the time was "not ripe" for rebellion. A directive was issued from Hanoi stating, "We must accumulate our forces and develop our apparatus . . . To ignore the balance of forces and rashly call for a general uprising is to commit the error of speculative adventurism, leading to premature violence and driving us into a very dangerous position."

But Vietcong activists in the south who were being decimated by Diem objected to such restraint. Their cause was supported in Hanoi by Le Duan, secretary-general of the Lao Dong Party and a native of central Vietnam. After visiting the south he returned to argue that the Vietcong structure would be completely destroyed unless it resorted to violence. As a result, the Central Committee in Hanoi issued new instructions, authorizing "armed struggle" in the south. The directive called for a campaign of terror against Diem officials and hamlet chiefs, whose popularity represented a threat to the communists.

In late January 1960, at the beginning of the celebration of Tet, armed bands sprang up throughout the south and attacked. Insurgents raided rubber plantations and government outposts. In Long An Province, south of Saigon, a wave of assassinations turned the holiday period into a time of terror. In the space of one week, 26 people were killed. In Long An's Can Duoc district, 90 out of 117 hamlet chiefs resigned, while others hid in market towns near government military outposts.

Between 1959 and 1961, the number of South Vietnamese government officials assassinated soared from 1,200 to 4,000 a year. Diem responded by appointing army officers to manage the rural bureaucracy so that, by 1962, soldiers pervaded the administration down to the district level. They not only neglected the economic and social needs of the local population, but also acted as if they were in enemy territory. They lived in fortified garrisons protected by blockhouses and barbed wire and ventured into the countryside only under heavy guard, often accompanied by American advisers. The villages were open to Diem's troops by day, but were run by the Vietcong at night.

THE NATIONAL LIBERATION FRONT

In December 1960, Hanoi decided that the moment had arrived to announce a new organization in the south, the National Liberation Front
(NLF). It was reminiscent of the formation of the Vietminh 20 years
before. As a "front," its aim was to bring together a disparate collection of groups opposed to Diem: Vietminh veterans, remnants of the
Cao Dai and Hoa Hao sects and the Binh Xuyen, university students,
farmers from the Mekong Delta, as well as army deserters, young men
fleeing conscription, leaders of splinter political parties and refugees
from the denunciation campaigns. Although North Vietnam claimed
the NLF was a southern movement and did not violate the Geneva
agreement, its leadership resided in the People's Revolutionary Party
and the Liberation army, which took their orders from the politburo in
Hanoi.

KENNEDY'S WAR

As his term neared its end, President Eisenhower was disturbed less
by the growing insurgency in Vietnam than by a crisis developing in
adjacent Laos. On January 19, 1961, on the eve of his retirement, Eisenhower warned his successor, John F. Kennedy, that Laos was "the
key to the entire area of Southeast Asia" and at some point might
even require the introduction of combat troops. They did not discuss
Saigon or Diem, or the NLF or the Vietcong. Later, Kennedy would
recall that final meeting to an aide: "Eisenhower never mentioned it,
never uttered the word Vietnam."

In his inaugural address, Kennedy promised to continue assisting
countries in the Third World, especially those, like Vietnam, threatened by the communists: "To those new states whom we welcome to
the ranks of the free, we pledge our word that one form of colonial
control shall not have passed away merely to be replaced by a far
more iron tyranny." U.S. assistance to those trying to "help themselves," he said, would continue "for whatever period is required, not
because the communists may be doing it, not because we seek their
votes, but because it is right."

Soon after his inauguration, the situation in South Vietnam came
forcibly to the attention of the new president: first in the form of a
Counter-Insurgency Plan (CIP) developed during the last months of
the Eisenhower administration, and then in a report by Colonel Edward Lansdale, who had just returned from a mission there.

The Counter-Insurgency Plan called for additional U.S. aid to support a 20,000-man increase in the Army of the Republic of Vietnam (ARVN) (up to 170,000 men) and to train, equip and supply a 32,000-man addition to the Civil Guard (up to 68,000). In return, Diem would be asked to expand his government to include opposition leaders in the cabinet, curb corruption and launch "civic action" in the countryside to win the loyalty of the peasants. It was a modest proposal to help the South Vietnamese help themselves, and Kennedy approved the CIP on January 28, 1961, virtually without discussion.

Four days later, Kennedy reviewed Lansdale's report, which offered a far graver analysis of the situation than had the CIP. South Vietnam was in a precarious condition. The insurgents had extended their control over larger sections of the countryside and were now close to a takeover. The South Vietnamese military command was in disarray and the administrative bureaucracy was crumbling. The Diem government was totally unprepared to fight the increasing level of insurrection it now confronted. Lansdale stressed that a revolutionary war was being conducted along the lines laid down by Mao and Giap. If South Vietnam was to survive, it would have to confront the enemy with the tactics and strategy of unconventional warfare.

The "Special War"

In response to Lansdale's assessment, Kennedy decided to develop the Army Special Forces into a major counterinsurgency force. At the president's direction the Special Warfare Center began preparing soldiers to confront guerrillas in the jungles and mountains of the Third World. Training centers in Panama, Okinawa and West Germany were expanded. By the end of 1961 a Special Group (Counterinsurgency) had been established to coordinate the nation's ability to wage guerrilla warfare.

In April 1961, Kennedy created a "task force" to prepare economic, social, political and military programs directed at preventing communist "domination" of South Vietnam. The task force recommended a plan for a two-division increase in the South Vietnamese army, and for the deployment of U.S. advisers to train the new ARVN soldiers. Kennedy accepted its proposals and agreed to send an additional 100 American military advisers to Vietnam, bringing the total up to nearly 800. Although the Geneva agreement specified that foreign military personnel could be assigned to Vietnam only as replacements, Secretary of State Dean Rusk recommended that they be deployed without consulting Britain, cochairman of the Geneva Conference, or the Inter-

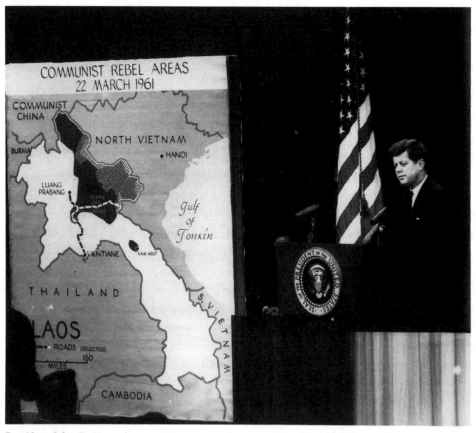

President John F. Kennedy at a 1961 press conference with a map of Vietnam. Courtesy of the National Archives.

national Control Commission, which was supposed to monitor the accords. Rusk suggested that the advisers "be placed in varied locations to avoid attention."

Kennedy's decisions did not commit the United States significantly further than had the Eisenhower administration. He had not gone beyond the program in Laos—advisers, materiel and some covert combat assistance. From the administration's point of view, it was a minimal response. Kennedy was determined to move forward, but cautiously. He wished to see what the Vietnamese would do for themselves.

In early May 1961, Kennedy dispatched Vice President Johnson to visit Saigon. After meeting with Diem at the presidential palace, Johnson told reporters, "President Diem is the Churchill of the decade . . . He will fight communism in the streets and alleys, and when his hands are torn he will fight it with his feet." Back in Washington, Johnson reported to the president that Diem had shown no interest in a bilateral treaty and that American troops were neither required nor desired. Johnson concluded that the fundamental decision was "whether to meet the challenge of Communist expansion in Southeast Asia or throw in the towel."

Despite the new equipment, the Special Forces advisers, and the training of South Vietnamese forces, NLF military units continued to push forward. By midsummer the front controlled at least a quarter of the villages in the Mekong Delta and had won nocturnal control of nearly 70% of the countryside. Attacks more than tripled, from 150 a month to over 450 in September. When the rebels launched a heavy attack in Darlac Province on September 22, 1961, an atmosphere of crisis took hold in Vietnam. "It's no longer a guerrilla war," Diem told the National Assembly, "but a real war."

In mid-October, Diem reversed his decision on American combat soldiers and told Ambassador Frederick Nolting he would welcome the troops as a "symbolic" presence; he also requested a bilateral defense pact between the United States and South Vietnam.

THE TAYLOR MISSION

The question of dispatching U.S. troops reached center stage in Washington. The Joint Chiefs of Staff estimated that 40,000 U.S. soldiers would be required to "clean up the Vietcong threat," and another 128,000 in the event of active North Vietnamese or Chinese communist intervention. The State Department guessed that only three divisions of 13,750 men each would be the ultimate force required to defeat the insurgents. Kennedy announced on October 11, 1961, at a National Security Council meeting that his military adviser, General Maxwell Taylor, would visit South Vietnam to make a personal assessment of the situation there.

After a two-week tour of South Vietnam, Taylor reported to the president that "if Vietnam goes, it will be exceedingly difficult if not impossible to hold Southeast Asia," and that he doubted if Diem's methods could defeat the NLF. He recommended an increase in the number of U.S. military advisers and urged that three squadrons of helicopters, manned by American pilots, be deployed in Vietnam to give mobility to Diem's forces. Taylor believed that the weakness of Diem's regime could be overcome if enough Americans—civilian and military alike—took an active role in showing the Vietnamese how to win the war. Moreover, he suggested that the United States should offer the South Vietnamese an American military force of between 6,000 and 10,000 troops. They would be disguised as logistical personnel for flood control in the Mekong Delta. The U.S. soldiers would "act as an advance party of such additional forces as may be introduced."

Defense Secretary Robert McNamara and the Joint Chiefs of Staff rejected Taylor's proposal as inadequate and urged the deployment of six U.S. divisions—some 200,000 men. Kennedy had misgivings about both proposals, and confided to adviser Arthur Schlesinger, "The troops will march in, the bands will play, the crowds will cheer, and in four days everyone will have forgotten. Then we will be told we have to send in more troops. It's like taking a drink. The effect wears off, and you have to take another."

The U.S. Commitment Begins

Kennedy persuaded McNamara to join Rusk in drafting a less aggressive memorandum (November 15, 1961) that approved more aid to Diem, but deferred any decision to commit combat ground forces to South Vietnam. The possible military courses of action were divided into two phases. In Phase A, the United States would immediately dispatch support troops and equipment, including helicopters, along with advisers necessary for training and operations. Phase B consisted of studying the feasibility of deploying major ground forces at a later date. The Rusk-McNamara memo of November 15 guided policy for the next two years and expanded America's involvement in South Vietnam.

The introduction of combat troops was deferred, but they were not ruled out as a future alternative. Kennedy escalated his rhetoric on stopping communism in Southeast Asia but carefully avoided any formal commitment. Eager to portray an image of decisiveness in the wake of the Bay of Pigs fiasco, the Vienna summit with Khrushchev and the Laos crisis, Kennedy adopted the strategy of doing what was minimally necessary to forestall a communist takeover of South Vietnam: He authorized an increase of aid and advisers. The number of advisers in South Vietnam, less than 800 when Kennedy took office, grew to 3,000 by December 1961, and to 11,000 by late 1962.

No conflict in history was studied in such detail while it was being waged. Military and civilian agencies conducted surveys in Vietnam, along with scores of private think tanks, like the RAND Corporation and the Stanford Research Institute. They included weapon technicians, economists, sociologists, political scientists, anthropologists, biologists, chemists and public opinion pollsters. They visited villages and interviewed peasants. They interrogated enemy defectors and prisoners. Captured communist documents were analyzed and statements from Hanoi were scrutinized.

But the missing factor in this "quantitative measurement" that guided McNamara and other U.S. policymakers was the element that could not easily be documented: There was no way to measure the motivation of the Vietcong guerrillas.

The Strategic Hamlet Program

After two years of mounting insurrection, the South Vietnamese government had no national plan for pacification. With more American troops and equipment came increased pressure on the Diem government to devise a counterinsurgency program. The strategy that eventually emerged, the "strategic hamlet" program, came from neither the Americans nor the South Vietnamese, but from a British advisory mission headed by Sir Robert Thompson, a veteran of the British victory over communist insurgents in nearby Malaya.

Thompson's plan was to corral peasants into armed stockades, thereby depriving the Vietcong of their support. They would be protected first by ARVN and then by locally trained self-defense militia units. The strategic hamlets would offer the rural population economic and social programs to win the hearts of the people for the government cause. However, Diem and his brother Nhu saw the strategic hamlet program as a means essentially to spread their influence rather than to rally the peasants against the Vietcong.

American soldiers and civilians in Vietnam criticized the strategic hamlet scheme. They voiced concerns that the defensive nature of the hamlets would tie down Vietnamese forces that could better be used

South Vietnamese Army troops in combat operations against communist Vietcong guerrillas in 1961. Courtesy of the National Archives.

in an offensive role. However, the plan received strong support among senior Kennedy administration officials. Roger Hilsman, director of intelligence for the State Department, called it "an effective strategic concept," and McNamara praised its progress in "countering subversion."

But the strategic hamlet program soon collapsed. Peasants were ordered to move or rebuild their hamlets, without incentive, compensation or pay, often at a new location far from ancestral graves. Nothing in the program, such as meaningful land reform, bound the peasants to the hamlets or to the South Vietnamese government. As Saigon lacked the military resources to police every hamlet by force, communist cadres soon reestablished contact with the peasants.

ADVICE AND SUPPORT

In 1962, the introduction of U.S. helicopters and other equipment into Vietnam seemed to turn the tide—for a while—despite the failure of the strategic hamlet program. The helicopters, piloted by Americans, ferried South Vietnamese troops into action, and at times attacked the battlefield with machine guns and rockets before landing. Terrifying as they were to the Vietcong, the American helicopters were not invulnerable. As early as April 1962 there were already regular reports of helicopters returning from patrols nicked by guerrilla gunfire. In July one of the ships of the 93rd Division was shot down near the Laotian border, with three Americans killed. Although it made few headlines back in the States, American casualties were beginning to mount in Vietnam.

The heliborne deployments initially set back the Vietcong, whose remote bases could now be penetrated, but the guerrillas gradually adapted to the new warfare. They dug trenches and tunnels as shelters against helicopter raids, and they practiced assaults against full-scale models of choppers constructed in jungle clearings. They also acquired more sophisticated weapons, either from North Vietnam or by ambushing South Vietnamese patrols.

By the end of 1962, while officials in Washington were enthusiastically announcing to the American public that U.S. aid to South Vietnam had begun to tip the balance against the guerrillas, there were a few American military leaders in the field who were more circumspect. "We are now doing a little better than holding our own," was the cautious assessment of General Paul Harkins's deputy, Major General Charles Timmes. But Harkins was convinced that the Vietnamese had seized the initiative and that the balance was beginning to swing in favor of the South Vietnamese government.

The Battle of Ap Bac

But the shortcomings of Diem's army became dramatically apparent in January 1963 near Ap Bac, a village in the Mekong Delta 40 miles southwest of Saigon. In late December 1962, intelligence reports began coming into ARVN 7th Division headquarters of heavy Vietcong concentrations in western Dinh Trong Province. Lieutenant Colonel John Paul Vann, the top U.S. adviser with the 7th Division, urged Colonel Bui Dinh Dam to move on January 1, 1963. For more than a year the continuing elusiveness of the Vietcong had been a source of mounting frustration to Vann. Ap Bac would be the place for a traditional battle in which ARVN forces could bring to bear their vastly superior firepower. Vann once boasted that the Vietcong guerrillas could be defeated "if they would only stand and fight." Ap Bac was the golden opportunity that the U.S. military command was waiting for.

The South Vietnamese Seventh Division outnumbered the Vietcong by a ratio of 10 to one. A three-pronged attack was planned. Infantry and Civil Guard battalions would advance on Ap Bac from the north and south, while a company of armored personnel carriers would attack from the west, with three additional South Vietnamese companies remaining in reserve. The entire force also had artillery and air support. By any measure, the Vietcong should have been doomed.

Waiting until the ARVN troops came into their sights, the Vietcong guerrillas held their fire as the first three waves of helicopters lifted the infantry regiment into the zone. Then, as the fourth wave arrived bearing reserves, the Vietcong opened up with automatic weapons. By noon, five choppers had been downed, and for the next three hours, despite pleas by his American adviser, the South Vietnamese armored commander refused to rescue the crews. When he finally did move, he deployed vehicles so slowly that they were easy targets for the guerrillas, who killed 14 of the South Vietnamese machine gunners. Three Americans, all helicopter crew members, also died.

Though the ARVN called airplanes, helicopters, armed personnel carriers and U.S. advisers to its assistance, it suffered 165 casualties and lost five helicopters, while the Vietcong escaped with fewer than 12 dead. The battle at Ap Bac revealed the failings of the South Vietnamese army and demonstrated the growing gap between the official optimism in Washington and the grim reality of the war on the ground.

In the wake of Ap Bac the guerrillas overran three government outposts in the Mekong Delta, killing over 300 defenders and making off with American rifles, machine guns and mortars. In March 1963, fighting reached south of Saigon, and the guerrillas captured enough weapons to arm two companies. American Special Forces were able to stabilize the situation in the Central Highlands, but the Mekong Delta was quickly falling into Vietcong hands.

OPTIMISTIC REPORTS

As management of the Vietnamese situation passed to the advisers in the field, Washington became increasingly dependent on the assessments of American civilian and military officials in Saigon. The U.S. ambassador to South Vietnam, Frederick Nolting, continued to express confidence in the Diem government. Impressive statistics, such as "kill ratios," "body counts," "weapons lost/weapons captured ratios" and "incident counts," flowed from MACV via the Pentagon. Unfortunately, both the embassy and MACV based their judgments on information supplied primarily by the Vietnamese government.

There was talk in Washington even of reducing the number of advisers from 12,000 in 1964 to only 1,500 four years later, and decreasing aid as well. McNamara announced, "There is a new feeling of confidence that victory is possible," and Admiral Harry D. Felt, the U.S. commander in chief, Pacific (CINCPAC), predicted "victory in three years."

Officially, the war in Vietnam was being won, but underneath the optimistic rhetoric of the top command a few respected political leaders were already beginning to raise serious questions about the progress of the war. One of the most determined voices belonged to Mike Mansfield, the new Senate majority leader. After visiting Vietnam in late 1962, he reported his frank conclusions to President Kennedy. The United States had spent $2 billion in seven years, yet "substantially the same difficulties remain if, indeed, they have not been compounded." He had serious reservations about the Diem regime and its failure to share political power. He warned Kennedy that deeper American involvement could eventually draw the United States into a position similar to the one once occupied by the French.

President Kennedy attacked Mansfield's report as defeatist. "For us to withdraw," he told reporters, "would mean a collapse not only of South Vietnam but Southeast Asia. So we are going to stay." Later, Kennedy intimated to Kenneth O'Donnell, one of his aides, that he planned to withdraw Americans from Vietnam after his reelection in 1964, even at the risk of being called "a Communist appeaser." Despite his private comments, Kennedy's actions and statements at the time reflected a strong position toward continued American involvement in Southeast Asia.

GROWING DOUBTS ABOUT DIEM

In early 1963, Kennedy received a troubling report on the situation in Vietnam from Roger Hilsman, assistant secretary of state for Far Eastern Affairs. After visiting Vietnam, Hilsman concluded that although the war was "going better than it was a year ago," the strategic hamlets were a failure. In an "Eyes Only" (for the president only) secret addendum to his report, he gave a pessimistic assessment of the corrupt and inept Diem regime. This low opinion of Diem was shared widely among top White House and State Department officials as well as by some members of the CIA, including many at the CIA station in Saigon.

The Kennedy administration urged Diem to appease his enemies, expand his government and crack down on corruption, but to no avail. Diem's resistance to change was due not just to his natural obstinancy, but to his belief that to accept U.S. advice would have confirmed his opponents' charge that he was a "puppet." To bolster his own claim as a rightful ruler he chose the path of appearing defiant.

THE BUDDHIST CRISIS

The downfall of the Diem regime began with the "Buddhist crisis" that first erupted on May 8, 1963, in the former imperial capital of Hue. Diem had prohibited the monks from flying their religious flags to celebrate the 2,527th birthday of the Gautama Buddha, and the Buddhists marched to the city radio station in protest. When they refused to disperse, government troops opened fire on the demonstrators, killing eight people, including one child, and wounding scores more.

Diem's regime charged that the incident had been provoked by "foreigners and the Vietcong." The Buddhists demanded that Diem lift the ban on religious flags, compensate the families and punish those responsible. Diem ignored their protests.

The Buddhists soon organized, and demonstrations in Saigon became almost a daily occurrence. For South Vietnam's 10.5 million Buddhists the dispute with the Diem government was not merely over whether they could fly religious banners, but over a perceived pattern of discrimination and hostility that they had endured for nearly a century. Buddhists complained that under the Diem regime Catholics received the best civil service jobs, preferential treatment in army promotions and the choicest land redistributed by the government.

Buddhism, however, was a secondary issue for most of the people who took part in the demonstrations, and even for many of the monks as well. The controversy quickly crystallized the growing popular resentment against the regime. In the guise of "defending Buddhism," the monks articulated a broad popular yearning to get rid of Diem.

At the core of the movement was a militant faction of the Unified Buddhist Church, under the leadership of Thich Tri Quang. Tri Quang had sided with the Vietminh against the French and Japanese and considered himself a revolutionary noncommunist. He toured South Vietnam to enlist support for his cause, and met covertly with U.S. officials, informing them: "The United States must either make Diem reform or get rid of him. If not, the situation will degenerate . . ."

Washington warned Diem that, if the South Vietnamese government continued its repression of the Buddhists, the United States would publicly disassociate itself from the regime's policies. But Diem refused to back down.

On the morning of June 11, the Buddhists engaged in a protest that soon turned world opinion against President Diem's regime. At a busy Saigon intersection, a motorcade pulled up, and Thich Quang Duc, a Buddhist monk, climbed out of one of the cars. He sat down on the pavement and crossed his legs as other monks and nuns encircled him, and then one of them doused him with gasoline while another ignited him with a lighter. As Thich Quang Duc sat motionless, without a cry of pain, a monk repeated into a loudspeaker over and over again, first in Vietnamese and then in English, "A Buddhist priest burns himself to death. A Buddhist priest becomes a martyr." The next morning a photograph of the horrific spectacle appeared on the front page of virtually every newspaper in the world.

THE COUP

Despite the self-immolation and repeated American entreaties, Diem refused to curtail his repressive policies. More popular protests against Diem occurred during the summer of 1963 as well as more public burnings by Buddhists. The loyalty of the army was also growing increasingly uncertain. The raids of August 21 on Buddhist temples and sanctuaries in Saigon by troops loyal to Diem, but disguised as regular soldiers, convinced key ARVN officers that Diem had to go. Chief-of-Staff Tran Van Don contacted American CIA agent Lou Conein on August 23 and indicated that planning for a coup was underway.

Washington had just sent a new ambassador, Henry Cabot Lodge, to replace Nolting, who had come to be regarded as too "pro-Diem." After studying the State Department files on Vietnam before leaving Washington, Lodge had concluded that Diem was going to be his main problem. In the new American ambassador, the generals found a man receptive to their plans.

Accounts of what followed differ mainly over the degree of U.S. involvement. According to General Don, the plotters kept their plans to themselves until the last moment and acted without encouragement from the United States. However, on August 28, Lodge sent a cable to Washington: "We are launched on a course from which there is no respectable turning back: the overthrow of the Diem government. There is no turning back because there is no possibility the war can be won under a Diem administration. The chance of bringing off a generals' coup depends on them to some extent: but it depends at least as much on us." Kennedy promptly approved Lodge's recommendations, giving him complete discretion to suspend U.S. aid to Diem. In effect, Lodge was given the mandate to change American policy, and as he defined it, the new goal was the toppling of the Diem regime.

The circle of plotters quickly widened to include General Duong Van "Big" Minh, who began his career under the French and had risen swiftly by commanding troops that crushed the sects, and General Tran Thien Khiem, one of Diem's most trusted generals and commander of the 7th Division. Except for their lack of ties to the old aristocratic mandarinate of Annam, the coup group differed little in social background from the Diem regime. They were repulsed by Diem's treatment of Buddhists but were more concerned with Diem's efforts to establish his personal control over the army.

At 1:30 in the afternoon of November 1, 1963, South Vietnamese marine, airborne and army battalions, backed by nearly 40 tanks, marched into Saigon and surrounded the presidential palace. While the palace guards held off the attack, Diem called Ambassador Lodge. It was the last conversation that any American would have with Ngo Dinh Diem.

Diem and his brother Nhu rejected the generals' repeated calls to surrender. Later that evening, they escaped from the palace through secret tunnels. The next morning, they were found hiding in a suburban church. Their hands tied behind them with metal wire, Diem and Nhu were forced into an armored personnel carrier and then shot by two of General Minh's aides. When news of the assassination was given to President Kennedy during a cabinet meeting in the White House, he was visibly shaken. "Why did they do that?" he asked bitterly. While Diem's death alarmed Kennedy, it brought jubilation to Saigon.

Crowds in Saigon tore up Diem's portrait and slogans. Political prisoners emerged from jails. In the countryside, peasants demolished the strategic hamlets. A few days after the coup, Lodge cabled Kennedy: "The prospects now are for a shorter war."

Another assassination occurred three weeks later in Dallas, Texas. On November 22, 1963, at 1:20 P.M. central standard time, Kenneth

O'Donnell, President Kennedy's appointment secretary, announced in the examining room at Parkland Hospital, "He's gone." Ten minutes later Vice President Lyndon Johnson was sworn in as president in a somber ceremony aboard Air Force One.

PREPARATIONS FOR A WIDER WAR

Two days later, on November 24, Johnson held a briefing on Vietnam with Ambassador Henry Cabot Lodge, Secretary of State Dean Rusk, Undersecretary of State George Ball, Secretary of Defense Robert McNamara, National Security Adviser McGeorge Bundy and CIA Director John McCone. While Lodge expressed cautious optimism, McCone was less encouraging. Johnson asserted he was ". . . not going to lose Vietnam" and "was not going to be the President who saw Southeast Asia go the way China did."

The new president made his first formal decision on Vietnam with a National Security Action Memorandum, NSAM 273, which reaffirmed the U.S. commitment to Vietnam and the continuation of Vietnam programs and policies of the Kennedy administration. The "action memorandum" also called for further South Vietnamese clandestine operations against the north.

Since Diem's overthrow the situation in South Vietnam had deteriorated, especially in the Mekong Delta region, the rice basket of South Vietnam, where 40% of the population lived. These gloomy reports from the field motivated Defense Secretary McNamara to make a two-day visit to Vietnam just before Christmas. He returned to report, "The Vietcong now control very high proportions of the people in certain key provinces, particularly those south and west of Saigon." He believed that unless current trends were reversed within two or three months, they would lead to "a Communist-controlled state."

While McNamara recommended expanded counterinsurgency activities, some members of the Joint Chiefs of Staff proposed more forceful moves, such as Air Force Commander General Curtis LeMay, who advocated bombing North Vietnam. Johnson subscribed to the maxim that "wars are too serious to be entrusted to the generals." But as he prepared for the 1964 presidential election, he was especially sensitive to those opponents who might label him as "soft on communism" if he were to back away from American involvement in Vietnam. As a politician, he assuaged the Pentagon with promises he may never have intended to keep. At a White House reception on Christmas Eve 1963, for example, he told the Joint Chiefs of Staff: "Just let me get elected, and then you can have your war."

December 2: Following a trip to Vietnam at President Kennedy's request, Senate Majority Leader Mike Mansfield (D–Mont.) becomes the first major U.S. official to refuse to make a positive public comment on the progress of the war.

December 31: U.S. forces in Vietnam total 11,300.

1963

January 2: First major defeat of the South Vietnamese army—Army of the Republic of Vietnam (ARVN)—by Vietcong units at the battle of Ap Bac, 30 to 50 miles southeast of Saigon.

February 24: A U.S. Senate panel reports that annual American aid to South Vietnam totals $400 million and that 12,000 Americans are stationed there "on dangerous assignment."

February 26: U.S. helicopters are ordered to shoot first at enemy soldiers while escorting ARVN troops.

April 17: Diem broadcasts an "Open Arms" (Chieu Hoi) appeal, promising clemency and material benefits to Vietcong guerrillas if they abandon the war against his government.

May 8: Buddhists begin to stage demonstrations and revolts against the Diem regime.

June 11: Buddhist monk Quang Duc publicly burns himself in a plea for Diem to show "charity and compassion" to all religions. More Buddhist monks immolate themselves during the ensuing weeks.

June 27: President Kennedy appoints Henry Cabot Lodge, his former Republican political opponent, to succeed Frederick Nolting as ambassador to Vietnam.

July 4: General Tran Van Don informs Lucien Conein of the CIA that certain officers are planning a coup against Diem.

August 20: Diem declares martial law.

August 21: Disguised as regular soldiers, troops loyal to Diem attack Buddhist temples and sanctuaries in Saigon, Hue and other cities.

August 24: Ambassador Henry Cabot Lodge receives a State Department cable stating that the U.S. can no longer tolerate Ngo Dinh Nhu's influence in President Diem's regime.

August 26: Ambassador Lodge meets with Diem for the first time. Diem refuses to drop Nhu and refuses to discuss reforms.

October 2: Defense Secretary McNamara predicts that most of the 15,000 U.S. troops in South Vietnam can be withdrawn by the end of 1965.

November 1: Dissidents organized by the key generals of the South Vietnamese army lay siege to the presidential palace. Diem is unable to summon any support, but he and Nhu escape.

November 2: Diem begins negotiating with the generals. He is assured his life will be spared and agrees to surrender along with Nhu. At General Minh's orders, Diem and Nhu are murdered on their way to staff headquarters.

November 4: The U.S. recognizes the new provisional government of South Vietnam. Former Vice President Nguyen Ngoc Tho, a Buddhist, becomes premier, but the real power is held by the Revolutionary Military Committee headed by General Duong Van Minh.

November 22: President Kennedy is assassinated in Dallas, Texas. Vice President Lyndon Johnson assumes the presidency.

November 24: President Johnson confirms the U.S. intention to continue military and economic support to South Vietnam.

December: Hanoi decides to start sending regular army troops into the south.

December 31: U.S. forces in Vietnam total 11,300.

EYEWITNESS TESTIMONY

Indications are growing that the VC [Vietcong] are mounting a special campaign aimed at undermining the Diem Government. According to CAS [Controlled American Source, a term used for the Central Intelligence Agency] sources, VC armed cadre strength has increased to about 3,000 in the southwest, double the number in September. VC groups now operate in larger strength, and their tactics have changed from attacks on individuals to rather frequent and daring attacks on GVN security forces. A recent CAS report has indicated a VC intention to press general guerrilla warfare in South Viet-Nam in 1960, and indicates the VC are convinced they can mount a coup d'état this year. President Diem also told me late February about the capture of a VC document indicating their intention to step up aggressive attacks all over the country, including Saigon, beginning in the second quarter.

Ambassador Elbridge Dubrow, to Secretary of State Christian A. Herter, telegram of March 7, 1960, in U.S. Department of Defense's United States-Vietnam Relations *(1971).*

I sense how deeply the Vietnamese value their country's independence and strength and I know how well you used your boldness when you led your countrymen in winning it. I also know that your determination has been a vital factor in guarding that independence while steadily advancing the economic development of your country. I am confident that these same qualities of determination and boldness will meet the renewed threat as well as the needs and desires of your countrymen for further progress on all fronts.

Although the main responsibility for guarding that independence will always, as it has in the past, belong to the Vietnamese people and their government, I want to assure you that for so long as our strength can be useful, the United States will continue to assist Viet-Nam in the difficult yet hopeful struggle ahead.

President Dwight D. Eisenhower, to President Diem, message of October 25, 1960, in Public Papers of the Presidents of the United States.

For the third time my life turned to war again. For the liberation of our compatriots in the south, a situation of boiling oil and burning fire is necessary! A situation in which husband is separated from wife, father from son, brother from brother is necessary. Now, my life is full of hardship. Not enough rice to eat, not enough salt to give taste to my tongue, not enough clothing to keep myself warm. But, in my heart, I keep loyal to the [Communist] Party and to the people.

Du Luc, Vietcong soldier, diary entry of December 1960, in Time *(December 15, 1961).*

We cannot let Laos fall to the Communists, even if we have to fight, with our allies or without them.

President Eisenhower, to National Security Council, statement of December 31, 1960, in Waging Peace *(1965).*

Let every nation know, whether it wishes us well or ill, that we shall pay any price, bear any burden, meet any hardship, support any friend, oppose any foe to assure the survival and the success of liberty.

President John F. Kennedy, to the nation, inaugural address of January 20, 1961, in Public Papers of the Presidents of the United States.

The enemy are barefoot or wear sandals. They wear black pajamas, usually, with tatters or holes in them. I don't think you'd recognize any of them as soldiers, but they think of themselves that way. The people that are fighting them, on our side, are being supplied with weapons and uniforms and good shoes and all of the best that we have; and we're training them. Yet, the enemy's licking our side.

Colonel Edward G. Lansdale, to Secretary of Defense Robert S. McNamara, after visiting South Vietnam, briefing of January 1961, in Gibbons' The U.S. Government and the Vietnam War *(1985).*

The present South Vietnamese regime is a camouflaged colonial regime dominated by the Yankees, and the South Vietnamese Government is a servile government, implementing faithfully all the policies of the American imperialists. Therefore, this regime must be overthrown and a government of national and democratic union put in its place composed of representatives of all social classes, of all nationalities, of the various political parties, of all religions;

patriotic, eminent citizens must take over for the people the control of economic, political, social, and cultural interests and thus bring about independence, democracy, well-being, peace, neutrality, and efforts toward the peaceful unification of the country.

National Liberation Front (NLF), to the people of South Vietnam, radio broadcast of February 1961, in U.S. Foreign Broadcast Information Service's Daily Report of February 13, 1961.

The security of all Southeast Asia will be endangered if Laos loses its neutral independence.

President John F. Kennedy, to the nation, television address of March 23, 1961, in Public Papers of the Presidents of the United States.

Watching Americans in the field who are organizing this effort, you get a feeling of tremendous drive and efficiency.

An American with a jungle pack, lightweight weapons, iodine tablets to purify water and tropical medicines is able to go anywhere his Asian counterpart can. He eats rice and dried beef, sleeps in his jungle uniform . . .

Robert P. Martin, journalist, on a U.S. Army Special Forces team, in U.S. News and World Report article of April 1961.

Both Governments recognize that under circumstances of guerilla warfare now existing in free Vietnam, it is necessary to give high priority to the restoration of a sense of security to the people of free Vietnam. This priority, however, in no way diminishes the necessity, in policies and programs of both Governments, to pursue vigorously appropriate measures in other fields to achieve a prosperous and happy society . . .

Vice President Lyndon Johnson and President Ngo Dinh Diem, joint declaration of May 13, 1961, in U.S. Department of State Bulletin of June 19, 1961.

The fundamental decision required of the United States—and time is of the greatest importance—is whether we are to attempt to meet the challenges of Communist expansion now in Southeast Asia by a major effort in support of the forces of freedom in the area or throw in the towel . . . at some point we may be faced with the further decision of whether we commit major United States forces to the area or

cut our losses and withdraw should our other efforts fail.

Vice President Johnson, to President Kennedy, after visiting Vietnam, report of May 24, 1961, in U.S. Department of Defense's United States-Vietnam Relations.

Now we have a problem in making our power credible, and Vietnam looks like the place.

President Kennedy, to James Reston, journalist, after the president had met with Premier Nikita Khrushchev, remark of June 1961, in Halberstam's The Best and the Brightest (1972).

The operation began when a reinforced regiment of infantry under a Vietnamese commander with an American adviser sealed off an area roughly fifteen miles long and five or six wide. The only normal means of access to the villages in the center of this zone is by small boat along the canals that irrigate the rice fields. Since the canals are small and easily defended, the region has become a Viet Cong sanctuary, complete with what communists call combat villages. It was like a big game hunt, with the beaters on the side driving the prey into the center for the guns. In this case, the hunters were fifteen amphibious and armored troop carriers made of an aluminum alloy and designed to skate along at twenty miles an hour or more across paddy fields.

Denis Warner, journalist, on accompanying a 1961 operation in the Mekong Delta, in a Reporter article of September 13, 1962.

As for Vietnam, it is agreed we must move quite radically to avoid perhaps slow but total defeat. The sense of the town is that, with Southern Laos open, Diem simply cannot cope.

Presidential adviser Walt Rostow, to President Kennedy, message of October 5, 1961, in Gibbons' The U.S. Government and the Vietnam War.

. . . we pressed ahead with our operations throughout the country and with our operations against the North. Flights left Danang in the dusk headed north with Vietnamese trained and equipped to land in isolated areas, make cautious contact with their former home villages and begin building networks there. Boats went up the coast to land others on the beaches, and we started leaflet drops and radio programs designed to raise questions in North

Vietnamese homes about their sons being sent to South Vietnam to fight and about the vices of Communist rule. We lost one plane, which did not give the crack radio signal that it had passed the coastal checkpoint, and a few weeks later Hanoi issued a press release containing confessions by the crew and team that they had been trained by Americans and sent by South Vietnam. No plausible denial there.

CIA Saigon station chief William Colby, on CIA operations in 1961, in Colby and Forbath's Honorable Men: My Life in the CIA *(1978).*

We are facing pro-Communist guerrillas who have perfected the technique of subversive warfare during the past fifteen years . . . In some ways, we are learning more about guerrilla warfare than we are teaching.

Captain Harold Ross, USA, to journalist Francois Sully, in Newsweek *(July 31, 1961).*

It is recommended . . . That upon request from the Government of Vietnam (GVN) to come to its aid in resisting the increasing aggressions of the Viet-Cong and in repairing the ravages of the Delta flood which, in combination, threaten the lives of its citizens and the security of the country, the U.S. Government offer to join the GVN in a massive joint effort as a part of a total mobilization of GVN resources to cope with both the Viet-Cong (VC) and the ravages of the flood. The U.S. representatives will participate actively in this effort, particularly in the fields of government administration, military plans and operations, intelligence, and flood relief, going beyond the advisory role which they have observed in the past.

General Maxwell Taylor, USA, to President Kennedy, after visiting South Vietnam, cablegram of November 1, 1961, in U.S. Department of Defense's United States-Vietnam Relations.

The sending of American armed forces to Viet Nam may be the wrong way and probably would be, in present circumstances . . . If American combat units land in Viet Nam, it is conceivable that the Chinese Communists would do the same. With shorter lines of communication and transportation, with much more manpower available, South Viet Nam, on that basis, could become a quicksand for us. Where does an involvement of this kind end even if we can bring it to a successful conclusion? In the environs of Sai-

gon? At the 17th parallel? At Hanoi? At Canton? At Peking?

Senator Mike Mansfield (D–Mont.), to President Kennedy, memorandum of November 2, 1961, in Gibbons' The U.S. Government and the Vietnam War.

The Vietnamese is a good soldier. But his officers don't like contact. They would rather stay in their pillboxes than be out in the jungle hunting for a scrap.

Anonymous U.S. military adviser, in U.S. News & World Report *article of November 6, 1961.*

. . . the Vietnamese nation now faces what is perhaps the gravest crisis in its long history. For more than 2,000 years my people have lived and built, fought and died in this land. We have not always been free. Indeed, much of our history and many of its proudest moments have arisen from conquest by foreign powers and our struggle against great odds to regain or defend our precious independence. But it is not only our freedom which is at stake today, it is our national identity. For, if we lose this war, our people will be swallowed by the Communist bloc, all our proud heritage will be blotted out by the "Socialist society" and Vietnam will leave the pages of history. We will lose our national soul.

President Diem, to President Kennedy, letter of December 7, 1961, in Gravel's The Pentagon Papers *(1971).*

Your letter underlines what our own information has convincingly shown—that the campaign of force and terror now being waged against your people and your Government is supported and directed from the outside by the authorities at Hanoi. They have thus violated the provisions of the Geneva Accords designed to ensure peace in Viet-Nam and to which they bound themselves in 1954.

At that time, the United States, although not a party to the Accords, declared that it "would view any renewal of the aggression in violation of the agreements with grave concern and as seriously threatening international peace and security." We continue to maintain that view.

In accordance with that declaration, and in response to your request, we are prepared to help the Republic of Viet-Nam to protect its people and to preserve its independence. We shall promptly increase our assistance to your defense effort as well as help relieve the destruction of the floods which you describe. I have already given the orders to get these programs underway.

President Kennedy, to President Diem, letter of December 14, 1961, in Public Papers of the Presidents of the United States.

This is a grubby, dirty method of fighting . . . If we could just corner all the Vietcong on the highland on open ground we could lay them flat in two minutes. But it takes weeks to find even 50 of them.

Anonymous U.S. Army colonel, statement of December 1961, in Newsweek *(January 1, 1962).*

Q. Mr. President, are American troops now in combat in Vietnam?

The President: No.

President Kennedy, to a news conference of January 15, 1962, in Public Papers of the Presidents of the United States.

The helicopter jounced down into the paddy, water coming up nearly to the doorframe. The troops began leaping out, each getting a friendly whack on the

An American adviser shows Vietnamese infantrymen how to get out fast from a U.S. helicopter after it has brought them to a battle scene, 1962. Courtesy of the U.S. News & World Report Collection, Library of Congress.

shoulder from the American door gunner. As they jumped up, they ran, hip deep in mud and water, holding their rifles high. The fifth soldier out of the helicopter took only ten steps before his face abruptly turned into a mass of red jelly, and slumped to the ground. All twelve soldiers were out now, and the machine gun was back in firing position. The first few shots headed toward the tree line, and then the arc of fire swept aimlessly up into the sky. The gunner was hit.

Malcolm W. Browne, journalist, recalls a helicopter operation in the Mekong Delta in 1962, in The New Face of War *(1965).*

This is not a game. We—two battalions of Vietnamese paratroopers and their two American military advisers from the U.S. 101st Airborne Division—are not waking up in the humid darkness just to prove that we can. Here, near the Cambodian border in the heart of southeast Asia, we are going out to hunt down live human beings. Human beings who otherwise, tonight or a decade from now, will hunt us down here or perhaps somewhere closer to home . . .

How can it be that in this nuclear age, with all the disarmament negotiations, all the arts of modern diplomacy, and all the world's will for peace, the real course of history is still being written by strong young men betting their lives at hide-and-seek on foot in darkness?

Dickey Chapelle, journalist, article of February 1962 in Reader's Digest.

We have increased our assistance to the [South Vietnamese] government—it's logistic; we have not sent combat troops there, although the training missions that we have there have been instructed if they are fired upon—they would of course, fire back, to protect themselves. But we have not sent combat troops in the generally understood sense of the word.

President Kennedy, to news conference of February 14, 1962, in Public Papers of the Presidents of the United States.

. . . the United States is now involved in an undeclared war in South Vietnam.

James Reston, newspaper columnist, editorial of February 14, 1962, in The New York Times.

. . . my wife sat up in bed and said, "Bombs or close-in artillery!" "It's only a thunderstorm," I muttered, but quickly realized she was right.

A South Vietnamese soldier with a submachine gun checks for signs of Vietcong, August 1962. Courtesy of the National Archives.

The telephone rang. A Marine guard at the Embassy reported aircraft dropping bombs on the President's Palace. "Whose aircraft?" In the dim light and fog, the Marine first thought they were Chinese planes, then American, and finally he recognized their South Vietnam markings. The planes circled slowly at a low altitude over the Palace, dropping their bombs and strafing with 20mm guns. Antiaircraft fire soon opened up—from Vietnamese Navy craft in the Saigon River, as it turned out. After a short time of intense firing, the racket ceased.
Ambassador Frederick Nolting, on the attempted coup against Diem on February 27, 1962, in From Trust to Tragedy *(1988).*

The Vietcong live like us, look like us, share our homes. How can we inform on them?
Anonymous Vietnamese peasant, statement in Time *(February 9, 1962).*

. . . the Viet Cong stopped my bus to check the identity cards of the passengers. They arrested two men and dragged them off the bus. They said . . .

"We've warned you many times to resign from your job but you haven't obeyed us. So now we have to carry out the sentence."

They cut off the heads of the two men and pinned the verdicts to their shirts. The verdicts were already written out. They were police agents.
Anonymous Vietnamese bus driver, Long Kanh province, statement of March 1962, in Rose's U.S. News & World Report *article of April 8, 1962.*

Guerrilla warfare is a means of fighting a revolutionary war, which relies on the heroic spirit to triumph over modern weapons.
General Vo Nguyen Giap, 1962, in People's War, People's Army *(1962).*

Department increasingly concerned over constant implications in press generally of U.S. participation and direction, rather than purely support and training.
Assistant Secretary of State W. Averell Harriman, to Ambassador Frederick Nolting, message of April 4, 1962, in Gravel's The Pentagon Papers.

Now, I agree [political negotiations are] a very hazardous course, but introducing American forces, which is the other one—let's not think there is some great third course—that also is a hazardous course, and we want to attempt to see if we can work out a peaceful solution.
President Kennedy, to news conference of May 9, 1962, in Public Papers of the Presidents of the United States.

It's a dirty, nasty little war . . . and nobody knows anything about it. But [Captain] Terry [Cordell] and the others are just as dead, and they died just as gallantly, as if it were a declared war.
Susan Cordell, on the death of her husband, shot down while flying as a U.S. adviser on a reconnaissance mission in the Central Highlands of South Vietnam, in Martin's Saturday Evening Post *article of November 24, 1962.*

This is a difficult war to cover . . . You never know where to go. We are never told of what's going to happen. American officials act as if they are afraid of newsmen.
Homer Bigart, Southeast Asia correspondent for The New York Times, *statement in* Newsweek *(July 2, 1962).*

I believe in a free press . . . but I'll admit we'd be better off propaganda-wise if there were no American journalists there.

Anonymous Pentagon official, statement in Newsweek *(July 2, 1962).*

I never heard a single Vietnamese voice raised in defense of the Diem regime. High and low, government officials, professors, army officers, and students condemned it and yearned for a change—a coup d'etat which would rid them of Diem before the Communists crushed him.

Visiting University of Saigon Professor Stanley Millet, in Harper's *article of September 1962.*

Our present objective is to find the enemy's forces, fix them, fight them, and finish them. Thorough pacification will come later.

Colonel Pham Van Dong, South Vietnamese army, statement in Newsweek *(September 3, 1962).*

About a hundred yards away we came upon a dead peasant lying in the yard of his hut with a poncho spread over him. Two huts farther on, a desperately frightened old man of eighty was genuflecting in front of the American and Vietnamese officers and telling them that he had never heard of the Vietcong. How many times had this old man had to tell Government troops that he knew no Vietcong? How many times had he had to tell the Vietminh or Vietcong that he knew no Government troops? "The war," a young Vietnamese said to me bitterly later, "only lasts a lifetime."

David Halberstam, New York Times correspondent, in the Mekong Delta in October 1962, in The Making of a Quagmire *(1965).*

Within five years, we could have three hundred thousand men in the paddies and jungles and never find them again.

Undersecretary of State George Ball, to President Kennedy, statement of November 1963, in Gibbons' The U.S. Government and the Vietnam War.

There was a patronizing, holier-than-thou tone in the official attitude toward the press corps. We re-

Saigon street, 1962. Courtesy of the U.S. News & World Report Collection, Library of Congress.

Secretary of Defense Robert S. McNamara (right) and General Lyman L. Lemnitzer, chairman of the Joint Chiefs of Staff (second from left, foreground), accompanied by American and Vietnamese officers, visit units of the U.S. Military Assistance Command in May 1962. Courtesy of the National Archives.

peatedly received cables from Washington using expressions like "tell the correspondents" to do so and so, or "explain how they were wrong" to write such and such. This was like trying to tell a New York taxi driver how to shift gears.

USIA officer John Mecklin, Saigon Mission, on briefing the press corps in 1962, in Mission in Torment *(1965).*

. . . it seems to me most essential that we make crystal clear to the Vietnamese government and to our own people that while we will go to great lengths to help, the primary responsibility rests with the Vietnamese. Our role is and must remain secondary in present circumstances. It is their country, their future which is most at stake, not ours.

To ignore that reality will not only be immensely costly in terms of American lives and resources but it may also draw us inexorably into some variation

of the unenviable position in Vietnam which was formerly occupied by the French.

Senator Mike Mansfield, to President Kennedy, a report of November 18, 1962, in U.S. Congress, Senate Committee on Foreign Relations' Two Reports on Vietnam and Southeast Asia to the President by Senator Mike Mansfield *(1973).*

Q. Mr. President, it was just a year ago that you ordered stepped-up aid to Viet-Nam. There seems to be a good deal of discouragement about the progress. Can you give us your assessment?

The President. Well, we are putting in a major effort in Viet-Nam. As you know, we have about 10 or 11 times as many men there as we had a year ago. We've had a number of casualties. We put in an awful lot of equipment. We are going ahead with the strategic hamlet proposal. In some phases, the military program has been quite successful. There is great difficulty, however, in fighting a guerrilla war. You need 10 to 1, or 11 to 1, especially in terrain as difficult as South Viet-Nam.

So we don't see the end of the tunnel, but I must say I don't think it is darker than it was a year ago, and in some ways lighter.

President Kennedy, to news conference of December 12, 1962, in Public Papers of the Presidents of the United States.

We landed there, amid twirling clouds of red dust, and were met by crowds of montagnard troops in green American field uniforms and a group of American Special Force advisors, looking lean and fit in their fatigues, jungle boots, and green berets. The troopers, although larger than the lowland Vietnamese, still appeared to be midgets next to the tall Americans.

One of the group was a sturdy, blond-mustached captain named Stanley Hyrowski (of Youngstown, Ohio). He led us along a dirt road into a cleared area, where in sandbagged outpost positions, montagnard troops were preparing to fire rifle grenades . . . "We're building command teams," he said. "The teams will go out and seek out the Viet Cong. We teach them submachine gun, carbine, hand grenades. We try to stress offensive actions."

Richard Tregaskis, journalist and author, journal entry of December 15, 1962, in Vietnam Diary *(1963).*

In Saigon I was staying at the Majestic Hotel and having my meals at the Rex . . . I was sitting on the roof of the Rex there, in a sweet kind of sunrise. Then going down to Bac Lieu, getting on an H-21, which is a rattletrap of a helicopter, and going into a rice paddy landing zone. Getting out and cruising around in the brush with a U.S. sergeant and some Vietnamese. Then getting picked up after a day in the paddies, and ending up that night on the roof of the Rex.

Lieutenant General John H. Cushman, USA, commander of the 21st Infantry Division advisory team, on operations with the strategic hamlet program in 1963, in Maurer's Strange Ground: America in Vietnam *(1989).*

Better to fight and die than run and be slaughtered.

Anonymous Vietcong commander, anticipating defeat at the battle of Ap Bac, diary entry of January 1963, in Karnow's Vietnam: A History *(1983).*

These people may be the world's greatest lovers, but they're not the world's greatest fighters. But they're good people, and they can win a war if someone shows them how.

Lieutenant Colonel John Paul Vann, top U.S. adviser with South Vietnam's 7th Infantry Division, to David Halberstam, New York Times *Southeast Asia correspondent, after the South Vietnamese army failed to defeat a Vietcong guerrilla force at the battle of Ap Bac, statement of January 1963, in Sheehan's* A Bright Shining Lie *(1988).*

. . . we got a fix on one machine-gun position and made 15 aerial runs on it . . . Every time we thought we had him, and every time that damned gunner came right back up firing.

Anonymous U.S. military adviser, on the battle of Ap Bac, in Time *(January 11, 1963).*

The lack of will to fight for their own independence that Vietnamese troops displayed at the battle of Ap Bac . . . merits fundamental Administration review of its current policy of military aid to South Vietnam.

Arthur Krock, editorial of January 8, 1963, in The New York Times.

Anyone who criticizes the fighting of the Armed Forces of Vietnam is doing a disservice to the thousands of gallant and courageous men who are fighting in the defense of their country.

General Paul Harkins, USA, MACV commander, to the Saigon press corps, January 10, 1963, in the Washington Star *(January 11, 1963).*

We went out on an operation the other day, and as soon as we lost one man my counterpart—a Vietnamese battalion commander—wanted to call it off and come back.

Anonymous U.S. military officer, in U.S. News & World Report *article of January 21, 1963.*

Barring greatly increased resupply and reinforcement of the Viet Cong by infiltration, the military phase of the war can be virtually won in 1963.

MACV report of April 1963, in Gravel's The Pentagon Papers.

. . . we saw that the U.S. support base was growing like a goddamned mushroom. Everytime we'd take a trip back to Nha Trang, Danang, or Cam Ranh

General Paul D. Harkins (front), the first commander of the U.S. Military Assistance Command in Vietnam, is accompanied by Vietnamese officers during an inspection of an anti-guerrilla training camp in 1963. Courtesy of the National Archives.

Bay we could see this tremendous buildup coming. More and more permanent-type installations were being built. The hospitals weren't operating in tents anymore, they were in quonset huts. I figured, "Something is going to happen, we're going to be here a long time."

Chuck Allen, USA, Special Forces (An Sanh and Khe Sanh, October 1962–April 1963), in Santoli's To Bear Any Burden *(1985).*

Before closing my eyes to Buddha . . . I have the honor of presenting my words to President Diem asking him to be kind and tolerant toward his people to enforce a policy of religious equality.

Buddhist monk Quang Duc, last will and testament before burning himself in protest against the Diem regime on June 11, 1963, in Time *(June 21, 1963).*

Wrench selves from mud pile. Thunderstorm begins. Capture swamp which obviously is base of VC-trained mosquitos. Too tired to brush them off. Fall flat in muck three times. Who cares? Wade small canal. Water is temperature of urine and smells same. So what? Mosquitos break off action. No contact. Rain continues with lightning accompaniment. Cig-

arettes soaked, last solace gone. Fall flat in mud. . . . [U.S. Army Lieutenant] Friedal points out possible spike traps as I fall in mud again. Downpour continues.

Robert MacCabe, journalist, on an operation with the South Vietnamese Seventh Division, diary entry of July 1963, in Newsweek *(July 15, 1963).*

The Vietcong are losing because we are steadily decreasing their areas of maneuver and the terrain over which they can move at will.

General Paul Harkins, statement in The New York Herald-Tribune *(August 28, 1963).*

Barbecues . . . Let them burn, and we shall clap our hands.

Madame Ngo Dinh Nhu, wife of Diem's brother and chief political adviser, about Buddhist self-immolations, statement of August 8, 1963, in Karnow's Vietnam: A History.

I declare a state of siege throughout the national territory. I confer upon the army of the Republic of Vietnam this responsibility to restore the security and public order so that the state may be protected,

Communism defeated, freedom secured, and de-mocracy achieved.

President Diem, to the nation, radio address of August 20, 1963, following the Buddhists' re-bellion, in Time *(August 30, 1963).*

US Government cannot tolerate situation in which power lies in Nhu's hands. Diem must be given chance to rid himself of Nhu and his coterie and replace them with best military and political person-alities available.

If, in spite of all of your efforts, Diem remains obdurate and refuses, then we must face the possi-bility that Diem himself cannot be preserved.

U.S. State Department, to Ambassador Henry Cabot Lodge, Saigon, top secret cablegram of August 24, 1963, in Gravel's The Pentagon Papers.

The entire contingent of Americans in Vietnam was so thinly spread out that there probably weren't more than five hundred in any one place. Tan Son Nhut had the highest concentration. And it was becoming apparent that the ARVN might turn on us. That became a real worry in the summer of 1963. It became rather apparent from discussions going on that there was going to be a coup. I recall going to Saigon several times and hearing this undercurrent in bars where Vietnamese officers would be.

Radio technician Jan Barry, 18th Aviation Company, USA, in Santoli's Everything We Had *(1981).*

We are launched on a course from which there is no respectable turning back: the overthrow of the Diem government. There is no turning back in part because U.S. prestige is already publicly committed to this end in large measure and will become more so as the facts leak out. In a more fundamental sense, there is no turning back because there is no possibil-ity in my view, that the war can be won under a Diem administration, still less that Diem or any mem-ber of the family can govern the country in a way to gain the support of the people who count, i.e., the educated class in and out of government service, civil and military—not to mention the American people.

Ambassador Henry Cabot Lodge, to Secretary of State Dean Rusk, top secret cablegram of Au-gust 29, 1963, in Gravel's The Pentagon Pa-pers.

The strategic hamlets look like the stockades the American pioneers built to defend themselves against the Indians, except that the Vietnamese use bamboo instead of logs. Most peasants have not been physi-cally moved from their old homes. Rather, defense works—bamboo moats—are erected around a group of closely situated villages.

Marguerite Higgins, journalist, article in The New York Herald-Tribune, *Sept. 1, 1963.*

Mr. [Walter] Cronkite: Mr President, the only war we've got running at the moment is of course the one in Viet-Nam, and we have our difficulties there, quite obviously.

THE PRESIDENT: I don't think that unless a greater effort is made by the Government to win popular support that the war can be won out there. In the final analysis, it is their war. They are the ones who have to win it or lose it. We can help them, we can give them equipment, we can send our men out there as advisers, but they have to win it, the people of Viet-Nam, against the Communists.

We are prepared to continue to assist them, but I don't think that the war can be won unless the people support the effort and, in my opinion, in the last 2 months, the government has gotten out of touch with the people.

President Kennedy, to Walter Cronkite, on a CBS News television program of September 2, 1963, in Public Papers of the Presidents of the United States.

Some of us are being killed or wounded every week. Anything that holds back the war effort keeps us Americans out here that much longer. Anyway, you don't win this kind of war with guns, you win it with people. And Diem no longer has the people with him.

Anonymous U.S. military officer, in U.S. News & World Report *article of September 9, 1963.*

South Vietnam is not worth the life of a single American boy.

Senator Wayne Morse (D–Ore.), to the U.S. Senate, speech of September 26, 1963.

Across the water-filled rice paddies, plumes of smoke and showers of debris marked the targets of the Vietnamese Army's artillery. An American-pi-loted B-26 made repeated passes over a banana grove where guerrillas were dug in.

This was the end of the engagement. On one side of the road the bodies of five Communist guerrillas sprawled in death. On the other side, a young Vietnamese soldier cradled his rifle in his lap while he stroked the head of his dead buddy.

A few yards away was the burned-out hulk of an American armored amphibious carrier and, to one side of it, the bodies of 17 more dead Communists. The road was lined with U.S. Army trucks and fighting vehicles, but the only movement was of a woman carrying off a pig in the battle.

Robert P. Martin, journalist, U.S. News and World Report *article of September 30, 1963.*

We would go into a village with a medical team, right in the middle of VC-controlled areas. Even if they didn't like you, two or three hundred people would flock to the village. We made a medical run up and down the canals every day. The people were very appreciative of getting medicine. The Special Forces pacification program was working out well.

But if we spread out too thin and our soldiers moved out of the village we pacified, the Viet Cong came right back in again. It was the old problem: We controlled the daytime, but the night belonged to Uncle Charlie.

The guy who might have been your cook during the day, or the guy across the street cutting hair . . . that night he'd put his black pajamas on and bring his AK-47 out from under his mattress. He went out to your camp and was shooting at you.

Dan Pitzer, USA, Special Forces, recalls the Mekong Delta in 1963, in Santoli's To Bear Any Burden.

Secretary McNamara and General Taylor reported their judgment that the major part of the U.S. military task can be completed by the end of 1965 . . . by the end of this year, the U.S. program for training Vietnamese should have progressed to the point where 1,000 U.S. military personnel assigned to South Vietnam can be withdrawn.

President Kennedy, to a news conference of October 2, 1963, in Public Papers of the Presidents of the United States.

[W]e certainly cannot be in the position of stimulating, approving, or supporting assassination, but on the other hand, we are in no way responsible for stopping every such threat of which we might receive even partial knowledge. We certainly would not fa-

vor assassination of Diem . . . Consequently believe best approach is hands off.

CIA Director John McCone, to CIA station in Saigon, cable of October 5, 1963, in U.S. Senate's Report on Assassination Plots *(1977).*

In my contacts here I have seen no one with the strength of character of Diem, at least in fighting Communists. Certainly there are no Generals qualified to take over in my opinion.

I am not a Diem man per se. I certainly see the faults of his character. I am here to back 14 million SVN people in their fight against communism and it just happens that Diem is their leader at this time. Most of the Generals I have talked to agree they can go along with Diem, all say it's the Nhu family they are opposed to.

General Paul Harkins, to General Maxwell Taylor, cablegram of October 30, 1963, in Gravel's The Pentagon Papers.

> We are winning, this we know;
> General Harkins tells us so,
> In the delta, things are rough;
> In the mountains, mighty tough.
> But we're winning, this we know;
> General Harkins tells us so,
> If you doubt that this is true,
> McNamara says so, too.

Song—sung to the tune of "Twinkle, Twinkle, Little Star"—popular among low-level U.S. military advisers in 1963, in Dareff's Story of Vietnam *(1971).*

We do not accept as a basis for U.S. policy that we have no power to delay or discourage a coup . . . But once a coup under responsible leadership has begun . . . it is in the interest of the U.S. government that it should succeed.

National Security Adviser McGeorge Bundy, to Ambassador Henry Cabot Lodge, message of October 30, 1963, in Gravel's The Pentagon Papers.

We finally decided on Friday, November 1, 1963, as the historic day for overthrowing Diem's despotic regime. This day had special significance in several aspects. In the first place, it corresponded to September 16 of the Year of the Cat, according to the lunar calendar. That day would appeal to the Vietnamese masses because it was considered to be favorable. And, since November 1 was a Friday, we could expect both President Diem and Nhu to be present since Diem never left Saigon on Friday and Nhu would be presiding over his weekly strategic hamlet meeting. That same day was also All Saints Day for the Catholics, and civil servants had half a day off. We thought, therefore, that not many people would be aware that a coup was taking place.

General Tran Van Don, SVA, in Our Endless War *(1978).*

Give up in five minutes, or the palace will be bombed.

Lieutenant General Duong Van "Big" Minh, to President Diem, telephone conversation of November 1, 1963, in Time *(November 15, 1963).*

Diem: Some units have made a rebellion and I want to know what is the attitude of the U.S.?

Lodge: I do not feel well enough informed to be able to tell you. I have heard the shooting but I am not acquainted with all the facts. Also it is 4:30 A.M. in Washington, and the U.S. government cannot possibly have a view.

Diem: But you must have some general ideas. After all, I am a chief of state. I have tried to do my duty. I want to do now what duty and good sense require. I believe in duty above all.

Lodge: You have certainly done your duty. As I told you only this morning, I admire your courage and your great contributions to your country. No one can take away from you the credit for all you have done. Now I am worried about your physical safety. I have a report that those in charge of the current activity offer you and your brother safe conduct out of the country if you resign. Had you heard this?

Diem: No. [A pause] You have my telephone number.

Lodge: Yes. If I can do anything for your physical safety, please call me.

Diem: I am trying to reestablish order.

President Diem, to Ambassador Henry Cabot Lodge, telephone conversation of November 1, 1963, in Gravel's The Pentagon Papers *[Diem and his brother Nhu were murdered shortly after this conversation.]*

There was heavy firing throughout the city during the night. The siege of the palace began as the cathedral's bells tolled 4:00 A.M. Sixteen anti-Diem tanks churned up the streets radiating from Gia Long, lobbing shots into the building, red-and-white tracer bullets splintered trees and smashed shop windows.

When the white flag was raised over the palace, the population went wild.

Beverly Deepe, journalist, on the coup against the Diem regime on November 1, 1963, in Newsweek *(November 11, 1963).*

. . . if the news is true, if really my family has been treacherously killed with either official or unofficial blessing of the American Government, I can predict to you all that the story of Vietnam is only at its beginning.

Madame Ngo Dinh Nhu, to press conference of November 2, 1963, in The New York Times *(November 3, 1963).*

We are swatting flies when we should be going after the manure pile.

General Curtis E. LeMay, chief of staff, USAF, advocating the bombing of North Vietnam, statement of November 1963, in Hilsman's To Move a Nation *(1967).*

I have changed my opinion about the VC. They are not ornery little fellows. They are mean, vicious, well-trained veterans. They are killers and are out to win. Although this is called a "dirty little war" and it is far from the shores of old U.S.A., it's a big, mean war. We are getting beat. We are undermanned and undergunned. The U.S. may say they are in this, but they don't know we need help over here . . .

If the U.S. would really put combat people in here we could win, and win fast. It seems to be the old story of a half-hearted effort.

Captain Edwin Gerald "Jerry" Shank, USAF, to his wife and family, letter of November 27, 1963, in U.S. News & World Report *(May 4, 1964).*

We are now at the breakeven point between winning and losing . . . At best we are winning the war more slowly than a year ago . . . but the war can still be lost. We can win every military engagement in the field but still lose the political war. It is a tossup with even money on both sides.

Anonymous U.S. military adviser, November 1963, in Newsweek *(December 2, 1963).*

Viet Cong progress has been great during the period since the coup, with my best guess being that the situation has in fact been deteriorating in the countryside since July to a far greater extent than we realize because of our undue dependence on distorted Vietnamese reporting. The Viet Cong now control very high proportions of the people in certain key provinces, particularly those directly south and west of Saigon. The Strategic Hamlet Program was seriously overextended in these provinces, and the Viet Cong have been able to destroy many hamlets, while others have been abandoned or in some cases betrayed or pillaged by the government's own Self Defense Corps. In these key provinces, the Viet Cong have destroyed almost all major roads, and are collecting taxes at will.

Secretary of Defense Robert McNamara, to President Lyndon Johnson, after visiting South Vietnam, memorandum of December 21, 1963, in Porter's Vietnam: A History in Documents *(1979).*

Well, here goes. I got shot down yesterday. We were escorting a C-123 and I picked up three slugs in my airplane. One went into my fuel strainer and I lost all my fuel. I made it to a field called Pan Tho and landed safely. Me and the airplane are both okay, not a scratch except the three bullet holes. No sweat . . .

Captain Edwin Gerald ''Jerry'' Shank, USAF to his wife and family, letter of December 30, 1963, in U.S. News & World Report *(May 4, 1964). [Captain Shank was killed while flying a mission on March 24, 1964.]*

3. Year of Decision: 1964

THE COMMUNIST RESPONSE

The Vietnamese communist leaders in late 1963 grimly concluded that Lyndon Johnson had no intention of abandoning the American commitment to South Vietnam or negotiating a settlement acceptable to them. They figured that he would continue to defend the Saigon regime with American advisers and equipment and might deploy as many as 100,000 U.S. combat troops in Vietnam. But, like the American public during that period, they considered that possibility as remote. The Vietcong determined that they could not meet the challenge alone. Up until then, many Vietcong leaders were experienced cadres, most of them southern veterans of the war against the French who had gone north after the Geneva agreement. Now they decided their only alternative was to send larger North Vietnamese detachments into the south.

The expanded conflict would involve great economic and social sacrifices on the part of North Vietnam's general population. Yet over the years, they had painfully learned that the battlefield was decisive. They concluded it was necessary to prepare for a people's war similar to the one waged against the French. Although guerrilla warfare was to be the primary mode of attack "for a long time to come," their main forces would be built up for the purpose of eventually "annihilating" regular South Vietnamese units. The North Vietnamese declared: "The key point at present is to make outstanding efforts to strengthen rapidly our military forces in order to create a basic change in the balance of forces between the enemy and ourselves in South Vietnam."

THE HO CHI MINH TRAIL

Like their counterparts in Washington, the senior communist commanders rarely acted without consulting studies and analyses from their advisers. In late 1963, a survey team investigated the feasibility of using the Ho Chi Minh Trail to transport hundreds of thousands of tons of weapons, ammunition, food and other supplies necessary for

A U.S. Army officer and a Vietnamese unit commander observe operations at a training camp in Vietnam in 1964. Courtesy of the National Archives.

conducting major battles in the south. In the spring of 1964, after five months in the south, the "fact-finding" mission reported to the Hanoi high command that it was possible to turn the Ho Chi Minh Trail into a modern logistical network.

The immense project began in the middle of 1964 and continued until hostilities ended a decade later. Engineer battalions equipped with modern Soviet and Chinese machinery built roads and bridges that could handle heavy trucks and other vehicles. Anticipating heavy American aerial bombing, sophisticated antiaircraft defenses were erected. Underground barracks, workshops, hospitals, storage facilities and fuel depots were created. Platoons of drivers, mechanics, radio operators, traffic managers, doctors, nurses and other personnel were recruited to support the North Vietnamese army in the field.

A PLAN FOR ACTION

While the communist leaders in Hanoi felt in 1964 that only a swift military victory could crush their South Vietnamese enemies, Washington during the same period was concerned that the wavering Saigon government would collapse at any moment. Neither side was willing to compromise, since each sought to strengthen its bargaining position.

On January 30, 1964, a 37-year-old field commander, General Nguyen Khanh, overthrew the junta that had ousted Diem only three months before. Although surprised by the coup, many Washington officials privately were relieved. Military security had collapsed, and General Minh's committee government had proven ineffective; American officials hoped that Khanh might be more competent. Khanh pledged to spur the war effort, and in return, President Johnson gave full U.S. support for the new regime.

Following his March visit to Vietnam, Defense Secretary Robert McNamara reported that the situation had "unquestionably been growing worse" since his last trip. About 40% of the countryside was now under Vietcong "control or predominant influence." South Vietnamese army desertions were "high and increasing," while the Vietcong was "recruiting energetically." McNamara recommended that the United States should finance an increase in the size of the South Vietnamese army and provide more modern aircraft and other equipment. Johnson approved these proposals, which were formally restated in a National Security Council "action memorandum."

The National Security Council document, NSAM 288, redefined the strategic goals of the United States in Vietnam. Until then, the United States had limited itself to helping the Saigon government defeat the Vietcong. Now more was involved than just South Vietnam or even Asia. A communist victory would damage the reputation of the United States throughout the world. The conflict was a "test case" for America's ability to deal with a communist "war of liberation," and the entire U.S. foreign policy faced a trial.

By the middle of 1964, the United States had formed in South Vietnam the largest military and civilian advisory team ever assembled abroad in "peacetime." American experts in the provinces were instructing Vietnamese peasants in how to breed pigs, dig wells and construct houses. Covert American operatives were involved in several secret intelligence networks. Military personnel were training South Vietnamese soldiers in how to use advanced weapons, such as high-velocity rifles and infrared cameras that peered through camouflage.

Despite the increased military aid, Johnson had not given up on a negotiated settlement with the north. He initiated several secret diplomatic attempts to induce North Vietnam to halt the war in the south. Johnson offered to provide the communists with economic aid and even diplomatic recognition if they agreed to cease their support for the Vietcong and end the conflict. If not, they could anticipate American air and naval attacks against North Vietnam. But only a complete withdrawal of American forces from Vietnam and the participation of the Vietcong in a neutral South Vietnamese coalition government was acceptable to North Vietnam. North Vietnam's Prime Minister Pham Van Dong told Johnson's confidential emissary, J. Blair Seaborn, chief Canadian delegate to the International Control Commission, "I suffer to see the war go on, develop, intensify, yet our people are determined to struggle."

THE DESOTO PATROLS

Various clandestine actions were also being taken at the time to bring greater pressure on the north; the most provocative were the 34-A raids and DeSoto patrols. The 34-A raids on coastal areas of North Vietnam were being carried out by highspeed boats manned by commandos from South Vietnam who were supported and led by the CIA. DeSoto patrols, which had been approved by President Kennedy in 1962, were highly classified missions off the coast of North Vietnam by U.S. Navy destroyers equipped with specialized electronic gear, which was manned by personnel from the National Security Agency (NSA, the U.S. government's communications intelligence agency). The purpose of the patrol was to gather information on North Vietnam's radar systems, as well as various other kinds of military intelligence, and to conduct a "show of force."

On the night of July 30, 1964, while 34-A South Vietnamese and other commandos, led by American advisers, raided the North Vietnamese islands of Hon Me and Hon Niem in the Gulf of Tonkin, about 120 miles away the U.S.S. *Maddox* was headed toward the same area to conduct its DeSoto patrol the following day. The *Maddox* had been given a scanty briefing on these 34-A raids, and in the communications center, technicians intercepted coded and uncoded radio traffic indicating that the Hanoi military was in an uproar. The monitors heard an order positioning a defensive ring of PT boats around the islands to prevent a recurrence of the attacks.

THE TONKIN GULF INCIDENTS

Early on the morning of Sunday, August 2, 1964, the *Maddox* was attacked in the Gulf of Tonkin by three North Vietnamese torpedo boats. The *Maddox*, as well as planes from the carrier U.S.S. *Ticonderoga*, returned their fire, reported sinking one PT boat and damaging if not sinking the other two. The skirmish, the first direct combat between the United States and North Vietnamese forces, had lasted exactly 37 minutes.

Washington is 12 hours behind Vietnam, and reports of the incident reached President Johnson on the morning of the same day. Johnson gathered his advisers at noon. Intelligence officers suggested that the

North Vietnamese might somehow have confused the *Maddox* with the 34-A operations. Gradually that explanation was accepted. Since no Americans had been hurt, Johnson specifically rejected reprisals against North Vietnam. In his first use of the "hot line" to Moscow, he sent a personal message to Premier Khrushchev stating that he had no wish to widen the conflict but hoped that North Vietnam would not molest U.S. vessels in international waters. At the same time, however, Johnson directed the *Maddox* and another destroyer, as well as protective aircraft, to return to the Tonkin Gulf. Orders were given to "attack any force that attacks them."

With the destroyer *C. Turner Joy* trailing 1,000 yards astern of the *Maddox*, the DeSoto patrol steamed back into the Gulf of Tonkin on August 3. On the night of August 3, another 34-A raid was made on the coast of North Vietnam.

By midmorning of August 4, Commander John Herrick, captain of the *Maddox*, intercepted messages that persuaded him of his precarious position. He advised his Pacific commanders that North Vietnam considered the destroyers part of the 34-A operations, hence as enemy craft. Herrick requested that the patrol be terminated. This was rejected by Admiral Thomas H. Moorer, commander in chief of the Pacific Fleet, who said that to terminate the mission so soon "does not in my view adequately demonstrate United States resolve to assert our legitimate rights in these international waters." He ordered Herrick to continue the patrols.

About eight o'clock in the evening on August 4, the *Maddox* intercepted radio messages from the North Vietnamese that gave Captain Herrick "the impression" that their patrol boats were planning an attack. Herrick called for air support from the *Ticonderoga* again, and eight Crusader jets soon appeared overhead. In the darkness, neither the pilots nor the ship crews could see any enemy craft, but about an hour later the sonar operators reported torpedoes approaching. The two destroyers started firing in the direction of the radar contacts. Officers reported sinking two or perhaps three North Vietnamese craft during the engagement. But hardly had the shooting stopped than Herrick and his crew began to have second thoughts. Herrick immediately communicated his doubts to his superiors and urged a "thorough reconnaissance in daylight."

After being badgered with cables from the Pentagon asking him to verify the attack, Herrick revised his report to conclude that "details of action present a confusing picture although [I am] certain that original ambush was bona fide." Captain Herrick's upgraded report went to Admiral Ulysses S. Grant Sharp, Jr., the CINCPAC, who reassured Defense Secretary Robert McNamara that the "ambush was bona fide."

Although the information was sketchy, President Johnson announced to key congressional leaders on the morning of August 4 that the U.S. destroyers in the Tonkin Gulf had definitely been subject to a second unprovoked attack. This time, he said, he would retaliate against North Vietnam by ordering reprisal air strikes, and he would ask Congress for a resolution of support.

THE U.S. RETALIATES

At 11:37 P.M., Lyndon Johnson appeared on television to report to the nation that "repeated acts of violence against the armed forces of the United States must be met not only with alert defense, but with positive reply. That reply is being given as I speak to you tonight."

The reprisals were described by Johnson spokesmen as "limited in scale." American aircraft flew 64 sorties against four North Vietnamese patrol boat bases and practically destroyed a major oil storage depot. An estimated 25 PT boats were sunk, more than half of North Vietnam's fleet. Two U.S. airplanes were shot down and two others were damaged. Struck over Lach Chao, Lieutenant Richard Sather of Pomona, California, ditched his Skyraider into the gulf and died. Lieutenant (j.g.) Everett Alvarez of San Jose, California, ejected from his Skyhawk after it was hit over Hon Gai. His jet crashed, and Alvarez became the first American pilot taken prisoner by the North Vietnamese.

THE TONKIN GULF RESOLUTION

On August 5, Johnson sent the proposed Gulf of Tonkin resolution to Congress. Two congressional leaders, Senator J. William Fulbright, chairman of the Senate Foreign Relations Committee, and Representative Thomas E. Morgan, chairman of the House Foreign Affairs Committee, acted as the bill's sponsors. The resolution would give the president authority to "take all necessary measures to repel any armed attack against the forces of the United States and to prevent further aggression . . . including the use of armed force, to assist any member or protocol state of the Southeast Asia Collective Defense Treaty."

Opinion polls showed that 85% of the American public stood behind the administration and so did the senators. Only one senator, Wayne Morse of Oregon, an independent politician who had been both a Democrat and Republican, demanded more detail about the incidents in the Gulf of Tonkin. Having received a tip from a Pentagon source about the 34-A raids, Morse asked the secretaries of State and Defense if there was any connection with the incidents in the Gulf of Tonkin. McNamara replied, "Our Navy played absolutely no part in, was not associated with, was not aware of any South Vietnamese actions, if there was any . . . I say this flatly. This is a fact."

After discussing the resolution for less than two hours, the Foreign Relations Committee took a roll call and voted nearly unanimously in favor of the bill, with only Senator Morse issuing a solitary "no." The resolution passed to the full Senate, and debate continued through the following morning. Morse's doubts were ignored by his colleagues. By the afternoon of August 6, 1964, Morse was speaking to an almost empty chamber. He asserted that the resolution was giving the president "warmaking powers in the absence of a declaration of war. I believe that to be a historic mistake." Only one other senator joined Morse in his opposition to the resolution, Senator Ernest Gruening of Alaska.

On August 7, 1964, the Senate, by a vote of 82–2, and the House of Representatives, 416–0, overwhelmingly approved Public Law 88-408, which became known as "The Tonkin Gulf Resolution." Morse predicted that its supporters "will live to regret it." The resolution became increasingly controversial among senators and representatives as President Johnson used it to expand the U.S. commitment to the war in Vietnam. By May 1970, the resolution was repealed.

A Crisis in the South Averted

Taking advantage of the mood of crisis surrounding the events in the Gulf of Tonkin, General Khanh declared a state of emergency in South Vietnam, reimposing press censorship and other controls. He justified these measures by announcing that the nation was threatened by the communists. He ignored the various drafts that had been proposed for a new constitution and unveiled a new constitution for South Vietnam that promoted himself to the presidency and dismissed his rival, General Duong Van Minh, the nominal chief of state, whom the United States had advised him to include in the government.

In late August, students and Buddhist factions opposed to Khanh's repressive actions took to the streets in a series of violent demonstrations. As marchers and rioters plunged Saigon and nearby cities into anarchy, Khanh capitulated. On August 27, after two heated sessions with the Military Revolutionary Council, he withdrew the charter and resigned from office. With rumors of a coup swirling, he left Saigon. But on September 3, he returned to announce a triumvirate government consisting of himself, General Minh and General Tran Thien Khiem that would eventually evolve into a civilian government. For the time being, the crisis ended.

For the next several weeks, the government of South Vietnam was in a state of suspension as the political crisis settled and a new constitution was drafted. At the end of October, the High National Council selected respected elder statesman Phan Khac Suu as chief of state and former Saigon mayor Tran Van Huong as prime minister. General Khanh stepped down to become commander-in-chief of the armed forces and pledged to keep the army out of domestic politics.

Talking Peace, Planning War

Three days before the U.S. presidential election, a detachment of Vietcong raiders infiltrated the U.S. air base at Bien Hoa, 12 miles north of Saigon, and launched a heavy mortar attack, killing four Americans and destroying five B-57 light bombers and damaging eight others. After inspecting the damage, Ambassador Maxwell Taylor concluded that the attack demonstrated a turning point in Vietcong tactics. He argued that the attack was instigated by Hanoi, and he recommended to Washington that immediate reprisals be made against North Vietnam.

President Johnson and his advisers decided not to retaliate. Throughout his campaign Johnson had contrasted his restraint versus policies of escalation advocated by Senator Barry Goldwater of Arizona, his Republican opponent. With the presidential election only a few days away, Johnson was wary of any dramatic action that might offend voters, that they might interpret as a move to meet Goldwater's call for escalation.

On November 3, 1964, soon, after the polls confirmed his landslide victory, Johnson formed a "working group" composed of eight middle-level State Department, Pentagon and CIA officials, to study "immediately and intensively" the U.S. options in Southeast Asia. By the end of November, the Working Group had produced a report that outlined three options: to continue the present policy of moderation; to launch bold attacks against North Vietnam immediately; and to conduct graduated bombing against infiltration targets, first in Laos, then in North Vietnam.

On December 1, President Johnson conferred with Dean Rusk, Robert McNamara, McGeorge Bundy and other advisers about the next step for U.S. involvement in Vietnam. He chose to continue the current policy of moderation, but, in the event more reprisals became necessary, the planning had already been done. The first phase would be Barrel Roll, a secret bombing campaign against the communist infiltration routes in southern Laos, to be conducted from aircraft carriers in the South China Sea. The second phase would involve air strikes against selected targets in North Vietnam.

THE VIETCONG ATTACK IN THE SOUTH

The communists, meanwhile, believed that they might step up the offensive without provoking Johnson into American involvement. In December, they launched a coordinated series of attacks throughout South Vietnam, the largest against Bien Gia, a Catholic village only 40 miles southeast of Saigon. It was the first time that Vietcong troops were deployed in such numbers. Two battalions and support units comprising more than 2,000 men occupied the village of Bien Gia for eight hours on the night of December 28, 1964, then faded into the jungle to elude pursuit. One senior U.S. officer commented at the time, ". . . the big question for me is how its troops, a thousand or more of them, could wander around the countryside so close to Saigon without being discovered. That tells me something about this war."

U.S. officials were even more stunned on the afternoon of Christmas Eve, when Vietcong terrorists planted a bomb in Saigon's Brinks Hotel, which housed U.S. officers. The explosion killed two Americans and injured 58 others. Ambassador Taylor and General William Westmoreland urged President Johnson to authorize retaliatory raids against North Vietnam, but Johnson refused.

In an unusually long cable to Taylor, Johnson explained that the war would not be won from the air and went on to state that he was considering a U.S. combat troop commitment. ". . . It seems to me that what is much more needed and would be more effective is a larger and stronger use of rangers and special forces and marines, or other appropriate military strength on the ground and on the scene . . . I know that it might involve the acceptance of larger American sacrifices [but] I myself am ready to substantially increase the number of Americans in Vietnam if it is necessary to provide this kind of fighting force against the Vietcong."

CHRONICLE OF EVENTS

1964

January 2: President Johnson receives a report prepared by Major General Victor H. Krulak, USMC, special assistant for counterinsurgency and special activities for the Joint Chiefs of Staff. It outlines a series of clandestine operations against North Vietnam. Known as Oplan 34-A, it will go into effect February 1.

January 13: Vietcong overrun strategic hamlets in Pleiku Province, burning 135 houses and kidnapping seven officials.

January 14: Lieutenant General William Westmoreland is appointed deputy commander MACV (U.S. Military Assistance Command Vietnam).

January 17: Five U.S. helicopter crewmen are killed and three are wounded while supporting a major ARVN attack on communist bases in the Mekong Delta.

January 30: Major General Duong Van Minh is ousted in a bloodless coup led by Major General Nguyen Khanh, commander of the ARVN First Corps.

South Vietnamese troops unload ammunition from a U.S. Marine helicopter in 1964. Courtesy of the National Archives.

February 1: President Johnson says he has General Khanh's pledge to continue the war effort, and he will in turn give full U.S. support for the new regime.

Oplan 34-A, the counterinsurgency plan, officially goes into effect.

February 8: General Khanh announces the formation of a new Vietnamese government with himself as premier; General Duong Van Minh is named chief of state, a titular position without authority.

February 19: The Vietcong shoot down two Vietnamese planes, and one U.S. pilot is killed.

March 8–12: Defense Secretary McNamara and General Taylor, chairman of the Joint Chiefs of Staff, visit Vietnam on a fact-finding mission.

March 17: After Johnson meets with McNamara and Taylor at a National Security Council meeting, a public statement is issued saying U.S. will increase military and economic aid to support Khanh's fight against the Vietcong. Various secret decisions are also taken, including a plan to launch retaliatory USAF strikes against North Vietnamese military and guerrilla bases inside the Laotian and Cambodian borders.

March 29: Defense Secretary McNamara announces that the U.S. will provide South Vietnam with $50 million annually to finance expansion of its armed forces (in addition to the current annual aid of $500 million).

April 8: South Vietnamese troops kill some 75 Vietcong in capturing a guerrilla base in Kontum Province, 300 miles north of Saigon; the base is an important distribution point for arms and personnel coming down the Ho Chi Minh Trail.

April 11–15: In the longest and heaviest battle to date, at Kien Long, 135 miles south of Saigon, South Vietnamese forces retake their original position, but 70 South Vietnamese guardsmen and 55 ARVN are killed, along with 175 Vietcong.

April 14: It is announced that the U.S. Military

Advisory Group (MAG) will be combined with the Military Assistance Command (MAC) to reduce duplication of effort and make more efficient use of U.S. personnel.

May 15: Premier Khanh signs a decree that abolishes restrictions imposed by the Diem regime on Buddhists, grants them same rights as Catholics.

May 18: President Johnson, in a special message to Congress, asks for $125 million more for economic and military aid to Vietnam.

June 1–2: At a conference in Honolulu, Rusk, McNamara and other top U.S. officials concerned with war gather for two days of meetings. The discussion focuses on the projected air war against North Vietnam.

June 20: General Westmoreland replaces General Harkins as commander of MACV.

June 23: President Johnson announces Henry Cabot Lodge has resigned as ambassador to South Vietnam and will be replaced by General Maxwell Taylor.

July 7: General Maxwell Taylor arrives in Saigon.

July 30–31: South Vietnamese naval forces carry out raids on islands near the coast of North Vietnam.

August 2: North Vietnamese patrol boats attack the *Maddox*, an American destroyer in the Tonkin Gulf.

August 4: U.S. destroyer *C. Turner Joy* reports attacks by North Vietnamese patrol boats. President Johnson orders air strikes against the patrol boats and their support facilities.

August 7: By a vote of 82–2 in the Senate and 416–0 in the House, the U.S. Congress passes the Tonkin Gulf Resolution authorizing "all

necessary steps, including the use of armed forces" in Southeast Asia.

General Khanh declares a state of emergency in South Vietnam.

August 21–25: Student demonstrations against Khanh and military government mount; rioting occurs in Saigon.

September 13: Bloodless coup against Khanh's government by General Lam Van Phat is aborted.

September 30: First major demonstrations by students and faculty opposed to the U.S. role in the war in Vietnam takes place at the University of California at Berkeley. But polls show a majority of Americans support the president's effort.

October 30: Vietcong attack Bien Hoa Air Base. Six U.S. B-57 bombers are destroyed, five U.S. servicemen and two Vietnamese are killed; about 76 are wounded.

October 31: Tran Van Huong, former mayor of Saigon, is named premier of South Vietnam.

November 3: President Johnson is elected by a landslide over Senator Barry Goldwater.

December 5: The first Congressional Medal of Honor awarded to a U.S. serviceman for action in Vietnam is presented to Captain Roger Donlon.

December 8–20: Student and Buddhist demonstrations threaten the stability of military-supported government of Tran Van Huong.

December 14: U.S warplanes begin bombing the Ho Chi Minh Trail in Laos.

December 31: U.S. forces in Vietnam total 23,300. 147 U.S. military personnel have been killed in action, with 1,039 wounded and 11 missing.

EYEWITNESS TESTIMONY

Neutralization of South Vietnam would only be another name for a Communist take-over . . . The United States will continue to furnish you and your people with the fullest measure of support in this bitter fight . . . We shall maintain in Vietnam American personnel and materiel as needed to assist you in achieving victory.

President Lyndon Johnson, to General Duong Van Minh, chairman of the Military Revolutionary Council, South Vietnam, New Year's message of January 1, 1964, in Public Papers of the Presidents of the United States

The Communists' basic military threat could be eliminated in one year . . . that means none of this 8-a.m.-to-8-p.m. five-day-a-week fighting. Viet Cong attacks are at night. Ours should be, too.

Lieutenant Colonel John Paul Vann, USA, statement in Newsweek *(January 4, 1964).*

Flying into Tan Son Nhut airport on the fringe of Saigon in a commercial airliner in late January 1964 was a strange experience, a swift plunge from a comfortable, peaceful world into an alien environment, neither peace nor war but with the trappings of war. Because enemy fire had hit a commercial plane a week or so earlier, pilots of Pan American airways DC-707s had taken to making incredibly steep, stomach-churning descents to the runways. As the plane taxied to a stop, the accountrements of war were conspicuous. It seemed odd that the pretty stewardess, the other passengers, and I, all dressed in civilian clothes, some obviously tourists going on to other destinations, should be set down abruptly in such a setting.

General William C. Westmoreland, on first arriving in South Vietnam, in A Soldier Reports *(1976).*

What gets me most is that they won't tell you people what we do here. I'll bet you that anyone you talk to does not know that American pilots fight the war. We—me and my buddies—do everything. The Vietnamese "students" we have on board are airmen basics [raw recruits]. The only reason they are on board is in case we crash there is one American "advisor" and one Vietnamese student.

Captain Edwin "Jerry" Shank, USAF, to his wife and family, letter of January 20, 1964, in U.S. News & World Report *(May 4, 1964). [Captain Shank was killed while flying a mission on March 24, 1964.]*

I cannot think of a greater mistake that this country could make than to seek to escalate the war in South Vietnam by using conventional American forces in North Vietnam or in any other areas to the north of South Vietnam.

I say to the American people, from the floor of the Senate this afternoon, "You have the right to ask your Government now, Do you have plans for sending American boys to their deaths by the tens of thousands in escalating the South Vietnam war above South Vietnam?"

Senator Wayne Morse (D–Ore.), to the U.S. Senate, speech of March 4, 1964.

The 15,500 U.S. military personnel in Viet Nam are divided into two camps—the "Hawks" and the "Doves."

The Hawks believe the war should be fought as war. Their solution to South Viet Nam's problem is to kill the Viet Cong.

The Doves believe this war is different. They say it can be won only by winning the people. They believe in something called "civic action."

The Doves call the Hawks "military minds."

The Hawks call the Doves "Peace Corps types," or "State Department boys."

Jim Lucas, Scripps-Howard correspondent, dispatch of March 9, 1964, in Dateline: Vietnam *(1966).*

Mr. [Eric] Sevareid [CBS News]: "Mr Kennedy said, on the subject of Vietnam, I think, that he did believe in the 'falling domino' theory, that if Vietnam were lost, that other countries in the area would soon be lost."

The President: "I think it would be a very dangerous thing, and I share President Kennedy's view, and I think the whole of Southeast Asia would be involved and that would involve hundreds of millions of people, and I think it's—it cannot be ignored, we must do everything that we can, we must be responsible, we must stay there and help them, and that is what we are going to do."

President Johnson, to news conference of March 15, 1964, in Public Papers of the Presidents of the United States.

Why can't we make up our minds to win down there? We never hear the President say we will win; he only says we will contain them.

Senator Barry Goldwater, Republican presidential candidate, to a campaign reception at Lampson Airport, near Clearlake, California, speech of March 18, 1964, in The New York Times *(March 19, 1964).*

Southeast Asia has great strategic significance in the forward defense of the United States. Its location across east-west air and sea lanes flanks the Indian subcontinent on one side and Australia, New Zealand, and the Philippines on the other and dominates the gateway between the Pacific and Indian Oceans. In Communist hands this area would pose a most serious threat to the security of the United States and to the family of free-world nations to which we belong. To defend Southeast Asia, we must meet the challenge in South Viet-Nam.

Secretary of Defense Robert McNamara, statement of March 26, 1964, in U.S. Department of State's Bulletin *(April 6, 1964).*

I'd drop a low-yield atomic bomb on the Chinese supply lines in North Vietnam, or maybe shell 'em with the Seventh Fleet.

Senator Barry Goldwater, quoted in an article of May 20, 1963, in Newsweek.

We the Undersigned.

Are Young Americans of Draft Age. We understand our obligations to defend our country and to serve in the armed forces but we object to being asked to support the war in South Vietnam.

Believing that the United States' participation in the war is for the suppression of the Vietnamese struggle for national independence, we see no justification for our involvement. We agree with Senator Wayne Morse, who said on the floor of the Senate on March 4, 1964, regarding South Vietnam, that

President Johnson and his leading military and civilian advisers meet at his ranch in Texas in mid-1964. After months of doubt and hesitancy, the president began to prepare for war. Courtesy of the Lyndon Baines Johnson Library.

"We should never have gone in. We should have stayed in. We should get out."
The May 2d Movement, an antiwar protest group, 1964 pledge, in Lynd's We Won't Go *(1968).*

My solution? Tell the Vietnamese they've got to draw in their horns . . . or we're going to bomb them back into the Stone Age.
General Curtis LeMay, chief of staff, USAF, to National Security adviser McGeorge Bundy, statement of May 6, 1964, in Pettit's The Experts *(1975).*

The VC hold the initiative and continue to develop their strength among the population.
CIA Saigon Station Chief William Colby, to CIA Director John McCone, report of May 11, 1964, in Gravel's The Pentagon Papers *(1971).*

When they stop their aggressions and the freedom of mainland Southeast Asia is assured, there will be no further need for any American military presence. We have never sought and we do not desire any base or other military position in South Vietnam—or Laos or Cambodia.

Our forces in Southeast Asia are there solely in response to the threat and reality of aggression from the North.
Secretary of State Dean Rusk, to the American Law Institute, speech of May 22, 1964, in the U.S. Department of State Bulletin *of June 8, 1964.*

They call it the "war of no thanks." They say nobody back home knows what's going on, and doesn't give a damn.
Robert L. Moore Jr., journalist, on the GI view, article in U.S. News & World Report, *June 18, 1964.*

Yesterday it was Korea; tonight it is Vietnam. Make no bones of this. Don't try to sweep this under the rug. We are at war in Vietnam . . . extremism in the defense of liberty is no vice . . . moderation in the pursuit of justice is no virtue.
Senator Barry Goldwater, Republican presidential candidate, to the G.O.P. convention in San Francisco, speech of July 16, 1964, in The Washington Post *(July 17, 1964).*

It does not appear there can be a military solution in South Vietnam . . . since war cannot bring a solution, one must make peace. This implies a return to the agreements made ten years ago and that, this time, it should be respected, in other words that in North Vietnam, South Vietnam, Laos and Cambodia, no foreign power intervenes in any way in these unfortunate countries.
President Charles De Gaulle, to a Paris news conference of July 23, 1964, in The New York Times *(July 24, 1964).*

General quarters! General quarters! This is not a drill!
Anonymous U.S.S. Maddox *shipman, to the crew, alert of August 2, 1964, 2:00 P.M., on sighting five North Vietnamese patrol boats approaching, in U.S. Senate Foreign Relations Committee's* The Gulf of Tonkin, 1964 Incidents *(1968).*

I am being approached by high-speed craft with apparent intention of torpedo attack. I intend to open fire in self-defense if necessary.
Commander John Herrick, USN, commanding officer aboard the U.S.S. Maddox, *to CINC-PAC [Commander-in-Chief, Pacific], "flash" cable of August 2, 1964, 2:40 P.M., in U.S. Senate Foreign Relations Committee's* The Gulf of Tonkin, 1964 Incidents.

While on routine patrol in international waters at 020808 GCT (1608 local time), the U.S. destroyer MADDOX underwent an unprovoked attack by three PT-type boats in latitude 19-40 North; longitude 106-34 East; in the Tonkin Gulf.

The attacking boats launched three torpedoes and used 37 millimeter gunfire. The MADDOX answered with five-inch gunfire. Shortly thereafter four F-8 (Crusader) aircraft from the USS TICONDEROGA joined in the defense of MADDOX, using ZUNI rockets and 20 millimeter strafing attacks. The PT boats were driven off, with one seen to be badly damaged and not moving and the other two damaged and retreating slowly

No casualties or damage was sustained by MADDOX or the aircraft.
U.S. Defense Department, press release of August 2, 1964, in Gravel's The Pentagon Papers.

The United States must take a firm course so that North Vietnam knows it is not a "paper tiger."
Premier Nguyen Khanh, South Vietnam, to a news conference of August 2, 1964, in Saigon, in Newsweek *(August 17, 1964).*

It is apparent that DRV has thrown down the gauntlet and now considers itself at war with the United States . . . [DRV boats] will be treated as belligerents from first detection . . .

Rear Admiral Robert B. Moore, USN, commander of the Ticonderoga Task Force, to Commander John Herrick, commanding officer aboard the USS Maddox, cable of August 3, 1964, in U.S. Senate Foreign Relations Committee's The Gulf of Tonkin, 1964 Incidents.

We believe that present OPLAN 34-A activities are beginning to rattle Hanoi, and MADDOX incident is directly related to their effort to resist these activities. We have no intention yielding to pressure.

Secretary of State Dean Rusk, to Ambassador Maxwell Taylor (South Vietnam), top secret telegram of August 3, 1964, in Porter's Vietnam: A History in Documents (1979).

Review of action makes many reported contacts and torpedoes fired appear doubtful. Freak weather effects on radar and overeager sonarman may have accounted for many reports. No actual visual sightings by *Maddox.* Suggest complete evaluation before any further action.

Commander John Herrick, to CINCPAC, "flash" cable of August 4, 1964, 1:27 P.M., in U.S. Senate Foreign Relations Committee's The Gulf of Tonkin, 1964 Incidents.

Turner Joy also reports no actual visual sightings or wake . . . Entire action leaves many doubts except for apparent attempt to ambush at beginning. Suggest thorough reconnaissance by aircraft at daylight.

Commander John Herrick, to CINCPAC, "flash" cable of August 4, 1964, 1:54 P.M., in U.S. Senate Foreign Relations Committee's The Gulf of Tonkin, 1964 Incidents.

Certain that original ambush was bonafide. Details of action following present a confusing picture.

Commander John Herrick, to CINCPAC, "flash" cable of August 4, 1964, in U.S. Senate Foreign Relations Committee's The Gulf of Tonkin, 1964 Incidents.

The initial attack on the destroyer *Maddox,* on August 2, was repeated today by a number of hostile vessels attacking two U.S. destroyers with torpedoes. The destroyers and supporting aircraft acted at once on the orders I gave after the initial act of aggression. We believe at least two of the attacking boats were sunk. There were no U.S. losses . . .

But repeated acts of violence against the Armed Forces of the United States must be met not only with alert defense, but with positive reply. That reply is being given as I speak to you tonight. An air action is now in execution against gunboats and certain supporting facilities in North Vietnam which have been used in these hostile operations.

President Johnson, to the American people, nationwide television and radio address of August 4, 1964, in Public Papers of the Presidents of the United States.

Today was a momentous day . . . On Tuesday, Lyndon always has lunch with the Secretary of Defense, the Secretary of State, and McGeorge Bundy . . . Today they stayed a long time. As McGeorge Bundy passed me in the hall afterward, he was looking extraordinarily grave. I remember asking him something which brought forth a portentous answer—one which left me apprehensive, of what, I did not know.

Lady Bird Johnson, wife of President Johnson, diary entry of August 4, 1964, in A White House Diary (1970).

Here is a vast expanse of international waters in which we have a perfect right to be. We had to strike immediately because we didn't expect to ask those ships to run a continuing gauntlet of torpedoes on their way back to the Gulf of Tonkin where their mission was completed, nor were we prepared to have them denied international waters in the Gulf of Tonkin.

Secretary of State Dean Rusk, to NBC News correspondent Elie Abel, interview of August 5, 1964, in U.S. State Department's Bulletin (August 24, 1964).

As I have repeatedly made clear, the United States intends no rashness, and seeks no wider war. We must make it clear to all that the United States is united in its determination to bring about the end of Communist subversion and aggression in the area . . . I recommend a Resolution expressing support of Congress for all necessary action to protect our Armed Forces . . .

President Johnson, to the U.S. Congress, address of August 5, 1964, in Public Papers of the Presidents of the United States.

Have we reached the point in American foreign policy where we are going to permit the President to

Senator Wayne Morse of Oregon. Only he and Senator Ernest Gruening of Alaska voted against the Tonkin Gulf resolution in August 1964. Courtesy of the National Archives.

send American boys to their death in the defense of military dictatorships, monarchies, and fascist regimes around the world with which we have entered into treaty obligations involving mutual security, no matter what the provocation and no matter what wrongs they may have committed that cause an attack upon them? Are we going to do that without a check by Congress by way of a declaration of war?

Senator Wayne Morse (D–Ore.), to the U.S. Senate, speech of August 6, 1964.

All Vietnam is not worth the life of a single American boy.

Senator Ernest Gruening (D–Alas.), to the U.S. Senate, speech of August 6, 1964.

I believe the joint resolution is calculated to prevent the spread of war, rather than the spread of it, as has been alleged by some critics of the resolution. I have considered every possible alternative, both those that have been suggested on the floor of the Senate and elsewhere, and I still have come back to my own conclusion that the action that was taken; the resolution adopted by the committee; and all other actions in this connection, are best designed to contribute to the deterrence of the spread of war.

Senator William J. Fulbright (D–Ark.), to the U.S. Senate, on the Tonkin Gulf Resolution, speech of August 7, 1964.

Some say that we should withdraw from South Viet-Nam, that we have lost almost 200 lives there in the last 4 years, and we should come home. But the United States cannot and must not and will not turn aside and allow the freedom of a brave people to be handed over to Communist tyranny. This alternative is strategically unwise, we think, and it is morally unthinkable.

Some others are eager to enlarge the conflict. They call upon us to supply American boys to do the job that Asian boys should do. They ask us to take reckless action which might risk the lives of millions and engulf much of Asia and certainly threaten the peace of the entire world. Moreover, such action would offer no solution at all to the real problem of Viet-Nam. America can and America will meet any wider challenge from others, but our aim in Viet-Nam, as in the rest of the world, is to help restore the peace and to reestablish a decent order.

President Johnson, to the American Bar Association in New York City, speech of August 12, 1964, in Public Papers of the Presidents of the United States.

This thing isn't going to be over in a year or two. Americans are too impatient. This thing is not going to be won by gimmicks. It's going to be won by soldiers on the ground. It's going to take a lot of hard work and lot of suffering.

Anonymous U.S. intelligence officer, in Army Times *(August 12, 1964).*

We don't want our American boys to do the fighting for Asian boys. We don't want to get involved in a nation with 700 million people and get tied down in a land war in Asia.

President Johnson, speech of September 25, 1964, at a dedication ceremony of the Eufaula Dam in Oklahoma, in Public Papers of the Presidents of the United States.

Our fleet is like the strong boy who comes to the aid of a smaller or weaker boy when he is attacked by a big bully. We are here as representatives of our great United States, to aid the small countries of South Vietnam and Laos against the Communist bully to the north—North Vietnam and Red China.

That is why some 15,000 men, including me, are here in the South China Sea instead of with our families in California—and all this is why the United States has a powerful Navy and why we are proud of the way it is used and proud that we are part of it . . .

Rear Admiral William S. Guest, commander of a U.S. Navy task force in the Tonkin Gulf, to his sons, letter of October 1964, in U.S. News & World Report *(October 19, 1964).*

The ability of the Viet Cong continuously to rebuild their units and to make good their losses is one of the mysteries of this guerrilla war . . . Not only do the Viet Cong units have recuperative powers of the phoenix, but they have an amazing ability to maintain morale. Only in rare cases have we found evidences of bad morale among Viet Cong prisoners or recorded in captured Viet Cong documents.

Ambassador Maxwell Taylor, to U.S. government officials concerned about Vietnam, briefing of November 1964, in Gravel's The Pentagon Papers.

Armed helicopters came in with their rockets and machine guns. That's what the Commies had been trying to avoid; why they were hiding. Now village after village caught fire, the flames leaping up in mushroom clouds of smoke. The sound was deafening as the rockets tore into the houses.

A Montagnard woman of the Rhade tribe dries rice in Darlac Province. The Rhade were the first uplanders to join in the civilian self-defense program. Courtesy of the National Archives.

The Viet Cong were in panic. But there was no place to run, no place to hide. Helicopter after helicopter came in, guns blazing. Many died where they fell. Others dived into the water and died there . . . Later we would try to count them.

Jim Lucas, Scripps-Howard correspondent, dispatch of December 14, 1964, in Dateline: Vietnam.

4. America Takes Over: 1965

GLOOMY REPORTS

During early January 1965 there was increasing concern among U.S. policymakers about the growing military and political strength of the communists. The CIA had concluded that the National Front for the Liberation of South Vietnam "had extended its influence if not its control, into every corner of South Vietnam." In early January, Ambassador Maxwell Taylor cabled Washington with a series of gloomy reports: "we are presently on a losing track" and "To take no positive action now is to accept defeat in the fairly near future." Taylor offered two options: either deploy American combat troops or step up the bombing of North Vietnam.

Taylor's argument reflected other reassessments taking place within the departments of State and Defense. Assistant Secretary of State William Bundy stopped short of recommending the bombing campaign but suggested looking for "an early occasion for reprisal action" and withdrawing U.S. dependents. In a memorandum to the president on January 27, 1965, National Security adviser McGeorge Bundy and Defense Secretary Robert McNamara stressed that the worst course was to continue "this essentially passive role." The United States could either negotiate and "salvage what little can be preserved" or resort to military power to "force a change" of communist strategy. They favored the military alternative, but added that other plans should be "carefully studied" and concluded that "the time has come for hard choices."

ATTACK ON PLEIKU

The conflict was propelled into a new phase on February 7, when the Vietcong launched a surprise attack against a U.S. base near the provincial capital of Pleiku, in the Central Highlands of South Vietnam.

Three hundred guerrillas slipped one by one beneath the barbed wire perimeter of Camp Holloway, evading a negligent cordon of South Vietnamese guards. At 2:00 A.M. mortar shells rained on the barracks, and guerrillas raced across the airstrip, blowing up parked helicopters and destroying 10 U.S. aircraft. Eight Americans died and more than 100 others were wounded. Not one of the 1,300 South Vietnamese troops at Holloway was injured; nearly all of the Vietcong guerrillas escaped. Found on the corpse of a communist casualty was a detailed map of the camp—indicating an ability for espionage and easing their escape.

The news of the attack was immediately relayed to Saigon, where General William Westmoreland convened an emergency predawn meeting with Ambassador Taylor and McGeorge Bundy, who was in Vietnam on a fact-finding mission, to discuss an appropriate American response. The United States had retaliated after the August 1964 Gulf of Tonkin incidents, and the mechanism for reprisal strikes, decided the previous March, was in place. They quickly agreed that it should be implemented. Bundy telephoned the White House to urge that American air raids against North Vietnam begin promptly.

LBJ GOES TO WAR

Johnson conferred with his National Security advisers, expanding the group to include Mike Mansfield, Senate majority leader, and John McCormick, speaker of the House of Representatives. The president used frontier images to express his anger. "We have kept our guns over the mantel and our shells in the cupboard for a long time, and what is the result?" he asked. "They are killing our men while they sleep in the night. I can't ask our American soldiers to continue to fight with one hand tied behind their back . . ." He announced that he was authorizing retaliatory raids. Most of those present concurred, except Mansfield and Vice President Hubert Humphrey.

Twelve hours after the first mortar fell on Pleiku, Operation Flaming Dart was under way, as the carrier *Ranger* launched its jets to bomb a North Vietnamese army camp near Dong Hoi, a guerrilla training facility 40 miles north of the 17th parallel dividing North and South Vietnam. The next day, a follow-up raid was conducted by South Vietnamese aircraft, led by Nguyen Cao Ky, the future prime minister of South Vietnam.

The two days of raids marked a costly turning point for the United States in its involvement with South Vietnam. Soviet Premier Kosygin, who was visiting Hanoi at the time, announced that the Soviet Union would increase its aid if the north were invaded. Previously, North Vietnam had relied almost exclusively on aid from China. There was speculation that the Vietcong deliberately timed their attack on Pleiku to force such a response by the United States, thus compelling Kosygin to give unconditional military aid. In any event, sophisticated Soviet surface-to-air missiles began to arrive at the port of Haiphong 10 days after Kosygin's return to Moscow.

As the war intensified in early 1965, Johnson tried to manage the nation's perception of his policies. Administration officials said that the bombing of North Vietnam after the Pleiku attack was "appropriate and fitting," which was how they had described the raid after the Tonkin Gulf incident six months earlier. Almost 70% of the nation gave LBJ a positive rating, with the same proportion supporting a bombing strategy as the only way to save Vietnam. Nearly 80% believed that an American withdrawal would open Southeast Asia to communist domination, and the same number favored a U.S. combat troop commitment to prevent that possibility.

On March 2, a continuous bombing program, known as Rolling Thunder (its name borrowed from the words of a hymn), began against North Vietnam. It was originally scheduled to last only eight weeks, but as it did not succeed in reducing North Vietnam's military capabilities or seriously damage its economy, the sustained bombing program would continue for the next three years.

With Rolling Thunder a continuing operation, the Joint Chiefs suggested improving "security and cover and deception measures" at U.S/Vietnamese air bases. General Westmoreland was especially concerned about the American airfield at Danang, which was vulnerable to attack by some 6,000 Vietcong guerrillas in the area. On February 22, 1965, Westmoreland asked Johnson for two Marine battalions to protect the base.

Ambassador Taylor had long opposed the commitment of American ground forces to Vietnam. In a cable to Washington he warned that, once the deployment began, "it will be very difficult to hold the line." Taylor emphasized that American soldiers were unsuited to "Asian forest and jungles," and he doubted they "could do much better" than the French. He added that there was also the problem of how American soldiers could "distinguish between a VC and friendly Vietnamese farmer." In deference to Westmoreland, and in recognition of the growing pressure for sending a Marine detachment to Danang, Taylor reluctantly agreed on the deployment of one Marine battalion for security purposes.

THE U.S. MARINES LAND

On the morning of March 8, Marines wearing full battle gear and carrying M-16s splashed ashore at Danang, the first American combat troops to set foot on the Asian mainland since the end of the Korean conflict. As they rushed onto the beach they were greeted by sightseers, ARVN officers and Vietnamese girls who distributed wreathes of flowers, and four American soldiers with a large poster: "Welcome to the Gallant Marines."

The Marines could hardly believe that this was a war-torn nation. Rice paddies and bamboo groves lay in the distance, as peasants in conical hats worked in the fields. "I scanned the countryside with my binoculars," wrote Lieutenant Philip Caputo, "but the only signs of war were our own Phantoms, roaring northward with their bomb racks full." The Marines soon learned that in Vietnam the war happened after sundown.

Although one of the crucial decisions of the war, the Marine deployment elicited hardly any response in Congress or in the American press. The Johnson administration skillfully described it as a short-term measure. Even the communists doubted that Johnson would authorize an enormous expenditure in money and materiel without being certain of victory.

Disappointed with the lack of success from the air strikes against the north, Johnson wanted new ideas from his military advisers. In response to a request from Westmoreland for additional troops, on April 1 at a high-level White House meeting, Johnson agreed to send two more Marine battalions as well as 18,000 to 20,000 support troops. The president also approved a tactical change in the use of U.S. forces. Westmoreland, arguing that "a good offense is the best defense," wanted the Marines out patrolling the countryside. Consequently, U.S. troops were authorized to engage in offensive operations in Vietnam, known as "search-and-destroy" missions. But Johnson concealed this major step from the public until June, when it was almost casually announced at the State Department.

THE CARROT AND THE STICK

Although at the time only a few in Congress opposed the war, Johnson decided to give a major policy speech that would allay the doubts of those who questioned U.S. involvement in Vietnam. On April 7, at Johns Hopkins University, Johnson asserted that the United States will not "withdraw, either openly or under the cloak of a meaningless agreement," but he appealed to the North Vietnamese to engage in "unconditional discussions" to settle the war. In addition, he offered North Vietnam a large share of a multibillion-dollar plan to develop the Mekong River Valley—after peace had been achieved in Vietnam.

Pham Van Dong, the North Vietnamese prime minister, insisted that peace discussions could not be held unless the U.S. bombing ceased;

During an April 1965 press conference at the Pentagon, Secretary of Defense Robert S. McNamara summarizes the results of the bombing campaign. Courtesy of the National Archives.

also, any settlement would require the formation of a coalition government that included Vietcong representatives. By May, Johnson's advisers had reached a decision to halt the bombing and extend new peace initiatives to Hanoi. The bombing pause, code-named Mayflower, was not publicly announced and began on May 12.

The U.S. ambassador in Moscow, Foy Kohler, was instructed to inform the North Vietnam legation that the United States expected "equally constructive" gestures in exchange. The message stated, "If this pause should be misunderstood . . . it would be necessary to demonstrate more clearly than ever, after the pause ended, that the United States is determined not to accept aggression without reply in Vietnam." Within two days, Radio Hanoi denounced the American bombing pause as "a worn-out trick of deceit and threat." In Hanoi's view, the peace initiative represented a brash demand for surrender. Soon thereafter Johnson decided to end the bombing pause, and on May 18 Rolling Thunder sorties were under way again.

After the failure of the May peace initiative it became apparent to Washington that bombing North Vietnam alone would neither force Hanoi to the negotiating table nor considerably improve South Vietnam's (and America's) bargaining position. Westmoreland believed that the enemy must be convinced that it would suffer a costly price in the north, and also that it could not win in the south. His long-standing proposal for more troops was now given more careful consideration by Defense and State department officials.

EXPANDING THE COMMITMENT

In early June, Westmoreland appealed to Johnson in an emergency cable that, in order to prevent South Vietnam's "collapse," he needed more than double the number of U.S. troops already approved. He said he needed an immediate increase of 45,000 troops, which would bring the total of U.S. forces to 123,000. He added, however, that 52,000 additional troops might be required, bringing the total to 175,000. And they would only be a "stopgap" measure to avert imminent catastrophe. Another 100,000 troops, perhaps more, would be required in 1966, and maybe even more afterward, "to seize the initiative from the enemy." His report to Johnson was gloomy: "I see no likelihood of achieving a quick, favorable end to the war."

The president's top advisers, including McNamara, Rusk, William Bundy, McGeorge Bundy, George Ball and Ambassador Taylor, convened to discuss Westmoreland's troop request. A consensus was reached that would give Westmoreland 25,000 of the requested 45,000 troops, with the remainder of his request postponed for future consideration. The new authorizations increased the American troop level to 100,000.

While Johnson had been seeking to avoid publicity over the use of U.S. forces in combat, the issue surfaced on June 8, when State Department press officer Robert McCloskey, in response to a question about whether America's mission in Vietnam had changed, said "American forces would be available for combat support together with Vietnamese forces when and if necessary." At the time, the American public was unaware of the decision made in National Security Action Memorandum 328 (April 6, 1965), which permitted the wider deployment of American troops.

The following day, the White House denied McCloskey's report, issuing a statement that said, "There has been no change in the mission of the United States ground combat units in Vietnam in recent days or weeks." This one incident opened up the credibility gap that plagued Lyndon Johnson for the remainder of his term.

In another decision withheld from the American public, on June 26, Westmoreland was granted even wider authority to use U.S. troops "in any situation . . . when, in COMUSMACV's [Westmoreland's] judgment, their use is necessary to strengthen the relative position of GVN forces." Westmoreland now had free rein to use American troops in any way he saw fit within the borders of South Vietnam. He pressed Johnson for more troops. The president summoned his advisers for their analyses.

George Ball, undersecretary of state, urged that the line be held below 100,000 troops. Shortly thereafter, he revised his recommendation to one calling for finding any means of negotiating America out of the war. In a memorandum to Johnson, he wrote, "If we can act before we commit substantial U.S. forces to combat in South Vietnam we can, by accepting some short-term costs, avoid what may well be a long-term catastrophe." McNamara urged that additional forces be sent but that efforts also be made to initiate negotiations with Hanoi. William Bundy argued for a middle course, a recommendation to wait and see how American troops performed in the field before making any further decision.

THE TURNING POINT

The president declined to make an immediate decision and instead ordered McNamara to visit Vietnam on July 15 for another firsthand look. But on July 9, in a news conference, LBJ implied how he was leaning. He indicated that more troops would likely be sent and even suggested that a call-up of the reserves might be necessary.

Upon meeting with American commanders, McNamara determined that they were confident of the abilities of the American combat forces and that the South Vietnamese leaders wanted more troops. He immediately cabled his findings back to Washington and within a few hours LBJ made his decision. On July 17, McNamara received a cable from the president, asking him to develop a plan for the deployment of a 44-battalion force, including such possible actions as congressional approval and a call-up of the reserves.

On July 21, Johnson's senior advisers met for a final time to approve the McNamara plan. McNamara's proposals called for: increasing U.S. strength in South Vietnam to 175,000 by November 1, 1965; calling up 225,000 U.S. reserves; increasing the strength of the Pacific command; raising the overall strength of the U.S. Army by 400,000 during the coming 12 months; and doubling U.S. draft calls.

Over the weekend of July 24–25, Johnson conferred exclusively with McNamara at Camp David. The president decided to make one major change in McNamara's program: He opted against calling up the reserves. Only with congressional approval could the president call up the reserves for longer than one year. By July 1965 it was clear that the war would last much longer.

On July 28, President Johnson made his decision known to the American public, in an afternoon press conference rather than in a highly visible prime-time presidential address. "We did not choose to be the guardians at the gate, but there is no one else," Johnson said, continuing to say that 50,000 additional troops would be sent now, with more sent later. He also announced that draft calls would be doubled. He asked for no congressional approval for these new deployments, but said he would ask Congress for an additional $1.7 billion appropriation for Vietnam. Johnson's political future now rested on his decision to involve the United States in a war in Vietnam.

WESTMORELAND'S STRATEGY

General Westmoreland had conceived a long-range military strategy even before Johnson had approved his request for more American troops. He would first deploy American troops to secure the U.S. air and supply bases along the South Vietnamese coast and around Saigon. Simultaneously, he would send units into the Central Highlands in order to prevent any attempt by the North Vietnamese and Vietcong to divide the country in two. Then, he planned to launch a series of "search-and-destroy" operations against the Vietcong.

He also relied on two other efforts for his plan's success. One was intensive bombing of North Vietnam, and the other was "pacification," or "winning the hearts and minds of the people," an economic and social program, under American sponsorship, which would help bring South Vietnam's rural population under the control of the Saigon government.

By August 1965, the Marines had secured the vicinity around Danang and had engaged in the first major American ground action of the war, destroying a Vietcong stronghold in the area. Two months later, the 1st Air Cavalry Division (Airmobile) defeated three North Vietnamese regiments in the Ia Drang Valley, a dense jungle area near Pleiku, and prevented the communists from launching an offensive through the Central Highlands down to the populated coast. Although it was the bloodiest battle of the war to date (300 Americans dead and nearly 2,000 Vietcong casualities), General Westmoreland was prompted to announce that his search-and-destroy mission could gradually wear down the enemy—if he was given the necessary number of battalions.

After their setback in the Ia Drang Valley, the high command in North Vietnam reexamined their strategy. The North Vietnamese decided to counter America's search-and-destroy operations by engaging in combat and suffering the inevitable consequences of U.S. firepower only when they felt the loss was justified. Their objective became one of gradually weakening America's will to fight by increasing its cost in manpower, money and time. They planned to make U.S. forces their main objective, to destroy U.S. morale and to set the stage for the day when American forces would leave and only ARVN troops would stand between North Vietnam and the liberation of the South. Hanoi was no longer seeking an immediate victory, but instead was aiming for a stalemate.

Assessing the Situation in the Field and at Home

Following a trip to Vietnam in late November, McNamara reported to Johnson that, although he was impressed with U.S. combat performance, he was worried about the heavy infiltration of North Vietnamese forces into the south. He believed the United States faced two options: to seek a compromise settlement and to keep further military commitments to a minimum, or to continue to press for a military solution, which would require substantial increases in U.S. troop strength and intensified bombing of North Vietnam. In conclusion, McNamara cautioned that even with more troops a military success could not be guaranteed. "U.S. killed-in-action can be expected to reach 1,000 a month," and he said, "and the odds are even that we will be faced in early 1967 with a 'no decision' at an even higher level."

Johnson was concerned about domestic dissent as he weighed his options. In response to increased draft quotas, student opposition to the war was spreading across college campuses and antiwar demonstrations were beginning to mount. A crowd of 20,000 protesters had encircled the White House for two hours on November 27, before moving on to the Washington Monument. Although surveys showed that an overwhelming majority of Americans supported the war effort if cease-fire initiatives failed, Johnson warned his staff, "The weakest chink in our armor is American public opinion."

McNamara urged Johnson to halt American air strikes against North Vietnam for three or four weeks before committing more troops. This would give the communists a chance to consider a diplomatic settlement and would also show the American public and the world that the administration had tried its best to end the war without escalation. A bombing pause began on Christmas morning and lasted for 37 days. During this period Johnson initiated a massive peace drive, as emissaries such as Vice President Hubert Humphrey, McGeorge Bundy and Ambassador-at-Large Averell Harriman were sent to more than 40 countries to persuade world leaders that the United States was interested in exploring a negotiated settlement. Johnson also invited the North Vietnamese to enter into negotiations without preconditions. Meanwhile, fresh American troops continued to arrive in Vietnam.

CHRONICLE OF EVENTS

1965

January 4: In his State of the Union message, President Johnson reaffirms the U.S. commitment to support South Vietnam in fighting communist aggression.

January 19–24: Buddhist demonstrations erupt in Saigon and Hue, demanding ouster of the Huong government.

January 27: The Armed Forces Council ousts Premier Huong and reinstalls General Nguyen Khanh. Buddhists stop their anti-government demonstrations.

February 7: Vietcong attack U.S. advisers' compound near Pleiku, killing eight U.S. servicemen. U.S. planes make reprisal strikes against targets in the north.

February 18: Bloodless military coup ousts General Khanh.

February 24: Operation Rolling Thunder begins, with sustained bombing of North Vietnam.

February 29: Hanoi government orders evacuation of the north's cities.

March 8–9: First U.S. combat troops land in Vietnam: U.S. Third Marine Regiment, Third Marine Division, deployed to Vietnam from Okinawa to defend Danang airfield.

April 2: U.S. announces it will send several thousand more troops to South Vietnam.

April 7: President Johnson, in a speech at Johns Hopkins University, offers North Vietnam a vast economic aid program in return for "unconditional discussions" to end the war.

April 8: North Vietnamese Prime Minister Pham Van Dong rejects President Johnson's offer, says settlement must be based on a Vietcong program.

May 13–18: U.S. begins a six-day bombing pause over North Vietnam.

June 8: State Department reveals U.S. troops are authorized to engage in combat.

June 11: Air Vice Marshal Nguyen Cao Ky becomes premier of South Vietnam.

While on a fact-finding mission in July 1965, Ambassador Henry Cabot Lodge (left) meets with Major General Nguyen Van Thieu (right). Secretary of Defense Robert S. McNamara is center. Courtesy of the National Archives.

July 8: Henry Cabot Lodge reappointed U.S. ambassador to South Vietnam to succeed General Maxwell Taylor.

July 28: President Johnson announces increased draft calls to allow buildup in Vietnam from 75,000 to 125,000, with more troops as needed.

August 18–21: Operation Starlight, the first major ground action fought only by U.S. troops, takes place. About 5,500 U.S. Marines destroy a Vietcong stronghold near Vantuong on a peninsula 16 miles south of the air base at Chu Lai.

September 11: The 1st Cavalry Division (Airmobile) begins to land at Qui Nhon, bringing U.S. troop strength up to about 125,000.

September 16: In their first strike over the Mekong Delta, B-52s bomb a Vietcong site in Vinbinh Province.

October 15–16: Protests against U.S. policy in Vietnam are held in some 40 American cities.

November 14–16: In the first big conventional clash of the war, U.S. forces defeat North Vietnamese units in the Ia Drang Valley.

November 24: U.S. casualty statistics reflect the intensified fighting in the Ia Drang Valley; 240 U.S. troops were killed and another 470 wounded.

December 8–9: In some of the heaviest raids of the war, 150 U.S. Air Force and Navy planes sever North Vietnamese transport routes at 117 points to reduce enemy infiltration.

December 24: U.S. begins second bombing pause.

December 31: 184,300 U.S. military personnel now in Vietnam; 1,369 killed in action, 6,114 wounded and 150 missing or captured during 1965. South Vietnam reports 11,100 killed, 22,600 wounded and 7,400 missing.

EYEWITNESS TESTIMONY

We are there, first, because a friendly nation has asked us for help against the Communist aggression. Ten years ago our President pledged our help. Three Presidents have supported the pledge. We will not break it now.

Second, our own security is tied to the peace of Asia. Twice in one generation we have had to fight against aggression in the Far East. To ignore aggression now would only increase the danger of a much larger war.

Our goal is peace in Southeast Asia. That will come only when aggressors leave their neighbors in peace.

President Johnson, to Congress, State of the Union Address of January 4, 1965, in Public Papers of the Presidents of the United States.

If we pulled out of Vietnam . . . All of the trusted islands in the Pacific as well as the Philippines are in danger.

Senator Everett M. Dirksen (R–Ill.), Senate minority leader, on NBC Television's Meet the Press *(January 24, 1965).*

On the ride into town I was struck by the crush of traffic: taxis, jeeps, U.S.-made cars, motorbikes, motorscooters, and the ubiquitous cycle-pousse, a sort of bicycle-driven rickshaw. Somehow, one doesn't expect to find traffic jams in a city fighting for its life, but nevertheless they exist.

William Tuohy, journalist, on first arriving in Saigon, in Newsweek *article of January 18, 1965.*

We were asleep when it started . . . We heard machine-gun fire and then the mortars thumped. I had just started putting on my pants when a mortar fragment came through the roof of the hut. It hit me in the back and both legs.

Spec. 4 Carl Clayton, USA, on February 7, 1965, Vietcong attack on the U.S. helicopter base at Camp Holloway, in Newsweek *(February 22, 1965).*

Any of the people in that hamlet over there could have warned us the Vietcong was around . . . But they didn't warn us.

Anonymous U.S. Army officer, on the Vietcong attack on an airfield at Pleiku, statement of February 7, 1965, in The New York Times *(February 8, 1965).*

As a result of this action, elements of the United States and South Vietnamese Air Force were directed to launch joint retaliatory attacks against barracks and staging areas in the southern province of North Vietnam.

Secretary of Defense Robert McNamara, to a news conference of February 7, 1965, on U.S. reprisals for raids on bases at Camp Holloway and Pleiku, in Gravel's The Pentagon Papers *(1971).*

TWO U.S. MARINE BATTALIONS TO BE DEPLOYED IN VIETNAM. After consultation between the governments of South Vietnam and the United States, the United States Government has agreed to the request of the Government of Vietnam to station two United States Marine Corps Battalions in the Da Nang area to strengthen the general security of the Da Nang Air Base complex.

The limited mission of the Marines will be to relieve Government of South Vietnam forces now engaged in security duties for action in the pacification program and in offensive roles against Communist guerrilla forces.

U.S. Department of Defense, press release of March 6, 1965, in Gravel's The Pentagon Papers.

. . . when either of us stops in a little town, twenty cents will buy the best protection from V.C. attack you ever saw. Because twenty cents will buy a fistful of candy. You give one piece to one little kid. Ye gads, the pied piper never had it so good! Immediately, about five hundred little urchins appear out of everywhere, all yelling "OK" (which they think means hello) at the top of their lungs. A V.C. wouldn't dare fire a shot or throw a grenade into that mob. It's really a bit dangerous when you go out to the off-beat hamlets, however. I don't mean dangerous because of the V.C. I mean that the little kids see so few Americans that in their enthusiasm they almost knock you over and trample you to death.

International Volunteer Service worker Roger Montgomery, to friends and relatives, letter of March 14, 1965, in Adler's Letters from Vietnam *(1967).*

A rifle company of the U.S. Army First Cavalry Division moves through a rice paddy in the coastal part of Binh Dinh Province on October 15, 1965. Courtesy of the National Archives.

An American in civilian clothes walked out of a nearby building carrying the body of a Vietnamese child. In his eyes was what U.S. Marines in World War II called "the thousand yard stare," acquired after seeing too much death and being unable to do any thing to help.

Robert P. Martin, journalist, on the bombing of the U.S. Embassy in Saigon on March 30, 1965, in U.S. News & World Report *(April 12, 1965).*

In the name of God, stop it! . . .

Mr. President, we plead with you to reverse this course. Let us admit our mistakes and work for an immediate cease fire . . .

Let us declare our intention to withdraw our troops, calling on other states to do the same, thereby allowing the Vietnamese the right of self-determination . . .

Clergymen's Emergency Committee for Vietnam, to President Johnson, advertisement of April 4, 1965, in The New York Times.

Vietnam is far away from this quiet campus. We have no territory there, nor do we seek any. The war is dirty and brutal and difficult. And some 400 young men, born into an America that is bursting with opportunity and promise, have ended their lives on Vietnam's steaming soil.

Why must we take this painful road?

Why must this Nation hazard its ease, and its interest, and its power for the sake of a people so far away?

We fight because we must fight if we are to live in a world where every country can shape its own destiny. And only in such a world will our own freedom be finally secure.

This kind of world will never be built by bombs or bullets. Yet the infirmities of man are such that force must often precede reason, and the waste of war, the works of peace.

President Johnson, at Johns Hopkins University, speech of April 7, 1965, in Public Papers *of the Presidents of the United States.*

Over the past ten years, the U.S. imperialists and their henchmen have carried out an extremely ruthless war and have caused much grief to our compatriots in South Vietnam. Over the past few months, they have frenziedly expanded the war in North Vietnam. In defiance of the 1954 Geneva Agreements and international law, they have sent hundreds of aircraft and dozens of warships to bomb and strafe North Vietnam repeatedly. Laying bare themselves their piratical face, the U.S. aggressors are blatantly encroaching upon our country. They hope that by resorting to the force of weapons they can compel our 30 million compatriots to become their slaves. But they are grossly mistaken. They will certainly meet with ignominious defeat.

President Ho Chi Minh, to the National Assembly of the Democrative Republic of Vietnam, address of April 15, 1965, in Fall's Ho Chi Minh on Revolution *(1967).*

Last night we were told to pack all our gear, and were told we are now on 72 hour standby-alert. We were told nothing definite, but according to rumour we are going to Viet Nam. I am attached to a helicopter assault battalion—that means at least I won't get wet when we land.

Pfc. Richard E. Marks, USMC, to Gloria and Sue Marks, his mother and sister-in-law, letter of April 21, 1965, from Okinawa, Japan, in The Letters of PFC Richard E. Marks *(1967).*

I have searched high and wide—and I am a reasonably good cowboy—and I can't even rope anybody and bring them in to talk and settle this by negotiation . . . and they say "We won't even talk to you . . ."

President Johnson, to congressional leaders, on North Vietnam's refusal to participate in peace negotiations, statement of May 4, 1965, in U.S. News & World Report *(May 17, 1965).*

Withdrawal . . . would involve a repudiation of commitments undertaken and confirmed by . . . three administrations . . . We must show Hanoi that it cannot win the war.

Senator Robert F. Kennedy (D–N.Y.), to the U.S. Senate, speech of May 4, 1965.

It's hard to sleep tonight. I don't mind who has to go to South Vietnam first. All my worry centers around the day of reunification and whether I will come back unscathed. How will the family be then?

NVA soldier Nguyen Quang Le, diary entry of May 11, 1965, in Newsweek *(May 9, 1966).*

Well, happy birthday to me. I am now 19. On day of my birthday it rained all day, and in the middle of all of it we had to hike about two miles to a new position. This is one birthday I most surely won't forget . . .

Pfc. Richard E. Marks, USMC, to Gloria and Sue Marks, his mother and sister-in-law, letter of June 2, 1965, in Letters of PFC Richard E. Marks.

As you know, American troops have been sent to South Vietnam recently with the mission of protecting key installations there. In establishing and patrolling their defense perimeters they come into contact with the Viet Cong and at times are fired upon. Our troops, naturally, return the fire. It should come as no surprise . . . that our troops engage in combat in these and similar circumstances. Let me emphasize that the Vietnamese government forces are carrying the brunt of combat operations. Those U.S. forces assigned as advisers to the armed forces of Vietnam remain in that capacity.

Anonymous U.S. State Department briefing officer, to a news conference, statement of June 5, 1965, in Hammond's Public Affairs, The Military and the Media *(1988).*

We have reached a point in Vietnam where we cannot avoid the commitment to combat of U.S. ground troops.

General William C. Westmoreland, to the Joint Chiefs of Staff, message of June 11, 1965, in Gravel's The Pentagon Papers.

General William C. Westmoreland. Courtesy of AP/Wide World Photos.

Well, come on all of you big strong men,
Uncle Sam needs your help again.
He's got himself in a terrible jam,
Way down yonder in Vietnam.
So put down your books and pick up a gun.
We're gonna have a whole lotta fun.

And it's one, two, three, what are we fightin' for?
Don't ask me I don't give a damn,
Next stop is Vietnam.
And it's five, six, seven open up the pearly gates.
There ain't no time to wonder why,
Whoopee we're all gonna die.

*Songwriter and singer Country Joe McDonald,
in "I-Feel-Like-I'm-Fixin'-to-Die Rag" (1965).*

Hey, hey, LBJ,
How many kids did you kill today?

*20,000 students to LBJ, a war protest chant
used for the first time at a demonstration in
Washington, D.C., in November 1965.*

You hold yourself stock-still in the jungle and you
can't see much. It's dark and there's only trees and
brush thick with vines. But you listen. Any sound
that's out of the ordinary means something. Every
insect noise change. Dogs in the village make telltale
noises, barking or yowling when something attracts
their attention and they can help or hurt you, de-
pending on who's doing the moving. A man can't
move through the jungle without making some kind
of noise or provoking some bug or animal to make
noise in the jungle—but so do the Vietnamese.

*Corporal D.G. Williams, USMC, 1st Battalion,
3d Marines, in Raymond's New York Times
Magazine article of July 25, 1965.*

The decision you face now, therefore, is crucial.
Once large numbers of U.S. troops are committed to
direct combat, they will begin to take heavy casualties
in a war they are ill-equipped to fight in a non-
cooperative if not downright hostile countryside.

Once we suffer large casualties, we will have started
a well-nigh irreversible process. Our involvement
will be so great that we cannot—without national
humiliation—stop short of achieving our complete
objectives. Of the two possibilities I think humiliation
would be more likely than the achievement of our
objectives—even after we have paid terrible costs.

*Undersecretary of State George Ball, to Presi-
dent Johnson, memorandum of July 1, 1965, in
Gravel's The Pentagon Papers.*

*In a village 15 miles west of Da Nang, a Marine of the First
Battalion, Third Regiment, takes a Vietcong suspect to the rear
during a search and clear operation on August 3, 1965. Photograph by Pfc. G. Durbin, USMC. Courtesy of the National Archives.*

As far as anything happening to me—you would
know in about 12 hours if I was seriously injured,
but don't worry about it. I do enough worrying for
both of us. If I'm gray the next time you see me don't
be surprised. I feel about 20 years old, and I'm sure
I must look the same.

*Pfc. Richard E. Marks, USMC, to Gloria and
Sue Marks, his mother and sister-in-law, letter
of July 30, 1965, in The Letters of PFC Richard E. Marks. [He was 19 years old when he
wrote this letter. Pfc. Marks was killed in action on February 14, 1966.]*

Some people say I am a dictator and everyone
speaks about democracy, equality and all that. Well,
if from time to time I have to resort to expedients
that aren't 100% democratic, it is not because I am a
military dictator. It is because of this corruption that

This Vietnamese couple was relocated from their village to a refugee center near Da Nang. Trying to separate neutral or friendly villagers from the Vietcong, U.S. Marines moved hundreds of thousands of peasants in 1965. Photograph by Sgt. H. Haeberle, USMC. Courtesy of the National Archives.

we've inherited, and because we have the Communists on our back . . .

Prime Minister Nguyen Cao Ky, South Vietnam, statement in Life *(July 23, 1965).*

My fellow Americans, not long ago I received a letter from a woman in the Midwest. She wrote,

DEAR MR. PRESIDENT: In my humble way I am writing to you about the crisis in Vietnam. I have a son who is now in Vietnam. My husband served in World War II. Our country was at war, but now, this time, it is just something that I don't understand. Why?

. . . . .

This is a different kind of war. There are no marching armies or solemn declarations. Some citizens of South Vietnam, at times with understandable grievances, have joined in the attack on their own government.

But we must not let this mask the central fact that this is really war. It is guided by North Vietnam, and it is spurred by Communist China. Its goal is to conquer the South, to defeat American power, and to extend the Asiatic dominion of communism.

There are great stakes in the balance.

Most of the non-Communist nations of Asia cannot, by themselves and alone, resist growing might and the grasping ambition of Asian communism.

Our power, therefore, is a very vital shield. If we are driven from the field in Vietnam, then no nation can ever again have the same confidence in American promise or in American protection.

President Johnson, to press conference of July 28, 1965, in Public Papers of the Presidents of the United States.

I hope you both realize that over half the men I knew at West Point have been or are here. I could never again face my buddies unless I came here. Call that pride . . . And there is something else, call it patriotism, and leave it at that.

Please hold your heads up and be proud of me.

Captain Ned Loscuito Jr., to his mother and father, letter of July 31, 1965, in Good Housekeeping *(December 1965). [Captain Loscuito was killed in action on August 20, 1965.]*

The VC are destroying battalions faster than they can be reconstituted and faster than they were planned to be organized under the buildup program. The RVNAF commanders do not believe that they can survive without the active commitment of US ground combat forces. The only possible US response is the aggressive employment of US regular together with

A Marine guards a Vietcong prisoner during Operation Golden Fleece in September 1965. Courtesy of the National Archives.

U.S. Marines landing at Danang on March 8, 1965. Courtesy of AP/Wide World Photos.

Vietnamese General Reserve Forces to react against strong VC/DRV attacks. To meet this challenge successfully, troops must be maneuvered freely, deployed and redeployed if necessary . . .
General William C. Westmoreland, to CINC-PAC, memorandum of June 13, 1965, in Gravel's The Pentagon Papers.

We came down off the *Boxer* on wet nets into these landing crafts. Everybody saw the movies going on in their heads, thinking we would be getting shot at. It was the movies, except it was real. We were carrying our duffel bags and saddle-up gear, but nobody'd been issued ammo. I thought, "What are we going to do when we hit the beach?" I came off the wet net very afraid. Everything I did seemed huge in that state of fear where everything seems to be so large and concentrated because you are making your-

self do it, forcing yourself to mechanically do it so the fear won't get you.

They opened the front of the craft. We started to charge in the water. All of a sudden I thought, "What the hell is going on here?" It was General Westmoreland and his whole brigade of generals. They were all lined up on the beach, saluting the Cav on the way into Vietnam.
Rifleman Thomas Bird, USA, First Cavalry Division, on arriving in Vietnam at An Khe, in August 1965, in Santoli's Everything We Had *(1981).*

I don't care about going. I care about coming back.
Anonymous U.S. Army Pfc., at Fort Benning, Georgia, in Newsweek *(August 9, 1965).*

You have to sit perfectly still and make no noise. None. So immediately you want a cigarette. You have to cough. Your throat starts to trickle and your nose itches. Your back aches, then your legs, then your shoulders, then your neck. When you do not react to this, but continue to sit still, the mind casts about for thoughts to amuse itself and pass the hours.

Captain James Morris, USA, on a patrol mission, in Morris' Esquire *article of August 1965.*

If you want to report a battle account you sniff around and try to find a helicopter pilot who has a mission. He'll say be at the airport at 5 a.m. You climb in and take off, only vaguely aware that your destination is such-and-such direction. He picks up his contingent of South Vietnamese troops and the operation begins, but usually the results are scanty.

William Tuohy, journalist, article of August 9, 1965, in Newsweek.

After surrounding the village . . . and receiving one burst of automatic fire from an unidentified direction, the marines poured in 3.5 rocket fire, 79 grenade launchers, and heavy and light machine-gun fire. The marines then moved in, proceeding first with cigarette lighters then with flame throwers, to burn down an estimated 150 dwellings.

CBS News correspondent Morley Safer, on a search and destroy mission at Cam Ne, television dispatch of August 3, 1965 ("Evening News with Walter Cronkite").

There is no new policy of toughness toward civilians. Our policy is still to bend over backward even at possible cost of U.S. lives . . . The U.S. Marine Corps has made a special effort in the Danang area. They have resettled some civilians, set up dispensaries for them and lost a number of marines killed just helping civilians.

Anonymous U.S. Defense Department official, statement of August 3, 1965 to The New York Times *(August 4, 1965).*

You're probably getting all the news that's fit to print, but let me give you some that's not fit to print: the Division has had a few guys killed, not from V.C. action, but from their own carelessness. Last night, for instance, during the raid at the airfield, a guy tossed a grenade "at something he heard," and it bounced off a tree, rolled right back at him, and killed him and his buddy . . . Also, several guys in the Division have been shot mistakenly by trigger-happy guards. Believe me, after dark, you don't

hardly step out of the tent. Consequently, there's this mad rush every morning to the latrine!

Spec. 5 William Keville, USA, 27th Maintenance Battalion, First Cavalry Division, to his family, letter of September 22, 1965, in Adler's Letters from Vietnam.

. . . in all other wars, you have been always been able to take a map and draw lines, you're here and the enemy's there. This is enemy territory, this is ours, and this is the battle line. It's not like that over there. Because, lord, one day we were 20 miles behind the lines, and the next day we were 20 miles in front of it. And you never know.

Staff Sergeant Bruce Whitten, USAF, statement of 1965 in a Challenge *newspaper article of 1966.*

You go out on patrol maybe twenty times or more and nothing, just nothing. Then, the twenty-first time, zap, zap, zap, you get hit—and Victor Charlie fades into the jungle before you close with him.

Anonymous U.S. Army sergeant, statement of September 1965, in Time *(September 24, 1965).*

It's no fun carrying 50 or 60 guys who are laid out on a stretcher moaning and crying and bleeding all over the place. It's a good thing that I am not home now, after all the bad stuff that I've seen over here. If anyone ever started talking about our position in Vietnam, and burning their draft cards, and all these protest marches—I swear I would kill him.

People don't realize what's going on over here. It is horrible, believe me, just plain rotten. These poor Army and Marine troops are living like animals and fighting for their lives every day that they are in the field. Some come back, but some don't. I've carried some of the ones that didn't, and it makes you sick. Every time I carry these bodies in canvas bags and wounded G.I.s I get sick inside. You may think that I'm like a baby when I tell you that I have cried when I've carried these guys, but it's no lie, and I'm no baby for doing it.

Airman Glen Kemak, USAF, to his family, on an air evacuation run to Clarke Air Force Base, letter of 1965, in Munson's Letters from Vietnam *(1966).*

I am a Marine, nineteen years of age, stationed in Chu-Lai, Vietnam. When people think of Vietnam they think of war. Let's stop and think of Vietnam in another sense. Through my eyes, Vietnam is a beautiful country.

I have seen her from the air and from the ground.

From the air, she has a beauty that few Americans see. Her mountains and valleys are patched in a hundred shades of green and brown, and between the shades you find an occasional strip of blue, where a river is cutting its way through the land on its journey to the sea.

You see miles and miles of flatlands where the green and brown blend together and produce a beautiful array of color.

Pfc. James Grandy, USMC, to Mrs. Ruth Parr, letter of 1965, in Munson's Letters from Vietnam.

The men woke me up to tell me that I had a letter from you. I must say that I have some good men, even though we do have some "trying" times. Never do they dispute my word when we are on patrol. There have been times when they have told me to be more careful and let them do some of the more dangerous assignments. I can't seem to do this, as I hate to take the chance of their losing their lives. My men mean a great deal to me, and when I lose one of them I wish it could have been me.

Sergeant George Carver, USMC, to his sister, letter of October 4, 1965, in Adler's Letters from Vietnam.

1:53 p.m. Given target by forward air controller in tiny plane below. He drops smoke bomb on suspected Vietcong mortar position right outside besieged camp.

Circle over Vietcong positions, turn left in stomach-wrenching peel-off, sweep in behind three other F-100Fs. I start to black out as we pull out. Bombs make brown puffs. Repeat the same run again. Can't see anti-aircraft fire. [1st Lieut.] Pete [Vanderhoef] says you hardly ever do until you're hit. Sharp peel-off. Going in again. Bright silver flashes show where our 20 mm-cannon fire is shredding the soil and snipers.

2 p.m. Level off, thank goodness. Head for Saigon.

Glenn Troelstrup, journalist, as a passenger on a sortie mission near a besieged Special Forces camp in Plei Me, journal entries of October 25, 1965, in U.S. News & World Report (November 22, 1965).

The helicopter came within 15 yards of where I was hiding . . . I ran out and dove right onto the floor of the chopper under a stretcher, and took off. I was a mighty happy fellow.

Captain Myron Whitney Burr, USAF, shot down in October 1965 while flying a combat mission over Plei Me, in Newsweek (November 8, 1965).

The kid stood stock still, his face frozen in a foolish grin.

The thing had come out of the elephant grass, nicking his side and burying itself in the earth.

It was a primitive spear, five feet long, its bamboo point needle sharp and hard as steel. The Viet Cong had planted them all about, lashed to bent saplings like bows and arrows and triggered when a man trips over a vine or a root.

They are fired silently and fly with a barely perceptible whoosh. They can go right through a man.

But so far we have been lucky.

Jim Lucas, Scripps-Howard News Service correspondent, on patrol with a U.S. Marine platoon, dispatch of November 2, 1965, from Plei Me, in Dateline: Vietnam (1966).

Restaurants where it was once possible to eat a leisurely meal and conduct a quiet conversation are now bursting with boisterous soldiers, and after five o'clock the bars are as crowded as New York subway cars in the rush hours.

Robert Shaplen, journalist, article of November 13, 1965, in The New Yorker.

You don't know me, but I truly hope that when you receive this letter it will find you and all your family in the very best of health. We received the cake you sent us a few days ago, and I speak for all the men in the first platoon by saying it was the best cake we ever tasted.

Your son was a proud member of this small unit. There isn't a man here who could say that he was anything less than a wonderful person to know and be with. I was his platoon sergeant and he was one of the best men I had. We were together most of the time. I believe he had the greatest respect for me, and I have nothing but praise for your son. Militarily speaking, also, you have every reason to be proud of him. We were together during the battle and in the face of the enemy and death. I want you to know that he handled himself like an American soldier.

I am Negro, Mrs. McClure. I think you might like to know that. To your son, I was his leader and I

A young Marine in South Vietnam in August 1965. Of the U.S. soldiers killed during the war, 3,104 were 18 years old or younger. Courtesy of the National Archives.

think that's the way he always thought of me. This is one of the reasons I can say that men like him just don't come any better.

Sergeant Samuel Vance, USA, 2d Battalion, 2d Infantry, to Mrs. McClure, letter of 1965, in The Courageous and the Proud *(1970).*

As I fell into the hypnotic rhythm of the patrol—we were moving between trees and cane fields, stepping high so we would not trip and clatter on the uneven ground—I was obsessed by a question that had plagued me on other walks in other wars: Why?

Why was it that humans still got along so badly that conflicts were settled like this, by young men betting their lives at hide-and-seek? Did I truly think I could, with the camera around my neck, help end the need for the carbine on my shoulder? Did I think I could make plain how warring really was, how

quickly the cutting edge of fear excised every human virtue, leaving only the need to live? Here, now, the supreme virtue was the ability to shoot fast. Or first.

Dickey Chappelle, journalist, with a U.S. and Vietnamese River Assault Group (RAG) in the Mekong Delta in 1965, in National Geographic *article of February 1966. [She was the first American correspondent to be killed in action in South Vietnam, on November 4, 1965.]*

When the war has ended and
the road is open again,
the same stars will course through the heavens.
Then will I weep for the white bones heaped
    together in desolate graves.
of those who sought military honors for their
    leaders.

Anonymous North Vietnamese soldier, diary entry of 1965, in Butterfield's New York Times Magazine *article of Feb. 4, 1973.*

Folks, by all rights I should be dead. The good Lord evidently saw fit to spare me, for some reason. I prayed, and prayed and prayed, some more, the three days we were in battle.

The many men that died, I will never forget. The odor of blood and decayed bodies, I will never forget. I am all right. I will never be the same though, never, never, never. If I have to go into battle again, if I am not killed, I will come out insane. I know I can't. The friends I lost and the many bodies I carried back to the helicopters to be lifted out, I will never forget.

The pen that I am writing this letter belongs to Stash Arrows, the boy that rode up to Winchester with me, on my emergency leave. Pop, remember him. He was hit three times in the back. I don't know if he is still alive or not. I hope and pray he is. God, I hope so.

Spec. 4 Kenneth Bagby, USA, First Cavalry Division (Airmobile), to his parents, letter of November 1965, written a few hours after the battle in the Ia Drang Valley, in The Winchester [Virginia] Evening Star *(November 17, 1965).*

We're running short of ammunition. Almost no food left. I have a shell fragment in my right leg. The wound hurts. There are still 14 of us, the remnants of an entire company. Hoang Ngoc Nhiem, one of my soldiers, is badly wounded . . . nothing to eat or drink. It's the thirst that bothers us most. I haven't swallowed a drop of water in four days.

Anonymous Vietcong commander, journal entry
of November 21, 1965, in Knoebl's Victor
Charlie *(1967).*

We have but two options, it seems to me. One is
to go now for a compromise solution . . . and hold
further deployments to a minimum. The other is to
stick with our stated objectives and with the war,
and provide what it takes in men and materiel. If it
is decided not to move now toward a compromise, I
recommend that the US both send a substantial number of additional troops and very gradually intensify
the bombing of NVN.

Secretary of Defense Robert McNamara, to
President Johnson, after visiting South Viet-
nam, report of November 30, 1965, in Gravel's
The Pentagon Papers.

Our people are determined to persevere in the
fight, and to undergo sacrifices for ten or twenty
years or a longer time, till final victory, because there
is nothing more valuable than independence and
freedom. We are determined not to flinch before
difficulties and temporary losses.

President Ho Chi Minh, to Felix Green, British
journalist, in the Vietnam Courier *(December*
16, 1965).

Before I start this letter, I want you to promise to
forget it, as soon as you've read it—but I've got to
talk to someone. Maybe, if I write about it, I'll be
able to understand it a little more.

I know that I shouldn't be "unloading" my problem on you, because God knows, you don't have an
answer for me; I guess nobody in this whole wide
world does.

I'll be true to my nature and be very blunt, and to
the point.

Yesterday I shot and killed a little 8- or 9-year-old
girl, with the sweetest, most innocent little face, and
the nastiest grenade in her hand, that you ever saw.

Myself and six others were walking along, when
she ran out to throw that grenade at us. Of course
there is always the old argument that it was us or
her, but what in hell right did I have to kill a little
child? All I can do is ask God to forgive me—I can't
forgive myself.

Anonymous U.S. Army sergeant, to a friend in
Toledo, Iowa, letter of 1965, in Munson's Letters from Vietnam.

The people here in North Vietnam are obsessed by
the bombings. Every aspect of life is animated by a
mood of embattlement and siege. It is tangible everywhere in the eerie emptiness of the daylight countryside, the emphasis on darkness, the air-raid shelters and foxholes, the rifles stacked at the corners of
the paddyfields and the edges of desks, the government painted posters everywhere proclaiming bitterness and defiance.

James Cameron, journalist, article of December
7, 1965, in The Evening Standard *[London].*

Again and again, a crowd of kids sees us approaching, on foot or in a car, and explodes into a chant,
almost in unison: "Okay! Okay! Hallo Hallo! Number
One!" . . .

In the hamlets, they want to hold your wrist, pluck
the hair on your arms; if you try to catch them to lift
them up, they dart just out of reach, till a brave one
tries it, then they all want to be swung. "Chao anh"
(Hello . . . to a child) brings thrilled looks, giggling
consultation.

Anonymous U.S. Embassy official in Saigon,
on visiting the countryside in 1965, article of
January 13, 1966, in the Reporter.

I would like the war to end because I hate hearing
shooting and artillery and planes and bombs . . . I
don't like to find bullet holes in my walls. I'm very
much afraid of getting killed when there is shooting.
I'm planning to dig a hole to take refuge in. I'm
always anxious and tense. I can't sleep well at night.
I've heard that a bomb was dropped on a hamlet
somewhere near here the other day . . . But my field
work is not affected by the war. If the crops are good,
I can make ends meet. If not, I have to beg the
landlord to lower the rent and borrow some money
so that my family will have enough to eat.

Nguyen Thi Lan, South Vietnamese peasant,
statement of 1965, in Sheehan's Ten Vietnamese *(1969).*

When I first toured Viet Nam in July, 1965, inter-
viewing servicemen, they all seemed to come from
Fayetteville, N.C., Columbus, Ga. and Junction City,
Kan., the towns that professional soldiers call home,
and almost to a man they insisted that they weren't
fighting "for Mom's apple pie." This wasn't that kind
of war, they said, and we didn't have that kind of
Army anymore. By the time Christmas rolled around,
the servicemen came from such nonmilitary meccas

as Queens and the Bronx and Stowe, Vt., and Shonkin, Mont., and Rose Lodge, Pa., and holiday shipments of Mom's apple pie and cookies had produced one of the greatest backlogs in the history of the Saigon post office. More than 100 ships were lying off Qui Nhon harbor waiting to be unloaded, some of them full of ammunition, some full of mail.

Hugh Mulligan, journalist, in No Place to Die *(1967).*

I wish those people who believe that we shouldn't be in Vietnam could see some of the things that the Vietcong has done to the South Vietnamese people. The strength we are demonstrating here is the only language the enemies understand; I'm proud of my uniform and glad that my being here will help keep this threat from our shores.

Helicopter Crew Chief John Murray, USA, 120th Aviation Company, statement of 1965, in Seventeen *(January 1966).*

Ed enclosed a picture of himself in his letter today. He looked tired and the sleeves of his dirty fatigues were rolled up. The children became very excited and looked at the picture for long periods of time. And they would study it and then say, "My Daddy, is that Daddy? My Daddy be back?" His little face was a picture of innocent dismay and longing. I've never watched anything that comes so close to breaking my heart. What is constant on this earth? I can really be sure of very little but maybe it's enough— there is God, there is love and there is loneliness.

Linn Boyt, wife of Captain Boyt, First Cavalry Division, diary entry of 1965, in Life *(December 10, 1965).*

We're down to the 19-year-olds . . . When young men reach 18 years and 10 months of age, we are processing them.

Anonymous Selective Service coordinator, in U.S. News & World Report *(December 13, 1965).*

Since I am unable to be with you and the child at Christmas, at least I'll be able to watch the Vietnamese children, to whom you have sent Christmas presents, opening their gifts on Christmas day. As they do, I'll be able to visualize Carol, Roger and Sandra opening and playing with theirs on Christmas morning . . . When I return home, we can make it up, no matter what time of year it is. We really have something to look forward to.

Be good, keep yourself and the child well and give them all a big hug and kiss.

J. C. Paierer, U.S. Army, to his wife and children, letter of December 1965, in Look *(December 28, 1965).*

5. Escalation: 1966

The Long War Begins

While the bombing pause and various diplomatic drives were under-way during January 1966, American commanders in Vietnam contin-ued to launch operations against the Vietcong. In late January, they waged the largest search-and-destroy operation to date, as the First Air Cavalry Division (Airmobile), ARVN and Korean forces began their sweep through Binh Dinh Province. These actions were not deliber-ately made to sabotage the peace efforts, since President Johnson mon-itored them closely himself, but they did little to generate an atmo-sphere for discussion. Nor did Johnson's State of the Union address, delivered to Congress on January 12: "The days may become months and the months may become years, but we will stay as long as aggres-sion commands us to battle."

With a bombing halt of 37 days and the peace initiatives heading no-where, Johnson announced to the nation in a televised address on Jan-uary 31 that the United States was resuming the air raids against North Vietnam. Consequently, Hanoi broke off all diplomatic contacts with the United States. It would be another 11 months before a U.S. official met again with a North Vietnamese representative.

Although surveys showed in 1966 that some 80% of the American people approved of the government's overall objectives in Vietnam, a substantial number did not necessarily assent to mounting a major ground war to achieve them. As far as Congress was concerned, in February 1966, during a lull in the bombing of North Vietnam, the time had come to address such basic questions as: Why had the United States become involved in Vietnam? How long would America stay in Vietnam? How many troops might have to be sent to fight there?

A War on Trial

The forum for Congress's discussion on Vietnam was the chamber of the Senate Foreign Relations Committee, chaired by Democratic Sena-

President Johnson greets American troops in Vietnam in 1966. Courtesy of the National Archives.

tor J. William Fulbright of Arkansas. The nationally televised hearings began on February 4. On the same date, Johnson, trying to divert attention from the hearings, announced his next-day departure for Honolulu to meet with South Vietnamese leaders. In an effort to detract attention from the military side of the war, Johnson directed the participants at the Honolulu conference to concentrate on economic, social and political projects for South Vietnam—the "pacification" programs.

The president's well-publicized departure grabbed headlines. News photos showed Johnson with his arm around Premier Nguyen Cao Ky's shoulders, the two vowing to launch a "social revolution" in South Vietnam. Amid all the hoopla and ceremonies was the president's announcement of an American troop increase in South Vietnam to 383,500 by the end of the year and a further goal of 425,000 by mid-1967.

When Johnson returned to Washington on February 7 the hearings were in full swing. Hostility had been building in the Senate toward the administration's almost single-handed approach to running the war. As a result the questioning of the White House advocates of the government's Vietnam policy took on an adversarial tone. During the hearings' first session, Fulbright announced that Defense Secretary Robert McNamara was refusing to testify. According to McNamara, he and Joint Chiefs of Staff Chairman General Earle Wheeler had decided that it was "not in the public interest to appear in public session." Fulbright asserted that the hearings would take place even if McNamara and other top officials would not appear. "If they don't wish to come," he stated, "there are other sources of information."

Those "other sources of information" would prove embarrassing to the administration. Lieutenant General James Gavin was the first important non-administration witness to face the committee. His credentials were impressive—an Army private who rose to the rank of brigadier general as commander of the famed 82nd Airborne Division in World War II. Before retiring in 1958 he had held several important positions, including chief of plans and operations for the Army.

In his testimony, Gavin suggested that the president's policy of continued escalation in Vietnam could lead to war with China. But the distinguished career officer could not be written off as a dove. Gavin told the committee that U.S. troops should remain in South Vietnam to hold areas under allied control while military and political alternatives to escalation were considered. He disapproved of the administration's aggressive search-and-destroy policy. Before he was through, he criticized the administration's "sacred cows," i.e., its strategic bombing of North Vietnam, and he argued that "the bombing of Hanoi would accomplish very little."

On February 17, the administration's two star witnesses appeared before the committee, former U.S. Ambassador to South Vietnam Maxwell Taylor and Secretary of State Dean Rusk. Taylor emphasized that the administration was interested in pursuing a limited war. But when asked about the "limit that the administration intended to put on the investment of United States forces," Taylor could not be specific. When Montana Senator Mike Mansfield pointed out that the conflict could escalate almost indefinitely, Taylor explained that the North Vietnamese could infiltrate only so many troops to support the Vietcong and would some day run out of replacements. When asked when that time would come, Taylor responded, "I wish I knew exactly where that ceiling is."

FULBRIGHT AND RUSK

Last to appear was Secretary of State Rusk. In his initial questioning, Fulbright challenged Rusk to defend the cornerstone of the administration's policy toward Vietnam. Fulbright remarked, ". . . it clearly began in my opinion as a war of liberation from colonial rule. Now, after 1956, the struggle then became a civil war between the Diem government and the Vietcong . . . I think it is an oversimplification . . . to say that this is a clear-cut aggression by North Vietnam." Rusk countered by stressing North Vietnam's "appetite to take over South Vietnam by force." He argued that the United States was simply asking for the North Vietnamese and the Vietcong to stop what they were doing. If they would not, Rusk warned, "There are some moments . . . when toughness is absolutely essential for peace."

Toward the end of Rusk's seven-hour marathon in the witness chair, an exchange occurred that revealed not only Rusk and Fulbright's differing views of the war but also those differences between the United States and North Vietnam, between North Vietnam and South Vietnam, and even between Washington and the antiwar protesters:

Fulbright: After all, Vietnam is their country. It is not our country . . . It seems to be the trigger that may result in world war.

Rusk: And none of us want it to happen . . . But when you say this is their country . . .

Fulbright: It is their country, with all its difficulties, even if they want to be Communists . . . Just like the Yugoslavs. I do not know why we should object to it.

On this note the hearings ended. In the aftermath of the Senate hearings, J. William Fulbright would emerge as one of the most outspoken opponents to Johnson's Vietnam policy.

DEBATE AND SUPPORT CONTINUES

Despite much criticism directed at the administration policy in the hearings, few senators were prepared to lessen their support for the White House. When Senator Wayne Morse introduced a bill a few days later to repeal the Tonkin Gulf resolution, his measure was defeated 92 to 5. The Senate then went on to approve a $21-billion military appropriation for the war.

From a long-term perspective, however, the hearings allowed the American press an opportunity to give in-depth coverage to basic questions about the nation's involvement in Vietnam. They also served to trigger public debate on the war. For the antiwar activists and the small group of dissenters in Congress, the testimony of Lieutenant General Gavin and former State Department official George Kennan dispelled the image of the activist as being on the radical fringe of American public opinion. They would be inspired to redouble their efforts to end the war in South Vietnam.

The Congress, and the nation as a whole, was beginning to divide into "hawks" and "doves," words that became prominent in the national vocabulary to describe those supporting President Johnson's war policy and those opposing it.

NATION BUILDING

While the United States dramatically expanded its military operations in Vietnam, it also had to cope with the problem of developing a viable South Vietnamese government. At the Honolulu conference, President Johnson had promised to extend his "Great Society" to Vietnam, to build democracy, improve education and health care, resettle refugees and reconstruct South Vietnam's economy. Johnson told Premier Ky, "We are determined to win not only military victory but victory over hunger, disease and despair." In return for economic aid, Ky promised to implement a sweeping program of reform.

When Ky returned to Saigon he announced that public employees who engaged in corruption and profiteering would be severely punished. But his message was ignored. As vast quantities of U.S. materiel arrived, much of it just as quickly vanished.

TURMOIL IN THE NORTHERN PROVINCES

The misused aid soon became a platform for renewed Buddhist dissent. The government had delayed on a promise of civilian elections, a pledge that had calmed the Buddhists. Now the most powerful Buddhist in the senior military, Lieutenant General Nguyen Chanh Thi, who commanded the northern region, including Hue and Danang, threatened that his provinces would secede unless the corrupt generals were removed. Instead, Ky, seeking to extend his control over central Vietnam, dismissed Thi. Within days of Thi's removal, Buddhists flowed into the streets of Hue to demonstrate, and the protests spread south to other coastal cities, including Danang, where dockworkers and civil servants went on strike. In Saigon, violence erupted as gangs of youths torched automobiles and smashed shop windows.

South Vietnam's military operations in the central provinces came to a halt as Thi's troops joined the resistance and took over Hue and Danang in an apparent act of secession. South Vietnam soon appeared to be engulfed by a civil war within a civil war. Attempting to quiet the protesters, Ky announced on March 25 a pledge to produce a new constitution and hold elections by the end of the year. However, these conciliatory moves failed to satisfy the Buddhists and their supporters, who demanded the immediate resignation of the military government.

The situation worsened in early April when Ky announced his intention to "liberate" Danang, which he claimed was "held by the Communists." Personally leading two Vietnamese marine battalions, Ky headed to Danang on April 5 for a planned dawn raid. Upon his arrival, he found Thi's dissident troops blocking the road into the city with machine guns. The U.S. Marine commander, in charge of the airport, intervened to avert a clash, leaving the two forces at a standstill. Ky decided against a confrontation and flew back to Saigon.

The United States wished to remain neutral in this internal crisis, but as the situation deteriorated, U.S. involvement became unavoidable, especially in the Danang area, where some sort of armed confrontation seemed imminent. Nearly 20,000 U.S. Marines were stationed there. On April 9, U.S. Marine General Lewis Walt dispatched Colonel John Chaisson to talk with Colonel Dam Quang Yeu, commander of a force of dissident I Corps soldiers. The rebel commander agreed to withdraw his troops, and a bloody showdown was avoided for the time being.

In mid-April, Ky held a private meeting with Buddhist leaders and pledged to dissolve the current ruling junta and hold elections for a constituent assembly with legislative powers within three to five months. But when Ky refused to announce publicly what he had guaranteed the Buddhists in private, the protest movement against his regime was revived. Ky and his generals were prepared this time to crush the dissidents with force.

On May 14, Ky moved on Danang and caught both the Americans and the rebel forces by surprise. Three-thousand Vietnamese marines steadily pushed back the 1,200 dissident I Corps troops and Buddhists, seizing the Danang City Hall and the radio station as well as other key installations. As the attack on Danang progressed, the fighting turned from sporadic and tentative to bitter and intense. The battle degenerated into a series of short sniper attacks as rebel forces abandoned all but a few strongholds and quit the city. The Buddhists gave way in the face of superior force and withdrew in protest.

The rebel officers in central Vietnam began to dissociate themselves from the Buddhist militants. General Thi was exiled to the United States with a generous allowance, and several Buddhist monks were permitted to remain, untouched, in their temples.

The breaking of the Buddhist uprising marked the end of the Buddhists as a dominant political force and crushed any hope for a civilian-based government in South Vietnam. Although elections were held in 1967, the military gained power with only 35% of the vote. As corruption increased so did desertions by ARVN troops. The Americans increasingly felt that they alone were doing the fighting. In 1966, 5,008 Americans died in battle, almost five times the previous year's toll.

THE BIG SWEEPS

As the defenses around I Corps (the areas of Quang Tri and Thua Thien) had become weakened due to the hostilities between the Buddhists and the government, the U.S. command suspected that Hanoi was preparing to seize these two provinces. In mid-May, about 200 NVA soldiers crossed a shallow section of the Ben Hai River, the demarcation line dividing North from South Vietnam. Their mission was not to fight but to engage in reconnaissance.

While the NVA division stood stalled in the DMZ, the American commanders monitored its activity and speculated about its intentions. Aerial observers spotted troops and trucks in the eastern sector of the zone. An NVA soldier who surrendered to an ARVN outpost provided further evidence that preparations for an invasion were underway.

In mid-July, a force of more than 8,500 U.S. Marines and 2,500 South Vietnamese troops launched a massive drive (Operation Hastings) in Quang Tri Province, in the vicinity of Cam Lo on east-west Route 9, below the DMZ. Pitched battles raged at Con Thien, Gio Linh, Camp Carroll, Rock Pile and Khe Sanh. Bitter fighting left U.S. and ARVN troops in control of the high ground, and the U.S. command claimed to have held off the "invading North Vietnamese."

Then in September one of the largest and longest U.S. offensives, Operation Attleboro (September-November 1966), took place in the heavily forested War Zone C, spreading north and west of Saigon toward the Cambodian border. The operation involved 22,000 men, 1,600 tactical air sorties and the dropping of 12,000 tons of bombs. U.S. commanders credited Attleboro with a very favorable "kill ratio" of nearly one-to-fifteen, the capture of large stocks of rice, weapons and supplies, and the foiling of the communist plans to attack the major population centers near Saigon and Danang. But, lacking sufficient forces to occupy the areas permanently, U.S. commanders admitted that communist troops and cadres soon returned to their positions.

THE BOMBING OF THE NORTH UNDER SCRUTINY

In December 1966, after much deliberation, the North Vietnamese leaders had finally decided to permit an American journalist to visit North Vietnam—Harrison Salisbury, the *New York Times* assistant managing editor. The U.S. air strikes against the North Vietnamese had recently been increased, and the Johnson administration claimed they were directed strictly at military objectives. On December 25, in the first of a series of reports from Hanoi, Salisbury disclosed that cities and towns had been hit and many civilians killed.

At first, Pentagon officials accused Salisbury of exaggerating his accounts of civilian damage, but later they admitted that, although air raids are confined to military targets, "it is sometimes impossible to avoid all damage to civilian areas."

Flying under radar control with a B-66 Destroyer, Air Force F-105 Thunderchief pilots bomb a military target through low clouds over the southern panhandle of North Vietnam, on June 14, 1966. Photograph by Lt. Col. Cecil J. Poss, USAF. Courtesy of the National Archives.

The Johnson administration was concerned with how Salisbury's reports would affect public opinion. In early 1967, Pentagon researchers were assigned to prepare rebutals, and their findings were leaked to rival newspapers such as *The Washington Post,* which reported that Salisbury's accounts matched those in a communist "propaganda pamphlet." Johnson himself entered the controversy and described the bombing as "the most careful, self-limited war in history." Despite the uproar that Salisbury's articles had caused in the White House and the Pentagon, many of those in Congress who questioned U.S. involvement in Southeast Asia continued to vote for appropriating the funds to fight the war.

CHRONICLE OF EVENTS

1966

January 19: President Johnson asks Congress for an additional $12.8 billion for the war in Vietnam.

January 24: Ho Chi Minh attacks American peace overtures in a statement demanding that Washington recognize the NLF "as the sole representative of the people of South Vietnam."

January 24: In the largest search-and-destroy operation to date—Operation Masher/White Wang/Thang Prong II—begins. The U.S. First Air Cavalry Division, ARVN and Korean forces sweep through Binh Dinh Province.

January 28: Defense Secretary McNamara receives a message from General Westmoreland that, in addition to the 443,000 troops already requested, he needs another 16,000 men by year's end.

January 31: President Johnson announces the resumption of American air strikes against North Vietnam.

February 4: The Senate Foreign Relations Committee begins televised hearings on the war.

February 6–9: President Johnson confers with South Vietnamese Premier Nguyen Cao Ky in Honolulu. A joint communique announces U.S. support for a pacification program in South Vietnam.

March 1: The Senate passes an emergency war funds bill after rejecting an amendment to repeal the Tonkin Gulf Resolution.

March 4–8: Operation Utah is conducted by U.S. Marine Corps and ARVN units in the vicinity of Quang Ngai city, against NVA and VC forces; there are 632 known enemy killed.

March 12: Buddhists and students begin demonstrations in Hue and Danang to protest the ouster of Corps Commander General Nguyen Chanh Thi. They demand elections for a new national assembly.

March 16–20: Mass Buddhist protests are staged in Saigon against the Thieu-Ky government.

March 23: General strikes occur in Danang and Hue.

April 1: Vietcong commandos set off explosives at a Saigon hotel housing U.S. troops, heavily damaging the building and killing three Americans and four South Vietnamese.

April 11: B-52s are used to bomb North Vietnam for the first time. Raids are directed against the Mugia Pass, the main route used to send supplies and infiltrators into South Vietnam from Laos.

April 12–14: "National Directorate" promises elections for a constituent assembly, and Buddhist demonstrations end.

May 1: U.S. forces shell communist targets in Cambodia.

Buddhist leader Thich Tri Quang leading a demonstration against the Saigon regime in June 1966. Courtesy of the U.S. News & World Report Collection, Library of Congress.

May 10: Operation Paul Revere/Than Phone 14 begins with 3rd Brigade, U.S. 25th Infantry Division units conducting a border screening and area control operations in Pleiku Province.

May 15: President Ky dispatches 1,500 troops to Danang to crush Buddhist and student rebellions.

June 11: Defense Secretary McNamara announces that another 18,000 troops will be sent to Vietnam, raising the U.S. commitment to 285,000 troops.

June 29: U.S. bombers conduct the first attack on oil installations near Hanoi and Haiphong, destroying an estimated 50% of North Vietnam's fuel supply.

July 15–August 3: Operation Hastings begins; a force of more than 8,500 U.S. Marines and 2,500 ARVN troops launch a massive drive in Quang Tri Province, below the DMZ. After losing 824 men, North Vietnamese troops withdraw from the area.

July 30–August 5: For the first time, U.S. planes intentionally bomb targets in the DMZ.

August 3: U.S. Marines begin a sweep south of the DMZ (Operation Prairie) against three battalions of North Vietnam's 324-B Division.

September 11: South Vietnamese voters elect a 117-member Constituent Assembly that is to draft a new constitution.

September 19–23: U.S. B-52 bombers carry out heavy raids against North Vietnamese targets in the DMZ and just north of it. Targets include infiltration trails, supply areas and base camps.

October 15–November 26: In Operation Attleboro, a heavy concentration of U.S. troops move into Tayninh Province near the Cambodian border, 40–60 miles north of Saigon, and search the area for Vietcong.

October 25: In Manila, the United States and five other nations assisting South Vietnam offer to withdraw their troops from South Vietnam six months after Hanoi withdraws its forces to the north and ceases infiltration of the south.

October 26: President Johnson visits U.S. troops in Vietnam.

November 5: At a press conference, Defense Secretary McNamara states that the troop buildup in Vietnam will continue in 1967.

November 24: Operation Attleboro in the Tay Ninh Province near the Cambodian border ends. U.S. and South Vietnamese troops engage in the biggest battles to date. At the height of the fighting, 20,000 allied troops are committed. Known enemy casualties total 1,106.

December 2: U.S. State Department decides to contact DRV representative in Warsaw about secret talks.

December 2–5: U.S. bombers carry out raids on truck depots, rail yards and fuel depots in the vicinity around Hanoi.

December 14–15: U.S. planes attack military targets two miles from Hanoi city limits.

December 26: Responding to reports by Harrison Salisbury of the *New York Times*, U.S. Defense Department officials concede that American pilots accidentally bombed North Vietnamese civilians during missions against military targets in Hanoi.

December 31: 385,300 U.S. military personnel are now in Vietnam; 5,008 killed in action and 30,093 wounded in the 1966 fighting. Total of 6,644 U.S. military killed in action and 37,738 wounded since 1961.

South Vietnamese forces increased to 735,900. SVNAF's combat fatalities totaled 19,110 during 1966, which brings the total to 43,582 since 1961.

EYEWITNESS TESTIMONY

A rapid solution to the conflict in Vietnam is not an immediate prospect. This would appear to be the case whether military victory is pursued or negotiations do, in fact, materialize.

Senator Mike Mansfield (D-Mont.), Senate majority leader, to Congress, after visiting South Vietnam, report of January 8, 1966, in The Vietnam Conflict: The Substance and the Shadow *(1966).*

Have spent four days in tunnel. About eight to nine thousand American soldiers were in for a sweep operation. The attack was fierce in the last few days. A number of underground tunnels collapsed. Some of our men were caught in them and have not been able to get out yet. . . . In the afternoon one of our village unit members trying to stay close to the enemy for reconnaissance was killed and his body has not been recovered.

Fifteen minutes ago, enemy jets dropped bombs; houses collapsed and trees fell. I was talking when a rocket exploded two meters away and bombs poured down like a torrent.

Vietcong soldier Tran Bang, diary entry of January 11, 1966, in Mangold and Penycate's The Tunnels of Cu Chi *(1985).*

We seek neither territory nor bases, economic domination nor military alliance in Vietnam. We fight for the principle of self-determination—that the people of South Vietnam should be able to choose their own course, choose it in free elections without violence, without terror, and without fear.

The people of all Vietnam should make a free decision on the great question of reunification.

President Lyndon Johnson, to Congress, annual State of the Union address of January 12, 1966, in Public Papers of the Presidents of the United States.

Some Do's and Don'ts in South Vietnam

Do be courteous, respectful and friendly,
Don't be overly familiar with the Vietnamese.
Do learn and respect Vietnamese customs;
Don't forget you are the foreigner.

Do be patient with the Vietnamese attitude toward time;
Don't expect absolute punctuality.

Do appreciate what the South Vietnamese have endured;
Don't give the impression the United States is running the war.

Do learn some useful Vietnamese phrases;
Don't expect all Vietnamese to understand English.
Do be helpful when you can;
Don't insist on the Vietnamese doing things your way.

Do learn what the South Vietnamese have to teach;
Don't think Americans know everything.

U.S. Department of Defense, to American military personnel, pamphlet of 1966, in DOD's A Pocket Guide to Vietnam *(1966).*

How many men who listen to me tonight have served their nation in other wars? How very many are not here to listen? The war in Vietnam is not like these other wars. Yet, finally war is always the same. It is young men dying in the fullness of their promise. It is trying to kill a man you do not even know well enough to hate.

President Johnson, to Congress, annual State of the Union address, January 12, 1966, in Public Papers of the Presidents of the United States.

. . . we believe that the South Vietnamese are entitled to a chance to make their own decisions about their own affairs and their own future course of policy . . . That they are entitled to make these decisions without having them imposed on them by force from North Vietnam or from the outside . . . If South Vietnam and the South Vietnamese people wish to pursue a nonaligned course by their own option, that is an option which is open to them . . . we do believe they are entitled not to have these answers decided for them on the basis of military force organized from Hanoi, initiated from Hanoi, in the leadership of a front which was organized in Hanoi in 1960 for the purpose of taking over South Vietnam by force.

Secretary of State Dean Rusk, to the U.S. Senate Committee on Foreign Relations, testimony of January 28, 1966, in U.S. Senate Committee on Foreign Relations' Supplemental Foreign Assistance—Vietnam *(1966).*

In the light of words and actions of the Government in Hanoi for more than 37 days now, it is our clear duty to do what we can to limit these costs.

Marines rush a badly wounded fellow Marine to a medevac helicopter after he was injured by a booby trap. Courtesy of the National Archives.

So on this Monday morning in Vietnam, at my direction, after complete and thorough consultation and agreement with the Government of South Vietnam, United States aircraft have resumed action in North Vietnam . . .

The end of the [bombing] pause does not mean the end of our pursuit of peace. That pursuit will be as determined and as unremitting as the pressure of our military strength on the field of battle.

President Johnson, to the nation, announcement of January 31, 1966, in Public Papers of the Presidents of the United States.

I'm writing this letter as my last one. You've probably already received word that I'm dead and that the government wishes to express its deepest regret.

Believe me, I didn't want to die, but I know it was part of the job. I want my country to live for billions and billions of years to come . . .

I can hold my head high because I fought, whether it be in heaven or hell. Besides, the saying goes, "One more GI from Vietnam, St. Peter; I've served my time in hell."

. . . Don't mourn me, Mother, for I'm happy I died fighting my country's enemies, and I will live forever in people's minds. I've done what I've always dreamed of. Don't mourn me, for I died a soldier of the United States of America.

Pfc. Hiram Strickland, USA, to his family, unmailed latter of 1966, in Adler's Letters from Vietnam *(1967). [Pfc. Strickland was killed while on patrol on February 1, 1966.]*

Fighting soldiers from the sky.
Fearless men who jump and die,
Men who mean just what they say,
The brave men of the Green Beret.

"The Ballad of the Green Berets," a 1966 hit
song by Sergeant Barry Sadler, U.S. Army
Special Forces.

In fact there are no real "lines" in Vietnam; and Saigon itself is an area of the most intense and regular fighting. Even in the center of the town where the main hotels are situated, one can hear the sound of bombings at most times of day. At night one is frequently woken up by the noise of bombs, artillery and machinegun fire. Flares often illuminate the city . . . There are many places in Vietnam where you could spend a month without hearing a shot or a bomb; in Saigon the war bangs continually in the eardrums.

Richard West, journalist, report of 1966, in
Sketches from Vietnam *(1968).*

I suspect that fear is the most intense and solitary of the emotions; love is fugitive by comparison. One tries to move forward, thinking that movement will help elude death, but knowing also that to move might be to invite it. We felt the ground shuddering under the concussion of artillery, and still the machine guns hammered. The earth seemed to reel. No one talked. And then, as suddenly as it had started, the firing stopped. We all lay still . . .

We rose to a squat. There was still firing on the far side of the village. We were squatting for a few minutes when we noticed the tall Negro.

He was lying still, facedown, his body jerked at an angle. We moved over to him. His body squirmed, but his eyes were still, and rolling backward into his head. I wondered how, back in Saigon, they would list him. One is never, after all, lightly dead, moderately dead, heavily dead; like chastity, death has no degrees.

Pete Hamill, journalist, article of February 4,
1966, in The New York Post.

There are special pleaders who counsel retreat in Vietnam. They belong to a group that has always been blind to experience and has been deaf to hope. We cannot accept their logic that tyranny 10,000 miles away is not tyranny to concern us, or that subjugation by an armed minority in Asia is different from subjugation by an armed minority in Europe. Were we to follow their course, how many nations might fall before the aggressors? Where would our treaties be respected, our word honored, and our commitments believed?

President Johnson, upon his arrival at Honolulu
International Airport to meet with Premier
Nguyen Cao Ky, speech of February 6, 1966, in
Public Papers of the Presidents of the
United States.

I am trying to look at this whole problem not from the moral standpoint but from the practical one. I see in the Viet Cong a band of ruthless fanatics, partly misled, perhaps by the propaganda that has been drummed into them, but cruel in their purposes, dictatorial, and oppressive in their aims. I am not conscious of having any sympathy for them. I think their claim to represent the people of South Vietnam is unfounded and arrogant and outrageous . . . But, our country should not be asked, and should not ask of itself, to shoulder the main burden of determining the political realities in any other country, and particularly not in one remote from our shores, from our culture, and from the experience of our people.

Former U.S. State Department official George
Kennan, to the U.S. Senate Committee on For-
eign Relations, testimony of February 10, 1966,
in U.S. Senate Committee on Foreign Relations'
Supplemental Foreign Assistance—Vietnam.

I saw on the road between Pleiku and Ban Me Thuot, they do not always travel by night. The road crosses the wild, sparsely inhabited Darlac plateau, where tigers are commonplace and wild peacocks scurry awkwardly out of the path of vehicles. It is a "liberated zone," and every few miles there are torn-up stretches of road and mined areas marked with bamboo stakes. (This is part of the confusing nature of the war. The road is mined, but the drivers who make regular runs know where the mines are and mark them off.)

Sanche de Gramont, journalist, report on the
Vietcong in the Central Highlands north of Sai-
gon, in Saturday Evening Post *article of Jan-*
uary 29, 1966.

Received another package from you—this one nothing broke open—a good omen I hope . . .

Don't send any more packages—we are suppose to be going on a 30 day operation real soon, and when I return it will be time for me to rotate. My plane leaves here on April 15, and if all goes according to schedule I will be on it.

Pfc. Richard Marks, USMC, to Gloria and Sue Marks, his mother and sister-in-law, letter of February 11, 1966, in The Letters of PFC Richard E. Marks *(1966). [Pfc. Marks was killed in combat on February 14, 1966.]*

. . . these people have planned to take over everything that borders on China, everything that borders on the Soviet Union, then everything that borders on everything that borders on that.

They are leapfrogging into Latin America, Africa. And if we have not got the courage to stand up here—where we are inflicting ten casualties on them for every one we are taking, and our nation is ten times as big as theirs—if we cannot stand fast here, are you sure we can hold Florida against Castro?

Senator Russell B. Long (D–La.), to the U.S. Senate Committee on Foreign Relations, statement of February 17, 1966, in the U.S. Senate Foreign Relations Committee's Supplemental Foreign Assistance—Vietnam.

The B-52 strikes now have been used on a scale supported by, I think, reasonably good intelligence, with the result that no [North Vietnamese] battalion is ever secure. We find from the prisoners—they complain about fatigue, of constantly moving for fear of a B-52 strike and from that point of view, I am sure, they are very effective. I would doubt if we would find many of the bombs hitting exactly where we would like them to go simply because of the fact this is area bombing, and, as I say, based on generalized intelligence; but the over-all effect has been very helpful.

General Maxwell Taylor, special consultant to President Johnson, to the U.S. Senate Committee on Foreign Relations, testimony of February 17, 1966, in the committee's Supplemental Foreign Assistance—Vietnam.

We are not asking anything from Hanoi except to stop shooting their neighbors in Laos and South Vietnam. We are not asking them to give up an acre of territory. We are not asking them to surrender a single individual, nor to change the form of government. All we are asking them to do is to stop sending armed men and arms, contrary to specific agreements and contrary to international law, into South Vietnam for the purpose of shooting somebody . . . We are not asking them to surrender a thing except their appetite to take over South Vietnam by force.

Secretary of State Dean Rusk, to the U.S. Senate Committee on Foreign Relations, testimony of February 18, 1966, in the committee's Supplemental Foreign Assistance—Vietnam.

No matter now modern its equipment, the American expeditionary corps cannot . . . escape the inevitable defeat which is likely to befall any aggressive army facing a whole nation resolute to resist them.

General Vo Nguyen Giap, commander of the North Vietnamese army, statement in Newsweek *(February 14, 1966).*

Rex Dula got hit in the leg the other day. It looks as though he will keep it, but the femur is broken,

U.S. Air Force Captain Wilmer N. Grubb is given first aid while being guarded by his North Vietnamese captors. Courtesy of the National Archives.

and he will probably go back to the States in a few days. Those of us who are healthy, and perhaps worthy, have mixed emotions about Rex. We hate like hell to see a good man hurt, but it's good also to see a good man go home to his life.

Captain John Sabine, U.S. Army scout helicopter pilot, to Deirdre Sabine, his wife, letter of March 4, 1966, in Brennan's Headhunters *(1987).*

I feel strange—I feel, somehow, that you, too, have been hurt or perhaps killed. Therefore, I am sort of empty of words—it's almost as though I am sitting here and writing to you to make you alive to me, to bring you here and close to me. Yet, I don't know what to say to you—no words can begin to describe how I feel right now. I only now realize that what I feel is fear, mostly of the unknown . . .

Deirdre Sabine, to Captain John Sabine, USA, her husband, letter of March 30, 1966 (written the same day her husband was killed at the battle of Chu Pong Massif), in Brennan's Headhunters.

The plain fact of life is there is no future for this poor, bedeviled place as long as we Americans refuse to crack any kind of whip, and look the other way while Vietnamese officials are mesmerized by the fascinating opportunity to build their personal fortunes.

Anonymous U.S. government official in Vietnam, to a friend in the United States, letter of April 1966, in U.S. News & World Report *(May 2, 1966).*

You could stroll out the guarded gates of the centre and head for the sound of the nearest fighting, edging closer to the fighting positions. During a lull it was possible to cross between the lines or infiltrate round the back over walls. I soon learned the new art of street fighting. It took someone a second to spot you and another to raise and fire his weapon. In two seconds you could leap up the street to the shelter of another doorway, ditch or wrecked car. Photographically I was working on bursts of frames, looting refreshments to quench a dried-out adrenalin surge not found in the boondocks. In the middle of a city, civilians get in the way and tank fire incinerates buildings.

News photographer Tim Page, on ARVN troops crushing the Buddhist rebellion in Danang in 1966, in Page After Page *(1988).*

We don't give a damn about students who demonstrate but those who violate the law with draftcard burnings and sit-ins go to the top of the list as draft delinquents.

Lieutenant General Lewis Hershey, director of the Selective Service System, in Newsweek *(April 11, 1966).*

No matter how fast we discharge them, the beds keep filling up. Some of the patients come from as far away as the Cambodian border or the lower Mekong Delta hamlets, perhaps even 100 to 200 kilometers away. Often this involves a trip of one to three days from deep within Vietcong territory. It is difficult to send patients like this back again, and yet they must go in order to make room for others.

Civilian Doctor Mark Hoekenga, diary entry of April 26, 1966, in U.S. News & World Report *(September 19, 1966).*

We are still acting like Boy Scouts dragging a reluctant old lady across streets when they do not want to cross. We are trying to remake Vietnamese society, a task which certainly cannot be accomplished by force and which probably cannot be accomplished by any means available to outsiders. The objective may be desirable, but it is not feasible.

Senator J. William Fulbright (D–Ark.), at Johns Hopkins University, speech of May 5, 1966, in U.S. News & World Report *(May 23, 1966).*

All I can say to you tonight is that the road ahead is going to be difficult. There will be some "Nervous Nellies" and some who will become frustrated and bothered and break ranks under the strain, and some will turn on their leaders, and on their country, and on our fighting men. There will be times of trial and tension in the days ahead that will exact the best that is in all of us. But I have not the slightest doubt that the courage and the dedication and the good sense of the wise American people will ultimately prevail. They will stand united until every boy is brought home safely, until the gallant people of South Vietnam have their own choice of their own Government.

President Johnson, to a Democratic Party dinner in Chicago, speech of May 17, 1966, in Public Papers of the Presidents of the United States.

There was a time when I didn't care much, one way or the other, whether I wore my helmet on

A Marine from Company G, 2nd Battalion, 4th Marines, holds his rifle chest-high as he crosses a stream. Courtesy of the National Archives.

patrol. That was for the first nine months I was out here. Now, with only three months to go, I make sure it's on my head every time.
Anonymous U.S. military officer, statement in
U.S. News & World Report *(April 4, 1966).*

It was weird. The first person that died in each battalion of the 9th Marines that landed was black. And they were killed by our own people. Comin' back into them lines was the most dangerous thing then. It was more fun sneakin' into Ho Chi Minh's house than comin' back into the lines of Danang. Suppose the Idiot is sleeping on watch and he wake up. All of a sudden he sees people. That's all he sees. There was a runnin' joke around Vietnam that we was killing more of our people than the Vietnamese were.
Rifleman Reginald "Melik" Edwards, USMC,
9th Regiment, Danang (June 1965–March
1966), in Terry's Bloods: An Oral History of
the Vietnam War by Black Veterans *(1984).*

The Vietcong are just like ghosts. You see them—and you see them fade away right before your eyes.
Anonymous U.S. Marine infantryman, state-
ment in U.S. News & World Report *(April*
4, 1966).

We were constantly out trying to find men who cried for help on the radio but who were totally hidden in the jungle. One company we tried to save

was completely wiped out as we flew above the canopy trying to find them. Their radio went dead, and they were gone.
Helicopter Pilot Robert Mason, USA, Company
B, 229th Assault Helicopter Battalion, First
Cavalry, on rescuing troops in 1966, in Chick-
enhawk *(1983).*

Give me voice or give me beeper.
Radio broadcast by American pilots, signaling
to find out if any of their crew had survived
after being shot down.

We have enough men here to keep from being pushed around—but not enough to win.
Anonymous U.S. military officer, statement in
U.S. News & World Report *(June 27, 1966).*

Due to the heavy volume of enemy fire and exploding grenades around them, a North Vietnamese soldier was able to crawl, undetected, to their position. Suddenly, the enemy soldier lobbed a handgrenade into Sp4c Santiago-Colon's foxhole. Realizing that there was no time to throw the grenade out of his position, Sp4c Santiago-Colon retrieved the grenade, tucked it into his stomach and, turning away from his comrades, absorbed the full impact of the blast . . .
Congressional Medal of Honor citation of Spec.
4 Hector Santiago Colon, USA, First Cavalry
Division, awarded posthumously for his actions
on June 28, 1966, in Quang Tri Province, in
U.S. Congress, Senate Committee on Veterans'
Affairs Vietnam Era Medal of Honor Recipi-
ents *(1973).*

I would hate to be an Army type down there, thrashing around in the bamboo and vines and snakes at 120 degrees in thick uniforms with heavy gear to lug through the woods—not to mention the humidity in a tropical rain forest.
South Vietnam is beautiful. From the air it looks a lot like Florida, all green and swampy. It's as easy for me to imagine that I'll soon be seeing Gainesville, Florida, as it is for me to picture the dying which must be occurring on that beautiful countryside. There is a redness of the soil that shows even through the foliage, and from the air, this red soil is the only striking difference from Florida.
Lieutenant Frank Elkins, U.S. Navy pilot,
journal entry of June 30, 1966, in The Heart
of a Man *(1973).*

They were so brave and they would come in . . . They were really hurting, and they were really afraid. Many of them hadn't had a good home-cooked meal or even a good meal . . . they'd been eating C-rations and stuff for such a long time—and their fatigues were so dirty . . . I think they were just so happy to be alive and to be somewhere safe that they would never complain about their pain.

U.S. Army nurse Pat Johnson, 18th Surgical Hospital, Pleiku, on treating wounded soldiers in 1966, in Walker's A Piece of My Heart *(1985).*

The worst are the leeches. They cling to our skin and suck blood avidly. We then have to burn them with a cigarette. A knife would be the easy solution, but leaves an indelible scar. Worst of all is that constant fear of running into an ambush. Everyone is obsessed by it. A suspicious sound, and we all fling ourselves flat on our stomachs, the men with their fingers on the triggers, me with mine on the camera release. False alarms!

Once, however . . .

"It's nothing. Only a cobra."

A cobra more than twelve feet long! "Only a cobra"—maybe so, but if we were not in a war that cobra would be the central figure in an adventure story.

Michele Ray, journalist, on patrol with U.S. Army Special Forces (the "Green Berets") in 1966, in The Shores of Hell *(1968).*

One man in each group stayed awake at all times. There would be no talking or smoking and the radio would be off. The jungle in Kontum goes dark before seven. The wetness comes as it grows black, and except for the chattering of small birds and animals it is silent; after a while the bird and animal sounds become part of the silence . . . We talked quietly of one thing and another, colleges, life on the West Coast, and then tried to sleep. I recalled a line from A. J. Liebling that when he was in an uncomfortable or dangerous spot during World War II, and he was trying to sleep, he thought about women. It seemed a sensible and distracting idea, so from nine that night until seven the next morning I thought about women.

Ward Just, correspondent of The Washington Post, *on patrol with a platoon from the 101st Airborne Brigade, in June 1966, in* To What End *(1968).*

We waded knee-deep across the river and at 1210 hours we set foot on South Vietnam soil. We then quietly walked through mountainous and heavily forested areas while [U.S.] aircraft buzzed crazily overhead. However, it was quite a rough route, going up and down; there weren't any level sections of more than a hundred metres. At 1400 hours we arrived at the rice depot and turned in the rice. We then began our return trip to our unit . . .

Anonymous NVA soldier, diary entry of June 20, 1966, in Shaplen's The Road from War *(1970).*

When I think about the hell I've been through the last few days, I can't help but cry and wonder how I am still alive. My company suffered the worst casualties—I believe something close to 50 dead and wounded. Friends who I took training with at Ft. Polk have been killed, and some are seriously wounded. In my squad of nine men, only four of us survived.

This was the worst battle as far as losses are concerned that this company has experienced. I'm not able to go into details now. I'm still in a slight state of shock and very weary and shaken from the last three days.

I just wanted you to know that I'm OK. How I made it I don't know.

Spec. 4 Kenneth Peeples, USA, to his mother and father, letter of July 3, 1966, in Edelman's Dear America: Letters Home from Vietnam *(1985).*

The men I attend are each day faced with the ultimate reality . . . the physical reality of death. I know now what every priest must know: the full meaning of compassion.

Father Thomas Confroy, U.S. Army Corps of Chaplains, statement in Castan's Look *article of July 12, 1966.*

That night while John pulled guard, I climbed to the watchtower, where a crew stood guard with two electronic devices. One was an instrument called a starlight scope, which could see in the dark by reading the differences in temperature. Warm things showed as white, cool as black. The other was a kind of ground radar that supposedly detected movement by reading subtle differences in the background noise.

Harold Martin, journalist, article of July 16, 1966, in The Saturday Evening Post.

Someone in the adjacent cell kept trying to make contact with me, and each time I'd try to determine the pattern of sounds to see if they contained any information. And then, early in the second week at the "Zoo," the key dawned on me. When the man in the next cell tapped on the wall again, I understood what he was trying to convey. The coded message was, "Who are you? I'm Dave Hatcher." I made several starts and stops in my response, but he was able to understand. I really felt great, because I was now in touch with an American. Within a very short time, Dave and I exchanged shootdown stories and brief biographies. I learned that Dave's home was near Winston Salem, North Carolina, that he had also been flying out of Takhli, and that he was shot down a couple of months earlier than I.

Captain Norman McDaniel, USAF, 432rd Tactical Reconnaisance Squadron (POW: July 29, 1966–February 12, 1973), at a North Vietnamese POW camp, in Yet Another Voice *(1975).*

Suddenly, I heard the helicopter, 200 feet above my head. The steel rope began falling slowly toward me. And there was the rescue harness; a slender device with three little arms folded into its side. I had to press the arms down to make a seat, but I couldn't unzip the plastic cover. I clawed at the harness and finally wrenched one arm free and gave a little signal. I was hanging sideways; I didn't know if I could hold on much longer. Everything was turning around. And I said, "God, don't let a bullet hit me now. Not after all this hell I've been through." Then I saw a leg and green pants standing in the chopper door. An American leg! I grabbed onto it and cried.

Lt. (j. g.) Dieter Dengler, U.S. Navy pilot, after escaping from a Pathet Lao POW camp in 1966, in his Saturday Evening Post *article of December 3, 1966.*

If we continue to push them [the North Vietnamese], to pursue them . . . pursue them back to the jungle areas . . . then some day they will stop fighting.

Premier Nguyen Cao Ky, South Vietnam, statement in U.S. News & World Report *(August 1, 1966).*

In Vietnam, if you are 30 years old, you feel an old man among youngsters. I was thinking about being 30 among youngsters when PFC Washburn leaned over and very quietly, very precisely, whis-

pered "grenade." Then he gave me a push. I don't remember the push, only a flash and a furious burst of fire. The grenade had landed a yard away and was the closest the North Vietnamese were to come to overrunning the CP [Command Post].

Ward Just, journalist, on a Vietcong ambush of Tiger Force (platoon from the 101st Airborne Brigade) in the Mekong Delta, article of July 17, 1966, in The Washington Post. *[Just was wounded in the ambush and returned a few days later as the* Post's *correspondent in Vietnam.]*

. . . the NVA were trying to get the ammo out of those three wrecked helicopters that were still lying there. Napalm got about twenty of them, and then another forty, in the middle of the landing zone. I remember one kid shouting, "Here comes some more Marines!" But they weren't Marines at all—they were NVA. And when they saw us, they ducked into the river on our flank. All we could see was their heads and their rifles above the water—it was like shooting pumpkins. The firing continued sporadically until dawn, and when it was over we figured we had killed more than five hundred. Our company was down from a hundred and thirty to eighty, and I had kids who were hit in five or six places.

Captain Modrzejewski, USMC, on a firefight during Operation Hastings in Quang Tri Province, I Corps, on July 18, 1966, in Shaplen's The Road from War.

. . . the great novelty of this war is the helicopter. It takes the Vietcong ten days to move three of its battalions. We can move five battalions in one day. The result is that ten Americans battalions can now fight 50 Vietcong battalions. Now the general can fly over the battalion and still be in constant contact with units by radio.

Major General William DePuy, USA, statement in Newsweek *(August 1, 1966).*

Before a resident correspondent left for reassignment elsewhere he was given the privilege of a day in the field with the commanding general on one of Westmoreland's regular trips by helicopter to visit American units. I took advantage of the privilege shortly before leaving for the Washington bureau of the *Times* in August 1966. At one point on the trip I asked the general if he was worried about the large number of civilian casualties from the air strikes and the shelling. He looked at me carefully. "Yes, Neil, it is a problem," he said, "but it does deprive the enemy of the population, doesn't it?"

Neil Sheehan, correspondent of The New York Times, *recalls August 1966, in* A Bright Shining Lie: John Paul Vann and America in Vietnam *(1988).*

It could take a million Americans to do what needs doing in all of South Vietnam . . . They way things are going, we are fighting no better than a standoff war.

Anonymous U.S. military officer, statement in U.S. News & World Report *(August 22, 1966).*

I hit the Red River and roared in almost to downtown Haiphong with Ralph on my wing. We received a warning that MIG's were coming after us. I swung south and on the way out found some barges on our alternate route. I let discretion go for a moment and hit them with rockets on the way out. Then the "Cottonpicker," Air Force radar jammers and radar warning aircraft, said more MIG's were taking off and SAM radars were tracking us. We made it to the coast just before the bad guys got there and headed out.

Lieutenant Frank Elkins, U.S. Navy pilot, journal entry of August 8, 1966, in The Heart of a Man.

When an article reads "structures destroyed" the definition means a straw-thatched hut. "Boat" means anything from a 12-foot one-man dugout to slightly larger sampans. "Bridge" means a bamboo foot-bridge or a pair of logs felled across a stream. "Pack animal" means a water buffalo, cow or even a pig or goat . . . The Vietcong are not anywhere strong enough to occupy any permanent dwellings, let alone operate any warships in the rivers . . . These targets must be hit to keep "Charlie" on the run, but at such cost?

Anonymous U.S. Air Force fighter-bomber pilot, editorial of September 19, 1966, in Aviation Week and Space Technology.

Ten casualties from a Vietcong's mortar attack arrive. One of the injured is a five-year-old boy with both his eyes blown out. An eight-year-old child with internal injuries needs an operation, as does a five-year-old boy with a smashed leg.

Civilian Doctor Joseph Weiss, journal entry of September 8, 1966, in Commentary *(May 1967).*

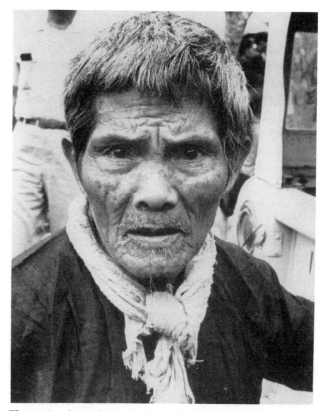

The strain of war shows clearly on the face of this Vietnamese farmer, ca. 1966. Courtesy of the National Archives.

A carbine round hit me where it would do the most good, right in the butt, the left buttock to be exact, exiting from the upper thigh. It hit no bones, blood vessels, nerves, or anything else of importance except my pride. It was, however, a little bit closer to my pecker than was comfortable. But that is as good as ever, although it is now going through a year's hibernation.

I am writing this letter in the hospital less than one hour after I got hit, so please don't worry—by the time you get this letter and can answer it, I will probably be back on my hill . . .

P.S. I am alright!!

Second Lieutenant Marion Kempner, Marine platoon leader, to his mother and father, letter of September 16, 1966, in Edelman's Dear America: Letters Home from Vietnam. *[Lt. Kempner recovered from these wounds; two months later he was killed by shrapnel from a mine explosion.]*

Nguyen Hoi pulled a small, worn notebook out of his shirt. The yellowed, graph-lined pages were crowded with sketches of traps, pitfalls, and the like, with instructions for waging guerrilla warfare in neat writing. A girl from one of the education teams had prepared it for the villagers. I leafed through the notebook and found information on ambushes, sketches of weapons, instructions on making mines from old tin cans, drawings of tunnels and trenches, data on how to protect fortifications with bamboo spikes and straps, on how to manufacture foot traps, and the best way of concealing them on paths and in rice paddies.

Kuno Knoebl, journalist, on meeting a Vietcong leader in a South Vietnamese village in 1966, in Victor Charlie *(1967).*

It makes me very angry to see my friends killed and wounded here and to put my own life on the line daily when you see the Vietnamese themselves are not trying and don't give a damn for your efforts and sacrifices. I see Vietnamese guys and their wives laughing and having a good time together. I see many young men not in the Vietnamese military. And I ask myself why I must be on the other side of the world from my wife, and I wonder why I must fight and risk death when many young Vietnamese men do not.

Anonymous U.S. Army soldier, to a friend in the United States, letter of 1966 in the Congressional Record *(1966).*

As I emerge in small clearing, there's deafening explosion. Followed by shouts of "Incoming mortar!" I run a few feet, see old artillery hole and fall in. Five Marines land on top of me. Mortar shells impact all around us. I can't move and have trouble breathing. Mercifully, shelling stops after four minutes. One Marine is lying with his head half severed three feet from a hole he didn't quite make. Everyone seems to be shouting at once: "Quick! More ammo forward!" "Corpsman!" and "John's got his foot blown off." "Where's Matthews?" someone calls—and is answered by "He's KIA, sir."

Arnaud de Borchgrave, journalist, on the battle for Hill 400, during Operation Prairie, south of the DMZ, in Newsweek *article of October 10, 1966. [He was slightly wounded in this battle.]*

When a man is kept at sea for nine months, often for periods of 30, 45 and 60 days without an in-port-call, he feels that it is unnecessary for the little effect he is having on the enemy. This man would much rather carry devastation to the enemy, end the con-flict, and return home to his family and friends. He is not interested in being utilized for setting records of on-station time, number of sorties, and continuous hours of operation merely to improve the image of his commanders.

Lieutenant Norde Wilson, USN, to Representative William Marshall of Ohio, letter reprinted in U.S. News & World Report *(October 31, 1966).*

I went to the launch crew's room. There, in near darkness, small model aircraft were being moved about on a mock-up of the carrier's flight deck to determine where each of the returning planes would be parked for the night. I noticed that two of the models had been pushed to one side and asked the reason.

"They never came back," I was told. There was a silence.

Winston C. Churchill, journalist and grandson of Sir Winston Churchill, on visiting the air-craft carrier U.S. Ranger, in Look *article of July 26, 1966.*

I was placed in a sitting position on a pallet, with my hands tightly cuffed behind my back and my feet flat against the wall. Shackles were put on my ankles, with the open ends down, and an iron bar was pushed through the eyelets of the shackles. The iron bar was tied to the pallet and the shackles in such a way that when the rope was drawn over a pulley arrangement, the bar would cut into the backs of my legs, gradually turning them into a swollen, bloody mess.

Commander Jeremiah Denton Jr., U.S. Navy pilot (POW: 1965–1973), at the "Hanoi Hilton" POW camp, in 1966, in When Hell Was in Session *(1976).*

I deeply regret to confirm on behalf of the United States Navy that your husband, Lt. Frank Callihan Elkins, 658100/1310, USN is missing in action. This occurred on 13 October 1966 while on a combat mission over North Vietnam. It is believed your hus-band was maneuvering his aircraft to avoid hostile fire when radio contact was lost. An explosion was observed but it could not be determined whether this was hostile fire exploding your husband's aircraft. No parachute or visual signals were observed and no emergency radio signals were received. You may be assured that every effort is being made with personnel and facilities available to locate your husband. Your great anxiety in this situation is understood and when further information is available concerning the results of the search now in progress you will be promptly notified . . .

Vice Admiral B. J. Semmes Jr., USN, to Mrs. Frank Elkins, telegram of October 13, 1966, in Elkins' The Heart of a Man.

The helicopter pilots have been shooting up the elephants and the jets have been dive-bombing because they reckon that only the V.C. would use them. We've been trying to get the word back but I still carry an American flag and as soon as I hear a plane I put that on the back of the elephant.

Captain Jerry Walters, U.S. Army Special Forces Civic Action officer, statement of 1966, in West's Sketches from Vietnam.

We're going to out-guerrilla and out-ambush the ambush . . . And we're going to learn better than he ever did because we're smarter, we have great mobility and firepower, we have more endurance and more to fight for . . . In war you have to pay a price.

General William C. Westmoreland, statement in Life (November 1966).

A 250,000-man French Expeditionary force came this way and was destroyed. Don't let it happen to you.

Sign posted by Vietcong on Route 4 in 1966, a twisting road dubbed by French soldiers as Rue sans Joie, "Street Without Joy."

The dead were kept in a fly tent adjacent to the division hospital. They were laid out on canvas stretchers, covered with ponchos or with rubber body-bags, yellow casualty tags tied to their boots—or to their shirts, if their legs had been blown off . . .

The interesting thing was how the dead looked so much alike. Black men, white men, yellow men, they all looked remarkably the same. Their skin had a tallowlike texture, making them appear like wax dummies of themselves; the pupils of their eyes were a washed-out gray, and their mouths were opened wide, as if death had caught them in the middle of a scream.

Lieutenant Philip Caputo, USMC, on his duty as a casualty reporting officer in 1966, in A Rumor of War (1977).

As for you, my beloved wife, once again you must bear the harsh burden of life's cross alone. Keep your faith and spirits, my darling. Our love can do nothing but grow stronger. Thank the good Lord for sparing my life. I love you all and miss you very much, and though I am a prisoner I remain ever with you in my thoughts and prayers. A happy and joyous Christmas. Love one another.

Commander James Mulligan Jr., U.S. Navy pilot (POW: 1966–1973), to his wife and children, letter of November 1966, in Hubbell's POW: A Definitive History of the American Prisoner-of-War Experience in Vietnam (1976).

The Company Commander broke the news to us today. We're to start packing for overseas. He didn't say where, but we all know—Vietnam. We were in formation when he told us. Why some of the guys were smiling is beyond me. All I could think was that they are either brainwashed or crazy.

Pfc. David Parks, USA, diary entry of November 12, 1966, in G.I. Diary (1968).

What we should do is to make up our mind that we are going to win, whatever the cost, and then buckle down and do it. If we cannot do this, we should get out just as quickly as possible—and getting out on any terms which are less than honorable is entirely unthinkable to me.

Senator John Stennis (D–Miss.), speech of November 30, 1966 at Meridian, Mississippi, in U.S. News & World Report (December 26, 1966).

Suddenly, a lone airplane appeared over the city and all of Hanoi seemed to concentrate its fire on it. The plane came so close that I could see the pilot. Then, either a blaze of sunlight on its fuselage or a flame spurted up and the Vietnamese shouted. But the plane flew off toward the sea.

Jacques Moalic, Agence France Presse Correspondent in Hanoi, dispatch of December 14, 1966, in Newsweek (December 26, 1966).

This correspondent is no ballistics specialist, but inspection of several dam sites and talks with witnesses make it clear that Hanoi residents certainly believe they were bombed by U.S. planes; that they certainly observed U.S. planes overhead and that damage certainly occurred right in the center of town.

Harrison Salisbury, correspondent, article of December 25, 1966, in The New York Times.

Our targets consisted mainly of a large transhipment area on the banks of the rivers; a fuel area on the delta east of town, and rail yards to the west . . . The North Vietnamese don't waste their antiaircraft batteries: They only put them around stuff they want to protect. Well, there must be at least 100 Triple-A around Nam Dinh, big 85s plus SAM's.

Commander Robert Mandeville, USN, Squadron 65, disputing New York Times *correspondent Harrison Salisbury's reports of American planes bombing civilian areas, statement of December 28, 1966, in* U.S. News & World Report *(January 9, 1967).*

We are using a "sledgehammer on gnats," if you want to use that description. But there seems to be no way around it. We'd never get anything done using a flyswatter here.

Anonymous U.S. military officer, statement of December 1966 in U.S. News & World Report *(January 2, 1967).*

It is impossible to avoid all damage to civilian areas especially when the North Vietnamese deliberately emplace their air defense sites . . . their radar and either military facilities in populated areas . . .

U.S. Department of Defense, press release of December 26, 1966, in response to reports of U.S. bombings of Hanoi, in The New York Times *(December 27, 1966).*

Twenty months of heavy American bombing has reduced all travel—road, rail and river—in North Vietnam to a crawl, and then only by night. Bridges have been destroyed, main roads cratered, railways pulverized. Highway 1, which hugs the coast, is so badly battered that peasants call it the "Road of Bygone Days." Rivers have to be crossed by ferry or on pontoons of bamboo. Everything is improvised.

Norman Barrymaine, journalist, article in Aviation Week and Space Technology *(Dec. 26, 1966).*

If the rail line was blocked by destruction of a bridge or trackage, bicycle brigades were called up. Five hundred men and women and their bicycle brigades would be sent to the scene of the break. They would unload the stalled freight train, putting the cargo on the bikes. Each bicycle would handle a six-hundred-pound load, balanced across the frame with a bar. The bicycles would be wheeled, not ridden, over a pontoon bridge, and on the other side

of the break a second train would be drawn up. The cargo would be reloaded and moved on south.

Meantime the work of repairing the trackage or the broken bridge would go forward.

Harrison Salisbury, correspondent of the New York Times, *on visiting North Vietnam in December 1966, in* Behind the Lines–Hanoi *(1967).*

These Marines had been on patrol and their point man had stepped on a mine. He was killed. The boy on the stretcher had been behind him, and his legs were in a sorry shape. All there was from hips to ankles was red hamburger. The bones were intact, or seemed to be. You could see them—the femur and shinbone—on his left leg. His buddies carried him to the landing zone in a poncho and the poncho, slimy with blood, was still crumpled under him. You could smell the blood and sweat and the muck of the paddy. When the corpsmen had cut away all his clothing you could see red holes in his arms, but these were ignored for the moment. The legs were the thing right now.

A soldier of the First Cavalry Division comforts a buddy after a firefight that took the lives of most of the men of his platoon during Operation Byrd in August 1966. Courtesy of the National Archives.

. . . After awhile the screaming stopped and the boy spoke one last sentence: "Mom! I'm dead!"

Martin Russ, journalist, on the triage center at Charlie Med, near Danang, journal entry of December 26, 1966, in Happy Hunting Ground *(1968).*

I was carefully smashing down the angled punji stakes when carbine bullets snapped the tips of the trees above my head. Enemy fire was coming from a mountain mass staring over the ridge on which we marched. A Huey gunship patrolling above charged the NVA riflemen at treetop level, burping a leaden vomit of machine gun fire and hiccuping an exploding chain of 40 mm grenades along the unfriendly slope. I ducked instinctively and turned my head to determine what course of action Lt. Earls would take in the face of the percolating firing. As I did so, I also thrust my left leg forward in a blind step directly into a pit bearing the uncompromising bamboo blade of a punji stake, a foot and a half of which struck menacingly out of its berth of earth and grass. A white-hot flash of pain exploded through my senses. The poisoning prong slashed deeply into the meat of my lower leg.

Sargeant Michael Clodfelter, USA, squad leader, walking point on December 30, 1966, in Clodfelter's Mad Minutes and Vietnam Months *(1988).*

It's a strange and dirty war—a booby trap and mine war . . . I'd rather be a hawk than a pigeon. I hope I won't have to go back next year, but if there is still a war, I have to go. It's an experience that defies description.

Bob Hope, entertainer, upon returning to Los Angeles after entertaining troops in Vietnam, statement in UPI news release of December 30, 1966.

6. An Expanding War: 1967

A War Without Front Lines

By 1967, intensive fighting was taking place across much of South Vietnam. Along the demilitarized zone (DMZ), Marines and North Vietnamese regulars were pounding each other relentlessly with artillery. Small American units were probing for the enemy in jungle areas. General Westmoreland was expanding large-scale search-and-destroy operations against enemy base camps.

In January, Operation Cedar Falls, the largest offensive of the war to date, sent about 16,000 U.S. and 14,000 South Vietnamese troops into the Iron Triangle, a 60-square-mile area believed to contain Vietcong base camps and supply dumps. U.S. infantrymen discovered a massive tunnel complex, apparently a headquarters for guerrilla raids and terrorist attacks on Saigon. Large numbers of specially trained combat forces were airlifted into the villages. After removing the population, bulldozers leveled the area, destroying the vegetation and leaving the guerrillas with no place to hide. The region was then bombed to destroy the miles of underground tunnels dug by the Vietcong.

According to the U.S. general in command, William E. Depuy, the operation was "a decisive turning point in the III Corps area . . . and a blow from which the VC in this area may never recover." Cedar Falls did destroy the area's physical structures and remove its population. But most of the communist forces headquartered in the Iron Triangle managed to escape as soon as the operation had begun. The operation also left vengeful villagers living in hastily constructed refugee camps.

Three months later, U.S. and ARVN troops returned to War Zone C to search for the communist forces that Operation Attleboro had supposedly crushed the previous year. Junction City, as the new operation was named, also was directed at making the area permanently insecure for the communists. It relied on surprise helicopter deployments, large infantry sweeps and immense firepower. It ended with the announcement of a high "body count" and large quantities of

Secretary of Defense Robert S. McNamara (right) is greeted by Ambassador Ellsworth Bunker (left) and General Westmoreland on his visit to Saigon on July 7, 1967. Courtesy of the National Archives.

seized weapons, supplies and documents. However, like previous operations, Junction City failed to deny the communist forces the use of War Zone C and the Iron Triangle. Lacking sufficient troops to hold the area, U.S. commanders had to admit that communist troops soon returned to their positions.

THE NUMBERS GAME

In a war without front lines and territorial objectives, the body count became the index of progress, "attriting the enemy" the major goal. Most authorities agree that the figures were unreliable. It was impossible to distinguish between Vietcong and noncombatants, and the destructiveness of combat made it virtually impossible to produce an accurate count of enemy killed in action.

There was heavy pressure from Washington to produce favorable figures in the field. Even if the body counts were inflated—sometimes as high as 30%—the United States inflicted huge losses on the enemy. By late 1967, official estimates placed the number as high as 220,000 dead. On the basis of these figures, the American military command insisted that the United States was winning the war.

In the north, air strikes were destroying hundreds of bridges, but virtually all of them were rebuilt or bypassed. Thousands of railroad cars, trucks and other vehicles had been destroyed, but North Vietnamese traffic was moving relatively smoothly. Although three-quarters of the country's oil-storage facilities had been bombed, there were no fuel shortages. Moreover, the morale of the communists had not been weakened, and they were continuing to supply their forces in the south.

The North Vietnamese and Vietcong remained extraordinarily elusive and were able to avoid combat when it suited them. They engaged American and ARVN troops at times and places of their own choosing and on ground favorable to them. If their losses reached unacceptable levels, they could simply fade away into the jungle or retreat into sanctuaries in North Vietnam, Laos and Cambodia.

Despite the impressive body counts, it was apparent to many observers by mid-1967 that the hopes of a quick military victory had been overestimated. The United States had nearly 450,000 troops in Vietnam. Westmoreland conceded that even if his request for an additional 200,000 troops was granted, the war might go on for as long as two years. If not, he warned, it could last five years or even longer.

NEARING A STALEMATE OR VICTORY?

General Westmoreland's troop request would be reviewed by Defense Secretary Robert McNamara and his staff of systems analysis specialists, known in Washington as the "whiz kids." Systems analysis was a relatively new management and research process at the Pentagon, an outgrowth of the computer age dawning in American industry and business. If Westmoreland's request was to be approved, it had to agree with the whiz kids' projections.

After his visit to South Vietnam in October 1966, McNamara's hope for a victory in the ground war was beginning to diminish. In his report to President Johnson, he stated that although "we have by and large blunted the Communist military initiative [I see] no sign of an impending break in enemy morale." McNamara expressed the concern that the situation was approaching a stalemate, that the strategy of attrition was not working.

In the spring of 1967, however, General Westmoreland and the Joint Chiefs of Staff did not share McNamara's pessimism about the strategy of attrition. Westmoreland insisted that the war was grinding down the enemy and that the death toll had doubled from the previous year, to 8,000 a month, with a kill ratio of four to one in favor of the U.S. and ARVN troops. He also pointed to the demolition of thousands of Vietcong bunkers, underground hospitals, food caches, ammunition dumps and camps.

While Military Assistance Command–Vietnam (MACV) interpreted its numbers as signs that a victory was on the horizon, the Defense Department systems analysis took a negative view of the future: "An end to the conflict is not in sight and major unresolved problems remain," they wrote. The systems analysts concluded that the enemy was able to minimize his losses so as "to fight indefinitely."

While Westmoreland and the systems analysts in the Pentagon debated the number of troops needed, in the jungles of South Vietnam the fighting continued. In early May 1967, in a valley north of Khe Sanh, 35,000 North Vietnamese troops were dug in on three hills, 881 North and South and 861. A 12-day battle ensued that was reminiscent of the famous Pork Chop Hill assault of the Korean War. Marines moving up the slopes of 861 and 881 were confronted with crossfire from well-placed NVA bunkers. After the Marines pulled back, B-52s bombed the hills into a "moonscape of craters." The NVA withdrew, leaving nearly 200 U.S. Marines dead and 800 wounded.

By the summer of 1967, President Johnson was frustrated by his lack of success in Vietnam, torn between his advisers, and unsure which way to turn. The military demanded more bombing. "Bomb, bomb, bomb—that's all you know," Johnson is said to have complained on several occasions to the Joint Chiefs of Staff. He was troubled by Westmoreland's request for more troops. "When we add divisions, can't the enemy add divisions?" he asked Westmoreland in April. "If so, where does it all end?" Johnson remained firmly opposed to mobilizing the reserves and expanding the war, which would increase domestic opposition. Johnson also feared a confrontation with the Soviet Union or China. "I am not going to spit in China's face," he later confided to an aide.

Johnson decided to hold a middle ground between the extremes of his advisers. He rejected Westmoreland's request for 200,000 additional troops, approving an increase of only 55,000. He turned down McNamara's proposal to limit or stop the bombing. To satisfy the Joint Chiefs and the congressional hawks, he significantly expanded the list of targets, authorizing strikes against bridges, railyards and bases within the Hanoi-Haiphong vicinity and against formerly restricted areas along the Chinese border.

A Nation Dividing Against Itself

As Johnson escalated the war, antiwar rallies and demonstrations drew larger crowds in 1967, and the participants became more outspoken in their opposition. Protesters marched daily around the White House chanting "Hey, hey, LBJ, how many kids did you kill today?" The most dramatic single protest occurred on October 21, 1967, when as many as 100,000 antiwar demonstrators gathered in Washington and an estimated 35,000 at the Pentagon.

During 1967 public support for the war dropped sharply. By October, approval of Johnson's handling of the war dropped to 28%. A number of major metropolitan newspapers shifted from supporting the war to opposing it. Although members of Congress found it impossible to vote against funds for American forces in the field, some began to openly criticize the president. The nation was dividing against itself.

To counter the antiwar movement, the Johnson administration mounted an intensive public relations campaign to shore up support for the war. Favorable government reports on the war were distributed to the media. Statistics and captured enemy documents were distributed to correspondents in Saigon to prove that the war was being won. Johnson toured military bases and naval installations around the country to promote his cause.

Minister of defense and third-ranking member of the North Vietnamese politburo, General Vo Nguyen Giap in the summer of 1967 began planning the offensive that he hoped would shorten the war. Courtesy of the Indochina Archives.

In mid-November, Johnson summoned Westmoreland home to revive the country's sagging spirit. He was steered away from meeting with Senator William Fulbright and other doves, and met with the more sympathetic Senate and House Armed Services committees. Speaking to an audience at the National Press Club, Westmoreland said, "We have reached an important point when the end begins to come into view." He challenged the communists to stage a massive attack. "I hope they try something," he said, "because we are looking for a fight."

THE NORTH SHIFTS ITS STRATEGY

So was General Vo Nguyen Giap. Since the summer, a major offensive was in the works. A North Vietnamese document captured on November 6, 1967, contained an outline of Hanoi's preparations for a 1968 offensive. The document described four principal objectives: annihilate major U.S. units forced to disperse in search of guerrillas and "disintegrate a large part of the Puppet Army"; improve combat technique; liberate areas for political struggle; and achieve unity and political-military coordination in the south. At the time, most U.S. military intelligence officers, as well as many American reporters, rejected the idea of a nationwide offensive as "implausible."

CHRONICLE OF EVENTS

1967

January 8–26: Operation Cedar Falls conducted jointly by about 16,000 U.S. and 14,000 South Vietnamese troops against Vietcong headquarters in the Iron Triangle. U.S. troops discover a massive tunnel complex, apparently a base for guerrilla raids and terrorist attacks on Saigon. Operation ends with 711 of the enemy reported killed and 488 captured.

January 10: President Johnson in his annual State of the Union message to Congress, asks for the enactment of a 6% surcharge on income taxes to help support the war.

February 7: The U.S. halts the bombing of North Vietnam during Tet. British Prime Minister Harold Wilson, acting on behalf of President Johnson, meets with Soviet Premier Alexei Kosygin in an effort to stop the bombing permanently and begin peace talks.

February 11: Tet cease-fire ends and allied ground forces resume operations in South Vietnam. Sixteen separate operations in South Vietnam are launched by the United States and South Vietnam.

February 22: Operation Junction City, an effort to crush the Vietcong's War Zone C stronghold near the Cambodian border, begins with a force of over 25,000 U.S. and South Vietnamese troops. It is the war's largest offensive to date.

March 21: The North Vietnamese press agency reports that an exchange of notes took place in February between President Johnson and Ho Chi Minh. It is reported that Ho rejected peace talks unless the United States unconditionally halted bombing and all other acts of war against North Vietnam.

April 15: Massive antiwar demonstrations take place throughout the United States. 100,000 antiwar protesters rally in New York.

April 20: U.S. planes bomb two power plants in Hanoi for the first time.

April 24: U.S. planes attack two North Vietnamese MIG bases for the first time.

May 1: Ellsworth Bunker replaces Henry Cabot Lodge as U.S. ambassador in South Vietnam.

May 13: Premier Ky announces he might respond "militarily" if a civilian whose policies he disagreed with is elected president.

May 15–23: U.S. ground forces just south of the DMZ come under heavy fire, as Marine positions between Dong Ha and Con Thien are attacked by North Vietnamese artillery. More than 100 Americans are killed or wounded during heavy fighting along the DMZ.

June 2: In Operation Union II, the 5th Marines in Quong Tin Province undertake a fierce battle with two North Vietnamese regiments that ends in bunker-to-bunker fighting.

June 22: A 130-man company of the 173rd U.S. Airborne Brigade is virtually wiped out by a

The strain of constant patrolling and combat shows on the face of this Marine from Company F, 2nd Battalion, 7th Marines. Courtesy of the National Archives.

North Vietnamese ambush near Dak To, Kontum Province, 28 miles northeast of Saigon. Eighty Americans are killed and 34 wounded, with 106 North Vietnamese fatal casualties.

June 30: Under pressure from other military leaders, Ky withdraws from the presidential race and agrees to run as vice-presidential candidate with Thieu.

July 2–14: B and C companies of the 9th Marines are heavily attacked, with serious losses, near Con Thien. 159 Americans are killed, 45 wounded. North Vietnamese losses are estimated at 1,301 dead.

July 23: In a five-hour battle, the U.S. 4th Infantry Division virtually wipes out a North Vietnamese company four miles south of Ducco in the Central Highlands. North Vietnamese forces lose at least 148 of their 400-man force.

August 13–19: U.S. B-52s carry out raids against the southern part of North Vietnam. The bombings are directed against North Vietnamese troops and installations in the DMZ and in the sector just north of the buffer.

August 31: The Senate Preparedness Investigating Committee calls unanimously for intensification of the bombing against North Vietnam and closing the port of Haiphong.

September 3: Thieu-Ky slate is elected, with 35% of the vote.

September 4–7: In a fierce four-day battle in the Queson Valley, 25 miles south of Danang, 114 men of the U.S. 5th Marine Regiment are killed; there are 376 North Vietnamese casualties.

September 11: U.S. jets carry out heavy raids on Haiphong and its suburbs in a major effort to isolate the port area from the rest of the country.

September 29: President Johnson, in a televised speech in San Antonio, Texas, announces that the United States will stop bombing in exchange for "productive discussions."

September: Base at Khe Sanh established as a potential launch point for ground operations to cut the Ho Chi Minh Trail.

October 12–14: U.S. Navy planes attack Haiphong shipyards and U.S. officials report heavy damage, claiming direct hits on drydocks west of the city.

October 21–23: More than 50,000 antiwar protesters participate in massive demonstrations in Washington, including an orderly procession around the Pentagon. A force of 10,000 troops surrounds the Defense Department.

November 3–23: One of the bloodiest and most sustained battles of the war is fought by U.S. and North Vietnamese troops in the Central Highlands around Dak To. In the 19 days of fighting, North Vietnamese fatalities are estimated at 1,455 while 285 U.S. men are killed, 985 wounded and 18 missing.

November 21: Gen. William Westmoreland, in a speech at the National Press Club, says the war has reached the point "when the end begins to come into view."

November 29: President Johnson announces Robert McNamara will resign as secretary of defense to become president of the World Bank.

December 21–22: U.S. forces launch a drive in and around the DMZ to thwart plans for what Hanoi calls "the winter-spring offensive." About 1,000 Marines land by boat and helicopter along the coast of Quang Ngai Province and exchange fire with entrenched communist forces.

December 30: South Vietnam announces a 36-hour New Year's truce. A Vietcong cease-fire also goes into effect.

December 31: 485,600 U.S. military personnel are now in Vietnam. 9,377 have been killed in action and 62,024 wounded in 1967. A total of 16,021 U.S. military have been killed in action and 99,762 wounded since 1961.

South Vietnamese forces have been increased to 798,000; 60,428 SVNAF have been killed in action to date.

EYEWITNESS TESTIMONY

If we are to reach an acceptable military decision in Vietnam, we must not permit our operational tactics to reflect the reticence which currently characterizes some bodies of public and official opinion. Our ground forces must take the field on long term, sustained combat operations. We must be prepared to accept heavier casualties in our initial operations and not permit our hesitance to take greater losses to inhibit our tactical aggressiveness. If greater hardships are accepted now we will, in the long run, achieve a military success sooner and at less overall cost in lives and money.

Admiral Ulysses S. Grant, USN, to Generals
William C. Westmoreland and Earle Wheeler,
message of January 3, 1967, in Gravel's The
Pentagon Papers *(1971).*

I lost track of the days after awhile. Each day was the same as the ones either side of it: you walked all day, up hills and down hills and between hills and across flooded uncultivated overgrown fields and through thickets and forests and wild meadows; and sometimes it rained and sometimes it didn't; and at night you took off your boots and burned the leeches from your feet and legs with a cigarette, and then you put up your one-man poncho tent and dug your fighting hole and tried to sleep for a few hours; and the next day you did it all over again.

Corporal William Ehrhart, USMC, recalls a
1967 patrol, in Vietnam-Perkasie: A Combat
Marine Memoir *(1983).*

Though I walk through the Valley of Death, I will fear no evil—because I'm the meanest mother in the valley.

U.S. infantrymen, saying of 1967, in Wintle's
The Dictionary of War Quotations *(1989).*

How many years? What I used to tell our friends was that the younger generation will fight better than we—even kids just so high. They are preparing themselves. That's the situation . . . How many years the war goes on depends on you and not on us.

Premier Pham Van Dong, North Vietnam,
statement of January 3, 1967, in The New
York Times *(January 4, 1967).*

At times the government had been penetrated all the way from the palace down to small units in the field. When I first visited the 25th ARVN Division headquarters at Duc Hoa, the division commander would discuss only trivial matters in the office; he took me outside well away from any building, with only the two of us present. Here he explained that he strongly suspected that his own Division G-2 (intelligence officer) was a Viet Cong agent; thus he did not dare discuss operational matters in his own command post.

General Bruce Palmer Jr., USA, recalls 1967,
in The 25-Year War: America's Military
Role in Vietnam *(1984).*

We used the most sophisticated electronic measures known to keep from killing civilians with our bombs. Our gear cross-check and double-check everything an airplane does up North.

Anonymous U.S. government official, state-
ment of January 7, 1967, in The New York
Times *(January 8, 1967).*

In the children's ward of the Qui Nhon province hospital I saw for the first time what napalm does. A child of seven, the size of our four-year-old, lay in the cot by the door. Napalm had burned his face and back and one hand. The burned skin looked like swollen, raw meat; the fingers of his hand were stretched out, burned rigid. A scrap of cheesecloth covered him, for weight is intolerable, but so is air.

Martha Gelhorn, journalist, Ladies Home
Journal *article of January 1967.*

Keeping low, the men I was with ran single file out into the center of the little plot, and then, spotting a low wall of brushes on the side of the plot they had just left, ran back there for cover and filed along the edges of the bushes toward several soldiers who had landed a little while before them. For a minute, there was a silence. Suddenly a single helicopter came clattering overhead at about a hundred and fifty feet, squawking Vietnamese from two stubby speakers that struck out, winglike, from the thinnest part of the fuselage, near the tail. The message which the American soldiers could not understand, went, "Attention, people of Ben Suc! You are surrounded by Republic of South Vietnam and Allied Forces. Do not run away or you'll be shot as V.C. Stay in your homes and wait for further instructions."

Jonathan Schell, journalist, with a joint surprise assault on a South Vietnamese village in 1967, in The Village of Ben Suc *(1967).*

Sixteen years ago we and others stopped another kind of aggression—this time it was in Korea. Imagine how different Asia might be today if we had failed to act when the Communist army of North Korea marched south. The Asia of tomorrow will be far different because we have said in Vietnam, as we said 16 years ago in Korea: "This far and no further."

President Lyndon Johnson, to Congress, State of the Union address of January 16, 1967, in Public Papers of the Presidents of the United States.

The guys on our track are a strange mixture, but they know their business. Sciosia talks all the time about his girl, his mother, his home. Zerman never lets you forget he went to college; it's always what he and the other guys did at the dorm, or the great proms he attended, etc. Christensen is just a down-to-earth soldier who doesn't seem to give a damn about anything but driving his track. I'm the only new replacement, but this battalion only arrived ten days before we did, so they haven't had too much experience with Charlie yet.

Pfc. David Parks, USA, diary entry of January 12, 1967, in G.I. Diary *(1968).*

We have to get all of our water out of streams, ponds, rice paddies or anything available. We have to put purification tablets in the canteens so we can drink it. I sure wish we could see our enemy. We have to stand guard every night. I hope you can read this as I borrowed some paper and a pen and am using a C-ration box for a table.

I guess I won't get any mail for about two more weeks. It is going to be a long 12 months. I wish I could be home so bad but that's life I guess. Well this all the paper I have so I better go. Wish I could be with you all. Tell everybody hello and that I'm trying my best to make it back.

Pfc. Gary Murtha, USMC, to his mother, letter of January 13, 1967, in Timefighter *(1985).*

Tonight was dark, a velvety crumbling dark, no firing, no earth-lighting flares swinging from their parachutes. No, it was dark and it was quiet. Once in a while a searchlight would stab through, waggle and go out. There are always lights on a dark night even if our eyes have to invent them. But out on the upland thick with small trees and elephant grass taller than a man, there were really lights, perhaps the glow of a family lantern. When you look at such a light steadily it begins to move erratically, it makes spirals and little dives and sometimes disappears entirely.

Author John Steinbeck, article of January 28, 1967, in (Long Island) Newsday.

It would be unthinkable for us to leave Vietnam on any terms except those which are entirely honorable. By going in, we made a direct issue with the Communists not only in South Vietnam but also in all Southeast Asia. We cannot back out now.

Senator John Stennis (D–Miss.), statement in U.S. News & World Report *(January 23, 1967).*

We have made one proposal after the other. We would like to have a cease-fire. We would be very glad to stop our bombing, as we have on two previous occasions, if we could have any indication of reciprocal action.

President Johnson, to press conference of February 2, 1967, in Public Papers of the Presidents of the United States.

I am prepared to order a cessation of the bombing against your country and the stopping of further augmentation of US forces in South Vietnam as soon as I am assured that infiltration into South Vietnam by land and by sea has stopped. These acts of restraint on both sides would, I believe, make it possible for us to conduct serious and private discussions leading toward an early peace.

President Johnson, to President Ho Chi Minh, secret letter of February 8, 1967, in Gravel's The Pentagon Papers.

If the U.S. Government really wants these talks, it must first of all stop unconditionally its bombing raids and all other acts of aggression against the D.R.V. It is only after the unconditional cessation of the U.S. bombing raids and all other acts of war against the D.R.V. that the D.R.V. and the United States would enter into talks and discuss questions concerning the two sides.

The Vietnamese people will never submit to force, they will never accept talks under the threat of bombs.

President Ho Chi Minh, to President Johnson, secret letter of February 10, 1967, in Gravel's The Pentagon Papers.

Immediately scores of screaming, hysterical peasants jumped on me. Some held me while others started beating me with hoes, rakes, and rifle butts and tearing off my clothes and survival equipment . . . One old peasant woman in particular got my attention immediately. Standing about ten feet away and dipping her hand into a slimy rice paddy, she was coming up with great globs of mud and throwing them at me—and she wasn't missing. She could have made a first-class pitcher on any major league team . . . They had been bombed by our aircraft for a long time; they had their homes destroyed, their crops and animals destroyed, and some of their family killed. It was no wonder that they were very angry . . . the military, while they hated us every bit as intensely, had been instructed very carefully on how important POWs were for information and especially as barter items for a peace treaty. Their orders were to capture us alive and keep us alive—just barely.

Lieutenant Colonel Jay Jansen, USAF pilot and POW (1967–1973), recalls his capture on February 18, 1967, in Six Years in Hell *(1974).*

The VC are hiding somewhere, just yards away. I know that I have to keep busy snapping pictures and taking notes. Otherwise I'll start worrying about the bullets that occasionally whine out of the bamboo. Giant red ants fall from the trees onto our necks; and their sting is supposed to drive a man mad.

Francois Sully, journalist, on patrol with the U.S. Army's First Cavalry Division during Operation Junction City, *notebook entry of February 1967, in* Newsweek *article of March 6, 1967.*

. . . now the chopper which can be heard in the background is probably our supply chopper—it's coming in—we have no supplies since yesterday and no water since yesterday and after a second day of march everybody much is pretty short—I kept my water down to the end so I've still got some water left and part of a C-ration and tomorrow we're going to get resupplied. So—everybody now cleans his weapons and Captain files his report via radio and another day has gone by on The Street Without Joy . . . first in the afternoon about 4:30—shadows are lengthening and we've reached one of our phase lines after the fire fight and it smells bad—meaning it's a little bit suspicious . . . Could be an amb . . .

Bernard Fall, author and journalist, with a U.S. Marine platoon north of Hue, along Route 4 ("Street Without Joy"), tape-recorded report of February 21, 1967, in Last Reflections on a War *(1967). [Fall was killed by a Vietcong land mine while filing this report.]*

Now as to bombing civilians, I would simply say that we are making an effort that is unprecedented in the history of warfare to be sure that we do not. It is our policy to bomb military targets only . . .

We hasten to add, however, that we recognize, and we regret, that some people, even after warning, are living and working in the vicinity of military targets and they have suffered.

President Johnson, to a joint session of the Tennessee State Legislature, speech of March 15, 1967, in Public Papers of the Presidents of the United States.

We can knock this off in a year or two at the most if we intensify and accelerate the war. We could use several more divisions . . . We could bomb North Vietnam more effectively, and really cripple their lines of communication and war-supporting industry. My guess is that with between 500,000 and 700,000 men, we could break the back of the Communist main forces by 1968–69.

Anonymous U.S. Army general, statement in Newsweek *(March 27, 1967).*

It was an eerie scene. The mortar rounds kept pounding in, many of them landing on tanks and personnel carriers, and the surrounding darkness was red with tracer fire. Meantime, under cover of night, the Vietcong had advanced within 50 yards of the U.S. position, screaming "You die, American."

John Bethelson, journalist, on a firefight 30 miles north of Saigon, article of April 3, 1967, in Newsweek.

Old men and women would sit by the side of the trail saying, "Oh hello GI, hello GI." And they'd count and count. They'd tell the local VC cadre that 50 Americans just went that way. Before the GIs ever got to where they were going, the word had spread. Well, do you shoot an old man sitting by the side of the trail? Whether he's a trail watcher or not? Do you shoot him? My viewpoint is that I am an infantry soldier, I seek out, engage, close with, and destroy

A Vietcong prisoner awaits interrogation at the A-109 Special Forces detachment in Thuong Doc, 15 miles west of Da Nang on January 27, 1967. After interrogation, captured VCs were turned over to the ARVN, which frequently executed them. Photograph by Pfc. David Epstein, USA. Courtesy of the National Archives.

the enemy. The enemy is not an old man sitting by the side of the trail.
Infantryman Steve Hassna, USA, 101st Airborne Division, C Company (March 1967–March 1968), in Smith's The Short-Timer's Journal *(1980).*

Everyone is thinking of mortars. There is a bunker next to your tent, but it holds only five men and your cot is the farthest from the door. "Don't bother to go there—it'll be full," a Marine captain says. "Throw yourself in the ditch. It doesn't matter how wet and cold it is. Once those mortars start coming in, you'll never notice the chill or dampness."
David Reed, journalist, on spending a night with a U.S. Marine platoon along the DMZ in 1967, in Up Front in Vietnam *(1967).*

Somehow this madness must cease. I speak as a child of God and brother to the suffering poor of Vietnam and the poor of America who are paying the double price of smashed hopes at home and

death and corruption in Vietnam. I speak as a citizen of the world, for the world as it stands aghast at the path we have taken. I speak as an American to the leaders of my own nation. The great initiative in this war is ours. The initiative to stop must be ours.
Reverend Dr. Martin Luther King Jr., civil rights leader, sermon of April 4, 1967, to a congregation at Riverside Church in New York City, in Ramparts *(May 1967).*

Hell no, we won't go.
Antiwar slogan, 1967.

U.S.A. Love it or leave it.
Pro-war slogan, 1967.

Greenfield got it today. It was our first day on Operation Hammer, a search-and-destroy deal . . . There was a cracking sound to my left. I turned just in time to see blood gushing through a hole in Greenfield's helmet. He'd been hit and his head disappeared beneath the top of the track. I jumped down beside him, but Lt. Wyeth was already reaching for a bandage to try and stop the bleeding . . .

Well, that's the way it went. What a hell of a way to start a mission. Poor Greenfield. Just a few more inches to the left and it would have been me. Maybe tomorrow will be my day. Who knows? Only yesterday he was talking about the girl back home he wanted to marry. He was a simple guy. He wanted to be a carpenter.
Pfc. David Parks, USA, diary entry of April 6, 1967, in G.I. Diary.

Our company commander and our battalion and brigade commanders told us that there is no sense trying to fool ourselves, we are going for sure. The only thing that makes me mad is how do they expect you to tell your parents. They act as though it is an everyday experience, and that we should feel that way. I don't mind going, but there are some guys here who just won't make it, and I don't think they will make it out alive. Tell Mom I wished I could have told her myself, but I just didn't know how.
Spec. 4 Robert Devlin, USA, 71st Infantry Detachment (Long Range Reconnaisance Patrol), to his father, letter of April 18, 1967, in Edelman's Dear America: Letters Home from Vietnam *(1985).*

Yesterday I took all my crates to town with all my electronic equipment in them to be mailed out by the

Army. Only one footlocker-size wooden crate is coming to Ft. Worth, the others are being sent directly to Ft. Bragg since if I sent them home I would never be able to carry them on to Ft. Bragg without a car and large trailer.

Captain Gerald Brown, USA, to his mother, on preparing for his return home after completing his tour of duty, letter of May 4, 1967 in No Sad Songs *(1973). [Captain Brown was killed in a combat operation on May 10, 1967.]*

When the plane exploded, it looked like I could reach out and touch the sea. I was that close. I'm willing to bet I wasn't three miles from the water. A minute and a half by air from the water. I could have touched it. I could smell it.

There was only one tree down there, too; one tree in a whole twelve-square mile area and I landed on it. Not a mark on me. There were two persons waiting for me that I could see, a very old guy and a younger one probably anywhere from 18 to 22; the old guy, jeez, he was 102.

The young guy had a machete. I got out of the chute sling; they didn't say anything and I didn't have anything to say. I was scared shitless. They were scared shitless, too. All of us standing there scared shitless.

Captain Richard Stratton, USAF pilot and POW (1967–1973) in Blakey's Prisoner of War: The Survival of Commander Richard Stratton *(1978).*

. . . a fellow at the end of the [prison] building I was in tapped a message through the wall to me. It said, "Lyndon Johnson is going to stop the bombing in North Vietnam tomorrow in order to make sure Hubert Humphrey gets elected president of the United States." My arms weren't working too well at the time, otherwise I would have put my fist through the wall. I was so outraged.

Colonel George E. "Bud" Day, USAF pilot and POW (1967–1973), in the U.S. Defense Information School's Vietnam: 10 Years Later *(1983).*

During the daily interrogations, after I had listened to two tapes, they wanted me to make similar tapes, denouncing the war. They insisted I write letters to the other members of my squadron. They wanted me to write a letter to Senator Fulbright. They wanted a signed confession, admitting I was a war criminal. They wanted to know how many and what kind of missions I had flown. They wanted the names of my squadron's pilots. Regularly, my answers were unsatisfactory. Just as regularly, I was put through the Ropes. After the twelfth time it was stupid to count the number of times Goose [North Vietnamese Prison Guard] triggered an agonizing cry of pain. At the end of a week of murderous torture they wanted me to write out a statement, telling the world the North Vietnamese were lenient and humane in their treatment of Americans. I refused.

Lieutenant Colonel John Arthur Dramesi, USAF pilot and POW (1967–1973), recalls the North Vietnamese POW camp of Hoa Lo (dubbed the "Hanoi Hilton" by American POWs) in 1967, in Code of Honor *(1975).*

Punishment was meted out almost capriciously. One one occasion they told me I would have to meet

North Vietnamese postage stamp depicting American prisoners of war, 1967. Courtesy of the National Archives.

with an unspecified delegation. When I refused to go, guessing it was another propaganda stunt, they again took me to the Carriage Shed, so named because it had swing doors through which they used to haul a wagon. There they made me kneel with my arms extended straight up. I must have knelt for four hours, during which the guard beat me persistently, especially when I had to drop my arms through sheer fatigue. Then they roped my ankles together and bound my arms behind my back. For two days I lay on the concrete, defenseless against the guard who burst in half a dozen times each day to punch me around.

Lt. (j.g.) Everett Alvarez Jr., USN pilot and POW (August 5, 1965 to 1973, first American pilot held captive), on the "Hanoi Hilton," in Alvarez and Pitch's Chained Eagle *(1989).*

Sheer desolation permeated the miserable dark cell I lived in twenty-four hours a day. I was absolutely convinced I would never get to leave that cell until the war was over. And I had no idea when that would be. What I was going through would continue for as long as I could think. I was not scared of anything they would put me through because I felt they had already done their worst. But I was terrified because I could not get rid of the panic. I would go to sleep only after I was completely exhausted, then awaken during the night—at twelve, two, three—and immediately jump up and start running. The instant I awakened, the shock of it would hit me—there I was, in the same place where I had gone to sleep. It was always going to be that way—until the end of the war.

Lieutenanat Colonel Robinson Risner, USAF pilot and POW (1965–1973), on his solitary confinement at the "Hanoi Hilton" in 1967, in Passing of the Night *(1973).*

We are being pulled step by step into a jungle quicksand that may claim our sons and that may claim sons of Asia for years to come—a fearful pain which our ablest generals have warned against for decades. "Anyone who commits American forces to a land war in Asia," said the late General Douglas MacArthur "ought to have his head examined."

Freedom is worth fighting for, but it cannot be achieved through an alliance with unpopular forces abroad that deny freedom.

Senator George McGovern (D–S.D.), to the U.S. Senate, speech of April 25, 1967.

Backed at home by resolve, confidence, patience, determination, and continued support, we will prevail in Vietnam over the communist aggressor.

General William C. Westmoreland, to a joint session of Congress, speech of April 28, 1967.

. . . we would continue to lose men to booby traps, and the people in the village who pretended not to know anything about these booby traps walked the same trails that we did day after day without stepping on them, it became obvious that these people were well informed by the VC where the booby traps were.

Corpsman Douglas Anderson, USMC, in Santoli's Everything We Had *(1981).*

We'd get through the wire in the black night and come into a village. There was always the smell of burning bamboo mixed with incense when we got near a village. We would walk down a street that might be a bustling marketplace in the daytime, but at night it would be empty. The grass doors on the hootches would be closed, but I could see through the wide crack. Inside the people would be sitting, and their heads would jerk around and look into the darkness where a little noise we had made had given us away. I could see the fear etched deeply in their faces. They didn't know which side was out there.

Pfc Jim Boros, USA, First Squadron, 9th Cavalry, in 1967, in Brennan's Headhunters *(1987).*

We left with 73 men in our platoon and came back with 19 . . . You know what killed most of us? Our own rifle.

Before we left Okinawa, we were all issued this new rifle, the M–16. Practically everyone of our dead was found with his rifle torn down next to him where he had been trying to fix it.

There was a newspaperwoman with us photographing all this, and the Pentagon found out about it and won't let her publish the pictures.

They say they don't want to get the American people upset. Isn't that a laugh.

Anonymous infantryman, USMC, to his family, letter of 1967, in U.S. News & World Report *(June 5, 1967).*

We don't have a declaration of war because the President doesn't dare to recommend one. And I maintain that if you can't justify a war declaration, then you can't justify the war.

Senator Wayne Morse (D–Ore.), statement in U.S. News & World Report *(May 22, 1967).*

The signers of this declaration, both Democrats and Republicans, share the conviction that the tragic war in Vietnam should be ended by negotiation of a mutually acceptable settlement. However, in the absence of such a settlement, we remain steadfastly opposed to any unilateral withdrawal of American troops from South Vietnam.

Senator Frank Church (D–Idaho), author of ''A Plea for Realism,'' declaration of May 17, 1967, in The New York Times *(May 18, 1967). [Signed by 16 senators, including Church, John Sherman Cooper, Robert Kennedy, George McGovern and Wayne Morse.]*

I believe that every Congressman and most of the Senators knew what that [Tonkin Gulf] resolution said. That resolution authorized the President—and expressed the Congress's willingness to go along with the President—to do whatever was necessary to deter aggression . . .

We think we are well within the grounds of our constitutional responsibility. We think we are well within the rights of what the Congress said in its resolution.

The remedy is there if we have acted unwisely or improperly.

President Johnson, to a news conference of August 18, 1967, in Public Papers of the Presidents of the United States.

I don't want to make any specific prediction, although I could say that within a year and a half we should have achieved enough success so that we could then consider the question of bringing American troops home.

General Harold K. Johnson, U.S. Army chief of staff, statement in U.S. News & World Report *(September 11, 1967).*

Homeward bound. Went across the thirteenth and going home on the thirteenth. Must be my lucky number. The white guy who sold me my ticket at the airport gave me some really dirty looks. He pitched my ticket at me like I was dirt. There is nothing like the army to make you conscious of such things. The ticket seller reminded me of how some of my white officers treated me. Well, I'm a Negro and I'm back home where color makes the difference . . . Thought I'd left all my problems behind. Hell, the new ones will just have to wait. I'm going to enjoy myself for a few days—just knowing Charlie won't be around to wake me up in the morning.

Pfc. David Parks, USA, diary entry of September 13, 1967, in G.I. Diary.

As we have told Hanoi time and time and time again, the heart of the matter is really this: The United States is willing to stop all aerial and naval bombardment of North Vietnam when this will lead promptly to productive discussions. We, of course, assume that while discussions proceed, North Vietnam would not take advantage of the bombing cessation or limitation.

But Hanoi has not accepted any of these proposals.

So it is by Hanoi's choice and not ours, and not the rest of the world's—that the war continues.

President Johnson, to the National Legislative Conference in San Antonio, speech of September 29, 1967, in Public Papers of the Presidents of the United States.

I know—I know probably as well as any man, save those who are fighting for us out there tonight, at this very hour—that it is a rough road to travel. But the road, I think, does lead to a free Asia—and the road does lead, I think, to a freer and a happier and a more secure United States.

I believe the American public will follow its course—not blithely, not cheerfully—for they all lament the waste of war; but they will follow it with a firm determination, now that we have begun it, to see it through all the way.

President Johnson, to a Democratic Party dinner in Washington, D.C., speech of October 7, 1967, in Public Papers of the Presidents of the United States.

. . . sometimes right in the middle of things, you think about what's going on back home. It was about two months ago, I guess, when I was out on operations. We ran into some enemy and two of our tanks got hit. I had a buddy from my company who got his leg blowed off him and another one got shot in the stomach with a 30-caliber machine gun. Seeing that happen right in front of me and thinking about people complaining back in the states doesn't seem to add up somehow.

Corporal Jerry Watson, USA, statement in the National Review *(November 28, 1967).*

First Division Marines debark from a UH-34D helicopter in the early morning of October 11, 1967, to begin Operation Medina. This search-and-destroy operation was a joint U.S.-South Vietnamese effort conducted in an area 12 miles south of Quang Tri city. Courtesy of the National Archives.

This is not Johnson's war. This is America's war. If I drop dead tomorrow, this war will still be with you.

President Johnson, to Washington Post *White House correspondent Chalmers Roberts, statement of October 13, 1967, in* Public Papers of the Presidents of the United States.

We can't sustain a shooting war on a non-emotional basis. Our support in this country seems to be slipping with respect to the war. Young people, subject to draft, need some stirring up. We should shift emphasis as to the reasons for our involvement—away from helping South Vietnamese to helping ourselves and the free world to combat the "new" Communist technique of conquest by infiltration and subversion. We should take or make an early opportunity to state, emphatically, that we're going to see this through to a successful conclusion . . . This country has never left the field of battle in abject surrender of cause for which it fought. We shall not do so now.

Supreme Court Associate Justice Abe Fortas, to President Johnson, letter of October 14, 1967, in Berman's Lyndon Johnson's War *(1989).*

At point you were walking alone. You walked fifteen meters ahead of the rest of the squad. You looked for signs of a booby trap or an ambush. Often you were the one who tripped the booby trap or walked into the barrel of Charlie's rifle before the enemy opened up the ambush. In a 15-second fire fight, the life expectancy of the point man was 0.8 seconds. Short-timers, men with just a few months left before they were to return home, avoided the point. So point fell to those less experienced or with less time in country . . . Stones or sticks piled off the trail in a certain way indicated a booby trap or an ambush. A piece of green plastic meant a booby trap. I'd walked point now for over twelve weeks. I felt good out in front. I trusted my instincts and I was slow and careful. I'd found several booby traps before and, more important, the others trusted me.

Pfc. Richard Eilert, USMC, recalls 1967 in For Self and Country *(1983).*

Though I walk through the valley of the shadow of Death, I fear no evil, because I'm the meanest son of a bitch in the valley.

Inscription on a grunt's (U.S. infantryman) flak jacket, 1967.

One moment you engage in a heart-to-heart conversation with a young man and the next you write his parents a letter expressing your regrets about the untimely passing of their courageous son. Another witnesses the deaths of four of his buddies within the space of a few minutes. He escapes with minor wounds to live another day and to pose the heart-rending question, "Why?" He waits with the look of bewildered pain for my answer. These and hundreds of other similar questions and experiences pierce into the flexible commentary of my challenging hours of service to the men I love and deeply respect.

Chaplain Raymond Johnson, USN, to his wife, letter of 1967, in Postmark: Mekong Delta *(1968).*

I met this kid from Miles City, Montana, who read the *Stars and Stripes* every day, checking the casualty lists to see if by some chance anybody from his town had been killed. He didn't even know if there was anyone else from Miles City in Vietnam, but he checked anyway because he knew for sure that if there was someone else and they got killed, he would be all right. "I mean, can you just see two guys from a raggedy-ass town like Miles City getting killed in Vietnam?" he said.

Michael Herr, journalist, report of 1967, in Dispatches *(1977).*

We are convinced that this war which Lyndon Johnson is waging is disastrous to our country in every way, and that we, the protesters, are the ones who may help to save our country if we can persuade enough of our fellow citizens to think and vote as we do.

Dr. Benjamin Spock, antiwar activist, to a rally at the Lincoln Memorial in Washington, D.C., speech of October 21, 1967, in The New York Times *(October 22, 1967).*

My name is Gary Rader, I'm twenty-three years Company B hold your line. Nobody comes, nobody goes. I was in the Special Forces Reserve Company B hold your line and I quit and I want nobody comes nobody goes I want to tell you what led me up to

that Company hold your line what led me up to that decision nobody comes nobody goes we will be heard . . .

Gary Rader, antiwar protester and former Army Green Beret, to U.S. troops surrounding the Pentagon, at antiwar demonstration on October 21, 1967, in Zaroulis and Sullivan's Who Spoke Up? *(1984).*

Make Love Not War.

Chant by antiwar protesters at a demonstration in Washington, D.C., October 21–23, 1967.

A girl confronted a soldier, "Why, why why?" she asked. "We're just like you. You're like us. It's them," she said pointing to the Pentagon. She brought her

Members of the military police keep back antiwar protesters during their "sit-in" at the Mall Entrance to the Pentagon on October 21, 1967. Courtesy of the National Archives.

two fingers to her mouth, kissed them and touched the soldier's lips. Four soldiers grabbed her and dragged her away, under arrest. The soldier she had spoken to tried to tell them she hadn't hurt him.

Norman Mailer, author, on the antiwar demonstration outside the Pentagon on October 22, 1967, in Armies of the Night *(1968).*

Support Our G.I.'s . . . Bring Them Home Now.

Antiwar protestors, banner-borne message carried October 21–23, 1967, at a demonstration in Washington, D.C.

Wouldn't it be wonderful right now to be able to walk down a freshly plowed furrow behind a tractor? One never forgets the smell. I wonder whether when I get home I will remember what size plates to put in the planter box, or if I will be able to set it right the first time.

One night we got to arguing while sitting around the foxhole. Someone asked, "Would you shoot a woman if you had to?" Well, I don't know, guess it would be different if she had a weapon. I don't really know, would you?

Captain James Landing, USA, to the editor of Farm Journal, *letter of October 1967.*

We went on a C.A. (combat assault) the other day—to another area of the same valley I've been in all along. It's really kinda exciting. Helicopters landed in our company perimeter, atop a hill, in waves of three. Each helicopter loads up seven guys and flies to the assault area or LZ (landing zone). I was in the second wave (seven waves in all). The choppers fly in low and fast—at the last minute they slow down and move over the LZ about six feet above the ground. That's when we jump out (much fun). No shots were fired—no one hurt, one fellow lost his pride in a water buffalo dropping (I should say pile). Please don't worry about me over here (sure is safer than freeways) . . .

The jar of Tang you sent me got smashed in the mail—damn. How about a plastic container of bourbon, Kool-Aid (presweetened), self-sealing envelopes (using borrowed one now) and some canned fruit?

Gotta go now—heading out on another patrol— really, they're quite boring!!

I'm pretty dirty but healthy . . .

Pfc. James Rowe Jr., USA, First Cavalry (Airmobile), to his family, letter of November 16, 1967, in Prescott's Love to All, Jim *(1989).*

There was another guy in our unit who had made it known that he was a card-carrying Ku Klux Klan member. That pissed a lot of us off, 'cause we had gotten real tight. We didn't have racial incidents like what was happening in the rear area, 'cause we had to depend on each other. We were always in the bush.

Well, we got out into a fire fight, and Mr. Ku Klux Klan got his little ass trapped. We were goin' across the rice paddies, and Charlies just start shootin'. And he jumped in the rice paddy while everybody else kind of backtracked.

So we laid down a base of fire to cover him. But he was just immobile. He froze. And a brother went out there and got him and dragged him back. Later on, he said that action had changed his perception of what black people were about.

Combat Engineer Harold "Lightbulb" Bryant, USA, First Cavalry Division, An Khe, in Terry's Bloods: An Oral History of the Vietnam War by Black Veterans *(1984).*

I'd heard the MACV [Military Assistance Command-Vietnam] briefings referred to as the "5 O'Clock Follies," but I went in with an open mind. A multipaged release was given out. Then a major stepped to a microphone and started reading what sounded like stock quotations. He'd mention an operation and then refer the assembled newsmen to item so and so on page such and such. The information was far from complete, and I got the feeling this was the way MACV wanted it. As a G.I. I could understand the classification problems, but to newsmen trying to make a living the rules had to hurt.

Information Specialist Larry Hughes, USA, on attending a military press briefing in 1967, in You Can See a Lot Standing Under a Flare in the Republic of Vietnam: My Year at War *(1969).*

The eyes of the men who were left were staring and glazed. All you could read in them was total exhaustion and the agonizing fear of death. Their uniforms hung in tatters on their bodies. The bulletproof waistcoats were the only things that had stood up to the ravages of the undergrowth. Darkness fell and our teeth chattered with cold. All through the night the F-100s circled over Hill 875 making an unholy, ear-splitting din. The perimeter was lit up like daylight. The napalm had set entire hillsides ablaze and the jungle burned and crackled around us.

Peter Scholl-Latour, journalist, on the battle for Hill 875 in the Central Highlands in November 1967, in Death in the Rice Fields: An Eyewitness Account of Vietnam's Three Wars, 1945–1979 *(1979).*

The stretchers started coming down the hill past me once more. On one was a G.I., dead of a hideous wound at chest and shoulder level; I recognized him as a tall, red-haired machine gunner I had walked behind on the lower slope. Scattered all over the hill were vestiges of the battle, abandoned packs, charred helmets and scraps of uniform, both American and North Vietnamese. Lying outside one bunker was a gray-green object which puzzled me. I looked more closely, and a wave of horror suddenly hit me. It was a man's shoulder and the stump of an arm. Nearby was a charred boot with black burnt flesh attached.

Edward Behr, journalist, on the capture of Hill 875 by the 173rd Airborne during the battle around Dak To in the Central Highlands in November 1967, in Newsweek *(December 14, 1967).*

My decision to challenge the President's position, and the administration's position, has been strengthened by recent announcements out of the administration—the evident intention to intensify the war in Vietnam and, on the other hand, the absence of any positive indications or suggestions for a compromise or for a negotiated political settlement. I am concerned that the administration seems to have set no limits to the price that it is willing to pay for a military victory . . . there is growing evidence of a deepening moral crisis in America; discontent and frustration, and a disposition to take extra-legal—if not illegal—action to manifest protest. I am hopeful that this challenge I am making . . . may alleviate to at least some degree this sense of political helplessness, and restore to many people a belief in the process of American politics and American government.

Senator Eugene McCarthy (D–Minn.), Democratic presidential primary candidate, speech to a Washington, D.C. press conference of November 30, 1967, in The Year of the People *(1969).*

On the first stretcher lay a boy whom, earlier in the day, any coach would have wanted as a tackle

This South Vietnamese soldier is engrossed in his thoughts moments before parachuting from an Air Force C-130 Hercules into a Vietcong stronghold in the Mekong Delta in December 1967. Courtesy of the National Archives.

or a defensive end. But now, as he lay on his back, his left thigh pointed skyward and ended in a red brown, meaty mass of twisted ligaments, jellylike muscle, blood clots, and long bony splinters. There was no knee, and parts of the lower leg hung loosely by skin strips and fascial strings. A tourniquet had been placed around his thigh, and a corpsman was cutting through the strips of tissue with shears to remove the unviable dangling calf. Lying separately on the stretcher was a boot from which the lower leg still protruded.

Lieutenant John Parrish, USMC doctor, on first arriving at a triage center in Phu Bai in 1967, in 12, 20 & 5: A Doctor's Year in Vietnam *(1972).*

In one big bang they have taken it all from me, in one clean sweep, and now I am in this place around all the others like me, and though I keep trying not to feel sorry for myself, I want to cry. There is no shortcut around this thing. It is too soon to die even for a man who has died once already.

I try to keep telling myself it is good to still be alive, to be back home. I remember thinking on the ambulance ride to the hospital that this was the Bronx, the place where Yankee Stadium was, where Mickey Mantle played. I think I realized then also that my feet would never touch the stadium grass; I would never play a game in that place.

Sergeant Ron Kovic, USMC, on being severely wounded in action in 1967, in Born on the Fourth of July *(1976).*

The rain drums hard on the roof of your tent. The monsoons have begun. It has rained steadily for ten days. There is a sudden splash on the end of the footlocker you are sitting on. A leak. You move to your cot to read the letters.

You lie on your back on the cot and stare at the gray sheets of water falling outside. The rain is coming straight down and you have rolled up the sides of the tent to get as much air as you can. You feel the long ridges of the rubber mattress pressing into your back . . . You remember talking with Peggy about the future and what you would do. You remember how soft the touch of her hand was and how her hair used to get in the way when you kissed. She would brush it aside and smile at you and laugh softly. And how blue her eyes were.

Captain Charles Coe, USMC, on patrol in 1967, in Young Man in Vietnam *(1968).*

We have reached an important point where the end comes into view.

General William C. Westmoreland, to the National Press Club in Washington, D.C., speech of November 21, 1967, in Porter's Vietnam: A History in Documents *(1981).*

You could tell the living from the dead not from their faces, all gray with the agony, but because the living could move. The living dived unashamedly for cover of tiny bunkers; the wounded crawled to the inhospitable shelter of blasted trees.

Peter Arnett, journalist, on the battle for Hill 875, at Dak To in the Central Highlands, Associated Press dispatch of November 22, 1967.

The pendulum has swung over to the other side, so that the well-motivated, the well-led and the capable territorial units now are in the majority.

I feel that the South Vietnamese soldier is a talented, heroic little soldier. He is not as big and he is not as strong and he cannot carry as much as the average American. But for his size and his capability, I repeat, he is a talented and heroic little fighter.

General Creighton Abrams, USA, deputy commander in Vietnam, statement in U.S. News & World Report *(December 4, 1967).*

Thanks a lot for the Christmas presents. They were great. Yesterday I went up Thunder Road on a guarded truck convoy to see the Bob Hope USO Christmas show. It was really a good time and very moving. One of the girls started crying while she was singing "Silent Night" to us and got interrupted by a barrage of artillery going off nearby. If you see pictures of it I'll be sitting just to the left of two tanks with "Merry Christmas" painted on them. . . .

Pfc. John M.G. Brown, USA, First Aviation Battalion, to his family, letter of December 25, 1967, in Rice Paddy Grunt *(1986).*

I had never been away from home more than a week in my life. I knew I wasn't cut out for the

Pfc. Frank Bunton, USMC, tries to get into the Christmas spirit in spite of his surroundings, December 1967. Courtesy of the National Archives.

heroics I saw on "Combat," but I could work on trucks and cars. I was scared and confused. Three years. Three years ago I had been a sophomore in high school. It seemed long ago. Three years from now I should be making good money. God, I was scared. I didn't want to shoot anybody, and I didn't want anybody to shoot me. I had to make a decision soon, or not get my guaranteed army training . . . I called the recruiter. Could I at least stay home for the holidays? . . . I would have to go in December 30. I signed the papers. The agony was over. I didn't like the outcome, but the terrible question was answered.

John Ketwig, on enlisting in the U.S. Army in 1967, in And a Hard Rain Fell *(1985).*

7. The Tet Offensive: 1968

The Attack on Saigon

At 2:30 A.M. on January 30, 1968, a 19-man Vietcong suicide squad blasted a large hole in the wall surrounding the United States Embassy in Saigon and rushed into the courtyard of the compound. For the next six hours the guerrillas held a section of the embassy building until they were routed by an assault force of U.S. paratroopers, who landed by helicopter on the building's roof. Meanwhile, some 84,000 North Vietnamese and Vietcong forces moved toward their targets in South Vietnam's seven largest cities and attacked 30 provincial capitals ranging from the Mekong Delta to the DMZ. One of the largest and best coordinated assaults of the war, known as the Tet Offensive, was under way.

It had been customary during the war to observe a cease-fire during the Tet holiday, a celebration of the lunar new year in Vietnam. While reports had been received by American and South Vietnamese intelligence agencies that the NVA and Vietcong might take advantage of the holiday truce to launch an attack, intelligence officers of the U.S. military command regarded the captured documents as part of a propaganda campaign designed to boost the morale of communist troops. MACV (Military Assistance Command, Vietnam) simply did not believe the communists capable of synchronizing major attacks throughout South Vietnam. However, General Earle Wheeler, chairman of the Joint Chiefs of Staff, warned on December 18, 1967, that "it is entirely possible that there may be a Communist thrust similar to the desperate effort of the Germans in the Battle of the Bulge in World War II." Also, in a military briefing on January 15, 1968, General William Westmoreland foresaw "a sixty/forty chance" that the communists would launch a major assault of some kind before or around Tet. However, the beginning of the siege of Khe Sanh 10 days before Tet distracted the White House and possibly the military command.

The Tet Offensive sent instant shock waves across the United States. Early wire service reports exaggerated the success of the raid on the embassy; some even indicated that the Vietcong had occupied several floors of the building. ''What the hell is going on? I thought we were winning the war!'' the veteran newsman Walter Cronkite is said to have commented. Americans watched the battle of Saigon on television as U.S. and South Vietnamese soldiers tried to drive out the assailants. Scenes of dead bodies lying amid the rubble and exchanges of automatic gunfire brought the war into the living rooms of millions of Americans.

The communists made an assault on Saigon from the north, the west and the south. Four to five thousand local troops had infiltrated the city in the days just prior to Tet. Outside Saigon the communists formed a ring of fire. The Vietcong hit the giant U.S. and Vietnamese bases throughout the city. Their principal targets also included the presidential palace and the national radio station.

The Vietcong hoped to seize the station and broadcast tapes announcing the ''General Uprising'' and proclaiming the liberation of Saigon. Although they managed to blast their way into the compound, their plans were thwarted by a government technician who signaled to

General William Westmoreland talks with military personnel in the American embassy after an unsuccessful Vietcong attack during the Tet Offensive, January 31, 1968. Courtesy of the National Archives.

the crew at a transmitter 14 miles away to shut down the lines to the downtown studio. Several hours later a company of ARVN paratroopers arrived and shot the guerrillas as they fled.

Rocket and mortar fire thundered into Tan Son Nhut air base, the site of MACV headquarters and the U.S. 7th Air Force. Other major targets hit during the Tet Offensive included the South Vietnamese Joint General Staff headquarters, Navy headquarters, ARVN's Armored Command headquarters and Artillery Command headquarters. But in each case the attacks failed. After a week of intensive fighting the infiltrators were dislodged. By February 10 the offensive in Saigon was largely crushed.

THE BATTLE FOR HUE

Meanwhile, the most bitter fighting of the war continued to unfold in Hue, the former imperial capital of Vietnam, located halfway between Danang and the DMZ. The city was dominated by the massive Imperial Citadel of the Nguyen emperors, known for its elegant boulevards and pagodas. Hue was the most exotic city in Vietnam. Up until the Tet Offensive, Hue had been treated almost as an open city, for the Vietcong had regarded it with respect and hardly any fighting occurred within its borders.

At 3:40 A.M. on January 31, 1968, a barrage of rockets slammed into the Imperial Citadel, signaling the moment of attack for the communist troops who had been waiting outside the city. Communist forces invaded Hue from three directions, encountering little resistance from the ARVN division based there. They ran up the yellow-starred Vietcong flag atop the Citadel, after which their political cadres proceeded to initiate one of the worst bloodbaths of the war.

The communist planners had compiled two lists; one detailed 200 targets, including such installations as government bureaus, and the other list contained the names of civilian servants and army officers and nearly anybody else linked to the South Vietnamese regime. Immediately after seizing the city, Vietcong teams conducted house-to-house searches for these people.

During the weeks and months following the battle, South Vietnamese authorities and American soldiers discovered a series of shallow mass graves in and around the city of Hue containing the remains of 2,800 people. Many of the victims had been shot in the head or bludgeoned to death; others had apparently been buried alive. Saigon and U.S. propaganda blamed communist terrorism for the deaths, while some scholars suspect that a campaign of political warfare by the Saigon government may have been responsible.

The full story of what happened in Hue between January 31 and February 25, 1968, may never be known. But the preponderance of evidence, including the testimony of many survivors, indicates that the communist forces did in fact carry out systematic assassinations. Whenever communist forces took over a country village or hamlet, they usually eliminated key government personnel in order to undermine the authority of the GVN and remind the local population of the price of "collaboration."

The estimated 7,500-man assault force, consisting mostly of NLF regulars, entrenched itself behind the well-fortified walls of the Imperial Palace for nearly one month. After a few days of bitter fighting, U.S. and ARVN forces realized that it would require a great deal of force to drive the enemy from Hue. American commanders called in artillery strikes while helicopter gunships and tactical aircraft strafed and napalmed the enemy.

U.S. Marines accustomed to fighting in jungles and open rice fields had to learn the tactics of urban fighting on the spot. During the fight for the Citadel, as in the other battles for South Vietnam's towns and cities, television crews were present. Their overnight filmed transmissions brought the drama of the war into the homes of millions of Americans. A correspondent asks a Marine while he is firing from behind a stone wall, "Have you lost any friends?" The Marine pauses and then answers, "Quite a few. We lost one the other day. The whole thing stinks, really."

House-to-house assaults were necessary to drive out the entrenched North Vietnamese troops. "Four men cover the exits of a building, two men rush the building with grenades, while two men cover them with rifle fire," explained one Marine lieutenant colonel.

In many instances the Americans found it more expedient and less costly to the lives of the Marines to simply destroy buildings. Commanders in the field contended that they made every effort to limit the damage to Hue, but the street-to-street fighting did take its toll on the city. By the end of the second week of fighting, large sections of Hue had been reduced to rubble. The streets of the old city had shattered buildings, bullet-riddled walls and rotting corpses.

On February 24, the U.S. Army First Calvary Division linked up with the ARVN First Division at the walls of the Citadel. The ARVN troops overran the NLF forces along the south wall of the Citadel and secured the main flagpole at the Midway Gate of the Imperial Palace. They tore down the NLF flag and replaced it with the yellow-and-red banner of the Republic of Vietnam. The following day ARVN soldiers entered victoriously into the Imperial Palace, only to find that the enemy had fled during the night.

Both sides claimed victory in the battle for Hue. Communist forces were proud of their hold on the city for more than three weeks. The U.S. and ARVN command pointed to the communist losses of 5,000 killed and 89 captured. Nearly 500 U.S. and ARVN troops died in the bitter door-to-door fighting, artillery shelling and aerial bombardment.

The sure losers in the last major engagement of the Tet Offensive were the city and citizens of Hue. It was officially estimated that more than 50% of the city had been damaged or destroyed, leaving 100,000 civilians homeless out of a population of 140,000. Although eventually the houses and monuments would be repaired or restored, the old imperial capital would never again be the same.

THE SIEGE AT KHE SANH

As the Tet Offensive raged across South Vietnam, 3,500 U.S. Marines and 2,100 ARVN troops at the U.S. Marine base at Khe Sanh were pinned down in their bunkers and trenches by an incessant barrage of long-range artillery fire from surrounding NVA forces. The siege at Khe Sanh, a northern outpost located 14 miles below the DMZ and six miles from the Laotian border, had begun on January 21, when hundreds of mortar rounds, artillery shells and rockets slammed into the combat base, hitting its main ammunition dump and detonating 1,500 tons of explosives. For the next 77 days one of the most controversial battles of the war would be fought.

In the summer of 1967, General Westmoreland had made the decision to reinforce the Khe Sanh base as a potential jumping-off point for clandestine operations into Laos that would cut off the Ho Chi Minh Trail, a main enemy infiltration and supply route. While the decision to move into Laos was pending in Washington, the NVA began to build up its forces in the Khe Sanh area. By December 1967, U.S. intelligence reports indicated that between 20,000 and 40,000 NVA troops were within striking distance of Khe Sanh. Frustrated by years of chasing an elusive enemy, Westmoreland was pleased that finally the communists would be forced to engage in a set-piece battle and forced to stand and fight.

During the first week of January 1968, Westmoreland moved 6,000 Marines into the Khe Sanh area and began to effect his plan for overwhelming the enemy; code-named Operation Niagara, it would be one of the most concentrated applications of aerial firepower in the history of warfare. Two-thousand strategic and tactical aircraft were assembled to implement a campaign of round-the-clock bombardment.

Meanwhile in Washington, there were fears that the communists intended to reenact another Dien Bien Phu. President Johnson was so concerned with a repetition of the French defeat that he pored over Defense Department maps and aerial photos, read the latest cables from the war zone and met with his advisers on the Khe Sanh situation. In an unprecedented request by a president, Johnson insisted that the Joint Chiefs of Staff sign a written guarantee that the Marines could hold Khe Sanh.

The president's chief military adviser, retired General Maxwell Taylor, had misgivings about holding the Marine base. He pointed out the isolation of Khe Sanh and emphasized that any defensive position can be taken if the enemy is willing to suffer the cost. Taylor recommended that withdrawal ought to be considered. While Johnson weighed this advice, the NVA forces struck not at Khe Sanh, but everywhere in South Vietnam. With the shock of the Tet Offensive, the debate over holding Khe Sanh came to an abrupt halt.

Westmoreland believed that there was little similarity between Khe Sanh and Dien Bien Phu. Although both bases were isolated, Dien Bien Phu had been in a valley while Khe Sanh rested upon a plateau. The French lacked aircraft, while the Marines could rely on the B-52s, which would deluge the surrounding North Vietnamese and Vietcong troops. Most of all, the French airstrip had been closed on the first day of the siege; Westmoreland was confident that the runway would remain open at Khe Sanh.

While Khe Sanh was pounded by artillery, on February 6, a nearby U.S. Army Special Forces camp at Lang Vei was overrun by NVA regulars and nine Soviet tanks, the communists' first use of tanks in South Vietnam. A few survivors fought their way out, crept through NVA lines, and made it to Khe Sanh. After the fall of Lang Vei, NVA ground probes subsided, and the battle for Khe Sanh became one of opposing artillery. Every day the North Vietnamese shells and rockets hammered the base, and every day Americans countered with massive air strikes. During the siege, U.S. planes dropped 5,000 bombs daily, exploding the equivalent of five Hiroshima-sized atomic bombs in the area.

In early April, the relief of Khe Sanh began with Operation Pegasus, as the First U.S. Air Cavalry Division (Airmobile) relieved besieged Marine units. The siege was finally lifted on April 6, when the cavalrymen linked up with the 9th Marines south of the Khe Sanh airstrip. In the battle for Khe Sanh, 205 American Marines lost their lives. While accurate North Vietnamese losses are not available, they are estimated to be between 10,000 and 15,000 men dead.

Why did the North Vietnamese and Vietcong submit their forces to such huge losses? Communist officers have said that they never intended to overrun Khe Sanh, but used the fighting as a diversionary tactic to draw the Americans away from South Vietnam's major population centers. Also, they succeeded in depriving the Americans of a quick victory. But despite all of their successes, the communists failed to achieve their primary goal: to instigate a popular national uprising against the GVN. However, General Vo Nguyen Giap, the North Vietnamese commander, believed that he had forced the Americans to commit themselves to a protracted war. Although the war might last "five, ten, twenty or more years," he wrote, if the communists continued to fight, eventually the Americans would leave.

DISSENSION AT HOME

For two years prior to Tet, American public support for the war had been slipping as casualties mounted, taxes rose and there seemed to be no end in sight. A Gallup survey conducted in early January 1968 had indicated that 47% of the public disapproved of Johnson's handling of the war. By mid-February that figure had climbed to 50% and by the end of the month to 58%. There was also an increasing percentage of people who believed that the U.S. had made a "mistake" in sending troops to fight in Vietnam—from 45% in December 1967 to 49% in late February 1968.

Congressional calls for a change in American policy were mounting. Senator Robert Kennedy of New York declared that the Tet Offensive had "finally shattered the mask of official illusion with which we have concealed our true circumstances, even from ourselves." The rising antiwar sentiment on Capitol Hill propelled Senator Eugene McCarthy, a scholarly senator from Minnesota, into the limelight. He had announced in December 1967 that he would challenge Johnson for the presidency, and his platform called for a negotiated settlement of the war. After Tet, Democratic Party regulars feared that McCarthy's growing "peace vote" was a real threat to Johnson's reelection.

By early March the Johnson administration was being criticized loudly by both sides. Hawks called for further escalation and a widening of the war while the doves clamored for deescalation and negotiation. The controversy was further intensified on Sunday, March 10, when *The New York Times* reported on its front page that General Westmoreland had requested 206,000 more troops for Vietnam, "stirring a divisive internal debate within high levels of the Johnson administration."

The official optimism of years past suddenly seemed to indicate either incompetence or outright deception on the part of the Johnson administration. Moreover, there was no guarantee that additional troops would result in a military solution or force Hanoi into submission.

In mid-March, Senator McCarthy, the "peace candidate," won 42% of the vote in the New Hampshire primary, which inspired Robert Kennedy to join the presidential race on an antiwar platform. Although Johnson won the New Hampshire primary, he sensed ultimate defeat. If he ran for reelection, the campaign would divide the nation, and so on March 31, Johnson announced he would not seek nomination for another term. He also declared a bombing halt over North Vietnam, except in the areas immediately north of the DMZ, and asked Hanoi to participate in peace talks. Formal talks between the United States and North Vietnam began in Paris in May. For the next five years the talks would drag on, as more Americans would be killed in Vietnam than had died there previously. The United States would continue to face its worst internal upheaval since the Civil War.

During 1968, campus unrest mounted significantly, with some 200 demonstrations erupting in the first half. The most violent occurred at Columbia University in New York, where 1,000 police wielding nightsticks forcefully broke up a mass sit in. The assassination of Martin Luther King Jr. in April brought latent racial unrest to the surface and led to rioting throughout the urban areas of the country. U.S. Army units had to be stationed in the nation's capital to maintain order. The assassination of presidential candidate Robert Kennedy in June dashed the hopes of those who believed that one man could bring the nation together and possibly end the war.

CONFRONTATION IN CHICAGO

The bloody events at the Democratic Convention in Chicago in late August dramatized the extent to which the nation had become divided against itself. Some 10,000 youthful antiwar protesters had converged on Chicago. Fearing that their demonstrations would disrupt the city, Mayor Richard Daley had mobilized 12,000 police and Illinois National Guardsmen to maintain security. Some of the National Guard troops deployed to the city waited in armories, while others set up machine-gun emplacements along the city's most luxurious boulevard, Michigan Avenue. The convention site itself—the old International Amphitheater—had been turned into a fortress surrounded by a one-square mile security area into which no one was admitted without proper credentials.

On August 28, while delegates inside the convention hall debated the party's platform on the war, Chicago police and National Guardsmen clashed with the antiwar protesters on the streets as they tried to prevent them from marching on the Internationl Amphitheater. The bloody confrontation was brought into the homes of millions of Americans via live television. Protesters were chased through the downtown area, some were attacked with clubs, rifle butts and tear gas, while other demonstrators hurled rockets and bottles at the police and the National Guardsmen.

General Creighton W. Abrams, U.S. commander in South Vietnam, discusses the military situation in Vietnam with President Johnson and his advisers at the White House on October 29, 1968. Courtesy of the National Archives.

During the nominating process, delegate after delegate denounced the violence. Senator Abraham Ribicoff of Connecticut accused the police of engaging in "Gestapo tactics in the streets of Chicago." Mayor Daley defended his police force and accused the protestors of instigating the mayhem. Regardless of who was to blame for the confrontation in Chicago, it was clear that division would plague the nation as long as the Vietnam War continued.

The convention nominated President Johnson's preferred candidate, Vice President Hubert H. Humphrey, who outdistanced McCarthy by more than 1,000 votes. The question of war and peace became the decisive issue in the campaign. Humphrey was unable to shake his identification with Johnson's war policies and lost the election by a narrow margin to Richard M. Nixon, who promised throughout his campaign to "end the war and win the peace."

DEBATING FORMALITIES IN PARIS

Meanwhile at the Paris peace talks, the dominating issue was not the war, but the shape of the conference table. The North Vietnamese sought a seating arrangement that would give "legitimacy" to the NLF as an independent party to the talks; the South Vietnamese wanted a table that would reflect their belief that the NLF was simply a puppet of Hanoi; and the United States was willing to approve any arrangement that would get the talks underway without antagonizing Saigon. For nearly two months various proposals of the shape and arrangement of the table were discussed: square, oblong, elliptical and circular. Finally, on January 25, 1969, all four sides sat down to discuss the questions of war and peace at a circular table.

CHRONICLE OF EVENTS

1968

January 1: DRV announces that it will hold talks with the United States if all bombing and "other acts of war" against North Vietnam are halted.

January 3: Minnesota Senator Eugene McCarthy announces his candidacy for the Democratic presidential nomination.

January 21: Khe Sanh is besieged by North Vietnamese Army forces. Located 14 miles below the DMZ and six miles from the Laotian border, the base is used by the U.S. Marines as a staging area for forward patrols. An incessant barrage of artillery fire keeps Khe Sanh's Marine defenders pinned down in their trenches and bunkers. The base must be resupplied by air, and it is not until mid-April that the siege is finally lifted.

January 30–31: During the Tet holiday, Vietcong and North Vietnamese troops launch simultaneous attacks on major South Vietnamese cities, including an invasion of the U.S. Embassy grounds in Saigon. Twenty-nine of the 44 provincial capitals are attacked, as well as 25 airfields.

February 1: Richard M. Nixon announces his candidacy for the presidency.

February 1–25: Vietcong and North Vietnamese forces massacre 2,800 civilians in Hue.

February 7: North Vietnamese troops overrun the U.S. Special Forces camp at Lang Vei, southwest of Khe Sanh.

February 10–17: All-time-high weekly rate is set for U.S. casualties—543 killed in action, 2,547 wounded in action.

February 20: The Senate Foreign Relations Committee begins hearings on the events leading to the passage of the Tonkin Gulf Resolution.

February 25: U.S. and South Vietnamese forces recapture Hue after 25 days of occupation by communist troops. This is the last major engagement of the Tet Offensive.

February 27: The Joint Chiefs of Staff forward Westmoreland's request for 206,000 additional troops to the president.

March 1: Clark Clifford replaces Robert McNamara as secretary of defense. After having doubts about continuing the war, McNamara has resigned and has taken a position as president of the World Bank.

March 11: Operation Quyet Thang, the largest to date, is initiated in the Saigon area and five surrounding provinces by elements of the U.S. First, Ninth and 25th Divisions, and ARVN Fifth and 25th Divisions, airborne battalions and South Vietnamese Marine Corps Task Forces—a total of 22 U.S. and 11 ARVN battalions.

March 12: In the New Hampshire Democratic primary, Eugene McCarthy wins a surprising 42% of the vote against Johnson's 48%.

March 16: New York Senator Robert Kennedy announces his candidacy for the Democratic presidential nomination.

March 16: In what will later become the most publicized war atrocity committed by U.S. troops in Vietnam, a platoon from Charlie Company, First Battalion, 20th Infantry, Americal Division, massacres Vietnamese civilians at the hamlet of Mylai-4. The hamlet is located in a heavily mined region where members of Charlie Company had been killed or maimed during the preceding month.

March 22: President Johnson announces that General Westmoreland is to be recalled to become chief of staff of the U.S. Army. General Creighton Abrams will assume command of U.S. forces in Vietnam.

March 31: In a televised speech to the nation, President Johnson declares a partial bombing halt, calls for peace talks and announces he will not run for reelection.

April 1–15: Operation Pegasus/Lam Son 207 is conducted by the U.S. First Cavalry Division (Airmobile) with U.S. Marine and ARVN airborne battalions to relieve the siege of Khe Sanh.

April 3: North Vietnam agrees to preliminary peace talks.

In Hue, Walter Cronkite (holding the microphone) of CBS News interviews a battalion commander of the 1st Marines on February 20, 1968. Upon returning to the United States, the dean of American newscasters declared in a controversial televised report that the Vietnam War was a stalemate. Courtesy of the National Archives.

April 4: Rev. Dr. Martin Luther King Jr. is assassinated by a white sniper in Memphis, Tennessee. The assassination precipitates racial unrest and rioting in 100 cities throughout the country.

April 11: Defense Secretary Clifford announces the troop ceiling for U.S. troops has been raised to 549,500.

April 26: Massive antiwar demonstrations take place on college campuses throughout the nation. 200,000 protesters in New York City demonstrate against the war.

April 27: Vice President Hubert Humphrey announces his candidacy for the Democratic presidential nomination.

May 3: Hanoi and Washington agree to hold preliminary talks in Paris.

May 5–13: The second large-scale communist offensive of the year begins with the simultaneous shelling of 119 cities, towns and military barracks. U.S. and ARVN forces suppress all attacks.

May 12: Vietnam peace talks begin in Paris.

May 25–June 4: The Vietcong launch their third major assault of the year on Saigon. U.S. and South Vietnamese forces use helicopters, fighter-bombers and tanks to dislodge deeply entrenched Vietcong infiltrators.

June 5: Senator Robert Kennedy, a leading critic of administration policy in Vietnam, is shot after making a statement announcing his victory in California's Democratic presidential primary; he dies the next day.

June 27: U.S. troops withdraw from their base at Khe Sanh after a 77-day siege that began on January 21.

July 3: The U.S. command in Saigon releases figures showing that more Americans were killed during the first six months of 1968 than in all of 1967.

August 8: In his speech accepting the Republican presidential nomination, Richard Nixon pledges to "bring an honorable end to the war in Vietnam."

August 29: Vice President Hubert Humphrey wins the Democratic nomination for president in Chicago amid antiwar protests and riots outside the convention hall.

September 13–October 1: The largest sustained allied drive inside the DMZ opens when U.S. and ARVN infantry and armored troops, supported by planes, artillery and U.S. Navy ships, move two miles into the buffer zone.

October 31: President Johnson announces a complete halt to bombing of North Vietnam; U.S. Air Force Operation Rolling Thunder ends.

November 2: President Thieu announces his government will not attend the Paris negotiations.

November 6: Richard Nixon is elected president of the United States with 43.40% of the popular vote.

November 12: Defense Secretary Clifford warns that if South Vietnam does not agree soon to participate in the talks, the U.S. may conduct negotiations without them.

December 23: NLF representative in Paris Tran Buu Kiem rejects any direct negotiations between the NLF and Saigon and insists on holding talks only with the United States.

December 31: 536,100 U.S. military personnel now in Vietnam; 14,589 killed in action and 92,818 wounded in the 1968 fighting. Total of 30,610 U.S. military killed in action and 192,580 wounded since 1961.

South Vietnamese forces have been increased to 820,000; 88,343 killed in action to date.

EYEWITNESS TESTIMONY

We expect our gains of 1967 to be increased many-fold in 1968 . . . [Pacification] is expected to gain considerable headway during the next six months. Impact on the enemy should be increased casualties, desertions, sickness and lowered morale . . . His in-country recruiting potential will be reduced by acceleration of our military offensive and pacification efforts . . . Our forces have been able to detect impending major offensives and to mount spoiling attacks . . . The enemy did not win a major battle in 1967.

General William Westmoreland, classified report of January 1, 1968, in The New York Times *(March 21, 1968).*

The bombing would stop immediately if talks would take place promptly and with reasonable hopes that they would be productive.

President Lyndon Johnson, to Congress, annual State of the Union message of January 17, 1968, in Public Papers of the Presidents of the United States.

We have left our sandbag huts on the hilltop and now we live in trenches just off the skyline, like World War I. We each dug a bunnyhole at the bottom of the trench that is big enough to curl up and sleep in. We stand 100-percent watch at night and sleep all day. It is safer because we usually get rockets and mortars during the day. I just stay in my little bunnyhole until dark. I don't come out for anything unless I hear "Corpsman, up," and then I crawl on my hands and knees.

Corpsman David Steinberg, USMC, to his wife, letter of January 27, 1968, in Hammel's Khe Sanh: Siege in the Clouds *(1989).*

We get bombarded every day, and at night we get sniper fire. The company on the hill next to us loses a man or more a day. Our company has not lost anyone yet. I have lost about fifteen pounds. We work all day in the hot sun and get so little to eat and drink. But I'm in real good health. I'm fine and I watch everything I do, so don't worry.

Pfc. Mike Delaney, USMC, Echo Company, to his mother and father, letter of January 28, 1968, in Hammel's Khe Sanh: Siege in the Clouds.

When I die, I'll go to heaven, for I've gone through hell in Vietnam.

Marine slogan, written on lighters, key rings and even tattooed on their arms.

I never head the explosion. Black powder and dirt flew by me. My eardrums were ripped. My body was flying through the air. I threw my arms in front of me in a reflex motion to balance myself. My eyes registered the horror of a brilliantly white jagged bone sticking out of the stump of arm above where my left elbow had been. Ragged, bloody flesh surrounded the splintered bone. My mind cursed as utter helplessness and despair overwhelmed me.

Another part of my body coolly calculated what had caused the explosion—it had been a land mine. But what kind would blow off my arm instead of my legs? Of course! It had to be a "Bouncing Betty," a mine that flies up out of the ground after being tripped and explodes waist high. That would do it!

Lieutenant Frederick Downs Jr., USA, on patrol on January 11, 1968, in The Killing Zone *(1978).*

The ward was pathetic and on bad days when the enemy struck somewhere it got worse as wounded were flown in. If a man was brought through the doors of our Quonset hut we knew the wound was serious and we would crane our necks around as he was rolled in. We asked questions of each other and the medical staff to find out who he was: Is he a friend? What unit is he from? What kind of attack was it? How did he get hit? When was he brought in? Where was he? What kind of wound does he have?

Yes, what kind of wound was it—we all wanted to know. No other question ever asked by a soldier is so full of dread.

By the answer we would know the man's future.

Lieutenant Frederick Downs Jr., at the 85th Evacuation Hospital, Qui Nhon, in January 1968, in Aftermath: A Soldier's Return from Vietnam *(1984). [Lt. Downs' left arm was blown off when he stepped on a "Bouncing Betty" land mine.]*

Well, what's new in The World this morning? I don't feel any different today. Just hungry, and I need some water. Some ice-cold water would be fine.

Well, it's been a good day so far. I'm still alive, and I think that's enough to be happy about. People back in the States don't know how lucky they've got it. People take too much stuff for granted. A little letter to me makes me so happy. I can't wait to get back to the States.

Pfc. Mike Delaney, USMC, Echo Company, to his mother and father, letter of January 30, 1968, in Hammel's Khe Sanh: Siege in the Clouds.

You never know when it's coming, so why worry about it. If it's got your name on it, you won't know what hit you anyway.

Anonymous U.S. Marine, statement of 1968 on the siege at Khe Sanh, in Dougan and Weiss' Nineteen Sixty-Eight *(1983).*

A B-52 strike was truly awesome. There would be no hint of a strike arriving until the bombs exploded. The bombs fell in a staggered pattern. First one bomb, then another to the right and front of the first explosion, then another to the left and front of the second explosion, and so forth. The bombs created a long pattern of craters, churned up earth, and blasted trees. After the bombs had exploded, I would be able to hear the planes.

Pfc. Robert Harrison, USMC, Alpha Company, on the siege of Khe Sanh in January 1968, in Hammel's Khe Sanh: Siege in the Clouds.

This spring shines far brighter than any before. Happy news of victory blooms across the land. South and North challenge each other to fight the U.S. aggressors. Forward! Total victory will be ours.

President Ho Chi Minh, to the nation, proclamation broadcast over Radio Hanoi in January 1968 in Newsweek *(January 11, 1968).*

I scurried from tree to tree and came to the edge of Cathedral Square [Saigon]. In the instant before starting the long, dangerous run across the open square, the early morning sunlight seemed to etch every detail of the scene in my mind—the gray paving stones of the street, the pale terra cotta bricks on the basilica wall. The feeling of deja vu was strong. I had seen all this a 100 times before in every movie about the fighting during World War II in the streets of Paris. But now, the soldiers crouching along the wall were real soldiers, and the shots coming from the Vietcong snipers hiding behind trees were definitely not Hollywood blanks.

John Donnelly, journalist, on January 31, 1968, in Newsweek *(February 12, 1968).*

Explosions, bangs, thumps crashed all around me. I slammed the heavy, wooden Embassy doors shut, and as I did so, a rocket hit the window and the side of the door, wounding my buddy in the arms, face and legs, and throwing me to the ground.

Sergeant Ronald Harper, USMC, on the Vietcong attack on the American Embassy in Saigon on January 31, 1968, in U.S. News & World Report *(February 12, 1968).*

What the hell is going on? I thought we were winning the war?

Walter Cronkite, CBS Television Evening News anchor, inadvertent broadcast remark of February 1, 1968, in Oberdofer's Tet! The Turning of the Vietnam War *(1983).*

If I've lost Walter Cronkite I've lost Mr. Average citizen.

President Johnson, to an aide, remark of February 1968, in Wintle's The Dictionary of War Quotations *(1989).*

Every morning I walk into the situation room and shudder at the changes on the map overnight. We've vastly underestimated the number of troops North Vietnam has poured into the Northern areas. Their weapons are the best they've ever had. They have detail maps of all our positions and they've been digging in beautifully all around us.

Anonymous U.S. official, statement in U.S. News & World Report *(February 12, 1968).*

I don't want any damned Dien Bien Phu.

President Johnson, to the Joint Chiefs of Staff, at a White House meeting on the siege at Khe Sanh, remark of February 1968, in Time *(February 9, 1968).*

And at night, all of it seemed possible. At night in Khe Sanh, waiting there, thinking about all of them (40,000, some said), thinking that they might really try it, could keep you up. If they did, when they did, it might not matter that you were in the best bunker in the DMZ, wouldn't matter that you were young and had plans, that you were loved, that you were a noncombatant, an observer. Because if it came, it would be in a bloodswarm of killing, and credentials would not be examined . . . You came to love your life, to love and respect the mere fact of it, but often you became heedless of it in the way that somnambulists are heedless. Being "good" meant staying alive, and sometimes that was only a matter of caring enough at any given moment.

Michael Herr, journalist, on the siege at Khe Sanh in February 1968, in Dispatches *(1977).*

You learn to distinguish the size and type of hit by the sonic boom. 61 mm mortar is a jab of a sound, unless it's right over you. An 82 mm mortar jolts you. The 152 mm shots from Co Roc seem to lift the entire bunker and slam it down again. The sound is so great that it ceases to be perceived as just sound. It is concussion. Too many shots in a row and you go out just like a guy who's down on the ropes.

Despite all the sound of battle, however, the human sound always seems to get through—the screams of a guy going out badly. Your ears are always so wide open when it happens. Those screams etch themselves like unwanted grooves on a record, forever dominating memory.

Lieutenant Ernest Spencer, USMC, on the siege at Khe Sanh in 1968, in Welcome to Vietnam, Macho Man: Reflections of a Khe San Vet *(1987).*

The nine blocks ahead of us to the wall are defended by what seems like a small but fantastically

well dug-in and well-supplied Communist force . . . You can hear the whine of the snipers' bullets and the eerie whoosh of B-40 rockets and feel the thunder of mortar rounds chewing up houses.

Alvin Webb Jr., UPI correspondent, on the block by block fighting in Hue during the Tet Offensive, dispatch of February 1968, in Braestrup's Big Story *(1977).*

At dawn, the new masters of the city went through the streets in groups of ten. In each group, there was a leader who spoke to the people through a bullhorn . . . The other members of the team . . . knocked on doors and passed out pamphlets and leaflets. Joking and laughing, the soldiers walk in the streets and gardens without showing any fear . . . They give an impression of discipline and good training . . . Numerous civilians brought them great quantities of food. It didn't seem that these residents were being coerced in any way.

Francois Mazure, correspondent of Agence-France, on the NLF occupation of Hue during the Tet Offensive, dispatch of February 2, 1968, in Braestrup's Big Story.

The Viet Cong had people all over this town . . . they were everywhere . . . They had apparently

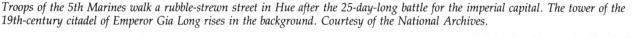

Troops of the 5th Marines walk a rubble-strewn street in Hue after the 25-day-long battle for the imperial capital. The tower of the 19th-century citadel of Emperor Gia Long rises in the background. Courtesy of the National Archives.

infiltrated into most of the town; they were probably living with the people. It was Tet and there were plenty of strangers in town.
Major Philip Canella, USA, on the fighting in Ben Tre, Kien Hoa Province, during the Tet Offensive, statement of February 1968, in Braestup's Big Story.

I am writing this on notebook paper by the illumination of a penlight under a blanket. Hue is completely blacked out. I came into Hue on a Marine convoy Saturday. The streets were littered with the debris of war—twisted street signs, fallen power lines and trees, cars and jeeps riddled with bullets.
Alvin Webb Jr., UPI correspondent, dispatch of Feburary 4, 1968.

The Saigon suburb of Nhonxa, which lies less than a mile from the city airport looks like Stalingrad with palm trees today . . . Row after row of concrete houses have been destroyed by the battle that has walked back and forth since early Tuesday.
Charlie Mohr, New York Times correspondent, dispatch of February 3, 1968, in The New York Times *(February 4, 1968).*

The enemy has met with an extremely heavy military setback.
U.S. Ambassador Ellsworth Bunker, to President Johnson, cable of February 4, 1968, in Gravel's The Pentagon Papers *(1971).*

As invisible high-flying B-52s sent great grey clouds of smoke up from ridges to the south, or jets roared in to throw bombs at Hill 1015, or helicopter gunships rocketed the tree lines to the south, the Marines [at Khe Sanh] barely took notice. It was all "outgoing," not incoming, they listened for incoming.
Peter Braestrup, Washington Post correspondent, dispatch of February 5, 1968, in The Washington Post *(same date).*

For days now, they've been fighting their way, bloody inch by inch, down Le Loi Street [in Hue]. And all that time they could see down the street a flagpole, and on it was a Vietcong flag. Much is left in shambles as the Marines advance building after building, the North Vietnamese retreat building after building, giving up nothing without a fight.
Don Webster, CBS News correspondent, report of February 7, 1968, in Braestrup's Big Story.

It became necessary to destroy the town to save it.
Anonymous U.S. Army major, on the battle for Ben Tre in the Mekong Delta, statement of February 7, 1968, in Associated Press dispatch (February 7, 1968).

For the sake of those Americans fighting today, if for no other reason, the time has come to take a new look at the war in Vietnam; not by cursing the past but by using it to illuminate the future.
Senator Robert F. Kennedy, statement in U.S. News & World Report *(February 8, 1968).*

A sign—and symbol—of the jauntiness of the hilltop Leathernecks [at Khe Sanh] can be found on 881 South, where daily a tattered American flag is raised and a bugle plays "To the Colors." The Marines stand at attention and salute during the rapid ceremony, and then dive for cover. They have it timed so they will be prone in their trenches by the time the North Vietnamese mortar shells begin falling again.
John Wheeler, journalist, dispatch of February 12, 1968, in the Associated Press.

From foxholes just inside the wire that makes up Khe Sanh's vulnerable perimeter, it was easy today to spot an occasional North Vietnamese soldier within 150 yards.
Anonymous London Times correspondent, dispatch of February 14, 1968, in The London Times *(February 15, 1968).*

I live in an underground bunker [at Khe Sanh] with a roof made of huge logs we cut with a machete and with a double layer of sandbags on top of that. Inside it is lined with a camouflaged parachute. The airstrip is closed for repairs so all our supplies are dropped by parachute, and we keep all damaged ones.

That's about all there is to say right now. The next time you hear from me, it'll probably be in person. I've got less than two months left in Vietnam.
Sergeant George Storz, USMC, to his family, letter of February 16, 1968, in Edelman's Dear America: Letters Home From Vietnam *(1985). [Sergeant Storz was killed in action on March 8, 1968, one month before he was due to return home.]*

They are hurt very severely in North Vietnam after three years of bombing, and they have lost many countryside areas, so they have difficulty to recruit men, to have supplies, and, most important, they are believing now, they are like fish thrown out of water because they have no people in the countryside . . . I believe the VC have met with complete failure with the Tet offensive . . . In three weeks they have suffered 40,000 casualties.

President Nguyen Van Thieu, statement of February 23, 1968, on CBS News' Face the Nation *(February 25, 1968).*

Care of the wounded within Khe Sanh and medical evacuation pose grave problems. It is an open secret that few of the bunkers are secure against shellfire. With the "bleeding" type operations now being conducted by the enemy, the hospital might do well enough for a week or so. But it was not built to care for the numbers of wounded that would result from a major protracted attack, "Dig a foot a day" is the order. It is more honored in the breach than in the observance. One looks in vain for the communication trenches.

Denis Warner, journalist, at Khe Sanh on February 25, 1968, in The Reporter *(March 21, 1968).*

Room for rent . . . Home is where you dig it.

Sign, along roadway leading to Khe Sanh.

Enemy losses have been heavy; he has failed to achieve his prime objectives of mass uprisings and capture of a large number of the capital cities and towns. Morale in enemy units which were badly mauled or where the men were oversold the idea of a decisive victory at Tet probably has suffered severely. However, with replacements, his indoctrination system would seem capable of maintaining morale at a generally adequate level. His determination appears to be unshaken.

General Westmoreland, report of 1968, in Gravel's The Pentagon Papers.

Returned to Charlie-Med. There were two patients from Echo Company, 2/26, on Hill 861A. One had a head wound, the other will lose his right arm and right leg and possibly will be blind. It was a very ghastly sight—black, charred flesh hanging down from a ripped-open area of the leg, to the bone. The hand was off; the arm was a stump. One corpsman walked to where I was: "I don't want to look at that, but I have to," he said resignedly, and walked back to aid the patient.

Lieutenant Ray Stubbe, USMC, battalion chaplain, on the siege at Khe Sanh, diary entry of February 26, 1968, in Hammel's Khe Sanh: Siege in the Clouds.

To say that we are closer to victory today is to believe, in the face of the evidence, the optimists who have been wrong in the past. To suggest we are on the edge of defeat is to yield to unreasonable pessimism. To say that we are mired in stalemate seems the only realistic, yet unsatisfactory, conclusion . . . it is increasingly clear to this reporter that the only rational way out then will be to negotiate, not as victors, but as an honorable people who lived up to their pledge to defend democracy, and did the best they could.

Walter Cronkite, CBS Evening News anchorman, to the nation, on the Tet Offensive, report of February 27, 1968, on CBS' "Who, What, When, Where, Why: Report from Vietnam by Walter Cronkite."

I saw Marines [at Khe Sanh] give up that last canteen cup of water—we only got three a day, and sometimes only two, for 24 hours. That's to eat, cook, wash and drink, and . . . we'd have a night attack, and a guy gets blown away—his buddy's dying—and I've seen him take that last canteen cup of water and give it to his buddy and then have to clean up his body, take all the dirt out of his eyes, because he's dead now, clean him up as best he could and put him in that bag . . .

Corpsman Richard Blanchfield, USN, in Columbia University's Vietnam Veterans Oral History Project.

Khe Sanh is physically and emotionally a miserable place, a noisy, dirty, dangerous hell. The men who live there have a special gait known as the "Khe Sanh double step"—a crouching swiveling of the head. The point of the Khe Sanh double step is to make sure that there is always a hole within easy reach.

Merton Perry, journalist, report in Newsweek *article of March 18, 1968.*

Helicopters would land on the runway and pick up the dead and wounded. Each time they landed, the NVA gunners would pound the airstrip with incoming rounds . . . The helicopter had so many wounded Marines aboard that it actually had to get a running start to get off the ground . . . I can remember vividly looking out the helicopter door as we circled Khe Sanh and seeing the trenchlines and bomb-scarred terrain become smaller as the helicopter flew higher. I thanked God for allowing me to be wounded in order to escape that hellhole.

Lieutenant Colonel Charlie Thorton, on March 10, 1968, in Hammel's Khe Sanh: Siege in the Clouds.

. . . the night was again split by the sounds of incoming. This time we weren't lucky. Running toward the bunker, I heard the whistle of a shell overhead, growing louder and louder. Suddenly, the sound evaporated. Someone had once told me that this would be a sign that a round was going to land on me. In the fury and the fear I recalled that warning and hurled myself to the ground . . . If I had remained on my feet, I have no doubt that I would have been killed. The explosion wasn't twenty yards away. I was showered by chunks of earth. When I got to my bunker, my colleagues said my body had been tossed into the air like a rag doll . . . A round hit, right in front of us. Someone to my right was crying for his mother. "Mom? Mom? Where are you Mom?"

Pfc. John Ketwig, USA, on a Vietcong attack on his base in March 1968, in And a Hard Rain Fell *(1985).*

We are there not just to save the South Vietnamese . . . if we lose there, before you know it, they would be up to the beaches in Hawaii.

Senator Strom Thurmond (R–S.C.), statement in U.S. News & World Report *(March 14, 1968).*

I have some good news and some bad news for you. First the good news: I'll be home soon. The bad news is that I no longer have one leg below the knee, or one of my arms. . . . Even though these things have happened to me, I am not disheartened. I still intend to do all the things I planned: swim, teach, political science and enter politics.

Anonymous U.S. Marine, wounded at the siege at Khe Sanh, to his parents, letter of March 20, 1968, in Odom's American Journal of Nursing *article of September 1986.*

You go into a house and ask if everyone is healthy, and the people smile and nod, and if the weather has been good for the crops, and they smile and nod, and then you ask: "Are there any VC around?" and they shake their heads gravely and say: "No, no," and so you leave and everyone smiles and bows, and you walk on a hundred meters past the house and one of your men loses both legs from a VC mine that those same people knew all about and probably set themselves.

Anonymous U.S. Marine lieutenant, statement of 1968, in Gannon's America *article of August 31, 1968.*

One of our platoons went out on a routine patrol today and came across a 155-mm artillery round that was booby trapped. It killed one man, blew the legs off two others, and injured two more.

And it all turned out a bad day made even worse. On their way back to "Dotti" they saw a woman working in the fields. They shot and wounded her. Then they kicked her to death and emptied their magazines in her head. They slugged every little kid they came across.

Why in God's name does this have to happen? These are all seemingly normal guys; some were friends of mine. For a while they were like wild animals.

Pfc. Gregory Olsen, USA, Charlie Company, First Battalion, 20th Infantry, to his father, letter of March 14, 1968, in Hersh's My Lai 4 *(1970).*

We were all pysched up, and as a result when we got there the shooting started, almost as a chain reaction. The majority of us had expected to meet Vietcong combat troops, but this did not turn out to be so. First we saw a few men running . . . and the next thing I knew we were shooting at everything. Everybody was just firing after they got in the village, I guess you could say the men were out of control.

Pfc. Dennis Conti, USA, Charlie Company, on the massacre of civilians at the hamlet of My Lai on March 16, 1968, in Hersh's My Lai 4.

He [Calley] told [Paul] Meadlo to take care of that group. Meadlo said yes and he continued watching them. Calley came back. A few minutes later he returned. He yelled at Meadlo, "Why haven't you wasted them yet?" Meadlo stood there astonished. As I made a turn in the trail, I heard firing to my rear.

Pfc. James Dursi, USA, Charlie Company, to Army court-martial (1971) of Lt. William Calley Jr., on the events at My Lai on March 16, 1968, in Hersh's My Lai 4.

A U.S. soldier, a "tunnel rat," crawls into a captured North Vietnamese bunker in 1968. Courtesy of the National Archives.

. . . I was ordered to go in there and destroy the enemy. That was my job on that day. That was the mission I was given. I did not sit down and think in terms of men, women and children. They were all classified the same, and that was the classification that we dealt with, just as enemy soldiers.

Lieutenant William Calley Jr., USA, to Army court-martial of 1971, on the events at My Lai on March 16, 1968, in Hammer's The Court-Martial of Lt. Calley *(1971).*

I am concerned that, at the end of it all, there will only be more Americans killed, more of our treasure spilled out; and because of the bitterness and hatred on every side of this war, more hundreds of thousands of Vietnamese slaughtered, so that they may say, as Tacitus said of Rome: "They made a desert, and called it peace." . . . can we ordain to ourselves the awful majesty of God—to decide what cities and villages are to be destroyed, who will live and who

will die, and who will join the refugees of our creation?

Senator Robert Kennedy, Democratic presidential primary candidate, to the students and faculty of Kansas State University, speech of March 18, 1968, in The New York Times *(March 19, 1968).*

While flying over the base, at altitudes ranging from several hundred to several thousand feet, I got a clear picture of the countless trenches that the North Vietnamese are building, some of which run almost to the edge of the airstrip.

Robert Shaplen, journalist, on the siege at Khe Sanh on March 23, 1968, in The Road From War *(1970).*

Instead of simply dumping in artillery and mortars on us constantly he's starting to maintain a withering blanket of machine-gun and rifle fire across the whole base. At some times, it's virtually impossible for anyone in the perimeter to stand up and get out of their holes.

Anonymous U.S. military officer, on the siege at Khe Sanh, statement of March 1968, in Deepe's Christian Science Monitor article of March 26, 1968.

A shell came right in this man's trench and what they had to send home would probably fit inside a handkerchief.

Anonymous U.S. Marine, on the siege at Khe Sanh, statement of 1968, in Maclear's The Ten Thousand Day War (1981).

For the most part nobody is particularly wild with patriotic feeling for the war . . . most people generate their enthusiasm for two reasons: one is self-preservation—if I don't shoot him, he'll eventually shoot me—and the other is revenge. It's apparently quite something to see a good friend blown apart by a V.C. booby trap, and you want to retaliate in kind.

Second Lieutenant Robert Ransom Jr., to his mother and father, letter of March 27, 1968, in The New Yorker (July 27, 1968). [Lt. Ransom died on May 11, 1968, from wounds received eight days earlier from an enemy mine.]

Today we moved 5 kilometers to join up with the rest of our battalion. My platoon had point. Hardest I've ever worked—yelling, threatening, swearing, keeping my men in formation. We were in a wedge shape as we moved—extremely difficult to control but perfect when you expected an ambush up ahead.

The battalion perimeter is an assembly area for our move north. We're going 7 miles from Khe Sanh. Each man will cary 6 sandbags, 1 mortar round, a gallon of water and 1 case (12 rations) of C-rations.

It's getting rough again.

Sergeant James Rowe Jr., USA, First Cavalry (Airmobile), diary entry of March 29, 1968, on patrol 15 miles northwest of Hue, in Prescott's Love to All, Jim (1989).

Tonight, I renew the offer I made last August—to stop the bombardment of North Vietnam. We ask that talks begin promptly, that they be serious talks on the substance of peace. We assume that during those talks Hanoi will not take advantage of our restraint.

We are prepared to move immediately toward peace through negotiations.

So, tonight, in the hope that this action will lead to early talks, I am taking the first step to deescalate the conflict. We are reducing—substantially reducing—the present level of hostilities.

President Johnson, to the American people, television address of March 31, 1968, in Public Papers of the Presidents of the United States.

With America's sons in the field far away, with America's future under challenge right here at home, with our hopes and the world's hopes for peace in the balance every day, I do not believe that I should devote an hour or a day of my time to any personal partisan causes or to any duties other than the awesome duties of this office—the Presidency of your country.

Accordingly, I shall not seek, and I will not accept, the nomination of my party for another term as your President.

President Johnson, to the American people, television address of March 31, 1968, in Public Papers of the Presidents of the United States.

It never changes. Every day is the same. You walk some more. You have some contact. Maybe you lose a few guys. And a couple of months later you're back again on the same hill.

Anonymous U.S. Army sergeant, statement of 1968, in Weinraub's New York Times Magazine article of October 20, 1968.

Today is a bad day for the 2nd Lieutenant. Early this morning, he steps on a booby trap, while on patrol near Danang. He is lucky, the device fails to explode. The sweep continues and he again takes the point. A short while later, he trips another explosive device. This time, he is not as lucky. It takes 46 pints of blood and almost six hours' labor to save him. He has lost both legs above the knees and part of his right hand. What kind of man takes the point position for a second time? The kind of men who are so much in abundance here in Vietnam! The same kind of man, who clutches a live grenade to his breast to save his patrol or who flies an unwieldly C-130 into the Khe Sanh day after day. These are the men who are toiling in this far off place.

Lieutanent Edward Briscoe, U.S. Army doctor, diary entry of April 11, 1968, in Diary of a Short-timer (1970).

A Marine wounded by a booby trap is comforted by another soldier. The Vietcong sowed trails and waterways with mines, grenades, tripwires and other lethal traps. Walking a patrol became a fearful, step-by-step search for any hint of these traps, which caused 11% of all American deaths during the Vietnam War. Courtesy of the National Archives.

I'm out! Khe Sanh has been left behind! Don't get me wrong. I'm not being cocky. Only the lucky get out Khe Sanh alive. Being good or talented doesn't help there.

Corporal Dennis Mannion, USMC, to a friend, letter of April 18, 1968, from Quang Tri, in Hammel's Khe Sanh: Siege in the Clouds.

As they removed articles from the body, I noticed a small piece of cloth, about three by five inches. It was red and white with a small patch of blue in one corner. Dirty, with some of his blood on it, it was between his chest and camouflage jacket. A small US flag. "He was a good Marine." And he thought enough of his flag to carry it on patrol with him. As it was taken from his young and now lifeless body I could not help but think of other young men, alive, who burn or try to burn our flag—the flag this young Marine died for.

I am in no mood for flag burners today.

Sergeant Major Jack Jaunal, USMC, First Reconnaissance Battalion, First Marine Division, journal entry of April 26, 1968, in Vietnam '68: Jack's Journal *(1981).*

There were booby traps all over the place. I was barefoot. We didn't want to make any boot prints.

We were walking along barefoot, and Americans don't go into jungles barefoot. I had no identification on me except for a morphine syringe around my neck. If I was hit, I'd shoot morphine. My number was 50, it was on all my clothes. My face was completely painted out black. Often I would wear a black pajama top. I learned how to walk like a Viet Cong, move like a Viet Cong, think like a Viet Cong.

Scout Mike Beamon, U.S. Navy Seal [Sea, Air, Land guerrilla warfare unit], recalls a mission in the Mekong Delta in 1968, in Santoli's Everything We Had *(1981).*

Night movement, that was a suicidal patrol. That was one of the worst patrols you could ever go out in. The purpose of it was for you to walk up on Charlie and for him to hit you, and then for our hardware to wipe them out. We were used as scapegoats to find out where they were. That was all we were—bait. They couldn't find Charlie any other way. They knew there was a regiment out there. They weren't looking for just a handful of VC. Actually, they'd love for us to run into a regiment which would just wipe us out. Then they could plaster the regiment and they'd have a big body count. The general gets another damn metal. He gets promoted.

Pfc. Stanley Goff, USA, 196th Light Infantry Brigade, recalls 1968, in Goff and Sanders' Brothers: Black Soldiers in the Nam (1982).

I pledge to you tonight that the first priority foreign policy objective of our next Administration will be to bring an honorable end to the war in Vietnam . . . My fellow Americans, the dark long night for America is about to end.

Republican presidential nominee Richard M. Nixon, to the Republican National Convention in Miami, Florida, acceptance speech of August 8, 1968, in U.S. News & World Report *(August 19, 1968).*

We droned through weeks of intermittent contact, receiving a steady trickle of reinforcements brought forward when the resupply helicopter came every fifth day. As a rule, our days were tediously boring; a hundred men carrying heavy loads silently through the steaming jungle. But every few days the tedium would be broken by moments of stark terror when we would bump into enemy forces; the noise of bullets screaming by kept that survival instinct alive and well oiled.

Lieutanent Tom Carhart, USA, platoon leader, recalls a patrol mission in 1968, in The Offering *(1987).*

I command 200 soldiers, mostly white . . . if I ever got out and went back to my hometown they would try to put a broom in my hand and fear in my heart.

Anonymous U.S. Army officer, statement in Johnson's Ebony *article of August 1968.*

So the next move must be theirs. In human affairs there is no more basic lesson than that it takes two to make a bargain and to make a peace. We have made a reasonable offer and we have taken a major first step. That offer has not been accepted. This administration does not intend to move further until it has good reason to believe that the other side intends serously to join us in deescalating the war and moving seriously toward peace. We are willing to take chances for peace but we cannot make foolhardy gestures for which your fighting men will pay the price by giving their lives.

President Johnson, to the annual convention of the Veterans of Foreign Wars, speech of August 19, 1968, in Public Papers of the Presidents of the United States.

I felt, I should think, as an American pilot must feel after he drops bombs on a defenseless village or a city. The only difference is that after his killing, he can fly away and not watch the destruction he caused. I couldn't fly away, I saw it. They lay down in pieces, men and women and children, and it was like a battlefield after the battle, and I covered my eyes . . . My duty is to fight Americans. This sometimes requires that I kill innocent people . . . there is no difference in firing a gun, dropping a bomb from an airplane or exploding two mines near a restaurant when people are eating.

Nguyen Van Sam, Vietcong soldier, on setting a bomb at a restaurant in South Vietnam in 1968, in Fallaci's Look *article of April 16, 1968.*

Now the waiting police were eager to move. Some youths fled from the [Lincoln] park. Most stayed. The police then lobbed cannisters of tear gas into the barricade. Coughing, gagging and stumbling, the demonstrators broke and ran, some throwing stones

An antiwar demonstrator confronts National Guard troops in front of the Chicago Hilton Hotel during the Democratic Convention of August 1968. Courtesy of AP/Wide World Photos.

as they retreated. Members of the Chicago police's elite Task Force Unit raced after the kids, and in the darkness of the park, ran scores of them to the ground like cowboys, bulldogging cattle. The sound of night sticks smashing into skulls resounded through the park; mixed with shrieks and screams.

Anonymous journalist, at the Democratic National Convention, report of August 28, 1968, in Newsweek *(September 9, 1968).*

The Whole World is Watching.

Antiwar demonstrators in Chicago, chant of August 1968.

Just to stop the bombing, without any indication that it will lead to anything but just stopping the bombing, I don't think is a very prudent act . . . I am not the President, gentlemen, and I don't think it helps to play President . . . I believe the war should be brought to a halt, but I don't believe it should be brought to a halt at the expense of the safety and the security of the people of South Vietnam . . . I don't see any prospect at all that we are going to be bogged down in Asia for 5 or 10 years. I don't see that as a possibility.

Vice President Hubert Humphrey, on ABC News' "Issues and Answers," statement of September 8, 1968.

The monsoons had a way of beating down a man's morale. The world seemed forever wet and gray. Dense fogs came and went, but always very slowly. And the moisture hung in the air like it was suspended on a string . . . Mud and water were inescapable, no matter where we went or how hard we fought to stay clean and dry. Fighting the monsoons was pure futility. Even the most determined man was finally overcome by the sheer length of the rainstorms and the deep mud. With every step a man's boots were sucked several inches into the ground, and the weight of his rucksack increased steadily as it took on the water. The enemy now became the weather, and sadly, there was no way to fight back. There was nothing to do but bear it, and to do that it took as much resolve as it did to pursue the VC in the jungle.

Pfc. Dale Reich, USA, recalls 1968, in Good Soldiers Don't Go to Heaven *(1979).*

Bring Home the GIs Now!

Antiwar demonstrators, protest sign at the Lincoln Memorial in Washington, D.C., on October 21, 1968.

I have now ordered that all air, naval, and artillery bombardment of North Vietnam cease as of 8 A.M., Washington time, Friday morning.

I have reached this decision on the basis of the developments in the Paris talks.

And I have reached it in the belief that this action can lead to progress toward a peaceful settlement of the Vietnamese war.

President Johnson, to the American people, television address of October 31, 1968, in Public Papers of the Presidents of the United States.

I'm twenty-nine, old enough to be a big sister, and a young mother myself, now feeling their fears and

apprehensions. These kids aren't old enough to come into the night clubs we played back home, much less be sent out to kill somebody, and not even knowing why. Then their "tough" red-head sergeant, who isn't much older than his men, walked up. He wanted four men to ride shotgun with us back to the highway . . .

We moved down the dirty road with ease this time in an armored personnel carrier . . . Our new friends waved goodbye, and I wondered if we'd ever see them again, or would their families? The Mexican boy was still waving as we turned out the gate, and I felt sorry for him, and I was nearly crying.

Nancy Noel, entertainer, diary entry of 1968, in Saigon for a Song *(1987).*

We got hit with our own artillery one night. I was laying there, sleeping out in the open. It was slightly raining. I remember that just as I got into this little niche on the side of the hill, I pulled some landing planks over so I had a little shelter. All of a sudden on top there is this big pshboom. I realized a 155

Spec. 5 Frank Moffitt, USA, a soldier in the First Cavalry Division (Airmobile) has marked off months of service on his short-timer's helmet. Courtesy of the National Archives.

artillery round had landed right on top of the mountain. I took one look at that and said, "U-oh, I know what's going to come now. We're going to get hit with a large barrage." But that didn't last very long. The lieutenant was yelling over the phone, "No! No! Wrong! Wrong!" And they got that straightened out.

Pfc. Donald Smith, USA, 101st Airborne Division, in 1968, in Santoli's Everything We Had.

The hospital was full of guys that were hurting. Hopping around the hospital . . . I saw just about everything . . . I used to go in places you weren't supposed to go . . . I saw guys with no privates, no penis. I saw guys with no legs, with one leg, one arm. Once they destroyed some part of your body, then it takes a lot just to go on. Guys do it, though!

Pfc. Robert Sanders, USA, 173rd Airborne Brigade, recalls his stay at the 8th Field Hospital in Nha Trang in 1968, in Goff and Sanders' Brothers: Black Soldiers in the Nam.

As I stepped from the plane, I stood in the early-morning rain and soaked up the emotional rush of finally being back home. A lump rose in my throat and my eyes misted over as I realized that through my personal determination and faith in God, I had made it through a full year of living in Hell. As I moved among the small crowds of sleepy early-morning travelers, I felt pride and personal accomplishment in the medals and battle ribbons decorating my chest. But suddenly I realized that no one really gave a damn—I was just another GI, in transit from point A to point B. I had the urge to shout, "Hey, look at me! Don't you know what I've just been through?" Picking up my duffle bag and the old K-44 carbine I had brought back, I made my way out the front doors of the terminal to flag down a taxi.

Pfc. Charles Gadd, USA, 101st Airborne Division (Screaming Eagles), recalls arriving back in the United States ("the world"), in Line Doggie: Foot Soldier in Vietnam *(1987).*

8. Fighting for Time: 1969

THE ROAD TO PARIS

President Richard M. Nixon, elected to office by a narrow margin, claimed to have a "secret plan to end the war." The 37th president of the United States was well aware that his political future hinged on preventing "Johnson's war" from becoming "Nixon's war." "The greatest honor history can bestow is the title of peacemaker," Nixon declared in his inaugural address of January 20, 1969, and he stated, "This honor now beckons America—the chance to help lead the world at last out of the valley of turmoil and onto that high ground of peace that man has dreamed of since the dawn of civilization."

His presidential campaign described nothing more specific than "de-Americanization" and "peace with honor," but Nixon's inaugural words were interpreted as an intent to disengage quickly from Vietnam. His hopes for a quick settlement were soon dashed as the war reached a double stalemate on the battlefield and at the negotiating table in Paris. In fact, Nixon had no "secret plan" to end the war. Moreover, the Nixon administration persisted in trying to achieve an independent, non-communist Vietnam. This goal was to be reached primarily by a massive buildup of South Vietnamese forces and by applying military pressure against North Vietnam. These measures had already been tried before in various forms and had failed. The result was four more years of bloody warfare and a marked increase in domestic strife.

By mid-1969, the Nixon administration was publicly pursuing a two-pronged approach: the negotiations in Paris and the "Vietnamization" of the war itself so that the South Vietnamese would take over the fighting and American troops could return home. As an improvement upon the term *de-Americanization*, the new secretary of defense, Melvin Laird, had coined the word *Vietnamization*.

The men he selected to be his senior foreign policy advisers would determine how Richard Nixon would handle the legacy of Johnson's war. German-born Harvard professor Henry Kissinger, appointed as the president's National Security adviser, would play a major role in

President Richard M. Nixon (left, front), accompanied by Secretary of Defense Melvin R. Laird and General Earle G. Wheeler, chairman of the Joint Chiefs of Staff, visits the Department of Defense for an orientation briefing shortly after taking office in January 1969. Courtesy of the National Archives.

negotiating an end to a war he had once openly supported. Although Nixon and Kissinger recognized that the war must be ended, both men insisted that it must be ended "honorably." Simply to pull out of Vietnam would be a reckless abandonment of those South Vietnamese who had depended upon American protection and would be unfitting of a great nation.

An honorable settlement had to meet several criteria. The American withdrawal from Vietnam must be implemented in a way that avoided even the slightest appearance of defeat. Kissinger rejected the idea of a coalition government, which, he said, would "destroy the existing political structure and thus lead to a Communist takeover." The Nixon administration's goal was set on a settlement that would preserve the independence of South Vietnam, or at least give South Vietnam a reasonable chance to survive.

WIDENING THE WAR

Within a month of assuming the presidency, Nixon had decided on his first move to pressure North Vietnam into taking part in serious negotiations. This was Operation Menu—the secret bombing of Cambodia. By the mid-1960s, North Vietnamese and Vietcong units had established base areas in eastern Cambodia and were using them to move supplies into position. With the tacit agreement of Prince Norodom Sihanouk, the Cambodian ruler, President Nixon ordered the "secret" bombing of these Cambodian bases on March 18, 1969.

Nixon and Kissinger realized a key ingredient to the operation's success was total secrecy. If they admitted to ordering bombing raids against a neutral country, they might cause an international crisis. The North Vietnamese did not dare complain, since protesting would have confirmed the illicit deployment of their troops on Cambodian soil.

Although elaborate measures were taken to keep the plan secret, an enterprising *New York Times* correspondent, William Beecher, published a story about the bombings in May. Despite the Nixon administration's fears that the revelation would fuel antiwar protests, the scoop resulted in no public reaction, but it infuriated Nixon and Kissinger. Wiretaps were placed on the telephones of several journalists and government officials, including members of Kissinger's own staff. The first abuses of authority, later to result in the Watergate scandal, had begun.

Over a 15-month period, 3,630 B-52 raids were flown, dropping more than 100,000 tons of bombs on Cambodia, quadruple the tonnage dropped on Japan in World War II. Despite damaging the communists' rear bases, the bombing failed to modify the North Vietnamese stand in negotiations. The NLF unveiled 10 points on May 8 that reiterated their demands for unconditional U.S. withdrawal and a coalition government excluding President Thieu.

One week later, on May 14, President Nixon made his first full-length television address to the American people on the Vietnam War. He responded to the 10-point plan offered by the NLF with his own eight-point plan. The first four points detailed a phased withdrawal of American and North Vietnamese troops from South Vietnam over a 12-month period, and the others concerned military issues: an international body to supervise a cease-fire, release of prisoners of war and an agreement to abide by the Geneva accords of 1954. The proposal Nixon offered was little more than a revision of President Johnson's October 1966 plan, known as the "Manila formula," in which the United States stated the withdrawal of U.S. forces would be completed within six months after the North Vietnamese left South Vietnam.

The response from North Vietnam was, as expected, negative. Hanoi was not going to redeploy their troops to the north, since the Vietcong alone was no match for the South Vietnamese army. Although they maintained they were not involved in the south for diplomatic purposes, they considered it their right to resist any foreign invaders anywhere in Vietnam. Their principal demand was the resignation of Thieu and the installation of a coalition government that included the

Vietcong, which they knew Nixon would never accept. With mounting antiwar sentiment in the United States, Hanoi was in no hurry to participate in serious negotiations.

In an effort to silence domestic criticism and deprive Hanoi of its hope that the U.S. people would press for peace on communist terms, Nixon announced the first withdrawal of 25,000 troops in June. One month later, in what became known as the Nixon Doctrine, he expressed the opinion that the United States in the future should not involve U.S. troops in limited wars between Asian states.

As plans were made for troop withdrawals, the fighting continued throughout the south and along the DMZ. By the time Nixon had entered office, 30,000 Americans had been killed in Vietnam, and nearly 10,000 more were to perish there during his first year as president. On February 22, following the end of the Tet cease-fire, communist forces staged an offensive throughout South Vietnam, firing rocket and mortar rounds into Saigon and approximately 70 other cities and allied military positions.

But Tet '69 bore little resemblance to the general offensive of 1968. Although the enemy struck at exactly the same number of provincial capitals—29 out of 44, as they had a year earlier—significant improvements in allied intelligence prevented the Vietcong from repeating its previous performance. This time they avoided attacks against civilian populations, but struck rather at American military installations, in a deliberate attempt to inflict as many casualties on U.S. troops as possible.

In the first three weeks of the offensive, 1,140 Americans were killed in action, a total that almost equaled American losses in the same period of the 1968 offensive. However, enemy losses were only one-third of the previous year's high. The enemy's tactics may have changed in 1969, but they were just as deadly as in previous years.

THE BATTLE FOR HAMBURGER HILL

In May, a massive search-and-destroy operation was begun in I Corps, the northernmost provinces of South Vietnam. Its purpose was to keep pressure on the NVA units in the A Shau Valley, preventing them from mounting an attack on the coastal provinces. For ten days American and South Vietnamese forces fought one of the fiercest battles of the war to capture Apbia Mountain, located one mile from the Laotian border. Because the battle turned into a "meat grinder," the clash became known as the battle of "Hamburger Hill."

After heavy allied air strikes, artillery barrages and 10 infantry assaults, the communist stronghold was captured in the 11th attack, on

May 20, when 1,000 troops of the U.S. 101st Airborne Division and 400 South Vietnamese fought their way to the summit. Because the human cost of taking the hill was so high, 56 Americans killed and 420 wounded, the battle stirred further criticism of the war at home.

After the hill was taken, a landing zone was constructed to facilitate the search of the area. Captured documents proved that the hill was indeed a regimental command post. As was often done during the war, the hill was abandoned, and it was reoccupied by the NVA a month later. Near the landing zone, one soldier posted a memorial to the battle, a cardboard sign bearing the scrawled message, "Hamburger Hill. Was it worth it?"

As a grim reminder that the war was far from finished, *Life* magazine published the pictures of 241 U.S. soldiers who were killed in less than a week. The battle for Hamburger Hill immediately triggered controversy in the United States, especially in Washington, where Senator Edward Kennedy declared that the battle was "senseless and irresponsible."

The general who had ordered the taking of the hill defended his decision by pointing to the 630 enemy KIAs, almost a 3-to-1 ratio. Hamburger Hill marked the point where victory would no longer be determined by "body count." General Creighton Abrams, commander of U.S. forces in Vietnam, was quietly ordered to avoid such large-scale battles. For now on, the concentration would be on "Vietnamization" rather than combat operations.

THE LULL

Fearing that rising dissatisfaction with his handling of the war would sabotage his efforts to pressure North Vietnam into a settlement, Nixon approved a go-for-broke strategy. In July, he sent a personal message through French intermediaries to President Ho Chi Minh, reiterating his desire for a "just peace," but adding an ultimatum: Unless some progress toward a settlement was made by November 1, he would have no choice but to resort to "measures of great consequence and force."

Nixon's ultimatum had no effect on North Vietnam. But Hanoi did agree to conduct secret peace talks. On August 4, in the first of a long series of meetings, Kissinger met privately with North Vietnamese diplomat Xuan Thuy. Kissinger reiterated Nixon's peace proposals and ultimatum, but Xuan Thuy insisted that the United States would have to withdraw all of its troops and abandon Thieu in order to reach an agreement. Ho Chi Minh's formal response, written shortly before his death on September 3, restated the same message, and was in Nixon's words, a "cold rebuff."

Nixon was tempted to strike back, but Secretary of Defense Melvin Laird and Secretary of State William Rogers implored him not to undertake any action that would ignite the opposition at home. Moreover, after careful analysis, the National Security Council had concluded that air strikes and a blockade of northern ports might not force concessions from Hanoi or even set back its ability to continue the war in the south. For the time being, Nixon abandoned his plans for "savaging, punishing blows," and decided that if he continued to furnish large-scale military and economic assistance to the south, Hanoi would forsake its goal of national unification and agree to a Vietnam permanently divided, like another Korea.

On September 16, Nixon announced a second troop withdrawal as well as a reduction in draft calls. Although he had considerable support for his approach to Vietnam, an approval rating of 71% in October, Nixon continued to face opponents of the war on Capitol Hill who called for an accelerated peace. Senator Charles Goodell, an independent New York Republican, proposed legislation to bring all the troops home by the end of 1970. Antiwar sentiment was also spreading throughout the nation, especially among influential people such as press commentators, corporate executives, labor leaders, clergy and other well-known figures.

A DIVIDING NATION

Late in the summer of 1969, various different antiwar factions were organizing massive nationwide protests. Sam Brown, a 25-year-old former divinity student who had campaigned for Senator Eugene McCarthy, had concluded that moderate antiwar demonstrations would be more effective in communities rather than on college campuses. He and other antiwar activists began organizing a series of "moratoriums" to begin in various parts of the country.

Brown helped found and became coordinator of the Vietnam Moratorium Committee (VMC), an umbrella organization of antiwar activists. The committee took out a full-page advertisement in *The New York Times* of September 21 to announce the October 15 moratorium against the war. The VMC won the endorsement of politicians, civic, religious and labor leaders and many community organizations.

Sam Brown argued that "it's not just a small group of tired old peaceniks or a fringe percentage of radicals that are willing to protest the war. It's millions of Americans in every part of the country, even places like Mississippi—all they need is a little push and the right channel." The VMC gained the support of "establishment" figures, among them John Kenneth Galbraith and labor leader Walter Reuther. Forty members of Congress endorsed the moratorium, and a group of legislators tried to keep the House in session the entire night of October 14 in recognition of Moratorium Day.

Responding to a question on the upcoming protests, President Nixon said on September 27, "Under no circumstances will I be affected whatever by it." The administration's indifference only motivated the antiwar activists to greater action.

On October 15, demonstrations occurred throughout the country. It was estimated that the number of participants was 1 million, but in fact, they were uncounted and uncountable. *Time* magazine pointed out that "the significance of M-day was less in the numbers of participants than in who the participants were and how they went about it." In contrast with the mayhem that occurred at the Democratic convention in Chicago, the demonstrations were largely sober affairs, with many of the protesters being middle-class citizens. Across the country, church bells tolled, the names of American war dead were read at candlelight services, and participants quietly called out their antiwar chant, "Give Peace a Chance." The largest demonstrations took place in such cities as San Francisco, Boston and New York, and participants included those dressed in blue jeans as well as those in business suits.

Although Nixon had put out the word that he had been conducting "business as usual" on October 15, he was alarmed that demonstrators had besieged him in the White House, just as protesters had once done to Johnson. Nearly two weeks before the next moratorium, he delivered his most expansive report to date on the Vietnam War before a nationwide television audience on November 3.

Nixon defended the American commitment in Vietnam, warned that a complete withdrawal would result in a bloodbath, and stressed that the world's confidence in American leadership depended upon the outcome in Vietnam. He emphasized that all this required time and openly appealed for public support: "To you, the great silent majority of my fellow Americans—I ask for your support. Let us be united for peace. Let us be united against defeat. Because let us understand: North Vietnam cannot defeat or humiliate the United States. Only Americans can do that."

The public response to Nixon's "silent majority" speech was overwhelmingly successful. The White House received thousands of telephone calls, telegrams and letters of support. Nixon shrewdly appealed to the patriotism of his audience and placed his opponents on the defensive. The job of assailing Nixon's critics fell to Vice President Spiro Agnew. In a series of speeches, Agnew labeled the antiwar protesters as "an effete corps of impudent snobs who characterize themselves as intellectuals," and attacked the news media as "a small and unelected elite" that "do not—I repeat not—represent the view of America."

The moratorium of November 13–15 was even bigger than the demonstrations of the month before. In Washington, the ceremonies began on November 13 with a dramatic "March Against Death," in which a single file of 40,000 people walked in silent vigil from Arlington National Cemetery to the White House and Capitol. Each marcher carried a candle and a placard bearing the name of an American soldier killed in Vietnam or a Vietnamese village destroyed in the war.

On Saturday, November 15, in the freezing cold, 250,000 to 300,0000 participants marched from the Capitol down Pennsylvania Avenue to the Washington Monument. Some marchers bore placards reading "Silent Majority for Peace." The demonstrations surpassed the planners' expectations, and for the most part their peacefulness defied all dire predictions. Although the antiwar movement made it known that it was alive and growing, it as yet had no effect on changing Nixon's policy.

My Lai

By mid-November the public was being exposed to troubling moral questions about the war. On November 13, about 30 newspapers published a story written by journalist Seymour Hersh about an incident that had occurred the previous year at the hamlet of My Lai in Son My village. On the morning of March 16, 1968, a platoon from Charlie Company, First Battalion, 20th Infantry, of the newly formed Americal Division, under the command of Lieutenant William Calley Jr., rounded up unarmed Vietnamese civilians—old men, women, children and babies—and herded them into a ditch. At least 200 civilians were then gunned down.

Thirteen officers and enlisted men were charged by the U.S. Army with war crimes, and an additional 12 were charged with covering up the incident. Of the 25 men charged, only Calley was found guilty of war crimes—specifically, the murder of 22 unarmed civilians—and sentenced to life imprisonment. After enormous public pressure was expressed on his behalf, Calley's sentence was reduced to 10 years. He served only one-third of his term and was paroled in 1974 and given a dishonorable discharge.

The My Lai incident was certainly a controversial issue. Those on the left believed that the atrocities vindicated their charges that the war was illegal, immoral and unjust, while some on the right saw Calley as a victim of the antiwar movement. The public's support for Calley despite his conviction as a mass murderer "compounded the tragedy," as Colonel Harry G. Summers Jr., a battalion and operations officer in Vietnam, has stated, "for it rendered a major disservice to the overwhelming majority of American combat soldiers who risked their lives to protect—not harm—the men, women and children of South Vietnam."

THE WAR'S NEW FACE

Vietnamization was in full swing by the end of 1969. The South Vietnamese force level, about 850,000 when Nixon took office, was approaching 1 million, and the United States was giving them huge quantities of the latest weapons: more than a million M-16 rifles, 12,000 M-60 machine guns, 40,000 M-79 grenade launchers and 2,000 heavy mortars and howitzers. Almost overnight the South Vietnamese army had become one of the largest and best-equipped forces in the world.

Although opposition to the war was now more openly expressed in Congress, the polls continued to show that a majority of Americans supported President Nixon's policies in general. His pitch to the "silent majority" had been successful in containing the antiwar movement, for the present, but the war in Vietnam was now "Nixon's war."

CHRONICLE OF EVENTS

1969

January 16: The United States and DRV announce agreement on a round conference table for the Paris peace talks.

January 20: Richard Milhouse Nixon is inaugurated as the 37th president of the United States.

January 22-March 18: The U.S. 9th Marine Regiment (Reinforced) conducts military operations, known as Dewey Canyon, north of Ashau Valley in Quang Tri Province. Enemy casualties are reported at 1,335.

January 25: Four-party peace talks open in Paris. Participants include the United States, South Vietnam, North Vietnam and the National Liberation Front.

February 23–24: Communist forces launch mortar and rocket attacks on 115 targets in South Vietnam, including Saigon, Danang, Hue and the American base at Bien Hoa. It becomes known as the "post-Tet" offensive.

March 18: Operation Menu, secret bombing of Cambodia, begins by the U.S. Air Force. These strikes continue for the next 14 months.

March 19: "Vietnamization" of the war is announced by Secretary of Defense Melvin Laird.

March 26: Women Strike for Peace rally is held in Washington, D.C., the first large antiwar demonstration since Nixon's inauguration.

April 5–6: Thousands of antiwar demonstrators march through New York City to Central Park demanding the United States withdraw from Vietnam. The weekend of antiwar protests ends with demonstrations in Los Angeles, San Francisco, Washington, D.C., and other cities.

April 30: U.S. military personnel in Vietnam reaches peak strength of 543,400.

May 8: NLF unveils a 10-point peace plan that demands unconditional U.S. withdrawal and a coalition government excluding GVN President Nguyen Van Thieu.

Two men of the 26th Marine Regiment huddle under their ponchos during Operation Bold Mariner in January 1969. Photograph by Lance Cpl. W.R. Schaaf, USMC. Courtesy of the National Archives.

May 10–20: U.S. and South Vietnamese forces battle North Vietnamese troops for Apbia Mountain (Hill 937), one mile east of the Laotian border. Due to the intense fighting and high loss of life (U.S. casualties are listed at 56 killed and 420 wounded), it is dubbed the battle of "Hamburger Hill."

May 12: The Vietcong and NVA launch their largest number of attacks throughout South Vietnam since the Tet offensive of 1968.

May 14: President Nixon responds to the 10-point peace plan offered by the NLF. He calls for a simultaneous withdrawal from South Vietnam of American and North Vietnamese forces. The NLF announces it is opposed to any partial acceptance of their peace plan.

June 8: President Nixon announces the withdrawal of 25,000 troops from Vietnam by August. He emphasizes that U.S. forces will be replaced by South Vietnamese forces.

July 25: At a briefing in Guam, President Nixon announces a policy dubbed the "Nixon Doctrine." While the U.S. will have primary responsibility for the defense of allies against nuclear attack, the non-communist Asian nations must bear the burden of defense against conventional attack and responsibility for internal security.

August 4: National Security adviser Henry Kissinger meets covertly in Paris with North Vietnamese representative Xuan Thuy. Xuan Thuy insists on the NLF's 10-point plan as the only way of settling the war. An agreement is reached to keep open the new secret channel of communication.

August 26-December 31: The ARVN 5th Regiment conducts operation Lien Kat 531 in Quang Tri Province. A total of 542 enemy casualties are reported.

September 3: President Ho Chi Minh of North Vietnam dies at the age of 79.

September 14: The U.S. command reports that North Vietnamese regular army units have moved into the Mekong Delta for the first time in the war. This movement is reported to have taken place in the four weeks since U.S. troops departed the region as part of President Nixon's withdrawal plan.

September 16: President Nixon announces the withdrawal of 35,000 more troops.

September 26: Speaking at a news conference, President Nixon points to "some progress" in the effort to end the Vietnam war, and urges the American public to give him the time and the support he needs to end the war honorably.

October 15: National Moratorium antiwar demonstrations involve hundreds of thousands of people around the United States.

November 3: In his second major address on Vietnam, President Nixon appeals to the "silent majority," arguing that withdrawal would lead to a "disaster of immense magnitude."

November 15: More than 250,000 protesters gather in Washington, D.C., to participate in the largest antiwar demonstration in the nation's history.

November 16: The My Lai massacre, which took place on March 16, 1968, is revealed. A platoon from Charlie Company, First Battalion, 20th Infantry, is reported to have killed between 200 and 500 unarmed villagers at the hamlet of My Lai-4.

November 24: The U.S. Army announces that Lieutenant William Calley Jr. has been ordered to stand trial at a general court-martial for the premeditated murder of 109 Vietnamese civilians.

December 1: The first draft lottery since 1942 is held at Selective Service headquarters; those 19-year-olds whose birthdate was September 14 and whose last name began with "J" would be the first called.

December 4: The Louis Harris survey reports that 46% of those polled indicated sympathy with the goals of the November antiwar Moratorium demonstrations, while 45% disagreed with its goals.

December 7: Operation Randolph Glenn is begun by U.S. 101st Airborne Division (Airmobile) in coordination with ARVN First Infantry Division to provide a shield of security on the periphery of the populated lowlands of Thua Thien Province, I Corps.

December 15: President Nixon announces a third U.S. troop reduction of 50,000 men by April 15, 1970.

December 31: U.S. military personnel in Vietnam decline to 475,200; 9,414 are killed in action and 70,216 wounded in action in the 1969 fighting. A total of 40,024 U.S. military personnel have been killed in action and 262,796 wounded since 1961.

South Vietnamese forces have been increased to 897,000; 110,176 killed in action to date.

EYEWITNESS TESTIMONY

In making your study of Vietnam I want a precise report on what the enemy has in Cambodia and what, if anything, we are doing to destroy the buildup there. I think a very definite change of policy toward Cambodia probably should be one of the first orders of business when we get in.

President-elect Richard Nixon, to National Security adviser Henry Kissinger, message of January 8, 1969, in Kissinger's The White House Years *(1979).*

Should you put your foot to that flat rock or the clump of weeds to its rear? Paddy dike or water? You wish you were Tarzan, able to swing with the vines. You try to trace the footprints of the man to your front. You give it up when he curses you for following too closely; better one man dead than two. The moment-to-moment, step-by-step decision-making preys on your mind. The effect is sometimes paralysis. You are slow to rise from rest breaks. You walk like a wooden man. . . . with your eyes pinned to the dirt, spine arched, and you are shivering, shoulders hunched.

Sergeant Tim O'Brien, USA, recalls walking patrol in 1969, in If I Die in a Combat Zone, Box Me Up and Ship Me Back Home *(1973).*

Soldiers of the 101st Airborne Division rush toward UH-1D helicopters arriving to carry them out of Fire Base Saber on October 12, 1969. Courtesy of the National Archives.

It seemed like every day somebody got hurt. Sometimes I would walk point. Everybody was carrying the wounded. We had 15 wounded in my platoon alone. And the water was gone.

First Lieutenant Archie "Joe" Biggers, USMC, platoon leader, in 1969, in Terry's Bloods: An Oral History of the Vietnam War by Black Veterans *(1984).*

Some days you felt you'd lived a lifetime in just a week. Because Vietnam was not John Wayne on the beach at Iwo Jima. It was not ketchup on make-believe wounds. It was more like a grotesque form of "can you top this," because each time you thought you'd seen the ultimate, something else would come along.

I remember one young man with beautiful blond hair who came in blinded and missing one of his arms and both of his legs. He also had a belly wound. Well, thank God he couldn't see my face when he said, "Nurse, today's my twenty-first birthday." Because that was one of those times when you just couldn't have let them see it. When you smiled and smiled while you were there taking care of them so that afterward you could go home to your hootch and cry.

Nurse Ruth Sidisin, USAF, 21st Casualty Staging Flight, stationed at Tan Son Nhut (December 1968–December 1969), in Marshall's In the Combat Zone: An Oral History of American Women in Vietnam *(1987).*

They were gathering to leave when one of them, perhaps as a reluctant afterthought, decided to crawl into our brambled thicket. The young soldier was no more than three feet away when he cocked his .45 automatic pistol and let out a yell. It sounded like a hundred guns were cocked on command . . .

The major in command of the unit was very proud while we stood there in our mud-covered black pajamas. Back inside the walls of the Zoo, before being separated, [USAF Captain] Ed [Atterberry] shook my hand and said quietly, "We tried."

Lieutenant Colonel John Dramesi, USAF pilot and POW (1967–1973), on his escape attempt and recapture in 1969, in Code of Honor *(1975).*

I think it is not helpful in discussing Vietnam to use such terms as "cease-fire" because cease-fire is a term of art that really has no relevance, in my opinion, to a guerrilla war.

When you are talking about a conventional war, then a cease-fire agreed upon by two parties means that the shooting stops. When you have a guerrilla war, in which one may not even be able to control many of those who are responsible for the violence in the area, the cease-fire may be meaningless.

President Richard Nixon, to press conference on January 27, 1969, in Public Papers of the Presidents of the United States.

As they continued on, we heard the roar of an antitank mine blowing up. To our horror we watched as one of the men from the mine sweep team was lifted high into the air amidst smoke, dirt and debris. He fell back to earth as limp as a rag doll, minus both legs and God knows what else . . . He was alive, but just barely, and I don't think he had a prayer for survival. Dear god, if that ever happens to me I hope somebody puts a .45 to my head and puts me out of my misery.

Sergeant Toby Brant, USA, recalls a tank patrol in February 1969, in Journal of a Combat Tanker, Vietnam, 1969 *(1988). [Sgt. Brant was wounded in action later that year, losing both of his legs. After several operations and months of rehabilitation he was fitted with artificial limbs, which he uses successfully.]*

The last couple of weeks have been unbelievably busy. I've been working at least sixteen to eighteen hours a day without a day off in almost three weeks. I know we will get some time off when this is over, but for now, I'm beat. There's no one particular thing going on, just a lot of little things coincidentally happening at the same time. One day it's a chopper crash, next day a Lambretta (Vietnamese bus) accident. Then a mine explodes in a convoy or something else happens. Plus, there are always the guys who are wounded in battle. It's now 10:30 P.M. and I've been scrubbed since 7 A.M. My fingers are wrinkled. But I'm finished for the night. There are still two operating rooms running. The night crew can handle the rest. I just hope we don't have to get up again.

Lieutenant Lynda Van Devanter, U.S. Army nurse, to her mother and father, letter of 1969, in Home Before Morning *(1984).*

Every three or four days we would get resupplied by helicopter. With our rations and our ammunition and our medical supplies would come a large red sack of mail, which each squad leader passed out with a running commentary, much of it obscene. But every now and then someone got a Dear John, which was almost as bad as stepping on a mine. Then all the laughter stopped and everyone moved away, leaving the victim to read and reread the letter alone. After a while, some close buddy would come up with a deck of cards and maybe a C-ration delicacy like peaches and pound cake with melted chocolate. The two of them would talk quietly and everyone else would clean their rifles or dry their socks in silence. A Dear John was a calamity for the whole platoon. It took days to recover.

Lieutenant William Broyles Jr., USMC, recalling 1969, in Brothers in Arms: A Journey from War to Peace *(1986).*

We have not moved in a precipitate fashion, but the fact that we have shown patience and forebearance should not be considered as a sign of weakness. We will not tolerate a continuation of a violation of an understanding. But, more than that, we will not tolerate attacks which result in heavier casualties to our men at a time that we are honestly trying to seek peace at the conference table in Paris.

An appropriate response to these attacks will be made if they continue.

President Nixon, to press conference of March 4, 1969, in Public Papers of the Presidents of the United States.

We have to change the emphasis so that American forces in Vietnam can move forward to train and modernize the South Vietnamese forces, rather than fighting so much of the war themselves.

Secretary of Defense Melvin Laird, statement in U.S. News & World Report *(April 7, 1969).*

The Americans still have a considerable role to play. We have to go on dealing with the North Vietnamese and Vietcong main forces. It's an essential part of the war, but not the most important. We must also have an interest in the people. That has to be our front burner.

General Creighton Abrams, U.S. commander in Vietnam, statement in Lester's Life *article of April 25, 1969.*

The feeling of the men is that if there must be a war, it should be a total war supported by everybody—or no war at all.

Captain Richard Gayle, U.S. Army surgeon, statement in Newsweek *(April 28, 1969).*

The whole area was littered with chicoms [grenades], pieces of flesh, skin; we found a leg down the trail. There were quite a few of them out there. One machine gun hole had 13 gooks stacked up in front of it; the nearest one was about ten feet away. That one machine gun probably saved us from being overrun; they were right on us. The area was literally infested with them all over the place. We had numerous sightings from our position on the high ground; we could see them crossing rivers and milling around the area below.

First Lieutenant James Rigoulot, USMC, to the commandant of the Marine Corps, message of April 15, 1969, in Smith's U.S. Marines in Vietnam: High Mobility and Standdown *(1988).*

What kind of settlement will permit the South Vietnamese people to determine freely their own political future? Such a settlement will require the withdrawal of all non-South Vietnamese forces from South Vietnam and procedures for political choice that give each significant group in South Vietnam a real opportunity to participate in the political life of the nation.

To implement these principles, I reaffirm now our willingness to withdraw our forces on a specified timetable. We ask only that North Vietnam withdraw its forces from South Vietnam, Cambodia and Laos into North Vietnam, also in accordance with a timetable.

President Nixon, to the American people, television address of May 14, 1969, in Public Papers of the Presidents of the United States.

The day the United States decides to withdraw its forces, all other problems will be solved and the Paris deadlock will be broken. It is this decision we demand and it is the key to all other issues.

Premier Pham Van Dong, North Vietnam, statement of May 17, 1969, in The New York Times *(May 18, 1969).*

There is a severe burning feeling when you are hit, and it feels like your buttock has been set on fire. I tried not to scream, but involuntary noises came out after seven or eight whacks, no matter how hard I tried hold back. Oddly enough, the more torture a man takes, however, the more he can take. The best thing is to try to learn how to screw them out of their fun, because for them to get real kicks, the

victim must be screaming. This excites the crazies even more, and then they really lay it on you. Not yelling or screaming is easier said than done. I tried hard as I could to cheat them out of any pleasure they got from beating me.

Major Larry Guarino, USAF pilot and POW (1964–1973), recalling the POW camp dubbed by American POWs as ''the Zoo,'' 1969, in A P.O.W.'s Story: 2801 Days in Hanoi *(1990).*

As far as this business of solitary confinement goes—the most important thing for survival is communication with someone, even if it's only a wave or a wink, a tap on the wall, or to have a guy put his thumb up. It makes all the difference . . . During one period while I was in solitary, I memorized the names of all 335 of the men who were then prisoners of war in North Vietnam. I can still remember them.

Lieutenant Commander John S. McCain III, USN (POW: 1967–1973), in U.S. News & World Report *article of May 14, 1973.*

I was mad at having to sit shirtless in that human oven called the Mekong Delta with the sweat from my arms smearing over the print of the goddamned computer printout sheets I was working on. I was mad because the guys who would take that report and feed it back into a computer would have an air-

U.S. Marine Pfc. Joseph Big Medicine Jr., of the Cheyenne tribe from Watonga, Oklahoma, writes a letter home in July 1969. Photograph by Lance Cpl. John A. Gentry, USMC. Courtesy of the National Archives.

conditioned office in Saigon. They would be doing the paper-pushing for some staff officer who would have his own air-conditioned office. That officer would file his report to the air-conditioned Pentagon . . . It was obvious to me that I was the only one in the entire chain without an air-conditioner, and I sat there thinking that I was the only one who had even the vaguest idea of what the hell was going on!

First Lieutenant David Donovan, USA, on an operation in 1969, in Once a Warrior King *(1985).*

You may not be able to read this. I am writing it in a hurry. I see death coming up the hill.

Anonymous U.S. Marine, to his family, on the battle at "Hamburger Hill," near the Laotian border, letter of May 1969, in Zaffiri's Hamburger Hill *(1988).*

This is my third war and I haven't bumped into a fight like this since World War II. This crowd must have gotten the word from Uncle Ho.

Colonel Joseph Commy Jr., USA, on the battle at "Hamburger Hill," statement of May 19, 1969, in The New York Times *(May 20, 1969).*

That damn Blackjack [Colonel Honeycutt's radio codename] won't stop unless he kills every damn one of us.

Anonymous U.S. Army paratrooper, statement in the Associated Press (May 19, 1969).

. . . those gooks aren't stupid—they know exactly how much damage a B-52 raid does, how deep the bombs blow. They build their bunkers to withstand that. That's what they've done out there.

Anonymous U.S. Army intelligence officer, on the battle at "Hamburger Hill," statement in the Associated Press (May 19, 1969).

I could be standing on the doorstep on the 8th [of June] . . . As you can see from my shakey printing, the strain of getting "short" is getting to me, so I'll close now.

Anonymous U.S. Marine, to his family, letter of May 1969, in Life *article of June 27, 1969. [He was killed in action at the battle of Hamburger Hill in May 1969.]*

The paratroopers came down from the mountain, their green shirts darkened with sweat, their weap-

ons gone, their bandages stained brown and red—with mud and blood.

Jay Sharbutt, journalist, on the battle of "Hamburger Hill," report of May 19, 1969, in the Associated Press.

Hamburger Hill. Was it worth it?

Cardboard sign, posted near the landing zone of Hill 937, as a memorial to the battle, May 1969.

President Nixon has told us, without question, that we seek no military victory, that we seek only peace. How then can we justify sending our boys against a hill a dozen times or more, until soldiers themselves question the madness of the action? The assault on "Hamburger Hill" is only symptomatic of a mentality and policy that requires immediate attention. American boys are too valuable to be sacrificed for a false sense of pride.

Senator Edward Kennedy (D–Mass.), to the U.S. Senate, speech of May 20, 1969.

It's a myth that if we don't do anything, nothing will happen to us. It's not true. If we did pull back and were quiet, they'd kill us in the night. They come in and crawl under the wire and they drop satchel charges in the bunkers and they mangle and maim and kill our men. And the only way I can in good conscience lead my men and protect them is to insure that they aren't caught in that kind of situation.

Major General Melvin Zais, USA, statement of May 22, 1969, in The New York Times *(May 23, 1969).*

. . . we think about last week at "Hamburger Hill." . . . I don't suppose any war has ever been pleasant, nor has anyone suggested it to be. So while watching my partner under the "buddy system" get shot six times in both legs going up the hill, or seeing one guy in my foxhole get shot in the mouth, when we finally reached the top I was simply more depressed than angered. For if we are indeed going to fight a war, all the horrors are certainly going to be there too. No, the test must be whether the war, with all of its attendant insanity, is worth the price. That this war has not ever been, is not now, and can never be, worth the colossal price we have paid, in a thousand different ways . . .

At a mass funeral near Quang Tri City, friends and relatives mourn 60 civilian victims of the 1968 Tet Offensive. The victims' bodies had been found in shallow mass graves east of the city in 1969. Photograph by Cpl. Trygg Hansen, USMC. Courtesy of the National Archives.

Anonymous U.S. Marine, to Senator Edward Kennedy, letter of June 1969, in Sheehan's Harper's *article of November 1969.*

Being a medic is a strange thing, because you've got to be everything to a unit. Like, when guys got "Dear John" letters, I was the guy that sat and talked to them. I was older than a lot of the guys, I was all of twenty-two. Most of the guys were nineteen or so, so it was like being a father, confessor, psychologist, everything. Sometimes it was really easy, like putting a bandage on. Sometimes, it was really hard, like deciding when somebody was dead, and just moving on.

Medic Stephen Gubar, USA, noncombatant service CO (1969–1971), in Gioglio's Days of Decision *(1989).*

It may drag on. Our compatriots may have to face new sacrifices in property and life. Whatever may happen, we must keep firm our resolve to fight the U.S. aggressors till total victory.

Our rivers, our mountains, our people will always be;

The American aggressors defeated, we will build a country ten times more beautiful.

Whatever difficulties and hardships may be ahead, our people are sure of total triumph. The U.S. imperialists shall have to quit.

President Ho Chi Minh, declaration of May 1969 (his last public statement before his death on September 3, 1969), in Porter's Vietnam: the Definitive Documentation of Human Decisions *(1979).*

. . . after five years of fighting in which more and more Americans have been sent to Vietnam, we have finally reached the point where we can begin to bring Americans home from Vietnam.

This does not mean that the war is over. There are negotiations still to be undertaken. There is fighting still to be borne, until we reach the point that we can have peace.

President Nixon, to the nation, upon returning from his meeting at Midway Island with President Thieu of South Vietnam, statement of June 10, 1969, in Public Papers of the Presidents of the United States.

We've done as much as possible to get them ready without actually taking over command of the division. It's time to see if they'll get off their tails and carry the load. If they don't, then there's nothing we can do about it—and we will have failed in Vietnam.

Anonymous U.S. military officer, statement in Newsweek *(June 30, 1969).*

I realize that it is difficult to communicate meaningfully across the gulf of four years of war. But precisely because of this gulf, I wanted to take this opportunity to reaffirm in all solemnity my desire to work for a just peace. I deeply believe that the war in Vietnam has gone on too long and delay in bringing it to an end can benefit no one—least of all the people of Vietnam.

President Nixon, to President Ho Chi Minh, secret letter of July 15, 1969, in U.S. Congress' Background Information Relating to Southeast Asia and Vietnam *(1970).*

I was airlifted to Bien Hoa this morning. Last night we had an incoming ground attack. I almost went crazy my last night out there and BAMB—it was an all night shootout. Charlie fought past the guard bunkers at one position and got into the base camp. There were still enemy inside the barbed wire when I hastily boarded the chopper this morning.

I hated parting with Sergeant So that way. I shall always pray for his welfare. Alabama is traveling home with me.

Pfc. Dominick Yezzo, USA, First Cavalry Division, diary entry of August 11, 1969, in A G.I.'s Vietnam Diary *(1974).*

It was pitch black on the rivers, and often there was so much jungle growth that it looked like shadow upon shadow. We had to keep glancing at the boat radar to see where the riverbanks were, because radar was all we had to guide us. We hoped every little blip we saw on the radar did not turn out to be some VC sampan just waiting to fire at us. We had

the feeling that we were in a dark closet, with the door closed, and someone was in there with a gun trying to kill us.

Lieutenant Elmo Zumwalt III, recalling a nighttime river patrol in 1969, in My Father, My Son *(1986).*

It's all over, my war is finished. I felt real sad about parting with my friends. We went through so much together.

I'm on my way back to the U.S. right now. Flying on a huge Air Force C-141. I cannot help but look back over all that's happened to me in the past year. All the hurt and suffering, all the stupidity and pity I saw, all the good I remember. There were many wonderful and new experiences in that small foreign land . . .

Now it's all past, the good and the bad, and I'm going home to my family . . . I'm truly sorry for all the dead young men I leave behind. I made it and they didn't. Why? Thank you, Lord, for keeping me.

Dominick Yezzo, USA, diary entry of August 16, 1969, in A G.I.'s Vietnam Diary.

I am sorry, sir, but my men refused to go—we cannot move out . . . Some of them simply had enough—they are broken. There are boys here who have only 90 days left in Vietnam. They want to go home in one piece. The situation is psychic here.

Lieutenant Eugene Shurtz Jr., USA, Company A, 196th Light Infantry Brigade, to Lieutenant Colonel Robert Bacon, battalion commander, on his company's refusal to move on an assault against North Vietnamese bunkers and trench lines 30 miles south of Danang, message of August 24, 1969, the Associated Press (August 26, 1969).

Our Vietnamese people are deeply devoted to peace, a real peace with independence and real freedom. They are determined to fight to the end, without fearing the sacrifices and difficulties in order to defend their country and their sacred national rights.

President Ho Chi Minh, to President Nixon, letter of August 25, 1969, in U.S. Congress' Background Information Relating to Southeast Asia and Vietnam.

I can't believe that a fourth-rate power like Vietnam doesn't have a breaking point.

Henry Kissinger, National Security adviser, statement of 1969, in Wintle's The Dictionary of War Quotations *(1989).*

A medic attached to a company of the 501st Regiment, 101st Airborne Infantry Division, bandages paratroopers wounded in a firefight east of Tam Ky on June 26, 1969. Photograph by Spec. 5 Stephen Klubock, USA. Courtesy of the National Archives.

In my clouded mind, I kept thinking the helicopter would leave without me and never come back. I was crying, babbling, whimpering about that. Finally, the four of them grabbed corners of the poncho liner and forced their way through the underbrush, up the pathway. They slipped and stumbled, jostling me against the rocks. I shrieked again.

They set me down on top of the ridge and sank to their knees exhausted. I looked up at the helicopter's turning blade. "Thank you, Lord."

I was the second man to leave the firefight, and last to arrive at the secured claiming area. It had taken six hours to move two miles. It was midnight.

Pfc. Rocky Bleier, USA, after being wounded in a firefight on August 29, 1969, in Fighting Back *(1975). [Bleier recovered from his shrapnel wounds, rehabilitated himself and played football for the Pittsburgh Steelers.]*

Given the history of over-optimistic reports on Vietnam the past few years, it would be practically impossible to convince the American people that the other side is hurting and therefore with patience, time could be on our side. . . . we are not sure about our relative position—we have misread indicators many times before. . . . Finally, to a large and vocal portion of the dissenters in this country, the strength of the allied position is irrelevant—they want an end to the war at any price.

Henry Kissinger, National Security adviser, to President Nixon, memorandum of September 11, 1969, in White House Years *(1979).*

We have engaged in the wrong war, in the wrong place, at the wrong time and we have embraced a wrong-headed concept of American power and responsibility in the world. At inordinate sacrifice, we have for 6 years given the people of South Vietnam their option of freedom from North Vietnam. It is now for them alone to exercise that option. Now, it is for them alone to rally their people for war or peace. It is time for the South Vietnamese to make hard and realistic decisions without the protective mantle of American troops. It is time we told the South Vietnamese leaders that 1 year from now they will be on their own.

Senator Charles Goodell (R–N.Y.) to the U.S. Senate, on his resolution (defeated) to withdraw all U.S. troops from Vietnam by December 1970, speech of September 25, 1969.

. . . before I came here this last time, I was in Boston and saw Leinsdorf conduct Beethoven's *Fifth*. Now, that's the way the war should be run. He calls on his strings—and he gets a little bit of strings. He calls on his drums—and he gets a little bit of drums. That's the way we should do it—a little bit of air support just when it's needed, not a goddamned hour of air support; a little bit of artillery, not a goddamned hour of artillery.

General Creighton Abrams, U.S. commander in Vietnam, statement of October 5, 1969, in Buckley's New York Times Magazine article of October 5, 1969.

There comes a time when it becomes a "sink or swim" proposition. Here in Vietnam, we never will truly know how good we South Vietnamese are until we have been pretty much left on our own. We know if we fail, it will be very difficult to get American troops back here because of political pressures in the United States.

Anonymous ARVN general, statement in U.S. News & World Report (October 6, 1969).

I'm not going to be the first American President who loses a war.

President Nixon, to Republican congressional and party leaders, statement in Time (October 10, 1969).

Although Hanoi has not been bombed in 19 months and the U.S. air war was halted almost a year ago, there are no signs of any official willingness to acknowledge the change . . . everywhere I traveled I saw again the same posters urging the people to remain war conscious and warning against any relaxation while the "enemy" still threatens. In Hanoi, the same bomb shelters still clutter almost every street. Outside the city the same anti-aircraft guns are pointed at the skies, manned by the same set of alert-looking soldiers that I saw last year.

Marc Ribaud, French photographer, statement in Newsweek (October 20, 1969).

President Nixon has a program to end the war in Vietnam. That program is Vietnamization.

Melvin Laird, secretary of defense, statement of October 29, 1969, in The New York Times (October 30, 1969).

The enemy always has the advantage, as I see it, of operating in the jungle, in the canopy. You only get a point to point contact. You cannot maneuver on a broad front, so you are on a parity with him as far as the infantry is concerned. Since your observation is limited and your fields of fire are limited, it is difficult to make use of supporting arms in which we have a distinct advantage. And the enemy can always break contact and he can always evade. And so this being the case, we are just about equal; we have no advantage.

Colonel James Ord Jr., USMC, statement of November 3, 1969, in Smith's U.S. Marines in Vietnam: High Mobility and Standdown (1988).

I wouldn't wear conventional camouflage fatigues in the field. I wore a dark-green loincloth, a dark-green bandana to blend in with the foliage, and a little camouflage paint on my face. And Ho Chi Minh sandals. And my grenades and ammunition. That's the way I went to the field.

I dressed like that specifically as the point man, because if the enemy saw anyone first, they saw myself. They would just figure I was just another jungle guy that was walking around in the woods. And I would catch them off guard.

Spec. 4 Arthur "Gene" Woodley Jr., USA, combat photographer, on walking on patrol in 1969, in Terry's Bloods: An Oral History of the Vietnam War by Black Veterans.

And so tonight—to you, the great silent majority of my fellow Americans—I ask for your support.

I pledged in my campaign to the Presidency to end the war in a way that we could win the peace. I have initiated a plan of action which will enable me to keep that pledge.

The more support I can have from the American people, the sooner that pledge can be redeemed; for the more divided we are at home, the less likely the enemy is to negotiate at Paris.

President Nixon, to the American people, television address of November 3, 1969, in Public Papers of the Presidents of the United States.

At the end of 1970 we will replace all American combat troops.

Vice President Nguyen Cao Ky, South Vietnam, statement of November 5, 1969, in The New York Times *(November 6, 1969).*

Hour after hour names were called out onto the night, slicing through the cold rainy air across the helmets of the marines guarding their President from the people, then bouncing with just a faint, faint echo off the wet, white walls of the White House. Charles Green, Jr. . . . Robert James . . . Karl Rollins . . .

Clarence Funnye, journalist, on the Moratorium demonstration of November 13–15, 1969, in Washington, D.C., in Village Voice *article of November 20, 1969.*

It's difficult to understand how we can be losing these boys the way we are and not accomplishing anything, especially since we've been there so long. Our neighborhood is flooded with 15- and 16-year-old kids, and the way things are going, their parents are afraid they could be over there in a few years.

Mrs. Florence Chotiner, antiwar demonstrator in Los Angeles, California, statement of November 13, 1969, in The New York Times *(November 14, 1969).*

I'm here on behalf of the fellows that never made it back and will never make it back.

Antiwar demonstrator Don Smith, Vietnam veteran, at the Moratorium demonstration in Washington, D.C., statement of November 13, 1969, in The Washington Post *(November 14, 1969).*

We feel the administration must know that many, many people, those of us who have lost our sons, feel we should get out of this involvement.

Mrs. Ransom, antiwar demonstrator and mother of Army 2nd Lt. Robert Crawford Ransom Jr. (KIA, May 1968), at the Moratorium demonstration in Washington, D.C., statement of November 13, 1969, in The Washington Post *(November 14, 1969).*

I can say as I stand here today . . . that we will achieve a just peace in Vietnam, I cannot tell you the time or date, but I do know this: That when peace comes . . . it will come because of the support that we have received not just from Republicans but from Democrats, from Americans in this House and in the other body and throughout the nation.

President Nixon, to Congress, speech of November 13, 1969, in Public Papers of the Presidents of the United States.

Now how is the network news determined? A small group of men, numbering perhaps no more than a dozen anchormen, commentators and executive producers, settle upon the twenty minutes or so of film and commentary that's to reach the public . . . How many marches and demonstrations would we have if the marchers did not know that the ever-faithful tv cameras would be there to record their antics for the next tv show?

Vice President Spiro Agnew, to the Midwest Regional Republican Committee at Des Moines, Iowa, speech of November 13, 1969, in The New York Times *(November 14, 1969).*

At 10:25 a.m.—twenty-five minutes after the appointed hour—the mass march began. Three drummers, their instruments muffled in black crepe, set the pace. Behind them came an honor guard of next-to-kin to those who had died in Vietnam carrying the ten coffins. Behind them, a man dragging a 300-pound wooden cross. And then the front row of marchers, seventeen abreast, bearing the banner SILENT MAJORITY FOR PEACE . . .

By early afternoon the mall was a solid mass of people stretching from the Washington Monument down the gentle, grassy slope to 17th Street where the speaker's stand was set up.

Paul Hoffman, journalist, on the Moratorium demonstration of November 15, 1969 in Washington, D.C., in Moratorium: An American Protest *(1970).*

They came down the great [Pennsylvania] Avenue and down the Mall in a seemingly endless cascade—thousands after thousands after thousands.

The Washington Post, *on the Moratorium demonstration of November 15, 1969, in Washington, D.C., in an article of November 16, 1969.*

We who are here today do not claim that we are a majority. Neither do we deny that we are a majority. We are here to witness in person by our presence . . . our position in opposition to the war.

Senator Eugene McCarthy (D–Minn.), to anti-war demonstrators, speech of November 15, 1969, at the Mall in Washington, D.C., in The Washington Post *(November 16, 1969).*

What do we want?
Peace.
When do we want it?
Now.

Antiwar protesters, chant at the Moratorium demonstration of November 15, 1969, in Washington, D.C.

Peace Now! Peace Now!

Antiwar protesters, chant at the Moratorium demonstration of November 15, 1969, in Washington, D.C.

GIs Against the War.

Vietnam Veterans Against the War (VVAW), banner carried at the Moratorium demonstration of November 15, 1969, in Washington, D.C.

The marchers did not move in mass. They walked slowly and in single file. Each carried a placard bearing the name of an American soldier killed or a village destroyed in Vietnam. When it was dark, most carried candles.

U.S. News & World Report, *on the Moratorium demonstration of November 15, 1969 in Washington, D.C., in an article of November 24, 1969.*

The worst thing in the world is [having] to wait for a rifle bullet to smash into you [before you can] fight back and influence the final outcome of your little duel. We took scattered potshots on the LZ extraction but got out safely with the help of some Cobra gunships. When we extracted, we could hear our friends in back of us yelling and scrambling for cover as the Cobras lined up for their runs. You'll never know how much a man can fall in love with a machine till you've stood on the ground with your head in a noose and had the rope cut at the last minute by a Huey's rotor blades. I'd marry one of those helicopters if it could scratch my back and cook a respectable meal.

After a five-hour march to Hill 190 northwest of Danang, men of the 1st Platoon, Company L, 3rd Battalion, 26th Marines, rest along a stream in December 1969. Courtesy of the National Archives.

The 1st Battalion, 9th Marines, waits to board the amphibious transport Paul Revere *at Danang, initiating the first phase of the withdrawal of American forces from Vietnam. Courtesy of the National Archives.*

Spec. 4 George Olsen, USA, Company G, 75th Infantry (Ranger), Americal Division, to a friend, letter of November 15, 1969, in Edelman's Dear America: Letters Home From Vietnam *(1985). [Olsen was killed in action on March 3, 1970.]*

The change I am talking about represents not only increased funding for modernization of the armed forces of South Vietnam; it also represents the establishment of a new objective for this modernization which has not previously existed, namely, the effective assumption by the R.V.N.A.F. [Republic of Vietnam Armed Forces] of a larger share of combat operations from American forces.

Melvin Laird, secretary of defense, to the Senate Armed Services Committee, testimony of November 19, 1969, in The New York Times *(November 20, 1969).*

Miniskirts. Jesus! I check my bag, get my seat assignment, and am shown to the plane . . . The stewardess leads me back to my seat, on the aisle next to a businessman in a suit. Eyeing my uniform, he whispers to the stewardess and moves to another seat. I fall into the window seat, eager for the plane to lift off so I can lean the seat back and catch some sleep. Strange, there is no real excitement; just fatigue, accumulated over two years, or was it three? The stewardess smiles, offers a miniature pillow and a blanket. God, she smells good! I close my eyes, try to picture my family. Will I recognize them? Will they recognize me? We rush into the air, the lights are dim, and I nod off.

Pfc. John Ketwig, USA, recalls going home in 1969, in And a Hard Rain Fell *(1985).*

We have had success this year in Vietnamizing the war . . . Infiltration is below 1968 . . . Vietnamization . . . has been moving along on schedule and we are very pleased . . . It is moving forward on a very progressive basis . . . I am not going to get into any predictions or forecasts. I think we have had too much of that . . . We are moving forward.

Melvin Laird, secretary of defense, statement of December 14, 1969, on ABC's "Issues and Answers."

The leaders in Hanoi have declared on a number of occasions that division in the United States would eventually bring them the victory they cannot win over our fighting men in Vietnam. This demonstration of support by the American people for our plan to bring a just peace has dashed those hopes.

Hanoi should abandon its dreams of military victory. It is time for them to join us in serious negotiations. There is nothing to be gained by delay.

If Hanoi is willing to talk seriously, they will find us flexible and forthcoming.

President Nixon, to the American people, television address of December 15, 1969, in Public Papers of the Presidents of the United States.

9. Vietnamizing the War: 1970–1971

OPERATION PHOENIX

By early 1970, about two-thirds of the estimated 125,000 communist regulars in the south were North Vietnamese. They were deployed to replace the Vietcong troops who were decimated during the Tet Offensive two years earlier. As a result of the Phoenix program, one of the more controversial American operations of the war, the Vietcong political structure was also coming under attack. Although formally initiated by President Thieu in mid-1968, in the wake of the Tet Offensive, it did not really get off the ground until 1969, when the government of South Vietnam finally provided an organizational basis for the program to exist.

Phoenix was not a military program. It was instead an intelligence-gathering, sharing and coordinating effort designed to identify the estimated 70,000 members of the Vietcong infrastructure (VCI)—the VC political leaders—so that armed Vietnamese forces and National Police could take action against them. Members of the VCI could be "neutralized" through either arrest or execution. By centralizing the U.S. and South Vietnamese intelligence activities, it was believed that the rural population, which the Vietcong relied on for recruits, food, money and asylum, could be crushed. The title for the program, Phoenix, is a near translation of *phung hoang,* a mythical Vietnamese bird endowed with omnipotent powers.

The Phoenix operation was labeled as a "mass murder" program by American antiwar activists. But participants involved in Phoenix suggest that it was instead a program plagued with inefficiency, corruption and abuse. South Vietnamese officials protested at working with Americans, appropriated U.S. aid set aside for the operation, and were so receptive to bribes that 70% of the Vietcong suspects captured were able to buy back their freedom.

Despite its flaws and excesses, William Colby, the CIA executive who ran Phoenix, claimed in his congressional testimony that some 17,000 VCI sought amnesty, 28,000 were captured and 20,000 were killed (some 85% in military actions). The effectiveness of the Phoenix

Marines patrol a valley just three miles west of Danang. The incongruity of war and peace is vividly demonstrated as the seemingly unconcerned farmer employs a crude plow and a water buffalo to work his plot. Courtesy of the National Archives.

Program was confirmed after the war by the Vietcong themselves. In his 1981 visit to Hanoi, Stanley Karnow, author of *Vietnam: A History*, was told by Madame Nguyen Thi Dinh, a veteran Vietcong leader, "We never feared a division of troops, but the infiltration of a couple of guys into our ranks created tremendous difficulties for us." Nguyen Co Thach, Vietnam's foreign minister after 1975, "admitted that the Phoenix effort 'wiped out many of our bases' in South Vietnam, compelling numbers of North Vietnamese and Vietcong troops to retreat to sanctuaries in Cambodia."

THE CAMBODIAN "INCURSION"

The overthrow of Cambodia's neutralist Prince Sihanouk on March 18, 1970, by a pro-American regime headed by Prime Minister Lon Nol presented an opportunity for President Nixon to demonstrate to Hanoi the United States' serious commitment to South Vietnam. It also paved the way for the possibility of accomplishing a short-term military objective: disabling the communists' sanctuaries along the Cambodian border.

Nixon had hoped that the demonstrations of public support that followed his November 3, 1969, speech would persuade the North Vietnamese to negotiate. But there had been no breakthrough in Paris, and the president recognized that the announcement of additional troop withdrawals would probably encourage North Vietnam to delay further. Also, with the communists closing in on Phnom Penh, the Cambodian capitol, Nixon feared that the entire country would be overrun by the North Vietnamese.

The possible U.S. military involvement in Cambodia, whether by ARVN or American forces, was a subject of heated debate in Washington. By late March, General Creighton Abrams was pressing for stepped-up measures, while Secretary of Defense Melvin Laird expressed his concerns in a memorandum to Secretary of State William Rogers: "We will be in a difficult position if Cambodia asks the U.S. government to become militarily involved in that country." Caution was also pervading Capitol Hill, where senators Frank Church and John Sherman Cooper began to draft legislation to forbid American forces from entering Cambodia.

President Nixon's decision to send American troops into Cambodia became one of the most important and controversial decisions of his presidency. Although he realized the move into Cambodia would cause "a hell of an uproar at home," Nixon reasoned that the "incursion" would demonstrate to the North Vietnamese the president's determination. Preoccupied throughout his career with the importance of responding to crises, Nixon grasped this opportunity to show his courage under fire and to demonstrate to his domestic and foreign adversaries that he would not be intimidated. On April 30, at five o'clock in the morning, Nixon had finished drafting his speech to the nation, and he said to his National Security adviser Henry Kissinger, "Now that we have made the decision, there must be no recrimination among us—not even if the whole thing goes wrong."

On Thursday, April 30, at 9:00 P.M., Nixon revealed the Cambodian "incursion" in a televised address. He justified the action as a response to North Vietnamese "aggression" and as a necessary measure to protect American forces in Vietnam. The real target of the operation, he explained, was the Central Office for South Vietnam (COSVN), the "nerve center" of North Vietnamese military operations, although the Defense Department had made it clear to him its uncertainty as to where COSVN was located or whether it actually existed.

Nixon denied any intention of widening the war and stressed the wider strategic and political ramifications of his decision: breaking the deadlock at the peace talks, continuing the American withdrawal and upholding the credibility of the president and the United States. "I would rather be a one-term president," he stated, "than be a two-term president at the cost of seeing America . . . accept the first defeat in its sound 190 years' of history."

As Nixon spoke, an allied force of 20,000 men, supported by American aircraft, was pushing into the Fishhook area, where it was believed the two main North Vietnamese and Vietcong bases in Cambodia were located. Meeting only little resistance, the allied forces uncovered sprawling complexes of living quarters, mess halls, training sites and storage depots. Thousands of weapons, millions of rounds of ammunition, tons of rice and hundreds of vehicles were seized. But the incursion set back North Vietnamese offensive capabilities only temporarily, and COSVN turned out to be only a few empty huts. An intelligence analyst ridiculed the idea of a consolidated headquarters, describing COSVN as "a kind of permanent floating crap game of Communist leaders," a highly mobile, widely dispersed operation.

TRAGEDY AT KENT STATE

The unexpected expansion of a war that the president had promised to wind down generated controversy at home and triggered the biggest antiwar protests to date, especially on college campuses. At Kent State University in Ohio, demonstrations had grown in strength day by day, with students occupying the faculty buildings, as they had all across the country. On May 4, the Ohio National Guard, with loaded rifles, surrounded the campus at Kent State. Harassed by rock-throwing students, the Guardsmen fired into the crowd, killing four students and wounding 11.

Two of the dead, Jeffrey Miller and Alison Krause, had actively participated in the rally. A third, William Schroeder, an ROTC cadet, had spent the weekend in a moral struggle over his increasing misgivings about the war. The fourth victim, Sandy Scheuer, was merely passing by on her way to class.

Five days earlier Nixon had referred to students who had set fires at Berkeley, Yale and Stanford universities as "bums." In a sorrow that reached across America, the father of one dead girl said, "My child was not a bum." The Kent State killings generated protests across the country. More than 400 universities and colleges closed down as students and professors staged strikes, and nearly 100,000 protesters peaceably demonstrated in Washington on May 9, demanding the withdrawal of U.S. military forces from Vietnam.

CHALLENGING THE PRESIDENT

The Cambodian incursion also generated the most serious congressional challenge to presidential authority since the beginning of the war. In a symbolic act of defiance, the Senate voted overwhelmingly in

June to terminate the Tonkin Gulf Resolution of 1964. An amendment sponsored by senators John Sherman Cooper of Kentucky and Frank Church of Idaho proposed to cut off all funds for American military operations in Cambodia after June 30. An even more restrictive amendment sponsored by senators George McGovern of South Dakota and Mark Hatfield of Oregon would have required the administration to withdraw all American forces from Vietnam by the end of 1971.

The administration eventually rode out the Cambodian controversy. Nixon removed American troops from Cambodia by the end of June, depriving his opponents of their strongest issue, and the protests gradually subsided. Congress was not prepared to challenge the president directly or assume responsibility for ending the war. The Cooper-Church amendment was passed in the Senate, but defeated in the House; and the McGovern-Hatfield amendment could not secure a majority even in the Senate.

NIXON'S NEW PEACE INITIATIVE

Expecting to break the diplomatic stalemate in Paris by going into Cambodia, Nixon had merely hardened it. North Vietnamese and Vietcong delegates boycotted the formal Paris talks until the American troops had been withdrawn from Cambodia, and the secret talks lapsed for months. Hanoi now believed that it could afford to bide its time and was convinced that domestic pressure would eventually force an American withdrawal.

On October 7, 1970, Nixon unveiled what he described as a "major new initiative for peace." In a televised speech, President Nixon asked North Vietnam and the Vietcong to agree to a "ceasefire in place" throughout Indochina, but the proposal made no concessions on the fundamental issues. Hanoi promptly rejected the proposal and continued to demand a total U.S. withdrawal from Indochina and the removal of Thieu from South Vietnam.

A National Security Council study of late 1970 grimly concluded that the United States could neither persuade nor force Hanoi to withdraw its troops from the South. Opposition to the war in Congress was growing, and a revived antiwar movement was taking shape. Although the situation in South Vietnam remained stable, by the end of 1970, intelligence reports were indicating a marked increase in the infiltration of North Vietnamese troops and supplies into Laos, Cambodia and South Vietnam, posing a threat to the northern province of Hue, from which a significant number of American forces were being withdrawn.

THE CHANGING OF THE GUARD

Despite the protests of General Creighton Abrams, Nixon ordered the removal of 100,000 troops by the end of 1971, leaving 175,000 men in Vietnam, of whom only 75,000 were combat forces. Determined to secure a "just" peace and to counter the threat to Vietnamization by increasing North Vietnamese infiltration, Nixon increased military pressure against the north. U.S. aircraft mounted heavy attacks against supply lines and staging areas in Laos and Cambodia, and in February 1971, Nixon again expanded the war, approving a major ground operation in Laos.

The objective was the same as the Cambodian incursion—to destroy enemy supply lines along the Ho Chi Minh Trail and also to buy time for Vietnamization. But this time only ARVN forces would participate in the ground fighting, with the U.S. providing air and logistical support. The Cooper-Church Amendment, passed after the Cambodian incursion of 1970, barred American ground troops from entering Cambodia and Laos.

The operation was codenamed Lam Son 719, for a 15th-century Vietnamese victory over China. This test of Vietnamization began on February 8, 1971, when 5,000 ARVN troops marched down Route 9 into Laos. The United States provided logistical support from Khe Sanh. After pushing a few miles into Laos with little resistance, the attack stalled until reinforcements brought the ARVN forces up to 21,000. Meanwhile the weather had turned bad, making close air support and helicopter resupply along Route 9 almost impossible.

By early March, the ARVN forces had crossed 20 miles beyond the border and had reached the town of Tchepone, a major NVA and Vietcong supply center. The South Vietnamese army found the town already wrecked by earlier American air strikes. President Thieu announced the "objective" had been achieved and ordered the withdrawal of the assault forces. By then, the NVA, fearing their crucial supply lines threatened, struck back at the withdrawing ARVN on Route 9, assaulting outlying firebases, shelling Khe Sanh and setting up a network of anti-aircraft fire. While MACV/ARVN spokesmen called it an "orderly retreat," news photographers captured images of terrified ARVN troops dropping from the skids of overloaded helicopters. On March 24, the ARVN pulled its last troops out of Laos, suffering some 9,000 casualties, almost 50% of their force.

Only the deployment of every available U.S. helicopter to evacuate the ARVN prevented a greater tragedy. The operation not only failed to destroy the supply route along the Ho Chi Minh Trail, but also raised doubts about whether the ARVN would soon be able to fight without U.S. support. The battle also convinced the communists that the NVA could defeat the best ARVN units.

DISILLUSIONMENT AT HOME

By spring 1971, a survey showed that Nixon's support for his conduct of the war had slid to 34%. Another poll reported that public confidence in Nixon had dropped to 50%, his lowest rating since entering office. Antiwar protests were also becoming more militant, and some demonstrations were now being spearheaded by Vietnam veterans themselves.

In late April, a group organized as the Vietnam Veterans Against the War (VVAW) staged a moving protest in Washington, D.C. After days of marching, rallying and lobbying, a few hundred veterans clothed in faded combat fatigues and wearing their combat decorations along with peace symbols, hurled their medals onto the steps of the Capitol Building. Many of the veterans embraced each other and broke into tears. One veteran explained, "My parents told me that if I really did come down here and turned in my medals, that they never wanted anything more to do with me . . . [My wife] said she would divorce me if I came down here because she wanted my medals for our son to see when he grew up."

THE PENTAGON PAPERS

President Nixon responded to the antiwar demonstrations by stating that "while everybody has a right to protest peacefully, policy in this country is not made by protests." But the publication on June 13 by *The New York Times* of the so-called "Pentagon Papers," a history of the decision-making in Vietnam based on secret Defense Department documents, infuriated Nixon. Although the *Pentagon Papers* covered U.S. involvement in Vietnam only form 1954 to 1968, Nixon feared that they might further erode public support for the war. For the documents confirmed what critics of the war had long been saying, that both Kennedy and Johnson had consistently misled the public about their intentions in Vietnam.

Although Nixon was able to obtain an injunction against their publication, more and more newspapers defied the order with the justification that they did not endanger national security. *The New York Times* appealed to the Supreme Court on its right to publish the documents, and on June 30 the Court ruled in favor of the *Times.*

As a consequence of the *Pentagon Papers,* Nixon approved the creation of a clandestine group of "plumbers" to plug leaks within the government. These illegal activities and their subsequent cover-up became part of the Watergate scandal, ultimately resulting in President Nixon's resignation in August 1974.

Three Marines cool off by pouring water over their heads from their helmets, 1969. Courtesy of the National Archives.

GETTING NOWHERE IN PARIS

In late May 1971, Kissinger resumed his discussions with the North Vietnamese in Paris. For the next year the talks dragged on inconclusively, with the main obstacle being the status of the Thieu regime. From the start of the secret talks, the North Vietnamese had insisted that Thieu's removal was an essential precondition to any peace agreement.

Elections were scheduled to be held in South Vietnam in September. Thieu further complicated matters in August by forcing the removal of two opposition candidates, Nguyen Cao Ky and Duong Van Minh. Thieu ran unopposed and was reelected, while the United States declared its position as one of "neutrality." Kissinger attempted to revive the secret talks by offering a new proposal calling for elections to be held within 60 days after a cease-fire and providing that Thieu would withdraw one month in advance of the elections.

Although Hanoi considered the offer an improvement over earlier ones, it rejected the proposal on the basis that Thieu could still use the organization of the government to circumvent the elections. The secret talks once again stalled in late November. After 10 years of struggle, both sides were unprepared to make the necessary concessions to bring forth a peace. Each felt it could achieve its objectives by means other than compromise.

CHRONICLE OF EVENTS

1970

January 28: A Gallup Poll shows that 65% of those interviewed said they approved of President Nixon's handling of the war, his highest approval rating to date.

February 21: National Security adviser Henry Kissinger begins secret talks in Paris with North Vietnamese representative Le Duc Tho.

March 13: With Cambodian chief of state Norodom Sihanouk out of the country, the Phnom Penh government demands the immediate withdrawal of Vietnamese communist troops from Cambodian territory.

March 18: The Cambodian National Assembly deposes Sihanouk, installs General Lon Nol as chief of state.

March 23: Prince Sihanouk declares from Beijing that he will form a "national union" government with the communist Khmer Rouge. North Vietnam and the Pathet Lao immediately pledge their support to the new resistance government.

March 27–28: U.S-supported ARVN forces launch their first major military operation into Cambodia.

March 28: The White House announces for the first time that U.S. troops, at the judgment of their field commanders, are permitted to cross the Cambodian border in response to enemy threats. U.S. officials contend that this does not mean a widening of the war.

April 4: The largest Washington, D.C., prowar demonstration since America's involvement in Vietnam began, is held. About 15,000 people march up Pennsylvania Avenue to a rally at the Washington Monument.

April 8: Cambodian government forces are driven back by Vietnamese communist troops in heavy fighting nine miles from the South Vietnamese border.

April 11: A Gallup Poll shows 48% of the public approves of President Nixon's policy in Vietnam, while 41% disapprove.

April 20: President Nixon, in a televised speech, pledges to withdraw 150,000 more U.S. troops over the next year "based entirely on progress" of Vietnamization.

April 30: President Nixon announces in a nationally televised speech that American troops are attacking communist sanctuaries in Cambodia, with the immediate objective being the location of the Communist Central Office of South Vietnam (COSVN) in the Fishhook area, 50 miles northwest of Saigon.

Large antiwar protests erupt throughout the United States, especially on college campuses.

May 4: Ohio National Guardsmen fire on student demonstrators at Kent State University, killing four and wounding 11 students.

May 6: More than 200 colleges and universities shut down as thousands of students join a nationwide campus antiwar protest.

May 8: Helmeted construction workers break up a student antiwar demonstration on Wall Street in New York City, attacking demonstrators in a melee that leaves more than 70 persons injured.

May 9: Between 75,000 and 100,000 people gather in Washington, D.C., in a hastily organized protest against the U.S. invasion of Cambodia.

May 12: South Vietnam's Vice President Ky announces that allied naval vessels have begun blocking a 100-mile stretch of the Cambodian coastline to prevent communist forces from being resupplied by sea.

May 20: More than 100,000 construction workers, dockmen and office workers lead a parade in New York City supporting the policies of President Nixon.

June 3: President Nixon, in a televised speech, announces that the allied drive into Cambodia was the "most successful operation" of the war, and that he is now able to resume the withdrawal of U.S. troops.

June 24: U.S. Senate repeals the *Tonkin Gulf Resolution* in a vote of 81–10.

June 30: U.S. ground combat troops end two months of operations in Cambodia and return to South Vietnam. About 34,000 South Vietnamese troops remain in Cambodia.

June 30: U.S. Senate passes the Cooper-Church Amendment by a vote of 58–37, barring U.S. military personnel from further combat or advisory roles in Cambodia. The amendment represents the first limitation ever voted on the president's powers as commander-in-chief during a war.

September 1: The Senate rejects (55–39) the McGovern-Hatfield amendment, which set a deadline of December 31, 1971, for complete withdrawal of American troops from South Vietnam.

September 7: U.S. troops strength falls below 400,000 for the first time since early 1967.

September 26: A Gallup Poll shows 55% of the American people favor the recently defeated McGovern-Hatfield amendment to pull all U.S. troops out of South Vietnam by December 31, 1971.

October 7: President Nixon proposes a "standstill ceasefire" in all three countries of Indochina, and makes a new five-point proposal to end the war, including the eventual withdrawal of all U.S. forces, the unconditional release of all POWs and a political solution reflecting the will of the South Vietnamese people.

October 8: The communist delegation in Paris denounces Nixon's proposal and continues to demand an unconditional and total U.S. withdrawal from Indochina.

November 11: For the first time in five years, there are no U.S. combat fatalities in Vietnam.

November 12: Lieutenant William Calley Jr. goes on trial at Fort Benning, Georgia, for his part in the My Lai incident; he is charged with the premeditated murder of unarmed South Vietnamese civilians.

November 21: A U.S. rescue team raids Son Tay prisoner-of-war compound 20 miles west of Hanoi, but finds no U.S. prisoners.

December 10: Holding his first news conference in four months, President Nixon warns North Vietnam that he will order the bombing of military sites in North Vietnam if the level of fighting in South Vietnam increases.

December 31: U.S. military personnel in Vietnam decline to 334,600; 4,221 killed in action and 30,643 wounded in action in the 1970 fighting. Total of 44,245 U.S. military personnel killed in action and 293,439 wounded since 1961.

South Vietnamese forces have been increased to 968,000; 133,522 killed in action to date.

1971

January 1: Congress forbids the use of U.S. ground troops in Laos and Cambodia, but not the use of U.S. air power in those countries.

January 30–February 7: Operation Dewey Canyon II begins as the vanguard of the U.S. First Brigade, 5th Infantry Division, begins movement with an armored cavalry/engineer task force in the Khe Sanh area. Some 9,000 GIs support the move of 20,000 South Vietnamese troops to reoccupy 1,000 square miles of territory in northwest South Vietnam and to mass at the Laotian border in preparation for Operation Lam Son 719.

February 8: South Vietnamese troops, supported by U.S. heavy airpower and artillery fire, cross into Laos for an extensive assault on the Ho Chi Minh Trail, to destroy supplies and cut the infiltration routes.

March 24: Operation Lam Son 719, the South Vietnamese invasion of Laos, ends as the last ARVN units pull out with heavy casualties under heavy communist assaults.

March 29: Lieutenant William Calley Jr. is found guilty by the U.S. Army of the premeditated murder of 22 unarmed South Vietnamese civilians at My Lai. He is sentenced to life imprisonment, but his sentence is later reduced to 10 years. (Calley will be paroled in 1974 and given a dishonorable discharge.)

April 6: Operation Lam Son 719 officially ends. The 45-day toll is high for both sides. An Associated Press dispatch, citing privileged information, reports SVNAF casualty figures of

A Marine fires into a treeline at Vietcong, 1969. Courtesy of the National Archives.

nearly 50%—3,800 dead, 5,200 wounded and 775 missing. U.S. losses include 450 dead, 104 helicopters downed, 608 damaged and five planes destroyed. Saigon claims 13,688 NVA troops dead and 167 taken prisoner. President Thieu and the North Vietnamese both claim victory.

April 7: President Nixon announces the withdrawal of 100,000 more U.S. troops.

April 19–23: One thousand members of VVAW (Vietnam Veterans Against the War) demonstrate in Washington, D.C. The protest, called Dewey Canyon 3 after the February–March Laos drive, ends with some veterans throwing their combat ribbons, helmets and uniforms on the Capitol steps.

April 24: An estimated 200,000 people participate in a massive antiwar rally at the Mall in Washington, D.C.

May 13: Still deadlocked, the Vietnam peace talks in Paris enter their fourth year.

May 31: The U.S. secretly proposes to the DRV a deadline for the withdrawal of all American troops in return for the repatriation of American POWs and a cease-fire.

June 13: The New York Times begins its controversial publication of the *Pentagon Papers*, a secret Pentagon analysis of how the U.S. commitment in Indochina grew over three decades.

June 26: The DRV offers to release American POWs at the same time as the release of civilian prisoners and withdrawal of U.S. forces, but demands that the U.S. stop supporting Thieu.

June 30: The Supreme Court rules that articles based on classified Pentagon material, the *Pentagon Papers,* may be published.

July 8: U.S. Ambassador David Bruce informs the North Vietnamese that their new proposal is unacceptable, but concedes it has some new elements, and asks for a "fresh start" in secret negotiations.

July 9: The U.S. completes the DMZ turnover to the South Vietnamese, as some 500 U.S. forces of the First Brigade, Fifth Mechanized Division, at Fire Base Charlie 2, four miles south of the DMZ, hand the stronghold over to Saigon troops.

July 15: In a surprise announcement, President Nixon discloses that he will visit Beijing, China, before May 1972. The news stuns the world.

August 7: The last troops of the first U.S. Army unit to enter Vietnam combat in 1965—the 4th Battalion, 503rd Infantry of the 173rd Airborne Brigade—are pulled out of the field to return home.

August 20: Retired General Duong Van Minh withdraws from South Vietnam presidential race, leaving President Thieu to run unopposed.

October 3: President Thieu is elected to another four-year term.

October 11: U.S. makes a new proposal offering free elections by an independent body representing all political forces in the South, with

Thieu and his vice president resigning one month before the elections.

October 21: Five GIs killed in Vietnam in the previous week—the lowest weekly U.S. toll in six years.

November 1: U.S. troop strength in Vietnam drops to below 200,000.

November 12: President Nixon announces the withdrawal of 45,000 more troops and states that the U.S. troops are "now in a defensive position."

November 22: Some 25,000 South Vietnamese troops begin an offensive against a reported 5,000 communists in the Mekong Delta between the U Minh Forest and the Camau Peninsula. They encounter only light resistance.

December 9: For the first time since the Paris peace talks began, both sides fail to set another meeting date after the 138th session.

December 26–30: U.S. planes stage heavy attacks on targets in North Vietnam, striking at airfields, missile sites, antiaircraft emplacements and supply facilities. U.S. government refers to bombing raids as "protective reaction" strikes.

December 31: U.S. military personnel in Vietnam decline to 156,800; 1,381 killed in action and 8,936 wounded in action in the 1971 fighting. Total of 45,626 U.S. military personnel killed in action and 302,375 wounded since 1961.

South Vietnamese forces have been increased to 1,046,250; 156,260 killed in action to date.

Eyewitness Testimony

We're cautiously optimistic. So far, the program has worked out quite well, and we have reason to think that it will continue to work out successfully. But we are a little bit cautious about making predictions . . . South Vietnam is certainly not going to accept a coalition government . . . We are reasonably satisfied with the progress that has been made these last 12 months . . . The rate of infiltration is down. So the whole war has changed . . . It's working . . . It's quite satisfactory.

William Rogers, secretary of state, statement in
U.S. News & World Report *(January 26, 1970).*

If Nixon is going to withdraw, then let's all go home now. I don't want to get killed buying time for the gooks.

Anonymous U.S. Army infantryman, statement in Newsweek *(February 2, 1970).*

The best characterization of the atmosphere among top U.S. GVN officials in South Vietnam is one of cautious optimism. I was told on this visit, just as last March, that we now have and can retain sufficient strength to keep the enemy from achieving any kind of military verdict in South Vietnam. I was also told the South Vietnamese were making satisfactory progress in Vietnamization, especially on the military front.

Melvin Laird, secretary of defense, to President Nixon, memorandum of February 17, 1970, in Porter's Vietnam: A History in Documents *(1979).*

We have not invaded North Vietnam. We have not demanded any concessions from them—no territory, no seat in the Hanoi government and no surrender from the North. But I have made clear that we will not surrender and that they can never defeat us.

So it is better for Hanoi to ease its aggression. Then there can be some relationship between the North and South as two temporary Vietnams with two temporary administrations—two temporary parts of the country . . .

All we demand is that they stop fighting and killing.

President Thieu, statement in U.S. News & World Report *(March 16, 1970).*

A Marine carrying an M-60 machine gun plods over a slick and muddy rice paddy dike while participating in a search for suspected Vietcong infiltrators in a hamlet near Danang in 1970. Courtesy of the National Archives.

. . . as I see it the gut issue is the Vietnamese do not have the will to fight. Helicopters, modern equipment, and the endless search for the magic panacea . . . that will replace the well-led soldier is not the answer. Leadership is the only answer. And I just do not think the Vietnamese can produce the type of leadership that is required . . . so we can continue to pour in the dollars and our nation's blood. But it will all go into a bottomless pit that will eat and eat and eat and then finally collapse. I say the red, blue, and gold [the North Vietnamese flag] will fly over Saigon within three years after the last U.S. unit embarks for home.

Colonel David Hackworth, USA, to Ward Just, Washington Post correspondent, letter of April 7, 1970, in About Face *(1989).*

Cambodia now seeks neutrality. We can no longer tolerate the seizure of parts of our national territory by the Vietcong forces and those of North Vietnam. They must go. Their presence was tolerated—even encouraged and made possible by the former chief of state [Prince Norodom Sihanouk] who has now been irrevocably relieved of his functions. Now the foreign forces occupying our soil must leave it.

Cambodian Premier Lon Nol, statement in U.S. News & World Report *(April 13, 1970).*

We were ordered off the plane and everyone was supposed to lay down on the ground. So here I am with my dress uniform, stockings, shoes, and skirt, and suddenly I'm lying down on a cement pavement at Tan Son Nhut wondering, "My God, what did I get myself into?" The noise was so deafening . . . We eventually got inside this terminal building where there were all these guys waiting to get on the plane to go home. They were whooping it up, running around with signs saying things like: "Only one hour and 35 minutes left!" They saw us coming and one of them said, "Cheer up, the worst is yet to come." . . . When we got on the bus, all the windows were screened. I learned from the bus driver that this was to prevent the Vietnamese from throwing grenades in through the windows. I said, "But I thought the enemy was up north somewhere." He told me, "No, the enemy is all around you here. You never know who you're fighting."

Nurse Jacqueline Navarra Rhoads, USA, 18th Surgical Hospital, Quang Tri, on April 26, 1970, in Freedman's Nurses in Vietnam *(1987).*

The Vietcong are advancing by intimidation. They do not shoot. They just glower.

Anonymous Western diplomat in Phnom Penh, Cambodia, statement in U.S. News & World Report *(May 4, 1970).*

Tonight, American and South Vietnamese units will attack the headquarters for the entire Communist military operations in South Vietnam . . .

This is not an invasion of Cambodia. The areas in which these attacks will be launched are completely occupied and controlled by North Vietnamese forces. Our purpose is not to occupy the areas. Once enemy forces are driven out of these sanctuaries and once their military supplies are destroyed, we will withdraw.

We take this action not for the purpose of expanding the war into Cambodia but for the purpose of ending the war in Vietnam and winning the just peace we all desire.

President Richard Nixon, to the American people, television address of April 30, 1970, in Public Papers of the Presidents of the United States.

What confronts this nation in Indochina is not a question of saving face. It is a question of saving lives. The vital concern of this nation, and I use the word "vital" advisedly, must be to end our involvement in the war in Vietnam. It is not to become bogged down in another war in all of Indochina.

Senator Mike Mansfield, to the U.S. Senate, speech of May 1, 1970.

A few weeks ago I never thought I'd be in Cambodia. I suppose we're making history, but as far as I am concerned Cambodia is no different from Vietnam.

Sergeant Carl Holzschub, USA, First Cavalry Division (Airmobile), statement of May 1, 1970, in The New York Times *(May 2, 1970).*

We have widened the front in such a way that this has become a war without end. Never was so much sacrificed for so little.

Senator Frank Church (D–Idaho), on U.S. and South Vietnamese troops attacking communist sanctuaries in Cambodia, statement in U.S. News & World Report *(May 11, 1970).*

So this is Cambodia. It looks just like Vietnam. And it looks like Charlie don't fight here except when he wants to, just like in Vietnam.

Anonymous U.S. Army soldier, statement of May 1, 1970, in the Baltimore Sun *(May 2, 1970).*

You see these bums, you know, blowing up the campuses. Listen, the boys that are on the college campuses today are the luckiest people in the world, going to the greatest universities, and here they are burning up the books, storming around about this issue. You name it. Get rid of the war there will be another one.

President Nixon, to civilian employees at the Pentagon, statement of May 1, 1970, in The New York Times *(May 2, 1970).*

They're firing blanks, otherwise they would be aiming into the air or at the ground.

Anonymous Kent State University student, on Ohio National Guardsmen firing into a crowd of student antiwar demonstrators, on May 4, 1974, in Newsweek *(May 18, 1970).*

My God, they're killing us!

Anonymous young woman at Kent State University whose scream was the first voice heard after Ohio National Guardsmen fired upon student protesters on May 4, 1970, in Time *(May 28, 1970).*

The crackle of the rifle volley cut the suddenly still air. It appeared to go on, as a solid volley, for perhaps a full minute or longer . . .

When the firing stopped, a slim girl, wearing a cowboy shirt and faded jeans, was lying face down on the road at the edge of the parking lot, the blood pouring out onto the macadam, about ten feet from this reporter.

The youths stood stunned . . . A young man cradled one of the bleeding forms in his arms. Several girls began to cry.

John Kifner, journalist, on Ohio National Guardsmen firing into a crowd of students participating in an antiwar demonstration at Kent State University on May 4, 1970, New York Times *article of May 5, 1970.*

I don't blame 18-year-olds for not wanting to go to Cambodia. Look, I had a daughter, and now she's dead.

Doris Krause, mother of Alison Krause (Kent University student killed by Ohio National Guardsmen), statement of May 4, 1970, in Newsweek *(May 18, 1970).*

Have we come to such a state in this country that a young girl has to be shot because she disagrees deeply with the actions of her government?

Arthur Krause, father of Alison Krause (Kent State University student killed by Ohio National Guardsmen), statement of May 4, 1970, in Newsweek *(May 18, 1970).*

National Guardsmen toss tear gas into a crowd of antiwar demonstrators at Kent State University on May 4, 1970. Courtesy of AP/ Wide World Photos.

My husband is no murderer. He was afraid. He was sure that they were going to be overrun by those kids. He was under orders—that's why he did it.

Anonymous wife of Ohio National Guardsman, statement of May 4, 1970, in Time *(May 18, 1970).*

I am satisfied these troops felt that their lives were in danger. I felt I could have been killed out there . . . Considering the size of the rocks and the proximity of those throwing them, lives were in danger . . . Hell, they were three feet behind us . . . I do think, however, that under normal conditions, an officer would have given the order to fire.

General Robert Canterbury, Ohio National Guard, statement of May 4, 1970, in Newsweek *(May 18, 1970).*

As 105mm howitzers boomed shells out into the surrounding jungle, four members of Company D dug their bunker to the accompaniment of a tape recorder playing a rock song by The Animals. When the chorus to one song came around, they all joined in loudly:

We gotta get outta this place,
   if its the last thing we ever do;
We gotta get outta this place,
   Where there's a better life, for me and you.

James Sterba, journalist, with the U.S. Army's First Cavalry Division (Airmobile) at Landing Zone North One, Cambodia, in New York Times *article of May 5, 1970.*

They are trying to say that they want peace. They are trying to say that they want to stop killing. They are trying to say that they want to end the draft. They are trying to say that we ought to get out of Vietnam. I agree with everything that they are trying to accomplish.

I believe, however, that the decisions that I have made, and particularly this last terribly difficult decision of going into the Cambodian sanctuaries which were completely occupied by the enemy—I believe that that decision will serve that purpose, because you can be sure that everything that I stand for is what they want.

President Nixon, to a news conference of May 8, 1970, in Public Papers of the Presidents of the United States.

I think it's time that the American people recognize that the President doesn't have the power to declare war or make war alone.

Senator Charles Goodell (R–N.Y.), to the nation, television address of May 12, 1970, in U.S. News & World Report *(May 25, 1970).*

I've got to run a sort of carrot-and-stick operation. The idea I got in training was that I give an order and everyone would obey. But when I got out here, I realized things weren't that simple. I found I sort of had to negotiate things, if I did something for my men, they would do something for me.

Anonymous U.S. Army platoon leader, statement of May 1970, in Newsweek *(May 25, 1970).*

Don't these antiwar demonstrators know they're giving the enemy real comfort and support? If they think we're going to pull out they really hit us much harder. There are men getting hurt and killed out here because some creeps at home are waving Vietcong flags and spitting on our own. To me these guys are traitors, there is no other word.

Anonymous U.S. infantryman, recovering from his battle wounds at a Saigon hospital, statement of May 28, 1970, in Musgrove's (Jacksonville, Florida) Journal *article of May 29, 1970.*

It is strange that the events should seem to be in slow motion, but it is so. I can visualize very clearly the flares being dumped onto the ground and the grunts carrying the wounded and placing them into the aircraft. We couldn't have been on the ground more than 45 seconds to a one minute, although it seemed like forever. At one point I remember looking out at the tree-line and thinking how close it was and what a nice target we must be making.

Lawrence E. (Crash) Carter, U.S. Army helicopter pilot, 25th Aviation Battalion, diary entry of June 8, 1970, in Chinnery's Life on the Line: Stories of Vietnam Air Combat *(1988).*

I remember cutting off all his clothes and the horror of taking one of his boots off and his foot still being in the boot . . . I remember that nurse say, "Draw four tubes of blood, type-cross him, and get it over to the lab right away." I remember drawing the blood, and he begged me not to leave . . . After I drew the blood he said, "Please don't leave me." I said, "I just have to run across the hall to the lab. I promise I'll be right back." I was right back, and he had died in the time that I had left him alone . . . And I never forgot that; I never again left anyone, because you realize that when they say that, it's like they know that they are going . . .

Nurse Christine McGinley Schneider, USN, 95th Evacuation Hospital, Danang (June 1970– June 1971), in Walker's A Piece of My Heart (1985).

I kept thinking, "Here I am in the middle of a war zone." But I didn't see any dead bodies; no bombs exploded as I explored Saigon. To me, the war was the people I met . . . It was the little boy doomed to spend his sightless childhood with no one to love him. And it was the sound of distant mortar fire that I heard late at night as I slept in air-conditioned comfort.

Neale Godfrey, American high school student, article of June 1970 in Seventeen.

As I look around, dirt-caked infantrymen move about the trash-covered camp, stringing wire, filling sandbags with red clay, clearing brush, digging holes. Through trees to the north you can see Cambodia. Every ten minutes or so a big helicopter carrying supplies clatters down, so convulsing the camp in its rotor wash that men have to hold the headquarters tent down to keep it from blowing away. Trash, equipment and newspapers sail around as if driven by hurricane winds.

James Willwerth, journalist, on visiting a U.S. firebase near the Cambodian border, journal entry of June 25, 1970, in Eye in the Last Storm (1972).

The situation in Phnom Penh is very tense. The communists seem to be able to cut the roads wherever they wish, and for a time last week, Phnom Penh's only transportation links with the outside world were the air lanes and the Mekong River. Peasants have reported seeing North Vietnamese troops only seven miles from the capital.

Arnaud de Borchgrave, journalist, article of June 29, 1970, in Newsweek.

Visited one of the 18 refugee camps in Phnom Penh into which some 90,000 Vietnamese residents of Cambodia have been herded. The conditions are dreadful. Thousands of people in each camp are crowded into small areas with no sanitation facilities at all. The smell of human excrement is overpowering. These wretched people are waiting for boats from Saigon to take them out of Cambodia. But South Vietnam is short of refugee facilities and suspects

many are Vietcong. If they weren't VC before, they certainly must be now.

Arnaud de Borchgrave, journalist, diary entry of June 1970, in Newsweek (June 15, 1970).

We have eliminated an immediate threat to our forces and to the security of South Vietnam—and produced the prospect of fewer American casualties in the future . . .

We have guaranteed the continuance of our troop withdrawal program. On June 3, I reaffirmed that 150,000 more Americans would return home within a year and announced that 50,000 would leave Vietnam by October 15.

We have bought time for the South Vietnamese to strengthen themselves against the enemy.

President Nixon, to the American people, on the Cambodian "incursion," television address of June 30, 1970 in Public Papers of the Presidents of the United States.

. . . Radio Hanoi would deliver the day's maddeningly incomprehensible news. Then, after what I presumed was a propaganda pep talk delivered by Hoa, and what seemed to be a textbook self-criticism session by the other members of the squad, the radio would blare out an hour or two of doleful Vietnamese music. Finally everyone would drift off to sleep, oblivious, except for me, of the far-off rumble of the nightly B-52 strike, which with clocklike regularity came just before three-thirty A.M.

Robert Sam Anson, journalist, on his captivity by NVA soldiers in Cambodia in August 1970, in War News: A Young Reporter in Indochina (1989).

Every Senator in this chamber is partly responsible for sending 50,000 young Americans to an early grave, and in one sense this chamber literally reeks of blood. Every Senator here is partly responsible for that human wreckage at Walter Reed [Hospital] and all across the land—young boys without legs, without arms, or genitals, or faces, or hopes.

If we don't end this damnable war those young men will some day curse us for our pitiful willingness to let the executive carry the burden that the constitution places on us.

Senator George McGovern (D–S.D.), to the U.S. Senate, in support of the McGovern-Hatfield amendment, a bill (defeated) that would withdraw all U.S. troops from South Vietnam by December 31, 1971, speech of September 1, 1970.

These guys are no longer blindly following puppets. They're thinkers and they want intelligent leadership. It's not a democracy, but they want to have a say. If I ran this company like an old-time tyrant, I'd have a bunch of rebels. There are people in the company with more experience than I have, and if they think I'm doing something grossly wrong, I'm ready to listen.

Captain Brian Utermahler, USA, commanding officer of Alpha Company, First Battalion, 8th Cavalry, First Air Cavalry Airmobile, statement in Saar's Life *article of October 23, 1970.*

. . . we each made it a point to commit to memory the name of each POW and some brief biographical detail about him. We never knew what the future held, what circumstances might some day give some of us our freedom, and any one of us could have told who was in captivity and carried to a man's loved ones some news about him.

Captain Larry Chesley, U.S. Air Force POW (1966–1973), on his captivity in 1970, in Seven Years in Hanoi *(1973).*

I spent Christmas with some close friends (you'd be surprised how fast you meet "friends"), listened to Bob Hope on the radio—he was about 30 miles away—and went to a show they had on our firebase. I still haven't reached my final destination, so don't try to write yet. It will be another week before I find out what I'll be doing and where.

So far everything has been real quiet and everything is going fine. There are always rumors flying around though. The lifers say the war is over and everyone is pulling out. We were told we would be pulling out the 15th of January—that doesn't mean me, specifically—it means my division, the 1st Cavalry; no telling when they'll get to my company.

Pfc. Thomas Kingsley, USA, to his mother and father, letter of December 1970, in Harper's *article of June 1974.*

This is the year we throw away the statistical yardstick and face an intangible but far more important question: Are the South Vietnamese ready to go it alone?

Anonymous military adviser, statement in U.S. News & World Report *(January 4, 1971).*

One night I went out to check our perimeter and I found everybody—I mean everybody—asleep in five bunkers in a row. I just decided enough was

enough, and the last bunker, I woke the men up and took their names. I was walking away when I heard one of the guys yell, "I'm gonna kill you, mother f———." I heard him pull the pin, and I went down fast in the ditch. The frag sailed right past me and went off a few feet away. As soon as the dust cleared, I was right back on top of that bunker, and I really whaled on that guy. I think I could have killed him, but people pulled me off. The other men testified against the guy, and he's in the stockade now. I hope he stays there.

Anonymous U.S. Army captain, First Cavalry Division, statement in Newsweek *(January 11, 1971).*

Hell, I don't care if the kids let their hair grow or write "Peace" on their helmets. When I go to a fire-support base, I want to see that the men have a layer of sandbags for overhead protection and that their ammo is well dug in.

Anonymous U.S. Army colonel, statement in Newsweek *(January 11, 1971).*

. . . there are 120 U.S. choppers making 2,000 landings a day. You see them with their glass fronts blasted in, their sides and blades punctured with bullet holes, their seats splattered with blood. "It's getting real hot out there," a pilot said, pointing toward Laos. "The NVA usually won't attack our gunships. They let them go past and go for the Hueys when they come in with loads of [South Vietnamese] troops."

Tony Clifton, journalist, on the U.S. air-supported South Vietnamese ground offensive into Laos, in Newsweek *article of January 22, 1971.*

I have ordered the Armed Forces of the Republic of Vietnam to attack Communist North Vietnamese bases on the Laotian territory along the Vietnam-Laos border, in Military Region I. The operation is called Operation Lam Son 719. This is an operation limited in time and space, with the clear and unique objective of disrupting the supply and infiltration network of the Communist North Vietnamese in Laos, which territory has for many years been occupied by the North Vietnamese Communists and used as a base to launch attacks against our country . . . this is not an expansion of the war by the Republic of Vietnam, either. On the contrary it is an action

South Vietnamese troops in Laos in 1971 captured enormous quantities of materiel, including this Soviet 37mm antiaircraft gun. Courtesy of the National Archives.

taken to help end soon the war in Vietnam and restore peace in this part of the world.

President Nguyen Van Thieu, to the South Vietnamese people, address of February 8, 1971, in The Washington Post *(February 9, 1971).*

The invasion began at 7:42 A.M. There was little to see at the time. Tanks with Vietnamese soldiers sitting on top, tree branches attached for camouflage, crossed the border with no resistance. They were still doing this when I arrive, engines growling and treads clanking. The border is lined with encamped American and Vietnamese artillery units, surrounded by war's sickening ecological side effects—paper and metal garbage, smoky cooking fires, cardboard and candy wrappers strewn about, cracker-box outdoor toilets, rusty shell casings piled up, the funky smell of C rations and rice cooking over the fires. All around here are bones of bushes and trees burned away to discourage snipers.

James Willwerth, journalist, on the U.S.-supported South Vietnamese invasion of Laos, journal entry of February 8, 1971, in Eye in the Last Storm.

From what I've seen, the ARVN can't take over from us. We can't do the job with what we've got now. They're pulling men out; we're short of men, all the time, and now they're pulling more men out. It's just throwing the load even more on us that are left. It's like being driven back into a corner. There's just nowhere to go—except back home. It wouldn't be so bad if you felt you were fighting for something. And things are getting worse. At one time we used to get a hot meal every other day when we were out in the boonies. Now we're lucky if we get two or three in 15 days. They just can't get the stuff out to us.

Anonymous U.S. soldier, statement in Bacon's Christian Century *article of February 17, 1971.*

When they start opening up on you they often kill the very people you came to rescue. That's what happened to me yesterday. Two ARVN medics were carrying a badly wounded man to my ship when mortar shells started to land on us. They killed the wounded guy and hurt the medic badly. Four more people rushed out to help the medics, and they were hit too. We ended up lifting six people out of there, but none of them were the ones we had come for. This happens all the time.

Anonymous U.S. Army Medevac (medical-evacuation craft) pilot, on U.S. air-supported operations in Laos, statement in Newsweek *(March 15, 1971).*

How different they are, the captor and the captive. The water had cleared some of the dullness from my head, but not the thirst. The captor is master; the captive is slave. It isn't just the guns, though if the guns were not there, we would have been just eight people—two Vietnamese, four Cambodians, a Japanese, and me.

Running through the scrub, you could have stretched a romantic frame of mind and seen our appearance as dramatic—torn clothing, little blood bubble scratches over our faces and arms, fingers filthy from scrabbling for water. But now, once captured, we just looked shabby, chain-gangish, mindless, with feet beginning to go mushy.

Kate Webb, journalist, on her captivity by NVA soldiers in Cambodia in 1971, in On the Other Side *(1972).*

When my troops were getting massacred and mauled by an enemy I couldn't see, I couldn't feel and I couldn't touch—that nobody in the military system ever described them as anything other than Communists. They didn't give it a race, they didn't give it a sex, they didn't give it an age. They never

let me believe it was just a philosophy in a man's mind. That was my enemy out there.

And when it became between me and that enemy, I had to value the lives of my troops—and I feel that was the only crime I have committed.

Lieutenant William Calley Jr., USA, on his court-martial conviction for the premeditated murder of 22 Vietnamese civilians at My Lai in 1968, statement of March 30, 1971, The New York Times *(March 31, 1971).*

I saw one of my men wounded with shrapnel. He's the first guy I've ever seen wounded. Once we've decided to get out, and then keep fighting, it seems kind of worthless. Nobody wants to be the last guy to die in Vietnam.

Anonymous U.S. Army captain, statement in Kirk's New York Times Magazine *article of September 19, 1971.*

After being in the bush for a few long weeks, I had decided that we, the good old American draftees, were the bait. Whether we were nibbled on, chewed, or swallowed whole, depended on where we were dropped. Every 21 days we were pulled out, healed up, fattened up, patted on the back, and then dropped in a new place.

There were a lot of big battles fought. More enemy were killed than friendly, but in the jungle it was a different story. Survival was what mattered. Going back to the real world in one piece counted more than anything.

Lieutenant Donald Stephen, USA, 101st Airborne Division, on search-and-destroy missions near the Laotian border in 1971, in Bait: Vietnam, 1971 *(1986).*

If the United States should announce that we will quit regardless of what the enemy does, we would have thrown away our principal bargaining counter to win the release of American prisoners of war, we would remove the enemy's strongest incentive to end the war sooner by negotiation, and we will have given enemy commanders the exact information they need to marshal their attacks against our remaining forces at their most vulnerable time.

The issue very simply is this: Shall we leave Vietnam in a way that—by our own actions—consciously turns the country over to the Communists? Or shall we leave in a way that gives the South Vietnamese a reasonable chance to survive as a free people? My plan will end American involvement in a way that would provide that chance. And the other plan would end it precipitately and give victory to the Communists.

President Nixon, to the nation, address of April 7, 1971, in Public Papers of the Presidents of the United States.

Each day to facilitate the process by which the United States washes her hands of Vietnam someone has to give up his life so that the United States doesn't have to admit something that the entire world already knows, so that we can't say that we have made a mistake. Someone has to die so that President Nixon won't be, and these are his words, "the first President to lose a war."

We are asking Americans to think about that because how do you ask a man to be the last man to die in Vietnam? How do you ask a man to be the last man to die for a mistake?

John Kerry, Vietnam veteran, representative of VVAW and former U.S. Navy lieutenant (awarded the Silver Star, Bronze Star and three Purple Hearts), to the U.S. Senate Foreign Relations Committee, testimony of April 22, 1971.

This is for all the dudes in 1–9, 3d Battalion, Charlie Company, 9th Marines who didn't make it.

Anonymous Vietnam Veteran Against the War (VVAW) demonstrator, statement of April 23, 1971, after tossing his combat medals onto the Capitol steps during an antiwar demonstration in Washington, D.C., in the Baltimore Sun *(April 24, 1971).*

Let's try to make this country wake up once and for all.

John Kerry, VVAW representative and former U.S. Navy lieutenant, after tossing onto the Capitol steps his Silver Star, Bronze Star and Purple Heart during an antiwar demonstration in Washington, D.C., statement of April 23, 1971, in the Baltimore Sun *(April 24, 1971).*

If the South Vietnamese don't succeed from here on out, it cannot be blamed on the lack of U.S. support. The U.S. has been unstinting in its support of this country and our mutual objective here.

John Paul Vann, U.S. military adviser, statement in U.S. News & World Report *(May 31, 1971).*

A lot of people wonder what it is like being in Vietnam. To answer that question would take quite some doing. It is really hard to explain. Here are some of the answers one would get just by asking the lowly G.I. on the street. Vietnam is:

A beggar holding an emaciated child sitting on the sidewalk outside a gaudy Tu-Du bar.

The stony faced look of a peasant as your unit sweeps through his village.

A voice pleading "MEDIC, MEDIC" . . .

A fourteen-year-old VC captive . . .

R & R to Bangkok and a girl with the improbable name of "Judy."

A green rubber bag being loaded on the chopper with a big Red Cross on the nose.

Bob Hope at Christmas . . .

A letter from home that is read over and over again . . .

A guy yelling "SHORT."

The bewildered look on a new arrival's face.

Blisters and Jungle Rot.

That Damned idiot who yells: "GOOOODDD MOOORRRNNNIINNNGGG, Vietnam" on the radio every morning . . .

Anonymous GI, to the editor, letter in the Negro History Bulletin *(May 1971).*

We're getting out anyway. So why should I be the last man killed in this "no-good war?"

Anonymous U.S. Army infantryman, statement of May 1971, in U.S. News & World Report *(June 7, 1971).*

What I failed earlier to do is now happening. I am flattered to be suspected of having leaked it . . . I didn't think there were was a single page that would do grave damage to the national interest, or I wouldn't have released them . . . Ten years in prison is very cheap if that would contribute to ending this war.

Dr. Daniel Ellsberg, former Defense Department and RAND Corporation employee, on his federal indictment for having unauthorized possession of classified, top-secret documents (the Pentagon Papers), statement of June 28, 1971, in Newsweek *(July 12, 1971).*

In my view, far from deserving condemnation for their courageous reporting, The New York Times, The Washington Post, and other newspapers should be commended . . . In revealing the workings of a

Spec. 4 Richard Champion, a squad leader in the 23rd Infantry Division, shouts to his men after receiving sniper fire while patrolling southeast of Chu Lai in January 1971. His hat, beads and medallions, which would have been forbidden in 1965, were common in the fragmented American Army of 1971. Photograph by Pfc. Stephen Befeld, USA. Courtesy of the National Archives.

government that led to the Vietnam war, the newspapers nobly did precisely that which the founders hoped and trusted they would do.

Supreme Court Justice Hugo Black, concurring opinion of June 30, 1971 (The New York Times Company v. The United States of America), in the U.S. Supreme Court's Cases Adjudged in the Supreme Court (1972).

To me it is hardly believable that a newspaper long regarded as a great institution in American life would fail to perform one of the basic duties of every citizen with respect to the discovery or possession of stolen property or secret government documents. That duty I had thought—perhaps naively—was to report forthwith, to responsible public officers. This duty rests on taxi drivers, Justices and The New York Times.

Supreme Court Chief Justice Warren Burger, dissenting opinion of June 30, 1971 (The New York Times Company v. The United States of America), in the U.S. Supreme Court's Cases Adjudged in the Supreme Court.

I've seen colonels and generals pouring into Vietnam to get their tickets punched, to get the proper credentials or an easy medal, spending only six months, then running off and never understanding this war . . . We made a decision to get into this war and that was a tough decision to make. But an even tougher decision to make is to say: Hey, baby, we have erred. Let's get out.

Colonel David Hackworth, USA, statement of June 1971, in Newsweek (July 5, 1971).

South Vietnam has a reasonably good chance to hold against any effort that Hanoi can mount in the next four years.

U.S. Ambassador Ellsworth Bunker (South Vietnam), statement in U.S. News & World Report (July 5, 1971).

This terrible war makes so many strange thoughts race through my head. I would like to jump up for thousands of miles to get away from here, from this killing. Before, I did not know what it was to kill a man; now that I have seen it, I don't want to do it any more.

But it is the duty of a soldier to die for his country, me for our fatherland, the enemy for his. There is no choice.

NVA soldier Nguyen Van Minh, to his girlfriend in South Vietnam, letter of July 10, 1971, in Butterfield's New York Times Magazine article of February 4, 1973.

. . . the only thing you fightin' for is your own life. You fightin' to go back home, and you got to fight your way out of here. You can't go out there and just give it up. You fight for yourself, man . . . I'm fighting to go home.

You be out there in the bush fightin' the VC and NVA and you go to some city in Vietnam and then you be fighting the Vietnamese people.

Anonymous U.S. infantryman, First Cavalry Division, to Richard Boyle, journalist, statement of October 10, 1971, in Boyle's The Flower of the Dragon: The Breakdown of the U.S. Army in Vietnam (1972).

. . . the government sends you off to fight its war—again, it's not your war; it's the government's war. You go off and fight not only once, but twice, okay? And suddenly a decision is made, "Well, look, you guys were all wrong. You're a bunch of dirty bastards. You never should have been there!" Now this is going to make me think long and hard before I go off to war again . . . War is a profanity. It really is. It's terrifying. Nobody is more antiwar than an intelligent person who's been to war. Probably the most antiwar people I know are Army officers . . .

I hate what Vietnam has done to our country! I hate what Vietnam has done to our Army!

Lieutenant Colonel H. Norman Schwarzkopf, USA, to C.D.B. Bryan, author, statement of October 1971, in Bryan's Friendly Fire *(1976).*

With the publication of the Pentagon Papers and a growing public realization of the enormity of the deceit practiced upon the American people—and even the Congress—in order to get us involved in Vietnam—keep us there and justify our remaining there—it is no wonder that our servicemen rebel at being asked to stay behind to preserve the Thieu-Ky regime and to preserve the pride and prestige of a President who does not want to be the first American President to lose a war.

Representative Paul "Pete" McCloskey (R–Cal.), to the U.S. Congress, speech of October 28, 1971.

Companies all around us are running into contact, and I firmly believe that I will not leave here without being shot or injured first . . . And anyone who tells you the war is over is full of shit . . .

It's really hell, man. I saw a medevac operation after a company had been hit by our own artillery.

Four dead—everyone was injured, most just slightly. But it was sickening. They carry the dead by a rope hanging from a helicopter (the dead man is inside a plastic bag) and just lower him to the ground—then throw them on a truck!

The fourth one was still alive when he came in—he was in the copter and died a while later. He had no right leg at all; and seeing it just turned me to jelly, man—and guys just sitting around crying—it really shakes you up. And for no goddamn reason at all!

Pfc. Thomas Kingsley, USA, to a friend, letter of January 1971, in Harper's *article of June 1974. [Kingsley died on March 20, 1971, from a mine placed by friendly forces.]*

I remember when I was in high school I figured the war would be over by the time I graduated. Then when I got to college I figured it would be over by the time I graduated. I got out of college in 1970—and here I am. I can remember how we discussed Vietnam in civics class—should we be in Vietnam or not?

Spec. 4 David Minaar, USA, 117th Aviation Company, statement in Newsweek *(December 27, 1971).*

10. Peace Is at Hand: 1972–1973

THE NIXON-KISSINGER STRATEGY

By early 1972, President Nixon had withdrawn more than 400,000 GIs from Vietnam since he had entered office, and American battle deaths were down to fewer than 10 a week. He was indeed following through on his promise to reduce the U.S. combat role in Vietnam. In response to criticism that his administration was not making a serious effort to end the war, Nixon revealed to the American public for the first time in late January 1972 that National Security adviser Henry Kissinger had been conducting secret talks with the North Vietnamese. Kissinger had held 12 secret negotiating sessions between August 1969 and August 1971 in Paris with Le Duc Tho, North Vietnam's chief negotiator. In his public announcement, Nixon accused Hanoi of refusing to continue the secret sessions, which, unlike the formal talks, "until recently . . . showed signs of yielding some progress."

As Nixon tried to pacify domestic opposition to his Vietnam policies, Kissinger was losing his "bargaining chips" at the negotiating table in Paris. American forces were shrinking, and U.S. aid to South Vietnam would inevitably be reduced as Congress no longer felt obligated to vote for appropriations to support "our boys in the field."

With the negotiations in Paris at a standstill, Kissinger and Nixon decided to pursue an alternate route to settling the Vietnam War. American relations with China and the Soviet Union were about to undergo a dramatic reversal. By the end of 1971, summit meetings had been scheduled for both Peking and Moscow; perhaps peace in Vietnam could be achieved as part of these broader diplomatic maneuvers.

On February 21, 1972, President Nixon landed in Beijing and announced that his breakthrough visit to China was "the week that changed the world." Vietnam was high on the agenda in the talks between Nixon and Prime Minister Chou En-lai. Although the Chinese wanted a quick end to the war, they also had to avoid making any gestures that might drive the Vietnamese communists into the sphere of the Soviet Union, which was seeking to flank China on the south. Chou En-lai ambiguously urged an early peace and at the same time avoided endorsing North Vietnam's political demands. With Nixon's promise to reduce the U.S. military presence on Taiwan, North Vietnam feared that China and the United States might make a deal behind its back as had happened at the 1954 Geneva Conference. Although the Chinese had significantly increased their aid to North Vietnam since 1971, they had done so primarily to keep up with the Soviet Union.

The buildup presaged a new communist offensive, and reports reaching the U.S. command in Saigon indicated that it could match the Tet offensive of 1968. As early as fall 1971, truck convoys were spotted along the Ho Chi Minh Trail, probably transporting materiel to three North Vietnamese divisions deployed at the border between Cambodia and South Vietnam. NVA units were also massing above the demilitarized zone separating North and South Vietnam.

THE SPRING OFFENSIVE

Hanoi had resolved to make 1972 the year of "decisive victory." The communists could no longer be sure just how the emerging U.S. detente with the Soviet Union and China would affect them. Moreover, the upcoming U.S. presidential election and scheduled withdrawal of U.S. forces from ground combat presented an ideal opportunity. But above all, Hanoi's main objective was to demonstrate that Vietnamization would never enable the ARVN to fight on its own. The communists reasoned that, if they inflicted a devastating defeat on the South Vietnamese army, the United States' only recourse would be to end its involvement on terms dictated by Hanoi.

In the dawn of March 30, 1972, the communists launched a massive conventional invasion of the south. Spearheaded by Soviet tanks, 120,000 North Vietnamese troops and thousands of Vietcong guerrillas struck across the demilitarized zone, in the Central Highlands and across the Cambodian border northwest of Saigon. Achieving almost complete surprise, the North Vietnamese routed the thin lines of defending ARVN troops and quickly advanced toward the towns of Quang Tri in the north, Kontum in the highlands and An Loc, just 60 miles north of Saigon.

Hanoi's leaders had calculated correctly that Nixon would not return U.S. ground forces to combat. By now, only 6,000 of the 70,000 Americans remaining in Vietnam were combat troops, and their activities were restricted. But they underestimated the lengths to which Nixon was prepared to go, election year or not, to prevent an outright defeat while the U.S. reputation was still at stake. In April, Nixon quickly approved air strikes directed at military targets across the demilitarized zone and followed up in May with massive air attacks on fuel depots in the Hanoi-Haiphong area. For the first time since 1969, B-52s flew bombing missions over the north.

On May 1, some 8,000 ARVN troops fled Quang Tri and streamed southward on Route 1. Abandoning tanks, trucks and armed personnel carriers as they went, the retreating troops flooded Hue. Although some South Vietnamese troops often displayed uncommon courage, they would have collapsed without American air support and advisers to build up their ranks. "The real problem," Nixon wrote in his dairy, "is that the enemy is willing to sacrifice in order to win, while the South Vietnamese simply aren't willing to pay that much of a price in order to avoid losing."

In the Mekong Delta communist troop strength continued rising. Estimated at only 3,000 in 1971, communist forces in the Delta would number between 20,000 and 30,000 by September 1972, as approximately 1 million South Vietnamese came under communist control.

PRESSURING FOR PEACE

Meanwhile, Kissinger and Le Duc Tho held another secret meeting in Paris on May 2. The United States was now prepared to waive its long-standing demand for total mutual withdrawal of "Northern forces" from the south, but Tho was still confident of a complete victory. The North Vietnamese flatly rejected Kissinger's offer. Nixon was faced with a set of difficult choices. Pressing for the intensification of the bombing of the north and for the mining of Haiphong harbor, General Creighton Abrams warned Nixon that Hue and Kontum might soon fall and the "whole thing may be lost." On the other hand, secretaries Laird and Rogers warned that intensified bombing of the north could have adverse domestic consequences, and Kissinger expressed concern that the Soviets might cancel Nixon's upcoming summit in Moscow, affecting the outcome of negotiations on strategic arms limitations and other issues.

Nixon was unwilling to risk defeat in South Vietnam and was determined to strike back. Moreover, he concluded that he could not survive politically if he accepted defeat. In a televised address to the nation on May 8, Nixon announced that he had ordered the mining of all North Vietnamese ports and the intensified bombing of military targets and supply lines. He said these actions would continue until an internationally supervised cease-fire was put into effect and all U.S. POWs were returned.

A new round of protests and demonstrations erupted, but compared to the uproar over the "Cambodian incursion," they were quite mild.

Demonstrations took place on college campuses from Boston to San Jose, California, and although in some instances there were violent confrontations, for the most part the antiwar movement was losing its momentum with the steady withdrawal of U.S. troops from Vietnam. In Congress, another round of end-the-war resolutions were issued by Senate doves. Nixon's gamble had paid off. His public approval skyrocketed and he emerged in a much stronger position at home than he had been before the North Vietnamese offensive.

Code-named Linebacker I, the bombing and mining operation also appeared to have averted defeat in South Vietnam. In June alone, American planes dropped 112,000 tons of bombs on North Vietnam, including new "smart" bombs precisely guided to their targets by computers receiving signals from television cameras and laser beams. With the crucial support of American airpower, the ARVN managed to stabilize the lines in front of Saigon and Hue and even mounted a small counteroffensive.

However, both sides suffered heavily in the campaigns of summer 1972, the North Vietnamese losing an estimated 100,000 men and the South Vietnamese 25,000. Despite experiencing heavy casualties and suffering massive damage from sustained American air raids, the North Vietnamese retained substantial forces in the south. According to intelligence reports, they had the capacity to fight on for at least two more years.

SIGNS OF A BREAKTHROUGH

By fall 1972, both sides found compelling reasons to resume their talks at the Paris peace table. Pressures were mounting in the U.S. Congress to cut off funds for the war, and the Nixon administration regarded the war as a major obstacle to its grand scheme for a "generation of peace." As for Hanoi, it had failed to achieve its "decisive victory." Also, the Democrats had nominated Senator George McGovern of South Dakota, an outspoken dove whose extreme views had practically assured the reelection of Nixon. Hanoi possibly concluded that it could get better terms from Nixon before rather than after the November election.

Kissinger and Le Duc Tho resumed their talks in July. By late summer, both the North Vietnamese and the United States were moving toward a compromise. The U.S. had already indicated its willingness to allow North Vietnamese troops to remain in the south after a ceasefire, and now the North Vietnamese were no longer demanding the removal of Thieu. By October 8, all the elements of an agreement were in place: a standstill cease-fire over all of Indochina, U.S. withdrawal within 60 days, return of U.S. POWs and arrangements for the Vietnamese parties to consult among themselves about elections and the future of South Vietnam. As far as Kissinger and Tho were concerned, a deal was about to be made.

But Kissinger had miscalculated his ally, Nguyen Van Thieu. For years Thieu had taken little interest in the negotiations, believing that Hanoi's intransigence would leave the United States with no choice but to continue supporting his regime. Now, finally faced with a draft agreement between Hanoi and Washington, Thieu protested. The requirement that he "consult" with the North Vietnamese threatened his very existence. He insisted that he would never accept an agreement that permitted North Vietnamese troops to remain in the south and accorded the Vietcong sovereignty. Thieu knew that compromise in Vietnam was impossible. It was hardly realistic to expect the communists to share power with his regime. Thieu held that, if he did not eliminate the communists, they would eliminate him.

Concerned primarily with getting the United States out of Vietnam, Kissinger urged Nixon to sign the agreement without Saigon's approval. Nixon, on the other hand, was not about to abandon his quest for a "peace with honor," and like Thieu, he was also having second thoughts about the agreement. Certain of an "enormous mandate" in the upcoming election, Nixon decided to wait until after he had been reelected, at which point he could bargain for better terms.

Kissinger continued to project the appearance of an early settlement by stating at a White House press conference on October 26, "We believe that peace is at hand . . . We believe that an agreement is within sight." But Nixon's support of Thieu ensured the breakdown of the October agreement.

When negotiations resumed after the presidential election, which Nixon won in a landslide, Kissinger presented Thieu's demand for 69 changes. Although Thieu quickly withdrew half, the remainder were substantial enough to raise serious doubts in Hanoi about the United States' commitment to the October draft agreement. With rising congressional obsession with the fate of U.S. prisoners, Hanoi apparently calculated that it had nothing to lose by postponing the settlement.

Over the next few weeks, Nixon tried every available means to impose a settlement on both South and North Vietnam. He ordered immediate delivery to South Vietnam of more than $1 billion worth of military hardware, equipping Thieu with the fourth-largest air force in the world. He assured Thieu that if North Vietnam violated the peace agreement he would order "swift and severe retaliatory action." Nixon warned Thieu that this was the best possible peace that could be obtained and that the United States would sign the agreement without him. However, the South Vietnamese president continued to hold out, and he defiantly informed the press that he had rejected the American ultimatum.

THE BOMBING OF HANOI

Pulled between adversary and ally alike, Nixon decided, as the talks came to a close on December 13, to have an immediate final showdown with both. On December 14, he sent an ultimatum to North Vietnam to begin "serious negotiations" within 72 hours or it would face grave consequences. At the same time, Nixon ordered Admiral Thomas Moorer, chairman of the Joint Chiefs of Staff, to prepare massive air attacks against railroads, power plants, radio transmitters and other facilities around Hanoi and Haiphong. "I don't want any more of this crap about the fact that we couldn't hit this target or that one," Nixon told Moorer. "This is your chance to use military power to win this war, and if you don't, I'll consider you responsible."

Starting on December 18, 1972, and lasting for the next 11 days; excluding Christmas Day, the United States unleashed the most intensive and devastating attacks of the war. Code-named Linebacker II, the operation dropped more than 36,000 tons of bombs, exceeding the tonnage during the entire period from 1969 to 1971. Although "smart bombs" made the strikes the most accurate in the history of warfare, not all of the bombs hit only military targets; some, in the words of Washington military spokesmen, "spilled over" to civilian areas. Antiwar activists labeled Linebacker II as the "Christmas Bombing," charging that U.S. bombers were deliberately "carpet bombing" (completely covering) the city.

Hanoi had prepared for the bombing by evacuating over half the city's population in April, and on December 3, it had stepped up its preparations for the relocation of nonessential persons. The vast majority of Hanoi's buildings were never hit, and the destruction was nothing compared to that inflicted on European and Japanese cities in World War II. Still, the official North Vietnamese figure for Hanoi fatalities was 1,318.

The public response in the United States was relatively subdued, with almost all of the American troops withdrawn. Congress, adjourned for the holidays, was divided along party lines. Although a lone French correspondent, on the scene in Hanoi and Haiphong and cited in many American newspapers, referred repeatedly to "carpet bombing," Malcolm Browne of *The New York Times* reported from Hanoi soon afterward that the damage had been "grossly overstated," and other foreign journalists corroborated his reports. One argument that explains the low casualties is that the populations of Hanoi and Haiphong by then had been evacuated to the countryside.

By December 30, when the bombing stopped, the North Vietnamese had shot down 26 U.S. aircraft, including 15 B-52s, and had depleted all of their surface-to-air missiles. Four days earlier, replying to an American message, the North Vietnamese had indicated their willingness to resume negotiations as soon as the bombing halted.

THE FALSE PEACE

The bombing did not produce a settlement markedly different from the draft hammered out in October. Kissinger and Le Duc Tho met again in Paris on January 8, 1973. The atmosphere was businesslike, but this time both parties were committed to a settlement. After six days of marathon sessions, marked by compromise on both sides, Kissinger and Le Duc Tho resolved their differences. The changes from the October agreement were mostly cosmetic. Kissinger achieved wording changes that he claimed gave the United States the right to continue supplying Saigon with military assistance on an "unrestricted" basis. Hanoi was able to define the demilitarized zone as "only provisional and not a political or territorial boundary." Each side was able to claim that nothing had been given up.

It is open to question how much the bombing helped persuade Thieu to agree to the settlement. One day after the bombing, Nixon sent Thieu an ultimatum to "decide now whether you desire to continue our alliance or whether you want me to seek a settlement with the enemy which serves U.S. interests alone." Although Thieu did drop his objections to the political provisions of the draft agreement, he reiterated his opposition to the continued presence of North Vietnamese forces in the south. What finally convinced Thieu to go along with the agreement was a letter Nixon sent him on January 16, 1973, that threatened "an inevitable and immediate termination of U.S. economic and military assistance."

"We have finally achieved peace with honor," announced President Nixon to the American public in a televised address on January 23, 1973. The cease-fire went into effect on January 27, 1973, at 2400 Greenwich Mean Time, the same day the agreement was signed in Paris. The Paris Peace Accords proved to be only a temporary armed truce between North and South Vietnam. Prisoner exchanges began in February, the United States dismantled what remained of its bases, and America's eight years of combat and a military involvement of some 20 years came to a close on March 29, 1973. In Hanoi on that day the last American prisoners-of-war were released, and in Saigon

Henry Kissinger and Le Duc Tho, North Vietnam's principal negotiator, confer after initialing the Paris peace agreement on January 23, 1973. Courtesy of Center of Military History.

the last token handful of GIs boarded a flight for home. Only a Defense Attaché Office and a few Marine guards at Saigon's American Embassy remained. As far as the United States was concerned, the war was over.

But it was only a new phase of the war for the Vietnamese. The North Vietnamese continued to maintain substantial numbers of their regular armed forces in the south. Both sides ordered their armed forces to increase areas of control just before the cease-fire went into effect, enlarging claims that each was sure to contest. Like the Geneva Accords of 1954, the Paris Peace Accords of 1973 did not put an end to war in Vietnam but were merely an interlude in the 30-year struggle for the control of Vietnam.

In late June, Congress approved an amendment requiring the immediate cessation of all military operations in Indochina, including the bombing of Cambodia. The House upheld Nixon's veto, but the president eventually was forced to accept a compromise extending the deadline to August 15, 1973. For the first time, Congress had taken decisive action to end America's involvement in the war.

By summer 1973, Vietnam was no longer on the front pages. It had been replaced by the sensational revelations about the unfolding Watergate scandal. President Nixon had been publicly accused by his special counsel, John Dean, of covering up various illegal activities within his administration, and another aide, Alexander Butterfield, had revealed the existence of tapes recording White House conversations that substantiated Dean's accusations. Nixon's presidency was crumbling.

Watergate reduced Nixon's popular approval rating to an all-time low, and he was now fighting to save his political life. In November, Congress passed over the president's veto the War Powers Act, a direct response to the exercise of presidential authority in Vietnam. The legislation required the president to inform Congress within 48 hours of the deployment of American military forces abroad and obligated him to withdraw them in 60 days in the absence of explicit congressional approval.

Combined with Watergate and the vote terminating operations in Indochina, Nixon found his ability to take unilateral military action severely limited. But given the public's disgust with the Vietnam War at the time, it is unlikely that any support could have been generated for a renewed commitment to Thieu's government. The end of direct American military involvement in Vietnam was inevitable.

CHRONICLE OF EVENTS

1972

January 2: President Nixon announces continued troop withdrawals, but says 25,000 to 35,000 U.S. troops will remain until the North Vietnamese release all U.S. POWs.

January 13: President Nixon announces that withdrawals of 70,000 U.S. ground troops in the next three months will reduce U.S. troop strength in South Vietnam to 69,000 by May 1.

January 25: President Nixon discloses the details of National Security adviser Henry Kissinger's 13 secret trips to Paris to negotiate with the North Vietnamese; he also makes public the text of the last U.S. peace proposal, on October 11, 1971.

January 26: Radio Hanoi broadcasts DRV's rejection of President Nixon's proposals.

February 3: The Vietcong delegation to the Paris peace talks presents a revised version of their seven-point plan of 1971. They call for the immediate resignation of President Thieu and ask for the U.S. to set a specific date for its withdrawal.

February 5: The North Vietnamese formally reject President Nixon's eight-point peace plan, which was submitted privately to the North Vietnamese delegation in Paris.

February 16: A Gallup Poll finds that of those interviewed, 52% approve of President Nixon's handling of the war and 39% disapprove.

February 21–28: President Nixon visits the People's Republic of China.

March 10: U.S. 101st Airborne Division (Airmobile) withdraws from Vietnam.

March 23: United States declares an indefinite suspension of the Paris peace talks until the North Vietnamese and NLF representatives agree to participate in "serious discussions" on issues determined beforehand.

March 30: North Vietnamese launch the Easter Offensive, the heaviest military action since the sieges of allied bases at Con Thien and Khe Sanh in 1968. NVA troops attack and overrun South Vietnamese bases south of the DMZ.

April 6: As communist forces open a second front close to Saigon, U.S. resumes Operation "Rolling Thunder," the bombing of North Vietnam.

April 15: President Nixon authorizes the bombing of areas near Hanoi and Haiphong.

April 22: Antiwar demonstrators hold marches and rallies throughout the United States to protest new bombing of North Vietnam.

April 26: President Nixon announces that 10,000 troops per month will be withdrawn from Vietnam in the next two months, bringing the total remaining to 49,000 by July 1.

April 27: The Paris peace talks resume after a one-month break.

May 1: North Vietnamese forces capture Quang Tri, the northernmost provincial capital of South Vietnam.

May 4: The United States and the South Vietnamese announce an indefinite halt to the Paris peace talks after citing a "complete lack of progress."

May 8: President Nixon announces the mining of Hanoi and Haiphong harbors, as well as intensified bombing of North Vietnamese military targets, until Hanoi agrees to an internationally supervised cease-fire throughout Indochina and to returning all American POWs.

May 8–12: A wave of antiwar demonstrations takes place across the country in response to President Nixon's announcement of the mining of North Vietnamese harbors.

June 9: Senior U.S. military adviser John Paul Vann, considered by all sides to be the most controversial, dedicated and respected American in Vietnam, is killed in a helicopter crash, probably shot down by a North Vietnamese unit.

June 17: Five men are arrested for breaking into the Democratic National Committee offices at the Watergate Hotel in Washington, D.C.

June 28: President Nixon announces that no more draftees will be sent to Vietnam unless they volunteer for such duty.

June 30: U.S. military personnel in Vietnam drops to 47,000.

July 13: The formal Paris peace talks resume after a 10-week suspension.

Senator George McGovern (South Dakota) is nominated by Democrats on an antiwar platform.

August 12: At Danang, the last U.S. ground troops leave Vietnam. Remaining are 43,500 American service personnel in administrative and supply jobs, plus helicopter and air crews.

August 22: The Republican National Convention renominates President Nixon by a vote of 1,347 to 1.

August 28: President Nixon announces that the U.S. draft will end by July 1973.

September 15: South Vietnamese forces recapture the provincial capital of Quang Tri.

September 21: For the first time since March 1965, a week passes without an American combat death in Vietnam.

September 25–27: Henry Kissinger holds more secret talks with North Vietnamese representatives in Paris.

October 8: Le Duc Tho, the North Vietnamese representative in Paris, presents Kissinger with a "breakthrough" draft peace plan, in which two separate administrations would remain in South Vietnam and negotiate general elections.

October 22: Henry Kissinger meets with President Thieu in Saigon. Thieu opposes the draft agreement's provisions for permitting North Vietnamese troops to remain in the south and for providing a three-segment "administrative structure" to preside over the political settlement and elections.

President Nixon announces a halt to all bombing of North Vietnam above the 20th parallel.

October 26: Hanoi announces that secret talks in Paris have produced a tentative agreement on a nine-point plan to end the war; Henry

Kissinger says that "peace is at hand," and that only one more meeting is needed to complete the agreement.

November 1: President Thieu publicly announces his opposition to the draft peace treaty.

November 7: President Nixon is reelected in a landslide.

November 11: The U.S. logistical base, Long Binh, north of Saigon, is turned over to the South Vietnamese, marking the end of direct U.S. Army participation in the war.

November 16: President Nixon sends a letter to Thieu pledging to press Hanoi for changes demanded by Thieu.

November 20–21: Kissinger and Le Duc Tho begin another round of secret negotiations in Paris.

December 13: Paris peace talks break down.

December 18: President Nixon orders bombing of areas around Hanoi and Haiphong.

December 22: The White Houses announces that the bombing will continue until Hanoi agrees to negotiate "in a spirit of good will and in a constructive attitude."

December 26: Hanoi agrees to resume diplomatic talks when bombing stops.

December 30: President Nixon announces the cessation of bombing and the resumption of the Paris peace talks.

December 31: U.S. military personnel in Vietnam declines to 24,200; 300 killed in action and 1,221 wounded in action in the 1972 fighting. Total of 45,926 U.S. military personnel killed in action and 303,596 wounded since 1961.

South Vietnamese forces have increased to 1,048,000; 195,847 killed in action to date.

1973

January 8–12: Henry Kissinger and Le Duc Tho resume their secret talks in Paris.

January 15: President Nixon announces that all hostile actions against the North Vietnamese have ceased.

Henry Kissinger, national security adviser to President Richard Nixon. Courtesy of the National Archives.

January 23: President Nixon announces that Kissinger and Tho have initialed an agreement in Paris that day on ending the war in Vietnam; a cease-fire will begin January 27, and all POWs will be released within 60 days.

January 27: Cease-fire agreements are formally signed in Paris by representatives of the United States, South Vietnam, North Vietnam and the Vietcong.

Secretary of Defense Melvin Laird announces the end of the U.S. military draft.

February 12: The return of American POWs begins with North Vietnam's release of 142 of 590 U.S. prisoners at Hanoi's Gialam airport.

February 14: The first 20 POWs arrive at Travis Air Base in California to a low-keyed Operation Homecoming, and are quickly dispersed to homes and hospitals across the country.

March 28: The 60-day, first phase of Vietnam's cease-fire ends with continued fighting.

March 29: The last 67 American prisoners-of-war held by North Vietnam are released, and the last American troops leave South Vietnam. Only a Defense Attache Office and a few Marine guards at the Saigon American Embassy remain, although some 8,500 U.S. civilians stay on.

April 25: United States and North Vietnam publish their earlier exchange of formal notes charging each other with extensive cease-fire violations.

June 24: Graham Martin sworn in as ambassador to South Vietnam, replacing Ellsworth Bunker.

July 1: The U.S. Congress votes to end all bombing in Cambodia after August 15.

August 15: American bombing of Cambodia ends; thus, all direct American military involvement in Indochina ceases.

September 22: Henry Kissinger replaces Williams Rogers as secretary of state and continues as National Security adviser,

October 1: President Thieu declares that the communists are planning a "general offensive" in spring 1974 and calls for "preemptive attacks" against communist forces.

October 16: Henry Kissinger and North Vietnam's Le Duc Tho are awarded the Nobel Prize for peace for negotiating the Paris peace accords. Kissinger accepts the award, but Le Duc Tho declines to accept until peace is truly established in his country.

November: North Vietnamese tanks and troops seize two South Vietnamese camps near the Cambodian border in one of the fiercest battles since the January 28 cease-fire.

November 7: The U.S. Congress overrides the presidential veto of the War Powers Act, which limits the president's power to commit armed forces abroad without congressional approval.

November 15: The Military Procurement Authorization bill is passed by Congress, prohibiting the use of funds for any U.S. military action in any part of Indochina.

December 31: The U.S. military contingent in Vietnam is less than 250; 237 are killed in 1973 and 60 are wounded. Total of 46,163 U.S. military personnel killed in action and 303,656 wounded since 1961.

South Vietnamese forces have increased to an estimated 1,110,000; 223,748 SVNAF killed in action to date.

EYEWITNESS TESTIMONY

. . . our troop ceiling will be only 69,000 by May 1. This means that in three years we will have cut our troops strength in Vietnam by 87 percent. As we proceed toward our goal of a South Vietnam able to defend itself, we will reduce that level still further.

President Nixon, to Congress, State of the Union address of January 13, 1972, in Public Papers of the Presidents of the United States.

I can assure you that the vast majority of the battles will be won by the South Vietnamese forces. They have the capability, they have the equipment, they have the training through this Vietnamization program to do the job.

Secretary of Defense Melvin Laird, to press conference of January 13, 1972, in U.S. News & World Report *(February 24, 1972).*

The only thing this plan does not do is to join our enemy to overthrow our ally, which the United States of America will never do. If the enemy wants peace it will have to recognize the important difference between settlement and surrender.

President Nixon, to the nation, on the secret plan to end the war, television address of January 25, 1972, in Public Papers of the Presidents of the United States.

The great advantage of secret negotiations is that you can leapfrog public positions without the turmoil that any change in positions brings about internationally and domestically in some of the countries concerned.

National Security adviser Henry Kissinger, to press conference of January 26, 1972, in U.S. News & World Report *(February 7, 1972).*

If successful pacification is the yardstick, the war in Vietnam is already settled. We have won.

This conclusion stems from extensive observation and from interviews with United States and Vietnamese officials at all levels in Washington and throughout Vietnam.

The overwhelming judgment of these knowledgeable people is that, in the zero-sum contest of pacification—a battle by two sides for control over the same population—the Vietcong's back is broken.

Colonel Robert Heinl Jr., USA, article of February 1972 in Armed Forces Journal.

It seems as if the price of calm in South Vietnam is chaos in the rest of Indochina. Clearly the Indochina war is not a series of separate conflicts but a totality which, much like a balloon, may be compressed in one area and only to blow up in another.

Anonymous U.S. military adviser, statement of March 1972, in Newsweek *(April 3, 1972).*

As I was destroying trenches, a helicopter flew in so low that I thought it was going to land on the hill. But it circled the area twice and then flew away. As I was lying flat on the ground, I could clearly see an American in the helicopter look down at the hill; how panic stricken I was at that moment.

Luong Trung Tam, North Vietnamese infantryman, 320th North Vietnamese Division, diary entry of March 8, 1972, in Butterfield's New York Times Magazine *article of February 4, 1973.*

There's no question in my mind that they [South Vietnamese troops] can defend their country. It's whether they believe they can do it. The big thing about Vietnam is what the Vietnamese people believe they can do. The rate at which you take out forces cannot be faster than what the Vietnamese people believe they can handle. Hanoi is counting on them to not believe they can handle [it], but I believe they can.

General Creighton Abrams, statement of March 17, 1972, in the San Francisco Examiner *(March 17, 1972).*

It is nine days since we had a bath and shave. It is a day for rest and satisfaction. The enemy is still searching. We are only two kilometers from the enemy.

Nguyen Van Phuoc, NVA soldier, diary entry of April 13, 1972, in The Washington Post *(April 24, 1972). [He was killed by a Claymore mine on April 15, 1972.]*

Beggars are all over Saigon, and they range in age from three to three score and ten. Some are the children of refugees, and wander about with infant sisters or brothers strapped to their backs, and some are native Saigonese who have made a profession of begging during all the years of war. Many of them are crippled, either born so or maimed in battle, and they sit on street corners where Americans are most likely to pass, holding out their hats or cups, smiling and bobbing their heads.

Robert Shaplen, journalist, in New Yorker *article of April 15, 1972.*

The American people are holding the POW's over us as an issue to get the war stopped. Frankly, I'd like to see us go out and win this war. But that won't happen now. Our hands are tied.

Lieutenant Stephen Rudloff, U.S. Navy pilot, statement in U.S. News & World Report *(April 17, 1972).*

The people of this country want to get out of Vietnam. They want to return to the urgent problems here at home and in areas of the world which have some relation to America's legitimate national interest. They do not want to keep fighting in this senseless war. They are sick and tired of the bloodshed caused as a result of our activities. They are sick and tired of the "antiseptic" death that is being rained down on villages by American bombers at altitudes of 50,000 feet.

Senator John Tunney (D–Cal.), to the Senate, on the resumption of bombing against North Vietnam, speech of April 17, 1972.

. . . we are doing it to protect the American troops that are in South Vietnam—protect the lives of those troops while the President's withdrawal program continues. We are doing it to make certain that the withdrawal program that the President has announced can continue. And we're doing it to give the South Vietnamese a chance to defend themselves against massive invasions by the North Vietnamese.

Secretary of State William Rogers, to the Senate Foreign Relations Committee, on the mining and renewed bombing of North Vietnam, testimony of April 17, 1972, in the U.S. Congress's Hearings on the Foreign Assistance Act of 1972 *(1972).*

My Son and 45,000 (?) GIs Were Killed in Vietnam in Vain.

Antiwar demonstrator, protest sign carried at a New York rally on April 22, 1972.

The only way to sweep out the enemy's supply depots, convoys, troop columns and to block the road network is to use saturation bombing. And that means B-52s. One of these babies can do what it

would take a couple of dozen Phantom fighter-bombers to do—and do it more efficiently.

Anonymous U.S. military officer, statement in U.S. News & World Report *(April 24, 1972).*

I have ordered that our air and naval attacks on military installations in North Vietnam be continued until North Vietnam stops their offensive in South Vietnam. I have flatly rejected the proposals that we stop the bombing of North Vietnam as a condition for returning to the negotiating table. They sold that package to the United States once before—in 1968—and we are not going to buy it again in 1972.

President Nixon, to the nation, television address of April 26, 1972, in Public Papers of the Presidents of the United States.

Since I have come into office we have withdrawn half a million men in Vietnam. We have offered everything that could be offered except impose a Communist government on the people of South Vietnam, and their answer has been massive invasion of South Vietnam by the North.

President Nixon, to press conference of April 30, 1972, in Public Papers of the Presidents of the United States.

The enemy opened the most devastating artillery barrage that the brigade had ever received. We thought the whole world was falling apart around us. Our vehicles, bunkers, villages and guns were being demolished. All we could do was dig deeper—and pray.

Major Bob Sheridan, USMC, military adviser, recalling the battle for Quang Tri, the northern provincial capital of South Vietnam, in April 1972, in Turley's The Easter Offensive, Vietnam 1972 *(1985).*

I walked and drove for 30 kilometers along Route 1 north of Hue and passed a solid line of [ARVN] soldiers and refugees going in the opposite direction, limping along on bleeding feet, and most had thrown away their weapons. The road was littered with helmets, ammunition belts and, weirdly enough, hundreds of pairs of uniforms. Obviously, many of the troopers had discarded their uniforms and put on peasant clothes to pass as refugees and evade the very few military police roadblocks.

Tony Clifton, journalist, on the retreat from
Quang Tri in May 1972, in Newsweek (May
15, 1972).

The Americans were sincere, they tried to help the
Vietnamese Armed Forces, and from A to Z they
brought equipment here. But one thing the Americans cannot bring is leadership—they cannot bring
that in from their arsenal.

Anonymous South Vietnamese official, on the
ARVN retreat from Quang Tri, statement of
May 1, 1972, in The New York Times (May
2, 1972).

Commandeering civilian vehicles at rifle point,
feigning non-existent injuries, carrying away C-rations but not their ammunitions, and hurling rocks
at Western news photographers taking pictures of
their flight . . . No one tried to stop them; their
officers were running too.

Sidney Schanberg, journalist, on the ARVN retreat from Quang Tri, article of May 2, 1972,
in The New York Times.

I cannot emphasize too strongly that I have determined that we should go for broke. What we have
got to get across to the enemy is the impression that
we are doing exactly that. Our words will help some.
But our actions in the next few days will speak
infinitely louder than words.

President Nixon, to Henry Kissinger, on the
mining of North Vietnamese harbors, memorandum of May 1972, in RN: The Memoirs of
Richard Nixon (1978).

There are only two issues left for us in this war.
First, in the face of a massive invasion do we stand
by, jeopardize the lives of 60,000 Americans, and
leave the South Vietnamese to a long night of terror?
This will not happen. We shall do whatever is required to safeguard American lives and American
honor.

Second, in the face of complete intransigence at
the conference table do we join with our enemy to
install a Communist government in South Vietnam?
This, too, will not happen. We will not cross the line
from generosity to treachery.

President Nixon, to the nation, television address of May 8, 1972, in Public Papers of the
Presidents of the United States.

The time for whitewashing the atrocities, tactics,
and goals of the enemy is past . . .

The time for ignoring and downplaying the broken
promises of the Hanoi government is past.

The time for proposing a sellout of our Southeast
Asia allies is past . . .

Hanoi will abandon her goals of military conquest
of the South only if this Congress shows a solid
unified wall of support behind our President.

Senator Strom Thurmond (R–S.C.), to the Senate, supporting President Nixon's decision to
mine North Vietnam's harbors and intensify the
bombing, speech of May 9, 1972.

. . . what we are witnessing is not a shortening of
the war—although I hope devoutly that that is what
it turns out to be—but a lengthening of it, an expanding of it . . .

. . . the sooner this horrible, tragic war is brought
to a close and every American is brought home, the
better off I will feel, because to me 358,918 U.S.
casualties in a 12-year period is 358,918 too many in
a war in which we have no business and which is
not vital to the security of this nation, a war, which
in my opinion, is the greatest tragedy which has ever
befallen this Republic.

Senator Mike Mansfield (D–Mont.), Senate
majority leader, to the Senate, speech of May 9,
1972.

I know that the American people want to get out
of the war. I want to get out; every other Senator
here does. But if we scratch beneath the surface of
the American people, we will find that they do not
want, like a whipped dog to have to leave the scrap
he has been into . . . The American people do not
want all our sacrifices and loss of life to go down the
drain . . . I think that the American people will have
to go through a period of travail and bereavement
and disappointment and evaluation such as this generation has never had to do before.

Senator John Stennis (D–Miss.), to the Senate,
speech of May 13, 1972.

. . . one [smart] bomb can knock out a big petro-
leum storage tank or bridge span. We are knocking
out more targets in a day than we probably did in a
week of heavy bombing in 1967.

Anonymous Pentagon official, statement of May
1972, in Newsweek (June 5, 1972).

The bombing is an ongoing operation that never will be finished as long as the enemy has laborers to work all night and all day to repair cuts.

Anonymous U.S. military officer, statement of May 1972, in U.S. News & World Report *(June 5, 1972).*

We now believe that we have a nation of our own, that it is worth saving, and that it can be saved. We are going to save it.

Anonymous South Vietnamese army captain, statement in U.S. News & World Report *(June 12, 1972).*

At the outskirts of Haiphong there was the first scene of total devastation: hundreds of acres flattened by what the [North] Vietnamese said was B-52 "carpet bombing" on April 16. There had been military targets; an oil depot and rail yards could be seen. But just as clearly, many houses had gone down. In the vistas and rubble there stood an occasional small wall with a bit of a thatched roof oddly surviving.

A little further on were a ruined church and power plant. But my interpreter said with a laugh: "Oh no, that's old—Johnson." They identify bombings with Presidents.

Anthony Lewis, journalist, article of June 18, 1972, in the New York Times Magazine.

All day long, the emotional ups and downs continue: up with a message that a captured prisoner speaks with a North Vietnamese accent . . . up when South Vietnamese tactical bombers put half a dozen strikes right into dense trees when enemy troops are regrouping . . . down when other planes, including U.S. Phantom jets, blast empty rice fields . . . down when a South Vietnamese battalion commander is wounded seriously—minutes after jumping from his helicopter to lead an assault.

James Wallace, journalist, article of June 26, 1972, in U.S. News & World Report.

Militarily and politically, Hanoi is losing its desperate gamble. We are nonetheless prepared to settle the conflict on honorable negotiating terms which would not require surrender and humiliation on the part of anybody. We stand ready to cease acts of force currently underway against North Vietnam when

our prisoners of war have been returned, our missing accounted for and an internationally supervised ceasefire throughout Indo-China has begun. We will then proceed with a complete withdrawal of all American forces from Vietnam within four months.

President Nixon, article of June 26, 1972, in U.S. News & World Report.

I'm speaking to U.S. servicemen who are stationed on the aircraft carriers in the Gulf of Tonkin . . . One thing that you should know is that these weapons are illegal . . . And the use of these [U.S.] bombs . . . makes one a war criminal.

Jane Fonda, actress and antiwar activist, from North Vietnam, statement of July 1972, broadcast over Hanoi Radio, in the Christian Science Monitor *(July 17, 1988).*

We are still at Phuc Xuyen, a little place on the map, about 40 miles north of Can Tho. There is nothing out here except a small hamlet, and a lot of VC, up the canal, but they are behaving pretty good. Think we will be here a few more days . . .

Time is getting short for R&R, and it gives us something to look forward to . . .

Not much news, as you know,—still the same frustrations, dirty war, unenthused people, but I'm sure it will all be over in about two more months, so we must hang in there.

Remember who loves you and thinks of you all the time.

Lieutenant Colonel Oscar Herrgesell, USA, military adviser, to his wife, letter of July 2, 1972, in Dear Margaret, Today I Died . . . *(1974). [Herrgesell was killed in action on July 29, 1972, while on a helicopter mission.]*

In 1968, Americans voted to bring our sons home from Vietnam in peace—and since then, 20,000 have come home in coffins.

I have no secret plan for peace. I have a public plan.

As one whose heart has ached for 10 years over the agony of Vietnam, I will halt the senseless bombing of Indochina on Inauguration Day . . . Within 90 days of my inauguration every American soldier and every American prisoner will be out of the jungle and out of their cells and back home in America where they belong.

Senator George McGovern of South Dakota, Democratic presidential candidate in 1972. His platform called for an immediate end to the war in Vietnam. Courtesy of the National Archives.

And then let us resolve that never again will we shed the precious young blood of this nation to perpetuate an unrepresentative client abroad.

Senator George McGovern, to the Democratic Party convention, accepting the presidential nomination, speech of July 13, 1972, in The Washington Post (July 14, 1972).

The Vietcong usually run away after a long fight . . . The NVA never run away unless we kill them all. The ones we capture from the north—they have a slogan, "Sinh bac tu nam," or, "Born in the North, die in the South."

Major Nguyen Thai Buu, ARVN, statement of 1972, in Kirk's New York Times Magazine article of August 20, 1972.

I'm a Vietnam veteran . . . I gave America my all, and the leaders of this government threw me and the others away to rot in their VA hospitals. What's happening in Vietnam is a crime against humanity.

If you can't believe the veteran who fought the war and was wounded in the war, who can you believe?

Ron Kovic, disabled Vietnam veteran and former Marine infantryman, to CBS News correspondent Roger Mudd, on demonstrating against the war at the Republican National Convention in Miami, broadcast of August 23, 1972, on CBS Television News.

Standing in this convention hall four years ago, I pledged to seek an honorable end to the war in Vietnam. We have made great progress toward that goal. We have brought over half a million men home from Vietnam, and more will be coming home. We have ended America's ground combat role. No draftees are being sent to Vietnam . . . There are three things we have not and will not do: We will never abandon our prisoners of war. We will not join our enemies in imposing a Communist government on our allies—the 17 million people of South Vietnam. We will not stain the honor of the United States.

President Nixon, to the Republican Party Convention in Miami Beach, accepting the presidential nomination, speech of August 23, 1972, in The Los Angeles Times (August 24, 1972).

I am a Vietnam veteran, and I don't think the American people really, really understand [the] war and what's going on . . .

The Vietcong are bad. But that doesn't make it right for me to be bad, or for someone to say that we should send their son, or their husband, or their brother to go over there to be just as vicious . . . You go into a village that has had a 1,000-pound bomb—it's called the daisy cutter . . . You don't worry about taking prisoners because there are no prisoners. You don't know if you kill Vietcong because you can't put the people together . . . and you don't have any idea whether it's a human being or an animal [because of] what's been done to it.

Anonymous Vietnam veteran, to the "Jerry Williams Talk Show" (WBZ Radio, Boston), telephone call of September 1972, in Time (October 23, 1972).

This is a war of attrition. The North Vietnamese are willing to lose tens of thousands more if they can break the back of the South Vietnamese Army.

Anonymous U.S. military officer, statement in U.S. News & World Report (October 9, 1972).

Were you to find the agreement to be unacceptable at this point and the other side were to reveal the extraordinary limits to which it has gone in meeting the demands put upon them, it is my judgment that your decision would have the most serious effects upon my ability to continue to provide support for you and the Government of South Vietnam.

President Nixon, to President Thieu, letter of October 21, 1972, in Porter's Vietnam: A History in Documents *(1979).*

We believe that peace is at hand.

Henry Kissinger, to press conference of October 27, 1972, in the U.S. Department of State's Bulletin *(November 13, 1972).*

We have not agreed on anything yet, and yet the Communists boasted that there will be a cease-fire and are preparing for it. We are not afraid of a cease-fire and the peace. I am sure it will come. But it only will come when I personally sign the treaty for a cease-fire and peace. The Communists can use 10 hands and 10 legs to sign treaties; but without my signature, it means there has been no agreement by the people.

President Thieu, statement of October 27, 1972, in the Los Angeles Herald-Examiner *(October 28, 1972).*

I repeat my personal assurances to you that the United States will react very strongly and rapidly to any violation of the agreement. But in order to do this effectively it is essential that I have the public support and that your government does not emerge as the obstacle to a peace which the American public now universally desires. It is for this reason that I am pressing for the acceptance of an [cease-fire] agreement which I am convinced is honorable and fair and which can be made essentially secure by our joint determination.

President Nixon, to President Thieu, letter of November 14, 1972, in Porter's Vietnam: A History in Documents.

Henry talked rather emotionally about the fact that this was a very courageous decision, but I pointed out to him that there was no other choice—that we were going to be here for four years and that even though we made a good, cheap peace now, to have it break within a matter of a year or two would leave us with nothing to be proud of and beyond that

would leave us with terrible choices—much worse choices—later than we would have at the present time. We are going to face up to the music at this time with the hope that this will gain their attention and keep them from reacting to us later.

President Nixon, on his decision to bomb military targets in the Hanoi-Haiphong area, diary entry of December 14, 1972, in RN: The Memoirs of Richard Nixon.

We will not be stampeded into an agreement, and if I may say so, we will not be charmed into an agreement until its conditions are right.

National Security adviser Henry Kissinger, to press conference of December 16, 1972, in The New York Times *(December 17, 1972).*

. . . we are not going to allow the peace talks to be used as a cover for another offensive . . . the President will continue to order any action he deems necessary by air or by sea to prevent any build-up he sees in the South.

Ronald Ziegler, presidential press secretary, to the press, on President Nixon's decision to bomb North Vietnam above the 20th parallel and deploy more mines around Haiphong harbor, announcement of December 18, 1972, in The New York Times *(December 19, 1972).*

The airplane began to shudder and shake, and I heard other explosions as the other crew members ejected. I heard another loud blast. The wing was exploding . . . I rolled through the opening, and as soon as I thought I was free of the airplane, I pulled the ripcord on my parachute . . . Everything was quiet and eerie. There was a full moon, the weather was clear . . . I saw the airplane . . . It was exploding as it hit the ground . . . I got my feet down, hit the ground, and rolled over on my backside . . . It felt good to be alive.

Lieutenant Colonel Conner, USAF, B-52 commander, recalls ejecting after his bomber was hit by a SAM on December 18, 1972, in Alison's Linebacker II: A View From the Rock *(1979). [Conner was rescued by a Marine helicopter within 20 minutes.]*

The U.S. jets came in practically one by one. Some of the aircraft flew so low that as they passed over Hanoi, the doors and windows of the Hoa Binh Hotel, where the AFP [Agence France Presse] office is located, were set shaking. The sounds of bomb explosions and anti-aircraft fire added to the din.

Jean Thoraval, journalist, dispatch of December 19, 1972, in Agence France Presse.

. . . when the ground shook, and the plaster fell from the ceiling . . . the guards cowered in the lee of the walls, cheeks so ashen you could detect it even from the light of the fiery sky . . . By day, interrogators and guards would inquire about our needs solicitously. The center of Hanoi was dead—even though like our prisons, thousands of yards from the drop zone. We knew the bombers knew where we were, and felt not only ecstatically happy, but confident. The North Vietnamese didn't . . . They knew they lived through last night, but they also knew that if our forces moved their bomb line over a few thousand yards they wouldn't live through tonight.

Commander James B. Stockdale, USN pilot and POW (1965–1973), recalls December 18–29, 1972, in Sharp's Strategy for Defeat: Vietnam in Retrospect *(1978).*

The noise was unbelievable—the sharp racket of the antiaircraft guns, the boom and whoosh of SAM missiles, the dull thud of distant bombs. For the first time in my life the noise of jet engines ceased to be merely an annoyance and became the sound of death. Tracers and streaks of fire from missiles cut across the sky. Against the slowly reddening sky—which became still more red as the bombing intensified—black smoke billowed on the horizon. It all seemed unreal—until the next day when I saw the damage.

Michael Allen, American teacher visiting Hanoi, on the bombing of December 18–29, 1972, in Christian Century *article of January 24, 1973.*

Evacuation of the city [Hanoi] began soon after the first bombing attacks; and was in full swing by today. By truck, pedicab, bicycle and on foot, families and individuals depart for the greater safety of the countryside. Street traffic and crowds have dwindled to a fraction of the volume observed before the bombing began, and many shops are now closed and shuttered.

Telford Taylor, American author and law professor, on visiting Hanoi during the bombing, article of December 25, 1972, in The New York Times.

I didn't understand why—the Americans dropped bombs all over the place. The people in Hanoi had already gained a lot of confidence in the accuracy of the bombing, and large groups of them would gather to watch the attacks. At one point the pilots dropped a couple of beehive bombs on the Bach Mai and Hung Ky Street area, in the vicinity of the "Eighth of March" factory, and on Hue Street. These beehive bombs contained hundreds of little steel balls. A large number of civilians were unexpectedly killed . . . people began to hate the Americans. If the local authorities hadn't intervened, they would have beaten shot-down American pilots to death.

NVA Sergeant Nguyen Van Mo recalls the bombing of December 18–29, 1972, in Chanoff and Toai's Portrait of the Enemy *(1986).*

The bombing tactic is eight years old. It has not produced results in the past. It will not lead to a rational, peaceful settlement now. It is the "Stone Age" strategy being used in a war almost unanimously recognized in this nation as a mistaken one. It is a raw power play with human lives—Americans and others—and, as such, it is abhorrent.

Senator Mike Mansfield (D–Mont.), to a news conference of December 20, 1972, in The New York Times *(December 26, 1972).*

The United States hopes to bend the will of the Vietnamese people by mass-bombing North Vietnam. This will prove to be an illusory hope. Hanoi, Haiphong and other cities may be bombed and erased, but the Vietnamese people will never bend.

General Vo Nguyen Giap, minister of defense of North Vietnam, speech of December 21, 1972, in The New York Times *(December 23, 1972).*

We may call it a week of shock, dismay, and disbelief.

When it was announced on Monday that President Nixon had ordered a renewal of the bombing of Hanoi and Haiphong Harbor in the heaviest American air attacks of the war, the nation was stunned . . . The question asked over and over was, What has happened to the man we elected as our President on November 7th? Why did he lead us to believe that a peace settlement was at most only a few weeks away? Is he now determined to win a military victory to show the world that we are the strongest nation on earth?

Senator George Aiken (R–Vt.), diary entry of December 23, 1972, in Senate Diary *(1976).*

Bob Hope and singer-dancer Lola Falana perform at the last Bob Hope Christmas show in Vietnam, at Tan Son Nhut Air Force Base on December 24, 1972. Photograph by 2nd Lt. Edward J. McNamara Jr. Courtesy of the National Archives.

We figured the war would be over by the time we got here. But now they're arguing about the hotel bill in Paris.

Bob Hope, entertainer, to an estimated 5,000 servicemen at Tan Son Nhut air base, during his last annual Christmas show in Vietnam, December 24, 1972, in The New York Times *(December 25, 1972).*

As Haiphong passed off our left wing, we could see the Navy support forces were really working over the SAM [Surface-to-Air-Missile] and AAA [Antiaircraft Artillery] sites. The whole area was lit up like a Christmas tree . . . At bombs away, it looked like we were right in the middle of a fireworks factory that was in the process of blowing up. As the bomb doors closed, several SAMs exploded nearby. Others could be seen arcing over and starting a descent, then detonating.

Colonel James McCarthy, USAF, commander, 43d Strategic Wing, recalls the B-52 raid of December 26, 1972 (the largest of the Linebacker II campaign), in Alison's Linebacker II: A View from the Rock.

I have followed President Nixon through all his convolutions and specious arguments, but he appears to have left his senses on this . . . I can't go along with him on this.

Senator William B. Saxbe (R–Ohio), opposing the bombing of Hanoi, statement of December 28, 1972, in The Cleveland Plain Dealer *(December 29, 1972).*

. . . you (Americans) can probably afford the luxury of being easy in this agreement. I cannot. A bad agreement means nothing to you. To me, it's a matter of life and death. What do these 300,000 North Vietnamese mean to you? Nothing. What is the loss of South Vietnam if you look at it on the world's map? Just a speck . . . for me, for us, it isn't a question of choosing between Moscow and Peking. It's a question of choosing between life and death.

President Thieu, statement of December 30, 1972, in Fallaci's New Republic *Article of January 20, 1973.*

I have . . . irrevocably decided to proceed to initial the Agreement on January 23, 1973 and to sign it on January 27, 1973 in Paris. I will do so, if necessary, alone. In that case I shall have to explain publicly that your Government obstructs peace. The result will be an inevitable and immediate termination of U.S. economic and military assistance which cannot be forestalled by a change of personnel in your government.

President Nixon, to President Thieu, letter of January 14, 1973, in Kissinger's White House Years *(1979).*

We tend to think only in terms of what this war has cost us, the United States, but by comparison to what it has cost so many Vietnamese, our price pales . . . What the terms of any cease-fire will hold for them is a big question mark . . . Time will provide some answers to much of this, I guess.

Lieutenant Colonel William B. Nolde, USA, senior military adviser, to a friend, letter of January 1973, in The New York Times *(January 29, 1973). [Nolde was killed by an enemy artillery shell at An Loc on January 27, 1973, 11 hours before the truce took effect. He was the last American serviceman to die before the cease-fire.]*

We today have concluded an agreement to end the war and bring peace with honor in Vietnam and Southeast Asia.

Henry Kissinger, statement of January 23, 1973, in The Washington Post *(January 24, 1973).*

Now that we have achieved an honorable agreement, let us be proud that America did not settle for a peace that would have betrayed our allies, that would have abandoned our prisoners of war, or that

American prisoners of war begin their long journey home from North Vietnam in February 1973. Courtesy of the National Archives.

would have ended the war for us but would have continued the war for the 50 million people of Indochina. Let us be proud of the 2½ million young Americans who served in Vietnam, who served with honor and distinction in one of the most selfless enterprises in the history of nations. And let us be proud of those who sacrificed, who gave their lives so that the people of South Vietnam might live in freedom and so that the world might live in peace.

President Nixon, to the nation, television address of January 23, 1973, in Public Papers of the Presidents of the United States.

With the signing of the peace agreement in Paris today, and, after receiving from the Secretary of the Army that he forsees no need for further inductions, I wish to inform you that the Armed Forces henceforth will depend exclusively on volunteer soldiers, sailors, airmen and marines.

Melvin Laird, secretary of defense, announcement of January 27, 1973, in The New York Times *(January 28, 1973).*

Man for man, the South Vietnamese right now probably are stronger than the North Vietnamese.

They have shorter supply lines, and they have access to more manpower for replacements.

Anonymous U.S. military adviser, statement in U.S. News & World Report *(January 29, 1973).*

What kind of peace is a peace that gives the North Vietnamese the right to have their troops here? What kind of treaty is a treaty that de facto legalizes their presence? [Nixon and Kissinger] were too impatient to make peace, too impatient to negotiate and sign. When you deal with the Communists, you must never fix time limits. You must not tell them you want to repatriate your prisoners as soon as possible and reach peace as soon as possible. They only take advantage of you.

President Thieu, statement of January 31, 1973, in the Los Angeles Herald-Examiner *(February 1, 1973).*

It never was a conventional war. It will not be a conventional peace—and the way to lose the peace is to forget that one fact.

Anonymous U.S. military officer, statement in U.S. News & World Report *(February 5, 1973).*

Former American prisoners of war cheer as their aircraft takes off from an airfield near Hanoi during Operation Homecoming, February 1973. Courtesy of the National Archives.

The reality of Indochina is that the war is not over. That is known in Saigon and in Hanoi—no matter how this fact may be papered over in the near future in Washington.

Anonymous South Vietnamese government official, statement in U.S. News & World Report *(February 5, 1973).*

We were met at the door by three pretty young ladies, the first American girls we had seen in seven years. They were attractively dressed, well groomed, and smelled delightfully of perfume. We sat down in the seats and looked around. Everything seemed like heaven. Just like heaven. When the back doors of that C-141 closed there were tears in the eyes of every man aboard.

Captain Larry Chesley, USAF pilot and POW (1966–1973), recalls his release on February 12, 1973, in Seven Years in Hanoi *(1973).*

The bird surged forward, and in seconds we were racing down the runway; we were close . . . close . . . we all let out our breath in tumultuous scream-

ing . . . yelling . . . arms of the seats . . . We could feel the nose lift, as the pilot eased back on the stick . . . The bird rotated and stood on its main wheels, as if perched on its hind legs . . . then it leapt into the air, and we all went completely crazy . . . screaming, yelling, "We're off . . . we're up . . . we're out . . . we're out of that rotten place . . . we're really going home . . . WE'RE FREE . . . FREE . . . FREE!!!!!!"

Major Larry Guarino, USAF pilot and POW (1964–1973), on his release in February 1973, in A P.O.W.'s Story: 2801 Days in Hanoi *(1990).*

I told one guy that Miami won the Super Bowl and he said, "What's the Super Bowl?"

Anonymous pilot, transporting American POWs, statement in Newsweek *(February 26, 1973).*

We are happy to have the opportunity to serve our country under difficult circumstances. We are pro-

Commander Jeremiah Denton Jr., USN, one of the first U.S. prisoners to be released by North Vietnam after the 1973 peace agreement, waves to well-wishers at Hickam Air Force Base, Hawaii, during the final leg of his trip home. Courtesy of the National Archives.

foundly grateful to our Commander-in-Chief and to our nation for this day. God bless America.

Commander Jeremiah Denton Jr., USN pilot and POW (1965–1973), upon arriving at Clark Air Force base in the Philippines from Hanoi, statement of February 12, 1973, in U.S. News & World Report (February 26, 1973).

All you wonderful people, all of our dreams have come true. Somebody pinch me quick before I wake up and find out it's all a dream.

Captain Larry Chesley, USAF pilot and POW (1966–1973), upon arriving at Clark Air Force Base in the Philippines, statement of February 12, 1973, in Newsweek (February 26, 1973).

As the coastline came into view we could see a very beautiful sight—the Golden Gate bridge. We all started cheering, crying, and broke into song—"California Here I Come." We talked the pilot into making a low pass over the Golden Gate (with permission of

Dependents of U.S. Marines greet repatriated Marine prisoners of war, March 31, 1973. Courtesy of the National Archives.

course). That was a great feeling. You just can't imagine the love and emotion we felt for our country.

Lieutenant Colonel Jay Jensen, USAF pilot and POW (1967–1973), recalls February 1973, in Six Years in Hell *(1974).*

During the first days of the cease-fire, the supposed winding down of the war was far from apparent. At eight o'clock on the morning of January 28, the moment the cease-fire officially went into effect, I was in a car with a couple of other correspondents near the town of Trang Bang, on the way to Tay Ninh along Route 1 . . . the first of 26 five-hundred pound bombs were dropped by South Vietnamese fighter-bombers 100 yards ahead of us, on and near the road . . . The fight continued for several hours and we spent part of that time lying in a ditch to escape the cross fire of rifles, machine guns and mortars.

Robert Shaplen, journalist, article of February 25, 1973, in The New Yorker.

For us, this is a day of joy and pride. What could be more joyous than to be delivered from your enemies and delivered to your friends. And the pride that we have in our nation and our government could not be greater. And this day justifies our faith. P.O.W.'s never have a nice day, but we get one great day. Each of us thanks all of you for this unforgettable day.

Lieutenant Colonel James O'Neil, USAF pilot and POW (1972–1973), upon his arrival at Clark Air Force Base in the Philippines, statement of March 29, 1973, in The New York Times *(March 30, 1973). [O'Neil was one of the last 67 POWs released by the North Vietnamese.]*

The former American camps that dot Vietnam are beginning to crumble. Long Binh outside of Saigon, once the largest U.S. military base in the world, does look like a ghost town . . . Scavengers have begun to dismantle unused buildings in order to sell the tin roofing and the wood. What promises to be the lasting American monument is the thousands of miles of rusted barbed wire strung over the country.

Zalin Grant, journalist, article of May 19, 1973, in The New Republic.

Saigon is not the same city I left six years ago—and the changes run deep. No longer do the thump of artillery and the roar of jets punctuate the night; no longer do the diesel-belching army trucks rumble through the streets with air horns blasting . . . The sad flotsam of the war—the maimed children selling peanuts and jasmine, the crippled teenage peddlers pushing everything from lacquerware to pornography, the amputee war veterans begging alms from foreigners—all this is still painfully prominent.

Arthur Zich, journalist, article of June 18, 1973, in Newsweek.

Two kilometers north on Route 14 a cluster of bunkers marked the roadblock which was the forward line of the North Viet Army. At home it was easy to talk about the basic kindliness and good intentions of the VC and North Viets. Out here (I realized suddenly, perhaps more than I ever had) in Vietnam, they were the enemy. They would kill you if they could. Especially in a flimsy helicopter above their lines, they were the enemy.

Up here in the upper air, the constant Blat, Blat, Blat of the helicopter motor, loud even through the big earphone helmets, was comforting, but also discomforting, in that it constantly reminded you it was all that was keeping you up there. If it stopped, we would drop like a stone.

James Jones, novelist, following the cease-fire in 1973, in Viet Journal *(1973).*

11. The Fall of the South: 1974–1975

Vietnam Without the United States

By the end of 1973, the Paris agreements had become a dead letter. Discussions of a political settlement had begun in early 1973 and continued off and on throughout the year, but the key issue—the future of South Vietnam—was nonnegotiable. After the talks formally broke off in late 1973, South Vietnamese forces stepped up ground and air attacks on NVA bases and launched a series of land-grabbing operations in PRG (Provisional Revolutionary Government) strongholds along the eastern seaboard, in the Iron Triangle and in the Mekong Delta. President Thieu formally proclaimed in early January 1974 the start of the "Third Indochina War."

At first, the NVA and PRG suffered heavy losses during the campaign. However, by late spring, the communist went on the counteroffensive and scored success after success, mauling ARVN units in the Iron Triangle, recapturing much of the territory they had lost and seizing additional territory previously under Saigon's control.

By fall 1974, the military balance had shifted in favor of North Vietnam. By this time, the North Vietnamese and PRG had mobilized large armies in the south. They had stockpiled vast quantities of supplies and created a sophisticated logistics system, which enabled them to move regulars, along with tanks and artillery, to any battlefront within hours. Meanwhile, South Vietnam's economy was teetering on the brink of total collapse, partly as a result of the American withdrawal and partly from soaring oil prices triggered by the 1973 Middle East war.

The economic crisis had an especially dire effect on Saigon's one-million-man army, causing chronic shortages of vital military supplies, eroding morale and promoting further corruption. The payment of bribes for air and artillery support became commonplace. Some pilots even demanded bribes to evacuate wounded soldiers. Military officers were growing rich by selling stolen gasoline and other supplies, and desertions were reaching epidemic proportions. Compounding Thieu's problems was the growing Buddhist movement for peace and reconciliation with the communists, while the Catholics, the government's principal base of support, had launched a nationwide anti-corruption campaign directed at Thieu himself.

At the same time, the United States was undergoing a crisis of its own. The Watergate scandal had prompted the House Judiciary Committee to vote for impeachment proceedings against President Nixon. On August 9, 1974, Nixon resigned from office and thus spared the nation the agony of trying its chief executive. One of his last acts as president had been to sign into law a bill that imposed a ceiling of $1 billion on American military aid to South Vietnam for the next 11 months. Many legislators agreed with Senator Edward Kennedy, who said that the time had come to terminate America's "endless support for an endless war." In September, Congress voted to trim the actual appropriation to $700 million, half of which comprised shipping costs.

The vote reducing aid had a devastating impact on the South Vietnamese armed forces. Air force operations had to be cut back as much as 50% because of shortages of gasoline and spare parts. Ammunition and other supplies had to be severely rationed. ARVN troops already demoralized from North Vietnamese blows, now sensed that they were being abandoned by their once strongest ally.

THE MILITARY BALANCE

In early October 1974, North Vietnamese military commanders and members of the Politburo met in Hanoi to reassess the shifting military balance in the South. By then, the NVA had already infiltrated 10 full divisions into the south—some 200,000 troops—supported by 70 tanks and 450 long-range artillery pieces as well as 20 antiaircraft regiments with sophisticated surface-to-air missiles. Vast quantities of weapons, ammunition and supplies had been stockpiled, new training and hospital facilities built and the logistical network had been completed.

"Now that the United States has pulled out of the South," Le Duan, the Communist Party first secretary, declared, "it will be hard to jump back in. And no matter how they may intervene, they cannot rescue the Saigon administration from its disastrous collapse." What emerged from the October meeting was a document known as the Resolution for 1975, a two-year plan to "liberate" the south not through negotiations, but through military force.

During the first year, communist forces would move out of their jungle base camps and systematically eliminate exposed ARVN outposts. Large-scale attacks against cities and major ARVN garrisons would be launched in the following year, 1976, culminating in a "General Offensive" that would topple the Saigon regime, or at least force the acceptance of a coalition government.

In early December, army Chief of Staff General Van Tien Dung modified his plans after Lieutenant General Tran Van Tra, the commander of the communist forces in the lowlands–Mekong Delta region convinced the politburo to begin the campaign with a major assault on Phuoc Long Province, northeast of Saigon. The attack on Phuoc Long proved even more successful than Tra had anticipated. In mid-December, NVA main units and PRG regional forces attacked Phuoc Long, and within three weeks had killed or captured 3,000 South Vietnamese troops, seized huge quantities of supplies and "liberated" the entire province.

The politburo, encouraged by this sudden collapse, now revised its plans for Campaign 275, the previously planned push into the Central Highlands. New orders werre now drawn up for a series of surprise attacks on Ban Me Thuot, the capital of Darlac Province and the headquarters of the 23d ARVN Division. Le Duan told General Dung, "Never have we had military and political conditions so perfect or a strategic advantage so great as we have now," as he dispatched the general south to take personal charge of the highlands offensive.

When news of the fall of Phuoc Long reached Washington in early January 1975, President Gerald Ford had been in office only five months, and he was burdened by a host of domestic problems ranging from rising inflation and widespread unemployment to the possibility of a renewed war between Egypt and Israel in the Middle East. He was not about to risk his political standing by taking any forceful military action in Southeast Asia. Moreover, even if he had been inclined to do so, the Indochina Prohibition of 1973 and the War Powers Act of 1974 sharply limited his options. Ford decided that the only alternative was to seek a supplemental appropriation of $300 million in military aid for South Vietnam and an additional $222 million for Cambodia, where Khmer Rouge forces were rapidly closing in on the capital of Phnom Penh.

THE FINAL OFFENSIVE

While the president's supplemental-aid request was debated on Capitol Hill, the North Vietnamese army continued its offensive. General Dung deployed three NVA divisions, encircling the town of Ban Me Thuot in the Central Highlands on March 10, and took it by five o'clock in the afternoon. Many South Vietnamese troops began fleeing along with their families, who traditionally lived with the army.

The fall of Ban Me Thuot convinced Thieu that he would have to start trading land in order to gain time. At first, Thieu ordered his troops to abandon the northern provinces of South Vietnam and called for the evacuation of Pleiku and Kontum. Known as the "Convoy of

A seemingly endless chain of overburdened trucks and buses stall in a massive traffic jam between Hue and Danang in the northern part of South Vietnam in March 1975. Thousands of civilians and military personnel fled Hue, Vietnam's old imperial capital, following a government decision not to defend it against advancing North Vietnamese and Vietcong forces. Courtesy of AP/Wide World Photos.

Tears,'' 200,000 leaderless men, women and children began straggling down a treacherous road to the coast as the communists shelled them. Thieu then reversed his earlier decision, insisting that Hue be defended to the last man. By then, the communists had cut the major roads. The withdrawal turned into a rout, and it opened the way for an even greater catastrophe in the coastal cities of South Vietnam.

Hanoi now sensed for the first time that total victory could be achieved in 1975 and immediately implemented contingency plans for the conquest of all of South Vietnam. By late March, more than a million refugees were streaming toward Danang, seeking safety. On March 25, the day Hue fell, North Vietnamese rockets tore into downtown Danang, Vietnam's second-largest city. Within three days, 35,000 communists were encircling its suburbs, while terrified citizens jammed the airport, the docks and the beaches, attempting to flee. Thousands of civilians and renegade soldiers tried to board waiting boats and barges. Many civilians drowned or were trampled to death in the crush. Others were shot by South Vietnamese soldiers to make room for themselves.

On March 31, 1975, almost 10 years to the day after the U.S. Marines had splashed ashore at Danang, the city was in North Vietnamese hands. The following day, a flash telegram arrived at General Dung's command post near Ban Me Thuot, informing him that the politburo had reached a "historic decision." They had abandoned the two-year plan outlined the preceding fall, and the North Vietnamese leadership had decided to "liberate Saigon before the rainy season." Dung now committed all his forces to the southern front in the final phase of what had been designated as the Ho Chi Minh Campaign. The offensive against Saigon was to be launched no later than the last week of April.

The United States was stunned by the collapse of South Vietnam, but was resigned to its outcome. American intelligence had correctly predicted that the major North Vietnamese offensive was not planned until 1976, but the ability of the South Vietnamese to resist was over-estimated. On the same day that Ban Me Thuot fell, Congress rejected Ford's request for an additional $300 million in military aid for South Vietnam.

By early April, Cambodia appeared to be nearing collapse, and John Gunther Dean, the U.S. ambassador, was arranging to evacuate the American embassy staff and selected Cambodians by helicopter to an aircraft carrier in the Gulf of Thailand. On April 11, U.S. Marines were dispatched on an evacuation mission to get the last Americans out of Cambodia.

Meanwhile, Ambassador Graham Martin in Saigon was making contingency plans for a full-scale U.S. evacuation in the event that ARVN forces failed to hold the defense line centered around the garrison town of Xuan Loc, 35 miles northeast of the capital. Martin insisted on proceeding slowly, since he feared that any visible sign of a U.S. pull-out might precipitate the same kind of mass panic that had engulfed Danang. Consequently, out of a total population of more than 6,000 American civilians, only 1,285 left the country during the first two weeks of April.

As the North Vietnamese army tightened its grip around Saigon, Ambassador Martin came under increasing pressure to accelerate the pace of the U.S. withdrawal. On April 19, two days after the Senate Armed Services Committee formally rejected President Ford's aid request, Martin was informed that the U.S. presence should be reduced to no more than 1,100 as soon as possible. In the days that followed, the number of evacuees from Tan Son Nhut air base grew dramatically, from an average of 200 to more than 3,000 per day. DAO (Defense Attaché Office) officials also organized a series of ultrasecret "black flights" to ensure that especially "sensitive" Vietnamese, many of them former U.S. intelligence agents, could leave the country without the knowledge of the GVN.

Aware that the pace of the American withdrawal was accelerating, thousands of Saigonese converged on the U.S. Embassy and the DAO compound in a frantic search for some way out of their country. Everywhere Americans were accosted by Vietnamese waving letters postmarked from the States, missionary school diplomas and U.S.

Army discharges—any document that established some connection to the United States. In the *Saigon Post*, one classified advertisement read, "Fairly pretty high school girl, 18, of well-to-do-family seeks adoption or marriage with foreigner of American, French, British, German or other nationality who would take her abroad legally to enable her to continue her studies outside Vietnam at her own expense. Please telephone 45470."

On April 21, Thieu announced his resignation, hoping he would be replaced by a leader who might make a deal with the communists. In his 90-minute television address, the South Vietnamese leader often rambled and at times was choked with tears as he bitterly attacked the United States, recounting President Nixon's "solemn pledge" to "respond with full force . . . if North Vietnam renewed its aggression." He declared, "The United States has not respected its promises," and not until the end of his speech did he unveil his decision: "I am resigning, but I am not deserting." Four days later, Thieu fled Vietnam and eventually settled in Great Britain.

Thieu had abdicated to Tran Van Huong, his aged and enfeebled vice president, who immediately transferred his authority as chief of state to General Duong Van Minh, a self-styled "neutralist," who could possibly pave the way for a negotiated settlement with the communists. By now, the time for bargaining with the north had long since passed. On April 26, General Dung and his staff had completed the finishing touches on their plan for the last offensive of the Ho Chi Minh Campaign. At precisely 5:00 P.M. on April 27, the "final, decisive battle" of the Vietnam War—"the liberation of Saigon"—would begin.

THE FALL OF SAIGON

During the predawn hours of April 27, four heavy rockets slammed into Saigon, signaling the onset of the communists' final offensive. The NVA sent 130,000 soldiers on the attack, moving toward the capital on five fronts. As the news of the latest communist advances reached Washington, President Ford and his senior advisers quickly determined that the time had come for a total U.S. pullout. Ambassador Martin informed Secretary of State Henry Kissinger that, since no more than 1,000 Americans remained in Saigon and Tan Son Nhut air base seemed in no imminent danger, he was confident that he "could get a maximum number of Vietnamese and Americans out by the 30th."

On April 28, as General Minh was finishing his acceptance speech at the Independence Palace, the communists launched their first and only air strike of the war. Led by a former South Vietnamese pilot who had defected to the enemy earlier in the month, a group of five captured A-37 Dragonfly jets streaked over Tan Son Nhut and bombed a line of Vietnamese air force planes along the main runway. Pandemonium broke out as ARVN soldiers swarmed onto the tarmac and VNAF pilots fired up their aircraft in a desperate attempt to flee the country.

In the early morning hours of April 29, 1975, NVA rockets hit near the guard post of the DAO compound, killing U.S. Marine Lance Corporal Darwin Judge, of Marshalltown, Iowa, and Corporal Charles McMahon Jr., of Woburn, Massachusetts, who were both recent arrivals to Vietnam. They were the first American victims of the "Ho Chi Minh Campaign" and the last U.S. casualties of the war.

By the morning of April 29, it was clear that fixed-wing aircraft could no longer continue the evacuation. After Ambassador Martin telephoned the White House, President Ford at 10:51 Saigon time executed the order for Operation Frequent Wind, codename for an emergency evacuation. A short time later, operators at the American radio station in Saigon began playing a tape of Bing Crosby's "White Christmas," a prearranged signal that the final evacuation had begun.

Operation Frequent Wind was one of the biggest helicopter evacuations on record. Beginning at 3:00 in the afternoon, an average of 36 helicopters per hour landed at Tan Son Nhut, boarded more than 50 passengers each, and whisked them away to the armada of ships stationed off the coast. By 8:00 P.M. more than 6,000 people, 5,000 of them Vietnamese, had been evacuated. Only a U.S. Marine security force and an undetermined number of Americans and Vietnamese remained inside the U.S. Embassy.

Although Operation Frequent Wind was miraculously successful, its original plan for picking up Americans and Vietnamese at designated departure points around the city broke down after mobs of hysterical Vietnamese, clamoring to be evacuated, blocked the buses. Recalling his own harrowing journey that day, journalist Keyes Beech of the *Chicago Daily News* wrote, "At every stop Vietnamese beat on the doors and windows pleading to be let inside . . . Every time we opened the door we had to beat and kick them back." Even those Vietnamese who had been promised evacuation by their American employers were sometimes lost in the mad rush to flee Saigon.

By late afternoon, the entire city of Saigon seemed to dissolve into chaos. Huge angry mobs roamed the streets, overturning abandoned cars and setting fire to buildings. Looters were everywhere, sifting through the former residences of Americans and carrying away furniture, bathroom fixtures and anything that might have the remotest value. Thousands of others surged toward the American Embassy, screaming to be saved. Rumors of an impending communist slaughter were rampant, but in fact, the North Vietnamese were deliberately holding back their fire, no longer seeing any gain in unnecessary slaughter.

As midnight approached on April 29, 1975, U.S. Marine demolition teams placed bombs on the bottom floor of the DAO headquarters building, the former headquarters of the United States Military Command, Vietnam (USMACV), which had served for more than 10 years as a symbol of American commitment to prevent a communist takeover. At approximately 11:40 P.M., the Marines triggered the delayed-action fuses and then dashed for the helicopters. As they ascended and looked down they watched the structure disintegrate along with millions of dollars of secret equipment and barrels containing more than $3.5 million in U.S. currency.

A few hours later, at 4:58 A.M., Ambassador Graham Martin appeared on the U.S. Embassy's roof and climbed aboard "Lady Ace 09," and with his aid, Ken Moorefield, was lifted off by helicopter into the dark sky and headed for the U.S. Seventh Fleet. It was one of the last evacuation flights from Vietnam. The only Americans remaining at the U.S. Embassy were Major Jim Kean and his Marines. However, remaining in the parking lot were 420 Vietnamese and "third-country nationals" who had been promised evacuation. A few hours earlier, the White House had ordered that the operation be shut down, fearing that the embassy could become a bottomless pit of refugees.

The Marines filed up to the roof as the evacuees tried to break through the barricaded doors that were blocking their way. While waiting for the helicopters, the Marines periodically sprayed Mace through the broken glass to fend off the Vietnamese trying to get through. At 7:53 A.M. on April 30, the final helicopter arrived and as Master Sergeant Juan Valdez boarded he could still see Vietnamese evacuees trying to push their way to the rooftop door, waving papers to prove that they, too, should be taken along.

As the last American helicopter disappeared over the eastern horizon on the morning of April 30, 1975, an eerie quiet settled over Saigon. At 10:24 A.M., President Duong Van Minh went on national radio and called on his soldiers "to remain calm, to stop fighting, and stay put." The communists had planned a two-year campaign to capture the capital. It took only 55 days.

THE LONG WAR IS OVER

At midday, a convoy of tanks and trucks rumbled down Hong Thap Tu Street and turned left onto Thong Nhut Boulevard to face the presidential palace. Without slowing down, the lead tank crashed through the high front gate and came to a halt inside the courtyard. A second tank soon crashed through the gate, followed by the rest of the tanks, which formed a huge semicircle facing the steps. One of the crewmen raced up the steps and unfurled a huge red and yellow Vietcong flag from the balcony.

As North Vietnamese Colonel Bui Tin entered the palace, General Minh announced, "I have been waiting since early this morning to transfer power to you." "There is no question of your transferring power," replied Bui Tin. "Your power has crumbled. You cannot give up what you do not have." He then announced, "You have nothing to fear. Between Vietnamese, there are no victors and no vanquished. Only the Americans have been beaten. If you are patriots, consider this a moment of joy. The war for our country is over."

Indeed, the 30 years' war in Vietnam was over. But the cost was very high. In the past decade alone, one in every 10 Vietnamese had been a casualty of war. Nearly a million and a half Vietnamese were killed and three million wounded. American losses were nearly 60,000 dead and 300,000 wounded.

In the immediate aftermath of the war, the United States went into a kind of self-conscious, collective amnesia. Vietnam was practically ignored by the news media, and it was hardly mentioned in the presidential campaign of 1976. "Today it is almost as though the war never had happened," the columnist Joseph C. Harsch of the Louisville *Courier-Journal* wrote in October 1975. "Americans have somehow blocked it out of their consciousness. They don't talk about it. They don't talk about its consequences."

It was not until November 13, 1982, on Veteran's Day weekend, when the Vietnam Veterans Memorial in Washington, D.C., was dedicated, that there was any widespread national recognition for those who served in Vietnam and for the sacrifices of those who did not return. America was finally coming to terms with the Vietnam War. The fighting had lasted for nearly 10 years; the healing would take much longer.

CHRONICLE OF EVENTS

1974

January 4: President Thieu claims, "The war has restarted."

January 27: Since the January 1973 truce, 13,788 South Vietnamese soldiers, 2,159 South Vietnamese civilians and 45,057 communist soldiers have died in the fighting.

February: ARVN offensive operations encroach upon areas long under communist control; communists retaliate.

March: Heaviest fighting since the cease-fire.

April 4: The U.S. House of Representatives rejects the Nixon administration's request to increase military aid to South Vietnam.

April 12: RVN (South Vietnam) withdraws from Paris talks on political reconciliation with PRG (North Vietnam).

May 9: U.S. House Judiciary Committee formally begins inquiry into possible impeachment of President Nixon.

August 6: House cuts military aid appropriation for South Vietnam from $1 billion to $700 million.

August 9: Richard Nixon resigns as president; Vice President Gerald R. Ford becomes president.

December 31: U.S. military strength in Vietnam limited to 50 personnel.

1975

January 1: Khmer Rouge in Cambodia launch final offensive from siege ring around Phnom Penh.

January 8: North Vietnamese seize Phuoc Long Province north of Saigon; U.S. does not intervene with airpower.

March 10: North Vietnamese army conducts an offensive against Ban Me Thuot, provincial capital in Central Highlands.

March 14: President Thieu orders withdrawal of ARVN forces from Central Highlands.

March 19: Communist forces attack and capture Quang Tri, as ARVN withdrawal toward Danang turns into a rout, and the First Division disintegrates.

March 25: Hue falls to communist troops. More than one million refugees are streaming toward Danang, which is already under heavy rocket fire.

March 28: President Ford announces he has ordered U.S. Navy transports and "contract vessels" to assist in the evacuation of South Vietnamese coastal cities.

March 29: Danang falls to the communist forces without resistance. The remaining coastal cities are taken over from fleeing ARVN troops.

March 31: Hanoi directs General Van Tien Dung to push toward Saigon in the "Ho Chi Minh Campaign."

April 1: Cambodian President Lon Nol abdicates and leaves for exile in Hawaii.

April 8: General Frederick Weyand, U.S. Army chief of staff and former Vietnam commander, reports to Congress that South Vietnam cannot survive without additional military aid.

General Frederick C. Weyand, Army chief of staff. Courtesy of the National Archives.

April 8–21: The ARVN 18th Division in Xuan Loc begins battling two North Vietnamese divisions at the last South Vietnamese defensive line before Saigon; it will become the last battle in defense of the Republic of South Vietnam.

April 10: President Ford requests $722 million emergency military aid for Saigon. Congress rejects the request.

April 17: Cambodia falls as Khmer Rouge troops capture Phnom Penh and government forces surrender.

April 18: Secretary of State Henry Kissinger orders the immediate evacuation of Americans from Saigon.

April 21: President Thieu announces his resignation; he is replaced by Vice President Tran Van Huong.

April 23: President Ford announces the war is "finished."

April 25: Thieu leaves Saigon for Taiwan.

April 26: Fifteen NVA divisions begin maneuvers for the final offensive on Saigon.

April 28: President Tran Van Huong transfers authority as chief of state to Duong Van Minh.

April 29: NVA begins attack on Saigon.

Corporal Charles McMahon Jr., USMC, and Lance Corporal Darwin Judge, USMC, are last U.S. military personnel killed in action in Vietnam, struck by shrapnel from NVA rocket.

April 29–30: Operation Frequent Wind, the largest helicopter evacuation on record, begins removing the last Americans from Saigon, including U.S. Ambassador Graham Martin and selected South Vietnamese.

Saigon falls to North Vietnamese assault.

April 30: At 10:24 A.M. Saigon time, President Duong Van Minh announces an unconditional

A Marine holds a refugee baby, one of thousands of Vietnamese civilians rescued during the evacuation of Saigon in April 1975. Courtesy of the National Archives.

surrender. NVA Colonel Bui Tin accepts. The Vietnam War ends.

Total casualties of the Vietnam War (1959–1975): 58,183 U.S. military personnel killed, 303,713 wounded and 2,273 missing in action.

223,748 South Vietnamese forces killed, 570,600 wounded.

Estimated 660,000 North Vietnamese/Vietcong troops killed, wounded figure unavailable.

EYEWITNESS TESTIMONY

We should not allow the Communists a situation in which their security is guaranteed now in their zone so that they can launch harassing attacks against us and destroy our infrastructure, schools and bridges . . . As far as the armed forces are concerned, I can tell you the war has restarted.

President Thieu, to South Vietnamese Army troops at Can Tho in the Mekong Delta, speech of January 4, 1974, in Reuters.

. . . if they [South Vietnam] don't have the will or desire to protect their own in-country security, we should not do anything else. We have given them the tools . . . And I would not recommend to the Congress, and I'm sure Congress would reject, the idea of reinserting Americans—whether it be on the ground or in the air—in Southeast Asia.

Melvin Laird, secretary of defense, statement of January 15, 1974, in an interview on "Panorama," WTTG-TV, Washington, D.C.

Whether there is honor or not does not depend on how much we spend on military aid for South Vietnam, but how we treat our own people . . . Let's spend it on our own Vietnam veterans.

Representative Otis Pike (D–N.Y.), leading opposition to President Nixon's request for increasing military aid to South Vietnam, statement of April 4, 1974, in The Washington Post (April 5, 1974).

For an American reporter, even the attempt to enter the liberated zones brought revelation: it was to see for the first time the invisible geography of the war. In certain places in South Vietnam, the NLF zones were half a mile or less from American-built roads and GVN [South Vietnamese] outposts.

Frances Fitzgerald, journalist, article in The Atlantic (April 1974).

We must strengthen the ability of the peoples of Indochina to determine their own destiny. After a decade of war, and the loss of 50,000 American lives, some hesitate to give to South Vietnam—for whom the war has not yet ended—the help it so desperately needs to maintain itself as an independent nation. It would be tragic, it would break faith with all those Americans who have fought and died there, if we

now failed to make the relatively modest effort that the Administration has proposed to the Congress to enable South Vietnam to survive.

Henry Kissinger, to American Legion group, Miami Beach, address of August 20, 1974, in The New York Times (August 21, 1974).

Current United States policies are sending South Vietnam to its doom . . . When the time is ripe, Hanoi will strike.

Major General John Murray, USA, former senior military officer with the Defense Attaché Office (DAO) in South Vietnam after the U.S. withdrawal, statement in U.S. News & World Report (September 30, 1974).

I just want my government to stand up to the North Vietnamese and get the truth. I can take the truth—even if it turns out that my husband is dead. I've been prepared for that for a long time.

What I can't take is not ever knowing.

Caroline Standerwick, wife of Colonel Robert Standerwick (USAF pilot shot down over Laos in 1971 and listed as Missing in Action [MIA]), article of December 30, 1974, in U.S. News & World Report.

They're going to fall whether we give them money or not.

Senator Stuart Symington (D–Mo.), statement in U.S. News & World Report (February 17, 1975).

I am not willing to let go for nought the lives of 56,000 men we lost there, as well as the wounding and maiming of over 300,000 more, as well as our remaining MIAs.

Senator John Stennis (D–Miss.), supporting more aid for South Vietnam, statement in U.S. News & World Report (February 24, 1975).

The United States would pay an enormous cost, a cost in turning inward in a new kind of isolationism which would provide enormous dangers for the people of the United States and for the people of the world. My concern with Vietnam is not so much with the Vietnamese. My concern is what happens to us [Americans] as a people, the whole intricate power balance in the world, as the world perceives us and perceives our will to do what we said we'd do.

Ambassador Graham Martin, arguing against reducing or cutting aid to South Vietnam, statement in The Washington Post (March 15, 1975).

Nobody knows whether they can reach Phu Bon tonight with their feet. Perhaps many will collapse and die on the long road. On the way to Phu Bon, along Highway 14, villages and hamlets and buon [Montagnard villages] appear deserted. The desolation of the highway gives me an impression I find hard to express in words . . . I too, with a knapsack on my back, joined the exodus . . .

If I had a friend by my side, I would tell him: Dear friend, the sky has as many stars as there are sorrows in my heart.

Nguyen Tu, South Vietnamese journalist, on refugees fleeing Pleiku, article of March 1975 in the Saigon Post.

Only the fastest, the strongest and the meanest of a huge mob got a ride on the last plane from Danang Saturday.

People died trying to get aboard and others died when they fell thousands of feet into the sea because even desperation could no longer keep their fingers welded to the undercarriage.

It was a flight into a hell, and only a good tough American pilot and a lot of prayers got us back to Tan Son Nhut air base alive—with the Boeing 727 flaps jammed and the wheels fully extended.

Paul Vogle, journalist, dispatch of March 29, 1975, for United Press International.

In a large measure it's up to the United States. Will it be life for South Vietnam, or slow death by a thousand cuts?

Anonymous South Vietnamese officer, statement in U.S. News & World Report *(March 31, 1975).*

It's a pity to see those people who could not afford to ride on cars or trucks or whatever vehicles available. They are the miserable who can only use their feet, and they are the largest bunch—women, children, elders, walking as rapidly as they can but not having even a drop of water to quench their thirst.

Anonymous South Vietnamese journalist, on refugees fleeing from Pleiku, article of March 31, 1975, in U.S. News & World Report.

We picked up everything in bags and ran to the neighbor's home. Everyone was crying. What to do? What to do?

We ran to the airstrip where there were helicopters. We closed our eyes. We did not want to open them.

Everywhere there were bodies, there were shells flying.

Li Thi Tinh, South Vietnamese refugee, on fleeing from Ban Me Thuot in March 1975, statement of March 18, 1975, in The New York Times *(March 19, 1975).*

When the attack came we all started to run. I have never seen a Communist.

Li Thi Oanh, South Vietnamese refugee, on the NVA attack on Pleiku, statement in Newsweek *(March 31, 1975).*

Danang, now overcrowded with two million refugees from Quang Tri, Hue and Quang Tin, was practically under siege. The population began to panic when they saw the evacuation of U.S. personnel and Vietnamese employees from the U.S. Consulate General. People were fighting to board commercial and American ships to flee the city . . . Bands of children, hungry and thirsty, wandered aimlessly on the streets, demolishing everything which happened to fall into their hands. Danang was seized by the convulsion of hysteria.

Anonymous senior South Vietnamese army officer, recalls March 1975, in Hosmer, Kellen and Jenkins' The Fall of South Vietnam: Statements by Vietnamese Military and Civilian Leaders *(1980).*

We are seeing a great human tragedy as untold numbers of Vietnamese flee the North Vietnamese onslaught. The United States has been doing—and will continue to do—its utmost to assist these people.

I have directed all available naval ships to stand off Indochina, to do whatever is necessary to assist. We have appealed to the United Nations to use its moral influence to permit these innocent people to leave, and we call on North Vietnam to permit the movement of refugees to the area of their choice.

President Gerald Ford, to press conference of April 3, 1975, in Public Papers of the Presidents of the United States.

This is it—the big Communist push for the brass ring.

Anonymous U.S. senior diplomat in Saigon, statement in U.S. News & World Report *(April 7, 1975).*

Outside, in the Embassy compound, Marine guards were now pacing nervously along the walls. Countless hands groped at the latticework of the front gate as hundreds of Vietnamese begged to be let in, many shaking white slips of paper, undoubtedly some sort of claim to passage. Inside, several of their more fortunate countrymen, most of them cooks and chauffeurs who had shown up with their Embassy employers at sunrise, stood patiently to one side of the parking lot waiting for a bus ride to Tan Son Nhut. In the recreation area nearly a thousand more Vietnamese were wandering about in no particular order.

Frank Snepp, CIA analyst, recalls the fall of Saigon in April 1975, in Decent Interval *(1977).*

This ain't our war anymore.

Anonymous U.S. military officer in Saigon, statement in U.S. News & World Report *(April 7, 1975).*

Don't worry about all the junk in the newspapers. I'm fine. Don't worry.

Lance Corporal Darwin Judge, USMC, to his mother, letter of April 8, 1975, in The Washington Post *(May 1, 1975).*
[Judge was one of the last two American servicemen killed in action in Vietnam on April 29, 1975.]

Assistance to South Vietnam at this stage must be swift and adequate. Drift and indecision invite far deeper disaster . . . I am therefore asking the Congress to appropriate without delay $722 million for emergency military assistance and an initial sum of $250 million for economic and humanitarian aid for South Vietnam.

President Ford, to Congress, message of April 10, 1975, in Public Papers of the Presidents of the United States.

If you want to save lives, you'd better save them in a hurry. The President acted courageously, bluntly and cooperatively. He is telling the truth.

Senator Hugh Scott (R–Pa.), statement of April 10, 1975, in The Washington Post *(April 11, 1975).*

President Ford in this request does not reflect the convictions of the American people. They want this ill-fated war to cease.

Senator Jennings Randolph (D–W.V.), statement of April 10, 1975, in The New York Times *(April 11, 1975).*

As far as I'm concerned $700 million will fall on deaf ears . . . it's dead . . . I don't know of anybody on the Democratic side who would vote for it.

Senator Henry Jackson (D–Wash.), statement of April 10, 1975, in The Washington Post *(April 11, 1975).*

We're not going to start a new war over there again.

Representative Carl Albert (D–Okla.), speaker of the House, statement of April 10, 1975, in The Baltimore Sun *(April 11, 1975).*

The city [Saigon] looks as though it belongs to the Vietnamese, not to the Americans who once inhabited it on a Brobdingnagian scale and who have begun to meld into the scenery like the French before them.

James Markham, journalist, article of April 14, 1974, in The New York Times Magazine.

For despite the agony of this nation's experience in Indochina and the substantial reappraisal which has taken place concerning our proper role there, few would deny that we are still involved or that what we do—or fail to do—will still weigh heavily in the outcome. We cannot by our actions alone insure the survival of South Vietnam. But we can, alone, by our inaction assure its demise.

Henry Kissinger, to the Senate Committee on Appropriations, testimony of April 15, 1975, in U.S. Department of State's Bulletin *(May 5, 1975).*

The current military situation is critical and the probability of the survival of South Vietnam as a truncated nation is marginal at best. The GVN is on the brink of military defeat . . . Given the speed at which events are moving . . . the United States should plan now for a mass evacuation of some 6,000 U.S. citizens and tens of thousands of South Vietnamese and Third Country Nationals to whom we have incurred an obligation and owe protection.

General Frederick Weyand, U.S. Army chief of staff, to President Ford, report of April 1975, in Gro's Vietnam from Cease-fire to Capitulation *(1981).*

We have finally stopped wasting lives in Vietnam. We must now stop wasting American dollars there too.

Senator Alan Cranston (D–Cal.), statement of April 17, 1974, in The New York Times *(April 18, 1974).*

Should it be felt necessary for U.S. personnel to report to their designated assembled areas, a coded message will be broadcast over American Radio Service. This message will consist of a temperature report for Saigon of "105 degrees and rising" followed by approximately the first 30 seconds of "I'm Dreaming of a White Christmas."

United States secret memorandum distributed at the American Embassy in Saigon, April 1975, in Dawson's 55 Days: The Fall of South Vietnam *(1977).*

The sentiment of our military, DOD and CIA colleagues was to get out fast and now . . . we must be at or below 2,000 official and unofficial U.S. citizens by Tuesday, April 22.

Henry Kissinger, to Ambassador Graham Martin, message of April 17, 1975, in Butler's The Fall of Saigon *(1985).*

The second biggest problem we have here is how to play God.

Anonymous U.S. officer in Saigon, on evacuating South Vietnamese nationals, statement in U.S. News & World Report *(April 21, 1975).*

. . . we would go home at night from the office and there would be a line of people waiting to see us. They wanted out. And I'd wake up in the morning and there would be another half dozen . . . They'd range from government officials down to businessmen. And they were all there, asking: "Get me out of here."

Alan Carter, USIA chief in Saigon, recalls the American Embassy in April 1975, in Willenson's The Bad War: An Oral History of the Vietnam War *(1987).*

The ARVN were running, they were coming in, they were bypassing civilians, shooting civilians, trying to get out [of Saigon] first all the time. The best way to describe it was every man for himself. There were pregnant women going into labor right on the goddamn landing zone. I delivered a baby right on the chopper. And I also delivered two more on the ships. It was just bananas.

Corpsman Stephen Klinkhammer, USN, aboard the carrier Midway, *recalls April 1975, in Santoli's* Everything We Had *(1981).*

Assistance to South Vietnam at this stage must be swift and decisive. Drift and indecision invite far deeper disaster . . . And now I ask the Congress to clarify immediately its restriction on United States military force in Southeast Asia for the limited purposes of protecting American lives by insuring their evacuation, if this should be necessary.

President Ford, to Congress, message of April 21, 1975, in Public Papers of the Presidents of the United States.

If the Americans do not want to support us anymore, let them go, get out! let them forget their humanitarian promises!

No matter what we cannot accept, we are adults. We are going to continue to be insulted because Americans will not help us.

The Americans promised us—we trusted them. But you have not given us the aid you promised us. With that aid which you promised us, I would not be afraid of the Communists.

President Thieu, to the South Vietnamese people, resignation speech of April 21, 1975, from United Press International *(April 21, 1975).*

America can regain the sense of pride that existed before Vietnam. But it cannot be achieved by refighting a war that is finished as far as America is concerned. As I see it, the time has come to look forward to an agenda for the future, to unify, to bind up the Nation's wounds, and to restore its health and its optimistic self-confidence.

President Ford, to a Tulane University convocation, New Orleans, address of April 23, 1975, in Public Papers of the Presidents of the United States.

It's the 25th hour. Not even an able leader can rescue the Republic now. It's too late.

Anonymous South Vietnamese officer, statement of April 1975, in U.S. News & World Report *(May 5, 1975).*

Fellow citizens, in the past days you have wondered why so many people have quietly left the country. I want to tell you, dear citizens, that this is our beloved land. Please be courageous and stay here and accept the fate of God.

President Duong Van Minh, to the South Vietnamese people, inaugural address of April 28, 1975, from United Press International *(April 29, 1975).*

I'm at the Marine Statue in downtown Saigon. It is twenty minutes after six, Saigon time. President Minh has just been inaugurated . . . People are running in the streets. Yes, there's a plane in the air.

And we have antiaircraft . . . This is heavy fire now, tracers rising from positions on all sides of me, streaking up from behind the buildings . . . The sky is gray and sparrows are wheeling. Sparrows are wheeling in the sky, and the tracers, the red tracers, arc through them. It's extraordinary. The war has come to Saigon.

David Butler, journalist, NBC Radio broadcast of April 28, 1975.

They are filing past me on foot, their sandals scraping mournfully against their pavements, their heads hunched down against the driving monsoon rain that lashes them.

They are riding on motor scooters, in cars, in trucks, buses, oxcarts all piled with crates and suitcases and ragged bundles of clothes. Sometimes the noise of the vehicles is deafening, but not so deafening as to drown out the wind-rushing sound of an incoming rocket that whips over their heads to burst in the paddylands beyond the river.

Philip Caputo, journalist, on refugees retreating along Highway 1, article of April 28, 1975, in The Chicago Tribune.

The overloaded helicopter flew only a few hundred feet—then thumped heavily back to earth. As it touched down, still more refugees tried to cram aboard. The screaming was like a soundtrack of hell.

Nicholas Proffit, journalist, aboard a helicopter carrying refugees from Xuan Loc, 40 miles northwest of Saigon, article of April 28, 1975, in Newsweek.

On the two-lane American-built highway to Bienhoa Sunday thousands upon thousands of refugees could be seen pouring in toward the capital [Saigon]. With darkness descending, under a rain-swollen sky pierced by lightning, the column stretched away over the rolling countryside like a moving dragon in the reddish light of the passing day. Buses, cars, tractors and bicycles inched slowly forward with the noise of engines and clashing gears blending into a coughing growl.

H.D.S. Greenway, journalist, dispatch of April 28, 1975, in The Washington Post.

I thought of my sick old father and I wept. He did not want to go and be a burden on us. "Go and don't worry about me," he said. "Whatever happens I will still be happy because I know you have gotten out and you are having a better life in a better land." Maybe he can still be evacuated.

Vo Tuan Chin, journalist, on being evacuated from Saigon to Guam, article of April 28, 1975, in The New York Times.

As we flew over the city, the [ARVN gunners] just opened up on us. There was ground fire from every direction. It was like the 4th of July. So we started an immediate climb into a thunderstorm that was right over the city at the time. We finally got into the clouds and in the storm, which was no fun either, but it was better than being shot at.

Captain Ken Rice, USAF, 374th Tactical Airlift Wing, recalls piloting an evacuation mission aboard a C-130 out of Saigon on April 28, 1975, in Lavalle's Last Flight from Saigon (1978).

When I turned into the streets leading to the airport I was confronted with crowds of people in cars, on the backs of Hondas or just walking, holding onto their children and carrying suitcases. The traffic was moving in both directions. Some people were still trying to reach the airport in the hope of being evacuated; others had moved out of their homes surrounding the airfield as the Communist rocket attack intensified and the airport buildings caught fire.

Liz Thomas, civilian nurse, recalls the fall of Saigon on April 29, 1975, in Dust of Life (1977).

South Vietnam is living on borrowed time. The only thing left to be decided is when and how it surrenders.

Anonymous U.S. senior diplomat in Saigon, statement of April 1975, in U.S. News & World Report (May 5, 1975).

Some people rolled on the ground in fits of hysteria: some screamed the names of Americans, colonels, generals with whom they had been friends. Elegant women with large pieces of Samsonite luggage between their feet and children in their arms sobbed as if in a daze. There were officers in uniform who tried to get themselves recognized by someone on the other side of the railing and simple bar girls who had come only because they had once had a few American boy friends.

Tiziano Terzani, journalist, on the scene outside the American Embassy on April 29, 1975, in Giaphong: The Fall and Liberation of Saigon (1976).

Desperate Vietnamese struggle to scale the wall of the U.S. Embassy in Saigon in order to reach U.S. evacuation helicopters inside the compound, April 29, 1975. Courtesy of AP/Wide World Photos.

Once moved into that seething mass we ceased to be correspondents. We were only men fighting for our lives, scratching, clawing, pushing ever closer to that wall . . . I am one of them. But if I could get over that wall, I would be an American again . . . Somebody grabbed my sleeve and wouldn't let go. I turned my head and looked into the face of a Vietnamese youth. "You adopt me and take me with you and I'll help you," he screamed . . .

Keyes Beech, journalist, on his evacuation from Saigon on April 29, 1975, article of May 1, 1975, in the Chicago Daily News.

The driver drove us back to the [American] Embassy, through the lines of tightly parked cars and trucks. One woman tried to throw her baby into our bus. She missed, and the child was crushed under the wheels.

Wendell Merrick, journalist, evacuating Saigon on April 29, 1975, article of May 12, 1975, in U.S. News & World Report.

I collected a dozen or so flyers, and we all piled aboard my helicopter as I started the motors shirring. I had hardly time to glance back at my house, where so much had happened, where the youngsters had been laughing only the previous morning, before we were over the city looking down on the streets alive with scurrying figures, the orange flames of fires dotting the picture. It all passed quickly—my last sight of beloved Saigon—as we headed out toward the sea. Every size and shape of vessel, from puny rowboats to carriers, seemed to fill the blue waters. Switching my radio on to a rescue emergency frequency, I made crackling contact with the U.S. carrier *Midway*, lying just off the coast. Willing voices guided me down to the deck.

Nguyen Van Ky, evacuating Saigon on April 29, 1975, in Twenty Years and Twenty Days *(1976).*

We lifted immediately from the pad—a tennis-court area—and more or less held our breath for 20 minutes, for fear we might be hit by one of the deadly Russian-made heat-seeking missiles . . . we set down safely aboard the helicopter carrier *Okinawa*, and half an hour later a huge load of Vietnamese arrived. Old men and women hobbled off, their canes slipping over the deck, and then came a score or more of children and infants, who were completely bewildered as young Marines carried them off to prevent their being swept overboard by the wash of rotors and exhausts. The youngest was only 8 hours old . . .

Robert Shaplen, journalist, evacuating Saigon from the U.S. Embassy on April 29, 1975, article in The New Yorker *(May 19, 1975).*

Finally, we heard the order: "Okay, let's go." Just before I rushed aboard, I looked down toward the pool area. A couple of thousand Vietnamese were still waiting their turn. Soon, we were high over the dark Saigon River. A bright yellow flare arched up and hung in the air off to the east; the Long Binh ammunition dump was exploding. Red fire balls shot high into the night. Out of the rear bay, I saw the lights of Saigon distantly—for the last time.

Loren Jenkins, journalist, on evacuating the American Embassy in Saigon on April 29, 1975, article of May 12, 1975, in Newsweek.

I took off that night from the (U.S.) Embassy roof in a helicopter. On the way out I could see fires around the city, and I knew the North Vietnamese were on their way in . . . As I looked down on that city and knew we were leaving for good, all I thought was, "So it all comes down to this."

Ed Bradly, CBS News correspondent, recalls leaving Saigon on April 29, 1975, in Engel-mann's Tears Before the Rain *(1990).*

Our chopper was loaded in less than two minutes. And we lifted off at full power, climbing 6,000 feet, and headed south, skirting the Mekong Delta . . . Two young [U.S.] Marines hunched over the port

A South Vietnamese helicopter pilot and his family, safely aboard the U.S.S. Hancock, are escorted by a U.S. Marine security guard on April 29, 1975. Courtesy of the National Archives.

and starboard .50 caliber machine guns, scanning the terrain below. As we crossed the coast, the two young gunners eased their fingers off their triggers, broke into tight grins, and gave each other—and then the passengers—the thumbs up sign.

Nicholas Proffit, journalist, on leaving Saigon from Tan Son Nhut on April 29, 1975, article of May 12, 1975, in Newsweek.

. . . the jumbled tile roofs of the city began to spin below us as the pilot corkscrewed up through the haze to his assigned 5,500-foot altitude. About half the passengers were civilians, the rest mostly Western newsmen and photographers . . . We must have talked, during the long, sweaty wait in DAO [Defense Attache Office] and the ascent over Saigon. But when I thought about it later, I could not remember exchanging a single word with anyone from the time I walked out into the noon sun from the hotel lobby. It was as if I left Vietnam for the last time in complete silence, alone.

Arnold Isaacs, journalist, recalls April 29, 1975, in Without Honor: Defeat in Vietnam and Cambodia *(1983).*

South Vietnamese refugees come alongside the amphibious cargo ship U.S.S. **Durham** *in April 1975. Courtesy of the National Archives.*

I mean, it was bad. We thought that they were going to call off the operation when it became dark, because we never expected them to send us into such a bad situation to begin with, even if it was daytime. But, as you probably know, they continued the mission until nearly five o'clock in the morning. The night sorties were the worst, because we flew lights out. The tracers kept everybody on edge. To see a city burning gives one a strange feeling of insecurity.

Lieutenant Richard Van de Geer, USAF, helicopter pilot, to Richard Sandza, on flying evacuation missions out of Saigon on April 29, 1975, audio tape of April 1975, in Edelman's Dear America: Letters Home From Vietnam *(1985). [Van de Geer was killed in action on May 15, 1975, while flying a mission to rescue seamen from the S.S. Mayaguez, which had been seized in the Gulf of Siam, by the Cambodian Khmer Rouge. Officially, he was the last American to die in the Vietnam War.]*

As the helicopter flew over the city, the dawn was just beginning to break. The fires in the distance could have been Tan Son Nhut Air Base, could have been the MACV complex burning, or the fires further in the distance, Bien Hoa.

An almost eerie calm had descended over Saigon. There was very little, almost no noise at all. No sound of gunfire. No sense of what was about to take place . . . the dramatic change that was about to overcome that city and country.

Looking out to sea, as the sun began to come up, there were hundreds of small boats off the coast. It looked like an armada of refugee vessels, all sizes and shapes.

Ken Moorfield, special assistant to Ambassador Graham Martin, recalls Saigon on April 29, 1975, in Santoli's To Bear Any Burden *(1985).*

When we got to the [Saigon] river we had to hurry to get on the boat, and in the confusion I lost my bag. So I left the country without anything but the clothes on my back . . .

I was very scared as we went down the [Saigon] river. Some of the people on the boat stayed on the deck to get a last look at Vietnam. The last thing they saw was the beach at Vung Tau. But I did not look back. I was so sad. I was leaving everything behind. And I didn't know where I was going or what would happen to me.

Nguyen Thi Hoa, South Vietnamese refugee who left Saigon, at the age of 16, on April 29, 1975, in Engelmann's Tears Before the Rain.

This action closes a chapter in the American experience. I ask all Americans to close ranks, to avoid recrimination about the past, to look ahead to the many goals we share and to work together on the great tasks that remain to be accomplished.

President Ford, to the nation, statement of April 29, 1975, in Public Papers of the Presidents of the United States.

As from 11:00 A.M. E.D.T. we are getting no answer to calls in Saigon. We have checked constantly since then, but we have had no luck.

Anonymous AT&T spokesman, statement of April 29, 1975, in The New York Times *(April 30, 1975).*

Tanks could be in Saigon in a few hours. The ARVN soldiers, left behind, are firing at the U.S. evacuation planes. . . . BBC radio. . . . . said the Americans had all left, except for a few reporters and a few "hard core expatriates." That's us! Wonder how many of us there are tonight in Saigon.

Claudia Krich, American Friends Service Committee worker, diary entry of April 29, 1975, in MS. *article of July 1976.*

I think it will be a long time before Americans will be able to talk or write about the war with some dispassion . . . What lessons we should draw from it, I think we should reserve for another occasion. But I don't think that we can solve the problem of having entered the conflict too lightly by leaving it too lightly, either.

Henry Kissinger, to a press conference of April 29, 1975, in The New York Times *(April 30, 1975).*

We secured the final door on the roof. And people began coming up toward the roof. They had forced open the main door of the [U.S.] embassy and were appearing on the [roof's] heli pad . . . They never actually got on the main roof . . . We were up there pretty close to an hour before any birds showed up. The ARVNs down below were doing a lot of "cowboy shooting" . . .

Later I was told that every chopper participating in the evacuation had eight to ten bullet holes from ARVN soldiers. Nobody was hit.

I was the last Marine out . . . When we got on those birds, all we had was what was on our backs.

Master Sergeant Juan Valdez, U.S. Marine security guard at the American Embassy in Saigon, recalling April 30, 1975, in Barrett's Leatherneck *article of September 1975.*

It was mayhem down below. The Embassy compound looked like it had undergone a nuclear attack. Paper and weapons were strewn everywhere . . .

Finally, at eight in the morning our bird appeared and we ran all twelve at the copter as soon as it was down. I told the kids [the U.S. Marines] to open their [tear] gas canisters. No one had masks and we gassed ourselves and the pilot. Gas was billowing out from the top of the embassy . . .

After we lifted off the radio buzzed and a voice said "What kind of pizza do you want in Manila?" Everybody was so exhausted we just laughed and cried at the same time.

Major James Kean, USMC, recalls the evacuation by the U.S. Marine security detachment on April 30, 1975, in Willenson's The Bad War: An Oral History of the Vietnam War *(1987).*

All over the sea there were these eerie fires of boats burning and drifting in the sea. They lit up the water that night, and it looked like the South China Sea was starting to burn.

Nguyen Ngoc Binh, refugee and former acting chancellor of Mekong University in Saigon, recalls leaving Saigon on April 30, 1975, in Engelmann's Tears Before the Rain.

If we had kept our commitments we wouldn't have had to evacuate.

Ambassador Graham Martin, aboard the U.S.S. Blue Ridge, statement of April 30, 1975, in The Washington Post *(May 1, 1975).*

The Communists did not win, we beat ourselves. We are a country that destroyed itself.

Anonymous South Vietnamese Air Force pilot, who flew his helicopter to a U.S. carrier, statement of April 30, 1975, in Butterfield's New York Times Magazine *article of May 25, 1975.*

After the last marines had left, hundreds of civilians swarmed into the [American Embassy] compound and onto the roof of a nearby building that had also served as an emergency helipad, several hundred civilians huddled together, hoping there would be more helicopters to carry them away . . .

George Esper, journalist, dispatch of April 30, 1975, from the Associated Press.

Saigon fell with a whimper . . .

One street scene perhaps epitomized Saigon's fall—a Communist tank smashed through the main gates of the presidential palace, disregarding the attempts of an unarmed south Vietnamese soldier trying to open them first.

Minutes later, the flag of the Communist backed Provisional Revolutionary Government (PRG)—red and white with a gold star—was waving in the palace.

Anonymous French journalist, dispatch of April 30, 1975, from Reuters.

I, General Duong Van Minh, President of the Saigon government, appeal to the armed forces of the Republic of Vietnam to lay down their arms and surrender unconditionally to the forces of the National Liberation Front. Furthermore, I declare that the Saigon government is completely dissolved at all levels.

President Minh, to ARVN and the nation, radio broadcast of April 30, 1975, in the United States Air Force's The Fall and Evacuation of South Vietnam *(1978).*

At the front headquarters we turned on our radios to listen. The voice of the quisling president [Duong Van Minh] called on his troops to put down their weapons and surrender unconditionally to our troops. Saigon was completely liberated! Total victory! We were completely victorious! All of us at the headquarters jumped up and shouted, embraced and carried each other around on our shoulders. The sound of applause, laughter, and happy, noisy, chattering speech was as festive as if spring had just burst upon us . . . We were all so happy we were choked with emotion. I lit a cigarette and smoked. Dinh Duc

Separated during their flight to safety, mother and daughter are tearfully reunited aboard the amphibious cargo ship U.S.S. Durham, as grandmother looks on, in April 1975. Courtesy of the National Archives.

Crewmen of the amphibious command ship U.S.S. Blue Ridge *push a helicopter into the sea on April 28, 1975. Vietnamese pilots flew their helicopters to the ship in such large quantity that some had to be pushed into the sea to make room for more to land, during the evacuation operations for Vietnamese refugees. Courtesy of the National Archives.*

Thien, his eyes somewhat red, said, "Now if these eyes close, my heart will be at rest." This historic and sacred, intoxicating and completely satisfying moment was one that comes once in a generation, once in many generations.
NVA General Van Tien Dung, in Our Great Spring Victory *(1977).*

I have been waiting since early this morning to transfer power to you.
President Duong Van Minh, to NVA Colonel Bui Tin, statement of April 30, 1975, in Karnow's Vietnam: A History *(1983).*

There is no question of your transferring power. Your power has crumbled. You have nothing in your hands to surrender and so you cannot surrender what you do not possess.
Colonel Bui Tin, to President Minh, statement of April 30, 1975, in Karnow's Vietnam: A History.

The colonel showed me his police identification badge. I did not note his name. I glanced into his eyes. They were filled with despair.

"Fin! Fin!" he yelled in broken English.

It is finished.

The colonel fingered his holstered pistol.

I watched him out of the corner of my eyes. For a moment, I thought he was going to shoot me, resentful that the Americans had pulled out.

But instead he did a sharp about face . . . raised his pistol to his own head and fired.

I tried to yell, "Wait! Don't do it!"

The words caught in my throat. I was too late. It happened so fast.

George Esper, journalist, recalls Saigon on April 30, 1975, in the Defense Information School's Vietnam: 10 Years Later *(1983).*

Today thousands of Saigonese took everything from the abandoned [American] embassy, including the kitchen sinks.

The bronze plaque with the names of the five American servicemen who died in the embassy in 1968 was torn from the lobby wall. It lay amid piles of documents and furniture on the back lawn. We carried it back to the Associated Press' office.

Peter Arnett, journalist, dispatch of April 30, 1975, for the Associated Press.

We have got to remember it, study it and find out what happened in great detail. I think this is vitally important. Both our military and political mistakes have to be learned and analyzed before we can let this thing die.

Anonymous U.S. Army major, who had served in Vietnam, statement of April 30, 1975, in The New York Times *(May 1, 1975).*

12. Legacies and Reflections

THE EFFECTS ON VIETNAM

Every war ever fought has left behind a legacy for those who fought it. In Vietnam itself, the principal legacy has been continued human suffering. For those who remain in Vietnam there has been poverty, oppression and forced labor. An estimated 1.5 million former Saigon government officials and supporters were forcibly relocated to harsh rural development areas. Another 200,000 senior officials and military officers were sent to "re-education" camps for various periods.

Despite the unification of North and South Vietnam, the 30 years of war left the country in a state of economic deprivation. The economic growth rate has been around 2% instead of the 14% projected in Hanoi's five-year plan of 1975. Per capita income averages around $200 a year, making Vietnam one of the poorest nations on Earth.

The mass exodus from Vietnam has been one of the largest continuing migrations of modern times. More than 1.4 million South Vietnamese have fled the country since 1975. As many as 50,000 of the so-called "boat people" either died from exposure or drowned, and some are still confined to refugee camps scattered throughout Southeast Asia. Nearly a million Vietnamese have resettled in other countries, over 725,000 of them in the United States. Most of them had to give up their personal possessions to escape, and many left family members behind.

The prediction that Southeast Asia would collapse to the communists if they won in Vietnam did not come to pass; the "dominoes" did not fall. However, one of the consequences of the end of the Vietnam War was the heightening of tension within the communist regime of Cambodia. The Khmer Rouge, originally organized and trained by their Vietnamese comrades, became distrustful of their former allies and unsure of their hold on power. The brutal Pol Pot regime launched a grisly campaign to rebuild Cambodia from the "Year Zero," resulting in the death of as many as two million people. Thousands of middle-class citizens, branded as intellectuals merely because they wore glasses or spoke a foreign language, were systematically liquidated. The slaughter was halted only in 1979, when the Vietnamese drove out Pol Pot and the Khmer Rouge and established a pro-Hanoi and pro-Soviet puppet government.

However, for the next 10 years Vietnamese troops skirmished with a disparate coalition of three Cambodian factions backed by China, including Khmer Rouge rebels. Then in 1989, after a decade of occupation, Vietnamese troops withdrew from Cambodia. Exhausted after years of fighting, the Cambodian government and the three resistance groups, including the Khmer Rouge, agreed in 1991 to meet and discuss a negotiated political settlement to Cambodia's civil war. Although a formal peace treaty was signed in Paris in October 1991, it is believed that it will be some time before a permanent peace will be achieved in Cambodia.

THE EFFECTS ON VETERANS AND THEIR FAMILIES

In the United States, the legacies of the war have been largely spiritual. Some Americans expressed the hope that the nation could put the "senseless tragedy" aside and move on with the future, while others could not easily forget, especially those who had served and those who had lost loved ones. "What did he die for?" asked thousands of parents whose sons never returned.

The average age of the Vietnam soldier was just over 19, at least seven years younger than his celebrated counterpart of World War II and younger even than those who had fought in Korea. They were whisked home virtually overnight by the miracle of the jet age, to a nation that seemed either hostile to them or indifferent to their plight.

Although the vast majority of the three million GIs who served in Vietnam have adjusted well to civilian life, a greater number than in previous wars have experienced problems with substance abuse, unemployment, homelessness and Post-Traumatic Stress Disorder (PTSD), the modern term for what was earlier called "shell shock" or "battle fatigue." Veterans afflicted with PTSD sometimes actually reexperience traumatic incidents from the war—often as recurring nightmares or in the form of psychotic hallucinations. These problems are particularly acute for combat veterans, many of whom have had to wrestle with what have been called "invisible wounds." These disorders take the form of extreme restlessness, depression, nightmares, insomnia and, in some cases, suicide.

The 1981 *Legacies of Vietnam* study by the Veterans Administration estimated that as many as 700,000 Vietnam veterans suffer from some symptoms of PTSD. However, the causes and exact nature of the disorder remain a matter of controversy among psychiatrists and Vietnam veterans themselves. James Webb, a highly decorated, thrice-wounded

in 1980 for the Veterans Administration, 82% of former U.S. soldiers engaged in heavy combat in Vietnam believe that the war was lost because they were not permitted to win. Many senior American officers who served in Vietnam assert that defeat could have been averted had the war been waged more effectively. General William C. Westmoreland, who commanded the U.S. forces in Vietnam from 1965 to 1968, faults the policy of "graduated response" imposed on the military by its civilian leaders. He argues that had the United States brought to bear the full brunt of its conventional military power, the war could have been won.

Colonel Harry G. Summers Jr., an infantry veteran of the Korean and Vietnam wars and the author of *On Strategy: A Critical Analysis of the Vietnam War* (1982), argues that the focus was mistakenly concentrated on search-and-destroy missions against the guerrillas in South Vietnam, when the United States should have used its own forces against North Vietnamese regulars along the 17th parallel to isolate the north from the south. "You know," Colonel Summers told a North Vietnamese colonel after the war, "you never defeated us on the battlefield." His communist counterpart replied, "That may be so, but it is also irrelevant."

To some who opposed the war, such as J. William Fulbright, the former chairman of the Senate Foreign Relations Committee, the fundamental lesson of the Vietnam War is "that the United States should not intervene in other countries with military force unless that country is a serious threat to our own security." For others, the war clearly demonstrated the limits of American power and showed that American foreign policy must remain true to the nation's historic principles. Then there are those who point to the weakness of the South Vietnamese government, arguing that even a superpower cannot save allies who are unable or unwilling to save themselves.

Immediately following the victory of the U.S. and its allies over Iraq in the Persian Gulf War in 1991, President George Bush announced, "By God, we have kicked the Vietnam syndrome once and for all." As many Americans expressed a regained sense of pride in their nation, especially its military, a chorus of politicians and news commentators proclaimed that America had finally buried the disgrace of Vietnam in the sands of the Arabian Desert. Some charged that the war against Iraq proved that the United States could have won in Vietnam if the military had not been hindered by timorous civilians. But just as failure in Vietnam did not prove success to be impossible or too costly in the Gulf, success against Iraq does not prove that victory was achievable in Vietnam. The Persian Gulf War was fought between conventional armies on desert terrain; the Vietnam War, in contrast, was essentially a guerrilla war, a nationalist anti-colonialist struggle and a civil war fought largely in jungle terrain.

The greatest lesson of any success or failure in foreign affairs, diplomatic or military, may be to see each event as largely unique—whether it be the Korean War, the Cuban missile crisis or Vietnam—and to avoid elevating its "lessons" into policy dogmas, be they Truman Doctrines or Vietnam Syndromes.

THE MEMORIAL

While debates over the lessons, if any, to be gained from the Vietnam War are waged in classrooms and symposia and discussed in articles and books, the Vietnam Veterans Memorial in Washington, D.C., is visited daily by an unending stream of people. The memorial was the brainchild of Vietnam veteran Jan Scruggs, who, in 1979, founded the Vietnam Veterans Memorial Fund to raise money for the construction of the monument in Washington, D.C. Scruggs began the fund with a $2,500 donation of his own, and over the next three years raised $7 million for its construction.

A competition was launched to produce a design for the memorial. Some 1,420 designs were submitted to the contest, which was judged by an architectural committee. It was won by a 21-year-old architecture student at Yale University, Maya Ying Lin, in 1981. Her design consisted of two massive slabs of polished black granite cut into a hillside, upon whose surface the names of those servicemen and -women killed or missing in Vietnam would be engraved.

Maya Lin explained that she chose black because it acts as a boundary between the living and the dead. "White is like a wall, a barrier; it shuts the door," she said. "I found black a soothing, deep, deep color because you can look into it forever." Not only did the memorial have to be black, she also knew it had to be granite, because granite, when polished, is deeply reflective. When you look at the wall, you see yourself reflected behind the names of the dead. Maya Lin felt that if people could face the traumatic moment in their past, they would then be able to move forward.

On Veteran's Day weekend of November 1982, thousands of Vietnam veterans streamed into Washington, along with their families and the families of the dead, to dedicate the memorial. Some were paraplegics in wheelchairs, others amputees. Some wore fatigues or business suits and several came in full combat gear. There was a solemn service at the National Cathedral, where volunteers held a candlelight vigil through the week, reciting the names of the nearly 58,000 killed and missing in action, one by one.

The memorial stands not only as a tribute to the sacrifices made by the dead but also as a recognition of the service done by all those who survived. "We waited 15 years to get here, man," said one veteran, still wearing the patch of the 101st Airborne Division in his faded green fatigues, at the dedication ceremony. "But it's not too late. I'm just proud to be here. We made it. It's like coming home."

Two million Americans a year visit the stark V-shaped Vietnam Veterans memorial on the Mall—inscribed with the names of 58,183 service members who died or who remain missing in action, in the longest war in the nation's history. The memorial has become one of the most visited sites in the nation's capital. Photos of young soldiers and sometimes letters to them are left on the walls. Often a flower is inserted between the panels, near a name.

Presumably, this will continue for many years. Healing a nation, like uncovering the truth, is a long process. The Vietnam War, like the Civil War, will be with us for generations to come. It divided a nation. It is perhaps the most misunderstood war in American history. Its outcome raised new questions about America's role in the world, which continue to be debated to this day.

Justice Oliver Wendell Holmes Jr., who was wounded three times in the Civil War, said in his Memorial Day address of 1882, "[We] cannot live in associations with the past alone . . . if we would be worthy of the past, we must find new fields for action or thought . . ."

CHRONICLE OF EVENTS

1977

January 21: President Carter pardons almost all the draft evaders—about 10,000—of the Vietnam War era.

September 20: Vietnam is admitted to the United Nations.

1978

December: Thousands of "boat people" begin to flee Vietnam.

December 25: Vietnam invades Cambodia.

1979

Vietnam veteran Jan Scruggs founds the Vietnam Veterans Memorial Fund; its aim is to raise money for the construction of a Vietnam Veterans Memorial in Washington, D.C.

January 7: The Cambodian government of Pol Pot is overthrown when the capital of Phnom Penh falls to Vietnamese forces.

February 17: China launches an invasion of Vietnam, largely as a retaliation for Vietnam's invasion of Cambodia. Chinese troops withdrew after 16 days of fighting.

November 24: The U.S. General Accounting Office reports that thousands of U.S. troops deployed in South Vietnam were exposed to Agent Orange herbicide, despite previous Defense Department denials.

1982

November 13: The Vietnam Veterans Memorial in Washington, D.C., is dedicated.

December 24: A group of Vietnam veterans begins a round-the-clock candlelight vigil at the site of the Vietnam Veterans Memorial to call attention to U.S. servicemen still missing in action.

1984

April: Vietnam veteran Diane Carlson Evans founds the Vietnam Women's Memorial Proj-

ect, its aim being the construction of a monument to honor those women who served in the Armed Forces during the Vietnam Era. (Some 250,000 were in the military and an estimated 11,000 were in Vietnam. Eight servicewomen were killed there.)

May 7: Federal District Judge Jack B. Weinstein announces a $180 million out-of-court settlement against seven chemical companies that manufactured the defoliant Agent Orange, in a class-action suit brought by 15,000 Vietnam veterans.

May 28: On Memorial Day the only American Unknown Soldier from the Vietnam War is laid to rest at ceremonies at Arlington National Cemetery in Washington, D.C.

November 11: On Veteran's Day, a statue of three Vietnam War infantrymen, by sculptor Frederick E. Hart, is dedicated at the Vietnam War Memorial.

1985

March 7: Ten years after the Vietnam War ended, Vietnam veterans march up Broadway in New York City in their first major welcome-home parade.

May 7: The New York Vietnam Veterans Memorial is dedicated in lower Manhattan. The memorial is a transclucent glass-block structure 70 feet long and 16 feet high, etched with excerpts of letters sent to and from servicemen during the Vietnam War.

1988

October: The U.S. Congress approves the construction of the Vietnam Women's Memorial. The monument will be a bronze statue of a woman servicemember and it will be located near the Vietnam Veterans Memorial in Washington, D.C.

1989

February: After the end of all legal challenges, the first payments from the Agent Orange settlement fund are made to families of 172 Vietnam veterans whose deaths were linked to the defoliant.

September 26: Hanoi announces that it has pulled the last of its troops out of Cambodia (Kampuchea), ending 10 years of occupation.

1990

November 11: Eileen Barry, a sculptor, and Robert Lee Desmond, a landscape designer, are selected out of 317 entries to design the Vietnam Women's Memorial monument. Construction is expected to begin in 1992.

1991

February 6: President George Bush signs the Agent Orange Act of 1991. It permanently extends disability benefits to Vietnam veterans suffering from two types of cancer presumed to be caused by Agent Orange: non-Hodgkins lymphomania and soft-tissue sarcoma.

March 1: Following the United States victory against Iraq in the Persian Gulf War (January 16–February 28), President Bush announces, "We have kicked the Vietnam syndrome once and for all."

April 2: The U.S. State Department announces that one million dollars will be given to Vietnam for prosthetic aid for amputees in the South.

U.S. reiterates its position that initiation of full diplomatic relations or lifting of its trade embargo hinges on Hanoi's cooperation in acting to account for all missing American soldiers and in reaching a diplomatic settlement to the civil war in Cambodia.

July: The U.S. Defense Department opens a temporary office in Hanoi to resolve cases of American military personnel who were listed as missing in action (MIA) or taken prisoner during the Vietnam War. The first official presence in communist Vietnam represents a step toward normalizing relations with Hanoi.

August 2: The U.S. Senate establishes the Select Committee on POW/MIA Affairs to obtain a full accounting of American military personnel listed as missing in action (MIA) or as prisoner of war (POW) in Southeast Asia, including Korea and Vietnam.

September 12: Vietnam and China issue a joint statement announcing they will hold a meeting to discuss normalizing relations.

October 23: The Cambodian government and the three warring factions, including the Khmer Rouge, sign a peace treaty in Paris designed to end Cambodia's 13-year-old civil war. The United Nations will oversee a cease-fire and organize free elections. Secretary of State James A. Baker 3d announces that the United States is prepared to open talks with Vietnam on normalizing relations.

November 5–7: Senator John Kerry (D–Mass.), chairman of the Select Committee on POW/MIA Affairs and a highly decorated Vietnam veteran, holds hearings on the issue of living POWs and MIAs remaining in Vietnam.

November 5: Vietnam and China normalize relations.

November 11: United States restores a diplomatic presence in Cambodia after 16 years.

November 14: Prince Norodom Sihanouk returns to Cambodia after 20 years in exile as president of the Supreme National Council, the organization comprising representatives of the Cambodian government and the three rebel groups who signed the October 1991 peace treaty in Paris.

EYEWITNESS TESTIMONY

One thing worries me—will people believe me? Will they want to hear about it, or will they want to forget the whole thing ever happened?

Lt. j.g. Richard Strandberg, USN, River Patrol Section 522, Mekong Delta, to his wife, letter of May 16, 1968, from an inscription at the top of the New York Vietnam Veterans Memorial in New York City.

We erect monuments so that we shall always remember and build memorials so that we shall never forget.

Anonymous, after visiting the Vietnam Veterans Memorial in Washington, D.C., on November 13, 1982.

. . . the very first day I stepped in this park and I walked down in that Wall, and I started from the edge, and every plaque that had names printed on

The Vietnam Veterans Memorial in Washington, D.C., a wall of polished black granite bearing the names of 58,183 Americans who died or are missing in action in the Vietnam War, was dedicated on November 13, 1982. Courtesy of the National Park Service. Photo by Bill Clark.

it . . . they told me, "Welcome Home. Welcome Home." Every single panel.

Robert Bancroft, Vietnam veteran, on visiting the Vietnam Veterans Memorial in Washington, D.C., in August 1983, in Fish's The Last Firebase: A Guide to the Vietnam Veterans Memorial (1987).

The Vietnam War should probably be best remembered for being the colossal mistake that it was. The military and civilian leadership failed the country miserably as American soldiers fought with great valor and sacrifice. The country tried to forget the war and the soldiers who had served it so well, but a Memorial was built so that no one can forget.

Jan Scruggs, Vietnam veteran and founder of the Vietnam Veterans Memorial, to the author, 1991.

What America doesn't see are the surviving families that now dread the unspoken words and melancholy that surround their holidays. What America doesn't see are the 57,939 shrines of pictures and medals, in houses and apartments from Maine to Hawaii, Alaska to Puerto Rico to New Orleans. What America doesn't see are the hundreds of thousands wounded in Vietnam, men now without arms, eyes, spleens, kidneys. What America doesn't see are the 115,878 mothers and fathers, the 231,756 grandparents, the uncounted brothers, sisters, daughters, sons, friends, lovers . . .

Patrick Finnegan, Vietnam veteran (whose brother was killed in Vietnam in 1972), after visiting the Vietnam Veterans Memorial in Washington, D.C. in 1982, in Brandon's Casualties: Death in Vietnam, Anguish and Survival in America (1984).

From the wall, like a mirror reflecting through my blurry tears, I seemed to see the faces. Then I realized it was not the faces of the ones who died, but of the living, who were here, like me, to find the name of a loved one.

Anonymous mother (of a son killed in Vietnam), letter left at Vietnam Veterans Memorial in Washington, D.C., on November 10, 1982, in Scruggs and Swerdlow's To Heal A Nation (1985).

Your name is on a black wall in D.C., but I'm sorry to say that it's a little below ground—kind of like how Charlie was! You look over a nice green—a place

A mother holds her pilot son's picture near his name on the wall of the Vietnam Veterans Memorial. Photograph by Jeff Tinsley. Courtesy of the Smithsonian Institution.

like we used to play football on back home. A lot of people walk by all day—you can tell the Vets—we are the ones who don't have to ask the size or type of material used to make the wall. We just stand and look, not caring who sees us cry—just like no one cared who died.

Robert Shockley, Vietnam veteran, letter left at the Vietnam Veterans Memorial in Washington, D.C., in Palmer's Shrapnel in the Heart *(1987).*

Within the soul of each Vietnam veteran there is probably something that says, ''Bad war, good soldier.''

Max Cleland, Vietnam veteran and former director of the Veterans' Administration, statement in Time *(November 22, 1982).*

Tomorrow is your birthday. The only present I can give you is to have your family—Mom, Dad, Donna, Barry, Marianne and Mindy, plus your aunts, uncles, nieces, nephews and cousins, who all love you, come to this memorial, to see your name chiseled in marble [sic] for all to see until time is no more, and to remember you.

Eleanor Wimbush, to her son, William R. Stocks, who died in a helicopter crash on February 13, 1969, letter left at the Vietnam Veterans Memorial in Washington, D.C., on May 9, 1983, in McCall's *(June 1985).*

Dear Michael: Your name is here but you are not. I made a rubbing of it, thinking if I rubbed hard enough I would rub your name off the wall. And you would come back to me. I miss you so.

Anonymous, note left at the Vietnam Veterans Memorial in Washington, D.C., in Broyles' Reader's Digest *article of May 1987.*

I was carried off the hill in a stretcher to a low spot and medivaced to a ship somewhere off Vietnam's coast. It is only now that I am able to visit this austere shrine and ask my unanswerable question: who else died at Ashau Valley that June day in 1969? A part of me did. And I have only this wall to talk to. I miss that part of me that is gone and those who were there that day as only they remember the part of me I left behind. The part of me that I lost that day is now given to the wall in hopes to erase the hurt and be a benefit to all.

John Reynolds, USMC, Vietnam veteran, letter of June 12, 1986, left at the Vietnam Veterans Memorial in Washington, D.C., in Palmer's Shrapnel in the Heart.

Over the years I had fallen into a pattern of visiting the memorial at least twice a year, the first time on Memorial Day and again six months later on Veterans Day. On each occasion, despite some good-natured kidding from [wife] Toddy and our children, I would don my dusty bush hat with its fading ribbons and Marine Corps emblem, square my shoulders, and go off with a red rose to place at the apex of the memorial. Later, toward the end of my ritual, I would spend a few moments in remembrance of the dead whom I had known. Then, turning my back to those forever youthful ghosts memorialized in stone; I would go in search of the living among the holiday crowds with whom I might share some connection in the past.

Lt. Lewis B. Puller Jr., USMC, platoon leader, a highly decorated Vietnam veteran who was seriously wounded in 1968 after stepping on a land mine (losing both of his legs), in Fortunate Son *(1991).*

I went to Vietnam to heal
and came back silently wounded.
I went to Vietnam to heal
and discovered that I was not God.
To all of those whose names are on the wall
I am sorry that I could not be God.

Anonymous American servicewoman who served in Vietnam, poem in The New York Times *(November 12, 1990).*

"The Wall" is not only a fitting tribute to the men whose names are on it, but also—and maybe more—to the 2 million minds that remember the pain, the terror, the fear, the agony of at least one name in particular. "Why" is probably the largest hurdle that we have to face. "Why" did we get treated like dogs on our return?

Larry Pauley, Vietnam veteran, in Greene's Homecoming: When the Soldiers Returned from Vietnam *(1989).*

From the time I got shot I never cried . . . The hospital ship, the naval ship—the doctors and nurses and attendants cared. When I got to Kingsbridge [VA] hospital and saw that this was going to be where I was staying, it so overwhelmed me that I broke down and cried. My mother broke down and cried. It was overcrowded. It was smelly. It was filthy. It was disgusting.

Robert Muller, USMC lieutenant and founder of the Vietnam Veterans of America (VVA), wounded in action in 1967 and paralyzed from the chest down, in Weinraub's New York Times Magazine *article of May 27, 1979.*

The hardest thing to come to grips with was the fact that making it through Vietnam—surviving—is probably the only worthwhile part of the experience. It wasn't going over there and saving the world from Communism or defending the country. The matter of survival was the only thing you could get any gratification from.

Anonymous Vietnam veteran, in Baker's Nam: The Vietnam War in the Words of the Men and Women Who Fought There *(1981).*

The Vietnam combat veterans drew this lesson: you are alone, no one else shares your experience or cares about you—no one except your buddies.

William Broyles Jr., Vietnam veteran and former editor-in-chief of Newsweek, *in* Newsweek *(November 22, 1982).*

Coming home was perhaps the strangest experience. One day I was in the war zone; the next I was in the states. There was no welcome home like there had been after other wars . . . You go to the airport for a flight home, and people look at you funny. No one seems to care. Your family greets you, and they are glad you're home, but even they can't understand what you've been through. To this day I feel truly meaningful conversations on the war can take place only between veterans.

Heidi (Bud) Atanian, Vietnam veteran (crew chief, 282d Helicopter Company, Hue Section, 1967–68), in McCloud's What Should We Tell Our Children About Vietnam? *(1989).*

Upon my return from Vietnam in March 1969, I was assigned to duty in Detroit, Michigan. I was given the duty of notifying and providing assistance to the next-of-kin whose loved ones were killed in Vietnam . . .

While walking through a local shopping mall I was spat upon by other Americans. It was quite a shock to have people so hostile toward me. I felt rejected by my country, and still do. The same country that I was willing to die for, if necessary.

Fred Alderman, Vietnam veteran, in Greene's Homecoming: When the Soldiers Returned from Vietnam.

I consider myself an American, a patriot. I love my country very much. I'm still here after all these years. But for me the greatest legacy of the war in Vietnam is that I will never believe my government again . . . And, I'm not about to forget those things and if I can help it, I'd like to make sure that nobody can forget them either.

William Ehrhart, Vietnam veteran (USMC, 1967–68), in Cohen's Vietnam: Anthology and Guide to a TV History *(1983).*

There is for almost every Vietnam veteran the memory of the sound of helicopter rotor blades. That sound anywhere brings the mama St. Bernard that wrests our memory back to Vietnam . . . In memory I climb in under the rotors. I climb out. It is the

Vietnam sound. Primal sound, like a mother's heartbeat as I formed in the womb. That sound is associated with fear or relief or rescue.

John Wheeler, Vietnam veteran (1969–70), in
Touched with Fire: The Future of the Vietnam Generation *(1984).*

I would ask those who—from their safe editorial offices, their college campuses, and suburban living rooms—condemned the American soldier in Vietnam these questions: how would you have behaved in such an environment? What kind of person would you have become?

Philip Caputo, Vietnam veteran and author of
A Rumor of War *(1977), in* Playboy *article of January 1982.*

The . . . lesson [of Vietnam] is that America must never commit its power and authority in defense of a country of only marginal strategic interests when that country lacks a broadly based government, or the will to create one.

George Ball, undersecretary of state in the Kennedy and Johnson administrations, in Diplomacy for a Crowded World *(1976).*

Now, what lesson have we learned? An enormously important lesson: We must be absolutely certain, before we send troops to engage in armed conflict, that our national security is at stake.

Clark Clifford, Secretary of Defense in the Johnson administration, in Willenson's The Bad War: An Oral History of the Vietnam War *(1987).*

It should never be forgotten that the American officials who made the big decisions about Vietnam were woefully ignorant of Vietnamese history, politics, culture and society . . . We supported the French effort to recolonize Vietnam, ignoring decades of strong Vietnamese nationalism. We sent our troops to Vietnam to prevent a Chinese-led march of international communism, ignoring centuries of animosity between the Vietnamese and Chinese. We supported a corrupt, incompetent and highly unpopular government . . . Vietnam was the wrong war in the wrong place at the wrong time fought for the wrong reasons.

Marc Leepson, Vietnam veteran (USA, 1967–68), and columnist for The Veteran, *to the author, 1991.*

One comment Vietnam veterans make is, "I'm not going to fight another war unless you're going to let me win it." And that is probably going to have a serious impact on the military. Because the young officers who served in Vietnam are going to be generals very soon . . . And the lessons they learned in Vietnam will be reflected in the judgments they make throughout their careers.

Jim Noonan, Vietnam veteran (USMC, 1966–1967), in Santoli's To Bear Any Burden *(1985).*

Everyone hopes the United States will not have to fight another war like the Vietnam War. The best way for us to avoid such a war is to be unmistakable in our will and sure of our ability to fight one if we must. But getting over the Vietnam syndrome means more than standing ready to use American military forces. It means being willing to provide military aid to friends who need it . . . and, above all, having the wisdom and the vision to support nonmilitary programs to address the poverty, injustice, and political instability that plague so many Third World countries.

Richard Nixon, U.S. president (1969–74), in
No More Vietnams *(1985).*

. . . there is no cost-free foreign policy. We must answer this question: is there anything in this world other than an attack on the United States that we will resist by force? If the answer is "No," we will gradually be pushed back into fortress America, by definition.

Henry Kissinger, secretary of state in the Nixon administration, in Newsweek *(April 15, 1985).*

I don't know that any reasonable, sensible person thinks the Vietnam War was a good and righteous undertaking, but it is crucial that we come to understand the war as an event and expression of our national character, and accept our responsibility. Now we have to discover what it was—this epoch of arrogant greed and self-destruction—and be honest with ourselves.

Larry Heineman, Vietnam veteran and author of Paco's Story *(1987), in McCloud's* What Should We Tell Our Children About Vietnam?

War may be too serious a matter to leave solely to military professionals, but it is also too serious a matter to leave only to civilian amateurs. Never again must the president commit American men to combat without first fully defining the nation's aims and then rallying Congress and the nation for war. Otherwise, the courageous Americans who fought and died in the defense of South Vietnam will truly have done so in vain.

Colonel Harry Summers Jr., Vietnam veteran and author of On Strategy: A Critical Analysis of the Vietnam War *(1982), in Braestrup's* Vietnam as History *(1984).*

I have always thought that had we been able to conduct the bombing at the level we did at Christmas of 1972 for another six weeks, we could have gotten a commitment from Hanoi to withdraw its troops from South Vietnam

General Alexander Haig, USA, secretary of state in the Reagan administration, in Newsweek *(April 15, 1985).*

It is perplexing to me that one often reads that the American military lost the War in Vietnam when it is a fact that: the American military did not lose a battle of consequence; the Nixon administration withdrew our ground forces and they were out of the country by early 1973; the Case/Church in mid 1972 decreed that no money . . . would be used to buy any military items to support the South Vietnamese Army; [and] it was two years after our withdrawal that the North Vietnamese Army came down en masse and seized the South.

In short we abandoned the South Vietnamese government. The American military was not defeated in Vietnam.

General William C. Westmoreland, USA, to the author, 1991.

Westmoreland was wrong to expect that his superior firepower would grind us down. If we had focused on the balance of forces, we would have been defeated in two hours. We were waging a people's war—*a la maniere vietnamienne.* America's sophisticated arms, electronic devices and all the rest were to no avail in the end. In war there are two factors—human beings and weapons. Ultimately, though, human beings are the decisive factor.

General Vo Nguyen Giap, former minister of defense of North Vietnam, in Karnow's New York Times Magazine *article of June 24, 1990.*

So how do I classify the tragedy of Vietnam, if not a crusade, a mistake, a crime or conspiracy? I classify it as a misguided experience of the Harvard Business School crowd—the "whiz kids"—in achieving foreign policy objectives by so-called rational game theory, while ignoring the reality and obstinancy of human nature.

These were some of the policy lessons of Vietnam. You can't finesse human nature, human will, or human obstinancy, with economic game theory. And you should never let those who think you can, call the shots in a war!

Admiral James B. Stockdale, the highest-ranking naval officer held as a POW (1965–73) and one of the most highly decorated officers in the history of the service (including the Medal of Honor), in San Jose Mercury News *article of January 3, 1982.*

American combat forces should not have been sent to fight a war the South Vietnamese should have fought for themselves. The American government should have followed a 1951 Army War College study that stated, "Indochina did not warrant American forces to come to its defense."

Sergeant Major Jack W. Jaunal, USMC, Vietnam veteran and college history professor, to the author, 1991.

The whole war was a sham. There was no moral purpose, it was a fraud. There's one good thing though, there's one good thing that came out of the war. The survivors . . . We all pretty much, I think, felt used by that war and the lies that were told, but we survived even that.

Oliver Stone, Vietnam veteran (USA, 1967–68) and writer/director of Platoon *(1986) and* Born on the Fourth of July *(1989), in Perry's* Veteran *article of September 1987.*

I felt cheated, lied to, misled, deceived! . . . My best intentions, my innocence, my youth, my beautiful young spirit had been desecrated by men who never went where I went, men who would never have to go through what I was about to endure.

Ron Kovic (USMC, 1964–67), disabled Vietnam veteran and author of Born on the Fourth of July *(1976), in Seldenberg's* American Film *article of January 1990.*

When I'm talking to reporters, I sometimes accuse them of biased reporting. They jump up and say, "Biased reporting? What do you mean?" I'll mention some names, "Did you ever hear of Pat Brady or Mike Novosel," and four or five other Medal of Honor recipients out of Vietnam.

The reporters say, "No, never heard of them."

Then I'll ask, "Did you ever hear of William Calley?"

They say, "Oh, yeah, yeah."

I say, "I rest my case."

Chief Warrant Officer Frederick E. Ferguson, First Cavalry Division (Airmobile), Vietnam veteran and Medal of Honor recipient for his actions at the battle of Hue on January 31, 1968, in Lowry's And Brave Men, Too *(1985).*

The only trace of America I saw were a few wrecked planes at Tan Son Nhut . . . It's like we've never been there. There were only two occasions when anyone spoke English. The signs on the government buildings where there used to be South Vietnamese flags painted are all painted with the new Vietnamese flag, which is red with a gold star. They're all faded like they have been there forever.

Eddie Adams, Pulitzer Prize–winning Vietnam War news photographer, recalls his return to Saigon [Ho Chi Minh City] in 1983, in the Defense Information School's Vietnam: 10 Years Later *(1983).*

Life for the average Vietnamese today is no better than it was three or four decades ago, and in some respects it is worse. The colonial master is gone, along with the American dispenser of mixed bombs and bounty, but the country is steeped in poverty and much of it still lies in ruins. Oddly enough, both French and the Americans, as people, are regarded with more esteem and admiration nowadays than the Russians, who gave so much to the war effort and remain Vietnam's biggest benefactors.

Robert Shaplen, journalist, on his return to Vietnam in 1984, in Bitter Victory *(1985).*

The economic situation is unbelievable. The north is worse off. In the south there is no comparison with what we had before . . . Vietnam is now a country worse off than Bangladesh.

Tran Van Don, former South Vietnamese government official, now living in Orlando, Florida, in Newsweek *(April 15, 1985).*

I was tragically wrong . . . The North Vietnamese Communists, survivors of protracted, blood-drained campaigns against colonialism, interventionism and human oppression, became in their turn colonialists, interventionists and architects of one of the world's most rigid regimes.

Truong Nhu Tang, founder of the NLF and former minister of justice for the Vietcong, who fled Vietnam in 1979 as a "boat person" and has since lived in Paris, in The New York Review of Books *article of October 21, 1982.*

The Vietnam veteran brought home a different kind of wisdom. He learned that you can fight a bad war, that you can get killed for nothing, that it's a complicated world. In that sense, Vietnam can be a very good experience for Americans, and to some extent it already has been.

Neil Sheehan, New York Times correspondent in Vietnam and author of A Bright Shining Lie *(1988), in* U.S. News & World Report *(October 24, 1988).*

One of the oddest and most unsettling things about meeting Amerasians [American-Vietnamese children] is how strong dominant Western genes seem to have been. It's probably just the sharp contrast with all the Vietnamese faces on the street, but after one glance you feel as if you know exactly how their fathers looked. As we walked over to this group, I thought I could see the faces of four Americans, two black and two white, who had been in Saigon 20 years before.

James Fallows, journalist, on visiting Ho Chi Minh City [Saigon] in 1988, in Atlantic *article of December 1988.*

That war cleaves us still. But, friends, that war began in earnest a quarter of a century ago; and surely the statute of limitations has been reached. This is a fact: The final lesson of Vietnam is that no great nation can long afford to be surrendered by a memory.

President George Bush, to the nation, inaugural address of January 20, 1989.

We were very firmly impressed with the fact that we will probably barely rate a footnote in Vietnamese history even though [the war] was such a profound thing in our lives. We were amazed on how quickly they had almost already forgotten us.

Mike Cerre, USMC Air Reconnaissance officer and Vietnam veteran, on his visit to Vietnam in January 1985, in The Los Angeles Times *(July 5, 1990).*

It was to us a continuation of the war against French colonialism. Very few people know very much about communism and socialism; it was a fight for independence.

Nguyen Ngoc Hung, North Vietnamese infantryman, in The Washington Post *(November 22, 1990).*

On the basis of our Vietnam experience, one thing is certain: The days when the United States will go it alone on a major overseas commitment are over.

Dean Rusk, secretary of state in the Johnson administration, in As I Saw It *(1990).*

I really don't think Vietnam is going to shape this nation's role in the future, or constrain this nation from developing or contributing to the new world order . . . I think our nation to some degree has been liberated from this terrible trauma of Vietnam.

Robert McNamara, secretary of defense in the Kennedy and Johnson administrations, following the opening of the war in the Persian Gulf, statement in Time *(February 11, 1991).*

The majority of the fighting and the dying was done by the youngest soldiers who came from working class, hispanic and black neighborhoods. After the war, government forgot about them and what happened in Vietnam. Vets came home to no parades and no jobs. Our country acted as if they were responsible for the mistakes of others while the people who made the decisions were rewarded with cabinet positions, professorships, and book contracts.

The lesson of that period is that never again can we let one segment of society serve disproportionately on the frontlines and never again can we exempt a few from sacrifices.

Representative Lane Evans (D–Ill.), Vietnam veteran (USMC, 1969–1971) and cochairman of the Vietnam Veterans in Congress Committee (VVIC), to the author, 1991.

In my mind and the minds of many Americans, the unresolved issue of more than 2,000 men still missing in Southeast Asia is the most poignant legacy of the Vietnam War.

It saddens me that 17 years after the fall of Saigon, so many questions remain that will not allow many Americans to close the final chapter of the Vietnam War. It is incumbent on all of us to do what we can to resolve these lingering questions so that wounds of war can finally heal.

Senator John McCain (R–Ariz.), USN pilot and POW (1967–73), to the author, 1991.

Only those who were there stood a slight chance of understanding Vietnam; for the rest, it was a shadow play, in which flags of one color or another invariably cloaked the truth.

Malcolm W. Browne, journalist (who received a Pulitzer Prize for his reporting from Vietnam), to the author, 1991.

For understandable reasons, most Americans want to forget the Vietnam War, and so it has taken on mythological dimensions. The very word "Vietnam" evokes feelings of frustration, failure and loss, no matter which side of the war you were on. To lay these memories to rest will take more than victory over Iraq and a Presidential pronouncement that the "Vietnam syndrome" is dead.

Americans must understand, not bury, the Vietnam experience. We need normal relations . . . so that the metaphor "Vietnam" loses its charge and the country Vietnam takes on reality.

Pham Thanh, South Vietnamese refugee, seriously wounded in the Tet Offensive of 1968 and since living in the United States, editorial of April 19, 1991, in The New York Times.

The most important thing about the Vietnam War for Americans and their allies and friends in Asia is to understand it. The meaning of the Vietnam War was not understood during the war by many otherwise well informed persons. Indeed this might well be the epitaph for the American adventure in Vietnam: We lost the war because we did not understand it. Nor is it understood today.

Douglas Pike, U.S. Foreign Service officer in Vietnam (1960–74), director of the Indochina Archive at the University of California-Berkeley (since 1981), to the author, 1991.

Appendix A
List of Documents

1. Franco-Vietnamese Preliminary Convention and Annex, March 6, 1946.

2. Treaty of Independence of the State of Vietnam, June 4, 1954.

3. Geneva Cease-Fire Agreement, July 20, 1954.

4. Final Declaration of the Geneva Conference, July 21, 1954.

5. The Gulf of Tonkin Resolution, August 7, 1964.

6. Paris Peace Accords: Agreement on Ending the War and Restoring Peace in Vietnam, January 27, 1973.

7. War Powers Resolution, November 7, 1973.

1. Franco-Vietnamese Preliminary Convention and Annex

March 6, 1946

Between the High Contracting Parties hereafter designated: on the one side, the Government of the French Republic, represented by M. [Jean] Sainteny, delegate of the High Commissioner of France, properly commissioned by Admiral d'Argenlieu, the High Commissioner of France, depositary of the powers of the French Republic; and on the other side, the Government of Viet-Nam, represented by its President, M. Ho Chi Minh, and the special delegate of the Council of Ministers, M. Vu Hong Khanh, it is agreed as follows:

1. The French Government recognizes the Republic of Viet-Nam as a free State having its own government, parliament, army and finances, and forming part of the Indochinese Federation and the French Union.

Concerning the unification of the three "Ky," the French Government agrees to accept [*entériner*] the decisions taken by the population consulted by referendum.

2. The Government of Viet-Nam declares itself prepared to receive the French army amicably when, in conformity with international agreements, it relieves the Chinese forces.

An agreement annexed to this Preliminary Convention will settle the means by which the relief operations will be effected.

3. The provisions formulated above will enter into force immediately. Immediately after the exchange of signatures each of the High Contracting Parties will take all necessary measures to bring about an immediate cessation of hostilities, to maintain the military forces in their respective positions, and to create the favorable climate necessary to the immediate opening of frank and friendly negotiations.

These negotiations will deal in particular with the diplomatic relations of Viet-Nam with foreign states, with the future status of Indochina, and with the French economic and cultural interests in Viet-Nam.

Hanoi, Saigon or Paris may be chosen as the site of the conference.

> Done at Hanoi, March 6, 1946
> SAINTENY
> HO CHI MINH
> VU HONG K[H]ANH

2. Treaty of Independence of the State of Vietnam

June 4, 1954

ARTICLE I

France recognizes Vietnam as a fully independent and sovereign State invested with the jurisdiction recognized by international law.

ARTICLE II

Vietnam shall take over from France all the rights and obligations resulting from international treaties or conventions contracted by France on behalf or in the name of the State of Vietnam or all other treaties and conventions concluded by France in the name of French Indochina, insofar as these affect Vietnam.

ARTICLE III

France undertakes to transfer to the Vietnamese Government all jurisdictions and public services still held by her on Vietnamese territory.

ARTICLE IV

The present treaty, which shall come into force on the date of its signature, abrogates all earlier and contrary acts and dispositions. The instruments of ratification of the present treaty shall be exchanged immediately following approval by the qualified institutions of France and Vietnam.

> Done at Paris, June 4, 1954
> JOSEPH LANIEL   BUU LOC

3. Geneva Cease-Fire Agreement

July 20, 1954.

PROVISIONAL MILITARY DEMARCATION LINE AND DEMILITARIZED ZONE

ARTICLE I

A provisional military demarcation line shall be fixed, on either side of which the forces of the two parties shall be regrouped after their withdrawal, the forces of the People's Army of Vietnam [P.A.V., or Vietminh, forces—eds.] to the north of the line and the forces of the French Union to the south. [The line ran roughly along the 17th parallel.]

It is also agreed that a demilitarized zone shall be established on either side of the demarcation line, to a width of not more than 5 kms. from it, to act as a buffer zone and avoid any incidents which might result in the resumption of hostilities.

ARTICLE II

The period within which the movement of all forces of either party into its regrouping zone on either side of the provisional military demarcation line shall be completed shall not exceed three hundred (300) days from the date of the present Agreement's entry into force . . .

[Administrative details are omitted.]

ARTICLE V

To avoid any incidents which might result in the resumption of hostilities, all military forces, supplies, and equipment shall be withdrawn from the demilitarized zone within twenty-five (25) days of the present Agreement's entry into force.

ARTICLE VI

No person, military or civilian, shall be permitted to cross the provisional military demarcation line unless specifically authorized to do so by the Joint Commission.

ARTICLE VII

No person, military or civilian, shall be permitted to enter the demilitarized zone except persons concerned with the conduct of civil administration and relief and persons specifically authorized to enter by the Joint Commission.

ARTICLE VIII

Civil administration and relief in the demilitarized zone on either side of the provisional military demarcation line shall be the responsibility of the Commanders-in-Chief of the two parties in their respective zones. The number of persons, military or civilian, from each side who are permitted to enter the demilitarized zone for the conduct of civil administration and relief shall be determined by the respective Commanders, but in no case shall the total number authorized by either side exceed at any one time a figure to be determined by the . . . Joint Commission. The number of civil police and the arms to be carried by them shall be determined by the Joint Commission. No one else shall carry arms unless specifically authorized to do so by the Joint Commission.

ARTICLE IX

Nothing contained in this chapter shall be construed as limiting the complete freedom of movement—into, out of, or within the demilitarized zone—of the Joint Commission, its joint groups, the International Commission to be set up as indicated below, its inspection teams and any other persons, supplies, or equipment specifically authorized to enter the demilitarized zone by the Joint Commission. Freedom of movement shall be permitted across the territory under the military control of either side over any road or waterway which has to be taken between points within the demilitarized zone when such points are not connected by roads or waterways lying completely within the demilitarized zone.

PRINCIPLES AND PROCEDURE GOVERNING IMPLEMENTATION OF THE PRESENT AGREEMENT

ARTICLE X

The Commanders of the Forces on each side, on the one side the Commander-in-Chief of the French Union forces in Indochina and on the other side the Commander-in-Chief of the People's Army of Vietnam, shall order and enforce the complete cessation of all hostilities in Vietnam by all armed forces under their control, including all units and personnel of the ground, naval, and air forces.

ARTICLE XI

In accordance with the principle of a simultaneous cease-fire throughout Indochina, the cessation of hostilities shall be simultaneous throughout all parts of Vietnam, in all areas of hostilities and for all the forces of the two parties. . . .

[Section on precise timing of the cease-fire is omitted.]

From such time as the cease-fire becomes effective in North Vietnam, both parties undertake not to engage in any large-scale offensive action in any part of the Indochinese theater of operations and not to commit the air forces based on North Vietnam outside that sector. The two parties also undertake to inform each other of their plans for movement from one regrouping zone to another within twenty-five (25) days of the present Agreement's entry into force . . .

[Military details are omitted.]

ARTICLE XIV

Political and administrative measures in the two regrouping zones, on either side of the provisional military demarcation line:

(a) Pending the general elections which will bring about the unification of Vietnam, the conduct of civil administration in each regrouping zone shall be in the hands of the party whose forces are to be regrouped there in virtue of the present Agreement.

(b) Any territory controlled by one party which is transferred to the other party by the regrouping plan shall continue to be administered by the former party until such date as all the troops who are to be transferred have completely left that territory so as to free the zone assigned to the party in question. From then on, such territory shall be regarded as transferred to the other party, who shall assume responsibility for it.

Steps shall be taken to ensure that there is no break in the transfer of responsibilities. For this purpose, adequate notice shall be given by the withdrawing party to the other party, which shall make the necessary arrangements, in particular by sending administrative and police detachments to prepare for the assumption of administrative responsibility . . . The transfer shall be effected in successive stages for the various territorial sectors.

The transfer of the civil administration of Hanoi and Haiphong to the authorities of the Democratic Republic of Vietnam shall be completed within the respective time-limits laid down in Article 15 for military movements.

(c) Each party undertakes to refrain from any reprisals or discrimination against persons or organizations on account of their activities during the hostilities and to guarantee their democratic liberties.

(d) From the date of entry into force of the present Agreement until the movement of troops is completed, any civilians residing in a district controlled by one party who wish to go and live in the zone assigned to the other party shall be permitted and helped to do so by the authorities in that district.

ARTICLE XV

The disengagement of the combatants, and the withdrawals and transfers of military forces, equipment, and supplies shall take place in accordance with the following principles:

(a) The withdrawals and transfers of the military forces, equipment, and supplies of the two parties shall be completed within three hundred (300) days, as laid down in Article 2 of the present Agreement;

(b) Within either territory successive withdrawal shall be made by sectors, portions of sectors, or provinces. Transfers from one regrouping zone to another shall be made in successive monthly installments proportionate to the number of troops to be transferred;

(c) The two parties shall undertake to carry out all troop withdrawals and transfers in accordance with the aims of the present Agreement, shall permit no hostile act, and shall take no step whatsoever which might hamper such withdrawals and transfers. They shall assist one another as far as this is possible;

(d) The two parties shall permit no destruction or sabotage of any public property and no injury to the life and property of the civil population. They shall permit no interference in local civil administration;

(e) The Joint Commission and the International Commission shall ensure that steps are taken to safeguard the forces in the course of withdrawal and transfer . . .

BAN ON THE INTRODUCTION OF FRESH TROOPS,
MILITARY PERSONNEL, ARMS AND MUNITIONS,
MILITARY BASES

ARTICLE XVI

With effect from the date of entry into force of the present Agreement, the introduction into Vietnam of any troop reinforcements and additional military personnel is prohibited.

It is understood, however, that the rotation of units and groups of personnel, the arrival in Vietnam of individual personnel on a temporary duty basis, and the return to Vietnam of the individual personnel after short periods of leave or temporary duty outside Vietnam shall be permitted under the conditions laid down below:

(a) Rotation of units (defined in paragraph (c) of this Article) and groups of personnel shall not be permitted for French Union troops stationed north of the provisional military demarcation line laid down in Article 1 of the present Agreement during the withdrawal period provided for in Article 2.

However, under the heading of individual personnel not more than fifty (50) men, including officers, shall during any one month be permitted to enter that part of the country north of the provisional military demarcation line on a temporary duty basis or to return there after short periods of leave or temporary duty outside Vietnam.

(b) "Rotation" is defined as the replacement of units or groups of personnel by other units of the same echelon or by personnel who are arriving in Vietnam territory to do their overseas service there.

(c) The units rotated shall never be larger than a battalion—or the corresponding echelon for air and naval forces.

(d) Rotation shall be conducted on a man-for-man basis, provided, however, that in any one quarter neither party shall introduce more than fifteen thousand five hundred (15,500) members of its armed forces into Vietnam under the rotation policy.

(e) Rotation units (defined in paragraph (c) of this Article) and groups of personnel, and the individual personnel mentioned in this Article, shall enter and leave Vietnam only through the [designated] entry points . . .

(f) Each party shall notify the Joint Commission and the International Commission at least two days in advance of any arrivals or departures of units, groups of personnel, and individual personnel in or from Vietnam. Reports on the arrivals or departures of units, groups of personnel, and individual personnel in or from Vietnam shall be submitted daily to the Joint Commission and the International Commission.

All the above-mentioned notifications and reports shall indicate the places and dates of arrival or departure and the number of persons arriving or departing.

(g) The International Commission, through its Inspection Teams, shall supervise and inspect the rotation of units and groups of personnel and the arrival and departure of individual personnel as authorized above at the [designated] points of entry . . .

ARTICLE XVII

(a) With effect from the date of entry into force of any present Agreement, the introduction into Vietnam of any reinforcements in the form of all types of arms, munitions and other war material, such as combat aircraft, naval craft, pieces of ordnance, jet engines and jet weapons, and armored vehicles, is prohibited.

(b) It is understood, however, that war material, arms, and munitions which have been destroyed, damaged, worn out, or used up after the cessation of hostilities may be replaced on the basis of piece-for-piece of the same type and with similar characteristics. Such replacements of war material, arms, and ammunitions shall not be permitted for French Union troops stationed north of the provisional military demarcation line laid down in Article 1 of the present Agreement, during the withdrawal period provided for in Article 2 . . .

[Details on designated entry points are omitted.]

(d) Apart from the replacements permitted within the limits laid down in paragraph (b) of this Article, the introduction of war material, arms, and munitions of all types in the form of unassembled parts for subsequent assembly is prohibited.

(e) Each party shall notify the Joint Commission and the International Commission at least two days in advance of any arrivals or departures which may take place of war material, arms, and munitions of all types.

In order to justify the requests for the introduction into Vietnam of arms, munitions, and other war material (as defined in paragraph (a) of this Article) for replacement purposes, a report concerning each incoming shipment shall be submitted to the Joint Commission and the International Commission. Such reports shall indicate the use made of the items so replaced.

(f) The International Commission, through its Inspection Teams, shall supervise and inspect the replacements permitted in the circumstances laid down in this Article.

ARTICLE XVIII

With effect from the date of entry into force of the present Agreement, the establishment of new military bases is prohibited throughout Vietnam territory.

ARTICLE XIX

With effect from the date of entry into force of the present Agreement, no military base under the control of a foreign state may be established in the regrouping zone of either party; the two parties shall ensure that the zones assigned to them do not adhere to any military alliance and are not used for the resumption of hostilities or to further an aggressive policy . . .

[Technical details are omitted.]

PRISONERS OF WAR AND CIVILIAN INTERNEES

ARTICLE XXI

The liberation and repatriation of all prisoners of war and civilian internees detained by each of the two parties at the coming into force of the present Agreement shall be carried out under the following conditions:

(a) All prisoners of war and civilian internees of Vietnam, French, and other nationalities captured since the beginning of hostilities in Vietnam during military operations or in any other circumstances of war and in any part of the territory of Vietnam shall be liberated within a period of thirty (30) days after the date when the cease-fire becomes effective in each theater.

(b) The term "civilian internees" is understood to mean all persons who, having in any way contributed to the political and armed struggle between the two parties, have been arrested for that reason and have been kept in detention by either party during the period of hostilities.

(c) All prisoners of war and civilian internees held by either party shall be surrendered to the appropriate authorities of the other party, who shall give them all possible assistance in proceeding to their country of origin, place of habitual residence, or the zone of their choice.

MISCELLANEOUS

ARTICLE XXII

The Commanders of the Forces of the two parties shall ensure that persons under their respective commands who violate any of the provisions of the present Agreement are suitably punished . . .

[Details about recovery of deceased military personnel are omitted.]

ARTICLE XXIV

The present Agreement shall apply to all the armed forces of either party. The armed forces of each party shall respect the demilitarized zone and the territory under the military control of the other party, and shall commit no act and undertake no operation against the other party and shall not engage in blockade of any kind in Vietnam.

For the purposes of the present Article, the word "territory" includes territorial waters and air space . . .

[Operational details are omitted.]

ARTICLE XXVII

The signatories of the present Agreement and their successors in their functions shall be responsible for ensuring the observance and enforcement of the terms and provisions thereof. The Commanders of the Forces of the two parties shall, within their respective commands, take all steps and make all arrangements necessary to ensure full compliance with all the provisions of the present Agreement by all elements and military personnel under their command . . .

[Further operational details are omitted.]

Done in Geneva at 2400 hours on the 20th of July, 1954, in French and in Vietnamese, both texts being equally authentic.

For the Commander-in-Chief of the French Union Forces in Indochina:

[Henri] DELTIEL
Brigadier-General

For the Commander-in-Chief of the People's Army of Vietnam:

TA QUANG BUU,
Vice-Minister of National
Defense of the Democratic
Republic of Vietnam

4. Final Declaration of the Geneva Conference

July 21, 1954
[The Final Declaration was not signed by any of the participants, nor was it voted upon by the Conference.]

FINAL DECLARATION OF THE GENEVA CONFERENCE ON THE PROBLEM OF RESTORING PEACE IN INDO-CHINA, IN WHICH THE REPRESENTATIVES OF CAMBODIA, THE DEMOCRATIC REPUBLIC OF VIET NAM, FRANCE, LAOS, THE PEOPLE'S REPUBLIC OF CHINA, THE STATE OF VIET NAM, THE UNION OF SOVIET SOCIALIST REPUBLICS, THE UNITED KINGDOM AND THE UNITED STATES OF AMERICA TOOK PART

1. Conference takes note of the agreements ending hostilities in Cambodia, Laos, and Viet Nam and organising international control and the supervision of the execution of the provisions of these agreements.

2. The Conference expresses satisfaction at the ending of hostilities in Cambodia, Laos and Viet Nam; the Conference expresses its conviction that the execution of the provisions set out in the present declaration and in the agreements on the cessation of hostilities will permit Cambodia, Laos and Viet Nam henceforth to play their part, in full independence and sovereignty, in the peaceful community of nations.

3. The Conference takes note of the declarations made by the Governments of Cambodia and of Laos of their intention to adopt measures permitting all citizens to take their place in the national community, in particular by participating in the next general elections, which, in conformity with the constitution of each of these countries, shall take place in the course of the year 1955, by secret ballot and in conditions of respect for fundamental freedoms.

4. The Conference takes note of the clauses in the agreement on the cessation of hostilities in Viet Nam prohibiting the introduction into Viet Nam of foreign troops and military personnel as well as of all kinds of arms and munitions. The Conference also takes note of the declarations made by the Governments of Cambodia and Laos of their resolution not to request foreign aid, whether in war material, in personnel or in instructors except for the purpose of the effective defence of their territory and, in the case of Laos, to the extent defined by the agreements on the cessation of hostilities in Laos.

5. The Conference takes note of the clauses in the agreement on the cessation of hostilities in Viet Nam to the effect that no military base under the control of a foreign State may be established in the regrouping zones of the two parties, the latter having the obligation to see that the zones allotted to them shall not constitute part of any military alliance and shall not be utilised for the resumption of hostilities or in the service of an aggressive policy. The Conference also takes note of the declarations of the Governments of Cambodia and Laos to the effect that they will not join in any agreement with other States

if this agreement includes the obligation to participate in a military alliance not in conformity with the principles of the Charter of the United Nations or, in the case of Laos, with the principles of the agreement on the cessation of hostilities in Laos or, so long as their security is not threatened, the obligation to establish bases on Cambodian or Laotian territory for the military forces of foreign Powers.

6. The Conference recognises that the essential purpose of the agreement relating to Viet Nam is to settle military questions with a view to ending hostilities and that the military demarcation line is provisional and should not in any way be interpreted as constituting a political or territorial boundary. The Conference expresses its conviction that the execution of the provisions set out in the present declaration and in the agreement on the cessation of hostilities creates the necessary basis for the achievement in the near future of a political settlement in Viet Nam.

7. The Conference declares that, so far as Viet Nam is concerned, the settlement of political problems, effected on the basis of respect for the principles of independence, unity and territorial integrity, shall permit the Vietnamese people to enjoy the fundamental freedoms, guaranteed by democratic institutions established as a result of free general elections by secret ballot. In order to ensure that sufficient progress in the restoration of peace has been made, and that all necessary conditions obtain for free expression of the national will, general elections shall be held in July 1956, under the supervision of an international commission composed of representatives of the Member States of the International Supervisory Commission, referred to in the agreement on the cessation of hostilities. Consultations will be held on this subject between the competent representative authorities of the two zones from July 20, 1955, onwards.

8. The provisions of the agreements on the cessation of hostilities intended to ensure the protection of individuals and of property must be most strictly applied and must, in particular, allow everyone in Viet Nam to decide freely in which zone he wishes to live.

9. The competent representative authorities of the Northern and Southern zones of Viet Nam, as well as the authorities of Laos and Cambodia, must not permit any individual or collective reprisals against persons who have collaborated in any way with one of the parties during the war, or against members of such persons' families.

10. The Conference takes note of the declaration of the Government of the French Republic to the effect that it is ready to withdraw its troops from the territory of Cambodia, Laos and Viet Nam, at the request of the Governments concerned and within periods which shall be fixed by agreement between the parties except in the cases where, by agreement between the two parties, a certain number of French troops shall remain at specified points and for a specified time.

11. The Conference takes note of the declaration of the French Government to the effect that for the settlement of all the problems connected with the re-establishment and consolidation of peace in Cambodia, Laos and Viet Nam, the French Government will proceed from the principle of respect for the independence and sovereignty, unity and territorial integrity of Cambodia, Laos and Viet Nam.

12. In their relations with Cambodia, Laos and Viet Nam, each member of the Geneva Conference undertakes to respect the sovereignty, the independence, the unity and the territorial integrity of the above-mentioned States, and to refrain from any interference in their internal affairs.

13. The members of the Conference agree to consult one another on any question which may be referred to them by the International Supervisory Commission, in order to study such measures as may prove necessary to ensure that the agreements on the cessation of hostilities in Cambodia, Laos and Viet Nam are respected.

5. The Gulf of Tonkin Resolution

August 7, 1964
[Adopted August 7, 1964. Signed by President Johnson August 10, 1964. Senate vote, 88-2; House vote, 416-0.]

Whereas naval units of the Communist regime in Vietnam, in violation of the principles of the Charter of the United Nations and of international law, have deliberately and repeatedly attacked United States naval vessels lawfully present in international waters, and have thereby created a serious threat to international peace; and

Whereas these attacks are part of a deliberate and systematic campaign of aggression that the Communist regime in North Vietnam has been waging against its neighbors and the nations joined with them in the collective defense of their freedom; and

Whereas the United States is assisting the peoples of Southeast Asia to protect their freedom and has no territorial, military or political ambitions in that area, but desires only that these peoples should be left in peace to work out their own destinies in their own way: Now, therefore, be it

Resolved by the Senate and House of Representatives of the United States of America in Congress assembled, That the Congress approves and supports the determination of the President, as Commander in Chief, to take all necessary measures to repel any armed attack against the forces of the United States and to prevent further aggression.

Sec. 2. The United States regards as vital to its national interest and to world peace the maintenance of international peace and security in Southeast Asia. Consonant with the Constitution of the United States and the Charter of the United Nations and in accordance with its obligations under the Southeast Asia Collective Defense Treaty, the United States is, therefore, prepared, as the President determines, to take all necessary steps, including the use of armed force, to assist any member or protocol state of the Southeast Asia Collective Defense Treaty requesting assistance in defense of its freedom.

Sec. 3. This resolution shall expire when the President shall determine that the peace and security of the area is reasonably assured by international conditions created by action of the United Nations or otherwise, except that it may be terminated earlier by concurrent resolution of the Congress.

6. Paris Peace Accords: Agreement on Ending the War and Restoring Peace in Vietnam

January 27, 1973

The Parties participating in the Paris Conference on Viet-Nam,

With a view to ending the war and restoring peace in Viet-Nam on the basis of respect for the Vietnamese people's fundamental national rights and the South Vietnamese people's right to self-determination, and to contributing to the consolidation of peace in Asia and the world,

Have agreed on the following provisions and undertake to respect and to implement them:

Chapter I

THE VIETNAMESE PEOPLE'S FUNDAMENTAL NATIONAL RIGHTS

ARTICLE I

The United States and all other countries respect the independence, sovereignty, unity, and territorial integrity of Viet-Nam as recognized by the 1954 Geneva Agreements on Viet-Nam.

Chapter II

CESSATION OF HOSTILITIES—WITHDRAWAL OF TROOPS

ARTICLE II

A cease-fire shall be observed throughout South Viet-Nam as of 2400 hours G.M.T., on January 27, 1973.

At the same hour, the United States will stop all its military activities against the territory of the Democratic Republic of Viet-Nam by ground, air and naval forces, wherever they may be based, and end the mining of the territorial waters, ports, harbors, and waterways of the Democratic Republic of Viet-Nam. The United States will remove, permanently deactivate or destroy all the mines in the territorial waters, ports, harbors, and waterways of North Viet-Nam as soon as this Agreement goes into effect.

The complete cessation of hostilities mentioned in this Article shall be durable and without limit of time.

ARTICLE III

The parties undertake to maintain the cease-fire and to ensure a lasting and stable peace.

As soon as the cease-fire goes into effect:

(a) The United States forces and those of the other foreign countries allied with the United States and the Republic of Viet-Nam shall remain in-place pending the implementation of the plan of troop withdrawal. The Four-Party Joint Military Commission described in Article 16 shall determine the modalities.

(b) The armed forces of the two South Vietnamese parties shall remain in-place. The Two-Party Joint Military Commission described in Article 17 shall determine the areas controlled by each party and the modalities of stationing.

(c) The regular forces of all services and arms and the irregular forces of the parties in South Viet-Nam shall stop all offensive activities against each other and shall strictly abide by the following stipulations:

—All acts of force on the ground, in the air, and on the sea shall be prohibited;

—All hostile acts, terrorism and reprisals by both sides will be banned.

ARTICLE IV

The United States will not continue its military involvement or intervene in the internal affairs of South Viet-Nam.

ARTICLE V

Within sixty days of the signing of this Agreement, there will be a total withdrawal from South Viet-Nam of troops, military advisers, and military personnel, including technical military personnel and military personnel associated with the pacification program, armaments, munitions, and war material of the United States and those of the other foreign countries mentioned in Article 3 (a). Advisers from the above-mentioned countries to all paramilitary organizations and the police force will also be withdrawn within the same period of time.

ARTICLE VI

The dismantlement of all military bases in South Viet-Nam of the United States and of the other foreign countries mentioned in Article 3 (a) shall be completed within sixty days of the signing of this Agreement.

ARTICLE VII

From the enforcement of the cease-fire to the formation of the government provided for in Article 9 (b) and 14 of this Agreement, the two South Vietnamese parties shall not accept the introduction of troops, military advisers, and military personnel including technical military personnel, armaments, munitions, and war material into South Viet-Nam.

The two South Vietnamese parties shall be permitted to make periodic replacement of armaments, munitions and war material which have been destroyed, damaged, worn out or used up after the cease-fire, on the basis of piece-for-piece, of the same characteristics and properties, under the supervision of the Joint Military Commission of the two South Vietnamese parties and of the International Commission of Control and Supervision.

Chapter III

THE RETURN OF CAPTURED MILITARY PERSONNEL AND FOREIGN CIVILIANS, AND CAPTURED AND DETAINED VIETNAMESE CIVILIAN PERSONNEL

ARTICLE VIII

(a) The return of captured military personnel and foreign civilians of the parties shall be carried out simultaneously with and completed not later than the same day as the troop withdrawal mentioned in Article 5. The parties shall exchange complete lists of the above-mentioned captured military personnel and foreign civilians on the day of the signing of this Agreement.

(b) The Parties shall help each other to get information about those military personnel and foreign civilians of the parties missing in action, to determine the location and take care of the graves of the dead so as to facilitate the exhumation and repatriation of the remains, and to take any such other measures as may be required to get information about those still considered missing in action.

(c) The question of the return of Vietnamese civilian personnel captured and detained in South Viet-Nam will be resolved by the two South Vietnamese parties on the basis of the principles of Article 21 (b) of the Agreement on the Cessation of Hostilities in Viet-Nam of July 20, 1954. The two South Vietnamese parties will do so in a spirit of national reconciliation and concord, with a view to ending hatred and enmity, in order to ease suffering and to reunite families. The two South Vietnamese parties will do their utmost to resolve this question within ninety days after the cease-fire comes into effect.

Chapter IV

THE EXERCISE OF THE SOUTH VIETNAMESE PEOPLE'S RIGHT TO SELF-DETERMINATION

ARTICLE IX

The Government of the United States of America and the Government of the Democratic Republic of Viet-Nam undertake to respect the following principles for the exercise of the South Vietnamese people's right to self-determination:

(a) The South Vietnamese people's right to self-determination is sacred, inalienable, and shall be respected by all countries.

(b) The South Vietnamese people shall decide themselves the political future of South Viet-Nam through genuinely free and democratic general elections under international supervision.

(c) Foreign countries shall not impose any political tendency or personality on the South Vietnamese people.

ARTICLE X

The two South Vietnamese parties undertake to respect the cease-fire and maintain peace in South Viet-Nam, settle all matters of contention through negotiations, and avoid all armed conflict.

ARTICLE XI

Immediately after the cease-fire, the two South Vietnamese parties will:

—achieve national reconciliation and concord, end hatred and enmity, prohibit all acts of reprisal and discrimination against individuals or organizations that have collaborated with one side or the other;

—ensure the democratic liberties of the people: personal freedom, freedom of speech, freedom of the press, freedom of meeting, freedom of organization, freedom of political activities, freedom of belief, freedom of movement, freedom of residence, freedom of work, right to property ownership, and right to free enterprise.

ARTICLE XII

(a) Immediately after the cease-fire, the two South Vietnamese parties shall hold consultations in a spirit of national reconciliation and concord, mutual respect, and mutual non-elimination to set up a National Council of National Reconciliation and Concord of three equal segments. The Council shall operate on the principle of unanimity. After the National Council of National Reconciliation and Concord has assumed its functions, the two South Vietnamese parties will consult about the formation of councils at lower levels. The two South Vietnamese parties shall sign an agreement on the internal matters of South Viet-Nam as soon as possible and do their utmost to accomplish this within ninety days after the cease-fire comes into effect, in keeping with the South Vietnamese people's aspirations for peace, independence and democracy.

(b) The National Council of National Reconciliation and Concord shall have the task of promoting the two South Vietnamese parties' implementation of this Agreement, achievement of national reconcilia-

tion and concord and ensurance of democratic liberties. The National Council of National Reconciliation and Concord will organize the free and democratic general elections provided for in Article 9 (b) and decide the procedures and modalities of these general elections. The institutions for which the general elections are to be held will be agreed upon through consultations between the two South Vietnamese parties. The National Council of National Reconciliation and Concord will also decide the procedures and modalities of such local elections as the two South Vietnamese parties agree upon.

ARTICLE XIII

The question of Vietnamese armed forces in South Viet-Nam shall be settled by the two South Vietnamese parties in a spirit of national reconciliation and concord, equality and mutual respect, without foreign interference, in accordance with the postwar situation. Among the questions to be discussed by the two South Vietnamese parties are steps to reduce their military effectives and to demobilize the troops being reduced. The two South Vietnamese parties will accomplish this as soon as possible.

ARTICLE XIV

South Viet-Nam will pursue a foreign policy of peace and independence. It will be prepared to establish relations with all countries irrespective of their political and social systems on the basis of mutual respect for independence and sovereignty and accept economic and technical aid from any country with no political conditions attached. The acceptance of military aid by South Viet-Nam in the future shall come under the authority of the government set up after the general elections in South Viet-Nam provided for in Article 9 (b).

Chapter V

THE REUNIFICATION OF VIET-NAM AND THE RELATIONSHIP BETWEEN NORTH AND SOUTH VIET-NAM

ARTICLE XV

The reunification of Viet-Nam shall be carried out step by step through peaceful means on the basis of discussions and agreements between North and South Viet-Nam, without coercion or annexation by either party, and without foreign interference. The time for reunification will be agreed upon by North and South Viet-Nam.

Pending reunification:

(a) The military demarcation line between the two zones at the 17th parallel is only provisional and not a political or territorial boundary, as provided for in paragraph 6 of the Final Declaration of the 1954 Geneva Conference.

(b) North and South Viet-Nam shall respect the Demilitarized Zone on either side of the Provisional Military Demarcation Line.

(c) North and South Viet-Nam shall promptly start negotiations with a view to reestablishing normal relations in various fields. Among the questions to be negotiated are the modalities of civilian movement across the Provisional Military Demarcation Line.

(d) North and South Viet-Nam shall not join any military alliance or military bloc and shall not allow foreign powers to maintain military bases, troops, military advisers, and military personnel on their respective territories, as stipulated in the 1954 Geneva Agreements on Viet-Nam.

Chapter VI

THE JOINT MILITARY COMMISSIONS, THE INTERNATIONAL COMMISSION OF CONTROL AND SUPERVISION, THE INTERNATIONAL CONFERENCE

ARTICLE XVI

(a) The Parties participating in the Paris Conference on Viet-Nam shall immediately designate representatives to form a Four-Party Joint Military Commission with the task of ensuring joint action by the parties in implementing the following provisions of this Agreement:

[References to sections of Articles 2, 3, 5, 6 and 8 omitted.]

(b) The Four-Party Joint Military Commission shall operate in accordance with the principle of consultations and unanimity. Disagreements shall be referred to the International Commission of Control and Supervision.

(c) The Four-Party Joint Military Commission shall begin operating immediately after the signing of this Agreement and end its activities in sixty days, after the completion of the withdrawal of U.S. troops and those of the other foreign countries mentioned in Article 3 (a) and the completion of the return of captured military personnel and foreign civilians of the parties.

(d) The four parties shall agree immediately on the organization, the working procedure, means of activity, and expenditures of the Four-Party Joint Military Commission.

ARTICLE XVII

(a) The two South Vietnamese parties shall immediately designate representatives to form a Two-Party Joint Military Commission with the task of ensuring joint action by the two South Vietnamese parties in implementing the following provisions of this Agreement:

[References to sections of Articles 2, 3, 7, 8 and 13 omitted.]

(b) Disagreements shall be referred to the International Commission of Control and Supervision.

(c) After the signing of this Agreement, the Two-Party Joint Military Commission shall agree immediately on the measures and organization aimed at enforcing the cease-fire and preserving peace in South Viet-Nam.

ARTICLE XVIII

(a) After the signing of this Agreement, an International Commission of Control and Supervision shall be established immediately.

(b) Until the International Conference provided for in Article 19 makes definitive arrangements, the International Commission of Control and Supervision will report to the four parties on matters concerning the control and supervision of the implementation of the following provisions of this Agreement:

[References to sections of Articles 2, 3, 5, 6 and 8 omitted.]

The International Commission of Control and Supervision shall form control teams for carrying out its tasks. The four parties shall agree immediately on the location and operation of these teams. The parties will facilitate their operation.

(c) Until the International Conference makes definitive arrangements, the International Commission of Control and Supervision will report to the two South Vietnamese parties on matters concerning the control and supervision of the implementation of the following provisions of this Agreement.

[We omit further operational details of the International Commission of Control and Supervision in Articles 18 and 19 and the agreement regarding Laos and Cambodia in Article 20.—eds.]

Chapter VIII

THE RELATIONSHIP BETWEEN THE UNITED STATES AND THE DEMOCRATIC REPUBLIC OF VIET-NAM

ARTICLE XXI

The United States anticipates that this Agreement will usher in an era of reconciliation with the Democratic Republic of Viet-Nam as with all the peoples of Indochina. In pursuance of its traditional policy, the United States will contribute to healing the wounds of war and to postwar reconstruction of the Democratic Republic of Viet-Nam and throughout Indochina.

ARTICLE XXII

The ending of the war, the restoration of peace in Viet-Nam, and the strict implementation of this Agreement will create conditions for establishing a new, equal and mutually beneficial relationship between the United States and the Democratic Republic of Viet-Nam on the basis of respect for each other's independence and sovereignty, and non-interference in each other's internal affairs. At the same time this will ensure stable peace in Viet-Nam and contribute to the preservation of lasting peace in Indochina and Southeast Asia.

Chapter IX

OTHER PROVISIONS

ARTICLE XXIII

This Agreement shall enter into force upon signature by plenipotentiary representatives of the parties participating in the Paris Conference on Viet-Nam. All the parties concerned shall strictly implement this Agreement and its Protocols.

Done in Paris this twenty-seventh day of January, one thousand nine hundred and seventy-three, in English and Vietnamese. The English and Vietnamese texts are official and equally authentic.

FOR THE GOVERNMENT OF THE UNITED STATES OF AMERICA

William P. Rogers
Secretary of State

FOR THE GOVERNMENT OF THE DEMOCRATIC REPUBLIC OF VIET-NAM

Nguyen Duy Trinh
Minister for Foreign Affairs

FOR THE GOVERNMENT OF THE REPUBLIC OF VIET-NAM

Tran Van Lam
Minister for Foreign Affairs

FOR THE PROVISIONAL REVOLUTIONARY GOVERNMENT OF THE REPUBLIC OF SOUTH VIET-NAM

Nguyen Thi Binh
Minister for Foreign Affairs

PROTOCOL TO THE AGREEMENT OF ENDING THE WAR AND RESTORING PEACE IN VIET-NAM CONCERNING THE RETURN OF CAPTURED MILITARY PERSONNEL AND FOREIGN CIVILIANS AND CAPTURED AND DETAINED VIETNAMESE CIVILIAN PERSONNEL

The Parties participating in the Paris Conference on Viet-Nam,

In implementation of Article 8 of the Agreement on Ending the War and Restoring Peace in Viet-Nam signed on this date providing for the return of captured military personnel and foreign civilians, and captured and detained Vietnamese civilian personnel,

Have agreed as follows:

THE RETURN OF CAPTURED MILITARY PERSONNEL AND FOREIGN CIVILIANS

ARTICLE I

The parties signatory to the Agreement shall return the captured military personnel of the parties mentioned in Article 8 (a) of the Agreement as follows:

—all captured military personnel of the United States and those of the other foreign countries mentioned in Article 3 (a) of the Agreement shall be returned to United States authorities;

—all captured Vietnamese military personnel, whether belonging to regular or irregular armed forces, shall be returned to the two South Vietnamese parties; they shall be returned to that South Vietnamese party under whose command they served.

ARTICLE II

All captured civilians who are nationals of the United States or of any other foreign countries mentioned in Article 3 (a) of the Agreement shall be returned to United States authorities. All other captured foreign civilians shall be returned to the authorities of their country of nationality by any one of the parties willing and able to do so.

ARTICLE III

The parties shall today exchange complete lists of captured persons mentioned in Articles 1 and 2 of this Protocol.

ARTICLE IV

(a) The return of all captured persons mentioned in Articles 1 and 2 of this Protocol shall be completed within sixty days of the signing of the Agreement at a rate no slower than the rate of withdrawal from South Viet-Nam of United States forces and those of the other foreign countries mentioned in Article 5 of the Agreement.

(b) Persons who are seriously ill, wounded or maimed, old persons and women shall be returned first. The remainder shall be returned either by returning all from one detention place after another or in order of their dates of capture, beginning with those who have been held the longest.

ARTICLE V

The return and reception of the persons mentioned in Articles 1 and 2 of this Protocol shall be carried out at places convenient to the concerned parties. Places of return shall be agreed upon by the Four-Party Joint Military Commission. The parties shall ensure the safety of personnel engaged in the return and reception of those persons.

ARTICLE VI

Each party shall return all captured persons mentioned in Articles 1 and 2 of this Protocol without delay and shall facilitate their return and reception. The detaining parties shall not deny or delay their return for any reason, including the fact that captured persons may, on any grounds, have been prosecuted or sentenced.

THE RETURN OF CAPTURED AND DETAINED VIETNAMESE CIVILIAN PERSONNEL

ARTICLE VII

(a) The question of the return of Vietnamese civilian personnel captured and detained in South Viet-Nam will be resolved by the two South Vietnamese parties on the basis of the principles of Article 21 (b) of the Agreement on the Cessation of Hostilities in Viet-Nam of July 20, 1954, which reads as follows:

"The term 'civilian internees' is understood to mean all persons who, having in any way contributed to the political and armed struggle between the two parties, have been arrested for that reason and have been kept in detention by either party during the period of hostilities."

(b) The two South Vietnamese parties will do so in a spirit of national reconciliation and concord with a view to ending hatred and enmity in order to ease suffering and to reunite families. The two South Vietnamese parties will do their utmost to resolve this question within ninety days after the cease-fire comes into effect.

(c) Within fifteen days after the cease-fire comes into effect, the two South Vietnamese parties shall exchange lists of the Vietnamese civilian personnel captured and detained by each party and lists of the places at which they are held.

TREATMENT OF CAPTURED PERSONS DURING DETENTION

ARTICLE VIII

(a) All captured military personnel of the parties and captured foreign civilians of the parties shall be treated humanely at all times, and in accordance with international practice.

They shall be protected against all violence to life and person, in particular against murder in any form, mutilation, torture and cruel treatment, and outrages upon personal dignity. These persons shall not be forced to join the armed forces of the detaining party.

They shall be given adequate food, clothing, shelter, and the medical attention required for their state of health. They shall be allowed to exchange post cards and letters with their families and receive parcels.

(b) All Vietnamese civilian personnel captured and detained in South Viet-Nam shall be treated humanely at all times, and in accordance with international practice.

They shall be protected against all violence to life and person, in particular against murder in any form, mutilation, torture and cruel treatment, and outrages against personal dignity. The detaining parties shall not deny or delay their return for any reason, including the fact that captured persons may, on any grounds, have been prosecuted or sentenced. These persons shall not be forced to join the armed forces of the detaining party.

They shall be given adequate food, clothing, shelter and the medical attention required for their state of health. They shall be allowed to exchange post cards and letters with their families and receive parcels.

ARTICLE IX

(a) To contribute to improving the living conditions of the captured military personnel of the parties and foreign civilians of the parties, the parties shall, within fifteen days after the cease-fire comes into effect, agree upon the designation of two or more national Red Cross societies to visit all places where captured military personnel and foreign civilians are held.

(b) To contribute to improving the living conditions of the captured and detained Vietnamese civilian personnel, the two South Vietnamese parties shall, within fifteen days after the cease-fire comes into effect, agree upon the designation of two or more national Red Cross societies to visit all places where the captured and detained Vietnamese civilian personnel are held.

WITH REGARD TO DEAD AND MISSING PERSONS

ARTICLE X

(a) The Four-Party Joint Military Commission shall ensure joint action by the parties in implementing Article 8 (b) of the Agreement. When the Four-Party Joint Military Commission has ended its activities, a Four-Party Joint Military team shall be maintained to carry on this task.

(b) With regard to Vietnamese civilian personnel dead or missing in South Viet-Nam, the two South Vietnamese parties shall help each other to obtain information about missing persons, determine the location and take care of the graves of the dead, in a spirit of national reconciliation and concord, in keeping with the people's aspirations.

OTHER PROVISIONS

ARTICLE XI

(a) The Four-Party and Two-Party Joint Military Commissions will have the responsibility of determining immediately the modalities of implementing the provisions of this Protocol consistent with their respective responsibilities under Articles 16 (a) and 17 (a) of the Agreement. In case the Joint Military Commissions, when carrying out their tasks, cannot reach agreement on a matter pertaining to the return of captured personnel they shall refer to the International Commission for its assistance.

(b) The Four-Party Joint Military Commission shall form, in addition to the teams established by the Protocol concerning the cease-fire in South Viet-Nam and the Joint Military Commissions, a sub-commission on captured persons and, as required, joint military teams on captured persons to assist the Commission in its tasks.

(c) From the time the cease-fire comes into force to the time when the Two-Party Joint Military Commission becomes operational, the two South Vietnamese parties' delegations to the Four-Party Joint Military Commission shall form a provisional sub-commission and provisional joint military teams to carry out its tasks concerning captured and detained Vietnamese civilian personnel.

(d) The Four-Party Joint Military Commission shall send joint military teams to observe the return of the persons mentioned in Articles 1 and 2 of this Protocol at each place in Viet-Nam where such persons are being returned, and at the last detention places from which these persons will be taken to the places of return. The Two-Party Joint Military Commission shall send joint military teams to observe the return of Vietnamese civilian personnel captured and detained at each place in South Viet-Nam where such persons are being returned, and at the last detention places from which these persons will be taken to the places of return.

ARTICLE XII

In implementation of Articles 18 (b) and 18 (c) of the Agreement, the International Commission of Control and Supervision shall have the responsibility to control and supervise the observance of Articles 1 through 7 of this Protocol through observation of the return of captured military personnel, foreign civilians and captured and detained Vietnamese civilian personnel at each place in Viet-Nam where these persons are being returned, and at the last detention places from which these persons will be taken to the places of return, the examination of lists, and the investigation of violations of the provisions of the above-mentioned Articles.

ARTICLE XIII

Within five days after signature of this Protocol, each party shall publish the text of the Protocol and communicate it to all the captured persons covered by the Protocol and being detained by that party.

ARTICLE XIV

This Protocol shall come into force upon signature by plenipotentiary representatives of all the parties participating in the Paris Conference on Viet-Nam. It shall be strictly implemented by all the parties concerned.

Done in Paris this twenty-seventh day of January, one thousand nine hundred and seventy-three, in English and Vietnamese. The English and Vietnamese texts are official and equally authentic.

FOR THE GOVERNMENT OF THE UNITED STATES OF AMERICA:

William P. Rogers
Secretary of State

FOR THE GOVERNMENT OF THE DEMOCRATIC REPUBLIC OF VIET-NAM:

Nguyen Duy Trinh
Minister for Foreign Affairs

FOR THE GOVERNMENT OF THE REPUBLIC OF VIET-NAM:

Tran Van Lam
Minister for Foreign Affairs

FOR THE PROVISIONAL REVOLUTIONARY GOVERNMENT OF THE REPUBLIC OF SOUTH VIET-NAM:

Nguyen Thi Binh
Minister for Foreign Affairs

PROTOCOL TO THE AGREEMENT ON ENDING THE WAR AND RESTORING PEACE IN VIET-NAM CONCERNING THE CEASE-FIRE IN SOUTH VIET-NAM AND THE JOINT MILITARY COMMISSIONS

. . . Cease-fire in South Viet-Nam

ARTICLE I

The High Commands of the parties in South Viet-Nam shall issue prompt and timely orders to all regular and irregular armed forces and the armed police under their command to completely end hostilities throughout South Viet-Nam. . . .

ARTICLE II

(a) As soon as the cease-fire comes into force and until regulations are issued by the Joint Military Commissions, all ground, river, sea and air combat forces of the parties in South Viet-Nam shall remain in place; that is, in order to ensure a stable cease-fire, there shall be no major redeployments or movements that would extend each party's area of control or would result in contact between opposing armed forces and clashes which might take place.

(b) All regular and irregular armed forces and the armed police of the parties in South Viet-Nam shall observe the prohibition of the following acts:

(1) Armed patrols into areas controlled by opposing armed forces and flights by bomber and fighter aircraft of all types, except for unarmed flights for proficiency training and maintenance;

(2) Armed attacks against any person, either military or civilian, by any means whatsoever, including the use of small arms, mortars, artillery, bombing and strafing by airplanes and any other type of weapon or explosive device;

(3) All combat operations on the ground, on rivers, on the sea and in the air;

(4) All hostile acts, terrorism or reprisals; and

(5) All acts endangering lives or public or private property.

ARTICLE III

The above-mentioned prohibitions shall not hamper or restrict:

(1) Civilian supply, freedom of movement, freedom to work, and freedom of the people to engage in trade, and civilian communication and transportation between and among all areas in South Viet-Nam;

(2) The use by each party in areas under its control of military support elements, such as engineer and transportation units, in repair and construction of public facilities and the transportation and supplying of the population . . .

ARTICLE IV

In order to avert conflict and ensure normal conditions for those armed forces which are in direct contact, and pending regulation by the Joint Military Commissions, the commanders of the opposing armed forces at those places of direct contact shall meet as soon as the cease-fire comes into force with a view to reaching an agreement on temporary measures to avert conflict and to ensure supply and medical care for these armed forces.

ARTICLE V

(a) Within fifteen days after the cease-fire comes into effect, each party shall do its utmost to complete the removal or deactivation of all demolition objects, mine-fields, traps, obstacles or other dangerous objects placed previously . . .

ARTICLE VI

Civilian police and civilian security personnel of the parties in South Viet-Nam, who are responsible for the maintenance of law and order, shall strictly respect the prohibitions set forth in Article 2 of this Protocol . . .

ARTICLE VII

(a) The entry into South Viet-Nam of replacement armaments, munitions, and war material permitted under Article 7 of the Agreement shall take place under the supervision and control of the Two-Party Joint Military Commission and of the International Commission of Control and Supervision and through such points of entry only as are designated by the two South Vietnamese parties . . .

(b) Each of the designated points of entry shall be available only for that South Vietnamese party which is in control of that point. The two South Vietnamese parties shall have an equal number of points of entry.

ARTICLE VIII

(a) In implementation of Article 5 of the Agreement, the United States and the other foreign countries referred to in Article 5 of the Agreement shall take with them all their armaments, munitions, and war material . . .

ARTICLE IX

(a) In implementation of Article 6 of the Agreement, the United States and the other foreign countries referred to in that Article shall dismantle and remove from South Viet-Nam or destroy all military bases in South Viet-Nam of the United States and of the other foreign countries referred to in that Article, including weapons, mines, and other military equipment at these bases, for the purpose of making them unusable for military purposes . . .

[Article 10 concerning the operations of the Joint Military Commissions omitted.]

ARTICLE XI

(g) . . . With respect to Article 7 of the Agreement, the two South Vietnamese parties' delegations to the Four-Party Joint Military Commission shall establish joint military teams at the points of entry in South Viet-Nam used for replacement of armaments, mu-

nitions and war material which are designated in accordance with Article 7 of this Protocol . . .

[Articles 12 through 17 with further operational details of the Joint Military Commissions omitted.]

ARTICLE XVIII

The common expenses of the Four-Party Joint Military Commission shall be borne equally by the four parties, and the common expenses of the Two-Party Joint Military Commission in South Viet-Nam shall be borne equally by these two parties.

ARTICLE XIX

This Protocol shall enter into force upon signature by plenipotentiary representatives of all the parties participating in the Paris Conference on Viet-Nam. It shall be strictly implemented by all the parties concerned.

Done in Paris this twenty-seventh day of January, one thousand nine hundred and seventy-three, in English and Vietnamese. The English and Vietnamese texts are official and equally authentic.

FOR THE GOVERNMENT OF THE UNITED STATES OF AMERICA:

William P. Rogers
Secretary of State

FOR THE GOVERNMENT OF THE DEMOCRATIC REPUBLIC OF VIET-NAM:

Nguyen Duy Trinh
Minister for Foreign Affairs

FOR THE GOVERNMENT OF THE REPUBLIC OF VIET-NAM:

Tran Van Lam
Minister for Foreign Affairs

FOR THE PROVISIONAL REVOLUTIONARY GOVERNMENT OF THE REPUBLIC OF SOUTH VIET-NAM:

Nguyen Thi Binh
Minister for Foreign Affairs

7. War Powers Resolution

November 7, 1973
[Passed by the U.S. Senate over President Nixon's veto.]

§ 1541. Purpose and policy

(a) Congressional declaration

It is the purpose of this chapter to fulfill the intent of the framers of the Constitution of the United States and insure that the collective judgment of both the Congress and the President will apply to the introduction of United States Armed Forces into hostilities, or into situations where imminent involvement in hostilities is clearly indicated by the circumstances, and to the continued use of such forces in hostilities or in such situations.

(b) Congressional legislative power under necessary and proper clause

Under article I, section 8, of the Constitution, it is specifically provided that the Congress shall have the power to make all laws necessary and proper for carrying into execution, not only its own powers but also all other powers vested by the Constitution in the Government of the United States, or in any department or officer hereof.

(c) Presidential executive power as Commander-in-Chief; limitation

The constitutional powers of the President as Commander-in-Chief to introduce United States Armed Forces into hostilities, or into situations where imminent involvement in hostilities is clearly indicated by the circumstances, are exercised only pursuant to (1) a declaration of war, (2) specific statutory authorization, or (3) a national emergency created by attack upon the United States, its territories or possessions, or its armed forces.

EFFECTIVE DATE

Section 10 of Pub. L. 93–148 provided that: "This joint resolution [this chapter] shall take effect on the date of its enactment [Nov. 7, 1973]."

§ 1542. Consultation; initial and regular consultations

The President in every possible instance shall consult with Congress before introducing United States Armed Forces into hostilities or into situations where imminent involvement in hostilities is clearly indicated by the circumstances, and after every such introduction shall consult regularly with the Congress until United States Armed Forces are no longer engaged in hostilities or have been removed from such situations.

§ 1543. Reporting requirement

(a) Written report; time of submission; circumstances necessitating submission; information reported

In the absence of a declaration of war, in any case in which United States Armed Forces are introduced—

(1) into hostilities or into situations where imminent involvement in hostilities is clearly indicated by the circumstances;

(2) into the territory, airspace or waters of a foreign nation, while equipped for combat, except for deployments which relate solely to supply, replacement, repair or training of such forces; or

(3) in numbers which substantially enlarge United States Armed Forces equipped for combat already located in a foreign nation;

the President shall submit within 48 hours to the Speaker of the House of Representatives and to the President, pro tempore of the Senate a report, in writing, setting forth—

(A) the circumstances necessitating the introduction of United States Armed Forces;

(B) the constitutional and legislative authority under which such introduction took place; and

(C) the estimated scope and duration of the hostilities or involvement.

(b) Other information reported

The President shall provide such other information as the Congress may request in the fulfillment of its constitutional responsibilities with respect to committing the Nation to war and to the use of United States Armed Forces abroad.

(c) Periodic reports; semiannual requirement

Whenever United States Armed Forces are introduced into hostilities or into any situation described in subsection (a) of this section, the President shall, so long as such armed forces continue to be engaged in such hostilities or situation, report to the Congress periodically on the status of such hostilities or situation as well as on the scope and duration of such hostilities or situation, but in no event shall he report to the Congress less often than once every six months.

§ 1544. Congressional action

(a) Transmittal of report and referral to Congressional Committees; joint request for convening Congress

Each report submitted pursuant to section 1543(a)(1) of this title shall be transmitted to the Speaker of the House of Representatives and to the President pro tempore of the Senate on the same calendar day. Each report so transmitted shall be referred to the Committee on International Relations of the House of Representatives and to the Committee on Foreign Relations of the Senate for appropriate action. If, when the report is transmitted, the Congress has adjourned sine die or has adjourned for any period in excess of three calendar days, the Speaker of the House of Representatives and the President pro tempore of the Senate, if they deem it advisable (or if petitioned by at least 30 percent of the membership of their respective Houses) shall jointly request the President to convene Congress in order that it may consider the report and take appropriate action pursuant to this section.

(b) Termination of use of United States Armed Forces; exceptions; extension period

Within sixty calendar days after a report is submitted or is required to be submitted pursuant to section 1543(a)(1) of this title, whichever is earlier, the President shall terminate any use of United States Armed Forces with respect to which such report was submitted (or required to be submitted), unless the Congress (1) has declared war or has enacted a specific authorization for such use of United States Armed Forces, (2) has extended by law such sixty-day period, or (3) is physically unable to meet as a result of an armed attack upon the United States. Such sixty-day period shall be extended for not more than an additional thirty days if the President determines and certifies to the Congress in writing that unavoidable military necessity respecting the safety of United States Armed Forces requires the continued use of such armed forces in the course of bringing about a prompt removal of such forces.

(c) Concurrent resolution for removal by President of United States Armed Forces

Notwithstanding subsection (b) of this section, at any time that United States Armed Forces are engaged in hostilities outside the territory of the United States, its possessions and territories without a declaration of war or specific statutory authorization, such forces shall be removed by the President if the Congress so directs by concurrent resolution.

§ 1545. Congressional priority procedures for joint resolution or bill

(a) Time requirement; referral to Congressional committee; single report

Any joint resolution or bill introduced pursuant to section 1544(b) of this title at least thirty calendar days before the expiration of the sixty-day period specified in such section shall be referred to the Committee on International Relations of the House of Representatives or the Committee on Foreign Relations of the Senate, as the case may be, and such committee shall report one such joint resolution or bill, together with its recommendations, not later than twenty-four calendar days before the expiration of the sixty-day period specified in such section,

unless the House shall otherwise determine by the yeas and nays.

(b) Pending business; vote

Any joint resolution or bill so reported shall become the pending business of the House in question (in the case of the Senate the time for debate shall be equally divided between the proponents and the opponents), and shall be voted on within three calendar days thereafter, unless such House shall otherwise determine by yeas and nays.

(c) Referral to other House committee

Such a joint resolution or bill passed by one House shall be referred to the committee of the other House named in subsection (a) of this section and shall be reported out not later than fourteen calendar days before the expiration of the sixty-day period specified in section 1544(b) of this title. The joint resolution or bill so reported shall become the pending business of the House in question and shall be voted on within three calendar days after it has been reported, unless such House shall otherwise determine by yeas and nays.

(d) Disagreements between Houses

In the case of any disagreement between the two Houses of Congress with respect to a joint resolution or bill passed by both Houses, conferees shall be promptly appointed and the committee of conference shall make and file a report with respect to such resolution or bill not later than four calendar days before the expiration of the sixty-day period specified in section 1544(b) of this title. In the event the conferees are unable to agree within 48 hours, they shall report back to their respective Houses in disagreement. Notwithstanding any rule in either House concerning the printing of conference reports in the Record or concerning any delay in the consideration of such reports, such report shall be acted on by both Houses not later than the expiration of such sixty-day period.

§ 1546. Congressional priority procedures for concurrent resolution

(a) Referral to Congressional committee; single report

Any concurrent resolution introduced pursuant to section 1544(c) of this title shall be referred to the Committee on International Relations of the House of Representatives or the Committee on Foreign Relations of the Senate, as the case may be, and one such concurrent resolution shall be reported out by such committee together with its recommendations within fifteen calendar days, unless such House shall otherwise determine by the yeas and nays.

(b) Pending business; vote

Any concurrent resolution so reported shall become the pending business of the House in question (in the case of the Senate the time for debate shall be equally divided between the proponents and the opponents) and shall be voted on within three calendar days thereafter, unless such House shall otherwise determine by yeas and nays.

(c) Referral to other House committee

Such a concurrent resolution passed by one House shall be referred to the committee of the other House named in subsection (a) of this section and shall be reported out by such committee together with its recommendations within fifteen calendar days and shall thereupon become the pending business of such House and shall be voted upon within three calendar days, unless such House shall otherwise determine by yeas and nays.

(d) Disagreement between Houses

In the case of any disagreement between the two Houses of Congress with respect to a concurrent resolution passed by both Houses, conferees shall be promptly appointed and the committee of conference shall make and file a report with respect to such concurrent resolution within six calendar days after the legislation is referred to the committee of conference. Notwithstanding any rule in either House concerning the printing of conference reports in the Record or concerning any delay in the consideration of such reports, such report shall be acted on by both Houses not later than six calendar days after the conference report is filed. In the event the conferees are unable to agree within 48 hours, they shall report back to their respective Houses in disagreement.

§ 1547. Interpretation of joint resolution

(a) Inferences from any law or treaty

Authority to introduce United States Armed Forces into hostilities or into situations wherein involvement in hostilities is clearly indicated by the circumstances shall not be inferred—

(1) from any provision of law (whether or not in effect before November 7, 1973), including any provision contained in any appropriation Act, unless such provision specifically authorizes the introduction of United States Armed Forces into hostilities or into such situations and states that it is intended to constitute specific statutory authorization within the meaning of this chapter; or

(2) from any treaty heretofore or hereafter ratified unless such treaty is implemented by legislation specifically authorizing the introduction of United States Armed Forces into hostilities or into such situations and stating that it is intended to constitute specific statutory authorization within the meaning of this chapter.

(b) Joint headquarters operations of high-level military commands

Nothing in this chapter shall be construed to require any further specific statutory authorization to permit members of the United States Armed Forces to participate jointly with members of the armed forces of one or more foreign countries in the headquarters operations of high-level military commands which were established prior to November 7, 1973, and pursuant to the United Nations Charter or any treaty ratified by the United States prior to such date.

(c) Introduction of United States Armed Forces

For purposes of this chapter, the term "introduction of United States Armed Forces" includes the assignment of members of such armed forces to command, coordinate, participate in the movement of, or accompany the regular or irregular military forces of any foreign country or government when such military forces are engaged, or there exists an imminent threat that such forces will become engaged, in hostilities.

(d) Constitutional authorities or existing treaties unaffected; construction against grant of Presidential authority respecting use of United States Armed Forces

Nothing in this chapter—

(1) is intended to alter the constitutional authority of the Congress or of the President, or the provisions of existing treaties; or

(2) shall be construed as granting any authority to the President with respect to the introduction of United States Armed Forces into hostilities or into situations wherein involvement in hostilities is clearly indicated by the circumstances which authority he would not have had in the absence of this chapter.

§ 1548. Separability of provisions

If any provision of this chapter or the application thereof to any person or circumstance is held invalid, the remainder of the chapter and the application of such provision to any other person or circumstance shall not be affected thereby.

Appendix B
Biographies of Major Personalities

Abrams, Creighton William, Jr. (1914–1974)   U.S. Army General. Abrams won fame in World War II and in the Korean War as one of the Army's foremost tank commanders. He served as the deputy chief of staff for operations and vice chief of staff of the Army before becoming deputy to General William Westmoreland at MACV (Military Assistance Command, Vietnam) in 1967. Abrams was responsible for the rural pacification programs that relocated over two million people to "safe military areas." With the departure of Westmoreland in 1968, Abrams assumed command of MACV. He faced the formidable task of implementing the Vietnamization policies of the Nixon administration. He became Army chief of staff in 1972 and died in office two years later.

Acheson, Dean Gooderham (1893–1971)   U.S. secretary of state in the Truman administration, from 1949 to 1952. He was private secretary to Supreme Court Associate Justice Louis D. Brandeis (1919–21), then became a successful lawyer in private practice, and served as undersecretary of the treasury in the Roosevelt administration. Acheson persuaded President Truman to furnish aid to the French who were fighting in Indochina. By 1966 he began expressing serious reservations about U.S. involvement in Vietnam, and by 1968 he was urging President Johnson to stop escalating the war and to seek a negotiated settlement.

Agnew, Spiro Theodore (1918–)   Thirty-ninth vice president of the United States, 1969–1973. While governor of Maryland in 1968, he ran successfully as Richard Nixon's vice presidential running mate. As vice president, Agnew sharply attacked opponents of the Vietnam War as being disloyal and frequently accused the media of biased news coverage. He re-

signed in October 1973, following his indictment for tax evasion.

Aiken, George David (1892–1984)   As a Republican senator from Vermont, Aiken at first supported LBJ's Vietnam War policies, but by 1966 he joined the ranks of the doves. He publicly stated in that year that to save face the president simply should "declare the U.S. the winner and begin de-escalation." Aiken retired from the Senate in 1975 and returned to his farm in Vermont. He described some of his misgivings about the war in his memoirs, *Senate Diary* (1976).

Alvarez, Lt. (j.g.) Everett, Jr. (1937–)   American POW. A native of San Jose, California, Alvarez was a U.S. Navy pilot stationed on the carrier U.S.S. *Constellation* in the South China Sea at the time of the Tonkin Gulf incident in August 1964. Flying an A-4 Skyhawk, he was shot down over North Vietnam on August 5, 1964. He was captured by the North Vietnamese and transferred to the "Hanoi Hilton" prison, where he spent the next eight years as a POW. Alvarez was the first American pilot taken prisoner by the North Vietnamese. He described his ordeal in *Chained Eagle* (1989).

Anson, Robert Sam (1945–)   Journalist, Vietnam War correspondent for *Time* from 1970 to 1971. While traveling to Cambodia in August 1970, he was taken captive by North Vietnamese and Cambodian Khmer Rouge troops and was released unharmed three weeks later. He is the author of several nonfiction books, including *War News: A Young Reporter in Indochina* (1989), which includes an account of his captivity.

Arnett, Peter (1935–)   Journalist. Born and raised in Riverton, New Zealand, Arnett became a stringer for the Associated Press in Vietnam in 1961, and by 1963 he was AP's full-time Southeast Asia correspondent. For the next 10 years he reported from Vietnam, often accompanying combat troops into the jungles and rice paddies. Arnett won a Pulitzer Prize in 1966 for his reporting from Vietnam, and he was one of the few Western correspondents who remained behind after the fall of Saigon on April 30, 1975. In 1981, he joined the Cable News Network (CNN) as its foreign correspondent, and has since covered more than a dozen wars, including the civil war in El Salvador, the fighting in Lebanon and the Persian Gulf War.

Ball, George (1909–)   Undersecretary of state in the Kennedy and Johnson administrations, 1961–66. A strong critic of the Diem regime, Ball was one of those who favored a coup during the discussions before Diem's fall in November 1963. He opposed American involvement in Vietnam during the Johnson administration and argued against the spring 1965 decision to escalate the war. Convinced that he could not change Johnson's policy, Ball resigned in September 1966 and returned to his private law practice. Two years later, he was one of the council of "wise men" Defense Secretary Clark Clifford convened to advocate the de-escalation of the war to LBJ.

Bao Dai (1913–)   The last emperor of Vietnam. Bao Dai succeeded his father in 1925 at the age of 12, but did not ascend the throne until 1932. He cooperated with the Japanese during World War II and abdicated in 1945 to join the Vietminh briefly, then went into exile and returned under the French to rule as head of state from 1949 to 1955. After the Geneva settlement he created a separate South Vietnam. Prime Minister Ngo Dinh Diem ousted him in a rigged referendum in 1955, and Bao Dai retired to France.

Beech, Keyes (1913–1990)   Journalist. A Marine Corps combat correspondent in World War II, Beech joined the *Chicago Daily News* as a foreign correspondent in 1947, and for the next 30 years covered events in the Far East and Southeast Asia. Beech won the Pulitzer Prize for international reporting for his coverage of the Korean War in 1951. While covering the Vietnam War, he was known as a strong proponent of U.S. involvement. Beech remained in Saigon until its fall on April 30, 1975. He is the author of *Not Without the Americans* (1971), a personal account of his reporting from Southeast Asia.

Berrigan, Daniel (1921–)   Roman Catholic priest and antiwar activist. In May 1968, Berrigan, his brother Philip and seven other activists broke into a draft board office in Catonsville, Maryland, and set fire to the draft cards with homemade napalm. As one of the "Catonsville Nine," he was convicted of conspiracy and destruction of government property and was sentenced to three years in prison. He served 18 months in a federal prison, before being paroled for health reasons. After the war, the Berrigans became active in the antinuclear movement.

Berrigan, Philip Francis (1923–)   Roman Catholic priest and antiwar activist. Berrigan was drafted in 1943 and served with the U.S. Army infantry in World War II, receiving a battlefield promotion to second lieutenant. Ordained as a Roman Catholic priest in 1955, he became active in the civil rights movement and, in the 1960s, the antiwar movement. In October 1967, Berrigan entered the Selective Service office in the Baltimore Customs House and poured jars of duck blood onto the draft records. In 1968, while awaiting sentencing for this act, he and his brother Daniel and seven other antiwar activists broke into a draft board in Catonsville, Maryland, and destroyed draft files. Known as one of the Catonsville Nine, he was convicted along with the others of conspiracy and destruction of government property. After he was paroled in 1972, the federal government unsuccessfully prosecuted him for conspiring to kidnap Secretary of State Henry Kissinger and to blow up heating systems of federal buildings in Washington, D.C. After the war, he and Daniel became active in the antinuclear movement.

Braestrup, Peter (1929–)   Journalist, served in the Korean War with the Marines as a platoon leader, attaining the rank of second lieutenant. As a *New York Times* correspondent from 1960 to 1968, he covered events in Algiers, Paris, Bangkok and Washington, D.C. As the *Washington Post*'s Saigon bureau chief, Braestrup covered the siege at Khe Sanh, the 1968 Tet Offensive and the Easter Offensive of 1972. He is the author of the extensive two-volume study *Big Story: How the American Press and Television Reported and Interpreted the Crisis of Tet 1968 in Vietnam and Washington* (1977), a critical analysis of the role played by the media in reporting the Vietnam War.

Browne, Malcolm Wilde (1931–)   Journalist. While in the U.S. Army from 1956 to 1958, he was a Korean correspondent for the *Pacific Stars & Stripes.* He then was correspondent for the Associated Press in Vietnam, 1961–65, and for ABC News, 1965–66. For his Vietnam coverage, Browne won a Pulitzer Prize for international reporting in 1964. Since 1968, Browne has been a *New York Times* correspondent, covering events in South America, Southeast Asia and the Middle East. He is author of *The New Face of War* (1965), a classic journalistic account of the Vietnam War during the early 1960s.

Brown, Sam(uel) Winfred (1943–)   Antiwar activist; founder in 1969 of the Vietnam Moratorium Committee (VMC), an umbrella organization of antiwar groups. Brown organized nationwide "moratoriums" against the war that were held throughout the country on October 15 and November 13–15, 1969. The November "moratorium" was one of the largest antiwar demonstrations in U.S. history, with some 250,000 protesters in attendance at a rally on the Mall in Washington, D.C.

Bui Diem (1923–)   South Vietnamese ambassador to the United States (1966–72). A cousin of President Nguyen Van Thieu, Bui Diem was a northerner by birth, but in 1954, after the Geneva Accords, he fled to the south, where he published an English-language newspaper in Saigon. After the fall of South Vietnam in April 1975, he fled to the United States and opened a delicatessen in Washington, D.C. Bui Diem has since become a resident scholar with the American Enterprise Institute.

Bundy, McGeorge (1919)–)   National Security Affairs adviser in the Kennedy and Johnson administrations. Convinced that the United States must make a strong stand against communism, Bundy was a strong proponent of U.S. involvement in Vietnam. After resigning from office, principally because of his distaste for Johnson's personal style, he began to urge the president privately to wind down the war. Bundy was one of the "wise men" convened by Secretary of Defense Clark Clifford in March 1968 to promote the policy of de-escalation to LBJ.

Bundy, William (1917–)   Assistant secretary of state for Far Eastern Affairs in the Johnson administration and brother of McGeorge Bundy. He was the chief author of the Tonkin Gulf Resolution, which gave the president the right to use American military power without congressional approval, to support any Southeast Asian nation threatened by communist aggression. Bundy was one of the leading hawks of the Johnson administration; he advised against negotiations with North Vietnam and proposed instead a series of escalated military responses, including massive bombings and mining the harbors of the North. By 1967 he opposed further escalation and advised against mining Haiphong Harbor, but he still advised "sticking it out." Bundy resigned from government service in 1969 and later became editor of *Foreign Affairs*.

Bunker, Ellsworth (1894–1984)   U.S. ambassador to South Vietnam, 1967–73. After holding a series of diplomatic posts, Bunker succeeded Henry Cabot Lodge as ambassador to South Vietnam. Throughout his tenure he vigorously supported Johnson's war policy. After the Tet Offensive of January 1968, he declared a U.S. victory even though Vietcong commandos had penetrated his own embassy compound. Bunker supported the 1970 invasion of Cambodia, believing that the destruction of North Vietnamese bases there would give the South Vietnamese Armed Forces more time to take over from withdrawing U.S. troops. After advising at the Paris peace talks, Bunker resigned as ambassador in 1973. He later headed the U.S. team that secured the Panama Canal treaty of 1978.

Burrows, Larry (1926–1971)   Photojournalist. Born in London, Burrows first joined *Life* magazine in 1942, as a darkroom assistant in its London office, and by 1962 he was covering the war in Vietnam. For the next decade, his vivid photographs of men in combat and beleaguered Vietnamese civilians illustrated *Life* articles on the war. Burrows was twice awarded the Overseas Press Club's Robert Capa award for superlative photography. He was killed along with three other journalists in a helicopter crash in Laos on February 10, 1971. To this day, his gripping photographs appear in countless Vietnam War books, articles and documentaries.

Buttinger, Joseph (1906–)   Author and relief worker. Born in Reichersbeurn, Germany, Buttinger immigrated to the United States in 1939 and was active in European refugee relief organizations throughout the 1940s. He was director of the American Friends of Vietnam, a relief organization, from 1955 to 1965 and worked in Vietnam in 1954 and 1958. Buttinger wrote several books about Vietnam, including *Vietnam: A Dragon Embattled* (1967), a comprehensive two-volume history of Vietnam from its earliest beginnings to the fall of the Diem regime in 1963.

Calley, Lieutenant William Laws, Jr. (1943–)   Calley became a platoon leader in the Americal Division after graduating from Officers Candidate School. In 1971, he was convicted of the premeditated murder of Vietnamese civilians at My Lai in March 1968. Other officers and enlisted men were also court-martialed for their roles in the My Lai massacre, but Calley was the only one found guilty of murder in the incident. He was initially sentenced to life imprisonment and dismissed from the U.S. Army. After several appeals, Calley was released on parole in 1974 and given a dishonorable discharge.

Caputo, Philip (1941–)   U.S. Marine Corps officer, journalist and author. Commissioned a lieutenant, Caputo landed at Danang with a battalion of the 9th Marine Expeditionary Brigade on March 8, 1965, the first U.S. combat unit sent to Vietnam. After leaving the Corps in 1967, he became a correspondent for the *Chicago Tribune,* and in 1975 he returned to Vietnam to report on the fall of Saigon. Caputo is the author of *A Rumor of War* (1977), a powerful personal memoir of his tour as an infantryman in Vietnam.

Chapelle, Georgette Meyer [Dickey] (1918– 1965)   Journalist. As a freelance war correspondent, Chapelle had taken scores of gripping photographs of the fighting on the beaches at Okinawa and Iwo Jima during World War II, covered the Korean War and reported on the revolutions in Hungary and Cuba. Her articles appeared in magazines ranging from *Reader's Digest* to *Life* to *National Geographic.* She first arrived in Vietnam in 1961, and periodically reported from there until her untimely death in November 1965. Chapelle was killed after stepping on a Vietcong land mine while accompanying a large-scale U.S. Marine operation near Chu Lai. She was the first woman correspondent to be killed in Vietnam.

Church, Frank Forrester (1924–1984)   Idaho Democrat and senator (1956–80). As a member of the Senate Foreign Relations Committee, Church was critical of U.S. involvement in Vietnam. In 1970, he and Republican Senator John Sherman Cooper introduced an amendment to a foreign military sales bill that would have barred funds for future military operations in Cambodia. It was passed in the Senate but defeated in the House. A modified version was passed in December 1970 as part of a defense appropriations bill. The Cooper-Church Amendment was the first limitation ever passed on the president's power as commander-in-chief during the hostilities. In 1973, Congress passed a bill sponsored by Church and Republican Senator Clifford Case, authorizing a termination of funds for all U.S. combat operations in Indochina. Church was defeated in his bid for reelection in 1980 and died four years later of cancer.

Cleland, Joseph Maxwell (1942–)   Vietnam veteran and Veterans Administration (VA) director in the Carter administration. Cleland enlisted in the Army in 1965 and graduated from paratrooper training school; in 1967, he volunteered for duty in Vietnam. Cleland was only five weeks from completing his tour in 1968, when he was wounded by a grenade as he was jumping off a helicopter. He became a triple amputee, losing his legs and one arm. After 18 months in VA hospitals, he successfully ran for a state senate seat in Georgia, and in 1977 he became, at the age of 34, the youngest man to ever head the VA. Since 1981 he has been the secretary of state of Georgia.

Clifford, Clark McAdams (1906–)   U.S. secretary of defense in the Johnson administration (1968). After a fact-finding trip to Southeast Asia in 1967, Clifford began to question U.S. policy in Vietnam. He succeeded Robert McNamara as secretary of defense and was appointed chairman of the President's Ad Hoc Task Force on Vietnam, which was convened to study a request by the Joint Chiefs of Staff and General Westmoreland for more than 200,000 additional troops. In late March 1968, Clifford assembled a group of senior statesmen, known as the "wise men," to assess U.S. policy in Vietnam. This council met with Johnson on March 26, 1968, and recommended that the U.S. find a way to disengage itself from the war. Clifford returned to his private law practice in 1969, but continued to publicly call for a unilateral U.S. withdrawal from Vietnam.

Cogny, René (1904–1968)   French army officer. As the youngest brigadier general in the French army, Cogny first went to Indochina in 1951 as an aide to General Henri Navarre. He contributed to the planning that locked the French garrison at Dien Bien Phu into its untenable position in the spring of 1954. After commanding French forces in Morocco during the late 1960s, he retired from active service in 1964. Cogny was killed in a passenger jet crash in the Mediterranean on September 11, 1968.

Colby, William Egan (1920–)   Central Intelligence Agency (CIA) officer and later its director, Colby was posted to South Vietnam in 1959 as first secretary of the U.S. Embassy and CIA station chief in Saigon. He was involved in the strategic hamlet program and the recruiting of Montagnard tribesmen by U.S. Special Forces. Colby returned to Washington, D.C., in 1962 to head the CIA's Far Eastern Division, where he presided over the agency's programs throughout Southeast Asia. He returned to Vietnam in 1968 and became deputy commander of the U.S. Military Assistance Command Vietnam, responsible for CORDS (Civil Operations and Rural Development Support) and also for coordinating the Phoenix Program, which was directed at eliminating the Vietcong infrastructure. In 1971, he resigned his post because of the serious illness of his daughter. Colby became director of the CIA in 1973 and retired from the agency in 1976.

Collins, General Joseph Lawton [Lightning Joe] (1896–1987)   U.S. Army chief of staff (1948–53). As a special envoy to Vietnam in 1954, General Collins assisted the newly formed South Vietnamese government in establishing a military training program and in implementing agrarian reforms. He believed that Diem was incapable of successfully leading South Vietnam and recommended that the United States withdraw its support for him. The Eisenhower administration was inclined to continue supporting Diem, believing that there was no better alternative and fearing that replacing him might weaken U.S. influence in South Vietnam. Collins was replaced in May 1955, and he retired from the service a year later.

Conein, Lucien (1919–)   The French-born Conein first served in Vietnam with the OSS (Office of Strategic Services) during World War II. He later joined the CIA as an agent and "dirty tricks" expert. Conein served as a liaison between Ambassador Henry Cabot Lodge and the South Vietnamese generals who overthrew Diem in 1963.

Cooper, John Sherman (1901–1991)   Kentucky Republican and senator (1960–73). Cooper was elected to the Senate in 1960, where he established himself as a liberal Republican with an interest in foreign affairs. He was an early critic of the Vietnam War, and in 1966 he began to criticize the bombing of North Vietnam. He joined Senator Frank Church in 1970 to introduce an amendment to an appropriations bill that would have prohibited the president from spending any funds, without congressional approval, for U.S. troops fighting in Cambodia after July 1, 1970. The Senate passed the measure, but the House deleted the Cooper-Church Amendment from its version of the appropriation bill. A modified version of the amendment was passed by both houses of Congress in December 1970. Cooper retired from the Senate in 1973.

Cronkite, Walter Leland (1916–)   CBS news correspondent and television news anchorman. Cronkite was a war correspondent for United Press International (UPI) during World War II, joined CBS news in 1950, and soon became one of its most prominent reporters. During the Tet Offensive in early 1968, he visited Vietnam, for the first time since 1965, and shortly thereafter reported on nationwide television that the war was not being won and that the United States might have to accept a stalemate. Cronkite's assessment especially irritated President Johnson, who had regarded the distinguished newsman as an administration ally. Cronkite retired from CBS news in 1981 and handed over the evening news anchor chair to Dan Rather.

De Borchgrave, Arnaud (1926–)   Journalist. Born a Belgian count, de Borchgrave fled the Nazis in 1940 and enlisted in the British Navy at the age of 15. He

was a foreign correspondent for *Newsweek* in Vietnam (1951–56, 1963–66, 1971–73). He covered the climactic battle at Dien Bien Phu in 1953, and, although wounded while covering the battle of Hill 400 in September 1966, he managed to file an account of the operation. In 1985, he became managing editor of *The Washington Times*.

De Castries, Christian de la Croix (1902–1991)   French army colonel. He was twice wounded in World War II, captured by the Germans, then escaped from a prisoner-of-war camp on his fourth try. In 1946, as a lieutenant colonel he began his first tour of Indochina. Assigned to command at Dien Bien Phu in December 1953, he stubbornly defended the fortress until it was overtaken by the Vietminh in May of 1954. Colonel de Castries surrendered along with some 10,000 French troops. He was held as a prisoner-of-war for four months until France and the Vietminh came to a negotiated settlement in Geneva. He returned to France as a battlefield hero.

Denton, Admiral Jeremiah, Jr. (1924–)   U.S. Navy pilot and POW. When he was an attack squadron commander in Vietnam in 1965, Denton's jet was shot down in May during a raid 75 miles south of Hanoi. He bailed out and was captured by the North Vietnamese, who held him a prisoner of war for the next seven years. Like many of the other American POWs, he endured confinement in coffin-sized cells, beatings, starvation and years of solitary confinement. Throughout his captivity he remained uncooperative with his captors and ordered his fellow prisoners to do the same. During a televised interview that was shown in the West, Denton blinked the word "torture" in Morse code with his eyelids. Denton received the Navy Cross in 1974 and later went into politics, becoming the first Republican senator from Alabama since Reconstruction. He is the author of *When Hell Was in Session* (1976), a vivid account of his captivity.

Dewey, A. Peter (1917–1945)   Office of Strategic Services (OSS) officer. As a lieutenant colonel in the OSS, Dewey was assigned to Saigon at the end of World War II, where he headed the U.S. mission that cared for Americans interned by the Japanese during the war. He was accidentally killed by the Vietminh on September 26, 1945, when he was mistaken for a French soldier. Dewey was the first American to die in Vietnam.

Diem, Ngo Dinh (1901–1963)   President of South Vietnam (1955–63). Diem was active in Vietnamese politics during the French occupation, serving as chief of Quang Tri Province in 1930–31 and later as minister of justice. He was captured by the Vietminh in September 1945, but Ho Chi Minh personally released him. A devout Catholic, Diem left Vietnam in 1950 and lived for a while in a seminary in New Jersey and later in a monastery in Belgium. He returned to Vietnam in 1954 to become prime minister for Bao Dai, whom he ousted the following year in a rigged referendum. He refused to participate in the elections prescribed under the 1954 Geneva agreement. Diem's regime was troubled from the outset by its incessant struggle with the communists and other rivals for power and by its persecution of the Buddhists, who were a majority. Diem was overthrown and assassinated in November 1963, along with his brother Ngo Dinh Nhu, in a coup d'etat staged by his own generals. It is speculated that the United States, although not directly involved in the coup, did grant its tacit consent.

Don, Tran Van (1917–) South Vietnamese army general and minister of defense. Tran Van Don was one of the organizers of the coup d'etat that ousted President Ngo Dinh Diem in 1963; in 1964 he was appointed minister of defense and continued to hold that post until the fall of Saigon in April 1975, when he managed to escape to the United States. Tran has since worked as a headwaiter and a real estate salesman.

Dong, Pham Van (1906–) Prime minister of North Vietnam. Son of a mandarin, Pham was an early member of the Communist Party and at the age of 24 was imprisoned for seven years by the French for revolutionary activities. He was active in the Vietminh before and during their 1946–54 war with the French. Pham led the Vietminh delegation to the 1954 Geneva Conference and served as North Vietnam's prime minister from 1954 to 1975. He was appointed prime minister of the Socialist Republic of Vietnam in July 1976. Pham resigned as prime minister in 1986 and retired to private life.

Doumer, Paul (1857–1932) Governor-general of French Indochina. Appointed governor-general in 1897, in the next five years Doumer made the colony a profitable economic venture, building roads and bridges and raising revenues by creating an opium monopoly. Doumer was elected president of France in 1931 and a year later was assassinated.

Duan, Le (1908–1986) Senior North Vietnamese official. Born in the central Vietnamese province of Quang Tri, Le Duan quit his job as a railroad employee to become a professional revolutionary and rose swiftly in the Indochina Communist Party. In 1959, he was appointed secretary-general of the Lao Dong (Worker's Party). After the death of Ho Chi

Minh in 1969, he emerged as one of the leading members of the government of North Vietnam. During the war, he was occupied with military and intelligence operations in the south, and it was he who approved the campaign that finally captured Saigon in 1975.

Dulles, John Foster (1888–1959) U.S. secretary of state in the Eisenhower administration. As a strong anticommunist, Dulles favored full support for the French in Indochina. During the siege at Dien Bien Phu in 1954, he proposed using nuclear weapons to defeat the Vietminh. At the Geneva Conference in 1954 Dulles opposed a negotiated settlement that would divide Vietnam.

Dung, Van Tien (1917–) North Vietnamese general. Van Tien Dung became an active communist revolutionary in 1936 and fought in the Vietminh guerrilla movement against the French and Japanese during World War II. In 1954, he commanded the North Vietnamese Army's 320th Division in the siege of Dien Bien Phu. Van Tien was appointed chief of staff of the North Vietnamese Army in 1963 and promoted to senior general in 1974. He planned and led the invasion that conquered South Vietnam in 1975. After the war, he wrote a popular book about the campaign, *Our Great Spring Victory* (1977), and in 1980 he replaced General Vo Nguyen Giap as minister of national defense.

Durbrow, Elbridge (1903–) U.S. ambassador to South Vietnam (1957–61). Durbrow publicly expressed confidence in the Diem regime but privately warned of its lack of leadership. In April 1961, President Kennedy replaced him with Frederick Nolting, and Dubrow returned to the State Department, remaining there until his retirement in 1968.

Eisenhower, Dwight David (1890–1969) Thirty-fourth president of the United States (1953–61). As a U.S. Army general in World War II, Eisenhower won fame as the Supreme Allied Commander in Europe. As president, Eisenhower decided against intervening to help France during the siege at Dien Bien Phu in 1954. Lack of allied support, especially from Great Britain, and lack of congressional support played a major role in his decision. After the Geneva Conference, he dispatched economic and military aid to the government of South Vietnam and military advisers to the newly formed South Vietnamese Armed Forces.

Ellsberg, Daniel (1931–) U.S. Defense Department analyst. After working for the RAND Corporation, Ellsberg joined the Defense Department in 1964. In 1967, he participated in the group that compiled the "Pentagon Papers," a massive report commissioned by then-Defense Secretary Robert McNamara to study America's involvement in Southeast Asia. The study convinced Ellsberg that the war was unjust and had also been mismanaged by several U.S. presidents. He gave copies of the documents to *The New York Times*, which began publishing excerpts from them in 1971. He was tried twice for theft of government property and espionage, but all charges were dropped in 1973, when a second mistrial was declared because of government involvement in the burglary of his former psychiatrist's office and wiretapping of his telephone conversations.

Ely, Paul (1897–1975)   French general. As a high-ranking military officer who commanded French forces in Indochina in 1954, Ely flew to Washington, D.C., to request American support; he warned that the destruction of Dien Bien Phu was likely, but assistance was not forthcoming. He departed South Vietnam in spring 1955, then served as a chief staff officer for defense until his retirement in 1961.

Esper, George (1933–)   Associated Press correspondent in Vietnam from 1965 to 1975, and the wire service's Saigon bureau chief from 1973 to 1975. Esper was one of the few Western reporters who remained in Saigon on April 30, 1975, to cover the fall of South Vietnam. He received the Associated Press Managing Editors Association's annual top performance award in 1975 for his coverage of Saigon and its aftermath. Esper covered the Persian Gulf War in 1991 as a special correspondent for the AP.

Fall, Bernard B. (1926–1967)   Journalist. A native of France, Fall first visited Indochina in 1953 to observe the end of French rule there, and then settled in the United States, where he earned a doctorate in history from Syracuse University. Fall frequently returned to Vietnam to research seven books and some 250 magazine articles about Vietnam and Southeast Asia. His ambition was to become, in his own words, "the foremost military writer of my generation." As a journalist who always sought out firsthand experience, Fall chose to accompany a U.S. Marine patrol along a road in Vietnam known as "The Street Without Joy," where on February 21, 1967, he was killed by a Vietcong mine. Fall's best-known works include: *Street Without Joy: Insurgency in Indochina* (1961), *The Two Vietnams: A Political and Military Analysis* (1963) and *Hell in a Very Small Place: The Siege of Dien Bien Phu* (1966).

Fitzgerald, Frances (1940–)   Journalist. As a freelancer, Fitzgerald first went to Vietnam in 1966. She contributed articles on Vietnam to several magazines, including the *Atlantic*, *The New York Times Magazine* and *The New Yorker*. She is author of *Fire in the Lake: The Vietnamese and the Americans in Vietnam* (1972), a definitive book on Vietnamese culture and American involvement. Fitzgerald won the Pulitzer Prize for contemporary affairs writing and the Bancroft Prize for history in 1973.

Ford, Gerald Rudolph (1913–)   Thirty-eighth president of the United States. Elected to the U.S. House of Representatives in 1948, Ford served there until appointed vice president by President Richard Nixon in October 1973. He assumed the presidency when Nixon resigned on August 9, 1974. As the communists pushed toward Saigon in 1975 in violation of the 1973 Paris Accords, Ford made no serious attempt to intervene, although the United States had promised it would do so if the North Vietnamese violated the accords. By this time, a majority of the American public and Congress wanted to end U.S. involvement in Vietnam. In 1976, Ford was defeated for reelection by Governor Jimmy Carter of Georgia.

Fulbright, William James (1905–)   Arkansas Democrat and senator (1944–74). As chairman of the Foreign Relations Committee, Fulbright introduced the Tonkin Gulf Resolution in 1964 on behalf of President Johnson. Fulbright soon turned against the war, however, and voiced criticism of LBJ's Vietnam policy during televised hearings of the Senate Foreign Relations Committee in February 1966. Then in April 1966, he gave a series of lectures at Johns Hopkins University in which he referred to "the arrogance of power" demonstrated by the United States in Vietnam. Fulbright lost the Democratic senatorial primary to Governor Dale Bumpers in 1974. He returned to private law practice in Washington, D.C.

Gavin, James (1907–)   U.S. Army general. During World War II, Gavin rose through the ranks to the grade of lieutenant general, winning the Silver Star. He landed with the 82d Airborne Division at Normandy and commanded the division in airborne operations in the Netherlands. Gavin retired from active service in the early 1960s. As one of the few American military figures who voiced any real reservations about U.S. involvement in Vietnam, Gavin testified in 1966 before the Senate Foreign Relations Committee's hearings on Vietnam and expressed the view that LBJ should stop escalating the war.

Giap, General Vo Nguyen (1912–)   Commander in chief of the North Vietnamese army and minister of defense. Born in central Vietnam, Giap was one of the founding members of the Indochinese Communist Party in 1929. He became a history teacher and studied law at the University of Hanoi, while engaging in communist activities. He created the Vietminh military organization that defeated the French at Dien Bien Phu in 1954, which effectively won Vietnam its independence. Although known as a brilliant military strategist, he made his share of mistakes, including the Tet Offensive and his attempt to turn Khe Sanh into another Dien Bien Phu. After a series of failures during the 1972 Spring Offensive, Giap was eased out of power and replaced by NVA chief of staff, Senior General Van Tien Dung. In 1980, Giap was formally replaced as minister of defense by General Dung and has since retired from public life.

Goldwater, Barry Morse (1909–) Arizona republican and senator (1952–86). As the leading spokesman for the Republican Party's conservative wing, Goldwater ran for president in 1964 but lost the election to President Johnson by a landslide. Goldwater was one of the Senate's strongest proponents of U.S. involvement in Vietnam, opposing all congressional efforts to legislate an end to the war. In April 1975, as communist forces approached Saigon, he called for increased military assistance to South Vietnam, but the Senate Armed Services Committee rejected his proposals. Goldwater decided not to seek reelection in 1986 and retired from public life.

Gravel, Mike (1930–) Alaska Democrat and senator (1968–80). Gravel gained national attention in spring 1971 when he entered portions of the *Pentagon Papers* into the Senate record. In June 1972, the Supreme Court ruled 5 to 4 that Gravel could not be subpoenaed or indicted for reading the documents to the press. He continued to take an active role in opposing the Vietnam War, including supporting attempts to cut off funding for the war. In 1980, Gravel lost Alaska's Democratic senatorial primary.

Gruening, Ernest Henry (1887–1974) Alaska Democrat and senator (1959–68). Gruening was one of the earliest congressional critics of U.S. involvement in Vietnam. In August 1964, he and Senator Wayne Morse (D–Ore.) cast the only two votes against the Tonkin Gulf Resolution. Gruening, Morse and Senator Gaylord Nelson (D–Wisc.) consistently voted against military appropriations for the war, and were often the only senators opposing such expenditures from 1965 to 1968. In 1965, he addressed the first large-scale demonstration against the war in Washington, D.C. He believed that Vietnam was not essential to American security, and called for negotiations with Hanoi. At age 81, Gruening lost the 1968 Democratic senatorial primary.

Hackworth, David H. (1931–) U.S. Army colonel. Hackworth enlisted in the Army at the age of 15, and earned a battlefield commission at age 20 during the Korean War. In 1965, as commander with the 101st Airborne Division, he led the first U.S. paratroopers into Vietnam. He became the youngest full colonel in Vietnam, but refused further promotions, believing that he would better serve the military by remaining on the battlefield. He retired from the service in 1971, after his advice for using counterinsurgency operations, rather than conventional tactics, went unheeded. He also publicly criticized top military commanders for being more interested in their promotions than in winning the war. He was the author, with Julie Sherman, of *About Face: The Odyssey of an American Warrior* (1989), a vivid memoir of his Army career and also a critique of the military tactics used in the Vietnam War. Hackworth is the most decorated living soldier, with more than 100 military awards, 70 of which are combat-related.

Haig, Alexander (1924–) U.S. Army general and National Security staff aide. Haig saw action in Vietnam as commander of the First Battalion, 26th Infantry, in the mid-1960s. In 1970, as a military adviser on the National Security Council, he undertook a series of trips to Vietnam to provide President Nixon with a firsthand assessment of conditions there. During the final phase of the cease-fire talks in 1972, Haig was engaged in full-scale shuttle diplomacy between Washington and the Thieu government of South Vietnam. He is credited with finally convincing Thieu to acquiesce to the 1973 cease-fire. Haig served briefly as President Ronald Reagan's secretary of state in 1981 and ran unsuccessfully in the Republican presidential primaries in 1984 and 1988.

Halberstam, David (1934–) Journalist. As *The New York Times* correspondent in Vietnam from 1962 to 1964, Halberstam received national attention when he reported on the battle at Ap Bac in January 1963, during which a South Vietnamese division was defeated by the Vietcong. President Kennedy suggested to *Times* publisher Arthur Ochs Sulzberger that Halberstam should be reassigned because he was "too close to the story." Sulzberger refused to follow Kennedy's suggestion. For his reporting in Vietnam, Halberstam won a Pulitzer Prize in 1964. Halberstam's first book, *The Making of a Quagmire* (1965), is a personal account of military operations and political events in Vietnam during the Diem regime. He has gone on to write several bestselling and critically acclaimed non-fiction works, including *The Best and the Brightest* (1972), *The Powers That Be* (1979) and *The Next Century* (1991).

Harkins, Paul Donald (1904–1985)   U.S. Army general and first commander of the U.S. Military Assistance Command, Vietnam (COMUSMACV) (1962–64). He supervised the advisory effort in Vietnam ordered by President Kennedy and established the structure that would continue throughout the war. Harkins was a strong supporter of the Diem regime, while U.S. Ambassador Henry Cabot Lodge supported the generals who eventually deposed and assassinated Diem. He acquired notoriety for his insistence on sending optimistic reports from Saigon to Washington. In 1964, Harkins was replaced by his deputy, General William C. Westmoreland, and retired from the service that year.

Harriman, William Averell (1891–1986)   U.S. ambassador at large. From 1961 to 1963, Harriman served as assistant secretary of state for Far Eastern Affairs and was instrumental in authorizing American support for the overthrow of Diem in 1963. In 1965, President Johnson appointed Harriman ambassador at large with the primary responsibility of handling Southeast Asia affairs. He was the chief U.S. negotiator at the Paris peace talks from 1968 to 1969, when he was succeeded by Henry Cabot Lodge.

Hatfield, Mark Odum (1922–)   Oregon Republican and senator (1966–). Hatfield was elected to the U.S. Senate on an antiwar platform and during the Nixon administration, the Republican Hatfield was one of the outspoken doves in the Senate. In May 1970, he cosponsored with Democratic Senator George McGovern an amendment to an arms appropriation bill that would have cut off spending for the Vietnam War after December 31, 1971. The McGovern-Hatfield Amendment was defeated twice in the Senate. He also advocated replacing the draft with an all-volunteer army.

Hayden, Tom Emmett (1940–)   Antiwar activist. Hayden was one of the key organizers of the demonstrations outside the Democratic National Convention in Chicago in August 1968. He was subsequently indicted along with six others for crossing state lines with the intention to riot. As one of the so-called "Chicago Seven," he was found guilty along with all of the other defendants, but the convictions were eventually overturned. Hayden was once married to antiwar activist and actress Jane Fonda. He was elected to the California State Assembly in 1982 and was reelected throughout the 1980s and in 1990.

Herr, Michael (1946–)   Journalist. Herr covered the Vietnam War for *Esquire* magazine from 1967 to 1968. Ten years later, his book *Dispatches* (1977), based upon his *Esquire* articles, was published and was hailed by critics as perhaps the most stunning and brilliant personal account to have been written about the Vietnam War. Herr, with Francis Ford Coppola and John Milius, wrote the screenplay of the Vietnam War film *Apocalypse Now* (1979), inspired by Joseph Conrad's *Heart of Darkness.*

Higgins, Marguerite (1920–1966)   Journalist. As a war correspondent for the *New York Herald Tribune,* Higgins covered World War II and the Korean War. She was the first woman to win a Pulitzer Prize for foreign reporting, awarded her in 1951 for her coverage of the Korean War. In the early 1960s, she reported from Saigon, covering such stories as the Buddhist demonstrations. She was an outspoken supporter of Diem and of U.S. involvement in Vietnam, and she often criticized other reporters for giving negative assessments of the Diem regime and the war effort. Author of *War in Korea: The Reporting of a Woman Combat Correspondent* (1951), which was a bestseller, and *Our Vietnam Nightmare* (1965). She died on January 3, 1966, at the age of 45, from a tropical infection she had been exposed to in Vietnam.

Hilsman, Roger (1919–)   U.S. State Department official in the Kennedy administration. As director of the State Department's Bureau of Intelligence and Research, Hilsman was responsible for analyzing current foreign developments, including events in Southeast Asia. As one of the architects of Kennedy's Vietnam policy, he advocated counterinsurgency methods in Vietnam to win the hearts and minds of the people. At odds with President Johnson's Vietnam policy, he resigned in 1964.

Ho Chi Minh (1890–1969)   President of North Vietnam (1954–69). Ho Chi Minh ("He Who Enlightens") was one of the many aliases of Nguyen Tat Thanh, born in Nghe An Province in the French protectorate of Annam (central Vietnam). In 1912, he left Vietnam to travel the world, and in 1917 he moved to Paris, where, under the alias Nguyen Ai Quoc ("Nguyen, the Patriot"), he became a founding member of the French Communist Party in 1920. He went to Moscow four years later and became a communist agent in China in 1925. In 1930, he founded the Indochina Communist Party in Hong Kong, but did not return to Vietnam until 1941, when he created the Vietminh and adopted his most famous alias, Ho Chi Minh. He proclaimed Vietnam's independence from France in September 1945, then fought the French for the next nine years, finally defeating them at Dien Bien Phu. In 1954, he became president and premier of North Vietnam, and remained in that office until his death, directing the war effort against the United States and the south, as much as his health would permit, never wavering in his pursuit of his goal for reunification.

Hoffmann, Abbie (1936–1989) Antiwar activist. Known for his irreverent protest activities, Hoffman gained national attention in October 1967, when he participated in an antiwar march in Washington, D.C., and led a ceremony to "levitate" the Pentagon off its foundation. For his activities at the antiwar demonstrations in Chicago during the National Democratic Convention in 1968, Hoffman along with six others was indicted by a federal grand jury for crossing state lines with the intent to riot. As one of the so-called Chicago Seven, he was convicted after a tumultuous trial. In 1972, his verdict was overturned on appeals. Hoffman was arrested in 1973 on cocaine charges, then jumped bail and lived as a fugitive until 1980, when he surrendered to authorities. After serving a short prison term, he settled in Upstate New York, where he became an environmental activist. His death on April 12, 1989, was an apparent suicide.

Humphrey, Hubert Horatio (1911–1978) Minnesota Democrat and senator (1948–64, 1970–78) and vice president under President Johnson (1965–69). Although he privately expressed misgivings about LBJ's Vietnam policy, Humphrey promoted the president's war out of a sense of loyalty. In his 1969 bid for the presidency, Humphrey tried to distance himself from Johnson, but he lost to Richard Nixon by less than 1% of the popular vote. In 1970, he won the Senate seat vacated by Eugene McCarthy and was reelected in 1976, and died of cancer two years later.

Johnson, Lyndon Baines [LBJ] (1908–1973) Thirty-sixth president of the United States. Elected to the U.S. House of Representatives as a Democrat in 1938, Johnson served four terms there before being elected to the U.S. Senate in 1948; he eventually became Senate majority leader. In 1960, he was chosen by John F. Kennedy as his vice presidential running mate. Upon Kennedy's assassination in November 1963, Johnson assumed the presidency. During the first several months of his presidency, Johnson sought to continue the Southeast Asia policy that Kennedy had initiated, and he retained many of JFK's top foreign-policy advisers. An adherent of the "domino theory," he escalated the war in Vietnam from 1965 until March 31, 1968, when he announced a unilateral halt to air and naval bombardment of North Vietnam in the hopes of reaching a negotiated settlement with Hanoi. At the end of his speech, Johnson announced

his decision not to seek reelection. Three days later North Vietnam agreed to open negotiations in Paris. He died on January 22, 1973, five days before the Paris Agreement on Ending the War and Restoring Peace in Vietnam was signed.

Just, Ward Swift (1935–) Journalist. As a *Washington Post* foreign correspondent, Just covered Vietnam from 1965 to 1967. He was wounded in an ambush while on a reconnaissance patrol with American troops near the Cambodian border. After a few days of recuperation, Just returned to covering the war for the *Post*. Author of *To What End: Report from Vietnam* (1968), a classic journalist's account of the Vietnam War, and several novels, including *Stringer* (1974) and *Jack Gance* (1989). Since 1970, Just has devoted himself exclusively to writing fiction.

Karnow, Stanley (1925–) Journalist. As a correspondent for *Time* magazine, Karnow first went to Vietnam in 1959 and subsequently reported from there for *The Washington Post*. Karnow served as a chief correspondent for PBS's 13-part documentary film series "Vietnam: A Television History" (1983) and was the author of the program's bestselling companion book. Karnow's *Vietnam: A History* (1983) is considered one of the most comprehensive and fair-minded histories of the Vietnam War, by scholars, book reviewers and by many of its participants.

Kennan, George Frost (1904–) U.S. State Department official. As head of the State Department's newly created Policy Planning staff in the late 1940s, Kennan is credited with conceiving the policy of "containment," the idea that Soviet expansion could be thwarted by firm but measured Western resistance throughout the world. In the mid-1960s, Kennan emerged as an important critic of American policy in Vietnam. He explained in several articles and speeches that his "containment" policy did not apply to places like Vietnam, and he argued that Vietnam was not vital to American strategic or diplomatic interests. Kennan received national attention when he appeared before Senator Fulbright's Foreign Relations Committee during its televised hearings on Vietnam in 1966.

Kennedy, John Fitzgerald [JFK] (1917–1963) Thirty-fifth president of the United States. A World War II Navy hero, Kennedy was elected to the U.S. House of Representatives in 1946 and to the Senate in 1952. In 1960, Kennedy defeated Richard M. Nixon by less than 100,000 votes to become the first Roman Catholic ever elected president. Alarmed by reports of the deteriorating military situation in South Vietnam, Kennedy sent General Maxwell Taylor on a two-week tour of the country in 1961. When Taylor recommended sending some 8,000 combat troops to Vietnam, Kennedy at first resisted, fearing that the commitment might embroil the United States directly in the war. Concerned with losing South Vietnam to the communists, Kennedy eventually agreed to send military advisers, and by the time of his assassination in November 1963, there were some 16,000 U.S. personnel operating in Vietnam.

Kennedy, Robert Fitzgerald [RFK] (1925–1968)   New York Democrat and senator (1964–68). RFK served as chief counsel of the Senate Rackets Committee in the 1950s and became attorney general in 1961, after his brother John won the 1960 presidential election. Although he was initially a supporter of Johnson's Vietnam War policies, RFK became increasingly critical of the war effort following LBJ's resumption of the bombing of North Vietnam in 1966. In 1968, he ran in the Democratic presidential primaries, and on June 4, after defeating Senator Eugene McCarthy in the California primary, he was shot; he died two days later.

Kerry, John Forbes (1943–)   U.S. Navy officer, Vietnam Veterans Against the War (VVAW) representative and U.S. Democratic senator from Massachusetts (1981–). Kerry graduated from Yale University in 1966 and enlisted in the U.S. Navy that same year. From 1966 to 1968 he served as a lieutenant on a U.S. destroyer off the coast of Vietnam, earning both the Silver and Bronze stars for heroism in combat. Upon his return to the United States he became active in the antiwar movement as national coordinator of the Vietnam Veterans Against the War (VVAW). After the war, he graduated from Boston University law school, spent three years as an assistant district attorney and two years as a lieutenant governor of Massachusetts. In 1984, Kerry was elected to the U.S. Senate, then reelected in 1990. He is a member of the Vietnam Veterans in Congress (VVIC), a bipartisan caucus group that is active in ensuring recognition and benefits for Vietnamese veterans.

King, Martin Luther, Jr. (1929–1968)   Civil rights leader and antiwar activist. King helped establish the Southern Christian Leadership Conference in 1957 to coordinate civil rights protests in the South, and he became its first president. King began to speak out against American involvement in Vietnam in 1965, and in 1967 he was openly identified with the antiwar movement. King's protests against the war alienated him from President Johnson, who supported many civil rights reforms. King was assassinated by a sniper on April 4, 1968.

Kissinger, Henry Alfred (1923–)   National Security adviser and secretary of state in the Nixon and Ford administrations. While teaching government at Harvard University Kissinger gained recognition outside academic circles by writing on foreign affairs and defense issues. President Nixon appointed Kissinger as his National Security advisor in 1969. He was a central figure in the Paris peace talks, and intermittently held secret talks with North Vietnamese diplomats. He was named secretary of state by Nixon in 1973, and was awarded the Nobel Prize for peace that same year for his efforts in securing the Paris Peace Accords.

Komer, Robert William (1922–)   CIA analyst and deputy to the commander of MACV (1967–68). Komer was responsible for advising President Johnson on Vietnam. After studying the French efforts, he became convinced that the war could succeed if the United States gained the support of the Vietnamese people. In 1967, he organized the CORDS (Civilian Operations and Rural Development Support) and the Phoenix programs, operations aimed at identifying and killing known or suspected communist leaders or sympathizers.

Kovic, Ron (1946–)   Vietnam veteran and author. Kovic enlisted in the U.S. Marines in 1964, attained the rank of sergeant and was wounded in action in 1967, after refusing to retreat during a firefight. Left paralyzed from the midchest down, he was awarded the Purple Heart and a Bronze Star for trying to help another wounded Marine "with complete disregard for his own safety." After his release from a deteriorating VA hospital in New York City, he became active with the Vietnam Veterans Against the War (VVAW). After years of anguish and depression, Kovic wrote *Born on the Fourth of July* (1976), a powerful autobiographical account of his experiences in Vietnam and in VA hospitals after his return, and also about his growing involvement in the antiwar movement. He cowrote with director Oliver Stone, also a Vietnam combat veteran, the 1989 Academy Award–winning film of the same title, based on his book.

Krulak, Victor H. (1913–)   U.S. Marine Corps general. In 1962, Krulak was named special adviser to the Joint Chiefs of Staff for counterinsurgency and special activities, and in 1963 he went to Vietnam along with Joseph Mendenhall, a State Department official, on a fact-finding mission for President Kennedy. He reported to Kennedy that the South Vietnamese military was making some progress against the Vietcong, while Mendenhall described a government close to collapse. It was after this meeting that President Kennedy asked, "You two did visit the same country, didn't you?" In 1964, he was promoted to commanding general of the Fleet Marine Force in the Pacific, and he retired from the service in 1968.

Ky, Nguyen Cao (1930–)   Prime minister of South Vietnam (1965–67). Born in Son Tay, near Hanoi, in the French protectorate of Tonkin, Ky was drafted into the Vietnamese National Army (a French-supported force raised to combat the Vietminh) in 1950. He attained the rank of lieutenant and in 1954 graduated from flight school. Ky, known as a flamboyant pilot, then became a lieutenant general in the newly formed South Vietnamese Air Force. He served as prime minister of South Vietnam from 1965 until the elections of 1967, when he stepped down to become vice president under Thieu. He served in that position until 1971, when he chose not to run as an opposition candidate against President Thieu. On April 29, 1975, during Operation Frequent Wind, he flew from Saigon to join the U.S. evacuation fleet. Ky relocated to California, where he opened a liquor store.

Laird, Melvin Robert (1922–)   Secretary of defense in the Nixon administration (1969–72). Elected to the House of Representatives in 1952, Laird served there until he was appointed secretary of defense by President Nixon in 1969. He strongly favored American troop withdrawal from Vietnam and invented the term "Vietnamization." Laird chose not to serve in the second Nixon administration and returned to private life.

Lansdale, Edward Geary (1908–1987)   U.S. Army general. During World War II Lansdale served in the Office of Strategic Services (OSS) and as an Army Air Force officer in the Pacific Theater. From 1954 to 1956, under CIA auspices, he served as an adviser to Diem, helping the leader to consolidate his power. His methods for gaining the loyalty of the peasants included "psychwar," psychological warfare operations such as dropping leaflets and making loudspeaker broadcasts to lower the enemy's morale. He was notorious enough to be immortalized in Graham Greene's novel *The Quiet American* (1955). In 1965, Lansdale returned to Vietnam as assistant to Ambassador Henry Cabot Lodge. For the next three years he was involved in implementing rural pacification programs and directing counterinsurgency operations.

Lattre de Tassigny, Jean Joseph de (1889–1952)   French army general. He saw combat in World War I and fought with the French Underground in World War II. After the war, he became chief of staff and was the prime mover behind building the Vietnamese National Army (Vietnamese fighting against the Vietminh) in French Indochina. He returned to France in 1951 because of illness and died in January 1952.

Lin, Maya Ying (1960–)   Designer of the Vietnam Veterans Memorial in Washington, D.C. While a Yale University architecture student in 1981, Lin had her design for the proposed Vietnam Veterans Memorial chosen out of 1,420 entries. Her design called for two polished black granite walls cut into a hillside, with the names of those service men and women killed or missing in Vietnam engraved into the surface—nearly 58,000 names in all. The wall was dedicated on Veterans Day weekend, on November 13, 1982, and has become the most visited memorial in Washington. Lin has since designed the Civil Rights memorial in Montgomery, Alabama, which was dedicated in November 1989.

Lodge, Henry Cabot (1902–1985)   U.S. ambassador to South Vietnam (1963–67). After serving in the Army in Europe during World War II, Lodge was elected to the U.S. Senate in 1946 but was defeated by John F. Kennedy in 1952. He ran unsuccessfully as Richard Nixon's vice presidential running mate in 1960. Kennedy, seeking bipartisan support for his Vietnam policy, appointed Lodge U.S. ambassador to South Vietnam in June 1963. It is speculated that Lodge played a key role in the overthrow of the Diem regime. In March 1968, Lodge was named to the Senior Advisory Group, the council of "wise men" who ultimately persuaded President Johnson to deescalate the war. He was appointed by President Nixon in 1969 as chief negotiator at the Paris peace conference, and from 1970 until 1977, Lodge served as the President's Special Envoy to the Vatican.

Lucas, Jim Griffing (1914–1970)   Journalist. As a U.S. Marine Corps correspondent during World War II, Lucas covered the battles at Guadalcanal, Tarawa, and Iwo Jima, winning eight battle stars, the Bronze Star and the Distinguished Service Award. As a Scripps-Howard newspaper correspondent, he covered the Korean War for 26 months and was with French troops during the Indochina War of 1946–54. In the early 1960s, he was the official U.S. Embassy spokesman in Saigon. Lucas wrote several books about his experiences, including *Dateline: Vietnam* (1966).

McCarthy, Eugene Joseph (1916–)   Minnesota Democrat and U.S. senator (1952–71). McCarthy voted for the Tonkin Gulf Resolution in 1964 and avoided any public criticism of Johnson's war policy until a few years later. By 1967, he had emerged as one of the foremost critics of the Vietnam War and announced that he was running for the Democratic presidential nomination as a "peace candidate," calling for a negotiated settlement of the war. Crowds of young McCarthy campaign workers, dubbed the "children's crusade," spread into the primary states, and in March 1968, to the surprise of everyone, McCarthy came within a few hundred votes of beating LBJ in the New Hampshire primary. As a result of McCarthy's strong showing, Senator Robert Kennedy declared his candidacy, and two weeks later LBJ announced he would not seek reelection. McCarthy's campaign was soon overshadowed by Kennedy, who went on to win most of the Democratic primaries until his assassination in California in June. McCarthy was defeated by Hubert Humphrey at the Democratic National Convention in Chicago. He retired from the Senate in 1971.

McGovern, George Stanley (1922–) South Dakota Democrat and U.S. senator (1962–81). McGovern was an early, outspoken critic of the Vietnam War. In 1965, he proposed a negotiated solution, including a gradual withdrawal of U.S. troops and a UN-supervised truce. With Senator Mark Hatfield, in 1970 he appended an end-the-war amendment to a military appropriations bill that would have legislated the withdrawal of all U.S. combat troops from Southeast Asia by the end of 1971. It was rejected by the Senate in 1970 and again in 1971. McGovern won the Democratic presidential nomination in 1972 and ran on a platform calling for an immediate end to the Vietnam War. He was overwhelmingly defeated by President Nixon, who carried every state but Massachusetts. McGovern retired from the Senate in 1981.

McNamara, Robert Strange (1916–) U.S. secretary of defense (1961–68). As a Harvard Business School graduate who directed a statistical control system for the U.S. Army during World War II, McNamara became known as one of the "whiz kids" (young computer systems analysts), and joined Ford Motor Company after the war, becoming its president in 1960. As secretary of defense under Kennedy and Johnson, he was instrumental in shaping U.S. policy in Vietnam. Following attacks on U.S. bases in Vietnam in February 1965, he joined with other members of the National Security Council in advocating retaliatory air strikes against North Vietnam. In July of that year he approved General Westmoreland's request for 185,000 combat troops to be sent to Vietnam by the end of 1965. The issue of bombing increasingly became a source of controversy between McNamara

and the Joint Chiefs of Staff, who argued that the defense secretary placed unnecessary restrictions on U.S. air power. In October 1966, after visiting Vietnam for the eighth time, McNamara publicly supported LBJ's war policy, but privately expressed doubts about the military prospects. By 1967, he began, fruitlessly, to look for diplomatic solutions. McNamara resigned in 1968 to become president of the World Bank.

Mansfield, Mike [Michael] Joseph (1903–) Montana Democrat and U.S. senator (1952–76). A college professor turned politician, Mansfield became the Senate majority leader in 1961. Although he initially supported Johnson's Vietnam policy, he eventually turned against the war effort. Following a fact-finding trip to Vietnam in 1966, he privately tried to persuade LBJ that a military victory was not possible. When Johnson responded with escalation, Mansfield publicly criticized the war. During the Nixon administration he emerged as a leading Democratic critic of the president's Vietnam policy. Mansfield was particularly concerned about preserving Congress's constitutional war-making powers. In 1971, he introduced an end-the-war bill that passed in the Senate but failed in the House. Mansfield retired from the Senate in 1976, and in 1977 President Carter appointed him ambassador to Japan.

Martin, Graham Anderson (1912–1990) U.S. ambassador to South Vietnam (1973–75). Martin replaced Ellsworth Bunker in June 1973 at the Saigon post. Although he had been advised for weeks in early 1975 of the communist preparations for an attack on Saigon, he persisted in his belief that a political solution was still possible. Ignoring the signs of an inevitable communist victory, Martin failed to make adequate preparations for the evacuation of U.S. and South Vietnamese government personnel. The result was a chaotic pullout, in which many South Vietnamese who worked for the United States were abandoned. Martin was one of the last Americans to leave Saigon on the morning of April 30, 1975, after President Ford had canceled further evacuation.

Mecklin, John Marin (1918–1971) Journalist. As a war correspondent for the *Chicago Sun* during World War II, Mecklin covered the landings at Sicily and Normandy. He joined *Time* magazine as a foreign correspondent in the late 1950s and reported from the Mideast and West Germany. In 1961, he took a leave of absence from *Time* to become the U.S. Information Service press officer in Saigon. He returned to *Time* in 1964 and later became an editor at *Fortune*.

He is the author of *Mission in Torment: An Intimate Account of the U.S. Role in Vietnam* (1965), a memoir of his experiences in Vietnam.

Mendes-France, Pierre (1907–1982)   Prime Minister of France (1954–55). Mendes-France was elected prime minister in June 1954, a month after the fall of Dien Bien Phu and in the midst of the Geneva Conference. He promised to reach a settlement in Geneva within four weeks or to resign. In the final hour, he honored his pledge and made an agreement with the Vietminh. Nevertheless, a year later he was voted out of office.

Minh, Duong Van [Big Minh] (1916–)   South Vietnamese general. Known as "Big Minh" because of his size, the French-trained soldier first came into prominence in 1956, when as a Diem loyalist he was instrumental in breaking the Hoa Hao sect, an anti-Diem group, and executing its leader. By 1963, he had become disaffected with the Diem regime and joined the generals plotting the president's overthrow. He is reportedly the one who gave approval for Diem's assassination. After taking control of the South Vietnamese government as head of the Military Revolution Council, Minh himself was deposed two months later. For the next four years he lived in exile. In April 1975, he became briefly the nominal head of state, and as such surrendered to the communists entering Saigon on April 30, 1975. He was permitted to immigrate to France in 1983.

Mohr, Charles Henry (1929–1989)   Journalist. As a *Time* correspondent in Vietnam in 1963, Mohr resigned from the magazine after it refused to publish his reports because they conflicted with those issued by the government. He then joined *The New York Times* and covered Vietnam until 1970. He was the first correspondent wounded in the war—by shrapnel in the leg in 1965—and one of three awarded the Bronze Star for trying to rescue a severely wounded Marine under heavy fire during the Tet Offensive of 1968. Mohr was one of the few reporters who not only provided graphic accounts of the fighting taking place in the jungle outposts, but also analyzed the strategic conduct and policies of the war.

Moorer, Thomas Hinman (1912–)   U.S. admiral, named commander-in-chief in the Pacific Fleet on June 26, 1964, a few weeks before the Gulf of Tonkin incident. Moorer was promoted to commander-in-chief of the Atlantic Command in 1965, and in 1967, he became chief of naval operations. He was appointed chairman of the Joint Chiefs of Staff in 1970. As chairman, he played a major role in withdrawing U.S. forces from Vietnam and in the "Vietnamiza-tion" of the war. He also coordinated the mining of Haiphong Harbor and the bombing of Hanoi in 1972. Admiral Moorer retired from the service in 1974.

Morse, Wayne Lyman (1900–1974)   Oregon Democrat and U.S. senator (1942–68). Morse was one of the earliest and most outspoken critics of American military involvement in Vietnam. Only he and Senator Ernest Gruening of Alaska voted against the Tonkin Gulf Resolution in August 1964. Throughout the 1960s, he asserted that the conflict in Vietnam was a civil war and that the U.S. was intervening on behalf of a despotic South Vietnamese regime that had little popular support. He denounced LBJ for pursuing a war without congressional approval, and in 1966, he introduced an amendment to repeal the Tonkin Gulf Resolution, which was defeated. Morse lost his reelection bid in 1968.

Muller, Robert O. (1946–)   Vietnam veteran and founder of the Vietnam Veterans of America (VVA). Muller enlisted in the U.S. Marines in 1967, attained the rank of lieutenant, and was seriously wounded in action, becoming paralyzed from the waist down. After spending months in VA hospitals, he earned a law degree from Hofstra in 1974, and in 1978 he founded the Vietnam Veterans of America. The VVA has grown into the largest national service organization devoted exclusively to Vietnam-era veterans. The congressionally chartered organization has nearly 500 chapters in 48 states, and it has successfully lobbied on behalf of its constituents.

Navarre, General Henri (1898–1954)   Commander in chief of French forces in Indochina (1953–54). Underrating his opponent, General Vo Nguyen Giap, Navarre failed to predict the big communist offensive on the garrison at Dien Bien Phu. During the battle itself, Navarre, comfortably ensconced in Saigon, failed to commit reinforcements and materiel to the besieged French forces, which were outnumbered. After the ensuing defeat in May 1954, the French government hastened its efforts to negotiate with the Vietminh.

Nhu, Ngo Dinh (1910–1963)   Head of the South Vietnamese government's secret police and younger brother of President Ngo Dinh Diem. He controlled the organization called the Cao Lao, which attempted to suppress any signs of disloyalty to the Diem regime. He was assassinated with his brother in the coup d'etat of November 1963.

Nhu, Madame Ngo Dinh (1924–)   Unofficial First Lady of South Vietnam. Daughter of an aristocratic and thoroughly Gallicized family, she married Ngo

Dinh Nhu, younger brother of President Ngo Dinh Diem, in 1944. She served as the first lady of South Vietnam, since the president was unmarried. Madame Nhu first attracted the world's notice with her considerable beauty and glamour, but her callous remarks about the anti-Diem self-immolations in 1963 brought her negative attention. After the assassination of Diem and her husband on November 2, 1963, she went into exile in Rome.

Nixon, Richard Milhous (1913–)   Thirty-seventh president of the United States. Nixon was elected to the House of Representatives in 1946 and the Senate in 1950, and served as vice president under President Eisenhower (1952–60). Defeated in his bid for the presidency in 1960 by John F. Kennedy, he ran successfully in 1968, defeating Senator Hubert Humphrey. Soon after taking office, he proclaimed a policy of "Vietnamization," slowly reducing U.S. troop strength while attempting to build up the South Vietnamese military. When Paris negotiations stalled in December 1972 over the future of South Vietnam, Nixon ordered an intensive bombing of Hanoi. After an 11-day air campaign, the North Vietnamese resumed talks, and on January 27, 1973, the Paris Peace Accords were signed. Implicated in the Watergate scandal, Nixon chose to resign from office on August 9, 1974, rather than face impeachment hearings. Since leaving office, Nixon has published several books, including his memoirs and *No More Vietnams* (1985), in which he coins the phrase, the "Vietnam syndrome," meaning a paralysis that prevents the nation from playing a decisive role in international affairs.

Nol, General Lon (1913–)   Premier of Cambodia (1970–75). As Cambodian defense minister, Lon Nol led the coup d'etat that ousted Prince Norodom Sihanouk from power in March 1970. Although he announced a policy of "active neutrality," Lon Nol lacked the ability to maintain Cambodia's neutrality. Ultimately, he did little to halt the advance of the Khmer Rouge, which launched a reign of terror upon one-third of the Cambodian population. Cambodia slid toward civil war and chaos. For a time, with massive U.S. aid his army was able to hold off the rebels, but in 1975 Phnom Penh fell, and Lon Nol fled to exile in Hawaii before the victorious forces of Pol Pot, architect of the worst genocidal bloodbaths in history, took control of Cambodia.

Nolting, Frederick Ernest, Jr. (1911–)   U.S. ambassador to South Vietnam (1961–63). From 1957 to 1961 Nolting was deputy chief of the U.S. delegation to NATO, then was appointed ambassador to South Vietnam in 1961 by President Kennedy. Unable to

convince Diem to implement reforms and to curb his attacks against Buddhist monks, Nolting was replaced by Henry Cabot Lodge in August 1963. He retired from government service in 1964.

O'Brien, Tim (1946–)   Vietnam veteran and author. O'Brien was drafted into the U.S. Army and from 1969 to 1970 served a tour of duty in Vietnam, most of it with an infantry platoon. He is the author of *If I Die in a Combat Zone, Box Me Up and Send Me Home* (1973), a personal memoir hailed by critics as the book that "brilliantly and quietly evokes the footsoldier's daily life in the foxholes and paddies." O'Brien has subsequently written three Vietnam War–related novels, which also have received much praise, including *Northern Lights* (1974), *Going After Cacciato* (1978) and *The Things They Carried* (1990).

Page, Tim (1944–)   Photojournalist. A native of England, Page began his career at the age of 18, covering the civil war in Laos and the communist guerrilla activities in Thailand for United Press International (UPI). He first arrived in Vietnam in 1965, and soon his graphic photographs began appearing regularly in *Time* and *Life*. Page was known as a photographer who would go anywhere, fly in anything, snap the shutter under any conditions, and when hit, as he was more than once, go at it again in bandages. He came close to death in 1969, when he was hit by shrapnel from an exploding land mine, but miraculously he recovered after spending 18 months in rehabilitation. To this day, Page's stunning combat photos continue to illustrate scores of Vietnam War articles, books and documentaries. He is the author of *Page After Page* (1988) a memoir of his experiences as a news photographer.

Patti, Major Archimedes L.A. (1913–)   Director of Office of Strategic Services (OSS) in Indochina during World War II. Patti assisted Ho Chi Minh's guerrillas in fighting the Japanese, and as an OSS representative, in late 1945 he spent several months with the communist leader and helped him draft the Vietnamese declaration of independence, based on America's own. His book *Why Viet Nam? Prelude to America's Albatross* (1981) discusses some of the earliest events that led up to full American intervention in Vietnam.

Pike, Douglas Eugene (1924–)   U.S. diplomat and author. Pike earned a B.A. from the University of California in 1953 and an M.A. from American University in Washington, D.C., in 1958. He was a U.S. Foreign Service officer in Saigon from 1960 until the early 1970s and was generally regarded as the U.S. government's leading analyst of Vietnamese communist affairs during the war. Pike is the author of several books on Vietnam; among the best known are *Viet Cong: The Organization and Techniques of the National Liberation Front of South Vietnam* (1966) and *War, Peace and the Viet Cong* (1969). Since 1981, he has been director of the Indochina Archive at the University of California at Berkeley, one of the world's largest collections of documentary materials on Vietnam, Laos and Cambodia.

Pol Pot (1928?–)   Cambodian premier (1975–78). Pol Pot is the pseudonym of Saloth (or Salot) Sar, a Cambodian communist leader, who in the mid-1970s led an almost unprecedented genocidal war on the people of his country (now called Kampuchea), slaughtering an estimated two million Cambodians. Pol Pot became secretary of the Cambodian Communist Party in 1963, the same year that he organized the Khmer Rouge, a communist guerrilla army that overthrew the Lon Nol government in April 1975. In an effort to make Cambodia an agricultural utopia and to eliminate "intellectuals," the entire population of Phnom Penh was forcibly evacuated by the Khmer Rouge and placed under forced labor in the countryside. Pol Pot was ousted from power by the Vietnamese invasion in late 1978.

Quang, Tri (1922–)   A Buddhist monk, Tri Quang headed Vietnam's Central Buddhist Association and led opposition to President Diem in 1963, including the self-immolation of monks. In 1966, he formed an alliance with opponents of Prime Minister Ky; as in 1963, there was violence in the streets. Tri Quang was arrested as a communist and soon thereafter the Buddhist movement lost its momentum. When the communists took control in 1975, he was put under house arrest and banished to a monastery.

Radford, Admiral Arthur William (1896–1973)   Chairman of the Joint Chiefs of Staff (1953–57). As a staunch anticommunist, Radford was a strong proponent of American intervention to rescue the French at the besieged garrison at Dien Bien Phu in spring 1954. He was overruled by President Eisenhower because of the lack of congressional and allied support. He retired from active service in 1955.

Rostow, Walt Whitman (1916–)   National Security adviser in the Johnson administration (1966–68). As an aide to National Security adviser McGeorge Bundy in the early 1960s, Rostow advocated a strong U.S. diplomatic and military role in Vietnam to combat communist insurgencies. As Johnson's National Security adviser he was an optimistic proponent of escalation and opposed any halt in the bombing of North Vietnam until LBJ proposed it in March 1968.

He returned to the academic community when Nixon took office in 1969.

Rubin, Jerry (1938–)   Antiwar activist. In 1968, he joined with Abbie Hoffman in forming the Youth International Party, or "Yippies," a group of anti-establishment revolutionaries and antiwar activists. As one of the so-called Chicago Seven, he was convicted of conspiracy to riot at the Democratic National Convention in Chicago in 1968, but in 1972 the verdict was overturned on appeal. By the early 1980s, Rubin had become a successful stockbroker on Wall Street.

Rusk, Dean David (1909–)   U.S. secretary of state in the Kennedy and Johnson administrations (1961–69). Rusk consistently favored strong American military involvement in Vietnam, including more troop commitments and more bombing, meanwhile opposing negotiations with Hanoi. Rusk was also a major public defender of Johnson's war policy, often appearing before Senate Foreign Relations Committee hearings on Vietnam. After leaving office in 1969, he became a professor of international law at the University of Georgia.

Safer, Morley (1931–)   Journalist. A native of Toronto, Canada, Safer worked for the Canadian Broadcasting Company (CBC) before joining CBS News as foreign correspondent in 1964. Reporting from Vietnam in August 1965, Safer reported that he had seen 150 dwellings in the hamlet of Cam Ne burned by the Marines. The story aroused controversy in the Johnson administration, and Pentagon officials contended that Safer "grossly exaggerated" the facts, insisting that American troops do not purposely harm Vietnamese civilians. Safer spent the next two years covering the Vietnam War, then in the late 1960s he was transferred to the Mideast and Europe. Since 1970, he has been a coeditor of the CBS News Program "60 Minutes." He published *Flashbacks* (1990), an account of his return visit to Vietnam in 1989.

Sainteny, Jean (1907–1978)   French ambassador at large. As a former banker and French colonial official in Hanoi, Sainteny was sent to Vietnam by de Gaulle in 1945 to negotiate on behalf of the French with Ho Chi Minh. Twenty-four years later, in 1969, Sainteny acted as an intermediary between the Nixon administration and Ho Chi Minh. He also arranged the secret talks between Kissinger and Le Duc Tho in Paris in 1972, which would finally end the war.

Salisbury, Harrison Evans (1908–)   Journalist. Salisbury was a *New York Times* foreign correspondent in Moscow (1949–54), winner of the Pulitzer Prize for international reporting in 1955 and assistant managing editor of the *Times* in the 1960s. Salisbury visited Hanoi in December 1966, and in his dispatches he mentioned that, contrary to American official accounts, the bombing was hitting nonmilitary targets and inflicting civilian casualties. His reports triggered an intense debate between government officials and the press. Johnson administration officials finally admitted that although U.S. policy was to attack only military targets, civilian areas were in fact accidentally struck. Salisbury is the author of several books, including *Behind the Lines: Hanoi, December 23, 1966–January 7, 1967* (1967).

Schanberg, Sidney Hillel (1934–)   Journalist. As a *New York Times* correspondent, Schanberg covered the Vietnam War and the fighting in Cambodia from 1973 to 1975. He won the George Polk Memorial Award for his coverage of the fall of Phnom Penh in 1975. The highly dramatic and realistic film *The Killing Fields* (1984), directed by Roland Jaffe, was based on Schanberg's reporting from Cambodia. Schanberg is author of *The Death and Life of Dith Pranh* (1985), a vivid memoir of his experiences covering Cambodia after the American evacuation and the savage advance of the Khmer Rouge.

Scruggs, Jan C. (1950–)   Vietnam veteran and founder of the Vietnam Veterans Memorial. Scruggs, an Army rifleman with the 199th Light Infantry Brigade (1969–70) who was seriously wounded in action, conceived of the idea for a Vietnam Veterans Memorial in 1979—then set out to raise money for the construction of a monument in Washington, D.C. He began the fund with a $2,500 donation of his own, then succeeded in gaining congressional authorization and raised $7 million for its construction. On Veterans Day weekend, on November 13, 1982, a memorial consisting of two polished black granite walls, engraved with the names of the nearly 58,000 service men and women either killed or missing in Vietnam, was dedicated. Designed in 1981 by 21-year-old Yale University architectural student Maya Ying Lin, the wall has become the most visited memorial in Washington, D.C.

Shaplen, Robert Modell (1917–1988) Journalist. Shaplen was a World War II Pacific correspondent for *Newsweek*, and he first visited Saigon in 1946. He began covering the Vietnam War as an Asian correspondent for *The New Yorker* in 1962, and for the next two decades he frequently reported from Southeast Asia. He is author of several well-known books on

the war, including *The Lost Revolution* (1965), *Time Out of Hand: Revolution and Reaction in Southeast Asia (1970)*, *The Road from War* (1970) and *Bitter Victory* (1986).

Sharp, Admiral Ulysses S. Grant (1906–)   Commander-in-chief of the Pacific Fleet (CINCPACFLT) in 1963, Sharp controlled the Seventh Fleet's aerial operations over North Vietnam and Laos. Promoted to commander-in-chief of the Pacific Command (CINCPAC) on June 30, 1964, a month before the Tonkin Gulf incident, Sharp vigorously promoted air raids against North Vietnam and was responsible for executing Operation Rolling Thunder. In July 1968, he retired from active duty, and he later criticized government officials for mismanaging the war, particularly Defense Secretary Robert McNamara. Sharp once proclaimed, "The war was lost in Washington, not on the battlefield."

Sheehan, Neil (1936–)   Journalist. Sheehan enlisted in the U.S. Army in 1958 and served in Korea and Japan as an Army journalist. He was United Press International's Saigon Bureau chief from 1962 to 1964 and a *New York Times* correspondent from 1965 to 1971, covering the Vietnam War from 1965 to 1966; the Pentagon from 1966 to 1968; and the White House from 1968 to 1969. In 1971, Sheehan obtained the "Pentagon Papers" for *The Times*. He is also author of the Pulitzer Prize–winning biography *A Bright Shining Lie: John Paul Vann and America in Vietnam* (1988).

Sihanouk, Norodom (1922–)   Cambodian premier (1947–70). Born into the royal family of Cambodia, the French-educated Sihanouk was enthroned as king of Cambodia in 1941. Following the French reoccupation of Indochina after World War II, Sihanouk announced a limited monarchy, and he was elected as head of state in 1947. Throughout the Vietnam War he worked tirelessly to preserve Cambodia's neutrality, but while he was traveling abroad in March 1970, his government was overthrown by Cambodian General Lon Nol. For the next 20 years he lived in exile in China. Then, in November 1991, Sihanouk returned to Cambodia as president of the Supreme National Council, the organization comprising representatives of the Cambodian government and the three resistance groups, including the Khmer Rouge, who signed the October 1991 peace treaty designed to end Cambodia's 13-year-old civil war.

Snepp, Frank Warren, III (1943–)   A CIA analyst, Snepp served two tours of duty at the U.S. Embassy in Saigon (1969–71, 1972–75), where he was responsible for directing an informant network, handling interrogations and conducting CIA briefings. Snepp remained in Saigon until its collapse on April 29, 1975. He resigned from the agency the following year, after making several futile attempts to generate interest in an official after-action report. Snepp's controversial book, *Decent Interval: An Insider's Account of Saigon's Indecent End Told by the CIA's Chief Strategy Analyst in Vietnam* (1977), describes in vivid detail the events leading up to and culminating in the fall of Saigon.

Spock, Benjamin McLaine (1903–) Pediatrician and antiwar activist. Spock, author of the phenomenal bestseller *The Common Sense Book of Baby and Child Care* (1946), was convicted in 1968 along with Yale University Chaplain William Sloane Coffin Jr. of counseling young men to resist the draft, but the convictions were overturned the following year. Spock was a key organizer and speaker at the November 15, 1969, demonstration in Washington, D.C.; one of the largest antiwar protests in the nation's history, it attracted some 250,000 people.

Stennis, John Cornelius (1901–) Mississippi Democrat and U.S. senator (1947–88). As chairman of the Armed Services Committee in 1969 and in the early 1970s, Stennis advocated intensified bombing of North Vietnam and expressed the opinion that the war effort should be managed by the military. Although he supported President Nixon's Vietnam policy, he feared that the war might set a precedent for the Executive to wage war without congressional approval. Consequently, he and Senator Jacob Javits cosponsored the resolution known as the War Powers Act in 1971. In November 1973, Congress overrode Nixon's veto and passed the resolution. Stennis retired from the Senate in 1988.

Stockdale, James Bond (1924–) U.S. Navy fighter pilot and POW. Stockdale was shot down in September 1965 while on a bombing mission over North Vietnam. As an air group commander, he was the highest-ranking naval officer held as a POW in Vietnam. During his captivity, he devised a simple tap code for communication with other American POWs. As a leader of secret resistance groups he was often subject to grueling torture and solitary confinement. He was awarded the Congressional Medal of Honor in 1976 for his "valiant leadership and extraordinary courage in a hostile environment." He retired from the service in 1979 as one of the most highly decorated officers in the history of the Navy.

Sully, Francois (1927–1971) Journalist. A native of France, Sully covered the French Indochina war for *Time* magazine and was one of the last correspondents to leave the besieged fort at Dien Bien Phu in 1954. He became a Southeast Asia correspondent for *Newsweek* in 1961 and was expelled from South Vietnam a year later by Diem because his reporting conflicted with the official account of events. Sully returned to Vietnam in 1964, and for the next decade covered the war with the unique perspective of having sources throughout Vietnamese society—from privates and officers to politicians inside the presidential palace. Sully was killed along with a top South Vietnamese commander in a helicopter crash on February 23, 1971. At the time of his death, he had been in Vietnam longer than any other correspondent.

Taylor, General Maxwell Davenport (1901–1987) Chairman of the Joint Chiefs of Staff (1962–64) and U.S. ambassador to South Vietnam (1965). During World War II and the Korean War Taylor won fame within the military for his innovative concept of airborne operations. As President Kennedy's favorite general, Taylor headed a fact-finding mission to Vietnam in 1961. His recommendations led to the first significant escalation of U.S. military involvement in the area. In March 1968, he was one of the members of the Senior Advisory Group convened to advise LBJ on the course of the war. Taylor was opposed to the policy of deescalation recommended by a majority of the "wise men." He returned to private life in 1969.

Thieu, Nguyen Van (1923–) President of South Vietnam (1967–75). Thieu played a role in the coup d'etat against Diem in 1963, and in another coup in 1965, in which he became military chief of state. With considerable back-stage maneuvering, he was elected president of South Vietnam in 1967 and 1971. Although he battled the communists with undeniable dedication, he failed to combat the corruption that crippled his regime. Thieu resigned on April 25, 1975, a few days before the fall of Saigon, and fled the country, eventually settling in Great Britain.

Tho, Le Duc (1912?–1990) North Vietnam's chief negotiator at the Paris peace talks (1968–73). Born in the French protectorate of Tonkin in northern Vietnam, Le Duc Tho was a founding member of the Indochina Communist Party. In the mid-1960s, Tho settled in the south, where he directed insurgency operations. In 1968, he became the chief negotiator for the North Vietnamese in the Paris peace talks. Henry Kissinger found Tho a tough bargainer, who was prepared if necessary to wait years for a favorable settlement. He was awarded the Nobel Prize for peace, with Kissinger, in 1973 for achieving the Paris Peace Accords, but Tho refused to accept the award, believing that his goal would be achieved only when North and South Vietnam were unified.

Thompson, Sir Robert (1916–)   British army officer and counterinsurgency consultant. Thompson advocated the concept of "strategic hamlets," which had proved successful in Malaya, and advised General Westmoreland to rely on counterinsurgency tactics rather than on large-scale military operations. Thompson's advice went unheeded by the U.S. military, which would have had to implement the program through the South Vietnamese government.

Thuy, Xuan (1912–1985)   North Vietnamese delegate at the Paris Peace talks. One of the old generation of nationalists, Thuy had fought the French, had been imprisoned by them and met them again as a diplomat. From 1963 to 1965 he was North Vietnam's foreign minister, and he headed the official North Vietnamese delegation to the Paris peace talks from May 1968 until the signing of the cease-fire agreement in January 1973. As Le Duc Tho's deputy, he periodically negotiated with Henry Kissinger.

Tin, Bui (1924–)   North Vietnamese army colonel. Bui Tin fought in major campaigns against the French, including the final battle at Dien Bien Phu. He was a member of the inner circle of the senior communists in Hanoi and rose to the rank of colonel in the North Vietnamese Army (NVA). He became deputy editor of *Quan Do Nhan Dan,* the official NVA newspaper; as a journalist, Bui Tin accompanied the communist forces in their final campaign against Saigon in April 1975. As the highest-ranking communist officer on the scene, Colonel Tin was the one who accepted the surrender of the South Vietnamese government from General "Big" Minh on April 30, 1975. In 1990, after criticizing Hanoi's failure to implement democratic reforms, Bui Tin defected and has since lived in exile in Paris.

Tra, General Tran Van (1916–)   North Vietnamese deputy commander of the Central Organization for South Vietnam (COSVN) (1963–75). As a young man, Tra worked on the railroad until he joined the Vietminh in their fight against the French at the end of World War II. Tra became an infantry commander in 1958 and then was made a major general. By 1963, he was a deputy commander of COSVN, coordinating Vietcong guerrilla attacks in the south, and in 1968, he directed attacks on Saigon during the Tet Offensive. After the fall of Saigon, he published an account that challenged the role played by General Dung's conventional forces in the final offensive of 1975. Soon thereafter the book was banned and Tra was purged for criticizing the communist leadership.

Truman, Harry S (1884–1972)   Thirty-third president of the United States. Elected to the U.S. Senate in 1939, Truman ran as Roosevelt's vice presidential running mate in 1944 and succeeded to the presidency upon Roosevelt's death on April 12, 1945. He established the Truman Doctrine, the policy that gave military aid to those countries threatened by communist expansion. In his second term, when North Korea attacked South Korea in June 1950, he ordered American troops into Korea and also sent the Seventh Fleet into the Taiwan straits to prevent an attack by communist China on Taiwan. Truman established the first U.S. military mission in Indochina in 1950, called the U.S. Military Assistance Advisory-Group-Indochina (MAAG-Indochina), whose mission was to aid the forces of France and the Associated States in Indochina. Thus Truman paved the way for events that would culminate 15 years later in a U.S. combat role in Vietnam.

Vann, John Paul (1924–1972)   U.S. Army lieutenant colonel and senior military adviser. Vann first arrived in Vietnam in 1962 to act as a military adviser to the South Vietnamese Armed Forces' (SVAF) Seventh Division in the Mekong Delta. He aroused controversy in South Vietnam and in the United States in January 1963, when he criticized the SVAF's Seventh Division for retreating before Vietcong forces at the battle of Ap Bac. Vann was reassigned to the Pentagon in 1964 and resigned from the Army that same year after his recommendations for increasing the war effort went unheeded. He returned to Vietnam in 1965 as an Agency for International Development (AID) pacification representative. In 1971, he became senior military adviser of II Corps, comprising the Central Highlands region, and was given authority over all U.S. military forces in that area. Unprecedented in the history of American wars, Vann was in effect a U.S. Army major general. He was killed in a helicopter crash on June 9, 1972, near Kontum in the Central Highlands. His life was the subject of Neil Sheehan's Pulitzer Prize–winning biography *A Bright Shining Lie: John Paul Vann and America in Vietnam* (1988).

Walt, Lewis W. (1913–)   U.S. Marine Corps general. During World War II Walt was a commander at Guadalcanal and twice won the Navy Cross for bravery. In June 1965, he assumed command of the Third Marine Division in Vietnam and supervised the buildup of I Corps until 1967. He returned to the United States and later served as assistant commandant of the Marine Corps. Walt retired from active duty in February 1971.

Webb, Catherine B. [Kate] (1943–)   Journalist. As United Press International's bureau chief in Phnom Penh, Cambodia, in April 1971, Webb was believed to have been killed while covering a battle, and obituaries of her death were published throughout the world. In fact, she had actually been captured by the Vietcong, and after being interrogated and spending nearly a month behind Vietcong lines, she was released unharmed. Webb described her ordeal in *On the Other Side: 23 Days with the Vietcong* (1972).

Webb, James Henry, Jr. (1944–)   Vietnam veteran and author. Webb graduated from the U.S. Naval Academy in 1968 and served in Vietnam with the U.S. Marine Corps from 1968 to 1972. He was an infantry platoon leader, attained the rank of captain and was twice wounded in action. He received the Navy Cross, Silver Star, two Bronze Stars, the National Achievement Medal and two Purple Hearts. Webb graduated from Georgetown University Law School in 1975 and served in the Reagan administration as assistant secretary of defense (1984–87) and secretary of the Navy (1987–88). He is the author of the powerful Vietnam War novel *Fields of Fire* (1978), which follows the progress of a single Marine platoon from its creation to its destruction in combat. His other novels include *A Sense of Honor* (1981) and *Something to Die For* (1991).

Westmoreland, General William Childs (1914–)   U.S. commander of Military Assistance Command, Vietnam (COMUSMACV) (1964–68). A decorated combat hero from World II and Korea, Westmoreland's plan for fighting the communists involved waging a war of attrition with "search-and-destroy" missions into the countryside and the use of helicopters for rapid deployment and evacuation. As the fighting dragged on, Westmoreland continued to give optimistic pronouncements and to request additional troops. In the wake of the Tet Offensive, which was a military victory for the allied forces but was portrayed by the U.S. media as a psychological victory for the north, Westmoreland's optimistic appraisal of the war came under review. When Johnson decided to deescalate the war in March 1968, Westmoreland was reassigned to Washington as chairman of the Joint Chiefs of Staff, a post he held until his retirement in 1972. In 1985, Westmoreland reached an out-of-court settlement with CBS over a news documentary it had aired in 1982 that implied that he had altered military intelligence data, particularly enemy troop strength and "body counts." In exchange for an apologetic statement by CBS, but not a retraction, Westmoreland withdrew the lawsuit.

Weyand, General Frederick Carlton (1916–)   U.S. commander of the Military Assistance Command, Vietnam (COMUSMACV) (1972–73). Weyand served as an intelligence officer during World War II and won the Silver Star for gallantry in action as a combat infantryman during the Korean War. As a general, he commanded an infantry division in Vietnam in 1966, and during the Tet Offensive in 1968, his forces played a major role in repelling the Vietcong attack on Saigon. He succeeded General Creighton Abrams as COMUSMACV in 1972, and as the last MACV commander, he was responsible for winding down the U.S. military presence in Vietnam. Weyand was named Army chief of staff in 1974 and in April 1975 was sent to Vietnam by President Ford to assess the military situation there. He retired from active duty in 1976.

Wheeler, General Earle Gilmore (1908–1975)   Chairman of the Joint Chiefs of Staff (1964–70). Although commissioned in the infantry, Wheeler had no combat experience in either World War II or Korea. As a protege of General Maxwell Taylor, he moved up through the ranks to become President Kennedy's Army chief of staff in 1962 and was named chairman of the Joint Chiefs of Staff in 1964 by President Johnson. Wheeler became the principal figure in Washington overseeing the war in Vietnam, urging escalation and advocating the bombing of the north. By early 1968, however, he concurred with the pessimistic assessment put forth by new Secretary of Defense Clark Clifford. Wheeler retired from active duty in 1970.

Zorthian, Barry (1920–)   U.S. press officer in South Vietnam (1964–68). As a former Voice of America (VOA) reporter, Zorthian headed the United States Information Agency's operations in Saigon and was, in effect, the chief press officer of the U.S. Mission in South Vietnam from 1964 to 1968. Since 1968, he has worked in the private broadcasting industry and as a consultant to foreign embassies.

Zumwalt, Admiral Elmo Russell (1920–)   U.S. commander of naval forces in Vietnam (1968–70). During World War II Zumwalt served on destroyers and minesweepers in the Pacific. As commander of U.S. naval forces in Vietnam, he was responsible for such operations as the River Patrol Force and the Riverine Assault Force as well as the SEABEEs of the Third Naval Construction Brigade. Zumwalt left Vietnam in 1970 to become chief of naval operations. He retired from active duty in 1974. His son Elmo R. Zumwalt III, a Navy officer who commanded a Navy patrol boat in Vietnam, died in 1988 from leukemia thought to be caused by exposure to Agent Orange, which Admiral Zumwalt had ordered sprayed on Vietnam's riverbanks to protect U.S. patrol boats from ambush. Zumwalt senior now speaks out on behalf of Vietnam veterans who were exposed to the defoliant.

Appendix C
Maps

Asian Independence Since 1945

The Burma Road and South China
Routes in the Mid-20th Century

North and South Vietnam

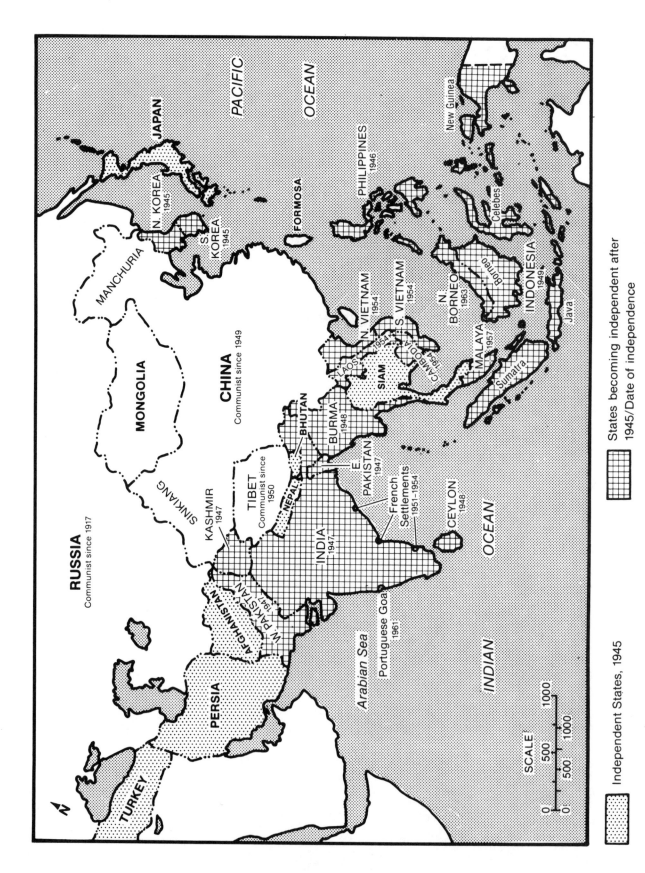

The Burma Road and South China Routes in the Mid-20th Century

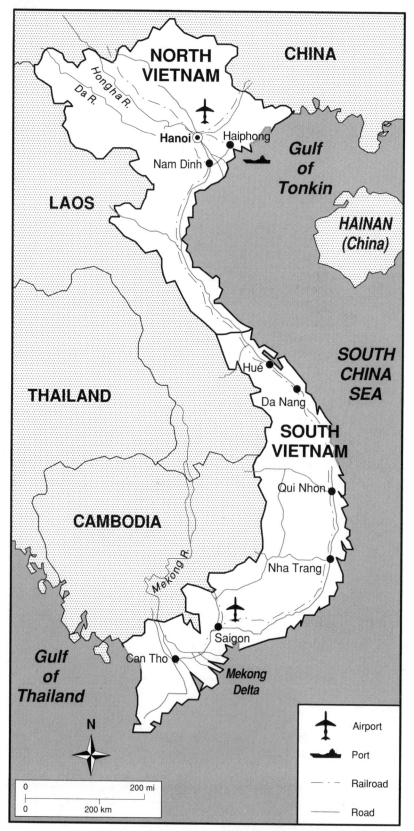

Appendix D

Statistics on the War

Americans who served: 3,330,000
Americans killed: 58,183;   in battle: 47,655
Americans wounded: 303,713

Americans taken prisoner: 839
      Returned: 691
      Escaped: 34
      Died in captivity: 114

Americans still classified as missing (1965–75):   2,273

Americans awarded the Medal of Honor: 239

American Aid to South Vietnam (1965–1975): $24 billion
Direct American expenditures for the war: $165 billion

The Aftermath

	KILLED	WOUNDED
U.S. military:	58,183	303,713
South Vietnamese military:	223,748	570,600
Other allied forces:	5,277	NA
North Vietnamese/Vietcong:	660,000	NA
Civilian:	587,000	3,000,000

Military and civilian dead (all forces):   1,534,208

Indochinese refugees generated: 9,000,000
Indochinese refugees resettled in the U.S. (4/90):   750,000

Living U.S. veterans with Vietnam service (4/85):   2,700,000
Vietnam veterans receiving government compensation (9/91):   650,000
Disabled U.S. Vietnam veterans: 519,000

Land defoliated: 5.2 million acres

All figures estimated
NA—not available
Note: Because of the nature of the Vietnam War and its aftermath, precise statistics on all aspects of the war are difficult to obtain. The figures cited above, many of them approximate, are based upon U.S. government estimates.

Appendix E
Glossary of Names, Acronyms and Terms

AAA Anti-aircraft artillery.

Ace Combat pilot credited with five or more victories over enemy aircraft.

AFVN Armed Forces Vietnam Network radio station.

Agent Orange A highly toxic defoliant sprayed on vegetation.

AID Agency for International Development.

Airborne Soldiers who are qualified as parachutists.

Air Cav Air cavalry; helicopter-borne infantry.

Airmobile Personnel or equipment delivered by helicopter.

Airstrikes Bombing attacks by planes.

Air-to-ground Gunnery or bombing from aircraft against surface targets.

AK-47 Russian-made Kalashnikov automatic rifle. It was the standard rifle of the North Vietnamese army.

All American Common nickname of the 82nd Airborne Division, taken from the two As on its shoulder patch.

Allies Those who fought on the side of the United States and South Vietnam.

Alpha Bravo Slang expression for ambush, taken from the initials AB

Alpha Strike A preplanned bombing mission against given targets in North Vietnam.

Ambush A surprise attack.

Ambush Alley Part of Highway Route 9 near Khe Sanh, nicknamed by U.S. soldiers because of numerous and treacherous Vietcong ambushes.

Annam Central section of Vietnam; French protectorate from 1893 to 1954.

AO A unit's area of operations.

APC Armored personnel carrier.

Arc Light Code term for B-52 bombing missions over North Vietnam. Bombs shook the earth as far as 10 miles away from the target area.

Artillery Weapons too large to be hand carried. The weapons are classified as light (up to a bore of 120mm), medium (121–160mm) and heavy (160mm). Artillery is often called the "king of battle" (from the game of chess).

ARVN Army of the Republic of South Vietnam.

AWOL Absent WithOut Leave, meaning to leave a post or position without permission.

Base camp Known as the rear area; a resupply base for field units and a location for headquarter units, artillery batteries and air fields.

Battalion 400 to 600 soldiers under the command of a lieutenant colonel.

BC Body count.

Beeper Emergency radio in every fighter-bomber crewmember's parachute pack; automatically activated upon ejection or bailout.

B-52 U.S. Air Force high-altitude superbomber, the Boeing Stratofortress, an eight-engine, swept-wing, heavy jet bomber.

Big R Rotation home.

Binh Xuyen The organized crime syndicate that controlled much of the Vietnamese underworld and Saigon police until ousted by President Ngo Dinh Diem's forces in 1955.

Bird Any aircraft; usually referring to helicopters.

Blood Black soldier.

Boat people Refugees fleeing Vietnam by boat after 1975.

Body Bag Plastic bag used for the retrieval of dead bodies from the battlefield

Body Count MACV term for the number of enemy killed, wounded or captured during an operation. It was used by Saigon and Washington as a means of measuring the progress of the war, or success in a mission.

Booby trap A hidden device, usually explosive, used to kill or maim enemy soldiers.

Boonies   The jungle, the field or the bush; short for boondocks.

Bought the farm   Killed.

Bought the ranch   Killed.

Bouncing Betty   A type of mine that, when triggered, is propelled into the air and explodes at groin to head level.

Brigade   2,000 to 3,500 soldiers, under the command of a colonel.

Bronze Star   U.S. military decoration awarded for heroic or meritorious service not involving aerial flights. Heroism is shown by a V on the ribbon.

Buddhism   The main organized religion in Vietnam.

Bush   An infantry term for the field or the "boonies."

Cache   Hidden enemy supplies.

Camp Carroll   A USMC combat base in I Corps named in honor of a U.S. Marine captain killed in action in 1966.

Cam Ranh Bay   A large seaport and an in-country R&R location in Khan Hoa Province, south of the city of Nha Trang in II Corps. A large U.S. Air Force base was located here.

Cao Dai   Religious sect formed in 1925 by a group of civil servants in Cochin China.

Care package   Slang for a package from home containing food and other needed items.

Caribou   Small cargo aircraft of the U.S. Air Force.

Casualty   A person lost to an organization. Battle casualties include dead, wounded or missing.

Cav   Nickname for air cavalry.

Central Highlands   The highlands area in Vietnam, in the western part of II Corps, populated mainly by Montagnard tribes.

Charlie   Vietcong, short for the phonetic representation Victor Charlie.

Cherry   A new, inexperienced soldier.

Chicom   Chinese communist, reference to Chinese-manufactured weapons.

China Beach   A recreational facility and in-country R&R spot. Infantry were given one day mini-R&R here.

Chinook   CH-47, a supply and transport helicopter.

Chopper   Helicopter.

CIA   Central Intelligence Agency or simply "The Agency" or "The Company."

CID   Counterintelligence division/detachment.

CIDG   Civilian Irregular Defense Group, South Vietnamese paramilitary force composed largely of Montagnards.

CINCPAC   Commander-in-chief, Pacific.

CIP   Counter-insurgency plan.

Claymore   An antipersonnel mine used by U.S. troops; when detonated it propelled many small steel cubes in a 60-degree fan-shaped pattern.

Clip   Ammo magazine.

Cluster bomb   A bomb used as an antipersonnel weapon. It held hundreds of pellets that burst outward to maim and kill.

CO   Commanding officer.

Cobra   Heavily armed Army helicopter, a gunship.

Cochin China   Southern section of Vietnam; French colony from 1863 to 1954.

Code of Conduct   Military rules for U.S. soldiers taken prisoner.

Combat Infantry Badge (CIB)   A U.S. Army award limited to infantry under fire in a combat zone.

Company   150 to 220 soldiers under the command of a captain.

Compound   A fortified military installation.

COMUSMACV   Commander, U.S. Military Assistance Command, Vietnam.

Contact   Firing on or being fired upon by the enemy.

CORDS   Civil Operations and Revolutionary Development Support, the U.S. pacification agency in Vietnam.

Corps   Two or more divisions, responsible for the defense of a military region.

COSVN   Central Office for South Vietnam. Communist Party headquarters in South Vietnam, overseen by Hanoi; changed location throughout the war.

Cowboys   Young, urban Vietnamese men who rode motor scooters and were often involved in petty crime.

CP   Command post.

C rations   Standard meal eaten in the field; provided in cartons containing 12 different meals, complete with instant coffee and three cigarettes.

Crispy Critter   Enemy soldier killed through burning to death.

Crunchies   Infantrymen; also, "Ground Pounders" and "Grunts."

Daisy Cutter   A 15,000-pound bomb, designed to clear helicopter landing zones in heavy jungle areas.

DAO   Defense Attache Office; part of the U.S. Embassy to South Vietnam, it replaced the Military Assistance Command, Vietnam.

Dead Man's Zone   Slang for the Demilitarized Zone (DMZ).

Dear John letter   A letter from a girlfriend at home, saying that she wanted to end the relationship.

Delta Tango   Phonetic alphabetization of DT, meaning defensive targets

DEROS   Dee-ros: date eligible for return from overseas; the date a person's tour in Vietnam was estimated to end.

De Soto patrols   U.S. destroyer patrols in Tonkin Gulf, specifically used for espionage.

Dien Bien Phu   Site of French defeat in 1954 signaling the end of their power in Vietnam. Located west of Hanoi on the Laotian border.

Dink   A derogatory reference to enemy forces or Vietnamese civilians.

Distinguished Flying Cross   An award for heroism or extraordinary achievement while participating in aerial flight. The second highest award in the U.S. Air Force.

Distinguished Service Cross   The second highest award for bravery, awarded by the U.S. Army for extraordinary heroism while in action against the enemy.

Distinguished Service Medal   Awarded to a person serving in the Army, Navy, Air Force or Coast Guard who distinguished himself or herself to the government in a duty of great responsibility. It ranks below the Distinguished Service Cross.

Division   An Army or Marine unit of 15,000 to 20,000 soldiers under the command of a general officer.

DMZ   Demilitarized zone, the boundary between North and South Vietnam; established according to the Geneva accords of 1954.

Doc   Affectionate title for enlisted medical aideman.

DOD   Department of Defense.

Doggie   Marine term for infantryman.

Door gunner   The soldier in a helicopter who fires the M-60 machine gun out the open door.

Doughnut Dollies   Red Cross girls.

Doves   Americans who opposed U.S. military intervention in Vietnam.

Downtown   Hanoi area.

Drop zone   Preplanned landing area for parachuted men or equipment.

DRV   Democratic Republic of Vietnam, or North Vietnam.

Dust-off   Medical evacuation by helicopter. The term came from the great amount of dust thrown up by the copter's rotors as the medevacs came in to land.

Elephant grass   Tall, sharp-edged grass found in the highlands of Vietnam.

EM   Enlisted man.

FAC   Forward air controller; coordinates air strikes from the ground and air.

Farmgate   Clandestine U.S. Air Force strike unit in Vietnam (1964).

Fatigues   Standard combat uniform, green in color.

Fireballing   Concentration of large amounts of artillery fire in an area.

Fire base   Temporary artillery encampment used for support of forward ground operations.

Firefight   Small-arms fire exchange with the enemy.

Five o'clock follies   Slang for the daily press briefings that reported enemy body count and allied victories.

Flak jacket   A heavy, fiberglass-filled vest worn for protection from shrapnel.

Flare   Illumination projectile; hand-fired or shot by artillery or mortar or from the air.

FNG   Most common name for newly arrived soldier in Vietnam. It was literally translated as a "Fuckin' new guy."

FO   Forward observer, responsible for calling for and adjusting artillery fire.

Fragging   Killing or attempting to kill a fellow soldier or officer, usually with a fragmentation grenade.

Freedom bird   Passenger airline returning troops from Vietnam to "the World."

Free Fire Zone   Area where artillery could target and fire without restriction. Any persons found within a free fire zone were presumed to be an enemy.

French Expeditionary Corps   Colonial army of France. Made up chiefly of soldiers from French colonies and commanded by an all-volunteer force from France.

Frequent Wind   Military plan for U.S. evacuation of Saigon.

Friendly Fire   Accidental attacks on U.S. or allied soldiers by other U.S. or allied forces.

Ghost Time   Free time off duty.

GI   "General issue" or "government issue"; slang for soldier, used since World War II.

Going Downtown   U.S. Air Force expression for flying a mission against Hanoi.

Good morning, Vietnam   Early morning greeting heard over the Armed Forces Vietnam Network (AFVN radio) in South Vietnam.

Gook   Derogatory term used to refer to a Vietnamese person, especially the enemy.

Gooney Bird   Nickname for C-47 aircraft.

Green   Used to signify "safe," such as Green LZ (safe landing zone).

Green Berets   Nickname for elite Special Forces of the U.S. Army, derived from the green berets of their uniforms.

Green Machine   Military bureaucracy of the U.S. Army.

Grenade   A hand-held bomb with a short delay fuse.

Ground Pounder   Infantryman.

Grunt   A popular nickname for an infantryman in Vietnam; supposedly derived from sound he made when lifting up his rucksack.

Guerrilla An armed element of a paramilitary movement; usually members of small bands of Vietcong soldiers who performed surprise and unconventional attacks. The word guerrilla comes from the Spanish word *guerra*, which means "war."

Gung ho Very enthusiastic and committed.

Gunship A helicopter armed with air-to-ground armaments. This combat helicopter, commonly a UH-1 Huey, was used primarily in support of infantry opeations.

GVN Government of South Vietnam.

Hamlet A small rural village.

Hanoi Hilton Nickname used by American prisoners of war to describe the Hoa Lo Prison in Hanoi.

Hanoi Jane After actress Jane Fonda posed next to an antiaircraft gun while visiting Hanoi in 1972, she was compared by some journalists and soldiers to World War II's "Tokyo Rose"; thus they dubbed her "Hanoi Jane."

Hawks Americans who supported the war effort or who wanted to expand the level of fighting in Vietnam.

Hoa Lo Prison A prison camp in North Vietnam where American POWs were held, also known as the "Hanoi Hilton."

Ho Chi Minh City Name given to Saigon following its takeover by the Vietnamese communists.

Ho Chi Minh Trail The infiltration route used by the North Vietnamese army to move troops and supplies from North Vietnam through Laos and Cambodia to all parts of South Vietnam.

Hootch A dwelling, either temporary or permanent, such as a tent or a Vietnamese home.

Hot Landing Zone A landing zone that was taking fire.

Huey Nickname for UH-1 series utility helicopters.

Humping Marching with a heavy load.

ICC International Control Commission; mandated by the Geneva Accords of 1954 to supervise implementation of the agreement.

I Corps "Eye" Corps, military region comprising five northern provinces of South Vietnam.

II Corps Two Corps, military region comprising Central Highlands and central coastal area of South Vietnam.

III Corps Three Corps, military region comprising provinces surrounding Saigon.

IV Corps Four Corps, military region comprising the Mekong Delta region.

Incoming Enemy artillery, mortars rockets, or grenades coming into a troop location. Used also as a shouted warning to take cover.

In country In Vietnam.

Infantryman A soldier, living and fighting out in the field. They were nicknamed Grunt, Line Doggie, Ground-Pounder, Crunchies, Dogface, Boonie Rat, Foot-Pounder, Foot-Slogger, Gravel-Crusher and Stump-Jumper.

In the field Any combat area or any area outside of an established base camp or town.

"It don't mean nothin' " A phrase said and heard frequently by servicemen, usually meaning the opposite. It was used, for example, on hearing that a buddy had gotten hurt or on receiving a Dear John letter.

Jacob's ladder A rope ladder dropped by a Chinook helicopter and used to descend through difficult foliage or onto rough terrain.

JCS Joint Chiefs of Staff; the senior officers of the U.S. Armed Services.

Jolly Green Giant Nickname for the largest helicopters used for transporting the troops and materiel supplied to American forces.

Jungle boots Combination combat boot and canvas sneaker worn by U.S. troops in tropical climates where leather would rot due to dampness.

Jungle busting Use of a tank or armored vehicle to cut trails through the jungle or other heavy vegetation.

JUSPAO Joint U.S. Public Affairs Office, the American press office in Vietnam.

Khmer Rouge "Red Khmers," the forces of the Cambodian Communist Party.

KIA Killed in action.

Killing zone The area within an ambush where everyone is killed or wounded.

Kit Carson scouts Vietcong defectors recruited by Marines to serve as scouts, interpreters and intelligence agents.

Klick Short for kilometer.

Landing zone (LZ) A small clearing secured temporarily for the landing of helicopters to unload men and cargo.

Lao Dong Party Vietnam Worker's Party, Marxist-Leninist party of North Vietnam. Founded by Ho Chi Minh in May 1951, it absorbed the Vietminh.

Las Vegas A section of Hoa Lo Prison, or the "Hanoi Hilton."

LBJ Ranch The Long Binh Stockade; the last word was changed to make a pun on the initials of President Lyndon Baines Johnson.

Leeches Bloodsucker worms that attached themselves to the human body and were common to parts of Vietnam.

Legs Term used by airborne troops for ground troops.

Lifer Career soldier.

"Light at the end of the tunnel" Term describing

the imminent demise of the Vietcong and North Vietnamese.

Line, the Being on duty with an infantry unit in the field.

Linebacker I Codename for U.S. bombing of North Vietnam resumed under President Nixon in April 1972.

Linebacker II Codename for full-scale U.S. bombing of North Vietnam in December 1972.

Line doggie Infantryman.

Listening post (LP) A position enabling one to detect any sound or movement that might disclose enemy activity in the area.

Long Binh Headquarters for the U.S. Army in Vietnam. This large complex just outside of Bien Hoa in III Corps was established in 1966–67. It was closed on November 11, 1972, ending direct U.S. participation in the Vietnam War.

Long green line Column of infantry advancing through jungle terrain.

LRRP Long Range Reconnaissance Patrol, an elite team usually composed of five to seven men who would go deep into the jungle to observe enemy activity without initiating contact.

Lt. Lieutenant.

Lurp A member of a LRRP (Long Range Reconnaissance Patrol).

LZ Landing zone.

MAAG Military Assistance Advisory Group, the precursor to MACV.

MACV Military Assistance Command, Vietnam; the headquarters that directed most of the American military and pacification effort.

Mamasan A mature Vietnamese woman.

MASH Mobile Army Surgical Hospital.

M-day Moratorium day, antiwar demonstrations.

Medal of Honor (Congressional) The highest award given for gallantry and risk of life above and beyond the call of duty in actions involving armed conflict with an enemy. During the Vietnam War, 238 Medals of Honor were awarded.

Medevac Medical evacuation helicopter used for the rapid evacuation of casualties from the battlefield.

Mekong Delta An area in the southern part of South Vietnam (IV Corps), with rivers, streams and canals.

MG Machine gun.

MIA Missing in action.

MiG All Soviet-built fighter-bombers supplied to the Hanoi Air Force.

Million-dollar wound A noncrippling wound serious enough to warrant return to the United States.

Montagnards Vietnamese term for several tribes of mountain people made up of roughly 60 ethnic groups and totaling about five million people altogether. They inhabited the highlands of Vietnam near the Cambodian border.

Mortar A muzzle-loading cannon that launched low muzzle-velocity shells at high angles.

MP Military Police.

M-16 Standard semi-automatic rifle used by U.S. and ARVN troops after 1966.

M-60 A light machine gun.

Nam, the Slang for Vietnam.

Napalm Incendiary used in Vietnam by French and Americans both as defoliant and antipersonnel weapon.

National Liberation Front (NLF) The South Vietnamese communist organization that led the fight against the Saigon government and its American allies.

Navy Cross The nation's second highest award for bravery. Awarded for extraordinary heroism in military operations against an armed enemy.

NCO Noncomimssioned officer, usually a squad leader or platoon sergeant.

Newbie New soldier.

Newmobe The New Mobilization Committee to End the War.

Next Soldier due for rotation to United States in a few days; also "Short."

NSA National Security Agency.

NSAM Naional Security Council Action Memorandum, presidential policy statements determining action on national security issues.

NSC National Security Council. Responsible for developing defense strategies for the U.S., it is situated in the White House.

Number One Vietnamese slang for the very best, pronounced "numba one."

Number Ten Vietnamese slang for the very worst, pronounced "numba ten."

NVA North Vietnamese regular army.

OP Outpost, manned during daylight hours to watch for enemy movement.

Operation Homecoming Code for the Pentagon procedures aimed at easing the transition of the American POWs from communist prison camps to their homes in the United States.

OPLAN Operations plan.

OPLAN 34 Program calling for covert action against North Vietnam, ordered by President Johnson soon after he took office in early 1964.

Option IV U.S. military plan for evacuation from Saigon.

OSS Office of Strategic Services, the World War II precursor of the CIA

Pacification Any of several programs of the South Vietnamese and U.S. governments to destroy enemy influence in the villages and gain support of civilians for the GVN and stabilize the countryside.

Paper pushers Slang for those with desk jobs.

Paris Agreement Agreement on Ending the War and Restoring the Peace in Vietnam, signed in Paris on January 27, 1963.

Pathet Lao The Laotian communists.

PAVN People's Army of Vietnam (North).

Pentagon East Slang for MACV (Military Assistance Command, Vietnam).

Pentagon Papers A once-secret internal Defense Department study of U.S.-Vietnam relations from 1945 to 1967. Made available to *The New York Times* in 1971 by Daniel Ellsberg and later released by the Pentagon.

PFC Private first class.

Phoenix Program A South Vietnamese intelligence-gathering program advised by CORDS, designed to neutralize the Vietcong infrastructure through identification and arrest of key party cadres.

Platoon 16 to 40 soldiers under the command of a lieutenant.

Point man The man in the lead of a squad or platoon on patrol; constantly exposed to the danger of tripping booby traps or being the first in contact with the enemy.

Poncho liner Nylon insert to the military rain poncho, used as a blanket.

POW Prisoner of war.

PRG People's Revolutionary Government, established in 1969 by the NLF.

Psyops Psychological warfare operations.

Psywar Psychological warfare.

PT Patrol boat.

PTSD Post-traumatic stress disorder.

Puff Nickname for U.S. Air Force fixed-wing gunships. "Puff" was derived from the song "Puff the Magic Dragon," since a gunship firing at night looked like a dragon spitting fire.

Punji stakes Primitive booby traps used by the Vietcong; sharpened bamboo stakes hidden at ground level and often smeared with excrement or poison.

Purple Heart A U.S. military decoration awarded to any member of the armed forces wounded by the enemy in action.

Rabbit Slang used by black soldiers for white soldiers in Vietnam.

R & R Rest and recuperation, a three- to seven-day vacation from the war, given to soldiers once during their one-year tours.

Rangers Elite infantry and commandos.

Reconnaissance (Recon) Small units going out into the jungle to observe and identify enemy activity.

Red Refers to the enemy, as Red (communist) North Vietnam.

Redleg Nickname for an artilleryman.

REMF Rear end [echelon] mother fucker, nickname given by front-line soldiers to men serving in the rear.

Rock 'n' roll To put an M-16 rifle on full automatic fire.

Rolling Thunder Codename for U.S. air campaign against North Vietnam from March 2, 1965 to October 31, 1968.

Rotate Return to the United States at the end of one year in Vietnam.

Rough rider Organized vehicle convoys, often escorted by helicopters and armored vehicles, using Vietnam's roads to supply Marine bases.

Round-eyes Slang used by American soldiers to describe western women.

RPG Rocket-propelled grenade; used by the NVA or VC.

RVN Republic of Vietnam (South)

RVNAF Republic of Vietnam (South) Air or Armed Forces.

Saigon tea An "alcoholic" beverage consisting primarily of Coca Cola.

SAM Surface-to-air missile.

Sampan A Vietnamese peasant boat.

Sapper A Vietcong or North Vietnamese army commando, usually armed with explosives.

Screaming Eagles Nickname for members of the 101st Airborne Division because of the eagle on their shoulder patches.

SDS Students for a Democratic Society.

Seabees Navy construction engineers.

SEALs Sea, Air and Land, the Navy's elite commando troops.

Search-and-destroy Operations designed to find and destroy enemy forces and their base areas and supply caches.

Search and rescue Missions to locate and rescue troops in trouble.

SEATO Southeast Asia Treaty Organization.

17th parallel The line that divided North and South Vietnam. The 17th parallel, flanked by a 15-mile buffer area, was called the Demilitarized Zone or DMZ.

Short, short-timer Having not much time left to serve in Vietnam.

Shrapnel Pieces of sharp, hot metal sent flying by an explosion.

Smart bomb   Laser-guided bombs and electro-optically guided bombs.

Sortie   One flight by one military aircraft.

Spec. 5   Specialist fifth class, equivalent to a sergeant.

Spec. 4   Specialist fourth class, an Army rank equivalent to a corporal.

Special Forces   U.S. soldiers trained in techniques of guerrilla warfare

Spook   Slang for a civilian intelligence agent.

Squad   8 to 10 soldiers under the command of a staff sergeant.

Steve Canyons   Pilots.

Strategic Hamlet Program   Begun in 1961, it concentrated rural villages into fortified villages to separate people from the Vietcong and to gain their allegiance.

Street Without Joy   Nickname for Highway 1, the main supply route in Vietnam.

SVNAF   South Vietnamese Armed Forces.

Tan Son Nhut   The large U.S. air base on the outskirts of Saigon.

Teach-ins   Night-long university meetings at campuses across America regarding Vietnam issues.

Tet   The Vietnamese lunar new year festival, celebrated as a national holiday.

Third force   Generic expression used to designate, especially after the Paris Peace Accords, all the various non-communist organizations in opposition to the regime of South Vietnamese President Thieu.

Ticket-punching   The policy of putting officers into the field for only a six-month period, which helped ensure their promotion but did not expose them to combat for too long a time.

Tiger cages   Term describing cells at the Con Son Correction Center on Con Son Island.

Tiger suits   Striped camouflage jungle fatigues.

Tin pot   Slang for the helmet that GIs were issued. It was also known as a steel pot.

TOC   Tactical Operations Center

Tonkin   Northern section of Vietnam; French protectorate from 1883 to 1954.

Tour of duty   Time spent in Vietnam by U.S. military personnel.

Tracer   Bullet or shell chemically treated to leave a trail of smoke or fire.

Triage   The procedure for deciding the order in which multiple casualties were to be treated in order to maximize the number of survivors.

Triple A   AAA, anti-aircraft artillery, referring to weapons used for shooting aircraft.

Trip wire   A wire or string, placed across a path or trail, which would set off an explosive charge.

Tunnel rat   A U.S. soldier who searched enemy tunnel systems with a flashlight.

Up north   North Vietnam.

USA   United States Army.

USAF   U.S. Air Force.

USAID   United States Agency for International Development.

USIA   United States Information Agency.

USMC   United States Marine Corps.

USN   United States Navy.

USNS   United States Naval Ship.

USO   United Service Organization.

VA   Veterans Administration.

VC   Vietcong.

VCI   Vietcong infrastructure, North Vietnamese army military term for the Vietcong's covert government.

Victor Charlie   Phonetic alphabet version of VC, the popular name for the Vietcong.

Vietcong   Originally a derogatory reference to the NLF, a contraction of Vietnam Cong Sam (Vietnamese communist).

Vietminh   Viet Nam Doc Lap Dong Ming Hoi, or the Vietnamese Independence League.

Vietnamization   President Nixon's program to gradually turn the war over to the South Vietnamese while phasing out American troops.

Vietnam Veterans of America (VVA)   A service organization for Vietnam and Vietnam-era vets. It is chartered by the U.S. Congress, and its main purposes include lobbying for veterans' rights and representing veterans in hearings involving the Department of Veterans Affairs (formerly the VA).

VMC   Vietnam Moratorium Committee.

VNAF   Vietnamese (South) Air Force.

VVAW   Vietnam Veterans Against the War, antiwar group formed in 1967 by veterans who opposed the war.

Wall, the   Nickname for the national Vietnam Veterans Memorial in Washington, D.C., erected in 1982; as of November 1991, inscribed with the names of 58,183 service members who died in Vietnam.

War Powers Act   Law passed in November 1973 that places a maximum 90-day limit on the U.S. president's use of troops abroad, or any substantial increase in the number of troops stationed abroad.

War Zone C   The major Vietcong guerrilla areas north of Saigon.

Wasted   Killed.

Waxed   Killed.

WIA   Wounded in action.

Wild Weasel   Fighter aircraft designed to seek out and destroy enemy defenses.

Wiley Pete   White phosphorus; an element used in grenades or shells for incendiary purposes.

Wise Old Men   The Senior Advisory Board on Vietnam during President Johnson's administration.

World, the   The United States or anywhere except Vietnam.

XO   Executive officer, the second in command of a military unit.

Yards   Montagnard soldiers.

Zap   To shoot at and hit, wound, kill or destroy.

Zippo   Flame-throwing device.

Zoo, the   Nickname for the North Vietnamese Cu Loc POW camp near Hanoi.

Zoomies   Air Force Academy graduates or jet pilots.

Zulu   Casualty report.

Bibliography

Ackers, Virginia Elwood, *Women War Correspondents in the Vietnam War, 1961–1975*. Metuchen: Scarecrow Press, 1988.

Adler, Bill (ed.), *Letters from Vietnam*. New York: E.P. Dutton, 1967.

Aiken, George, *Senate Diary: January 1972–January 1975*. Brattleboro, Vermont: Stephen Greene Press, 1976.

Alison, Lt. Col. George B., *Linebacker II: A View from the Rock*. Washington, D.C.: U.S. Government Printing Office, 1979.

Allen, Michael, "Sharing the Agony of Hanoi," *Christian Century*, January 24, 1973.

Alvarez, Everett, Jr. and Pitch, Anthony S., *Chained Eagle*. New York: Donald I. Fine, 1989.

Amter, Joseph A., *Vietnam Verdict: A Citizens History*. New York: Continuum, 1982.

Anonymous, "Letter from Nam," *Negro History Bulletin*, May 1971.

———, "Pilot Report From Vietnam," *Aviation Week and Space Technology*, September 9, 1966.

———, "The Yanks Come to Saigon," *U.S. News & World Report*, April 9, 1954.

———, "Vietnam Diary," *The Reporter*, January 13, 1966.

———, "Vietnam Diary; Notes from the Journal of a Young American in Saigon," *The Reporter*, January 13, 1966.

Anson, Robert Sam, *War News: A Young Reporter in Indochina*. New York: Simon & Schuster, 1989.

Bacon, Margaret, "Conversation at Chu Lai Hospital," *Christian Century*, February 17, 1971.

Baker, Mark, *Nam: The Vietnam War in the Words of the Men and Women Who Fought There*. New York: William Morrow, 1981.

Ball, George, *Diplomacy for a Crowded World*. Boston: Little, Brown, 1976.

Barrett, Tom, "The Last to Leave," *Leatherneck*, September 1975.

Barrymaine, Norman, "Bomb Damage in North Vietnam Described," *Aviation Week and Space Technology*, December 26, 1966.

Bater, Victor, *Vietnam, A Diplomatic Tragedy*. Dobbs Ferry, N.Y.: Oceana Publishing, 1965.

Beech, Keyes, *Not Without the Americans; a Personal History*. Garden City, N.Y.: Doubleday, 1971.

Berman, Larry, *Lyndon Johnson's War: The Road to Stalemate in Vietnam*. New York: W.W. Norton, 1989.

Berrigan, Darrell, "I Saw the French Losing Indochina," *The Saturday Evening Post*, March 18, 1950.

Blakey, Scott, *Prisoner of War: The Survival of Commander Richard Stratton*. Garden City, N.Y.: Doubleday, 1798.

Bleier, Rocky and O'Neil, Tony, *Fighting Back*. New York: Stein & Day, 1975.

Borchgrave, Arnaud de, "Cambodia: A Reporter's Diary," *Newsweek*, June 15, 1970.

————, "How Sad to Be a Cambodian," *Newsweek*, June 29, 1970.

————, "Indo-China: It's French by Day, Red by Night," *Newsweek*, April 20, 1953.

Boyle, Richard, *The Flower of the Dragon: The Breakdown of the U.S. Army in Vietnam*. San Francisco: Ramparts Press, 1972.

Braestrup, Peter, *Big Story: How the American Press and Television Reported and Interpreted the Crisis of Tet 1968 in Vietnam and Washington*. Boulder, Colo.: Westview Press, 1977.

————, *Vietnam as History: Ten Years After the Paris Peace Accords*. Washington, D.C.: Woodrow Wilson Center for Scholars, 1984.

Brandon, Heather, *Casualties: Death in Vietnam, Anguish and Survival in America*. New York: St. Martin's Press, 1984.

Brant, Toby, *Journal of a Combat Tanker, Vietnam, 1969*. New York: Vantage Press, 1988.

Brennan, Matthew, *Headhunters: Stories From the 1st Squadron 9th Cavalry in Vietnam, 1965–1971*. Novato, Calif.: Presidio Press, 1987.

Briscoe, Edward G., *Diary of a Short-timer*. New York: Vantage Press, 1970.

Brown, Gerald Austin, *No Sad Songs*. Fort Worth, Texas: Branch-Smith, 1973.

Brown, John M.G., *Rice Paddy Grunt*. New York: Regency Books, 1986.

Browne, Malcolm W., *The New Face of War*. New York: Bobbs-Merrill, 1965.

Broyles, William, Jr., *Brothers in Arms: A Journey from War to Peace*. New York: Alfred A. Knopf, 1986.

———, "The Wall That Heals," *Reader's Digest*, May 1987.

Bryan, C.D.B., *Friendly Fire*. New York: G.P. Putnam's Sons, 1976.

Buckley, Kevin, "General Abrams Deserves a Better War," *The New York Times Magazine*, October 5, 1969.

Butler, David, *The Fall of Saigon*. New York: Simon & Schuster, 1985.

Butterfield, Fox, "How South Vietnam Died by the Stab in the Front," *The New York Times Magazine*, May 25, 1975.

———, "Who Was This Enemy," *New York Times Magazine*, February 4, 1973.

Buttinger, Joseph, *Vietnam: A Dragon Embattled*. New York: Frederick A. Praeger, 1967.

———, "An Eyewitness Report on Vietnam." *The Reporter*, January 27, 1955.

Cameron, Allan W. (ed.), *Viet-Nam Crisis: A Documentary History*. Ithaca, N.Y.: Cornell University Press, 1971.

Caputo, Philip, *A Rumor of War*. New York: Holt, Rinehart & Winston, 1977.

———, "Running Again—the Last Retreat," *The Chicago Tribune*, April 28, 1975.

———, "The Unreturning Army," *Playboy*, January 1982.

Carhart, Tom, *The Offering*. New York: William Morrow, 1987.

Castan, Sam, "Father Tom Conroy: Church Is in His Combat Pack," *Look*, July 12, 1966.

Challenge, "G.I.'s in Vietnam Say: 'Get the Hell Out!'," New York: Challenge-Desafio, 1966.

Chanoff, David and Toai, Doan Van (eds.), *Portrait of the Enemy*. New York: Random House, 1986.

Chappelle, Dickey, "Water War in Viet Nam," *National Geographic*, February 1966.

———, "With the Paratroopers," *Reader's Digest*, February 1962.

Charlton, Michael and Moncrieff, Anthony, *Many Reasons Why: The American Involvement in Vietnam*. London: Scolar Press, 1978.

Chesley, Larry, *Seven Years in Hanoi: A POW Tells His Story*. Salt Lake City: Bookcraft, 1973.

Chieu, Ngo Van, *Journal d'un combattant Vietminh*. Paris: Editions du Seuil, 1954.

Chinnery, Philip D., *Life on the Line: Stories of Vietnam Air Combat*. New York: St. Martin's, 1988.

Churchill, Winston C., "Reports from Vietnam," *Look,* July 26, 1966.

Clodfelter, Michael, *Mad Minutes and Vietnam Months*. Jefferson, N.C.: McFarland & Company, 1988.

Coe, Charles, *Young Man in Vietnam*. New York: Four Winds Press, 1968.

Cohen, Stephen, *Vietnam: Anthology and Guide to a TV History*. New York: Alfred A. Knopf, 1983.

Colby, William E. and Forbath, Peter, *Honorable Men: My Life in the CIA*. New York: Simon & Schuster, 1978.

Collins, General J. Lawton, "What We're Doing in Indo-China: Interview with General J. Lawton Collins," *U.S. News & World Report,* March 4, 1955.

Corson, William R., *The Betrayal*. New York: W.W. Norton, 1968.

Cosmas, Graham A. and Murray, Terrence P., *U.S. Marines in Vietnam: Vietnamization and Redeployment*. Washington, D.C.: U.S. Government Printing Office, 1986.

Croft, Maj. A.J., "Dateline . . . Viet-Nam," *Marine Corps Gazette,* October 1963.

Dareff, Hal, *The Story of Vietnam*. New York: Avon, 1967.

Dawson, Alan, *55 Days: The Fall of South Vietnam*. Englewood Cliffs, N.J.: Prentice-Hall, 1977.

Deepe, Beverly, "Pressure for Khe Sanh Offensive," *Christian Science Monitor,* March 26, 1968.

Dengler, Dieter, "I Escaped From a Red Prison," *Saturday Evening Post,* December 3, 1966.

Denton, Rear Admiral Jeremiah A., Jr., with Edwin H. Broadt, *When Hell Was in Session*. New York: Reader's Digest Press, 1976.

Devillers, Philippe, *Histoire du Viet-Nam de 1940 a 1952*. Paris: Editions du Seuil, 1953.

Don, Tran Van, *Our Endless War: Inside Vietnam*. Novato, Calif.: Presidio Press, 1978.

Donovan, David, *Once a Warrior King*. New York: McGraw-Hill, 1985.

Dougan, Clark and Weiss, Stephen, *Nineteen Sixty-Eight*. Boston: Boston Publishing, 1983.

Downs, Jr., Frederick, *Aftermath: A Soldier's Return from Vietnam*. New York: W.W. Norton, 1984.

———, *The Killing Zone: My Life in the Vietnam War*. New York: W.W. Norton, 1978.

Dramesi, John A., *Code of Honor*. New York: W.W. Norton, 1975.

Dung, Van Tien, *Our Great Spring Victory: An Account of the Liberation of South Vietnam*. New York: Monthly Review Press, 1977.

Edelman, Bernard (ed.), *Dear America: Letters Home From Vietnam*. New York: W.W. Norton, 1985.

Ehrhart, William D., *To Those Who Have Gone Home Tired*. New York: Thunder's Mouth Press, 1984.

———, *Vietnam-Perkasie: A Combat Marine Memoir*. Jefferson: McFarland & Company, 1983.

Eilert, Rick E., *For Self and Country: A True Story*. New York: William Morrow, 1983.

Eisenhower, Dwight D., *Public Papers of the Presidents of the United States: Dwight D. Eisenhower, 1953–1961*. Washington, D.C.: U.S. Government Printing Office, 1954–1961.

———, *Waging Peace, 1956–1961: The White House Years*. Garden City, N.Y.: Doubleday, 1965.

Elkins, Frank C., *The Heart of a Man*, ed. Marilyn Roberson Elkins. New York: W.W. Norton, 1973.

Engelmann, Larry, *Tears Before the Rain: An Oral History of the Fall of South Vietnam*. New York: Oxford University Press, 1990.

Everett, Arthur, Johnson, Kathryn and Rosenthal, Harry F., *Calley*. New York: Dell, 1971.

Fall, Bernard B., *Hell in a Very Small Place: The Siege of Dien Bien Phu*. Philadelphia: J.B. Lippincott, 1966.

——— (ed.), *Ho Chi Minh on Revolution*. New York: Frederick A. Praeger, 1967.

———, *Last Reflections on a War*. Garden City, N.Y.: Doubleday, 1967.

———, *Street Without Joy*. Harrisburg, Penn.: Stackpole Company, 1961.

———, *The Two Vietnams: A Political and Military Analysis*. New York: Praeger, 1963.

———, *Vietnam Witness*. New York: Frederick A. Praeger, 1966.

Fallaci, Oriana, "An Interview with Oriana Fallaci: Thieu," *New Republic*, January 20, 1973.

———, "An Interview with a Vietcong Terrorist," *Look*, April 16, 1968.

Fallows, James, "No Hard Feelings?," *Atlantic*, December 1988.

Fish, Lydia M., *The Last Firebase: A Guide to the Vietnam Veterans Memorial*. Shippensburg, Penn.: White Maine, 1987.

Fitzgerald, Frances, *Fire in the Lake: The Vietnamese and the Americans in Vietnam*. Boston: Little, Brown, 1972.

———, "Vietnam Behind the Lines of the 'Cease-Fire' War," *Atlantic*, April 1974.

Ford, Gerald R., *Public Papers of the Presidents of the United States: Gerald Rudolph Ford, 1974–1977*. Washington, D.C.: U.S. Government Printing Office, 1975–1978.

Freedman, Dan and Rhoads, Jacqueline (eds.), *Nurses in Vietnam: The Forgotten Veterans*. Houston: Gulf Publishing, 1987.

Funnye, Clarence, "Give Peace a Chance," *Village Voice*, November 20, 1969.

Gadd, Charles, *Line Doggie: Foot Soldier in Vietnam*. Novato, Calif.: Presidio Press, 1987.

Gannon, Rev. Michael V., "Up Tight in Vietnam," *America*, August 31, 1968.

Gelhorn, Martha, "Suffer the Little Children," *Ladies' Home Journal*, January 1967.

Giap, Vo Nguyen, *Dien Bien Phu*. Hanoi: Foreign Language Publishing House, 1964.

———, *Nhiem Vu Quan Su Truoc Mat Chuyen Sang Tong Phan Cong [Immediate Military Tasks for Switching to the General Counteroffensive]*. Ha Dong: Resistance and Administrative Committee of Ha Dong Province, 1953.

———, *Orders of the Day*. Hanoi: Foreign Languages Publishing House, 1952.

———, *People's War, People's Army*. New York: Frederick A. Praeger, 1962.

———, *Trang Su Moi [A New Page of History]*. Hanoi: Hoi Van Cuu Quoc, 1945.

Gibbons, William Conrad, *The U.S. Government and the Vietnam War: Executive and Legislative Roles and Relationships, 1945–1960*. Washington, D.C.: U.S. Government Printing Office, 1984.

———, *The U.S. Government and the Vietnam War: Executive and Legislative Roles and Relationships, 1961–1964*. Washington, D.C.: U.S. Government Printing Office, 1985.

————, *The U.S. Government and the Vietnam War: Executive and Legislative Roles and Relationships, 1965*. Washington, D.C.: U.S. Government Printing Office, 1988.

Gioglio, Gerald R., *Days of Decision: An Oral History of Conscientious Objectors in the Military During the Vietnam War*. Trenton: Broken Rifle Press, 1989.

Godfrey, Neale, "My Visit to Vietnam," *Seventeen*, June 1970.

Goff, Stan and Sanders, Robert, with Clark Smith, *Brothers: Black Soldiers in the Nam*. Novato, Calif.: Presidio Press, 1982.

Gramont, Sanche de, "Under Vietcong Control," *Saturday Evening Post*, January 29, 1966.

Grant, Ulysses S., *Strategy for Defeat: Vietnam in Retrospect*. Novato, Calif.: Presidio Press, 1978.

Grant, Zalin B., "Vietnam Without GIs," *New Republic*, May 19, 1973.

Grauwin, Paul, *Doctor at Dien Bien Phu*. London: Hutchinson & Company, 1955.

Gravel, Senator Mike (ed.), *The Pentagon Papers*. Boston: Beacon Press, 1971.

Graves, Louise, *Let Us Remember: The Vietnam Veterans Memorial*. Washington, D.C.: Washington Memorial and History Association, 1984.

Greene, Bob (ed.), *Homecoming*. New York: G.P. Putnam's Sons, 1989.

Greene, Graham, "Indo-China," *The New Republic*, April 12, 1954.

Gro, Colonel William E., *Vietnam from Cease-fire to Capitulation*. Washington, D.C.: U.S. Government Printing Office, 1981.

Guarino, Col. Larry, *A P.O.W.'s Story: 2801 Days in Hanoi*. New York: Ballantine, 1990.

Hackworth, Col. David H. and Sherman, Julie, *About Face: The Odyssey of an American Warrior*. New York: Simon & Schuster, 1989.

Halberstam, David, *The Best and the Brightest*. New York: Random House, 1972.

————, *The Making of a Quagmire: America and Vietnam During the Kennedy Era*. New York: Random House, 1965.

Hammel, Eric, *Khe Sanh: Siege in the Clouds, An Oral History*. New York: Crow Publishers, 1989.

Hammer, Richard, *The Court-Martial of Lt. Calley*. New York: Coward, McCann and Geoghegan, 1971.

Hammond, William M., *Public Affairs: The Military and the Media*. Washington, D.C.: U.S. Government Printing Office, 1988.

Herr, Michael, *Dispatches*. New York: Alfred A. Knopf, 1977.

Herrgesell, Lt. Col. Oscar, *Dear Margaret, Today I Died . . .* , ed. Margaret Rowton Herrgesell. San Antonio: Naylor Company, 1974.

Hersh, Seymour M., *My Lai 4: A Report on the Massacre and Its Aftermath*. New York: Random House, 1970.

Higgins, Marguerite, *Our Vietnam Nightmare*. New York: Harper & Row, 1965.

———, "Vietnam: Fact and Fiction," *The New York Herald Tribune*, August 26– September 1, 1963.

Hilsman, Roger, *To Move a Nation: The Politics of Foreign Policy in the Adminis- tration of John F. Kennedy*. Garden City, N.Y.: Doubleday, 1967.

Ho Chi Minh, *Selected Works*. Hanoi: Foreign Languages Publishing House, 1961–1962.

Hoffman, Paul, *Moratorium: An American Protest*. New York: Tower Publica- tions, 1970.

Hogard, Jean, *Guerre revolutionnaire et pacifation*. Paris: Revue Militaire d'Information, 1957.

Hosmer, Stephen T., Kellen, Konrad and Jenkins, Brian M., *The Fall of South Vietnam: Statements by Vietnamese Military and Civilian Leaders*. New York: Crane, Russak and Company, 1980.

Hubbell, John G., *P.O.W.: A Definitive History of the American Prisoner-of-War Experience in Vietnam, 1964–1973*. New York: Reader's Digest Press, 1976.

Hughes, Larry, *You Can See a Lot Standing Under a Flare in the Republic of Viet- nam: My Year at War*. New York: William Morrow, 1969.

Hung, Nguyen Tien and Schecter, Jerrold L., *The Palace File*. New York: Har- per & Row, 1986.

Isaacs, Arnold R., "Peace Comes to Saigon," *Harpers*, March 1946.

———, *Without Honor: Defeat in Vietnam and Cambodia*. Baltimore: Johns Hop- kins University Press, 1983.

Jaunal, Jack W., *Vietnam '68: Jack's Journal*. San Francisco: Denson Press, 1981.

Jenkins, Loren and Proffit, Nicholas, "The Long Day of the Copters," *News- week*, May 12, 1975.

Jensen, Jay R., *Six Years in Hell: A Returned POW Views Captivity, Country and the Nation's Future*. Bountiful, Utah: Horizon, 1974.

Johnson, General Harold K., "End of Vietnam War in Sight?—Sized up by Army's Chief of Staff," *U.S. News & World Report*, September 11, 1967.

Johnson, Lady Bird, *A White House Diary*. New York: Holt, Rinehart & Winston, 1970.

Johnson, Lyndon Baines, *Public Papers of the Presidents of the United States: Lyndon Baines Johnson, 1963–1969*. Washington, D.C.: U.S. Government Printing Office, 1964–1969.

Johnson, Raymond W., *Postmark: Mekong Delta*. Old Tappan: Fleming H. Revell, 1968.

Johnson, Thomas A., "Negroes in 'The Nam,' " *Ebony*, August 1968.

Jones, James, *Viet Journal*. New York: Delacorte Press, 1973.

Just, Ward S., *To What End: Report from Vietnam*. Boston: Houghton Mifflin, 1968.

Karnow, Stanley, "Diem Defeats His Own Best Troops," *The Reporter*, January 19, 1961.

———, "Giap Remembers," *The New York Times Magazine*, June 24, 1990.

———, *Vietnam: A History*. New York: Viking/Penguin, 1983.

Kennedy, John F., *Public Papers of the Presidents of the United States, 1961–1963*. Washington, D.C.: U.S. Government Printing Office, 1962–1964.

Ketwig, John, *And a Hard Rain Fell*. New York: Macmillan, 1985.

Kifner, John "Four Kent State Students Killed by Troops," *New York Times*, May 5, 1970.

King, Martin Luther, Jr., "Declaration of Independence from the War in Vietnam," *Ramparts*, May 1967.

Kingsley, Thomas E., "Letters Home," *Harpers*, June 1974.

Kirk, Donald, *Tell It to the Dead*. Chicago: Nelson-Hall, 1975.

———, "How Major Buu of South Vietnam Fights His War," *New York Times Magazine*, August 20, 1972.

———, "Who Wants to Be the Last American Killed in Vietnam?," *New York Times Magazine*, September 19, 1971.

Kissinger, Henry A., *The White House Years*. Boston: Little, Brown, 1979.

Knoebl, Kuno, *Victor Charlie: The Face of War in Viet-Nam*. New York: Frederick A. Praeger, 1967.

Kovic, Ron, *Born on the Fourth of July*. New York: McGraw-Hill, 1976.

Krich, Claudia, "Vietnam Journal: Witness to the War's End," *MS.*, July 1976.

Ky, Nguyen Van, *Twenty Years and Twenty Days.* New York: Stein & Day, 1976.

Lancaster, Donald, *The Emancipation of French Indochina.* New York: Oxford University Press, 1961.

Lansdale, Edward G., *In the Midst of Wars: An American's Mission to Southeast Asia.* New York: Harper & Row, 1972.

Lavalle, A.J.C. (ed.), *Last Flight from Saigon,* by Thomas G. Tobin, Arthur E. Laehr, and John F. Hilgenberg. Washington, D.C.: U.S. Printing Office, 1978.

LeMay, Curtis, *Mission with LeMay.* New York: Doubleday, 1965.

Lester, Colin, "One Day They Will Go It Alone," *Life,* April 25, 1969.

Lewis, Anthony, " 'You Americans do not understand Vietnam!' they kept telling me . . . Journal of a Correspondent in North Vietnam," *New York Times Magazine,* June 18, 1972.

Life magazine eds., "Vietnam: One Week's Dead, May 28–June 3, 1969," *Life,* June 27, 1969.

Lindley, Ernest K., "An Ally Worth Having," *Newsweek,* June 29, 1959.

Linn, Hugh, *Vietnam: A Reporter's War.* New York: Stein & Day, 1985.

Lowry, Timothy S., *And Brave Men, Too.* New York: Crown, 1985.

Lucas, Jim G., *Dateline: Vietnam.* New York: Award House, 1966.

Lynd, Alice (ed.), *We Won't Go.* Boston: Beacon Press, 1968.

McCain, John S., "How the POW's Fought Back," *U.S. News & World Report,* May 14, 1973.

McCarthy, Eugene, *The Year of the People.* Garden City: N.Y.: Doubleday, 1969.

Maclear, Michael, *The Ten Thousand Day War, Vietnam: 1945–1975.* New York: St. Martin's Press, 1981.

McCloud, Bill (ed.), *What Should We Tell Our Children About Vietnam.* Norman: University of Oklahoma Press, 1989.

McDaniel, Norman A., *Yet Another Voice.* New York: Hawthorne Books, 1975.

McPherson, Myra, *A Long Time Passing: Vietnam and the Haunted Generation.* Garden City, N.Y.: Doubleday, 1984.

Mailer, Norman, *Armies of the Night.* New York: New American Library, 1968.

Mangold, Tom and Penycate, J., *The Tunnels of Cu Chi.* New York: Random House, 1985.

Mansfield, Mike, *The Vietnam Conflict: The Substance and the Shadow. Report of Senator Mansfield.* Washington, D.C.: U.S. Government Printing Office, 1966.

Markham, James, "Letter from Saigon: Not 10, Not 15, but 50 Rounds," *The New York Magazine,* April 14, 1974.

Marks, Richard E., *The Letters of PFC Richard E. Marks.* New York: J.B. Lippincott, 1967.

Marshall, Kathryn, *In the Combat Zone: An Oral History of American Women in Vietnam.* New York: Warner Books, 1987.

Martin, Harold H., "Fighting an Uneasy Enemy," *Saturday Evening Post,* November 24, 1962.

———, "My Son in Vietnam," *Saturday Evening Post,* July 16, 1966.

Martin, Robert P., "A Hard Choice for U.S.: Get Tough or Get Out," *U.S. News & World Report,* November 6, 1961.

———, "If GI's Go to Vietnam; the Way It Looks Out There," *U.S. News & World Report,* November 6, 1961.

———, "The Strange War the U.S. Is Not Winning—Eyewitness Report from the Front in Vietnam," *U.S. News & World Report,* September 30, 1963.

———, "Up Front with U.S. Guerrillas in Asia—An Eyewitness Report," *U.S. News & World Report,* April 24, 1961.

Mason, Robert, *Chickenhawk.* New York: Viking Press, 1983.

Maurer, Harry, *Strange Ground: America in Vietnam, 1945–1975: An Oral History.* New York: Henry Holt, 1989.

Mecklin, John, *Mission in Torment: An Intimate Account of the U.S. Role in Vietnam.* Garden City, N.Y.: Doubleday, 1965.

Millet, Stanley, "Terror in Vietnam," *Harper's,* September 1962.

Moore, Robert L., "I Fought in Vietnam: Interview with an American Observer," *U.S. News & World Report,* June 8, 1964.

Morris, James, "The Ambush," *Esquire,* August 1965.

Mulligan, Hugh A., *No Place to Die: The Agony of Viet Nam.* New York: William Morrow, 1967.

Munson, Glenn (ed.), *Letters from Vietnam.* New York: Parallax, 1966.

Murtha, Gary, *Timefighter.* Kansas City, Missouri: G.D.M. Publications, 1985.

Musgrove, Patches (Helen), "Wounded Florida GI's Dad Sees for Himself," [Jacksonville, Florida] *Journal,* May 29, 1970.

Navarre, Henri, *Agonie de l'Indochine*. Paris: Plon, 1956.

Nixon, Richard M., *No More Vietnams*. New York: Arbor House, 1985.

————, *The Public Papers of the Presidents of the United States: Richard Milhous Nixon, 1969–1974*. Washington, D.C.: U.S. Government Printing Office, 1970–1975.

————, *RN: The Memoirs of Richard Nixon*. New York: Grosset and Dunlap, 1978.

————, "The Road to Peace," *U.S. News & World Report*, June 26, 1972.

Noel, Reuben and Noel, Nancy, *Saigon for a Song: The True Story of a Vietnam Gig to Remember*. Phoenix: UCS Press, 1987.

Nolting, Frederick, *From Trust to Tragedy*. New York: Praeger, 1988.

Oberdorfer, Don, *Tet! The Turning Point of the Vietnam War*. New York: Da Capo, 1983.

O'Brien, Tim, *If I Die in a Combat Zone, Box Me Up and Ship Me Home*. New York: Delacorte Press/Seymour Lawrence, 1973.

Odom, James R., "The Vietnam Nurses Can't Forget," *American Journal of Nursing*, September 1986.

Page, Tim, *Page After Page*. London: Sidgwick & Jackson, 1988.

Palmer, Bruce, Jr., *The 25-Year War: America's Military Role in Vietnam*. Lexington: University of Kentucky Press, 1984.

Palmer, Laura, *Shrapnel in the Heart: Letters and Remembrances from the Vietnam Veterans Memorial*. New York: Random House, 1987.

Parks, David, *G.I. Diary*. New York: Harper & Row, 1968.

Parrish, John A., *12, 20 & 5: A Doctor's Year in Vietnam*. New York: E.P. Dutton, 1972.

Patti, Archimede L.A., *Why Viet Nam? Prelude to America's Albatross*. Berkeley: University of California Press, 1980.

Perry, Mark, 'First, They Have to Find You: the Return of Oliver Stone's Platoon," *Veteran*, September 1987.

Perry, Merton, "The Dust Agony of Khe Sanh," *Newsweek*, March 18, 1968.

Pettit, Clyde Edwin (ed.), *The Experts*. Secaucus, New Jersey: Lyle Stuart, 1975.

Pike, Douglas, *Vietcong: The Organization and Techniques of the National Liberation Front of South Vietnam*. Cambridge, Mass.: MIT Press, 1966.

————, *War, Peace and the Viet Cong*. Cambridge, Mass.: M.I.T. Press, 1969.

Porter, Gareth (ed.), *Vietnam: The Definitive Documentation of Human Decisions*. Stanfordville, NY: E.M. Coleman Enterprises, 1979.

————, *Vietnam: A History in Documents*. New York: New American Library, 1981.

Prescott, Gary Rowe (ed.), *Love to All, Jim: A Young Man's Letters from Vietnam*. San Francisco: Strawberry Hill Press, 1989.

Profitt, Nicholas, "Escape from Xuan Loc," *Newsweek,* April 28, 1975.

———— and Jenkins, Loren, "The Long Day of the Copters," *Newsweek*, May 12, 1975.

Puller, Lewis B., Jr., *Fortunate Son: The Autobiography of Lewis B. Puller, Jr.* New York: Grove Weidenfeld, 1991.

Ray Michele, *The Two Shores of Hell*. New York: David McKay, 1968.

Raymond, Jack, "When G.I. Joe Meets Ol'Charlie," *The New York Times Magazine*, July 25, 1965.

Reed, David, *Up Front in Vietnam*. New York: Funk & Wagnalls, 1967.

Reich, Dale E. *Good Soldiers Don't Go to Heaven*. Whitewater, Wisconsin: Garden of Eden Press, 1979.

Reinberg, Linda, *In the Field: The Language of the Vietnam War*. New York: Facts On File, 1991.

Ridgway, Matthew B., *Soldier: The Memoirs of Matthew B. Ridgway*. New York: Harper & Row, 1956.

Risner, Robinson, *Passing of the Night*. New York: Random House, 1973.

Rose, Jerry A., "The Peasant Is the Key to Vietnam," *U.S. News & World Report*, April 8, 1962.

Rusk, Dean, with Richard Rusk and Daniel S. Papp, *As I Saw It*. New York: W.W. Norton, 1990.

Russ, Martin, *Happy Hunting Ground*. New York: Atheneum, 1968.

Saar, John, "You Can't Just Hand Out Orders," *Life*, October 23, 1970.

Sadler, Barry, *I'm a Lucky One*. New York: Macmillan, 1967.

Safer, Morley, *Flashbacks: On Returning to Vietnam*. New York: Random House, 1990.

Salisbury, Harrison E., *Behind the Lines – Hanoi: Hanoi, December 23, 1966 – January 7, 1967*. New York: Harper & Row, 1967.

Samuels, Gertrude, "Passage to Freedom in Viet Nam," *National Geographic*, June 1955.

Santoli, Al (ed.), *Everything We Had: An Oral History of the Vietnam War by Thirty-Three American Soldiers Who Fought It*. New York: Random House, 1981.

———— (ed.), *To Bear Any Burden: The Vietnam War and Its Aftermath in the Words of Americans and Southeast Asians*. New York: E.P. Dutton, 1985.

Sareff, Hal, "Story of Vietnam," *Parent's Magazine*, 1971.

Schanberg, Sidney H., *The Death and Life of Dith Pranh*. New York: Penguin, 1985.

Schell, Jonathan, *The Village of Ben Suc*. New York: Alfred A. Knopf, 1967.

Scholl-Latour, Peter. *Death in the Rice Fields: An Eyewitness Account of Vietnam's Three Wars, 1945–1979*. London: Orbis, 1985.

Scruggs, Jan C. and Swerdlow, Joel L., *To Heal a Nation: The Vietnam Veterans Memorial*. New York: Harper & Row, 1985.

Seldenberg, Robert, "To Hell and Back," *American Film*, January 1990.

Shaplen Robert, *Bitter Victory*. New York: Harper & Row, 1986.

————, "Letter From Saigon," *The New Yorker*, November 13, 1965.

————, "Letter from Vietnam," *The New Yorker*, February 25, 1973.

————, *The Lost Revolution*. New York: Harper & Row, 1965.

————, *The Road From War: 1965–1970*. New York: Harper & Row, 1970.

————, *Time Out of Hand: Revolution and Reaction in Southeast Asia*. New York: Harper & Row, 1970.

————, "Saigon Exit," *New Yorker*, May 19, 1975.

————, "We Have Always Survived," *The New Yorker*, April 15, 1972.

Sharp, U.S.G., *Strategy for Defeat: Vietnam in Retrospect*. Novato, Calif.: Presidio Press, 1978.

Sheehan, Neil, *A Bright Shining Lie: John Paul Vann and America in Vietnam*. New York: Random House, 1988.

————, "Letters from Hamburger Hill," *Harpers*, November 1969.

————, "Vietnam, and the Battle for Reality," *U.S. News & World Report*, October 24, 1988.

Sheehan, Susan, *Ten Vietnamese*. New York: Alfred A. Knopf, 1969.

Shulimson, Jack, *U.S. Marines in Vietnam: An Expanding War*. Washington, D.C.: U.S. Government Printing Office, 1982.

Shulimson, Jack and Johnson, Charles M., *U.S. Marines in Vietnam: The Landing and the Buildup*. Washington, D.C.: Government Printing Office, 1978.

Simpson, Howard R., "Slow Boat to Saigon," *Comonweal*, January 21, 1955.

Smith, Charles R., *U.S. Marines in Vietnam: High Mobility and Standdown*. Washington, D.C.: U.S. Government Printing Office, 1988.

Smith, Clark (ed.). *The Short-Timer's Journal*. Berkeley: Winter Soldier Archives, 1980.

Snepp, Frank, *Decent Interval: An Insider's Account of Saigon's Indecent End Told by the CIA's Chief Strategy Analyst in Vietnam*. New York: Random House, 1977.

Spector, Robert, *U.S. Army in Vietnam, Advice and Support: The Early Years, 1941–1961*. Washington, D.C.: U.S. Government Printing Office, 1983.

Spencer, Ernest, *Welcome to Vietnam, Macho Man: Reflections of a Khe Sanh Vet*. Martinez, Calif.: Corps Press, 1987.

Standerwick, Caroline, " 'Missing in Action . . .' How Agony of Vietnam Lingers," *U.S. News & World Report*, December 30, 1974.

Steinbeck, John, "Letters to Alicia," [Long Island] *Newsday*, January 28, 1967.

Stephen, Donald E., *Bait: Vietnam, 1971*. St. Joseph, Ill.: self-published, 1986.

Sterba, James, "In the Field: Grunts, Groans and Jokes," *The New York Times*, May 5, 1978.

Stevens, Paul Drew (ed.), *The Navy Cross–Vietnam*. Forest Ranch: Sharp & Dunnigan, 1987.

Stockdale, James B., "The Most Important Lessons of Vietnam: Power of the Human Spirit," *San Jose Mercury News*, January 3, 1982.

Sully, Francois, "I Smell Charlies Around," *Newsweek*, March 6, 1967.

Summers, Col. Harry G., Jr., *On Strategy: A Critical Analysis of the Vietnam War*. New York: Dell, 1982.

———, *Vietnam War Almanac*. New York: Facts On File, 1985.

Tang, Truong Nhu, "The Myth of Liberation," *The New York Review of Books*, October 21, 1982.

Taylor, Telford, "Hanoi Is Reported Scarred But Key Services Continue," *The New York Times*, December 25, 1972.

Telfer, Gary L., Rogers, Lane and Fleming, V. Keith, Jr., *U.S. Marines in Vietnam: Fighting the North Vietnamese*. Washington, D.C.: U.S. Government Printing Office, 1984.

Terry, Wallace (ed.), *Bloods: An Oral History of the Vietnam War by Black Veterans*. New York: Ballantine, 1984.

Terzani, Tizoano, *Giaphong: The Fall and Liberation of Saigon*. New York: St. Martin's Press, 1976.

Thanh, Pham, "My Two Countries, My Flesh and Blood," *The New York Times*, April 19, 1991.

Thien, Nghiem Xuan, editorial of March 15, 1958, *Thoi-Luan* [South Vietnam newspaper].

Thomas, Liz, *Dust of Life*. London: Hamish Hamilton, 1977.

Tregaskis, Richard, *Vietnam Diary*. New York: Holt, Rinehart & Winston, 1963.

———, "Vietnam Visit," *Travel*, March 1959.

Trumbull, Robert, *The Scrutable East: A Correspondent's Report on Southeast Asia*. New York: David McKay, 1964.

Tuohy, William, "Sometimes It's Bad, Sometimes It's Good," *Newsweek*, January 18, 1965.

Turley, Colonel G.H., *The Easter Offensive, Vietnam 1972*. Novato, Calif.: Presidio Press, 1985.

U.S. Air Force, *The Fall and Evacuation of South Vietnam*. Washington, D.C.: U.S. Government Printing Office, 1978.

U.S. Congress, House Committee on Foreign Affairs, *Current Situation in the Far East*. Washington, D.C.: U.S. Government Printing Office, 1959.

U.S. Congress, House Committee on Veterans' Affairs, *Legacies of Vietnam: Comparative Adjustment of Vietnam Veterans and Their Peers*. Washington, D.C.: U.S. Government Printing Office, 1981.

———, *Report on Assassination Plots*. Washington, D.C.: U.S. Government Printing Office, 1977.

U.S. Congress, Senate, *Hearings before the Committee on Foreign Relations, 92nd Cong., 2nd Session*. Washington, D.C.: U.S. Government Printing Office, 1973.

U.S. Congress, Senate Committee on Foreign Relations, *Background Information Relating to Southeast Asia and Vietnam*. Washington, D.C.: U.S. Government Printing Office, 1967 and 1970.

———, *Current Situation in Vietnam*. Washington, D.C.: U.S. Government Printing Office, 1959.

————, *The Gulf of Tonkin, 1964 Incidents.* Washington, D.C.: U.S. Government Printing Office, 1968.

————, *Hearings on Causes, Origins and Lessons of the Vietnam War.* Washington, D.C.: U.S. Government Printing Office, 1973.

————, *Hearings on the Foreign Assistance Act of 1972.* Washington, D.C.: U.S. Government Printing Office, 1972.

————, *Report on Indochina, Report of Senator Mike Mansfield on a Study Mission to Vietnam, Cambodia, Laos, Committee Print, 83d Cong., 2d sess.* Washington, D.C.: U.S. Government Printing Office, 1954.

————, *Report on a Study Mission, 84th Cong., 2d sess.* Washington, D.C.: U.S. Government Printing Office, 1956.

————, *Supplemental Foreign Assistance–Vietnam.* Washington, D.C.: U.S. Government Printing Office, 1966.

————, *Two Reports on Vietnam and Southeast Asia to the President by Senator Mike Mansfield.* Washington, D.C.: U.S. Government Printing Office, 1973.

————, *The United States and Vietnam: 1944–1947.* Washington, D.C.: U.S. Government Printing Office, 1972.

————, *Vietnam and Southeast Asia.* Washington, D.C.: U.S. Government Printing Office, 1963.

U.S. Congress, Senate Committee on Veterans' Affairs, *Vietnam-Era Medal of Honor Recipients.* Washington, D.C.: U.S. Government Printing Office, 1973.

U.S. Department of Defense, *A Pocket Guide to Vietnam.* Washington, D.C.: U.S. Government Printing Office, 1966.

————, *United States-Vietnam Relations, 1945–1967.* Washington, D.C.: U.S. Government Printing Office, 1971.

U.S. Department of Defense Information School, *Vietnam: 10 Years Later.* Washington, D.C.: U.S. Government Printing Office, 1983.

U.S. Department of State, *American Foreign Policy 1950–1955: Basic Documents.* Washington, D.C.: U.S. Government Printing Office, 1957.

————, *American Foreign Policy, Current Documents, 1956.* Washington, D.C.: U.S. Government Printing Office, 1959.

————, *Bulletin,* Washington, D.C.: U.S. Government Printing Office, January 4, 1954; April 5, 1954; April 15, 1954; May 27, 1957; September 30, 1963; April 6, 1964; June 8, 1964; August 24, 1964; November 13, 1972; and May 5, 1975.

————, *Foreign Relations of the United States, 1945.* Washington, D.C.: U.S. Government Printing Office, 1967–1969.

———, *Foreign Relations of the United States, 1950*. Washington, D.C.: U.S. Government Printing Office, 1976.

———, *Foreign Relations of the United States, 1952–1955*. Washington, D.C.: U.S. Government Printing Office, 1982.

———, *Foreign Relations of the United States, 1958–1960, Vietnam*. Washington, D.C.: U.S. Government Printing Office, 1986.

United States Foreign Broadcast Information Service, *Daily Report*. Washington, D.C.: U.S. Government Printing Office, February 13, 1961.

U.S. Supreme Court, *Cases Adjudged in the Supreme Court at October Term 1970*, vol. 403. Washington, D.C.: U.S. Government Printing Office, 1972.

Vance, Samuel, *The Courageous and the Proud*. New York: W.W. Norton, 1970.

Van Devanter, Lynda, *Home Before Morning: The True Story of an Army Nurse in Vietnam*. New York: Warner Books, 1984.

Walker, Keith, *A Piece of My Heart: The Stories of Twenty-Six American Women Who Served in Vietnam*. New York: Ballantine, 1985.

Wallace, James, "One Day in Vietnam's War," *U.S. News & World Report*, June 26, 1972.

Warner, Denis, "Report From Khe Sanh," *The Reporter*, March 21, 1968.

———, *The Last Confucian*. New York: Macmillan, 1965.

———, "The Many-Fronted War in South Vietnam," *The Reporter*, September 13, 1962.

Webb, Catherine (Kate), *On the Other Side: 23 Days with the Vietcong*. New York: Quadrangle, 1972.

Weinraub, Bernard, "Footnotes on the Vietnam Dispatches," *The New York Times Magazine*, October 20, 1968.

———, "Now, Vietnam Veterans Demand Their Rights," *The New York Times Magazine*, May 27, 1979.

Weiss, Joseph J., "Vietnam—A Doctor's Journal," *Commentary*, May 1967.

West, Richard, *Sketches from Vietnam*. London: Jonathan Cape, 1968.

Westmoreland, General William C., *A Soldier Reports*. Garden City, N.Y.: Doubleday, 1976.

Wheeler, John, *Touched With Fire: The Future of the Vietnam Generation*. New York: Franklin Watts, 1984.

Whitlow, Robert H., *U.S. Marines in Vietnam: The Advisory & Combat Assistance Era*. Washington, D.C.: U.S. Government Printing Office, 1982.

Wilkenson, Kim, *The Bad War: An Oral History of the Vietnam War*. New York: New American Library, 1987.

Willwerth, James, *Eye in the Last Storm*. New York: Grossman, 1972.

Wintle, Justin (ed.), *The Dictionary of War Quotations*. New York: The Free Press, 1989.

Yezzo, Dominick, *A G.I.'s Vietnam Diary, 1968–1969*. New York: Franklin Watts, 1974.

Zaffiri, Samuel, *Hamburger Hill: May 11–20, 1969*. Novato, Calif.: Presidio, 1988.

Zaroulis, Nancy and Sullivan, Gerald, *Who Spoke Up? American Protest Against the War in Vietnam, 1963–1975*. Garden City, N.Y.: Doubleday, 1984.

Zich, Arthur, "That Was the War That Was," *Newsweek,* June 18, 1973.

Zumwalt, Admiral Elmo R., Jr., and Zumwalt, Lieutenant Elmo R., III, *My Father, My Son*. New York: Macmillan, 1986.

Credits

INDEX

Names and page numbers in bold refer to biographical entries in Appendix B; numbers in italics refer to illustrations and captions.

A

Abrams, Gen. Creighton W., Jr. 160, *171*, 173, 193, 202, 208, 215, 218, 239, 249, **321**
Acheson, Dean 35, **321**
Adams, Eddie 299
Advisers. *See military advisers.*
Agent Orange 62, 288, 292, 293. *See also Operation Ranch Hand.*
Agnew, Spiro 195, 209, **321**
Agreement on Ending the War and Restoring Peace in Vietnam 308–316. *See also Paris Peace Accords and Paris peace talks.*
Aiken, George 255, **321**
Albert, Carl 274
Alderman, Fred 296
Allen, Chuck 72
Allen, Michael 255
Alvarez, Lt. (j.g.) Everett, Jr. 82, 153–154, **321**
An Khe 111
An Loc 238
Annam 1, 9, 15, 16, 18
Anson, Robert Sam 229, **321**
Antiwar Movement xi, 89–90, 103, 107, 120, 152, 169, 192, 217, 219, 253
  against Cambodian incursion 216, 221, *227*
  Democratic National Convention (1968) 170–171, 175, *185*
  Demonstrators 90, *157*, *158*, *185*, 209, 210, 227, 253
  Moratorium Against the War 194–196, 199, 209–210
  Pentagon march 148, *157*
  rallies and marches 87, 104, 109, 145, 147, 170, 174, 198, 223, 239–240, 246
Ap Bac, Battle of 55–56, 71
Arnett, Peter 160, 283, **321–322**
Arrowsmith, Marvin 38
ARVN. *See South Vietnamese Armed Forces.*
A Shau Valley 192
Atanian, Heidi 296
Attleboro, Operation 123, 126, 141
Auriol, Vincent 39
Australia 23, 30, 89

B

Bagby, Spec. 4 Kenneth 114
Baie d'Along Agreement 29
Baker, James A., 3d 293
Ball, George 60, 69, 100, 101, 109, **322**
Ballad of the Green Berets, The 129
Bancroft, Robert 294
Bang, Tran 127
Ban Me Thuot 263, 264, 265, 270
Bao Dai, Emperor 4, 12, 30, 32, 42, **322**
  and Diem 25, 31
  France supports 17–18, 29
Barrel Roll, Operation 84
Barry, Eileen 293
Barry, Jan 73
Barrymaine, Norman 138
Bay of Pigs 52
Beamon, Mike 184
Beatrice, stronghold 22
Beech, Keyes 267, 277, **322**
Beecher, William 191
Behaine, Pierre Pigneua de 3
Behr, Edward 159
Ben Hai River 123

Ben Tre Province 61, 179
Berrigan, Daniel **322**
Berrigan, Philip **322**
Bethelson, John 151
Bien Gia 85
Bien Hoa 5, 28, 31, 84, 87, 198
Bigart, Homer 68
Biggers, Lt. Archie "Joe" 201
"Big Minh." *See Minh, Gen. Duong Van.*
Binh Dinh Province 107, 117, 125
Binh, Nguyen Ngoc 280
Binh Xuyen 25–26, 48
Bird, Thomas 111
Black, Hugo 234
Blacks in the military 113–114, **132**, 158, 184
Blanchfield, Richard 180
Bleier, Pfc. Rocky 207
Boat people 285, **287**, 292
Boros, Pfc. Jim 154
Boyle, Richard 234
Bradley, Ed 278
Braestrup, Peter 179, **322**
Brant, Sgt. Toby 202
Brinks Hotel (Saigon), attack on 85
Briscoe, Lt. Edward 183
Brown, Capt. Gerald 152–153
Brown, Pfc. John M.G. 160
Brown, Sam 194, **323**
Browne, Malcolm W. 67, 242, 300, **322–323**
Broyles, Lt. William, Jr. 202, 296
Bryant, Harold "Lightbulb" 158
Buddhists:
  protest movement 57–58, 63, 83, 104, 121–122, **125**, 126, 261
  self-immolation campaign 58, 63, 72
Bui Diem **323**
Bui Tin. *See Tin, Bui.*

Buis, Maj. Dale R. 28, 31
Bundy, McGeorge 60, 74, 84, 91, 95, 96, 100, 103, **323**
Bundy, William 95, 100, 101, **323**
Bunker, Ellsworth *142*, 147, 179, 234, 248, **323**
Bunton, Pfc. Frank 160
Burchett, Wilfred 41
Burger, Warren 234
Burr, Capt. Myron Whitney 113
Burrows, Larry **323**
Bush, George 289, 293, 299
Butler, David 276
Butterfield, Alexander 245
Buttinger, Joseph 44, **323**
Buu, Nguyen Thai 253
Byrd, Operation *138*
Byrnes, James 32

C

Cahart, Lt. Tom 184–185
Calley, Lt. William L., Jr. 182, 196, 199, 222, 232, **323**
Cambodia xiii, 23, 30, 90, 125, 126, 143, 214, 218, 222, 226, 238, 244, 248, 263, 265, 270, 271, 285, 292
  incursion into 214–217, 218, 221, 226, 228, 229
  peace treaty 286, 293
  secret bombing of 191, 198
Cameron, James 115
Cam Lo 123
Cam Ne 112
Cam Ranh Bay 71–72
Cao Bang Province 11
Camp Carroll 123
Camp Holloway 96, 106
Canada 24
Canella, Maj. Philip 179
Can, Nguyen Din 27
Canteburry, Gen. Robert 228
Cao Dai sect 25, 48

Caputo, Lt. Philip 98, 137, 276, 297, **324**
Carter, Alan 275
Carter, Jimmy 288, 292
Carter, Lawrence 228
Carver, Sgt. George 113
Catholicism/Catholics in Vietnam 2, 4, 5, 26, 30, 57, 87, 262.
See also missionaries.
Cedar Falls, Operation 141, 147
Cédile, Jean 13, 14
Central Highlands 56, 68, 95, 102, 129, 148, 159, 160, 238, 263, 270
Central Intelligence Agency (CIA) 30, 57, 58, 61, 63, 66, 80, 84, 95, 213

Central Office for South Vietnam. *See COSVN*
Cerre, Mike 299
Chaisson, Col. John 122
Chapelle, Georgette [Dickey] 67, 114, **324**
Chau, Phan Boi. *See Phan Boi Chau.*
Chesley, Capt. Larry 230, 258, 259
Chicago Democratic Convention (1968) xiii, 170–171, 175, *185*, 195
Chieu, Ngo Van 36
China xiii, xiv, 2, 7, 10, 15, 18, 19, 23, 30, 32, 51, 78, 96, 119, 144, 237, 238, 286, 292, 293
Chou En-Lai 237
Chu Lai 104
Church, Frank 155, 215, 217, 226, **324**
"Christmas Bombing" 242–243
Churchill, Winston 136
CIA. *See Central Intelligence Agency.*
Citadel, the (Hue) 165–166
Clayton, Spec. 4 Carl 106
Cleland, Max 288, 295, **324**
Clifford, Clark 173, 174, 175, 297, **324**
Clifton, Tony 230, 250–251
Clodfelter, Sgt. Michael 139
Clos, Max 45
Cochin China 5, 6, 10, 15, 18, 29

Coe, Capt. Charles 160
Cogny, Maj. Gen. René 41, 42, **324**
Colby, William 66, 90, 213, **324**
Colegrove, Albert 46
Collins, Gen. J. Lawton 31, *37*, **44**, **324–325**
Colon, Spec. 4 Hector Santiago 132
Combat Soldiers:
    French (First Indochina War) *21*, 24, 39, 42
    North Vietnamese (NVA and Vietcong) 36, 64, 108, *109*, *110*, 114, 127, *130*, 133, *152*, 185, 234, 249, 255, 299, 300
    South Vietnamese (ARVN) *53*, *67*, *86*, *159*, *231*, *252*, 253
    United States 66, *67*, 71, 72, 74, 88, 106, *107*, 108, 109, *110*, *111*–112, 113, *114*, 116, *128*, 130, 131, *132*, 133, 134, 135, 137, *138*, 139, *147*, 149, 150, 152, 154, 155, *156*, 158, *160*, 176, 177, *178*, 179, 180, 181, *182*, 183, *184*, *186*, *187*, *198*, *201*, 202, 203, 204, 206, 207, 208, *210*, 211, *214*, 220, 223, 225, 226, 228, 230, 232, 233, 234, 235, 250, 252, 294, 295, 296, 297, 298, 300
Communist Party (Vietnamese) 9, 10, 11, 27
Commy, Col. Joseph, Jr. 204
Conein, Lt. Col. Lucien 58, 63, **325**
Confroy, Thomas 133
Confucianism 2, 4
Con Thien 123, 147, 148
Conti, Pfc. Dennis 181
Continental Palace Hotel 14
"Convoy of Tears" 263–264
Cooper-Church Amendment 217, 218, 222
Cooper, John Sherman 155, 215, 217, **325**
Cordell, Susan 68
Cordell, Capt. Terry 68
COSVN (Central Office for South Vietnam) 215–216, 221

Counterinsurgency 49, 53–54
Counter-Insurgency Plan (CIP) 48–49, 61, 86
Cranston, Alan 274
Cronkite, Walter 73, 164, *174*, 177, **325**
C. Turner Joy 81, 87, 91
Cushman, Gen. John H. 71

D

Da Faria, Antonio 1
Dai, Bao. *See Bao Dai.*
Dak To 148
Daley, Richard 170, 171
Dam, Col. Bui Dinh 55
Danang xiii, 1, 2, 4, 5, 71, 97, 102, 123, 125, 126, 165, 247, 264, 265, 270
    and Buddhists rebellion 121, 122, 131
    and U.S. Marines land at (1965) 104, 106, *111*
D'Aregenlieu, Georges Thierry 15, 29
Darlac Province 51, 93, 263
Day, Col. George E. "Bud" 153
Dean, John 245
Dean, John Gunther 265
De Borchgrave, Arnaud 37, 136, 229, **325**
De Castries, Col. Christian *39*, 41, 42, **325**
Declaration of War. *See Tonkin Gulf Resolution and Gulf of Tonkin Resolution.*
De Garland-Terraube, Genevieve *21*
Deepe, Beverly 75
Deer Mission 12
Defense Attaché Office (DAO) 244, 248, 265, 268
Defoliants. *See Agent Orange and Operation Ranch Hand.*
De Gaulle, Charles 13, 32, 41, 90
De La Croix, Col. Christian 39
Delaney, Pfc. Mike 176, 177
Delayed Stress Syndrome. *See Post-Traumatic Stress Disorder (PTSD).*

Democratic National Convention (1968). *See Chicago Democratic Convention.*
Denton, Adm. Jeremiah, Jr. 136, *259*, **325**
DePuy, Gen. William 134, 141
Desmond, Robert Lee 293
DeSoto Patrols 80. *See also Tonkin Gulf incidents.*
Devlin, Pfc. Robert 152
Dewey, Lt. Col. A. Peter 29, **325**
Dewey Canyon, Operation 198, 222
Diem, Bui. *See Bui Diem.*
Diem, Ngo Dinh 30, 43, 45, 46, 47, 51, 53, *61*, 62, 65, **325–326**
    assassination of 59, 63
    and Binh Xuyen 25–26
    and Buddhists 57–58, 73
    and Catholics 58
    and French 25, 29
    and Kennedy 57, 66–67
    and opposition to 27, 48, 58–59, 61
    and overthrow of 58–59, 63, 74–75
    and U.S. support of xiv, 26, 27, 31, **44**, 49, 50, 52, 56
Dien Bien Phu:
    battle of *21*–23, 39–42, *39*
    Giap at *21*–22, 23, 30, *39*, 41
    Khe Sanh comparison 167, 168, 177
Dinh Trong province 55
Dirksen, Everett 106
DMZ (Demilitarized Zone) xiii, 24, 123, 126, 141, 147, 148, 163, 165, 167, 170, 173, 175, 192
Don, Gen. Tran Van 43, 58, 59, 63, 75, 299, **326**
Dong Ha 147
Dongkhe 19
Dong, Pham Van 11, 79, 149, **326**
    and peace negotiations 98, 104
Donlon, Capt. Roger 87
Donnelly, John 117
Donovan, Lt. David 203–204
Donovan, William J. 32
Doumer, Paul 326
Downs, Lt. Frederick, Jr. 176

Draft 101, 103, 104, 116, 131, 194, 199, 247
Dramesi, Lt. Col. John A. 153, 201
Duan, Le 47, 262, 263, **326**
Duc, Thich Quang 58, 63, 72
Dulles, John Foster 23, 39, 40, 42, 44, **326**
Dung, Gen. Van Tien 263, 264, 265, 266, 270, 281–282, **326**
Duong Van Minh. *See Minh, Duong Van.*
Durbrow, Elbridge 64, **326**
Dursi, Pfc. James 181
Dutch in Vietnam 1, 2

E

East India Company 3
Easter Offensive (1972) 246. *See also Spring Offensive.*
Edwards, Reginald "Melik" 132
Ehrhart, William 149, 296
Eilert, Pfc. Richard 156
Eisenhower, Dwight D. 40, 43, 48, 61, **326**
    Indochina policy xiv, 22–23, 26, 30, 31, 38, 39, 42, 46, 50, 64
Elkins, Lt. Frank 132, 135, 136
Ellsberg, Daniel 233, **326–327.** *See also Pentagon Papers.*
Ely, Gen. Paul 22, **327**
Elysée, Agreement (1949) 17–18, 29
Esper, George 280–281, 282–283, **327**
Evans, Diane Carlson 292
Evans, Lane 300

F

Faifo 1
Falana, Lola *256*
Fall, Bernard 37–38, 151, **327**
Fallows, James 299
Farm Gate, Operation 62
Felt, Adm. Harry 56
Ferguson, Frederick E. 298–299

Final Declaration of the Geneva Conference 27, 306–307. *See also Geneva accords and conference.*
Finnegan, Patrick 294
First Indochina War 16–24, 29
Fishhook 215
Fitzgerald, Frances 272, **327**
Flaming Dart, Operation 96
Fonda, Jane 252
Fontainebleau conference 15, 29
Ford, Gerald 263, 265, 266, 267, 270, 271, 273, 274, 275, 280, **327**
Fortas, Abe 156
France xiv
    attacks Haiphong 15–16, 29
    defeated in Indochina 23, 30
    at Dien Bien Phu 21–23, 39–42
    grants independence to Vietnam xiii, *29*
    occupation and rule in Vietnam 2–23, 26, 29–31, 34
    treaty with Vietnam 14–15, 24
    U.S. relations xi, xiii, 14, 17, 20, 22, 23, 30, 35
Franco-Vietnamese Preliminary Convention and Annex 301–302
French Foreign Legion 9–10, 14, 24, 35
French Union 15, 29
Frequent Wind, Operation 267, *271, 278, 279, 281, 282*
Fulbright, J. William 82, 92, 118, 120, 131, 146, 289, **327**
Funnye, Clarence 209

G

Gabrielle, stronghold 22
Gadd, Pfc. Charles 187
Galbraith, John Kenneth 194
Gama, Vasco da 1
Gavin, Lt. Gen. James 119, 120, **327**
Gayle, Capt. Richard 202
Geer, Lt. Richard Van de 279

Gelhorn, Martha 149
Geneva accords and conference (1954) xiv, 23–25, 26, 27, 30, 31, 43, 48, 49, 62, 66, 77, 191, 238, 244, 306–307. *See also Final Declaration of the Geneva Conference.*
Geneva Cease-Fire Agreement 302–306
Genouilly, Adm, Rigault de 5
Gia Dinh Province 5
Gia Long, Emperor (Nguyen Anh) 3–4
Giap, Gen. Vo Nguyen 11, 12, 16, 17, 32, 34, 41, 42, *145,* **327–328**
    and Dien Bien Phu 21–22, 23, 30, 39, 42
    on Khe Sanh 168–169
    war strategy 19, 20, 35, 49, 68, 130, 146, 255, 298
Gio Linh 123
Goff, Pfc. Stanley 184
Golden Fleece, Operation 110
Goldwater, Barry xi, 84, 87, 89, 90, **328**
Goodell, Charles 194, 207–208, 228
Gracey, Gen. Douglas D. 13–14
Gramont, Sanche de 129
Grandy, Pfc. James 113
Grant, Adm. Ulysses S. 149
Grant, Zalin 260
Grauwin, Paul 40
Gravel, Mike 328
Great Britain 5, 18, 23, 30, 31, 49
    in Vietnam 2
    occupation of South Vietnam 13–14
Green Berets. *See Special Forces.*
Green, Felix 115
Greene, Graham 40
Greenway, H.D.S. 276
Grubb, Capt. Wilmer *130*
Gruening, Ernest 83, 92, **328**
Grunts. *See combat soldiers (United States).*
Guarino, Maj. Larry 203, 258
Gubar, Stephen 205
Guest, Adm. William S. 93

Gulf of Tonkin 80–82. *See also Tonkin Gulf incidents.*
Gulf of Tonkin Resolution 307–308. *See also Tonkin Gulf incidents.*

H

Hackworth, Col. David H. 225, 234, **238**
Haig, Gen. Alexander 298, **328**
Haiphong *10,* 15–16, 29, 97, 126, 144, 239, 242, 246
Haiphong Harbor 148, 239, 246, 254
Halberstam, David 69, **328**
Halsey, William F. "Bull" 11
Hamburger Hill, Battle of 192–193, 199, 204
Ham Nghi, Emperor 6, 7, 16, 17
Hamill, Pete 129
Hanoi 2, 208
    attacks on 123, 126, 137–138, 144, 147, 239, 242–243, 246, 247, 254–255
    French in 16, 19, 20, 31
    celebration in 12
Hanoi Free School 8
Hanoi Hilton 136, 153, 154
Harkins, Gen. Paul 54, 62, 71, 72, 74, 87, **329**
Harper, Sgt. Ronald 177
Harriman, Averell W. 68, 103, **329**
Harrison, Pfc. Robert 177
Harsch, Joseph C. 269
Hart, Frederick 292
Hassna, Steve 151–152
Hastings, Operation 123, 126, 134
Hatfield, Mark 217, **329**
Hayden, Tom 329
Heiman, Larry 297
Heinl, Col. Robert, Jr. 249
Herbicides. *See Agent Orange.*
Herr, Michael 156, 177–178, **329**
Herrgesell, Lt. Col. Oscar 252
Herrick, Capt. John: and Tonkin Gulf Incident 81 90, 91
Hersh, Seymour 196
Hershey, Gen. Lewis 131
Herter, Christian 64

Higgens, Marguerite 73, **329**

Hill 937. *See Hamburger Hill.*

Hilsman, Roger 54, 57, **329**

Hoa Hao sect 25, 48

Hoa, Nguyen Thi 279–280

Ho Chi Minh 10–11, 18, 25, 26, 36, 41, 42, 177, 199
    background 8, **329–330**
    and China 9
    and Communist Party 29
    and France 14, 15, 16, 17, 30, 35
    and Geneva Agreement 45
    and peace negotiations 125, 147, 160, 193
    and U.S. 12, 32, 33, 34, 108, 205
    and war strategy 19, 47, 115

Ho Chi Minh Campaign 265, 266, 267, 270

Ho Chi Minh Trail 31, 77–78, 86, 87, 148, 167, 218, 222, 238

Hoekenga, Mark 131

Hoffman, Abbie 330

Hoffman, Paul 209

Holmes, Oliver Wendell, Jr. 291

Holzschub, Sgt. Carl 226

Homecoming, Operation (return of POWS) 248, *258, 259*, 260

Hon Gai 82

Hong My 62

Hon Me 80

Hon Niem 80

Honolulu conference (1966) 118, 121, 125, 129

Hope, Bob 139, *256*

Hue xiii, 6, 12, 57, 121, 125, 217, 239, 264, 270
    fighting in, during Tet Offensive 165–167, *173, 174, 178*

Hughes, Larry 158

Humphrey, Hubert 26, 96, 103, *171*, 174, 186, **330**

Hung, Nguyen Ngoc 300

Huong, Tran Van 84, 87, 104, 266, 271

I

Ia Drang Valley 102, 104, 114

I-Feel-Like-I'm-Fixin'-to-Die Rag 109

India 1, 24

Indochinese Communist Party (ICP) 9, 10, 29

International Control Commission (ICC) 24, 31, 49–50, 61, 79

Iraq xv, 289, 293

Iron Triangle 141, 142, 147, 261

Isaacs, Arnold 278

Isaacs, Harold R. 34

J

Jackson, Henry 40, 274

Jansen, Lt. Col. Jay 151, 259–260

Japan 7
    in Vietnam xiii, 1, 13
    surrenders in Indochina 12, 29, 32

Jaunal, Sgt. Maj. Jack W. 184, 298

Jenkins, Loren 278

"Johns Hopkins University" speech, Johnson's 98, 104, 107

Johnson, Gen. Harold K. 155

Johnson, Lady Bird 91

Johnson, Lyndon B. xi, 22, 41, 76, 77, 80, 81, 86, 143, 146, 156, *171*, 219, **330**
    and bombing policy xiv, 91, *96, 97*, 99, 123–124, 125, 128, 144, 148, 151, 170, 173, 175, 176, 183, 186
    and Gulf of Tonkin Resolution 82–83
    and Honolulu conference 118, 121, 125, 129
    and public opinion 103, 124, 145, 169, 177
    and Vietnam policy 60, 63, 79, 84, 87, 88–89, 92, 104, 106, 107, 108, 110, 120, 125, 127, 147, 150, 155, 185
    visits Vietnam 50, *61*, 65, *118*, 126
    war strategy 85, 88, 98, 100, 101–102, 117, 131, 167

Johnson, Pat 133

Johnson, Capt. Raymond 156

Joint Chiefs of Staff 22, 51, 143, 144, 168
    propose escalation 60, 97

Jones, James 260

Judge, Corp. Darwin 267, 271, 274

Junction City, Operation 141–142, 147

Just, Ward 133, 134, 225, **330**

K

Karnow, Stanley 46, 214, **330**

Kean, Maj. James 268, 280

Kemark, Glen 112

Kempner, Lt. Marion 135

Kennan, George F. 120, 129, **330**

Kennedy, Edward 193, 204–205, 262

Kennedy, John F. xi, 48, 57, 61, 64, 65, 66, 69, 80, 219, **330–331**
    and Diem 59, 66–67
    and assassination of 59–60, 63
    and communism 45
    and troop levels in South Vietnam xiv, 74
    and U.S. involvement in Vietnam 38, 41, 49, *50*, 51, 54, 56, 67, 68, 70–71, 73
    and Vietnam policy 62
    visits Vietnam 37

Kennedy, Robert F. 155, 169, 170, 173, 174, 179, 182, **331**

Kent State University xiii, 216, 221, 227

Kerry, John 233, 293, **331**

Ketwig, Pfc. John 160–161, 181, 211

Keville, William 112

Khanh, Gen. Nguyen 79, 83, 84, 86, 87, 90, 104

Khe Sanh 123, 144, 148, 218

Khe Sanh, Battle of xiii, 163, 167–169, 173, 174, 176, 177–181, 182, 183, 184

Khiem, Gen. Tran Thien 59, 83

Khmer Rouge 221, 263, 270, 271, 285, 286

Khrushchev, Nikita 52, 65, 81

Kiem, Tran Buu 175

Kienhoa Province 61

Kien Long 86

Kifner, John 227

King, Martin Luther, Jr. 152, 170, 174, **331**

Kingsley, Pfc. Thomas 235

Kissinger, Henry xi, 189, 190, 191, 201, 206, 207, 215, 251, 266, 271, 274, 275, 280, 297, **331**
    and peace negotiations 193, 199, 220, 221, 237, 239, 240, 241, 243, *244*, 246, 247, *248*, 249, 254, 256, 272

Klinkhammer, Stephen 275

Knoebl, Kuno 136

Kohler, Foy 99

Komer, Robert 331

Kontum Province 86, 148, 238, 239, 263

Korean War 20, 98, 144, 290

Kosygin, Aleksei 96, 97, 147

Kovic, Ron 159–160, 253, 298, **331**

Krause, Alison 216

Krause, Arthur 227

Krause, Doris 227

Krich, Claudia 280

Krock, Arthur 71

Krulak, Gen. Victor H. 86, **331–332**

Ky, Nguyen Cao 96, 104, 110, 118, 121, 122, 123, 125, 126, 129, 134, 147, 209, 220, 221, 277–278, **332**

L

Lach Chao 82

Laird, Melvin 189, *190*, 194, 198, 208, 211, 215, 225, 239, 248, 249, 257, 272, **332**

Lam Son, Operation 218, 222

Landing, Capt. James 158

Langson 19

Lang Vei 168, 173

Laniel, Joseph 42

Lan, Nguyen Thi 115

Lansdale, Gen. Edward 30, 43, 48, 49, 64, **332**

Lao Dong Party 47, 61

Laos 23, 30, 48, 50, 52, 62, 65, 84, 87, 90, 125, 143, 167, 217, 218, 222, 231

Lattre de Tassigny, Gen. Jean de 19–20, 36, 37, 332
Le Duan. *See Duan, Le.*
Le Duc Tho. *See Tho, Le Duc.*
Le dynasty 5
Leepson, Marc 297
LeMay, Gen. Curtis 60, 75, 90
Le, Nguyen Quang 108
Lemnitzer, Gen. Lyman L. 70
Lewis, Anthony 252
Lin, Maya Ying 290, 332
Lindley, Ernest K. 46
Linebacker Operations 240, 242
Lodge, Henry Cabot 58, 60, 63, 73, 74, 75, 87, 104, 332
Long An Province 47
Long Binh 247
Long, Russell B. 130
Lon Nol. *See Nol, Lon*
Loscuito, Capt. Ned, Jr. 110
Lucas, Jim G. 88, 93, 113, 332
Luc, Duc 64

M

McCain, John, III 203, 300
McCarthy, Eugene xi, 159, 169, 171, 173, 194, 210, **332–333**
McCarthy, Col. James 256
McCloskey, Robert 100
McClosky, Paul "Pete" 235
McCone, John 60, 74, 90
McCormick, John 96
McDaniel, Capt. Norman 134
McDonald, Country Joe 109
McGovern, George 154, 155, 217, 229, 240, 247, 252–253, **333**
McGovern-Hatfield Amendment 217, 222, 229
McMahon, Corp. Charles, Jr. 267, 271
McNamara, Robert xi, 64, 118, 300, **333**
  and air war *99*
  and bombing policy 87, 106, 144

in Johnson administration 60, 76, 81, 82, 84, 89
  in JFK administration 52, 54, 56, 63
  resigns 148, 173
  and troop levels 51, 100, 101, 115, 125, 126, 143
  visits Vietnam 62, *70*, 79, 86, 103, *104*, 142
  war strategy 95
MAAG. *See Military Assistance Advisory Group.*
MacCabe, Robert 72
MACV. *See Military Assistance Command, Vietnam.*
Mailer, Norman 157–158
Malacca 1
Mandeville, Robert 138
Mannion, Corp. Dennis 184
Mansfield, Mike 43, 56, 63, 66, 70, 96, 119, 127, 226, 251, 255, **333**
Mao Zedong 19, 49
Markham, John 274
Marks, Pfc. Richard E. 108, 109, 130
Marshall, William 136
Martin, Graham 248, 265, 266, 267, 268, 271, 272, 275, 280, **333**
Martin, Harold 133
Martin, Robert P. 65, 74, 107
Mason, Robert 132
Mayflower (code-name) 99
May 2d Movement 89–90
Mazure, Francois 178
Mecklin, John 70, **333–334**
Medal of Honor 87, 132, 347
Medevac *128*
Medical personnel xi, 49, 133, 135, 138–139, 159, 183, 201, 202, 205, *207*, 226, 228–229. *See also nurses.*
Medina, Operation *156*
Mekong Delta 27, 31, 48, 51, 55, 56, 60, 61, 65, 67, 74, 86, 104, 134, 163, 199, 224, 239, 261, 263
Mendes-France, Pierre 334
Menu, Operation (secret bombing of Cambodia) 191, 198

Merrick, Wendell 277
MIAs (Missing in Action) 293, 347
Military advisers 26, 28, 31, 46, 47, 50, 51, 52, 55, 56, 61, 62, 67, 68, 71, 77, 79
Military Assistance Advisory Group (MAAG) 26, 31, 37, 43, 45, 61, 62, 87
Military Assistance Command, Vietnam (MACV) 56, 62, 87, 144, 163, 165
Miller, Jeffrey 216
Millet, Stanley 69
Minaar, Spec. 4 David 235
Minh, Gen. Duong Van [Big Minh] 59, 63, 75, 79, 83, 86, 88, 220, 223, 266, 268, 269, 271, 275, 281, 282, **334**
Minh Mang, Emperor 4
Minh, Nguyen Van 234
Missing in Action. *See MIAs.*
Missionaries xi, 1, 2, 3, 4, 5
Moalic, Jacques 137
Moffat, Abbot Low 34
Mohr, Charles 179, **334**
Montagnards *93*
Montgomery, Roger 106
Moore, Adm. Robert B. 91
Moore, Robin L., Jr. 90
Moorer, Adm. Thomas 81, 242, **334**
Moorfield, Ken 268, 279
Moratorium Against the War 194–196, 199, 209–210
Morgan, Thomas 82
Morris, Capt. James 112
Morse, Wayne 41, 73, 82, 88, 89, 91–92, 120, 154–155, **334**
Mountbatten, Lord Louis 13
Mudd, Roger 253
Muller, Robert 288, 296, **334**
Mulligan, Hugh 116
Mulligan, James, Jr. 137
Murray, John 116
Murray, Maj. Gen. John 272
Murtha, Pfc. Gary 150
My Lai 173, 181, 182, 196, 199, 222, 232

N

Napoleon III 5
National Liberation Front (NLF) 51, 65, 95, 125, 198, 199
  formation of 48, 61. *See also Vietcong.*
National Security Action Memorandums: (NSAM 273) 60; (NSAM 288) 79; (NSAM 328) 100
Navarre, Gen. Henri 20, 21, 30, 38, 42, **334**
Navarre Plan 20–21
New York Times, The 169, 219, 223. *See also Pentagon Papers.*
The New York Times v. The United States of America 233–234. *See also Pentagon Papers.*
New Zealand 23, 31, 89
Nghe An Province 9
Ngo Dinh Diem. *See Diem, Ngo Dinh.*
Ngo Dinh Nhu. *See Nhu, Ngo Dinh.*
Ngo Dinh Nhu, Madame. *See Nhu, Madame Ngo Dinh.*
Nguyen Ai Quoc. *See Ho Chi Minh.*
Nguyen Anh 3
Nguyen Cao Ky. *See Ky, Nguyen Cao.*
Nguyen Dinh Can. *See Can, Nguyen Dinh.*
Nguyen Dinh Thuan. *See Thuan, Nguyen Dinh.*
Nguyen Dynasty 2, 3, 4
Nguyen Khan. *See Khan, Nguyen.*
Nguyen Van Thieu. *See Thieu, Nguyen Van.*
Nhu, Madame Ngo Dinh 75, **334–335**
Nhu, Ngo Dinh 27, 53, 59, 63, 72, 75, **334**
Nixon doctrine 192, 199
Nixon, Richard M. xi, xiv, 38, 61, 171, 173, 174, 184, 193, 198, 211, 222, 248, 256–257, 297, **335**
  and antiwar movement 195, 197, 216, 219, 226
  and bombing 191, 238–239, 247, 250
  and Cambodia 201, 214–217, 221, 228, 229

and Hanoi and
Haiphong bombing
242, 246, 247, 254
and peace proposals
190–191, 193, 199,
205–206, 209, 214, 217,
220, 222, 237, 240,
241–242, 243, 246, 252
and resignation of 219,
262, 270
and Thieu 243, 254, 256
and troop withdrawals
192, 194, 199, 200, 203,
218, 221, 223, 224, 237,
246, 249
and Vietnamization 20,
189–190
and visits China 223,
237, 246
and war policy
201–202, 206, 207–208,
232–233, 251, 253
and Watergate 245
Noel, Nancy 186
Nol, Lon 214, 221, 226,
270, **335**
Nolde, Lt. Col. William B.
256
Nolting, Frederick E., Jr.
51, 56, 58, 63, 68, **335**
Noonan, Jim 297
Norodom Sihanouk. *See
Sihanouk, Norodom.*
North Vietnam xii, 11, 27,
31, 48, 51, 80–81
and air war against xiv,
60, 82, 84, 87, 95, 96,
97, 99, 102, 103, 104,
115, 117, 119, 123, *124*,
125, 126, 128, 130, 135,
137–138, 143, 147, 148,
183, 224, 238–239, 240,
246, 254–255
and casualties in war
125, 148, 166–167, 168,
198, 199, 240, 271, 347
and formation of 23–24,
30
and invades South
Vietnam 61, 263–269
and peace negotiations
108, 117, 170, 173, 174,
175, 191, 198, 217, 220,
239, 240, 241, 243, 246
and war strategy 77, 85,
102, 167, 238, 262–263,
264–265
*See also NVA and
Vietcong.*
Nurses 21, 133, 201, 202,
226, 228–229
NVA (North Vietnamese
Army) xi, xiv, 108, 114,
123, 125, 126, 133, 141,

143, 144, 147, 163, 166,
167, 168, 173, 193, 199,
218, 234, 238, 249, 263,
266. *See also combat
soldiers (North
Vietnamese).*

O

Oanh, Li Thi 273
O'Brien, Tim 201, **335**
O'Donnell, Kenneth 56,
59–60
Office of Strategic Services
(OSS) 12, 29, 32, 33
Olsen, Spec. 4 George 211
Olsen, Pfc. Gregory 181
O'Neil, Lt. Col. James 260
Operation Vulture (French
Indochina War) 22
Operations:
Attleboro 123, 126, 134
Barrel Roll 84
Byrd *138*
Cedar Falls 141, 147
Dewey Canyon 198, 222
Farmgate 62
Frequent Wind 267,
271, *278, 279, 281, 282*
Golden Fleece 110
Hastings 123, 126, 134
Junction City 141–142,
147
Linebacker I 240
Linebacker II 242
Masher/White/Thang
Prong II 125
Medina *156*
Menu 191, 198
Niagara 167
Paul Revere/Than
Phone 126
Pegasus 168
Prairie 126, 136
Quyet Thang 173
Randolph Glen 199
Ranch Hand 62, 128
Rolling Thunder 97, 99,
104, 175, 246
Starlight 104
Union II 147
Utah 125
Oplan 34–A 80, 81, 82, 86,
91. *See also Tonkin Gulf
incidents.*
Ord, Col. James, Jr. 208
OSS. *See Office of Strategic
Services.*
Ovnand, M/Sgt. Chester
31

P

Pacification 17, 53, 62,
102, 118, 125. *See also
strategic hamlets.*
Page, Tim 131, **335**
Page, Adm.
Theogene-Francois 5
Palmer, Gen. Bruce, Jr.
149
Parks, Pfc. David 137,
150, 152, 155
Paris Peace Accords 243,
248, 261, 308–316
Paris peace talks 170,
171–172, 173, 174, 175,
198, 217, 220, 223, 224,
240, 243, 246, 247
Parrish, Lt. John 159
Patterson, James J. 39
**Patti, Maj. Archimedes
L.A.** 32, **335**
Pauley, Larry 296
Peace movement. *See
antiwar movement.*
Peeples, Spec. 4 Kenneth
133
Pegasus, Operation (Khe
Sanh) 168
Pentagon antiwar march
148, *157*
Pentagon Papers 219, 223,
233–234. *See also Ellsberg,
Daniel.*
Perfume River 6
Perry, Merton 180
Persian Gulf War xv, 289,
293
Pham Van Dong. *See
Dong, Pham Van.*
Phan Boi Chau 7
Phan Chu Trinh 7–8
Phat, Gen. Lam Van 87
Philippines 11, 23, 30, 34
Phnom Penh 215, 263,
270, 271, 292
Phoenix program 213–214
Pho Hien 1, 2
Phuoc Long Province 263
Phuoc, Nguyen Van 249
Phuoc Vinh 62
Pike, Douglas 300,
335–336
Pike, Otis 272
Pitzer, Dan 74
Plain of Jars 62
Pleiku 86, 95–96, 102, 104,
106, 126, 263
Poison Plot 7
Pol Pot 285, 286, 292, **336**
Poland 24
Pork Chop Hill 144

Portuguese in Vietnam 1,
2
Post-traumatic stress
disorder (PTSD) 286, 288
Potsdam Conference 13
Poulo Condore 5
POWs (Prisoners of War)
xi, xiv, 82, *130*, 134, 136,
137, 151, *153*–154, 191,
201, 203, 222, 230, 255,
293, 347
French 23, 30
and release of
(American) 239, 241,
243, 246, 248, 257, *258*,
259, 260. *See also MIAs.*
Prairie, Operation 126, 136
PRG (Provisional
Revolutionary
Government) 261
Prisoners of war. *See
POWs.*
Proffit, Nicholas 276, 278
Puller, Lewis, Jr. 296–296

Q

Quang Ngai Province 125
Quang, Thich Tri 58, 122,
125, **336**
Quang Tri Province 123,
198, 199, 238, 239
Qui Nhon 104
Quyet Thang, Operation
173

R

Rader, Gary 157
Radford, Adm. Arthur
22, 40, **336**
Ramadier, Paul 35
Ranch Hand, Operation
62, 288. *See also Agent
Orange.*
RAND Corporation 52
Randolph Glenn,
Operation 199
Randolph, Jennings 274
Ransom, Lt. Robert, Jr.
183
Ray, Michele 133
Reagan, Ronald xv
Reed, David 152
Refugees 30, 44–45, *110*,
121, 270
boat people 285, *287*,
292

evacuation of *264*,
267–268, 271, 273,
275–280, *281*
numbers of xiii, 285,
347
*See also Operation
Frequent Wind.*
Reich, Pfc. Dale 186
Reston, James 65, 67
Reuther, Walter 194
Reynaud, Paul 38
Reynolds, John 295
Rhoads, Jacqueline 226
Rhodes, Alexander de *2, 3*
Ribaud, Marc 208
Ribicoff, Abraham 172
Rice, Capt. Ken 276
Richards, Robert 40
Ridgway, Gen. Matthew
44
Rigoulot, Lt. James 203
Risner, Col. Robinson 154
Roberts, Chalmer 56
Rogers, William 194, 215,
225, 239, 248, 250
Rolling Thunder,
Operation 97, 99, 104,
175, 246. *See also North
Vietnam, air war against.*
Roosevelt, Franklin D. 32
Ross, Capt. Harold 66
Rostow, Walt 65, **336**
Rowe, Pfc. James, Jr. 158,
183
Rubin, Jerry 336
Rudloff, Lt. Stephen 250
Rusk, Dean xi, **336**
in Johnson
administration 60,
84, 87, 90, 91, 100,
119–120, 127, 130
in Kennedy
administration 49,
50, 52, 73
Russ, Martin 139

S

Sabine, Deirdre 131
Sabine, Capt. John 131
Sadler, Barry 129
Safer, Morely 112, **336**
Saigon xiii, *9*, 10, 11, 12,
13, 18, 25, 30, 31, *33*, *69*,
106, 123
attacks on U.S.
embassy 107, 163, 173
Buddhist
demonstrations in
57–58, 72, 83, 121, *125*
Diem overthrow in 59

evacuation of xi,
265–268, 271, 274–280.
*See also Operation
Frequent Wind.*
Fall of (1975) xiv,
265–269, 271, 274–283
French in 5, 14
in Tet Offensive xiv,
163–165, 173, 177
Sainteny, Gen. Jean 336
Salisbury, Harrison
123–124, 126, 137, 138,
336–337
Sam, Nguyen Van 185
Samuels, Gertrude 45
Sanders, Pfc. Robert 187
Sather, Lt. Richard 82
Saxbe, William B. 256
Schanberg, Sidney 251,
331
Schell, Jonathan 149–150
Scheuer, Sandy 216
Schlesinger, Arthur 52
Schneider, Christine 229
Schockley, Robert 295
Scholars' Revolt 6–7
Scholl-Latour, Peter 43,
158–159
Scott, Hugh 274
Schroeder, William 216
Schwarzkopf, Lt. Col. H.
Norman 234–235
Scruggs, Jan 290, 292, **337**
Seaborn, J. Blair 79
Search-and-destroy
operations xiv, 98, 102,
107, *109*, 112, 117, 119,
125, 141, *156*, 192, *225*
Semmes, Vice-Adm. B.J.,
Jr. 137
Sevareid, Eric 88
Shank, Capt. Edwin
"Jerry" 75, 76, 88
Shaplen, Robert 35, 113,
182, 249–250, 260, 278,
299, **337**
**Sharp, Adm. Ulysses S.
Grant** 81, **337**
Sheehan, Neil 134–135,
299, **337**
Sheridan, Maj. Bob 250
Sherman, William
Tecumseh xi
Shorr, Daniel 38
Shurtz, Lt. Eugene, Jr. 206
Sidisin, Ruth 201
**Sihanouk, Prince
Norodom** 191, 214, 221,
293, **337**
"Silent majority" speech,
Nixon's 195, 199,
207–208

Simpson, Howard R. 44
Smart bombs 240, 242, 251
Smith, Pfc. Donald
186–187
Snepp, Frank 273–274,
337
Son Tay (POW camp), raid
on 222
Southeast Asia Treaty
Organization (SEATO)
31
South Vietnam xiii, 3, 25,
26, 31
Buddhists in 57–58, 63,
83, 121–122, 125, 126
collapse of 263–269,
270–271
formation of 23–24, 30,
31
invasion of 63, 77, 85,
95, 123, 163–167, 173,
238
national elections 27,
31, 121–122, 125, 126,
220
peace negotiations 175
U.S. commitment to
xiv, 49, 52, 54, 63
U.S. troops arrive in
xiv, 97, 104, 106, *111*
*See also South Vietnamese
Armed Forces (ARVN).*
South Vietnamese Armed
Forces (ARVN) 49, 51,
53, 63, 79, 123, 141, 143,
147, *159*, 175, 218, *231*
and casualties/losses
55, 62, 86, 105, 126,
148, 167, 175, 200, 218,
222, 223, 224, 247, 248,
271, 347
and U.S. advisers 55,
67, 68, 71, *86*
and U.S. commitment
to 83, 104, 118, 121,
126, 197, 262, 265, 270,
271. *See also combat
soldiers (South
Vietnamese).*
South Vietnamese Seventh
Division 55, 59, 71, 72
Soviet Union xiv, 23, 30,
78, 96, 97, 144, 237, 238
Special Forces (Green
Berets) 49, 51, 55, 61, 62,
71, 72, 74, 133, 137, 168,
173
Spencer, Lt. Ernest 178
Spock, Dr. Benjamin xi,
·157, **338**
Spring Offensive (1972)
238–239, 246
Standerwick, Caroline 272

Stanford Research
Institute 52
Starlight, Operation 104
Steinbeck, John 150
Steinberg, David 176
Stennis, John 38, 39, 137,
150, 251, 272, **338**
Stephen, Lt. Donald 232
Sterba, David 176
Stettinius, Edward R. 32
Stockdale, Adm. James
255, 298, **338**
Stone, Oliver 298
Storz, Sgt. George 179
Strandberg, Lt. Richard
294
Strategic hamlets 53–54,
57, 62, 73, 76
Stratton, Capt. Richard
153
"Street Without Joy" 137,
151
Strickland, Pfc. Hiram 128
Stubbe, Lt. Ray 180
Student protest
movement. *See antiwar
movement.*
Sully, Francois 151,
338
Summers, Col. Harry, Jr.
196, 289, 297–298
Suu, Phan Khac 84
Symington, Stuart 272

T

Tadien (landless tenants) 9
Tam, Luong Trung 249
Tan Son Nhut Air Base
88, 165, 265, 266, 267
Tang, Truong Nhu 299
Taoism 2
Taum Gio 30
Taylor, Gen. Maxwell
62, 66, 74, 84, 86, 119, 168,
338
Ambassador
(1964–1965) 87, 91,
93, 104
on bombing 85, 95, 96,
130
on troop build-up 51,
97, 100
Taylor, Telford 255
Tayninh Province 126
Tay Son rebellion 3–4
Tchepone 218
Terzani, Tiziano 276
Tet Offensive (1968) xiii,
xiv, 163–165, 168, 169,
173, 177–179, 180, 213

Thach, Nguyen Co 214
Thailand 18, 23, 31, 62
Thanh, Pham 300
Thi, Lt. Gen. Nguyen
    Chanh 121, 122, 125
Thich Quang Duc. *See*
    Duc, Thich Quang.
Thien, Nghiem Xuan 46
Thieu, Nguyen Van *104,*
    148, 179–180, 191, 193,
    198, 213, 217, 218, 220,
    223, 224, 225, 230–231,
    240, 245, 246, 248, 261,
    262, 263, 264, 270, 272
    and peace negotiations
        175, 247, 241–242, 243,
        254, 256, 257
    resigns 266, 271, 275
Tho, Le Duc 221, 237,
    239, 240, 241, 243, 244,
    247, 248, **338–339**
Tho, Nguyen Ngoc 63
Thomas, Maj. Allison K.
    33
Thomas, Liz 376
Thompson, Sir Robert
    53, **339**
Thorovai, Jean 254–255
Thorton, Lt. Col. Charlie
    180–181
Thua Thien Province 122,
    200
Thuan, Nguyen Dinh 62
Thurmond, Strom 251
Thuy, Xuan 193, 199, **339**
Tin, Col. Bui 169, 271,
    282, **339**
Timmes, Maj. Gen.
    Charles 54
Tonkin 1, 5, 6, 7, 11, 15,
    16, 18, 19
Tonkin Gulf incidents
    80–82, 87, 90–91, 96
Tonkin Gulf Resolution
    82–83, 87, 92, 120, 125,
    155, 173, 217, 221,
    307–308. *See also Gulf of*
    Tonkin Resolution.
Tourane, Bay of 1, 4, 5
Tra, Gen. Tran Van 263,
    339
Tran Van Don. *See Don,*
    Tran Van.
Tran Van Huong. *See*
    Huong, Tran Van.
Trapnell, Gen. T.J.H. 37
Treaty of Independence of the
    State of Vietnam 302. *See*
    also France.
Tregaskis, Richard 71
Tri Quang. *See Quang, Tri.*
Trinh Dynasty 2

Trinh, Phan Chu. *See*
    Phan Chu Trinh.
Troelstrup, Glenn 113
Truman, Harry S. 34, **339**
    and Indochina policy
        xiii, 18, 30, 36
Trumbull, Robert 34
Tu Duc, Emperor 5, 6
Tu, Nguyen 273
Tunnel rats *182*
Tunney, John 250
Tuohy, William 106, 112

U

Union II, Operation 147
United Nations 22–23, 36
United States xii, 11–12,
    13
    aid to France in
        Indochina xi, xiii, 14,
        20, 22, 23, 30, 35–36
    casualties/losses during
        Vietnam War xiii, 31,
        46, 54, 62, 84, 85, 86,
        87, 96, 102, 104, 105,
        122, 125, 144, 167, 168,
        173, 175, 192, 193, 199,
        200, 222, 223, 224, 247,
        248, 269, 271, 347
    military advisers in
        Vietnam xiv, 26, 28,
        31, 46, 47, 49, 50, 51,
        56, 62, 67, 77
    troop
        commitment/levels in
        Vietnam 52, 67, 100,
        118, 126, 144, 147, 148,
        174
    Vietnam policy 13, 17,
        18, 50, 60, 62, 78–79,
        82, 91, 95, 97, 119–120,
        124, 130, 191, 265, 271
    See also specific generals
    and presidents.
U.S.S. Maddox 80–81, 87,
    90. *See also Tonkin Gulf*
    incidents.
U.S.S. Ticonderoga 80–81,
    90. *See also Tonkin Gulf*
    incidents.
Utermahler, Capt. Brian
    230

V

Valdez, M/Sgt. Juan 268,
    280
Valluy, Gen. Etienne 29,
    34
Vance, Sgt. Samuel 114

Vann, Lt. Col. John Paul
    55, 71, 88, 233, 246, **339**
Van Devanter, Lt. Lynda
    202
Van Tien Dung. *See*
    Dung, Van Tien.
Versailles Peace
    Conference 8
Veterans xi
    Agent Orange 62, 288,
        292, 293
    Memorial (New York
        City) 292, 294
    Memorial (Washington,
        D.C.) xiv, 269,
        290–291, 294–295
    Post-traumatic stress
        disorder (PTSD) 286,
        288
    statistics and problems
        286–288, 347
    Vietnam Veterans of
        America (VVA) 288
Viet Bac 16, 29
Vietcong xiii, xiv, 47, 51,
    52, 55–56, 60, 64, 68, 72,
    77, 85, 93, 102, *109, 110,*
    117, 126, 127, 129, 136,
    141, 142, 143, *152,* 174,
    185, 192, 199, 238
    at Bien Hoa 31, 84, 87
    and Brinks Hotel
        bombing 85
    and name 27
    and Phoenix program
        213–214
    at Pleiku 95–96, 97, 104,
        106
    and strategic hamlets
        53–54, 75–76, 86
    in Tet Offensive xiv,
        163–167, 173
    See also combat soldiers
    (North Vietnamese) and
    National Liberation
    Front (NLF).
Vietminh xi, 13–14, 15,
    58
    founded (1941) 11
    and Diem 48
    and French 16–23, 29–31
    and national revolution
        12
    in North Vietnam 26–27
    rebellion against
        French 24–42
Vietnam xi, xiii
    British in 2, 13–14
    Dutch in 1, 2
    French occupation
        2–23, 29–31
    independence 12, 29
    Portuguese in 1

    rebellion against
        French 6–12, 14,
        15–23, 29–31
    treaty with France
        14–15, 24, 29
    See also North Vietnam;
    South Vietnam.
Vietnam, Democratic
    Republic of (DRV) xiii,
    12, 14, 15, 17, 18, 23, 24,
    25, 29
Vietnam Doc Lap Dong
    Minh (Vietnamese
    Independence League)
    11. *See also Vietminh.*
Vietnam, Republic of
    (RVN) 17, 23, 31
Vietnamese Communist
    Party 8, 9, 10, 11
Vietnamization policy 20,
    189, 193, 197, 198, 208,
    218, 221, 238
Vietnam syndrome xv,
    289, 300
Vietnam Veterans Against
    the War (VVAW) 219,
    223, 233
Vietnam Veterans
    Memorial (Washington,
    D.C.) xiv, 269, 290–291,
    294–295
Vietnam Veterans of
    America (VVA) 288
Vietnam Women's
    Memorial Project 292,
    293
Vinbinh Province 104
Vo Nguyen Giap. *See*
    Giap, Vo Nguyen.
Vogle, Paul 273

W

Wallace, James 252
Walt, Gen. Lewis W. 122,
    339–340
Walters, Capt. Jerry 137
War correspondents xi,
    xii, xv, 34, 35, 37, 41, 42,
    65, 67, 68, 69, 71, 72, 74,
    88, 90, 93, 106, 107, 112,
    113, 114, 115, 116, 129,
    131, 133, 134, 136, 137,
    138, 139, 149–150, 151,
    152, 156, 158–159, 160,
    177, 178, 179, 180, 182,
    229, 230, 231, 232,
    250–251, 272, 273, 274,
    276, 277, 278, 281, 282,
    283, 299, 300. *See also*
    specific names.

Warner, Denis 65, 180
War Powers Act 245, 248,
  263, 316–319
War Powers Resolution
  316–319
War protest movement.
  See antiwar movement.
War Zone C 123, 141, 142,
  147
Watergate scandal 191,
  219, 245, 246, 262
Watson, Corp. Jerry 155
Webb, Alvin, Jr. 178, 179
Webb, James 286–287,
  340
Webb, Kate 232, **346**
Webster, Don 179
Weiss, Joseph 135
West, Richard 129
**Westmoreland, Gen.
  William** 85, 86, 87, 88,

96, *142*, 149, 173, 289, 298,
340
  assessment by 143, 146,
    148, 154, 176, 180
  on attrition 144
  strategy of 99, 102, 103,
    137, 141, 167, 168
  and Tet Offensive 163,
    164
  troop buildup 97, 98,
    100, *108*, 125, 169, 173
  on Vietcong 97
Weyand, Gen. Fred 270,
  274, **340**
Wheeler, Gen. Earle 118,
  149, 163, *190*, **340**
Wheeler, John 179,
  296–297
White, Frank M. 33
Whitman, Walt xi
Whitten, Sgt. Bruce 112
Williams, Corp. D.G. 109

Williams, Gen. Samuel T.
  45
Willwerth, James 229, 231
Wilson, Harold 147
Wilson, Lt. Norde 136
Wimbush, Eleanor 295
Women in U.S. military.
  *See nurses and Vietnam
  Women's Memorial Project.*
Woodley, Spec. 4 Arthur
  "Gene" 208
World War I 8
World War II xiii, xiv,
  10–11, 12, 13, 32

X

Xuan Loc 265
Xuan, Nguyen Van 29

Xuan Thuy. *See Thuy,
  Xuan*

Y

Yeu, Col. Dam Quang 122
Yezzo, Pfc. Dominick 206

Z

Zais, Maj. Gen. Melvin
  204
Zich, Arthur 260
Ziegler, Ronald 254
Zorthian, Barry 340
Zumwalt, Adm. Elmo
  340–341
Zumwalt, Lt. Elmo, III 206